ROSAMOND LEHMANN

By the same author

Nancy Mitford
Evelyn Waugh

Rosamond Lehmann

Selina Hastings

Chatto & Windus
LONDON

Published by Chatto & Windus 2002

2 4 6 8 10 9 7 5 3 1

Copyright © Selina Hastings 2002

Selina Hastings has asserted her right under the Copyright, Designs
and Patents Act 1988 to be identified as the author of this work

First published in Great Britain in 2002 by
Chatto & Windus
Random House, 20 Vauxhall Bridge Road,
London SW1V 2SA

Random House Australia (Pty) Limited
20 Alfred Street, Milsons Point, Sydney,
New South Wales 2061, Australia

Random House New Zealand Limited
18 Poland Road, Glenfield,
Auckland 10, New Zealand

Random House (Pty) Limited
Endulini, 5A Jubilee Road, Parktown 2193, South Africa

The Random House Group Limited Reg. No. 954009
www.randomhouse.co.uk

A CIP catalogue record for this book
is available from the British Library

ISBN 07011 65421

Papers used by Random House are natural,
recyclable products made from wood grown in sustainable forests;
the manufacturing processes conform to the environmental
regulations of the country of origin

Typeset by Deltatype Ltd, Birkenhead, Merseyside

Printed and bound in Great Britain by
Biddles Ltd, Guildford and King's Lynn

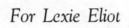

For Lexie Eliot

Contents

List of Illustrations

Acknowledgements

I owe an immense debt of gratitude to many people who have most generously helped me in the writing of this biography. Some unfortunately are no longer alive but I wish to record my thanks to them nonetheless. Among those who were particularly kind in lending letters and photographs, providing information, talking to me about Rosamond Lehmann, and giving me permission to quote are:

Peter Adam, Anne Balfour-Fraser, Frith Banbury, Paul Beard, Steuart Bedford, Sybille Bedford, Jacqueline Benedetti, Sir Isaiah Berlin, Jill Black (Royal Literary Fund), Lady Moorea Black, Michael Bloch, Helen Bradish-Ellames, Anita Brookner, Katherine Bucknell, Carmen Callil, Nina Campbell, Philip Caraman SJ, Christian Carrit, Colette Clark, Leo Cooper, J.A. Cowie, Quentin Crewe, Jill Day-Lewis, Sean Day-Lewis, Lady Devlin, the Duchess of Devonshire, Nina Drury, Alexandra Eliot, Trader Faulkner, Josephine Filmer-Sankey, Paul Fincham, Angela Flowers, Roy Foster, Edward Fox, Sue Fox, Shelagh Fraser, Margaret Gardiner, Martha Gellhorn, Barbara Ghika, Iris Goldsworthy, David Goudge, Valerie Grove, John Haffenden, Dorris Halsey (Reece Halsey Agency), Mary Hammersley, Henry Hardy, John Harris, Duff Hart-Davis, Sir Rupert Hart-Davis, Grizel Hartley, Francis Haskell, Doreen Hawkins, Lady Anne Hill, Derek Hill, Adrian House, Elizabeth Jane Howard, Bruce Hunter (David Higham Associates), Laura Huxley,

Elizabeth Jenkins, J.D.F Jones,. Patrick Kavanagh, Barbara Ker-Seymer, Lady Pansy Lamb, Jack Lander, C.H. Layman, Kathy Lee, Laurie Lee, James Lees-Milne, Jean-Noël Liaut, Andrew Lownie, Mary Lutyens, James MacGibbon, Jean MacGibbon, Andrew Malec, Derwent May, Lord Milford (Hugo), Lord Milford (Wogan), Lady Mosley, Elizabeth Mostyn-Owen, William Mostyn-Owen, Alexander Norman, Belinda Norman-Butler, Viscountess Norwich, Peter Parker, Frances Partridge, Lady Richard Percy, Gwenllian Philipps, Dudley Poplak, Lady Violet Powell, Stuart Preston, Kathleen Raine, Simon Raven, Jenny Rees, Matthew Ridley, Viscount Ridley, Barbara Roett, Kenneth Rose, Sir Joshua Rowley, Sir Steven Runciman, Viscount Runciman (Garrison), Viscount Runciman (Leslie), George Rylands, Lady Sandys, Norman Scarfe, Linda Shaughnessy (A.P.Watt Ltd), Francis Sitwell, Lady Spender, Sir Stephen Spender, John Sutherland, Lady Terrington, Colin Thubron, Patrick Trevor-Roper, David Twiston-Davis, Sir Laurens van der Post, Hugo Vickers, Margaret Vyner, Gillian Warrender, Patrick Woodcock, Adrian Wright, Francis Wyndham, Sebastian Yorke, Philip Ziegler

I am most grateful to the following institutions for allowing me access to their collections:

Trish Hayes and the BBC Written Archives Centre
Stephen Crook and the Berg Collection, the New York Public Library
The Bodleian Library
The British Library
Cambridge University Library
Jenny Lee and the College for Psychic Studies
Kate Perry and Girton College, Cambridge
Prof. T.F. Staley, Cathy Henderson and the Harry Ransom Humanities Research Center, University of Texas at Austin
Fiorella Gioffredi Superbi and the Harvard Center for Renaissance Studies, I Tatti, Florence
Rosalind Moad and King's College, Cambridge
The Karl Marx Memorial Library
Lori Curtis and the McFarlin Library, University of Tulsa
The National Library of Wales

Acknowledgements

Princeton University Library
Mike Bott and Reading University Library
Jeremy Crow and the Society of Authors
Vincent Giroud and the Beinecke Mss Library, Yale University

There are two collections which to my great regret it was not possible to locate, the archive of William Collins, Rosamond Lehmann's publisher, and the letters of Grizel Hartley, Rosamond's oldest friend, to whom she wrote regularly for nearly seventy years.

I would like to give particular thanks to Roland Philipps, Rosamond Lehmann's grandson and co-executor of her literary estate; to Julie Kavanagh and Tom Staley for a judicious reading of the work in progress; and to my editor, Jenny Uglow, whose criticism and encouragement I cannot rate too highly.

I would also like to give heartfelt thanks to Drue Heinz DBE whose bountiful hospitality both at Hawthornden Castle in Scotland and Casa Ecco in Italy provided me with weeks of the most comfortable and carefree working conditions.

Every effort has been made to trace the holders of copyright and I very much regret if inadvertent omissions have been made: these can be rectified in any future editions.

Selina Hastings 2002

1

Vestiges of Creation

On the evening of 8 June 1938 Rosamond Lehmann, in company with fifty other well-known writers, sat on the stage of the Queen's Hall in London. In her late thirties more beautiful than ever, Rosamond in a silvery skirt and purple chiffon blouse made a magnificent figure, with her pale complexion, imposing height and thick, prematurely white hair. The purpose of the meeting was to protest against Fascism, most pertinently Fascist involvement in the Civil War in Spain, and Rosamond herself, for over a decade a prominent member of the English literary scene, had been the event's prime mover, hiring the hall and writing to a large number of influential names for money and support. By inclination Rosamond shrank from political activity – 'I was not, never have been, a political animal,' she said once in an interview – but on this occasion she felt a special sense of commitment: her husband, Wogan Philipps, had twice gone out to Spain in support of the Republican cause, and her current lover, Goronwy Rees, 'that seductive semi-cad', as she later described him, was also a dedicated opponent of Fascism. Rees was with her that night on the platform. He spoke immediately after the poet Cecil Day Lewis, whose languid tones were in marked contrast to the stocky Welshman's emotional delivery. Although she had small inkling of it then, it was with Day Lewis that Rosamond, less than three years later, was to embark on the great love affair of her life.

By general agreement Rosamond's speech, on the Fascist threat to the freedoms of the next generation, was considered one of the most impressive, and when she stepped down to mingle with the audience she was warmly congratulated. One young man, John Guest, who had been brought to the meeting by his cousin, the writer Elizabeth Jenkins, noticed that Rosamond had left her handbag on the dais. Having retrieved it, he went up to return it to her. 'Thank you,' she said, smiling sweetly as she took it from him. 'Oh!' Guest exclaimed to his cousin, overwhelmed. 'I feel weak at the knees!'

Such a reaction was far from unusual. Men found Rosamond's lustrous beauty irresistible, coupled as it was with a gentle manner and an air of innocence and vulnerability. One of the most highly regarded novelists of her age – two of her novels, *Invitation to the Waltz* and *The Weather in the Streets*, were unquestionably among the most distinguished English fiction produced in the years between the wars – Rosamond frequently found herself in the uncommon position of having her looks reviewed in tandem with her work. Although by the standards of today such treatment might be considered an affront, by Rosamond it was accepted as entirely appropriate. For in an important sense her loveliness was central to her life. An incurable romantic, Rosamond was an intensely subjective writer, whose life closely informed her writing, and the fact that her marvellous beauty lay at the root of her failure to find happiness provided her with a powerful source of inspiration, her own story, of love deceived and innocence betrayed, compellingly narrated in varying form throughout her work. As a novelist she was subtle and perceptive, but in reality she never learned from her tumultuous adventures, driving through her personal dramas high on a sense of injury and injustice, pursuing her perfidious lovers like an avenging Fury.

Rosamond was one of a remarkable group of siblings, prominent among their generation, her brother John a distinguished editor and man of letters, her sister Beatrix renowned as an actress. Cyril Connolly wrote of them, 'Time was when the Lehmanns, like the Sitwells and Stracheys, were a well-knit family full of torque and thrust . . . a formidable clan . . . [who] rode through the arts like the Valkyrie.' All three enjoyed celebrity status, a status which in the view of some of their contemporaries encouraged an inclination towards self-importance. The trouble with the Lehmanns, remarked Stephen Spender who knew them all, is that they think they're the Brontë sisters, but in fact they're the Marx Brothers. This criticism could most accurately be applied to John, gifted, but a conceited, pompous man, while Rosamond, vain in other ways, tended to be modest about her professional achievements. Her first novel, *Dusty Answer*, published when she was 26, was a phenomenal success and made her name known to a reading public all over the world. Yet at the time such fame meant little to her. Her mentors, greatly loved and revered, were members of the Bloomsbury group, specifically Lytton Strachey and Virginia Woolf: it was to their standards that she aspired, and by their criteria that she tended somewhat harshly to judge herself.

An equally important touchstone was her father, Rudolph Lehmann. '[My father] stands behind everything I have ever written in my life, or ever will,' Rosamond wrote in middle age, long after he was dead. 'And if, in spite of it all, I have continued to believe . . . I would one day discover what to say and how to say it, I owe the belief now, as in the beginning, to my father.' Rudolph Lehmann was undoubtedly the dominating influence on his daughter's career, and yet his literary ability cannot begin to bear comparison with hers. A charming, cultivated man, his style was lightweight and ephemeral, and a dilettante's disposition coupled with a comfortable patrimony ensured that he never did very much with the talents he was fortunate enough to inherit from a distinguished ancestry.

Rudolph Chambers Lehmann was descended on both sides from notable families, the German Lehmanns and the Scottish Chamberses. His paternal grandfather, Leo Lehmann, born in 1779, was a leading miniature-portrait painter in Hamburg. Baptised a Christian in middle age, he was almost certainly in origin Jewish, a fact which became effectively obscured by his nineteenth-century descendants until proclaimed proudly in the twentieth. 'Of course the Lehmanns are of Jewish descent,' Rosamond declared. 'I think we owe to that what brains & looks we have.' (During the Second World War Leo Lehmann's name, together with those of Rosamond, her father and her brother John, appeared in Volume Six of the *Forschungen zur Judenfrage*, Hitler's notorious directory of European families with Jewish blood.)

Of Leo Lehmann's seven sons, two, Rudolf and Henri, studied in Paris under Ingres, both becoming well-known painters and exhibiting at the

Salon. A third, Frederick, Rosamond's grandfather, aged 18 emigrated in the early 1840s to England, and from thence to Scotland, where in Edinburgh he was introduced to the delightful Robert Chambers, celebrated writer and publisher, and editor of *Chambers's Encyclopedia*. Chambers's most famous work, however, had been published anonymously: *Vestiges of the Natural History of Creation*, probably the most important of the pre-Darwinian theories of evolution, had created a furore, attracting much vituperative condemnation particularly from religious bodies. When asked why he never publicly acknowledged such an important work, Chambers would point to his eleven children. 'I have eleven good reasons,' was the reply.

Of these eleven children, eight were girls, so young Frederick Lehmann was warmly welcomed at 1 Doune Terrace, especially as he was a talented amateur violinist, and the Chambers family was musical. Indeed the eldest daughter, Nina, was a pianist of professional standard; she was also vivacious, pretty and intelligent, and in November 1852 Frederick married her. The Lehmann–Chambers link was reinforced nine years later when brother Rudolph met and married Amelia, one of Nina's sisters, by whom he had a daughter, Elizabethna, better known as Liza Lehmann, the popular singer and composer. Rudolph prospered as a fashionable portraitist in London, and Frederick went into business with the iron and steel firm Naylor, Benzon & Co., first in Liverpool, then moving to the Midlands, where he took a house called Fieldhead on the outskirts of Sheffield. Here Rosamond's father, Rudolph, always known as Rudie, was born on 3 January 1856. Three years later the family moved to London. A town house was brought in Berkeley Square, and a country house in Highgate which provided a peaceful retreat from the hurly-burly of metropolitan society.

Nina gave birth to two more boys, Frederick (Freddy) and Ernst, and a daughter, also called Nina. The marriage was a happy one: the Lehmanns had a wide circle of acquaintance and entertained lavishly. While a bachelor Frederick had made friends among musicians, such as the violinist Joachim, Carl Hallé, Meyerbeer, Clara Schumann; through his painter brother Rudolf he had come to know Landseer, Millais and Lord Leighton. Nina, accustomed since girlhood to meeting at her father's house the great figures of the literary world, was on familiar terms with, among others, Wilkie Collins and Charles Dickens, whose assistant editor on *Household Words* was married to Robert Chambers's sister. Both writers became regular guests in Berkeley Square, as did Robert Browning, Bulwer-Lytton and George Eliot. 'It's sad that I never knew my grandparents,' said Rosamond in old age, 'because I'm the real daughter of their time.'

As a child Rudie naturally remembered best those of his parents' friends who noticed and were kind to him. Once when he was taken backstage to see Dickens after one of his dramatic readings, the great novelist swung Rudie up in his arms and kissed him; Browning, grateful to Frederick Lehmann for buying an unlovely early painting by his son, Pen, offered to give Rudie a pony; and Wilkie Collins, plump, bearded and bespectacled, told the children stories and took them to the pantomime.

Rudie was educated at Highgate School and at Trinity College, Cambridge, where he distinguished himself both in politics and sport. Having decided on the law, Rudie was called to the Bar and went out on circuit, but his heart was not in it, the sole distinction of his short legal career the winning of a newspaper prize for the best-looking barrister. His father's fortune enabling him to do very much as he pleased, he then gave himself over to what he liked best, writing, rowing and politics. In the political arena he made little impression, unsuccessfully contesting Cheltenham (1885) for the Liberals, and Central Hull (1886) and Cambridge Town (1892) as a Gladstonian. In 1889 Rudie with a group of colleagues founded *The Granta*, as it was then known, a journal modelled closely on *Punch*, for which it soon established itself as a feeder, with many of *The Granta's* contributors graduating directly to *Punch*, among them Owen Seaman, F. Anstey, A. A. Milne and Rudie himself, who became a member of the *Punch* table in 1890.

Since boyhood Rudie had been a gifted athlete and dedicated sportsman. He fenced, rode, was an excellent shot and a fine amateur boxer; but his greatest love was for rowing and the river. He wrote three books about rowing, and was one of the first to write about boating as a sporting pastime on a level with hunting, shooting and fishing. His watery world was in the tradition of *Three Men in a Boat* and *The Wind in the Willows*, a world of river bank and shady shallows, where you either punted lazily along with a picnic hamper under the seat or, as described in one of Rudie's characteristic verses, skimmed the surface at speed in an exhilarating contest between two highly trained racing eights:

To make the rhythm right
And your feather clean and bright,
And to slash as if you loved it, though your muscles seem to crack;
And, although your brain is spinning,
To be sharp with your beginning,
And to heave your solid body indefatigably back . . .

Rudie's love of rowing decided him to move from London to Bourne End in Buckinghamshire, to the banks of the Thames, the 'dear lazy shining Thames', as he dotingly described it. Here he built himself a house called Fieldhead, after the house in which he was born, and here he was able to indulge to the full his lifelong passion. For two years, 1894 and 1895, he captained the prestigious Leander Club at Henley, and his reputation as a coach was unrivalled: he coached both the Oxford and Cambridge eights, as well as rowing clubs in Dublin and Berlin, and went twice to America to train the Harvard crew. Always fastidiously maintaining his amateur status – he fought for years to keep the Olympic Games out of the hands of professionals – he refused to accept any fee or expenses. At Harvard he was greeted as a hero and awarded an honorary degree, the ovation given him in Harvard Square 'one of the most spectacular scenes in the history of athletics at Harvard'. He was received in Washington by Mr Roosevelt and at the White House was presented to President McKinley. The 15-year-old Franklin D. Roosevelt wrote to his parents, 'Dear Papa and Mama, Last night Mr Lehmann, the English coach, gave us an informal talk on rowing. He went to Cambridge with Mr Peabody, and, as you probably know, he is about the greatest authority on rowing in the world.'

Frank Peabody, member of the large and influential tribe of Boston Peabodys, was an old friend of Rudie's from Cambridge, and it was at his house in Harvard in 1897 that Rudie met the girl he was to marry. The Peabodys had three daughters, and as tutor their mother had engaged a young woman from a good if impoverished New England family. Alice Marie Davis, 23 years old, was a clever, outspoken young woman with fine eyes, a flawless complexion and a slender figure, only a slightly too large chin spoiling her beauty. At 41 Rudie was handsome, witty and flirtatious, but at their first meeting he and Alice fell out over the question of equal education for women, Rudie dismissing the idea as ridiculous, Alice arguing hotly in favour. Soon, however, the two of them grew close, Alice attracted by his charm and sense of humour, he intrigued by her dignity and independence and by a firmness of purpose missing from his own somewhat indolent nature. Both were liberal in outlook and intensely interested in politics. Before long Rudie's attentions became so marked that Mrs Peabody felt obliged to have a word in his ear, warning him that she regarded Miss Davis almost as a daughter and did not want her hurt. Rudie listened politely, and then with his hand already on the door, or so family tradition has it, he quietly informed Mrs Peabody that, 'Miss Davis and I are already engaged.'

Alice Davis was born in Somersworth, New Hampshire, in 1874, the eldest of four children, three girls and a boy. Her father, Harrison Davis, a widower when he married her mother, died at only 45 as a result of the shock of a business failure: head of a small insurance firm, he lost most of his money after fire destroyed a large number of insured properties to whose owners he was obliged to pay compensation. One of Alice's uncles, Owen Gould Davis, was a Pulitzer Prize-winning playwright, while another, Harry Phillips Davis, became known as the father of American radio broadcasting. Her mother, Helen, was a Wentworth, descended from the eighteenth-century John Wentworth who had been Lieutenant-Governor of New Hampshire. After her husband's death, Helen Davis moved the family to Worcester, Massachusetts, where the children were educated at Worcester High School. Helen Davis, although strict, was a devoted mother. In winter she took the children on moonlit sled rides, and in summer moved the entire family to a small farmhouse in Northwood, New Hampshire, where they picnicked by Stonehouse Pond and gathered berries on the hillside.

At 18 Alice was enrolled in the women's section of Harvard University, Radcliffe, then a new college of only sixty students situated across the common from the main campus. Alice enjoyed her time at Radcliffe, she and her colleagues lodging with families in the town as there were no dormitories, and attending lectures given by Harvard professors, one of whom, Professor Archie Coolidge, lecturer in

7

European History, wrote in a testimonial that Alice was his 'best girl', awarding her a double A in the final examination in his course. When her three years were up she found a job lecturing in literature to classes of ladies in Worcester, an occupation she described as 'rather dull'. Then while on a visit to Boston she met Mrs Peabody, who asked her to come and live with them and teach her three children, 'a difficult trio', Alice recalled, 'but I was determined to stick it out for one year'.

Alice and Rudie were married on 13 September 1898, at Piedmont, near Worcester, Rudie supported by three menfriends from England, Alice attended by a sister and two of the Peabody girls. The wedding breakfast was at her mother's house, after which the newly married Lehmanns left by train for New York, sailing the following day for Liverpool on the White Star liner, *Majestic*. On arrival in London they travelled in a private car attached to the train at Paddington, stopping first at Maidenhead for the presentation of a silver tray by members of the Maidenhead Rowing Club, before being welcomed at Bourne End with a red carpet, a bouquet presented by the vicar's daughter and a speech delivered by the vicar. A carriage took them on the short journey from the station to Fieldhead, where they drove through a triumphal arch to be greeted by the servants lined up outside the front door.

Alice was very much in love with her husband, but however great her excitement at coming to England and beginning her married life, it cannot have been easy to face not only a foreign country but a new house, unknown servants, and her husband's numerous friends and relations, not all of whom were wholly in favour of the introduction into their midst of this American stranger. Rudie, although the eldest, was the last of Frederick Lehmann's children to marry, and his three siblings had become accustomed to having him to themselves, his sister, Nina Campbell, being particularly possessive of her bachelor brother and thus particularly resentful of the intruder; some of the wives of Rudie's rowing friends, too, susceptible to his glamorous good looks, found themselves unable to give more than a restrained welcome to his wife. To the young and inexperienced Alice almost every aspect of her new home was unfamiliar. On her first morning, going into the kitchen to interview the cook, she was met by the alarming sight of Mrs McCloud throwing bones and chunks of raw meat to a hungry group of sixteen dogs, including several puppies and a deerhound. Her sense of disorientation was increased when after only six weeks in England she became infected with typhoid, probably as a result of drinking contaminated milk at a dinner in Cambridge, and became so ill that her life was despaired of, the flag on one of the University boat-houses being flown at half-mast. However, by Christmas she was out of danger, and soon afterwards became pregnant, giving birth on 14 October 1899 to the first of her four children, a daughter called Helen, after her mother. Less than two years later another girl was born: as at the time Rudie was editor of a newspaper, the *Daily News*, it was suggested by a waggish member of staff that the baby be christened 'Dahlia'. Rosamond, however, was the name preferred by her parents.

The *Daily News* was Rudie's third and final venture as a newspaper editor. A lifelong Liberal and fervent admirer of Gladstone, Rudie was vehemently opposed to the imperialistic warmongering characteristic of the age, and in the late 1890s with a group of left-wing colleagues he had taken over the weekly gazette *The Speaker*, one of the few papers during the Boer War to be pro-Boer and anti-war. *The Speaker* failed to make its mark, and at the suggestion of Lloyd George, a member of the board, Rudie invested instead in the ailing *Daily News*, becoming editor in 1901. In spite of an explosive temper, Rudie was liked and respected by his staff; he was decisive, he knew men and affairs, and had a broad spectrum of interests; certainly he enjoyed working with such idiosyncratic contributors as Hilaire Belloc, G. K. Chesterton, H. W. Massingham and Harold Spender, father of the poet Stephen. But although he relished the idea of filling the editorial chair which Dickens had held before him, he lacked the temperament and ambition necessary to succeed at such a demanding career, and lacked, too, the experience to deal with the intrigues and complex managerial problems inherent in the newspaper world; most crucially, he was never able to grasp the economic aspects of the business. 'His mind', said his secretary, Archibald Marshall, 'was not on making the paper pay.' In 1902, after barely more than a year in office, Rudie was obliged to resign.

According to the opinion of one of his friends, Theodore Cook, editor of *The Field*, '[Lehmann] has never been in reality a true journalist at heart. . . . Why he became a proprietor of the *Daily News* I could never quite understand.' This view was shared by Archibald Marshall, who had been given the job of Rudie's secretary on *The Granta* on coming down from Cambridge, had gone with him to the *Daily News*, and continued to work for him after his resignation. Marshall was puzzled that such a charming, intelligent, gifted and cultivated man should be so deficient in drive, apparently content to spend his days doing very little of anything.

[He was] singularly unenterprising in providing himself with work, or even with amusement. Before his marriage, when I was very much with him at Bourne End . . . he would sit for hours in his big library, absolutely surrounded by books, and read nothing but the papers. We would take the dogs for a walk before lunch and in the afternoon, and that was his day, until we came to the evening, when there were usually others there. In the rowing season of course it was different, and for a year or two he had a shoot in Norfolk. He had his *Punch* work, and the weekly dinner, the affairs of the amateur rowing Association took up some of our attention, and during my time with him he wrote a book on rowing, which a publisher had asked him for. . . . Outside all of this one would have to say that his life was definitely an idle one.

It was as a member of the team at *Punch*, which he joined in 1890, that Rudie finally found a completely congenial occupation. It suited him that he could work at home rather than in a city office, he found stimulus in the quick sprint of writing to deadline, and on the whole he enjoyed the weekly dinners round the famous *Punch* table at 10 Bouverie Street, when the subject for the week's political cartoon was decided upon. Inevitably there were tensions: the editor, Owen Seaman, and the majority of writers and illustrators were Tory, and the atmosphere sometimes grew heated, with Seaman and Sir John Tenniel arguing their high Tory line against the Liberal Lehmann with his inflammable temper. (Another member of the table, E. V. Lucas, wrote years later to Rudie's youngest daughter that her father was 'a cherished (if sometimes feared) colleague of mine on *Punch*.') Nonetheless it was here that Rudie found his niche. In his day he was something of a pioneer, the supreme exponent of a relaxed and gently humorous style, retailing comic anecdotes in a comradely, gentlemanly fashion. Within the limits demanded by the journal, he was extremely versatile, turning out everything from hard-hitting political satire to the lightest of light verse about animals, daily life, sporting pursuits, and later the antics of his children. Among favourite subjects for versification were his beloved dogs, and his poem to his spaniel Rufus, immensely popular, was several times reprinted. True to Victorian tradition, he frequently favoured a lofty, archaic style, full of 'mayhap' and 'lo!', regularly veering between a luxuriant sentimentality and a tone of whimsical facetiousness; he was fond, too, of the mock heroic, in which he made humble objects the subject of acclamatory address ('I sing the sofa! . . .'). Equally character-istic was what his friend Alfred Noyes described as 'the Roman poet's note of sadness, that deep and quiet sadness of a happy man who longs for permanent values in a world where everything seems transitory'.

Rudie found contentment in his life at Fieldhead, although both he and Alice, hoping for a son, regarded the birth of two girls as something of a disappointment. When in 1903 Alice, at nearly 30, produced a third daughter, Beatrix, her sense of failure was so acute that she fell into deep depression. Her melancholy imposed a serious strain on the marriage, the undemonstrative Rudie being ill-equipped to deal with such a condition, and when Alice in despair went off to her mother in America there was for a time some doubt that she would return. While she was away Rudie missed her badly and wrote to her with rare expressions of devotion. 'I don't know if it will give you any pleasure to know, but it is the fact that I miss you most awfully and begin to think I was a perfect idiot to let you go. In spite of the children the house somehow seems quite desolate, the drawing-room being a particularly melancholy sight, and I'm beginning to hate my widowed bedroom.' And as the date for her sailing home drew near, he wrote excitedly, 'This is the last letter you'll get from me in the U.S. Expect the next at Queenstown – and then hurrah for our second Honeymoon!!' Four years later, to the joy of both parents, a boy eventually arrived.

Once back at Fieldhead Alice quickly settled down, running the household, supervising the nursery and acting as hostess for Rudie who loved entertaining his many friends from the literary, political and sporting worlds. 'No one', wrote one of his colleagues, 'could give a better dinner or lead the conversation as a better host on multitudinous topics, than could Rudie.' The organisational demands made on his young wife were considerable. In 1901 Rudie was appointed High Sheriff of Buckinghamshire, which during his year in office inevitably involved a great deal of hospitality, and sometimes he would invite the whole of the *Punch* table to dinner, once asking them all with their wives for a day on the river, an occasion which Alice admitted afterwards she had been far too nervous to enjoy. Among their neighbours the most congenial were the Hammersleys, who lived just down-river at Abney, a beautiful, wisteria-covered Georgian house. The wealthy Arthur Hammersley, bluff and blond, had a wife much younger than himself, a dark, Spanish-looking beauty with a thrillingly low voice. Violet Hammersley was sophisticated, well read and musical, with a marked taste for the dramatic. Perhaps unexpectedly she became a close friend of the commonsensical Alice, but the whole Lehmann family were fascinated by her, by her rich, eccentric clothes, her theatrical way of declaiming a story, and her memorable appearances on the river in her very own gondola ferried by Giulio, her very own gondolier. Late in life Rosamond wrote that as a child, 'I believed Violet Hammersley to be a witch. . . . My tastes too tuppence-coloured to admire that elegance of hers in the high Spanish style which made her one of nature's works of art. . . . I thought her very ugly. Her low-toned intensity in conversation troubled me; so did that hooded sombre gaze which impaled her interlocutor.'

In most of Rudie's occupations Alice took little or no part. He enjoyed above all rowing and the coaching of undergraduate oarsmen, which Alice privately regarded as a waste of his time and intellect. In winter he frequently went away to shoot, either with the Smiths at Hambleden or with Harry Cust at Preshaw in Hampshire, and he regularly rode with that paragon among sportsmen, Lord Desborough, owner of one of the local great houses, Taplow Court. Rudie had his work for *Punch*, but although Alice tried her hand, very creditably, with a few short stories, writing was never to become an area of common ground. In the mornings Alice coped with domestic matters, and in the afternoons drove out in the carriage to pay calls, while Rudie was either on the river or in the library fulfilling his week's work, dashing off an ode 'To a Brussels Sprout'.

Alice doted on her husband and there is no doubt that he was fond of her, but it was she who loved the more. In nearly every respect Rudie was a man's man, and all his close friends were men. Interestingly, there exists no hint of any love-affair previous to his meeting Alice, although such matters were spoken of in regard to other members of the family: it was common knowledge, for instance, that Rudie's brother Freddy had a mistress and a family of illegitimate children, while Alice made no secret of the fact that she had had proposals from two men before she accepted Rudie. Yet no rumour of this kind was attached to him. The strongest bond with his wife was a shared interest in their four children, but there is evidence that Alice longed for a more openly affectionate relationship. Strong-minded and forthright though she was, she suffered from his not infrequent outbursts of temper, and suffered, too, from his elusiveness, his emotional detachment, a reluctance to drop the teasing, the ironic tone in favour of sincerity and feeling. 'I know you'd rather die than tell the truth if it's agreeable,' she told him, and in a letter written during one of her triennial visits to America she wrote, 'I'm sailing on the 3rd [September] chiefly to be with you on our anniversary. I don't suppose you'd care a rap if I wasn't there then, but I care & you'll have to make the best of it. . . . Really life is too short for these separations. I hope you sometimes feel miserable too!'

The one area of Rudie's professional life in which Alice was able marginally to participate was the political, her interest in politics being equal to his own. On their first meeting at the Peabodys' house they had vigorously disagreed over women's education, and the subject of female emancipation continued to be a contentious issue between them. Rudie at the age of 50 had finally succeeded in being elected to Parliament, representing the Market Harborough division of Leicestershire after the Liberal landslide of 1906. When soon after the election women's suffrage was debated in the House of Commons, Alice, an ardent suffragette, wrote witheringly, 'I suppose you will deny your liberal principles and vote against the bill this p.m. . . . [Your] attitude is not due to all the difficulties which one foresees to the passing of a Women's Franchise Bill . . . but because you don't like the sex and think them inferior. This is in sorrow – not in anger this time.' As the movement continued to attract powerful opposition, Alice grew more openly critical of her husband's stand. 'You played a noble part on Tuesday night!' she wrote sarcastically. 'What rot you all talked – ready and eager to admit that a woman is capable of everything on earth except putting a cross on a voting paper.' When women were finally on the point of winning the right to vote Rudie commented in a typically facetious manner, making reference to it in *Punch* in what he called one of his 'Francescas'. This was a series of light-hearted pieces in which he retailed dialogue purportedly between himself, the genial, wise, long-suffering husband, and his wife, Francesca, with her adorable 'feminine' logic. Clearly inspired by actual exchanges with Alice, they are good-humoured, affectionate and gently patronising. The episode entitled 'The Vote' was written in July 1917.

> 'And now,' I said, 'that you've got your dear vote, what are you going to do with it?'
>
> 'If,' said Francesca, 'you'll promise to treat it as strictly confidential I'll tell you.'
>
> 'There you are,' I said. 'Unless you can make a secret out of it you take no pleasure in it. You're just like a lot of girls. . . .'

And so on.

This apart, however, their views on politics were similar, both of them liberal, humane, much concerned with social issues, in favour of supporting the victimised and impoverished. In 1899, a year after their marriage, the Boer War broke out. Rudie, an entrenched anti-imperialist, made several highly critical speeches while the fighting was still going on, which took courage. Alice, who whole-heartedly supported him – 'a hateful, bitter war', she called it – accompanied him on his speaking engagements whenever she could, and was shocked when on more than one occasion the two of them were forced to leave the platform with undignified haste. Later as an MP, Rudie concerned himself in the House with questions regarding the treatment of Kaffirs in Natal and of coolies in the Chinese compounds in the Transvaal. Esteemed by the Prime Minister, Sir Henry Campbell-Bannerman, he was on good terms, too, with Winston Churchill, who when at the Home Office had appointed him to a departmental committee to look into the treatment of foreign aliens on their arrival from abroad. 'Winston ignorant,' Rudie noted in his diary, 'but as quick to pick up as a bit of hot sealing wax.'

Nine months after the general election of 1910, Rudie after only four years in Parliament decided to stand down, preferring to take life at a more leisurely pace and spend a greater proportion of his time at home reading, writing and messing about on the river. No doubt this was a disappointment to Alice, who had followed her husband's career with passionate interest, often going with him on tours of his Leicestershire constituency and coming up to Westminster to hear him speak. The self-indulgent, lackadaisical side of Rudie's nature irritated her, and his less than driving ambition was a constant affront to her firmly held New England work ethic.

There was, however, one overriding advantage in having him more at home: his absorbed interest in his young family, providing for their mother an unfailing claim on her husband's attention and for the four children an inexhaustible source of drama, excitement and inspiration.

2

Prospero and His Magic Isle

Bourne End in Buckinghamshire is situated in one of the loveliest parts of the Thames valley, in that country of lush, low-lying pasture and wooded hills that lies between Marlow and Cookham. Here the banks of the river were edged with weeping-willow, with poplar, chestnut, elm and beech, the trees parting at discreet intervals to reveal the landing-stages and boat-houses belonging to the big riverside villas, each with its hedged-off 'river garden' sloping down to the water. As a young man to whom rowing and the river were of paramount importance, Rudie had bought a large field beside the Thames where in 1895 he built his house, Fieldhead, a rambling pile of gable and red brick, its style cumbersomely combining arts-and-crafts with stockbroker's Tudor. Extensively enlarged when he married, it was converted into a family house by the addition of a spacious library for himself and a separate wing for children and nursemaids. Bourne End itself, once a tiny hamlet, had recently been extended by a sprawl of pinched little houses constructed for the workers in the nearby paper mill. There was a modern church immediately opposite the Fieldhead front gate, a Methodist chapel, and a line of featureless shops grandly named The Parade. On one side of the house was a row of squalid cottages, whose urchin inhabitants were to become a source of ambivalent fascination to the Lehmann children gazing down on them from the nursery windows; on the other side was Bourne End station and shunting-yard, only partially screened by a line of poplars; and stretching across the river the great iron railway bridge, effortlessly dwarfing the Victorian gothic of the Fieldhead boat-house.

But the beauty of Fieldhead lay not with the house but in the garden. It was a large garden full of well-stocked beds, pretty walks and arbours, and a number of magnificent trees. Leading away from the house was a wide lawn planted with patches of woodland; there was a walnut tree, chestnuts, a weeping beech, under and around which grew drifts of violets, primroses and daffodils in spring, in summer roses, clematis, peonies and honeysuckle. There were rose beds and herbaceous borders, a lavender walk, a lily-pool teeming with goldfish, an orchard full of apple and pear trees, and a kitchen garden with greenhouses and a red-brick wall for the growing of peaches, nectarines, grapes and figs, beyond which were the gardeners' sheds and the dog-kennels. A gate at the far side of the lawn led to the river garden, the boat-house and the river itself, with its fast-flowing current, weedy smell, and the constant slap-slap of water against the bank as the busy riverine traffic plied to and fro.

It was at Fieldhead that Rosamond was born in the midst of a thunderstorm at one o'clock on the snowy morning of 3 February 1901, the day after the old Queen's funeral.[1] Alice in bed received cables and letters from family and friends, their expressions of congratulation tempered by tactful statements of commiseration. 'I am disappointed for you & Rudie that it is a girl,' wrote one on hearing of the arrival of a second daughter, while another explained that she could not quite send '*congrats* for I am so sorry it was not a boy'.

Although neither Alice nor Rudie was much interested in religion, they liked to support the established Church and observe the conventions, and so the baby was baptised on 13 April in the neighbouring village of Wooburn Green. Rosamond Nina joined 2-year-old Helen in the nursery under the charge of Mrs Pottle: whose regime came to a sudden end when she was discovered one night by Alice lying asleep dead drunk with her head on the nursery table. The nursery maid, lovely Lizzie Hildreth, was then promoted, with a new maid, Lucy, to work under her. Lizzie adored the new baby. 'You're *my* baby,' she would tell her, and the little girl returned her love, a mutually satisfying

---

[1] In her autobiographical work, *The Swan in the Evening*, Rosamond mistakenly claims to have been born on the day of the funeral itself, but in fact the funeral was on 2 February.

relationship which lasted until Rosie was four when Lizzie, pregnant, left to marry her young man.

Rudie and Alice paid their children more attention than was customary among many of their class and generation, yet during their early years all four Lehmann children, Helen, Rosamond, Beatrix and John, were closer to the servants than to their parents. In the nursery, Lizzie was succeeded by Lucy, with nursemaid Julia. Downstairs were the cook, Mrs McCloud, known as Cloudie (whose name made Rosamond puzzle over the rhyme, 'One misty moisty morning / When cloudy was the weather'); she, too, left when Rosie was 4, her place taken by Mrs Almond; there was a kitchenmaid, a head housemaid, Seymour, who also acted as maid to Alice and tonged her hair, and an under-housemaid; James the butler presided over the pantry assisted by a footman and a boot-boy. Every year, for several months at a time, Cloudie's seamstress sister, the tiny, lively, witty Mrs Slezina, known as 'Dickie', moved into the sewing-room at the top of the house. Out of doors were Moodie the coachman, who looked after the carriage horses, Yankee and Bruno, and three gardeners under the head gardener, Goodman, who lived with his family at the lodge.

In many ways Fieldhead was a paradise for children, and Rosamond always looked back to it with nostalgia as a lost Eden, with its large, beautiful garden, kindly servants and much-loved animals. These included rabbits, a cat called Topaze, and at one time a pair of pigs known as Marmaduke and Millicent, but heading the hierarchy were always the dogs. Rudie was a great dog-lover, and his tall, athletic figure was a familiar sight in the neighbourhood loping over the water-meadows in the afternoons surrounded by his canine pack, a varying assortment of Great Danes, spaniels, mastiffs, St Bernards and Pekinese, on all of whom he doted and at whose deaths he wrote copiously in his diary, often composing valedictory verses in grief-stricken commemoration. Rosie, when a very small girl, used to ride round the lawn on the back of a St Bernard, and when old enough to have a dog of her own was given a black Pekinese, which she adored. The dogs' cemetery in the garden, with its neat rows of engraved headstones, was regarded as a holy spot.

The children in those days saw little of their parents, who were frequently away from home. Alice supervised the running of the household but was not involved much in nursery routine, while Rudie was now extremely busy, his many interests and occupations detaining him most of the week in London, where Alice often joined him at their small flat in Ashley Gardens. During the four years of his parliamentary career, he spent much time in his Leicestershire constituency, and while Parliament was in session he was in regular attendance at the House. The little girls in their pinafores, Helen, Rosie and the youngest, Beatrix, would watch him walk down the garden to the door leading to the station dressed in his parliamentary uniform of top hat and frock coat looking wonderfully handsome and distinguished. On Sundays large gatherings of relations and friends came down to Fieldhead, among the most frequent visitors E. V. Lucas, A. A. Milne, Owen Seaman, G. K. Chesterton, the Hammersleys, Alfred Noyes, and George and John Drinkwater. Even during the summer holidays Rudie had little time to spare, depositing his family at Felixstowe, Rottingdean or Westgate-on-Sea before returning to London, reappearing only briefly for weekends of fresh air and games on the beach.

It was not that Rudie was indifferent to his children – on the contrary he engaged with them far more than did many an Edwardian paterfamilias – but the demands on his time were numerous. There was *Punch* and his political career, both of which required heavy social as well as professional commitment; he was besides a governor of Highgate School, and a member of the Thames Conservancy board, and he still regularly coached both the Oxford and Cambridge crews, and the Harvard crew when it came over in 1906; he went more than once to Germany at the invitation of the Berliner Ruder Club, and in summer acted as umpire at the various regattas on the Thames.

An important change took place at the end of 1910 when Rosie was 9 and her father decided against standing again for Parliament. He had come to find increasingly lonely and tiring the long political tours in his constituency, when he was sometimes away from home for weeks at a time: 'a nightmare (for me) of tedium, re-iteration, and dulness,' he wrote after one such tour, when he had had to attend thirty consecutive meetings. He was worried, too, that he could no longer afford it: after resigning his candidature he recorded, 'I could not face the enormous expense of another contested election (*at least* £2000). Besides membership of Parliament entails an annual expense of some £700. . . .

19

Moreover I am separated for the greater part of every week during the session from home and family. On the whole a relief – though not without counterbalancing losses.'

Anxieties over expense had intensified since 1907. In April of that year Rudie discovered to his horror that a stockbroker friend, Frank Boyd May, to whom he had entrusted his investments, had failed and lost all the securities, worth over £90,000, that Rudie had left in his hands. Before any plan of recovery could be put into action, Boyd May shot himself, leaving Rudie to break the news to Alice only hours before she gave birth to their fourth child and only son on 2 June. However, by September he had managed to retrieve £42,000 paid by the dead man's insurers, which as he himself admitted, '[was] on the whole not an unsatisfactory termination of a hateful business'. Although their standard of living remained very much as before, both Lehmanns were severely shaken; even Rudie, always inclined to be irresponsible with money, grew noticeably more careful, while Alice became positively stingy, cutting back on household expenses with a ruthless relish and refusing to buy the children new clothes except as an absolute necessity. Her puritanical policy of make-do-and-mend, vigorously pursued from this time on, came to be much resented by her daughters. That summer for the first time Fieldhead was let, with the family variously dispersed, Alice, Beatrix and the baby with Mrs Hammersley at Abney, and Helen and Rosie with their father in the London flat, before they all gathered in a cottage belonging to Aunt Nina at Rottingdean.

With their father more at home, the children enjoyed a much greater measure of his time and attention, and it was he, not their mother, who played the starring role in their lives. When Alice returned to America after Beatrix's birth in 1903, the two toddlers, Helen and Rosie, enjoyed almost unlimited access to their father, bringing him his letters first thing in the morning, eating breakfast with him, playing in his company most of the afternoon. 'Helen and Rosamond are like two great blush-roses,' he wrote to his wife. 'They really are wonderful children for companionship and fun and jokes. They take up everything as quick as lightning and are a most appreciative little pair. . . . This afternoon they were glued to Mr Noyes who was reading "The Jumblies" to them with immense fervour and pathos.' He found them infinitely entertaining, and was proud of their cleverness and ravishing appearance. When apart, he and Alice reported on them to each other, and in his diary Rudie described, often at length, their activities and sayings. At the end of 1909 he wrote,

> I must add a few words about the children. Except for a few 'seasonable' colds they have all been very well, and they are all developing rapidly in their own different ways.
>
> Helen is all candour and frankness. She couldn't think wrong of any human being if she tried; and, as to saying anything even remotely untrue, it would kill her. Her sense of justice is tremendous. . . .
>
> Rosie is more reserved, but she too is the soul of honesty. She longs for affection and expands under its glow. . . .
>
> Peggy [Beatrix], being the youngest, has 'come on' more than her sisters. She has left babyhood behind. She is an impishly clever little kitten – whimsical, affectionate, witty and amusing. And full of quaint sayings. . . .
>
> John is in splendid condition, a great stout sturdy, big-framed thick limbed paragon of a boy, devoted to his mother.

The children idolised their tall, handsome papa and were fascinated by his interests, in which they longed to be allowed to join. And here Rudie, when in the mood, was generous, devising entertainments for them and including them as much as possible in his own pursuits. He played tennis and rode with them, and took them on long walks with the dogs. In spring there was the annual expedition to pick primroses in the fields and copses of Winchbottom; in May bluebell-gathering in the Hedsor woods; at the end of summer blackberrying across the river on Cock Marsh, children, father and dogs plunging into the brambles, each person provided with a chipped enamel mug to hold the fruit; in winter skating on the frozen flood-water that lay at the bottom of Winter Hill, and paper-chases along the valley. At Christmas Rudie filled the stockings and in costume as Santa Claus distributed presents. Particularly exciting for the children was their father's enthusiasm for motoring. Very early on Rudie began buying cars, one of his first a little Humberette, purchased in 1905, in which he steered himself round the garden. This was succeeded by, in turn, a Packard, a Decauville, a

Cadillac and a Humber, in all of which Rudie loved to drive his family sometimes as far as Oxford or Brighton, Alice in hat and veil, the children in motoring caps. One day there was an accident: when steeply descending Hedsor Hill, the brakes failed and the car crashed into a high bank and turned over, throwing out Helen and Rosamond and pinning Rudie under the steering wheel. Luckily no one was seriously hurt.

Highlights for the children were their trips to London with their father, who was always well primed by Alice beforehand with practical instructions of the kind which, she knew, might not naturally occur to him.

> Don't forget the *one* thing needful in regard to Beatrix or you will have to take her out in the middle of the show. . . . If they could get the 4.50 it would be better . . . however, if you can arrange to give them tea – or hot buns & cocoa at Paddington – *no milk unless boiled* – it doesn't matter if they don't leave before 5.50. Also don't forget to send them all into the ladies' room as soon as they arrive at Paddington.

A keen theatre-goer himself, Rudie enjoyed taking his children to the pantomime at Drury Lane, to Hengler's Circus, to *Hamlet* and *Peter Pan*. When Rosamond was 8 she was taken to see Maeterlinck's *The Bluebird*, an experience of enchantment that stayed with her all her life. 'I was absolutely spell-bound and bewitched by it. . . . The marvellous scenery, and the children walking into a garden full of bright lilies, which seemed to me like paradise, and one of them saying, "But there are no dead." And I remember thinking, "Yes, I know that, I know that." ' The following year, 1910, Rudie took the two older girls up to London to watch the funeral procession of Edward VII, having access as a Member of Parliament to a window on Whitehall along the designated route. The two girls were wearing straw hats dyed black, and in the heat of the day the dye began to run down their faces, giving them a grotesque appearance by which their father, usually so proud of his pretty daughters, was not amused. For them, the most moving part of the day had been the sight of Caesar, the king's wire-haired terrier, trotting along behind the gun-carriage bearing the coffin, and afterwards they were given a harrowing little book called *Where's Master?* by Caesar the

King's Dog. Rudie wrote a heartrending poem about the bereaved animal for *Punch*: 'Hail, Caesar, lonely little Caesar, hail! . . .'

The most seductive element of life at Fieldhead was the river running at the bottom of the garden, 'the wax-skinned reed-pierced olive river', which was to exert such a powerful hold on Rosamond's imagination. For Rudie it was the centre of his existence, and thus a matter of priority to introduce his children as soon as possible to water-borne pursuits. One by one he taught them to swim by means of a halter attached to a boathook, recording in July 1911 that, 'This is a great day in Rosie's calendar, for she swam, for the first time, across the river, I accompanying in the skiff.' All summer the children played in the water and on the river banks, tugging up weed, picking the yellow lilies, and throwing crusts to the bad-tempered, hissing swans. On warm evenings they tore off their clothes and dashed screaming into the chilly dark-brown depths while their parents watched sitting in deck-chairs under the chestnut tree, the dogs beside them panting at their feet. When he bought the Fieldhead property, Rudie had build an ornate boat-house, now presided over by Oliver the boatman, in which was kept a large collection of fastidiously maintained craft, 'the single sculler, the pair oar, the four, the eight, poised on rafters and stretchers, like gold-brown giant hibernating insects'; there were also a catamaran, a canoe and light skiff, a big punt, and a huge family boat known as the 'Water-Baby' complete with enormous picnic baskets. Rudie would row the children one at a time up as far as Cookham Lock or Marlow, and as soon as they could hold the oars he taught them to scull. 'Both Helen & Rosie are now expert little scullers and, what is more, they scull in very pretty form,' he recorded in 1910.

On fine summer weekends the river traffic was swelled by pleasure craft from Salter's Boatyard, their rails lined with trippers, dance music booming from the deck. In June and July was the regatta season, when Rudie, chugging up- and down-river in a motor launch, was much in demand as umpire for regattas at Henley, Marlow, Cookham and – a sadly amateurish affair – Bourne End. Colourful crowds cheered on the races, and by night fireworks and a procession of gaudily illuminated boats were watched by the children with the maids from a punt moored to the bank and discreetly decorated with a few Chinese lanterns. Far more serious were the preparations for the Oxford and Cambridge boat race in March, when one or other of the university crews came down to Bourne End to be coached, the children watching in awe as the godlike young men lowered themselves into their fragile shell, to be pushed out midstream by Oliver and Godden while their coach followed in the launch.

But the river could be treacherous. In 1905 there was a tragic accident when the son of a neighbour, Major Burnham's little boy, was drowned, and once when Rosie was peacefully fishing for minnows she saw something like a giant puffball just beyond the bathing raft that turned out to be a water-logged corpse. Like most children, she was both drawn to and repelled by the concept of death, hearing with a delicious *frisson* the news that Dora from the sweetshop had had her throat cut by her young man, shaken and appalled when the adored 6-year-old daughter of Moodie the coachman died of diphtheria.

Rudie was a fascinating father mainly because he himself was fascinated by his children, whom he regarded as comic little characters. He made use of them for his humorous articles and light verse for *Punch*, drawing on the events of the domestic day, retailed in an arch, sprightly style – a picnic, a seaside holiday, preparing for bedtime.

Come, Peggy, put your toys away; you needn't shake your head,
Your bear's been working overtime; he's panting for his bed.
He's turned a thousand somersaults, and now his head must ache;
It's cruelty to animals to keep the bear awake. . . .

Describing himself leaving the house to catch a train for London he writes, 'In the garden I found the junior members of the family gathered together to escort me. When they saw me they assumed an air of profound solemnity and doffed imaginary hats in my honour. . . . "Will his lordship deign to take my humble arm?" said Rosie . . .' Servants are given comic dialect and bumpkin names, such as Glumgold the gardener: 'So I found Glumgold in among the cabbages and . . . he said he'd be gingered if he knew . . . and that was the question they was a-going to arst of us . . .' The verse, too, is often ponderously jaunty, such as this one describing 'A May Picnic':

I can't explain, though I wish I could,

Why everything tasted twice as good
As it does at home in the cheerful gloom
Of the old familiar dining-room.
Every picnicky thing was there,
Including the girls and the son and heir,
A red-cheeked frivolous knife-and-fork crew
Who hadn't forgotten, oh joy, the cork-screw! . . .

Yet the children loved it and admired their father unreservedly for his great gifts.

Tall, handsome and moustachioed, Rudie was indeed a glamorous figure. He was always laughing at and with his children, his favourite among them his third daughter, Beatrix, known as Peggy, who was a natural comedian. But all four worshipped him, trusted his benevolence and generosity, his unwavering sense of justice. 'He was never one to blame or to pass a moral sentence,' Rosamond wrote. 'The principle of his life was a humorous benevolence combined with a philosophical scepticism about humanity.' He was looked up to as an unrivalled source of interest and entertainment, telling stories, operating the magic lantern on winter evenings, and constructing magical effects to enchant them. One of his best, described by Rosamond, was of fairies dancing on the lawn.

'Daddy, will the fairies come tonight?'

'No – no. I don't think so. Not tonight.'

'Oh, why not? Why won't they? Mightn't they? It's not windy, it's quite dancing weather. Couldn't you whistle for them?'

Presently he lays down his newspaper, extinguishes his cigarette, and says: 'Well, we'll see. Just keep a sharp look-out. And mind, not a sound. They're very shy.'

He has to go upstairs alone, we know, to whistle for them; our stomachs turn over with the suspense and silence. We have almost begun to give up hope when – ah! down they all come like birds in a white flutter. Faintly illumined by my father's lit dressing-room above us, they dance on the lawn, they swirl and caper in a jerky, spirited, rollicking, rather than a graceful fashion. Then, as suddenly, they all spring upwards and vanish. One night, one fairy is left behind. When my father returns we draw his attention to the white shape sprawling motionless on the lawn. She must be dead.

'No, no,' he says, somehow sounding tickled. 'Fairies don't die. She's just a bit winded by all that prancing. You'll see – she'll be gone in the morning.' And she is.

One day, during one of his absences in his constituency, Helen asks me sternly if I can keep a secret. While exploring in his dressing-room she has seen something behind the wardrobe. What? A long pole with lots of strings attached to it, and on the end of each string a cut-out white paper doll. I do not twig, and she has to explain: the fairies! We are stunned. But chiefly I remember our pact to conceal from him and everybody else our prying and our shock.

We must somehow manage never to mention the subject again. No doubt he thought, with relief, that we had outgrown the fairies: and in the instant of our enlightenment, we had.

All this was enormous fun, yet the children were subliminally aware that while their father, the Prospero of their magic isle, could when inclined be the provider of the most deliriously enjoyable entertainment, such entertainment lasted only as long as he himself found it amusing. It was impossible for him to take them seriously. Emotionally he was undemonstrative and remote, and his interest in his progeny quickly evaporated if they were tired or tiresome or in some way under the weather, when the charm and good humour would quickly transmute into a mood of stern displeasure. 'As far as we were concerned,' said John, 'we were there to amuse him. . . . There was a kind of affectionate detachment about his attitude which made it difficult for him to see our misdemeanours as anything but absurd and entertaining.' Rosamond, who idolised her father, recalled, 'Everybody adored him, and he was very beautiful, but he was rather narcissistic, and cold perhaps.' In many respects he seemed very distant, 'as all Edwardian fathers were. He was very irritated with us if we weren't looking wonderful and amusing him. After his death I found one or two letters saying how worried he was about me because I was so vulnerable . . . but he never told me. . . . I felt I was not loved, but I was loved.' It was necessary to be wary, too, of this genial man's sudden rages, which if rarely directed against the children were nonetheless terrifying to witness. The two most frequent targets were James the butler, whose occasional misjudgements would cause his employer to turn literally white with anger, and of course Alice. More than once Rosamond was the wretched witness of her father's shouting at her mother, which she later described as 'one of the deepest traumatic memories of my childhood', and from an early age she was aware that her mother was 'very unhappy sometimes, very, very. But she was totally loyal.'

Rudie inspired in all his children a love of literature, reading aloud to them from his own favourites, the great Victorians, particularly Dickens, and helping them choose books from the library shelves. 'I had the run of my father's library,' Rosamond remembered. 'I was allowed to read anything, and did.' There was a bookcase in the hall where he would put books sent him for review, and from these Rosamond, graduating from her beloved Hans Andersen, E. Nesbit and *Les Petites Filles Modèles*, began to discover some of the more adult novelists, tell-tale gaps in the shelves indicating which of these had been considered unsuitable by Alice and removed. The children looked with awe at their father as he sat cigarette in hand reading in his big armchair beside the fire, or at his desk worked on pieces for *Punch*, beneath the gaze of Wilkie Collins and Robert Browning painted by Great-Uncle Rudolf. As a very small girl Rosamond was once introduced to Georgina Hogarth, Dickens's sister-in-law, an immensely stout old lady in voluminous black with thin white corkscrew curls, who kindly presented both Helen and herself with a miniature attaché case. As soon as they could read, Rudie encouraged the children to write. In May 1905 he noted in his diary, 'The three girls became afflicted with literature this morning. I had to make composition-books for them & they then set to work, Helen to write a story, Rosie a poem, and Peggy a fairy-tale.'

There was no doubt in Rosamond's mind that her father was a great poet and that one day she would be a great poet, too. Having inherited his copious facility for versifying, from the age of 8 she poured out an unstoppable stream of verse dramas, epics, lyrics and long narrative poems, spending whole mornings sitting in the fork of the walnut tree in the garden equipped with pencil, exercise book and bag of caramels.

No sooner tapped than the facile fount began to flow. No trouble at all in those days. Heather, weather, brim, dim, bloom, gloom and off we go: every rhyme rhyming, every fairy flitting, stars glimmering, moon beaming, wind sighing, buds breaking – never stumped for a subject, never uneasy about a sentiment, each completed work as neat, tinkling and bland as a poem by Wilhelmina Stitch, and quite satisfactory to myself.

The best poems of Rosamond Nina Lehmann were inscribed in a fat book bound in pink moiré, one, 'The Home of a Fairy', winning a prize from *Little Folks* magazine. 'I couldn't think what I was doing, quite, but I realised I was doing what I was born for,' she recalled years later. 'And then instead of being unsure of myself and often in floods of tears and feeling a strange despair, I felt I knew who I was.' Everything she wrote was shown to Rudie for his approval. Her literary ability was the one sure hold on his attention, one which she possessed pre-eminently and which her sisters did not, and therefore even more highly valued. Years later she was to state:

> [My father] helped me to start trying to select words for their accuracy and weight, and directed my voracious appetite for reading, and encouraged me with unfailing sympathy and patience. . . . The recollection of that fostering atmosphere in which my childish talent budded has never disappeared.

Rudie's criticism was detailed and constructive, his manner courteous, and only occasionally did he hurt his daughter's feelings by bursting out laughing at some particularly fragrant fancy about flowers or elves or woodland glades. Once Rosamond made up to amuse her sisters a frivolous account of a storm-tossed trip to the Isle of Wight entitled 'The Adventurous Voyage' ('It was, I remember, a windy day / On which we started for Totland Bay; / And if you've learnt your geography right / You'll find that this bay's in the Isle of Wight. . . .'). Rudie was so impressed that he had her copy it out for him to read aloud at one of the *Punch* dinners, a fact that although gratifying made her slightly uneasy: 'This was trivial stuff. Why not have presented one of my serious works – *Poppy Fields*, for instance, or *Fairy Gold*?'

Much of Rosamond's childhood was spent in the guise of a princess or a fairy, queening it in the rock-garden as Amaranth Aurora or Beryl Diamond, despatching her attendant fairy, Starstripe, to do her magic bidding. She and Helen gave dramatic performances in the nursery, and when she was nine she wrote a play, typically entitled 'The Fairy Queen's Farewell to her Ladies', which featured Helen in the lead as the Queen, Rosie herself as a courtier in a silvery dress with wings, and Beatrix as 'Prince John' in knickerbockers and knitted cap. 'I don't think I've ever laughed so much,' Rudie observed.

Such extravagant bursts of creativity found a less appreciative response in Alice. Kind and conscientious, she was true to her New England Puritan roots in disapproving of emotional expression and believing that it was good for children to have their self-esteem regularly punctured. She saw her maternal role as one of correcting, controlling and putting down. 'My mother had many a subtle way of deflating vanity,' Rosamond recalled. Once when Rosie was boasting of her poetical prowess to a group of her parents' friends, Alice interrupted with, 'Rosie writes doggerel,' a remark which, said her daughter, 'went through me like a sword-thrust'. Rosamond rarely confided in her mother or went to her to be comforted if upset: it was to her father she would rush with her woes, if he were there. The few occasions on which Alice allowed herself to show tenderness were remembered and treasured: one was when Rosamond, suffering from bronchitis, woke up in the middle of the night to find her mother sitting by her bed, and another was when she was ill with tonsillitis and allowed to curl up on her mother's knee, 'in a lovely white armchair covered with pink roses. . . . Never so happy in my life.' Alice herself had fragile health, and her frequent aches and pains tended to make her irritable. Rosie once drew a picture of her mother striding through the garden hitting out with a tennis racquet, a balloon coming out of her mouth saying, 'I HATE everybody'.

Strict, scrupulously fair and an efficient administrator of the household, Alice had little sense of humour or fun. Very occasionally something would strike her as comic and she would throw back her head and laugh till the tears ran, but this was unusual. 'People have no business to expect happiness in this world,' she would say dourly. Unlike Rudie, she never played with her children, and when with their mother most of their time was spent carrying out obligations of one kind or

29

another. Alice caused great misery by enrolling Helen and Rosamond in the Girl Guides, and when they were still very young she would take them with her in the carriage to leave cards on the neighbours, the little girls dressed in white beaver hats tied round with a Liberty scarf. Once Rosamond was taken to call on G. K. Chesterton at nearby Beaconsfield. Chesterton, rumpled, stout and asthmatic, talked to her amiably, and picking up a photograph asked if she recognised who the young man in it was. She did not. 'That's me,' he said. 'You wouldn't know it, would you?' Generally, Rosie was nervous of strangers, terrified that they would look either angry or ugly; it was a family joke that whenever she was introduced to somebody new, she had to be pushed into the room, anxiously asking her mother, 'What will their face be like?' She herself was accustomed to her own lovely features being admired. 'Isn't she beautiful!' lady visitors would exclaim.

Alice accompanied the girls to children's parties, occasions which were not always an unqualified success. Rosamond was given a party for her third birthday at which the ventriloquist's doll frightened her so much she had to be carried screaming from the room. On another occasion at a birthday party at Cookham where the children ran races on the lawn, she disgusted her mother by sobbing uncontrollably after coming last in the egg-and-spoon race. Much more fun were the weekly dancing classes, and the noisy, jolly tea-parties with the children of the family who owned the local paper mill, whose indulgent parents allowed them to play romping games of hide-and-seek through the attics of their big house on the hill. But for Rosie the greatest excitement came from the parties at Taplow given for the neighbourhood children by the rich and elegant Lady Desborough, 'Queen of the "Souls"'. Beatrix disliked going there because she felt they were being patronised, but for Rosamond it was a fine thing to be invited to Taplow Court. Her first visit, aged 8, was to a children's fancy-dress ball, and the grandeur of the great house and the luxury of her surroundings made an indelible impression. On that occasion the little girl, insignificant and anonymous, glimpsed a young man she was never to forget, Julian Grenfell, eldest of the Desboroughs' glamorous sons, proud and beautiful in all his glory, 'striding through the room like a god'.

Rosamond was a sensitive, self-absorbed child, thin-skinned and easily reduced to tears. On the one hand she was encouraged to believe herself exceptional, her vanity fed by being allowed to show off to her parents' friends with her poetic compositions, accustomed to flattering remarks about her exceptional beauty – large brown eyes, pink-and-white skin, thick, wavy dark hair. But at the same time she was well aware that she came first with nobody. This resulted in an imbalance that grew increasingly marked and which was to have injurious consequences throughout her adult life. Ever anxious and insecure, as a small child she suffered from a fear of being abandoned: if her mother had gone out and was later than expected returning to the house, Rosie would be sure she had met with a fatal accident, and would work herself up into a welter of uncontrollable sobbing, terrified that she would be left alone and unprotected. Craving love and attention, she felt she was missing both by her position in the middle of the family. Her mother, she knew, loved best the youngest, John. Rudie's favourite, far and away, was Beatrix, 'my beloved Peggy', who so amused him with her quaint antics and sayings. It is Beatrix about whom he writes most in his diary, and after her Helen, the conscientious little helper, who as she grew older became a trustworthy companion, allowed on occasion to go by herself with her father to town; then John, the son and heir; and last and patently least, Rosamond, who so longed to be first.

Even as a child Rosamond was aware that her happiness depended almost entirely on her standing with her father, whom she both feared and adored. 'He was very beautiful, and all my life I was in love with him. As a result, I have always been fatally attracted to good-looking men who resemble him,' she recalled in old age. If he were pleased with her, she blossomed; if displeased or, worse, distracted or indifferent, she was miserable.

My constant worry was that I was unable to amuse him as much as did my sisters. To be a joke-maker, a clown, a laughter-provoking kind of child seemed obviously the way to win his heart; whereas I was the little girl that cried the most and must inevitably lose status. He really did hate my tears, and used to sigh at me and say, 'Rosie, Rosie, turn the tap off'; or exclaim impatiently to my mother: 'What in Heaven's name is the matter with this child?' The 'matter' was him, I suppose – I didn't know it, couldn't have explained the cloud of nameless woe that sometimes overcame me.

31

During childhood Rosamond was closest to her elder sister. Helen, as fair as Rosamond was dark, was equally beautiful, equally clever; she was, however, a very different, much less vulnerable character, unsentimental, practical, outspoken, a talented seamstress, good with animals and interested in domestic economy. She preferred the real world to the world of imagination, and could hardly wait to grow up, having little time for fairy fantasies and only reluctantly taking part in the high-flown romances that Rosie staged in the nursery. The third sister, auburn-haired Beatrix, on the other hand, was never happier than when performing; although not a beauty like the other two, she was a born actress and a natural clown. Beatrix had had a difficult start, with her mother effectively abandoning her when she was only a few weeks old, and she later suffered torments of jealousy after the birth of John, from which time onward Alice had no time for her at all. Known at her own request as 'Peggy', after a beloved pony, she enjoyed dressing up and was much given to elaborate hoaxes. She was a tomboy who lived a vivid fantasy life on her own, running a make-believe shop in the laurels and setting up a 'field kitchen' in the Lovers' Walk. Where Rosamond was timid and preferred to stay within the confines of the garden, happily playing fairies in a disused dog-kennel festooned in pink gauze, Beatrix roamed the back lanes of Bourne End in the self-created role of Lone Scout, wearing a personally designed uniform fastened with a stiff leather belt stuck with knives, ropes and whistles. Her preferred playmates were the poor children from the slum cottages, with whom, unlike Rosamond who found them menacing and alien, she was on the easiest terms of familiarity.

John, born on 2 June 1907, the long-awaited boy, was doted on by his parents and spoilt by everyone, his blond curls and blue eyes clucked and cooed over as his nurse Julia pushed him in his pram, 'an infant version of Mithras, Sun God, rayed round by the layers of a broderie anglaise sun hat, tied in a dashing bow beneath his chins'. John for his part worshipped his sisters, always longing to join in and ready fervently to admire whatever they did, while they, Rosamond and Beatrix in particular, taking advantage of their seniority, teased him mercilessly.

When the time came, John was sent away to prep school, to Summer Fields on the outskirts of Oxford, but Rudie had a low opinion of school for girls and insisted on his daughters being educated at home, building a brick pavilion in the garden designed by the architect George Drinkwater to act as a schoolroom. A Froebel teacher, Miss Winifred Davis, blonde and willowy, was hired to teach a class which included Helen and half a dozen children from the village, as well as Imogen Grenfell who rode over on her pony from Taplow. The main room, lit by popping gas chandeliers hanging from the rafters, was equipped with desks and divided by a curtain, babies one side, older children the other, with a little room at the back where French lessons were given. The school opened in the first week of October 1905, and from the first day Rosamond, aged 4, insisted on joining in. 'I was brilliantly clever in some ways. I learnt to read in a flash, as if I'd always known how to read and was recognising something I'd already known. But sums, oh dear. Despair, despair. It was a family joke that I'd come in sobbing, "Sums are so uneasy, so uneasy". . . .' Unfortunately at the end of the first year, nice Miss Davis left to get married. She was mourned by the children, less so by Alice, who claimed to have found the young woman common. Her successor was a Belgian, Mlle Maria Jaquemin, 'an absolute fiend', with a sallow complexion and a decided antipathy to children. Bad-tempered and vindictive, Mlle Jaquemin had many a method of causing dread. She made the girls sew buttons on the sleeves of their overalls so that she could hear the click when they put their elbows on the table, and she was quick to hand out 'punitions', even to Rosie who was her favourite, her *'petite fille douce et bien élevée'*. It used to make their father laugh to overhear the girls at her mercy. Helen had a very long neck, and to annoy she would stretch it up as far as she could. *'Mon Dieu, Hélène, n'allonges pas ton cou comme ça,'* Mademoiselle would say. Then turning to Rosie, *'Voilà une petite fille qui a un joli cou!'*

They all loathed their lessons with Mademoiselle, and it was a happy day when in 1914 she went back to Belgium for her annual holiday and found herself unable to return. After a long interval a letter arrived describing the terrible time she and her family were having, a letter so harrowing that Alice burst into tears. But Helen, speaking for them all, muttered darkly, 'Serve her right!'

With Mademoiselle's departure, schooldays were much happier, the school itself growing in size until there were twenty-five pupils. All the children sat the Cambridge Junior and Senior examinations, which Helen and Rosie passed with first-class honours. Rosie was taught the piano, first by Mademoiselle, then by William Spencer, father of the painter Stanley Spencer, who was the organist at Hedsor Church. She was very musical, unlike Beatrix, who was uninterested, and Helen and John, who, like their mother, were tone deaf.

When the Pavilion school broke up for Easter and the summer, the Lehmanns usually went away. Rosamond's first holiday at 18 months old had been three weeks at St Peter Port on Guernsey, where all she remembered was her outrage at being picked up and kissed by the proprietor of the hotel, Mlle Sidonie, a child-loving spinster with a prickly moustache. Her first taste of abroad was in April 1912 when the three girls with their parents went to Paris for ten days, and in August the following year the whole family went to Château d'Oex in Switzerland.

In between, in August 1912, Rosamond, aged 11, accompanied her mother to America, where Alice went every three years to visit her family. They sailed from Southampton on RMS *Oceanic*, together with Violet Hammersley, who grew very excited at discovering among the crew several survivors from *Titanic* which had famously foundered in April that year. Having left Mrs Hammersley in New York, the Lehmanns arrived at Northwood, New Hampshire, a pretty little town where just before the turn of the century Helen Davis had bought Cliffhead, an old farm property at the foot of what was known locally as 'the Mountain'. This she had restored, renovating the old farmhouse and buildings, and constructing a 'summer house' beside it. The countryside of lakes and wooded hills was peaceful and Rosie spent contented days learning the zither from Mrs Davis's black cook and picking blueberries with her cousins. After several visits to friends and relations in the vicinity they sailed home from Boston at the beginning of September.

By far the most popular destination with all of them was the Isle of Wight, well known to Rudie from boyhood holidays. The first visit as a family was in 1910, to Totland Bay, a newly built village on the west coast of the Island, made up of houses fronted by beds of begonias where boys and girls in white flannels played tennis on smoothly mown lawns. It was the perfect resort for children, '[although] I was pleased to discover', Rosamond wrote later, 'that Totland was not so named, as I had feared, because of its amenities for tots and toddlers. It is very ancient, and means a sacred or holy piece of ground.' The undertaking was such a success that it was decided to make it an annual event, one which was greatly looked forward to: the journey by train from Bourne End to Lymington in Hampshire; the crossing of the Solent in the little paddle-steamer, then disembarking on the pier in Totland Bay and walking up the path to their lodgings, a comfortable boarding-house kept by a Mrs Scovell. In the mornings they swam and went shrimping among the rock pools and played on the sands, the girls in their brown holland frocks tucked into their knickers, long hair tied behind; in the afternoons they picnicked on the heathery downs or chipped off chunks of the variously coloured cliff at Alum Bay, taking the pieces back in jam jars to be ground down into sand. There were also expeditions by coach and four to Carisbrooke Castle and Osborne House, and explorations of the ruined Napoleonic forts from which you could gaze out at the Needles, at the sailing yachts and the huge grey Union Castle liners steaming slowly towards Southampton. At night could be seen on the mainland the lights along Bournemouth Pier.

For Rosamond the Island was an enchanted place which took hold of her imagination and remained with her always. In a broadcast made in 1946 she said of the holidays there, 'They were . . . as different from ordinary life as if we'd slipped through a gap onto another plane.'

When war broke out on 4 August 1914 the family were on the Island. A plan to send Helen and Rosamond to relations in Germany for the summer had been abandoned on account of the international situation, to the disappointment of the elder sister, the wild relief of the unadventurous younger. 'That's how I saw the outbreak of World War One – as a personal and miraculous reprieve. At the same time I was aware that this was wrong and shameful and prayed to become less cowardly and selfish,' Rosamond wrote. 'Of the world crisis, I remember only that sudden emptiness of the beach and the expression on my father's face as he sat reading the papers all day, and his saying to my mother: "It'll be over by Christmas."' Although most of the holiday-makers quickly departed, the Lehmanns stayed on. The children were excited by the sudden change, by barbed wire sprouting everywhere, soldiers in possession of the forts, and rumours of spies: Beatrix and John spent an entire afternoon shadowing across the downs a tall man in a straw boater, who turned out to be a literary gentleman walking harmlessly over from Freshwater to visit their parents for tea. At least

35

once a day somebody claimed to have sighted the periscope of a German submarine in the Solent. The family's German nursemaid, Maria Hasewitz, had to be taken by Rudie to the police station at Totland Bay to be registered as an enemy alien, and when disembarking at Lymington on the journey home they were all asked to state their nationalities, 'American,' said Alice, 'and was all but arrested for her pains'.

The war heralded the end of that sheltered Edwardian world which was all that the Lehmann children had known. For Rosamond it saw also the end of childhood, and the onset of a melancholy and emotionally turbulent adolescence. 'I was being shocked out of the enclosed, boundlessly self-centred state of childhood into a world with proportions; and I had no sense of proportion and no idea how to acquire it,' she wrote later. Even her writing failed her. Proud of having had a poem printed in *The Cornhill*, she continued relentlessly to submit her compositions until a tactful letter from the editor requested her to stop. 'That was a great blow to my vanity.' Then there were the normal disorders inseparable from that difficult age.

In my teens I nearly always felt most unwell.... That was one disgraceful secret; the other was the ghastly though thrilling fact of being always in love. I would have liked to lie all day in a hot bath, and stay safe in bed eating enormous meals brought to me, lovingly, on trays, reading novels and dreaming of the loved one of the moment. Instead I had to work for examinations and take exercise and generally pretend to be what I appeared to be: a cheerful, lucky, healthy, well-grown girl preparing to come to grips with life.

Life at that time was grim for everyone, not only for growing girls.

The bathwater was always cold, there was not much food, and everybody was totally miserable and it seemed interminable, and everybody was being killed. All my little friends' brothers, and my father's younger friends; and he was in total total despair. You couldn't have imagined this war. It was the end of all hopes.... [My parents] were very deeply-feeling people and the whole thing was an agony to them.

36

At first, however, the changes to the routine at Fieldhead were relatively minor, the children continuing very much as before, going up to London for the theatre, taking their summer holidays on the Isle of Wight, working in the Pavilion during term. But gradually international events began to impinge. A family of Belgian refugees came to stay for a few days, followed by a series of evacuees from London. The lawn sloping down to the river was ploughed up for potatoes. Alice went to work at the hospital organised by Lady Astor for the Canadian Red Cross at nearby Cliveden, while Rosamond helped at Abney which had been turned into a home for blinded officers, and Rudie joined the 3rd Voluntary Battalion of the Oxford & Bucks Light Infantry. As time passed and reports from the front grew more terrible, there were few who were unaffected. In the summer of 1915 came the shocking news of the death, within a few weeks of each other, of two of the Grenfell boys: their father, Lord Desborough, came over to see Rudie bringing with him Oliver Lodge's famous book about communicating with his dead son, a subject which Rudie, although appalled by his friend's tragedy, found distasteful in the extreme.

But despite hardships and disruption, the children's schooling continued uninterrupted, and Alice, who was a firm believer in higher education for girls, encouraged both Helen and Rosamond to try for Cambridge. Helen would much have preferred a London season, but it was wartime and there was no season, the very idea of which in any case Alice despised, and so in 1917 to Cambridge she went, her sister to follow a couple of years later. The vicar tutored Rosie for her university entrance in Latin and Greek, which she loved, and Algebra and Geometry, which she hated. On these papers, sitting for her 'Little-Go' in the pavilion with the vicar invigilating, she only just scraped through, but because she had done so well in other subjects she was awarded a scholarship.

Towards the end of the war, a new anxiety took root at Fieldhead regarding the deterioration of Rudie's health. He had been feeling vaguely out of sorts for some time, but put his lack of vigour down to exhaustion caused by the exercises and long route marches undertaken with the Volunteers. Apart from an occasional attack of gout, Rudie had always been extremely fit, but from the middle of 1917 he began to suffer from a mysterious shaking and an alarming loss of weight. Several Harley

Street specialists were consulted, although it was months before the correct diagnosis was made, of Parkinson's Disease. By the end of the war he was showing such alarming signs of mental disturbance that Alice reluctantly committed him to a nursing home, where he grew so agitated that he had to be discharged. From then on Alice dedicated herself to his care, determined that he should be nursed at home and never again be taken away. She was ready to structure her life round the demands of the disease, and she expected her daughters when at home to do the same. Over the following years, as the illness took hold and Rudie grew weaker and more incapable, their domestic lives revolved around their father's armchair, as they were required to feed him, read to him, push him round the garden in a bath-chair, and – particularly disturbing to Rosamond – escort him to the lavatory. Except for visits from neighbours, all entertaining ceased, which was hard for girls of their age. 'All the weekends of rowing friends and literary friends ended and we never saw anybody. It was a very, very sad time.'

On Armistice Day, Rosamond at 17 was at home after taking her scholarship examination for Cambridge. 'I went for a long, long walk over the hills by myself, thinking, Well, what do I do next? As *all* the young men have been killed, I shall never marry. There'll be nobody left to marry. I remember that quite acutely.'

3

The Castle of Otranto

In October 1919 Rosamond went up to Cambridge to join Helen at Girton. Although a Cambridge man himself, Rudie had been strongly opposed to his girls going to university: typically Victorian in his attitude to women, he would have preferred them to grow up like Trollopian heroines, spirited, pretty, filial, virtuous, retiring and domesticated; that they should wish for independence and perhaps even careers of their own did not fit the picture. Alice, in contrast, had always been determined that her daughters should enjoy the benefits of higher education. Before he fell ill she had persuaded her husband to go with her to meet the Mistress of Girton, a handsome woman of strong character and caustic wit who had made a great fuss of Rudie, and thus his objections reluctantly were overcome. Rosamond had won a scholarship worth £20 (the annual fee was £150), although this she was asked to waive on account of her family's well-to-do circumstances. In the weeks before her departure from Fieldhead she felt both excited and apprehensive. Reports sent home by her elder sister had on the whole been encouraging, although even the self-possessed Helen admitted she found herself considerably less experienced than her contemporaries. 'I am sure one gets more out of college life by being older – it isn't just the work. I feel I ought to know more about things generally!' she had written. Nothing, however, prepared Rosamond for the shock of what awaited her.

Girton College was founded in 1869, chief among its founders the pioneering Emily Davies, whose portrait by Rudolf Lehmann hung in pride of place. A vast, gloomy edifice set on fifty acres of land, Girton is grand in scale and massive in design, its handsome chapel, enormous dining-hall, turrets, towers, gate-house and gothic arches an eccentric mix of Norman, Tudor and Scottish baronial. Referred to by the wits as 'the Castle of Otranto', it stood isolated in a bleak stretch of countryside in the middle of fields three miles outside the centre of Cambridge, the village of Girton then undeveloped except for a few raw new houses opposite the college gates. In 1919, the first year after the war, there was an enormous increase in new students, the number of undergraduates in residence at the university having risen from 235 in 1916 to nearly 4,000. In common with the other colleges, Girton was bursting at the seams, as its student population swelled to an unprecedented 180. Entering this bewildering conglomeration of cloisters, courtyards and a maze of dimly lit, linoleum corridors teeming with life, Rosamond was appalled by the bustle and noise: everywhere girls were streaming in and out of their rooms, animatedly greeting each other, all seeming to know exactly where to go and what they were doing. With her newly adult appearance – her long hair was now worn up, parted in the middle and arranged in 'ear-phones' – she looked considerably more composed than she felt. But in truth, never having been away from her family before, nervous and insecure, Rosamond felt utterly lost. 'Coming straight from a very sheltered if liberally-minded home, equipped with an unbridled love of English literature, plus a moral outlook based on excessive shyness plus a high-minded romanticism plus total worldly ignorance, I was dazed by my first taste of community life and floored by the most elementary practical problems of my independence.' Apart from Helen, she knew no one, while all the other first-years seemed to have plenty of chums made during their years at Cheltenham, Wycombe Abbey and St Paul's. 'They thought I was queer as a coot – which I was,' she recalled. She was convinced she would never find her way anywhere, worried that she would never even discover the location of Hall in order to get something to eat. She was, she felt, living in a nightmare.

Although the war was over, provisions were scarce and conditions comfortless in the extreme. On the edge of the flat fen country, Cambridge in the winter months is damp and bitingly cold. The coal supply, already strictly rationed, had recently been cut, and first thing in the morning the contents of water jugs and ink-pots were regularly frozen over. The college itself was still in a comparatively primitive state of development: the original earth sanitation had only just been replaced by water closets, and not till the following year were gas and oil lamps made redundant by the installation of electricity. (In her second term, January 1920, Rosamond reported excitedly to her mother, 'We have a scuttle of coal a day!! – and electric light!!!') Girls were allowed only two baths a week, and the swimming-bath had been empty for five years because there was no coal to warm it. As Girton lay outside the city boundary, it had not only a separate electricity system but was responsible for its own fire safety precautions, enrolling a fire brigade every year from the student body. (For this Helen in an access of enthusiasm had signed up in her first term. 'Alas! when I joined I didn't realise that I should have to be down at 7.30 four mornings in the week to practise hosing and roping.')

There was no public transport into town, but the college laid on a motor-bus departing after breakfast and returning just before lunch, with taxis, provided by a legacy, to bring girls back when afternoon lectures were over. Girls could walk or bicycle into town, but hats and gloves had to be worn, and it was not permitted to carry parcels: books from Heffers' or meringues from Matthews' had to be delivered to the college direct from the shop. Dinner, the only formal meal of the day, was at 7 p.m., for which afternoon dress was required. Each student was allocated a small bedroom and sitting-room – the two divided sometimes only by a curtain – furnished with a desk and chair, a narrow iron bedstead and strip of carpet, as well as a coal scuttle, fire-irons and a copper kettle. Before breakfast a maid, known as a 'gyp', brought a can of hot water and later laid the fire. Every wing had a service-room with a gas-ring for making hot drinks.

Gradually with Helen's help ('I simply don't know *what* I should have done without Helen the first few days! It's been everything having her here'), Rosamond began to find her feet and take an interest in arranging her living quarters. Her rooms were really quite nice, she told her mother, 'fairly big, with (Thank heaven!) neutral-coloured walls'. Even the alarming, anonymous mob was beginning to look less alarming, its individual members turning out to be perfectly friendly, if not notably repossessing. 'Spotty complexions & greasy hair, and cotton blouses buttoned right up to their fat necks, & hats on the back of their heads, & oh! such unspeakable figures! Some, of course, are good-looking, & clever & nice (including myself) but I've only noticed two really pretty ones.' Of the fifty 'freshers', it was obvious that few came from a background as properous as her own. Jobs were scarce in the post-war years, and there was a large population of unsupported women desperate for qualifications which would equip them for work more highly paid than the merely clerical. The two women's colleges, Newnham and Girton, were thus in the main catering for the daughters of middle-class families of modest means hoping to become teachers, not a section of society likely to appeal to the refined Miss Lehmann.

Social life in college revolved round cocoa parties, known as 'jugs', the name deriving from the little white jug of milk allotted to each young woman for the making of a hot drink after the evening quiet period between 8 and 9 p.m. It was during these firelit gatherings over hot chocolate and cigarettes that it was customary, after a decent period of acquaintance, for girls to ask each other, 'May I prop?', in other words, 'May I propose that I use your Christian name?' Rosamond sometimes attended up to three 'jugs' in an evening, with the result that she spent much of the term in a state of chronic biliousness. More ambitious were the all-girl dances, and also the occasional private supper-parties, for which the hostess would provide in her sitting-room as many courses as she could contrive with only the gas-ring to cook on; however eccentric the results, they were much appreciated as a supplement to endless crumpets toasted over the fire and the appalling food served in Hall. 'I went to a supper-party in a girl's room the other night, & had haggis for the first time in my life!' Rosamond wrote to her mother during her second term. 'How good it is! It was followed by scrambled eggs, galantine, peaches & *lashions* of clotted cream, – raisins, nuts, coffee. After which, somewhat disturbed dreams, as you may imagine.'

Because of the coal shortage, girls were expected to share their fires, a practice which fostered a friendship which, although it lasted her university career, Rosamond found exasperating. 'Oh, the bitterness of having to share one's fire with the object of one's hatred! There is a girl here, Dorothy Torlesse by name, my next door neighbour . . . [who] is in my room all day, beginning at 7 a.m. & I get rid of her at, roughly, 10 o'clock. . . . She is what's known as a forward fresher, and not popular with the other years, so you can imagine I don't like to be seen about with her.' Dorothy, jealous and possessive, would not be shaken off, although Rosamond much preferred the company of others, such as Margery Runciman, daughter of the Liberal MP and shipping magnate, Sir Walter Runciman, and pretty Rosamond Wethered, 'a bit of a monkey . . . full of spirits and talk', daughter of Rudie's old rowing friend, Frank Wethered. She became fondest of all of Grizel Buchanan, a lively, eccentric girl, daughter of a distinguished senior civil servant and recently head girl of St Paul's. With her mass of red-gold hair, glowing good looks and larky high spirits she fascinated Rosamond, while the tomboyish Grizel, whose party trick was standing on her head while downing a mug of cocoa, was impressed by her new friend's cool beauty and air of grave sophistication. The two of them quickly became close. 'We had a very emotional friendship,' said Rosamond: Grizel was 'a temptation' to everyone, 'like a particularly heady wine'.

Unlike Helen who was reading French and Italian, Rosamond had only ever wanted to read English. But although she was allowed to sit the English Tripos and be classed, she would be denied a degree as women were not yet admitted to full membership of the university. The Mistress of Girton, Katharine Jex-Blake, was a member of a remarkable academic family (her father had been Dean of Wells Cathedral and Headmaster of Rugby, her sister was currently Principal of Lady Margaret Hall, Oxford), and she had taken an active part in fighting for the feminist cause. Public opinion about female emancipation had been profoundly affected by the war, and in 1919, the year in which Girton celebrated its Jubilee, there was a buoyant feeling in the air that this time when the matter was put before the Senate the women of Newnham and Girton would at last be accepted on the same terms as men. Oxford had just relented: surely Cambridge would do the same? But the motion was defeated. The *Cambridge Review* ran an article expressing the views of the masculine majority. 'Not that we wish in any way to appear unchivalrous or to minimize the good work often done by women students; but "so long as the sun and moon endureth" Cambridge should remain a society for *men*.'[1]

---

[1] And a society for men it remained until 1948, the last university in England to deny women a full degree.

The English Tripos was divided into two parts: Section A, which covered English literature, medieval and modern; and Section B, concentrating on early history and literature, predominantly Anglo-Saxon. Rosamond's tutors were Miss Murray, sister of the distinguished classicist, Gilbert Murray, 'a real old battle-axe whom I couldn't bear', and the lively, young Miss Tomkins. The work was demanding but '*most congenial*', and the college library a peaceful place in which to study. The lecture list that first term was a tempting one – 'Prof. Coulton is giving a series on "Life & Literature in the Middle Ages" . . . Prof. Downs began a course at Christ's to-day on "The Victorian Novelists" – ripping' – but women were allowed to attend only by courtesy of each individual lecturer. It was understood that they were there on sufferance and must sit on one side of the room, well away from the men (among whom, also reading for the English Tripos at the same time as Rosamond, were J. B. Priestley, Basil Willey and F. R. Leavis). The presence of women was never formally acknowledged, and even such a chivalrous personality as Sir Arthur Quiller-Couch, who was fond of the ladies and had something of a roving eye, always began his lectures, 'Gentlemen . . .'

Quiller-Couch, or 'Q' as he was universally known, Edward VII Professor of English, made an impression on Rosamond, not least, perhaps, because of literary and political leanings very similar to those of her father. 'I've got to read aloud my essay to "Q." next Tuesday,' she wrote to her mother towards the end of her first term. 'Oooo-oo-er! Just imagine it.' A courtly gentleman of the old style and a life-time Liberal, he was celebrated as a novelist, a critic, and as the compiler of an anthology, *The Oxford Book of English Verse*, to be found on the shelves of almost every cultivated home in the land. His enthusiastic promotion of literature as a subject to be enjoyed by normal human beings did much to raise the reputation of the newly established English Honours School, and he encouraged his pupils to write, impressing on them that 'Literature is not a mere science, to be studied; but an art, to be practised'. His lectures, urbane, amusing, sometimes sentimental, were extremely popular, a marked contrast in manner to the tedious droning of many of the drier dons. He was gregarious and enjoyed undergraduate society, particularly that of the prettier women students, to whom his manner was kindly and avuncular. Once during a lecture naughty

Pamela Paget from Newnham as a dare held out a cigarette, and 'Q', without a pause in what he was saying, bowed and lit it. Rosamond, with her dark-haired, statuesque beauty, became a favourite and was invited to a number of gatherings in his rooms at Jesus, where dressed like a country squire he strolled about dispensing wisdom while puffing on his pipe. 'Q''s parties were such funny affairs, she reported home.

> Crowds of long-haired 'literary blokes' come, & sit in corners & glower. Coffee is handed round, & chocolate biscuits; and people sing & play; & then we read obscure Irish drama, & finish up by dancing. None of the men will dance, & the girls revolve in bored couples. 'Q' asked me to 'act as hostess' ... [he] is a darling: he danced with me – round & round in circles till I wanted to lean against the wall & groan.

Immediately after the war Cambridge was a feverish, excitable, unorthodox place, full of older men returned from the trenches as well as pink-cheeked boys straight out of school. The post-war dance-craze was in full swing: Rosamond's first summer, 1920, saw the revival of May Week, with its luncheon parties, river picnics and college balls; there were weekly dance clubs like the Quinquaginta with its undergraduate jazz band, and several new dancing societies had recently been licensed by the proctors, to the expression of sour disapproval in many a senior common room. One don, interviewed in the *Evening Standard*, complained of the deleterious influence of women students, who, he said, had wormed their way in and done nothing except

> start a lot of dances. Before the war, the undergraduates would have nothing to do with them. They were fresh from school, you see, of that sound, honest age when boys have a healthy contempt for their sisters. . . . But now they go out for their elevens with the girls; go off to lunch with them. There are thés dansants at the Liberal Club and the Masonic Hall. You wouldn't believe it was the same place.

Under Helen's wing, Rosamond began going to dances, not only with undergraduates but with young naval officers whom the sisters met through a sailor cousin of theirs, one of a group currently up at Cambridge whose education had been interrupted by the sudden demands of active service. Helen remarked appreciatively on the atmosphere of jolly gaiety created by the navy, 'who seem to have an idea that they are on a jaunt and must have tea-parties & dances every day of the week'. Frances Marshall, a pretty, dark-haired girl from Newnham, a lively regular at the Quinquaginta, was impressed by Rosamond's deportment on the dance floor: she was taller than most of the girls, her manner both stately and demure, and she never allowed her partners to grip her in a clinch, as did some of the other, more liberated young women. The grander occasions were often preceded by dinner in one of the men's colleges, and in Rosamond's view, 'The Cambridge dances couldn't be beaten from the point of view of purely enjoying oneself'. There was a dance at St John's at which two of the royal princes were present, the future Duke of Gloucester (Prince Henry) and the future George VI (Prince Albert). 'I sat next to Pr. Henry after one dance, & listened to his astonishing lack of conversation. It's really awfully sad: I believe he's so stupid as to be really deficient. Albert is more intelligent, & a beautiful dancer.'

For the girls the possibilities of such a heady social life were limited by the rules of chaperonage. 'The amount of chaperonage was absolutely fantastic,' Rosamond recalled. Women were not allowed to visit men other than brothers in their colleges, although they could entertain them in their own rooms as long as there was at least one other girl present. In May 1919 there had been a new concession permitting a woman on her own to meet a man in a teashop, although it was still not possible for her to go on the river unaccompanied, unless with a brother or authorised fiancé. The following year the rules were further relaxed so that provided a tutor had given leave mixed-sex parties without chaperones could go on the river in punts or boats, although not in canoes. For pretty girls like Rosamond the cruellest restriction was that governing the time of return to college at night: curfew was 11 p.m., although an exeat till midnight could sometimes be obtained for a special occasion. To her mother she wailed, 'It's agony having to leave [a party] before twelve, when one's just getting properly settled into it. . . . That dance I'm going to on the 11th doesn't begin till 9.30, & I shall have to leave at 11.40 to be back here at 12. Oh, that hateful rule! I could cry. Only 2 hours dancing!' Resented through the rules were, there was no question of rebellion. Rosamond was never not back in time – 'That would have been unthinkable' – and she was stung when Alice once accused her of forward behaviour. 'I was thoroughly startled to hear you imagined I went to men's rooms unchaperoned. *No*, I do NOT, & feel most insulted.'

As a species Girton girls were considered by the more sophisticated undergraduates to be dim, dowdy creatures, beneath the notice of any smart young man. 'The grand people, older men like Lance Sieveking and Joe Ackerley, wouldn't have looked at Girton girls. We were supposed to be extremely infra dig.' Rosamond, however, with her tall, slender figure, her lovely face and almond-shaped eyes, was hardly typical of the bluestocking image, and she soon became aware of the attention she was attracting from the opposite sex. Men stared at her in the street and at lectures, and sometimes a note would be dropped at her feet, saying 'Meet me', which she never dared do. 'It was borne in on me that I had this tremendous effect on young men, and as a result was in a state of constant self-consciousness.' All this was extremely exciting, but also alarming, and recently emerged from the sheltered atmosphere of Fieldhead she was not best equipped to deal with it. At 18 when she came up to Cambridge her head was full of naive imaginings and she was completely ignorant about men and about sex. 'To have a sensible view of the opposite sex was something that was totally lacking in my day among my class of girls, and it caused a great deal of unnecessary suffering and disillusionment. Although cynicism is the worst possible view of the world, the romantic view is almost equally dangerous – and I had that in abundance.' The young men she met in her first year, like her regular 'boyfriend', Hugh Gordon, were too young to engage her emotionally, while the older men, the godlike figures in blazers and boaters whom she saw lounging by the river or walking arm in arm along King's Parade, were tantalisingly out of reach. The intensity of some male friendships, with their excluding, sometimes hostile vibrations, intrigued and vaguely troubled her, although she was unable to define the cause of her disquiet.

Cambridge, more even than Oxford, was a very masculine society. Not only had Oxford accepted the equal status of women, but Oxford undergraduates had easy access to London where they could keep company with sisters and girlfriends, go to parties and night-clubs, and (if they so wished) be back before the midnight curfew. Cambridge, still a country market town, lacked this metropolitan veneer, it was in any case further from the capital, and the nature of its undergraduate population was noticeably less sophisticated and more austere. The aesthete dandy element so prominent at that period at Oxford, personified by Harold Acton, Brian Howard, Robert Byron and Evelyn Waugh, was much less evident at Cambridge, where homosexual sections of society preferred in the main to express themselves with discretion and restraint, and often in secrecy, rather than in the public posturing popular among the more flamboyant members of the older institution. That secret élite, the 'Apostles', almost a Cambridge branch of Bloomsbury, which numbered among its members Lytton Strachey and Maynard Keynes, promoted the theory that the love of man for man was superior, morally and aesthetically, to that of man for woman, a theory summed up in one of the Apostolic private phrases, 'the Higher Sodomy'.

In letters home to her parents, Rosamond wrote guardedly about her social life ('Next week I'm going to 2 dances,' she told her brother John. 'Don't tell Mum!'), but with open enthusiasm about the various clubs and societies of which she became a member. Helen, considered by many a purer, more classical beauty than her sister, had had a great success in a production of Purcell's *Fairy Queen*, for which Margy Runciman's brother, Leslie, played in the orchestra. Lacking Helen's confidence, Rosamond never went on the stage but she took an enthusiastic part in the Girton English Club, of which she was secretary, as well as in an intercollegiate debating society and in the Modern Drama Club, which met, heavily chaperoned, in the rooms of a Mr Kerr at King's, for reading and acting contemporary plays. To her father she wrote about her term work, the poetry she was reading and with details about new publications. 'Do', she urged him, 'try to get hold of "The London Mercury", a new periodical edited by J. C. Squire. The first number has just appeared, & is quite excellent, – but I don't suppose it will keep it up. There are hitherto unpublished poems by Rupert Brooke & Thomas Hardy.' She proudly sent him her own literary efforts, poems which were published in *The Granta* and *The Cambridge Review*. One, entitled 'Defiance', was described by its author as 'a gloomy bit of verse':

Myself is knocking at your gates:
You shall not know she weeps and waits;
She clamours frenzied at your ear:
I laugh to see you do not hear;
Her wound is bitter . . .

It received some stringent criticism from Fieldhead. 'I'm sure you're right about the latest. It does need polishing. . . . It's very bad indeed, that middle verse. . . . I'm feeling a bit discouraged about poetry in general. I seem not to have written anything with any promise or life in it for ages.' She persevered none the less, encouraged by a young poet at St John's, E. L. Davison, who asked her to contribute to a book of Cambridge poets, and invited her to meet J. C. Squire himself and the poet and critic W. J. Turner, 'which really *is* exciting'. But gradually the suspicion grew that in spite of a copiously productive childhood, in spite of all those happy hours spent scribbling in the walnut tree, she was never going to be a poet. 'I began to realise my poems were simply awful. Some young man or other said they were like cream buns – which they were.'

In retrospect her three years at Cambridge seemed to Rosamond a confused, often unhappy time. Her feelings of self-doubt, an impression of failing to find her way through territory which to others appeared clearly mapped, undermined her pleasure in her achievements. 'I had this worrying feeling of being "different", not at home in the world,' she recalled. 'Other girls seemed to take for granted all sorts of things that seemed traumatic to me. I was haunted by a natural inability to cope.' Clever, popular and extremely attractive to men, Rosamond remained inwardly timid and unsure; as in childhood an inflated sense of superiority was inseparable from a profound insecurity. None of this, of course, was revealed in letters home, especially not in letters to her mother, who would have had little patience with any hint of self-pity. Writing to Alice, Rosamond focused chiefly on her social and scholastic life at the university and on domestic concerns at Fieldhead. Alice came to stay in Cambridge several times, as did Beatrix, each visit requiring a flurry of letters about train times and accommodation. Then there were frequent requests for news about her beloved dog, about John, now at Eton, and in particular for news of her father's deteriorating condition. Having determined that she would always look after her husband herself,

Alice had recently been forced to admit a measure of defeat and employ a full-time nurse. There was also cause for anxiety about Beatrix: with the departure of the two elder girls, the Pavilion classroom had been closed and Beatrix sent away to school. The experiment had not been a success, Bea having returned home indefinably unhappy and suffering from bouts of migraine. Increasingly she seemed to be withdrawing into herself, less ready to play the family clown, perhaps already suffering from what she later described as 'the brutal business of being *forced* to seem silly'.

A leitmotif in Rosamond's correspondence was the constant need for money and new clothes. Alice, still pleading wartime economy, kept both girls financially on a very short string – which accounted for their indignation when they discovered at the end of the war that she had saved the enormous sum of £3,000 out of the housekeeping money. Rosamond and Helen had an allowance of only £5 a term, which meant they were constantly in debt, forever begging their mother for advances and loans. With an increasingly demanding social life, the patch-and-darn policy instilled in her daughters by Alice became less and less satisfactory. Hours were spent repairing stockings and stays, and dancing was ruinous to the fabric of Rosamond's few evening dresses, which soon needed replacing. 'Alas for the peach satin! I fear that wretched New Year's dance did it in properly. Perhaps a milder colour would be best for a tea-gown, if I have one, – pale pink, or what they call madonna blue. . . . The pink voile doesn't look nice any more because of the rent, but could, I s'pose, be made to do. Oh d—— clothes!'

The summer term ended in a burst of perfect weather and Cambridge in full beauty, the river crowded with punts, people picnicking along the Backs, the smell of wallflowers in college gardens, and nightingales singing at full throttle in the cedars and limes of Girton. There were idyllic days walking through meadows rich with buttercups, luncheon parties at the University Arms, canoeing with a girlfriend to Grantchester for tea. Helen was taking her finals, calmly confident that she would come through and buoyed up by having fallen in love. Montague Bradish-Ellames was the soldier son of a near neighbour at Little Marlow who used to give children's dances to which the Lehmann girls were invited. 'Mounty', as he was known, wanted to marry Helen, but before any engagement could be made official he had been sent abroad with his regiment, the 8th Hussars, and Helen was having to rely on his infrequent letters. Rosamond for her part had also come to a decision about her future, she told her mother. 'I want to take Trip. next year, & devote my last year to French. . . . It seems absurd to drop the only subject I've ever excelled in. And I can't bear much more Anglo-Saxon or Icelandic.'

With her first year at Cambridge behind her, Rosamond spent the long vacation at Fieldhead, a dull summer interrupted only by a short visit to Paris in July with an aunt, staying at the Crillon, where to Rosamond's excitement fellow guests were Douglas and Mary Fairbanks. As well as sightseeing, going to the opera and to some first-class restaurants, they made a tour of the battlefields of the Pas de Calais, a disturbing experience which made a lasting impression. It was interesting but dreadfully sad, Rosamond wrote to her brother. 'We walked over a bit of the Hindenburg line that hasn't been restored. You never saw such a sight: shell-holes as big as the library, barbed-wire that you tripped over; old gas-masks. . . .'

Rosamond's second year was a great improvement on her first. She was more assured, had made friends, and better still she now had an escape route from the claustrophobic atmosphere of college life through an acquaintance with a 'perfectly sweet' young married couple living in town. Vivian and Maisie Burbury were as enchanted with her as she with them, and soon she was looking upon their house almost as a second home. 'I go to them whenever I like,' she told her mother. 'They've got a dear little house, and an atmosphere of home and comfort and books and nice clever people all round them. It makes a tremendous difference to have a place like that to run to.' It was with the Burburys that she met two delightful young men, both cousins of hers, Nigel Norman, whose mother was a first cousin of Rudie's, and Leslie Bedford, a son of Liza Lehmann's. Bedford was good-looking and fun as well as possessing that quality prized above all else, of being an accomplished dancer, while Nigel Norman, although perfectly agreeable, was as a dance partner an unfortunate combination of persistent and clumsy. Soon he was in love with Rosamond, a situation which, unknown to her, had been enthusiastically encouraged by his mother, the notorious Ménie Fitzgerald.

Under her maiden name, Ménie Dowie, Mrs Fitzgerald had written for the *Yellow Book* and was the author of a number of popular novels. She had married Sir Henry Norman, by whom she had Nigel, and had then run away with one of her husband's closest friends, a dashing Irish American, Edward Fitzgerald. Furious, the extremely respectable Sir Henry forbade her ever to see her son again, bringing Nigel up to believe his mother was a fallen woman who had heartlessly abandoned him. Rudie had supported the Normans over the affair, deeply disapproving of his cousin's scandalous behaviour. Ménie, however, who had never stopped scheming to see her son, wrote to Alice when she heard that Rosamond was at Cambridge, suggesting the two young people should meet, by which time Rudie was too ill to try to stop it.

Her father's illness as the dominating topic in news from home was temporarily supplanted by the announcement of Helen's engagement, followed rather quickly by the wedding, as Mounty had been posted to Egypt. Rosamond was pleased for her sister – 'My dear, I'm awfully, awfully glad' – while at the same time seizing an unrivalled opportunity to put in a familiar plea with her mother. '*Tell Helen*: any of her discarded clothes MOST gratefully received, particularly a few under-clothes, her brown taffeta dress, her fawn-coloured coat with the fur collar, her gray fur(!), all her stockings & her rust-coloured straw hat for next spring.' The wedding took place on 10 November 1920 at St Paul's, Wooburn Green, with the reception afterwards at Fieldhead. Rudie was only just well enough to give his daughter away, his nurse, Sister Lewis, in attendance. Helen, ravishing in white charmeuse and a train of ivory net, was followed up the aisle by five bridesmaids, among whom were Rosamond and Beatrix wearing frocks of peach-coloured satin, peach-coloured lace hats, and carrying bouquets of gold chrysanthemums.

The third and last year of Rosamond's Cambridge career saw her in possession of a much greater self-confidence, although she was still naive and emotionally immature. The year began with yet another attempt to persuade the authorities to accept women as full members of the university, an attempt that again met with defeat, except for the concession that female students could be awarded titular degrees. On 23 October 1921 Rosamond sent a stirring description of the occasion to her mother.

Thursday was an unforgettable day – but rather horrible . . . and oh! – I can't tell you what an uncomfortable position it was for us!

Lectures were an agony; & we had to set our teeth and lift our heads and sail unconcernedly through mob after mob of mischievously-inclined undergraduates. Kit [Miss Jex-Blake] announced the news in Hall at 8.30 p.m. & made a *perfect* speech which I wish some of our opposers could have heard. It was very sad. 'Many of you will see it through,' she said, 'but I never shall.' I think she's one of the finest women I've ever met. I wish you knew her better.

The whole of college was locked and barred and bolted, & we sat awaiting a rag – which never came – till about 11 p.m. Girton is too far out for even those adventurous spirits; but they went to Newnham, smashed the lovely memorial gates & did £700 worth of damage. And *that* is the superior sex!!

Of course we've got the *titular* degree. It seems to me more like d——d cheek than a concession.

As Rosamond had no desire to teach – 'Oh, *how* I want to publish a book!' she exclaimed to her mother later that term – whether or not she had the title of degree meant very little, but she was nonetheless determined to do well in her examinations. Devoting her final year to French, at which she knew she was more than proficient, she hoped that if she worked hard enough she might be awarded a first, an ambition that, fearful of failure, she was careful not to voice in public. 'I honestly don't think Trip. matters terribly, do you?' she asked with studied carelessness. However, her plan for a stint of serious study was scuppered by an attack of appendicitis, necessitating an operation and convalescence in a Cambridge nursing-home, a misfortune that was hardly at all ameliorated by learning that Helen, now pregnant and living in married quarters in Cairo, was almost simultaneously undergoing the same painful procedure.

Appendicitis was, if unfortunate, a wholly respectable reason for slacking off work. Less respectable was the new and raffish social life to which Rosamond had recently been introduced by her cousin, Nina Lehmann. Nina was everything Rosamond most admired, tiny, pretty and deliciously chic; with her big eyes and starry black lashes, she flirted outrageously, was always up to the minute with the latest slang and dance-step, and enviably confident of her own considerable powers of attraction. When they were children Nina on visits to Fieldhead used to tell the young Lehmanns details about the adult world of which their parents, had they known of it, would certainly never have approved. And indeed respectable matrons might have condemned her as fast if it had not been for a sweet girlishness that lulled even the straitest-laced among them, such as Alice, into believing that she was a perfect poppet, and that for all her silly talk there was no harm in her. Nina's mother, Rosamond's Aunt Bertha, married to Rudie's brother Freddy, had taken a house in Cambridge for a year, and here she entertained merrily, her house a popular resort for a group of glamorous undergraduates, those 'dazzling young men' that up to now Rosamond had seen only from a distance, men like David Keswick, Jack Talbot and the intimidatingly sophisticated Peter Murphy, an ex-Irish Guards officer, homosexual, close friend of 'Dickie' Mountbatten. Such society was irresistible, and in the eyes of the Dean of Girton the fact that everything took place under the patronage of Aunt Bertha made it entirely decorous. Rosamond was given permission to go there as often as she pleased ('Any aunt of *yours*, Miss Lehmann . . .'), with consequences that were as unhappy as they were unforeseen.

Soon in letters home the name of David Keswick began casually to appear, briefly referred to at a tea-party, encountered unexpectedly outside his college or as one of a shopping expedition with Peter Murphy. Keswick, son of a Dumfriesshire family of landed gentry, was at Trinity, an old Etonian, tall and slender with an attractive, puppyish face, witty, clever and flirtatious. Before she knew it, Rosamond found herself badly smitten; hungry for romantic love, she eagerly responded to his light-hearted attentions, innocently interpreting his amiable amorousness as signifying the most serious intent. In this she was egged on by cousin Nina. 'Wicked, wicked Nina. . . . She encouraged me like mad . . . [and] it was my undoing.' The weather that final summer term of 1922 was exceptionally beautiful, and with Dorothy Torlesse, who had recently become engaged, Rosamond broke off from an intensive period of revision to play tennis and go on the river, escorted by David Keswick and Dorothy's fiancé, 'Borris' Butler. The two women veered between increasingly panic-stricken periods of study and long leisurely afternoons with their young men. At one moment Rosamond was describing to her mother the hours spent poring over previous examination papers – 'White & trembling we passed from question to question – all in vain. . . . How false & futile & idiotic & pernicious is this system of examinations' – and the next, 'motoring to Granchester with D[orothy], Borris (her fiancé) & another young man, & having tea in the Orchard – a *mass* of apple blossom & thick warm sunny grass. Trip. seemed a delicious joke, a glorious farce. . . . To-day I'm again plunged into an abysm of woe & terror, & am rushing to Aunt B. & Nina for relief.'

The warm May weather, anxieties about Tripos, her ecstatic emotional state over David Keswick, all contributed to induce a heady atmosphere of unreality. The day before Tripos began, the weather was hot and sultry, and Rosamond spent all day on the river in a state of terror mingled with surges of blissful happiness over what appeared to be the prospect of a flawless future with the love of her life. The happy illusion was furthered by the fact that to a gentle and unrebellious nature such as hers it would be unthinkable to flout the strict rules of chaperonage, which ensured that she was never, not once, alone with Keswick, always with him as part of a group; on this occasion they were accompanied by Nina, Dorothy and Peter Murphy, who himself seemed infatuated with David. 'Such perfect weather! One is tempted to forget oneself and be happy,' she wrote home in soaring spirits.

At Girton it was the tradition to cosset the Tripos candidates. First-years took in early-morning tea to each examinee, and a little crowd of students and dons would wait at the gate to wave them off on their way to the Guildhall in the motor-bus. When they returned in the afternoon there was a special tea, and at dinner the cook would send up a dish of potatoes in the shape of a horseshoe for luck. Rosamond did well, but not well enough to earn her first; she was marked down, too, in her viva voce by the examiner, Mr Prior, as she clearly recalled over fifty years later. 'I spoke really marvellous French, much better than anybody else's, [but] as I went out, Mr Prior, who thought I was a spoilt arrogant hussy – which I was – said, Was I going to teach? I said with horror, "Good God, no. I'm going to be a writer, write novels." I scorned the idea of being a teacher. And he marked me down so I only just scraped through.' When Miss Jex-Blake wrote with the news that she had got a 2(1) rather than a first, she added consolingly, 'There is no doubt that it was the bad luck of appendicitis, and though it is very sickening for you, it ought not to stand in your light in the future, as your testimonials will show what your quality is.'

With Tripos behind her, the last couple of weeks could be dedicated to pleasure. With dances and river picnics, and Dorothy's wedding at which she was to be a bridesmaid, the need for money and new clothes was more pressing than ever. Rosamond had, she told her mother, managed to buy a yellow dress off Margy Runciman, but still there were things she desperately needed. 'I'm afraid I shall have to ask for more money, Mummie,' she wrote.

> I have NOT been extravagant: but I've had to contribute to the year present, to Kit's present, to the Russian Relief, to three birthdays, to the French Society – & have *had* to buy a pair of brown silk stockings because I hadn't any. The expenses I've got to face are: my contribution to Dorothy's present (a yellow lustre tea-set), flowers & gloves for my bridesmaid's outfit, & something to the Girton dance. . . . I do so want to keep my 2 nice cotton frocks & my white skirt for the Races & May Week.

She was living in a whirl, dancing almost every night, in a state of sleepless excitement over David Keswick, who was included in nearly all the social events she attended. 'I dined out last night with David Keswick & Nina & some other people. . . . Tonight we're both dancing . . .' she wrote happily to her mother. She had also received a proposal, not from David, but from the undiscourageable Nigel Norman. Tall, good-looking, the well-to-do heir to a baronetcy, Nigel seemed a promising prospect; he was one of the slightly older undergraduates who had come back from the war, an interesting and likeable young man but not, in Rosamond's eyes, attractive. In spite of some charming letters from his mother, Ménie, Rosamond knew she could never take him seriously: she was, too, made uneasy by a cruel streak she thought she detected and was annoyed by his crude persistence in trying to make physical love to her. She had told him that he stood no chance and he had appeared to give up the pursuit, before suddenly and unexpectedly asking her to marry him. 'I felt he'd deceived me – all the time pretending he'd long ago ceased to be in love with me, & that we were the best friends in the world. . . . However, it'll be all right. He's written me a very nice letter, which I suppose I must answer.'

And how could she think of Nigel Norman when there was David Keswick, who seemed so 'very, very smitten'? She suggested to her mother that David should be invited to Fieldhead for a house-party in June. Meanwhile she was seeing him every day and dancing with him at night, with Nina encouraging her 'to think it was all very thrilling and forbidden'. At the end of May Week, after she had moved out of Girton and was being put up by an acquaintance, a Mrs Granville Gordon, for her last night in Cambridge, she was taken to the Trinity ball by another man, but danced all evening with David. When the ball ended he took her back to where she was staying, and on the doorstep, no doubt intoxicated by the champagne and the dancing and the nearness of this lovely girl, he kissed her passionately. It was the first time they had been alone together. 'When will I see you again?' he asked urgently, and then, 'I'll write, I'll write,' as he dashed off into the dawn. Rosamond with her trunk and boxes returned to Fieldhead in a trance of happiness to await the letter. Yearning, romantic, hopelessly naive, it never crossed her mind that the kiss was anything but a declaration of undying love. She believed that she and David were now committed to each other and would marry. But when days, then weeks, went by without a sign she began to grow anxious, and finally, perplexed, she sent him a long, emotional letter begging him to let her know when they were going to meet again. His short reply was shattering. He had been engaged to a girl since he was at Eton, he wrote, and had no idea what she was talking about.

4

Into Marriage with a Sinking Heart

For Rosamond the despondency of returning home to Fieldhead with its nursing-home atmosphere – Rudie in his wheelchair, an oxygen cylinder in the bathroom, and Sister Lewis always to be met with on the landing – was thankfully alleviated by an invitation from Ménie Fitzgerald to accompany herself and her husband, Edward, on a trip to France. This was exactly the antidote Rosamond needed to counter the gloom engendered by her father's illness, by a bleak lack of prospects, and above all by the humiliating circumstances of her rejection by David Keswick which had painfully intensified Rosamond's innate insecurity. In August 1922 she and the Fitzgeralds spent a few days at the Ritz in Paris, where she was taken to the theatre, dancing at the Château de Madrid, and to dress shows, where the extravagant Ménie ordered quantities of new frocks for herself and her guest – little black frocks for the morning, delicate yellows, pinks and greens for the afternoon, straight sleeveless shifts, exquisitely cut, for the evenings. 'Oh Mummie!' Rosamond wrote ecstatically, 'I *never* saw such clothes.' After Paris they motored south to Vichy, Rosamond every day falling more deeply under the spell of the dark-haired, bewitching Ménie, admiring her elegance and chic, her air of bravado, hypnotised by the stories of her unconventional past. 'She was fascinating, brilliant, an actress, a liar – there was something wicked in her, though there was generosity and tenderness as well.'

At 18 Ménie had been briefly on the stage, then travelled alone through France and Germany to Ruthenia, where she had ridden through the Carpathian mountains with only a peasant horseman as guide, her subsequent book on the subject, *A Girl in the Karpathians*, becoming a sensational best-seller. After her marriage to Sir Henry Norman, by whom she had Nigel, she continued to travel widely, publishing witty articles about her experiences as well as three novels considered remarkably outspoken for their time. It was while on a visit to Russia with her husband and his close friend, Edward Fitzgerald, that Ménie began the adulterous affair with Fitzgerald that resulted in their running off together, in a scandalous divorce case, and in Ménie's being banned for years from seeing her only son. When Nigel was at school she would go down to Winchester and surreptitiously watch him on the playing-field, but never dared speak to him or in any way identify herself. 'You cannot possibly know', she wrote to Sir Henry's second wife, 'what the horror of being cut off from him has meant.' Ménie's charm and the resonances from this dark and adventurous past gave her an irresistible allure, her powerful personality sinking deep into Rosamond's subconscious, from which years later it would resurface in two novels (*The Ballad and the Source* and *The Sea-Grape Tree*) in the form of that sinister spell-binder, Mrs Jardine.

During their stay at Vichy, Ménie put herself out to enchant the gauche young woman, courting her with presents of clothes and jewellery, and bestowing on her affectionate nicknames – one of which, 'Sappho', made Rosamond distinctly uneasy. She had no need for anxiety in that quarter, however. Four days after they arrived, Nigel Norman suddenly appeared and everything fell into place: Ménie, desperate to re-establish herself in her son's affections and knowing of his feelings for Rosamond, had used her as a decoy to lure him down. The ploy may have served to improve his relationship with his mother, but it did nothing to further his cause with Rosamond. After 'a wild 4 days, motoring, playing tennis & dancing', she told Alice that in spite of his good looks and undoubted intelligence, Nigel still slightly repelled her. 'I wish I could like Nigel better. He gets on my nerves; and there are things about him, such as a sulky temper & a crabby turn of mind, which I hate.' Besides, by this time she was tired of hotels and ready to come home, anxious to see Helen and her newborn baby before they returned to Egypt, and John before he went back to Eton. Most of all, she was eager to start work.

Although her ambitions as a poet had evaporated while at Cambridge, Rosamond knew that she was 'bound to be a writer'. Moping about at Fieldhead, secretly nurturing her 'terrible state of depression and despair over David Keswick', she told her mother she could never fulfil herself as a writer while she remained at home, that it was essential she travel and see something of the world. Alice pointed out that the Brontës rarely left home and no one could say that they had failed to fulfil themselves as writers, a bracing reply which effectively put an end to that particular line of argument.[1] The portraits of Browning and Dickens and Wilkie Collins which hung in Rudie's library continued to exert a powerful influence. 'I sat under them and felt they were my ancestors and that I'd inherited all that – yet it was such a grand inheritance, and I wondered how I could possibly live up to it.' Once again it was Ménie who intervened, offering to show a couple of Rosamond's short stories to her friend, the popular novelist Berta Ruck. Ménie herself had always been flattering about Rosamond's compositions and was sure her old friend would be impressed, but Berta Ruck, although kind, was dismissive, and Rosamond, expecting praise, felt snubbed. 'I don't know that you'll ever be a writer,' said Miss Ruck, 'but you must write about things you know: these are just romances,' advice that left the recipient so dejected that for the time being she decided to give up altogether. But Berta Ruck was right, even if Rosamond was as yet unaware that in her own recent unhappy experience she was already incubating the nucleus of her first novel, a novel that would bring her acclaim and notoriety, and with which she would be inseparably associated for the rest of her life.

The longer she stayed at home, the more determined she became to find a way out. Her father's invalid state was a constant source of worry, and helping to look after him she found depressing, particularly as she was now the only one of the children left behind: Helen was a wife and mother; Beatrix, having won permission to train at the RADA (the Royal Academy of Dramatic Art), aimed at a career on the stage; and

---

[1] 'She was wrong,' Rosamond wrote years later. 'They were, all three of them, forced at one time or another, to leave home, and it was the anguish of that wrenching, of being torn from that uniquely nuturing womb of Haworth Parsonage, that was for each of them so catastrophic and creative'.

John was away at school. Privately she was beginning to panic that she would never find a husband. 'I had it lodged in my subconscious mind that the wonderful unknown young man whom I should have married had been killed in France.' Many of her Girton girlfriends, like Dorothy Torlesse, were already married, or about to be married, like Grizel Buchanan who was engaged to Hubert Hartley, a young man from St John's. Margy Runciman, however, was still unattached, and through her Rosamond began seeing something of her older brother, Leslie, whom she had known slightly at Cambridge. A scholar at Eton and Trinity, tall, athletic and strikingly handsome, Leslie Runciman was working for a firm of chartered accountants in the City as essential grounding for a career in his family's shipping business. Ménie Fitzgerald, in her accustomed position at the centre of the web, had lent Alice her town house in Mayfair so that she could give small dinner parties for Rosamond, and Leslie was one of the young men invited. Rosamond liked him, found him attractive, and asked him down to Bourne End for a couple of weekends, during which it became clear that Leslie was falling in love. One Sunday morning, he walked with her over the bridge spanning the river, and while they were sitting in the sun on a grassy knoll immediately opposite Fieldhead, he proposed and was accepted. 'It was pretty quick when it started with her and me,' said Leslie; adding with hindsight, 'Very much too quick.'

To begin with, the engagement had to be kept within the family because Leslie's parents were abroad and he must break the news to them before it could become public knowledge. Nervous of his father and easily overwhelmed by his domineering mother, this was an occasion to which he was not greatly looking forward. Alice, on the other hand, was delighted and welcomed him warmly, although Rudie was hardly capable of taking in the information at all – 'A nice boy, very handsome,' he was heard shakily to murmur – a sadly ironic state of affairs as it had been largely to please him that his daughter had agreed to the marriage. Rosamond was not in the least in love, but Leslie's father, Walter Runciman, a distinguished Liberal politician and keen oarsman, had been a colleague and friend of Rudie's since they had been at Trinity together. 'As I wanted above all things to marry somebody my father approved,' said Rosamond, 'I thought to marry a very handsome young rowing man who was the son of a Liberal MP would be the most marvellous thing I could do for him.' Still brooding over her rejection by Keswick, now almost a year ago, she had convinced herself that she would never love again and that her emotional life was over; it was, therefore, almost a matter of indifference whom she married, and she believed in time she would grow fond of Leslie, as could never have been the case with Nigel Norman. Most importantly, marriage would provide an immediate escape from Bourne End.

Leslie, meanwhile, was happily unaware of the state of his fiancée's true feelings. He had known of the Keswick affair but believed it to be long over, and was thrilled to have been accepted by this beautiful girl who had cut such a swathe through the young men at Cambridge. One of his Trinity friends congratulating him said, 'You appear to have waded through slaughter to a throne.' Now as he prepared to confront his parents on their return from India at the beginning of June 1923, his anxiety became increasingly obvious; if his parents had not been out of the country, he told Rosamond, he would never have dared get engaged, and in any event he was convinced his mother was unlikely to take to her. An evening was appointed for dinner with the family at their town house in Barton Street, near Westminster Abbey, an occasion which by Rosamond's account was so terrifying that she remembered little of it, only that Walter Runciman alone made any attempt to put her at ease, while the others, his wife Hilda and four younger children, did not. Although Leslie told her afterwards that, 'You went down so terribly well with Father,' she gained the distinct impression that she had not been considered good enough for their precious eldest son. 'Nobody was good enough to enter the family, was the feeling I was given.'

The family of which Rosamond was about to become a member was an interesting one. Leslie's grandfather, Sir Walter Runciman, having run away to sea at the age of 12, was now a wealthy ship-owner, chairman of the Moor Line based in Newcastle-upon-Tyne, with a fleet of twenty-three steamships. A lifelong Liberal, representing the Hartle-pool division in Parliament during the war, he was an ardent Methodist and a firm adherent of the temperance movement, a result, he claimed, of seeing so many vessels wrecked as a consequence of drunkenness: he refused to employ anyone on his ships unless they had first taken the Pledge. His only son, also called Walter, had followed closely in his powerful father's footsteps, joining the family firm and taking his seat as a Liberal Member of Parliament, appointed to Asquith's Cabinet, serving with distinction during the war as president of the Board of Trade. His wife Hilda Stevenson, mother of his five children, had read History at Girton, and was almost as active politically as her husband: in 1928 she was to be elected Liberal member for St Ives, thus providing the first instance of a married couple sitting together in the House of Commons. Both Methodists, they continued in the temperance tradition, making an exception only for Asquith himself, who when he came to stay was offered champagne in place of the non-alcoholic cider provided for everyone else. While Walter Runciman was a shy, austere man, with a gentle charm shown only to his intimates, his wife was a clever, complacent, managing woman, 'tough as an old boot, hugely stout with a mouth like a trap. I had never', said Rosamond, 'met anybody quite like her.' Of her five children, two boys and three girls, her favourite was her younger son, Steven, dark, good-looking, intellectually brilliant, and with a malicious sense of humour which found in his brother's callow fiancée an irresistible butt.

Although both sets of parents considered their children young for their years and not ready yet for marriage, Rosamond 22, Leslie a year older, no objection was formally made and preparations were soon under way during the autumn of 1923 for a December wedding. Alice's Maidenhead dressmaker was put to work on the trousseau, Rosamond an ideal client as her height and slender figure were shown to their best advantage in the graceful, flowing dresses of the early 1920s. Now that the news was public, congratulations were coming in: Helen wrote from Cairo, 'Oh! I'm so terribly excited and happy. . . . Isn't it a gorgeous feeling that, however annoying the petty present may be, the future is gloriously assured & full of excitement,' while Grizel Buchanan, her own wedding imminent, cheerfully expressed the hope that 'You're preparing some nice seductive underclothes, darling, opening upside down.' Leslie left Deloitte, the company for which he had been working in the City, to move to Liverpool and begin learning his trade in Holt & Co.'s Blue Funnel Line, writing to Rosamond almost daily and coming south for weekends in London or Bourne End whenever he could. Although Leslie later destroyed all Rosamond's letters, many of his survive, gauche, self-conscious, tortuous, sometimes pompous and patronising, but unvaryingly affectionate.

I'd never describe you as 'beyond all words – perfect' (a) because
you're not – at least I imagine an imperfection will appear some day
though at the moment I confess to being at a loss to name one (b)
because if I thought you were I shdn't be able to love you half as
much . . . but shall you be annoyed if I write, a little shamedly 'You
will mock (or weep?) to hear that I have been not inelegantly
caught by that Lehmann female (here insert a short note on you,
probably depreciatory). . . .'

It was amusing to learn that you felt shy about kissings. Was I
impetuous? I expected to be shy but when it came to the point it
seemed, & seems, obviously & naturally the thing to do. We
certainly don't know each other very much (though I shall no
doubt have to pretend to my parents otherwise, lest they rail at my
rashness) and it's going to be great fun finding out (unless we find
very miry pits by the way. D'you feel the risk great? I don't.). . . .

Do you know the feeling of a hot potato in the pocket on a cold
day. It's not unlike what I feel about you. . . .

Oh my dear, you are the only thing I really want to go on living
for. You may think that flattery but it is absolutely literally true.

As he began to feel more sure of himself and of her, Leslie wrote at
greater length about his interests and occupations. Formidably know-
ledgeable, he was even in his undergraduate days inclined to the
didactic, and sometimes his lengthy lectures could be boring. 'He really
should have been a don because he loves teaching,' said his brother
Steven, adding wearily, 'He's explained how cars work to me, I don't
know how many times.' Similarly Rosamond was told rather more than
she wished to hear about a number of topics, including Ancient Roman
and Greek literature and contemporary politics and economics, and
often she pretended to understand more than she did to save herself the
tedium of further explanation. For recreation away from the office, she
learned, her fiancé played racquets, went shooting with his parents on
their Northumberland estate, drove into the country in his beloved little
car, a Fiat nicknamed 'Gwen', and lunched and dined regularly with
fellows from the office. And the shipping business, although the endless
paper work was often dreary, had its interesting aspects. 'This afternoon I
spent on two of our passenger boats at the landing stage. One was sailing

to the Far East & tother to Australia. I can't help being a little excited even now to see a Blue Peter at the masthead & ships in themselves (apart from their management which spoils it rather) do thrill me.'

Occasionally he expressed qualms about his future wife's ability to adapt to life in the north. Grimy, wet Liverpool was not everybody's idea of an attractive location, but at first Leslie did his best to present it in an appealing light, writing encouragingly that, 'the little I have yet seen of this city convinces me that apart from the climate, which is damp cold & almost universally condemned, we could be very happy here. There does seem to be quite a reasonable amount of music & other arts & the people, though incorrigibly moral & religious, seem more cultivated than I had dared to hope.' As the weeks passed, however, and the weather deteriorated, he started referring to 'this revolting town', confessing that, 'I do feel the bloodiest beast bringing you into this place – & if it was for ever I wouldn't do it,' adding hopefully that 'longer days in the spring are bound to make some difference'. Reading his descriptions of his work and the new friends he was making, Rosamond came to resent Leslie's emphasis on his own concerns, prompting him to take seriously her complaint that once they were married and he was away working all day from nine to six she would have little to occupy her. He deserved all her reproaches: 'It was bloody & thoughtless of me ... & I'm terribly and burningly ashamed of not having realised more what you must be feeling with no surface occupation at all,' he wrote, slightly spoiling the apology by adding with fond facetiousness, 'Your life will be a long series of light hearted neglect & excessive though sincere contrition from me, but I do love you very dearly all the same and I do miss you terribly yearningly & achingly.'

With such obstacles already in their path it is unsurprising that Rosamond approached her marriage 'with a sinking heart'. But only gradually was the full extent of the engaged couple's disastrous incompatibility revealed. The first indication that Leslie would present more of a problem than could be accounted for by immaturity and a difference in upbringing came with the vehemence of his objections to any kind of religious service at the wedding. Rosamond cared very little what they did, and a civil ceremony would not unduly have worried her parents who regarded religion chiefly as convention and themselves had rarely attended church, expecting their children to go more as a courtesy to the vicar, whom they liked, than because they wished them to grow up practising Christians. Most of the Runciman family, on the other hand, took their low-church beliefs very seriously indeed. The old man, Sir Walter, was a noted Methodist lay-preacher, while his father, Leslie's great-grandfather, had become a Wesleyan preacher after retiring from the navy. Leslie, by contrast, was a committed atheist; not only did he not believe ('[my] own disbelief is a very definite sort of faith'), but the idea that there should be any spiritual content in the proceedings revolted him. 'I refuse flatly to regard the day on which we get married as anything more than the day after which we can be known to sleep in the same bedroom without the servants giving notice,' he stated uncompromisingly. 'A religious ceremony is fuss in very bad taste, and as for its dignity I can think of few positions less dignified than kneeling before a rather tiresome man with a book (whom in everyday life you almost always laugh at) and exposing the soles of your feet to the audience.'

The problem was that by marrying in a register office they would give profound offence to nearly all their relations, and, more crucially, would put at risk a marriage settlement of £400 a year promised by Sir Walter, bringing their expected annual income up to a comfortable £900. 'The more I think of a church the physically sicker I become,' Leslie wrote. 'If £400 a year is in the balance, such Paris is perhaps worth a mass, but I don't think that the monetary is really the cogent or deciding factor. . . . I am tired tonight & half inclined to throw up the sponge with a contemptuous gesture . . . but at the same time I am so deeply and passionately revolted by the thought of church that I am very loath to give in.' His brother Steven did his best to persuade him to relax his intransigent line, and in the end a compromise was reached by Leslie finding an accommodating Wesleyan minister, father of Grace Rattenbury, one of Rosamond's Girton friends, to whom he candidly explained the situation. Dr Rattenbury agreed to do the absolute minimum, and with this Leslie reluctantly professed himself content.

But now a far uglier problem emerged. When Rosamond accepted Leslie's proposal, it never crossed her mind that he did not share her wish to have children; she longed for babies, and assumed that he did, too. It was, therefore, a shock when Leslie revealed that he loathed children, they bored and repelled him, and he believed it morally wrong to bring the 'wretched objects' into the world at all. The more

Rosamond tried to coax him into changing his mind, the more certain he became that he never would, referring with all seriousness to his 'paedophobia', and talking enviously of an American acquaintance of Rosamond's who had been sterilised. 'If it were not that you, like her, would mind, I suppose, terribly, I should indeed be relieved if you had suffered your American friend's fate.' He asked her to set down on paper 'the pro children argument you promised' so that he could write a careful refutation of it, a refutation unencumbered, he said, by personal prejudice and founded on a philosophical conviction that it was a grave misfortune ever to have been born. '[While] it is impossible to exist in this world without being conscious of at least a little pain & unhappiness,' he wrote, 'I think it better not to exist at all. . . . To resolve the application of this to my own feelings about procreation, it makes me unhappy to think that a being should be made conscious through me who will certainly be at times more or less unhappy.' In a letter in which he combined his contempt for the Christian God with his deep disgust for the prospect of paternity, he used an image as startling as it was disturbing. 'My complaint against God is that he makes people just happy enough to go on living, & above the life line, so to say, plays cat & mouse with them,' he wrote. The only way to 'score off' such a cruel deity is one that he doubted his future wife would care for: 'namely to produce a child by you & then kill you & it just in your first flush of maternal generative joy. And as that is really the last thing that I could want to do . . . God has me all round. As you know I don't even want to die now myself, though I am convinced of the desirability of human life stopping altogether.'

Both Leslie and Rosamond were emotionally undeveloped ('If I was 14,' said Rosamond, 'Leslie was 10'), and perhaps for this reason Rosamond failed to feel any serious alarm over her fiancé's eccentric attitude. 'I used to think his terror of having children was just young and silly and it would all be quite different when we were married.'

In other areas, meanwhile, they continued peaceably and with affection. With Leslie a couple of hundred miles away, they had little chance to get to know each other, except by letter. It is clear from Leslie's side of the correspondence that he felt himself very much in love and that Rosamond, concealing her unhappiness, showed him genuine fondness, attentive and indulgent even during his most nihilistic moods.

Leslie having been brought up never to talk about his feelings (the Runcimans disapproved of what they called 'remorseless undressers in public'), it was a revelation for such an inhibited young man to be able to confide so openly. 'You were so easily the kindest & most sympathetic person I'd ever met,' he told his fiancée. 'Other people (in this case me) plague you with whining pessimisms & weak complainings & instead of brushing them aside & going cheerfully on alone, you stop & reason & sympathise & help with a patience & gentleness & attention which are far more than the case has any right . . . to claim or expect.'

Sexually, both were inexperienced. At university all Leslie's friends had been male, many of them homosexual, and he was an unquestioning subscriber to the Cambridge Apostolic belief that friendship between man and man was by its nature of a higher order than friendship between man and woman. Rosamond was affronted when she discovered that Leslie was virtually apologising to his Trinity chums for allying himself with her. 'He thought it was an intellectual disgrace to marry . . . and most of the letters he wrote to his friends said, I know you think it's pretty unforgiveable to have anything to do with a woman but she's got a mind like a man. Me, of all people!' She was ignorant of homosexuality, which had to be explained to her by Leslie, himself a non-participant. 'I never think of you without a delicious wiggly physical sensation,' he wrote, 'and as I'm generally thinking of you, my body gets almost as much excitement as my mind.' During his occasional weekends at Fieldhead he tentatively began to make love to her, recalling afterwards their rapturous sessions in the schoolroom.

> I'm missing you so horribly, my darling, that I can hardly bear it. . . . I've never felt the same about anything before; it was an exaltation and a fierce joy comparable with that of violent physical efforts like rowing a race or the wall game but different in quality & far intenser & more individual, with the passionate feeling all the time that it was you with whom I was sharing this & that you were loving it too, & that made it a thousand times more satisfying still.

So elated was he that 'little Lelly', as he began referring to himself, even considered braving public and parental disapproval by establishing 'prematrimonial cohabitation', a step wisely decided against on the grounds that it would cause too much unpleasantness, 'owing to the intolerance of others'.

The wedding was set for five days before Christmas, 1923. At the end of November Leslie came south to help his father campaign in Brighton for the December general election, speaking in support of the Liberal manifesto in favour of free trade. Rosamond, looking glamorous with her long hair newly bobbed, joined him for a couple of days, reporting to her mother how impressed she was by Leslie's performance on the platform and by Mr Runciman's skilful oratory, especially when addressing a mob of rowdy unemployed. She herself, she admitted, found the proceedings not particularly enjoyable. 'I go now to canvass. Ugh!'

Even for a young woman less avidly romantic than Rosamond, the days leading up to her wedding would have induced despondency. Leslie's attitude was one of barely concealed impatience at having to involve himself in such a tiresome and irrelevant business: as far as he was concerned, the sooner they were through with it the better. 'I'm all in favour of getting the thing over on Thursday morning,' he wrote briskly. 'There's nothing like cramming all the bother into one day. . . . As to Thursday night I have no real ideas . . . a play will no doubt help to take the day's taste away.' There were to be no photographs, as neither of them saw any point in recording the event, and only members of the immediate families would attend. It was Leslie who had been dealing with wedding presents and Leslie who had prepared the flat at 42 Princes Road into which they would move in Liverpool, so there was little for Rosamond to do except dread the parting from her parents and Fieldhead. She moved through the remaining hours like an automaton, 'numb with misery'.

With Rudie so ill, there was no question of having the wedding at Bourne End, and so Rosamond and Leslie were married on 20 December 1923 in a bleak Methodist chapel in Kingsway, a busy London thoroughfare in the middle of Holborn. The officiating minister, Dr Rattenbury, sweating copiously, enraged Leslie by going back on his promise and conducting a full religious service. Dr Rattenbury was heard afterwards to say that in his opinion it was a union unlikely to last, an ill-timed remark that was picked up by 'wicked, malicious' Steven and repeated to the bride. The wedding breakfast was given by Ménie Fitzgerald, who mischievously placed in front of the groom's place at table an ashtray with the motto '*Le Favorisé de Dieu Voyage sans sa Femme*'. A chaste wedding night was spent at the Goring Hotel near Victoria Station, during which Leslie, with his intellectual's respect for absolute accuracy, told his new wife that although he liked her and was currently in love with her, technically he was not sure he could say that he loved her, an unlooked-for item of information that reduced her to tears. The next morning they left for their honeymoon, a skiing holiday in St Moritz.

The young Runcimans began their married life on friable foundations, Leslie adamant in denying his wife the children for which she longed, Rosamond deliberately marrying a man with whom she was not in love mainly to get away from home. Fortunately for both, they had mutual affection, a number of interests in common – they were great readers, particularly of modern novelists such as Huxley, Lawrence and Gerhardie, and they loved music and the theatre – and Leslie's kindness and equable temper did much to support his wife through her periods of depression. At home in moments of intimacy he playfully adopted the role of little boy, 'little Lelly', longing to see 'wife . . . who do more & more love', all of which his Rosie found most endearing. But for Rosamond, child of the Thames valley, nothing could make palatable the fact that she had exchanged the soft, green Buckinghamshire countryside for Liverpool, that soot-blackened city of noise and fog. At least their residence there was temporary, as Leslie would shortly be leaving Holt's to join the family firm in Newcastle, but whether Newcastle would provide any visible improvement on Liverpool was in her mind a subject open to debate.

Meanwhile Rosamond found plenty to occupy her, engaging a cook and parlourmaid, shopping for furniture and utensils, and learning her housewifely duties. 'Leslie has bought me an account-book with 14 columns, and intends to keep a firm cold eye on me and it. Isn't he killing?' she wrote to her mother, adding a request for some recipes. 'Ham salad. Eggs à l'Aurore. Apple Meringue. Hot Apple Pudding. Chocolate Sponge. And that new soup with bits of vegetable in it.' They entertained a little, mainly business colleagues of Leslie's, attended a few dinner-parties and one or two modest dances, 'but they're very early ones. L'pool people are very nice, but mostly very unintellectual & rather provincial.' It was a comfort for Rosamond that Helen was living nearby, as Mounty's regiment, returned from Egypt, was now stationed in York. Unfortunately the Bradish-Ellames had taken a dislike to Leslie, so Rosamond usually drove over by herself to see her sister, who craved company. 'It's funny how she can't bear to be alone,' Rosamond remarked to Alice. 'Besides, she's *not* alone: she's got a perfectly good baby. It's not like me!'

But while Rosamond complained of passing most of every day in solitude at home, the situation was little better for Leslie. His natural bent was for the academic, and although he enjoyed the outdoor part of the shipping business, going into the docks, meeting homecoming ships on the Mersey and taking new vessels on sea-trials, the long hours he was obliged to spend in the office calculating pilotage returns and dealing with bills of lading bored him. Rosamond worried about her husband. 'It makes me angry to see anybody so naturally cheerful & adorable become dyspeptic & morose! . . . I get so angry with the office & all that business stands for & with his parents for pushing him into it, that I can hardly speak. I loathe the very word "business". . . . The very *minute* there's a chance in politics I shall make him take it.'

None of this, of course, could be revealed to Leslie's parents, whose relationship with their daughter-in-law remained wary: she seemed to them self-indulgent, lacking in fibre, and in private they doubted she had the backbone to make a go of her marriage; 'exotic', they called her between themselves, in a meaningful tone of voice. Although politics was the air they breathed, they were far from philistine, interested in music and literature, but to Rosamond the older generation of her husband's family were of a different species, one wholly incompatible with her own. 'I can't describe how grim they were, those Runcimans,' she said, confiding to her mother her fear and dislike especially of Hilda Runciman, with her red face and sharp turn of phrase. 'I simply perspire at the thought of that eye & tongue.' Of Leslie's father, on the other hand, she could see herself becoming fond, but chiefly because he appeared so susceptible to this ravishing young woman his son had married, with her soft, seductive charm. 'He really did sort of fall in love with me, as far as fathers-in-law do with their sons' wives. I was his very favourite person. He was the only one who made it human for me.' It was he who had insisted that Rosamond be presented at court at the same time as Margy, giving her a dress for the occasion. The three daughters seemed amiable enough, although Margy herself was too detached in manner to inspire much affection, while the two younger girls were still at school. The second son, Steven, had followed his brother to Cambridge; now a scholar at Trinity, he was making a name for himself in certain circles as something of an aesthete, wearing make-up, smoking Russian cigarettes and keeping a parakeet in his rooms. 'Steven is sure to be a monster,' Leslie had warned Rosamond, and so indeed he proved. 'Steven – God, he was so awful! He did everything he could to make me miserable and tease me.'

Leslie and Rosamond spent many of their weekends at Doxford, the family's Northumberland estate, where in spite of the dominant Runciman presence, the comfort, delicious food and beautiful country provided a welcome respite from the rough-shod domesticity at Princes Road. Rosamond's 16-year-old brother John was also invited to Doxford on one occasion, leaving a perceptive account of the experience in his diary. 'They [the Runcimans] are a chattery, "scory", & clever lot, and most of all, Mrs, and Steven. Mr I like. They don't make one feel pleasantly welcome, but rather on-edge and unsettled. . . . At dinner it feels a little better, and afterwards, during the Charades – Steven of course doing all the women's parts he can – I notice LR [Leslie] stands just slightly outside the family.' Later when staying with his sister, John noted a similar effect. 'Steven & Margie came to lunch, & quite changed Leslie, & made me feel thoroughly uncomfortable, with their sort of "showing off" & nervy flashiness – & squashiness! Rosamond confessed . . . that it affected her in the same way – & we had a heart-to-heart & vowed mutual protection.'

In July 1924 Leslie and Rosamond moved to Newcastle. A house had been bought as a wedding present by the Runciman grandparents, a spacious Victorian house in a pleasant suburb near to the wide-open spaces of the Town Moor. From the very first, Rosamond hated 3 Sydenham Terrace, hated its situation next to the tram lines, and hated its design and decor, although to begin with she tried to put on a brave face, telling her mother that,

I really think when the ornamental plaster-work, lincrusta, dados, linoleum & imitation brown marble mantelpieces are removed, and if we furnish with extreme care, it will be quite nice. Two more bathrooms are to be put in, and everything stripped & garnished. . . . The grandparents are going to furnish the drawing room – which is a vast & stately apartment. There is ample room for a family of 6 – but L. didn't seem to think that an advantage when I pointed it out.

The city itself was regarded in an equally unfavourable light, its grace and grandeurs obscured in her eyes by an all-pervading provincial shabbiness, by the ugliness of docks and factories, the scream and clang of trams along the dark, dismal streets; to her 'Newcastle seems much like any other nasty town'. When she complained to Leslie, telling him she could not bear to live in such a frightful place, he told her she was being unreasonable: eventually they would buy a nice house in the country, but while he was still making his way in the business, surely she could see that they had to be where the business was.

The move had been predictably chaotic, and Rosamond was worn down by having to deal with plumbers, painters, joiners and electricians. 'Oh!! how I hate it all. They seem to think I should enjoy it. Well, I don't.' Finding servants was another difficulty. Parlourmaids seemed impossible to come by, and the first husband-and-wife couple she engaged lasted almost no time at all. Mrs Turner was an excellent cook but her husband was discovered to be an alcoholic, and after one spectacularly catastrophic occasion, when Leslie had invited a group of shipping people to dinner, the Turners had had to be sacked. 'It was an *awful* evening . . . and [the next morning] he [Turner] was in such a state he wouldn't get up & I had to go & reason by his bedside for a good half hour before I could persuade him to don his clothes & come & help me make the beds.' After some more domestic ups and downs the Turners were replaced by a cook and two maids.

In retrospect there was almost nothing about her life in the north that gave Rosamond pleasure or satisfaction, but in fact at the beginning it was not all bad, and her later recollections were undoubtedly coloured by the extremes of misery she was soon to experience. Shortly after the move Alice and John came to stay, John noting in his diary that the three Lehmanns had thoroughly enjoyed themselves, Leslie had been full of beans, and Number 3 was delightful. 'The house is marvellous in its reds & oranges & old golds, & yellow & blues, & books &

pictures. . . . I was quite overwhelmed by the library. It's a happy, comfortable & intellectual room: Rosamond's bedroom too! What lovely taste.'

Leslie also was going through a difficult time and more than ever needed the support of his wife. Now working for the Moor Line, he was directly answerable to his grandfather, Sir Walter, known in the family as 'the Beast'. Originally one of the most enlightened of ship-owners, the canny old sea-dog had grown fanatically reactionary, an irascible tyrant hopelessly out of touch, who thought he knew it all and would listen to nobody, forcing Leslie to conspire with the office manager behind Sir Walter's back. 'There were moments', said Leslie, 'when I really wondered if I could stand it any longer, [but] as my father told me he'd had exactly the same experience at exactly the same age, I thought if he could see it through, so could I.' Rosamond helped him where she could, young Mrs Runciman, wife of the heir apparent, being much in demand at official functions, such as the launching on the Tyne of a new Moor Line ship. 'I christened my ship successfully on Monday and made a little speech which was kindly received, & listened to a great many other speeches full of gloom about the shipping-trade & the Russian treaty.' As Leslie had little time to make new friends, most of their social life involved business colleagues and their wives, the ladies in long dresses, the men in stiff white shirt-fronts, entertained to joyless little dinner-parties at Sydenham Terrace, soup, meat course, pudding and savoury, with only Cydrax on offer to drink. Leslie, like his parents, never touched alcohol, but once when he and Rosamond went out to dinner with some friends from work he was persuaded – 'Come *on*, old chap!' – to drink a glass of wine. When they got home Leslie broke down, sobbing uncontrollably, saying he could never look himself in the face again, that he had broken his vow and committed a terrible sin.

With her husband away all day, Rosamond was lonely. She could have made friends with other young shipping wives, but they were busy having babies, underlining the fact that she was not, and they tended to regard her reluctance to join in as stand-offish. 'It was wretched, really.' Sympathetic to the problem and wishing to provide her with companionship, Leslie bought her a dog, a dreadful little Aberdeen terrier, stupid and hysterically incontinent. 'Prudence continues to flood the house. She's quite unteachable,' Rosamond reported in despair. After ruining most of the new carpets, the puppy was found another home, replaced, much more successfully, by a descendant of one of the Fieldhead Pekineses. Whenever she could, Rosamond escaped, sometimes to Helen, now enviably the mother of two children, sometimes to London to see Beatrix if she were not on tour, sometimes to see her parents at Bourne End. 'While we were living in Newcastle I was always going back home because I was so miserable. The excuse was that I must see my father who couldn't do without me. That was one of the conditions on which I married.' Leslie was prepared to let her go if it made her happier, although he did not care for being in the house with only the servants to look after him. 'My darling Wiggles, I'm terribly glad you're coming back tomorrow, because I do miss you drefful,' he wrote. 'Wee I do miss you. Your drefful drefful loving L.'

The Christmas of 1924, the first after the move to Newcastle, was spent at Fieldhead, a cheerful occasion for Rosamond, in spite of the pathos of her father's condition. Her loathing for her mother-in-law had been substantially intensified when she overheard Mrs Runciman say that Rudie had taken to the bottle, and that he had developed the disease because he drank so much. 'I never forgave her for that. And it was ironic that her own husband died of Parkinson's.' The young couple seemed on excellent terms, and on their first wedding anniversary on 20 December, Rosamond told her mother that, 'Leslie says he's bound to admit it's been all right so far'. But at the most profound level it was not all right: Leslie absolutely refused to change his mind about having children, although Rosamond still believed she could bring him round. That she was mistaken about this became shockingly clear a few days later when she discovered that she was pregnant.

The physical side of the marriage had always been far from ideal. 'Our sex life', said Rosamond later, 'was a disgrace to sex.' Leslie had had no previous experience, and was lacking in confidence, he confided to his wife, as a result of an operation in childhood on a tubercular testicle, which had left him violently traumatised. 'I remember him saying, "My God, they nearly castrated me!" and I didn't even know what "castrated" meant.' Leslie had conducted some careful research into methods of birth control, all distasteful to Rosamond, who found none of them compatible with enjoyable sexual relations, infrequent at the best of times because of Leslie's terror of impregnating his wife. Aware that he was unlikely to greet the news with rapture, Rosamond none the less was totally unprepared for the violence of his reaction. When informed that she was expecting a child, Leslie lost his head. He went berserk, circling furiously round her like a maniac, incapable of talking rationally, frantically insisting that she could not possibly have the baby and that if she would not agree to an immediate abortion she must leave his house for ever. So great was his anguish that he lost nearly ten pounds' weight in a week. Eventually he calmed down sufficiently to make one concession: he would be prepared to let her stay and have the child, but only on condition that she swore it was not his.

Appalled, frightened and desperately unhappy, but realising she had little choice, Rosamond, as before at Cambridge, turned to her cousin Nina, her only close confidante, to whom she felt she could speak with a candour not possible even with her sisters. Nina, worldly and unshockable, was still unmarried, still leading a gay social life, 'trotting round race meetings and hunt balls'. She herself had had an abortion, in those days strictly illegal, and knew just the man to go to, a Mr Osborne, a successful physiotherapist in the West End, who ran a flourishing practice on the side for fashionable ladies. Rosamond had already announced her pregnancy and her parents-in-law were thrilled, delighted at her suggestion that she should come up to London for a few days and stay at their house in town. From there Nina took her in a taxi to Harley Street, where they were admitted by a manservant who checked off the name in a little black book. Between them the two women had concocted a plausible story, Rosamond explaining that she was about to go abroad with her husband and that she could not possibly have a baby just then, although of course they intended to have children later. Mr Osborne, smooth and civil in his morning suit, nodded sympathetically – 'These accidents will happen. Nature's a wily dame' – and asked her to lie down on the couch. The little intervention was quickly made, the envelope containing £100 discreetly pocketed, and Rosamond returned to Barton Street to await the result, which was easily passed off a few hours later as an unfortunate miscarriage.

It was some time before Rosamond, weepy and unwell, could bring herself to return to Newcastle, staying first in a nursing-home in London, then retreating to Bourne End. She knew her marriage was effectively over, although as yet she had no idea how she would make her escape. 'I thought, I'm married to a hopeless cripple, and I must get out of this as soon as I can.' Physically she could not bear Leslie to come near her, indeed would never let him make love to her again, and yet she still felt fond of him and pitied him, her thwarted maternal instinct responding to her husband as a little boy. Leslie, meanwhile, although sorry for his wife's unpleasant ordeal, appeared to understand little of its consequences.

> The more I think that Rosie is betterer . . . & all clear & clean inside & on the road to being properly well again at last the gladder I get. You know I try to feel self reproachful at moments about it all & I do feel always terribly sorry for you & very humbled, but I'm so convinced that you & the infant as well as myself wd have been made wretched by its continuance, that I can only be conscious of an almost moral satisfaction. . . . But anyhow I do love you more 'n ever. And miss you something drefful.

As far as he was concerned, it had been a disagreeable business, but it was over now, and the sooner they both returned to normality the better. 'Don't think I'm unhappy, I'm not,' he wrote to reassure her. 'A few weeks for each of us, for you getting well, for me rushing about, to let the sediment sink & clear the liquid, ought to help a lot.' But as days, then weeks went by and still his wife did not return, he began to grow plaintive, entreating her not to leave him any longer alone, promising that if only she would come back, 'somehow I'll make you happy in Newcastle and somehow I'll get you often to London (& come too). . . . Come soon & cheer up Lellie who does so want & so love.'

When finally Rosamond did return, she found that the conditions of her exile were in some substantial respects improved. The bitter northern winter was nearly over, her husband had been promoted to a directorship, which meant an increase in income, and there was a new employee in his office who was proving exceptionally agreeable. Leslie had several times made mention in his letters of 'Philipps', heir to a baronetcy and eldest son in a shipping family, who had recently arrived to learn the business in Newcastle with Walter Runciman & Co., just as Leslie had done his apprenticeship in Liverpool with Holt. Wogan Philipps, a couple of years younger than Leslie and like Leslie an old

Etonian, although he had gone on not to Cambridge but to Magdalen College, Oxford, was entertaining company and an accomplished sportsman, and soon the two young men were playing squash, rowing on the Tyne, dining together and sharing a box at the Empire for the music hall. 'I do really rather like him,' Leslie reported. 'For one thing he's the only person . . . whom one can apparently say what one likes to & he has certainly, as they say, seen life.' Wogan's first meeting with Rosamond was not propitious. On returning from the office one evening Leslie informed his wife that he had invited his new chum, Philipps, to dinner, an announcement that was badly received as Rosamond's adored Pekinese had just been run over and she was in her bedroom in tears. The guest was already downstairs, however, and so with face unbecomingly swollen she was obliged to make the best of it and play hostess to this attractive young man, on whom, it was dismayingly clear, she made no impression whatever.

Before long Wogan Philipps became a frequent visitor to the house, an agreeable haven for him from his impersonal rooms at the Northern Counties Club in the centre of town. With his charm, easy manner and dark, dazzling good looks, the newcomer, already widely acquainted, was much in demand. 'Everybody in Northumberland fell for him.' Indeed it was through Wogan that the Runcimans began to see a couple of friends of his who were to play a considerable part in all their lives. Matthew and Ursula Ridley ('Lord & Lady', as Rosamond was careful to emphasise) lived only a few miles outside Newcastle at Blagdon, a large, handsome Georgian house surrounded by terrace and lawns, with a lake, woods and an extensive park. They were a glamorous couple, recently married, with a small baby: Matt Ridley, tall and distinguished-looking, scion of an old Border family, was an inventor as well as land-owner, while Ursula, dark, chic, rather febrile in manner, was a daughter of the architect Sir Edwin Lutyens. The Ridleys were lively, intelligent and infinitely hospitable, providing the kind of patrician society, grand but informal, luxurious yet highly literate, to which Rosamond immediately responded. Here was a world to which she felt she should by rights belong, Blagdon an oasis of sophistication and refinement a thousand times more congenial than the Newcastle commercial circles in which up till then she and Leslie had almost exclusively moved. 'They are delightful,' Rosamond reported. '[We] both feel we have found kindred spirits at last.'

As spring gave way to summer there were more opportunities to spend time away from Sydenham Terrace. Not only were there delicious days at Blagdon – swimming in the lake, dining among ancestral portraits by candle-light – but also weekends at Doxford, walking, playing tennis, sometimes motoring over to luncheon with Lord Grey at Fallodon; and recently the Runcimans had bought the island of Eigg, off the west coast of Scotland, for the fishing and snipe-shooting. 'Eigg is rather a marvellous place – quite unreal, with its lochs and heather & mountain-peak & sheep roaming wild.' The Runcimans were keen sailors, and Leslie's parents had the frequent use of Sir Walter's famous three-masted yacht, *Sunbeam*. Rosamond was among the party aboard *Sunbeam* for Cowes week ('the great yachts, including the king's yacht, came sweeping right past "Sunbeam" all day – the most beautiful sight in the world') and also, with Wogan Philipps a member of the party, for a trip to Scandinavia. Both of these expeditions she enjoyed, revelling in the immaculate service and the 'gorgeous & colossal meals', although even on such a large vessel there were inevitable drawbacks. 'It's a wonderful yacht – my cabin is most comfortable, and everything beautifully arranged except ——!! – which is worked with sort of pumps, & resounds from end to end of the vessel. I'm wounded in all my susceptibilities by the very thought of it. If only nature would grant me complete suspension till next Monday!'

In spite of these pleasant distractions, however, Rosamond was privately determined that she would not, could not, remain in Newcastle, that somehow she must terminate her marriage. She tried to persuade Leslie to buy a house near Bourne End, but he refused to consider it. 'South Bucks has its attractions but I won't tie myself to any place & have to nurse it & so forth yet. I can't possibly afford it myself & grandparental or paternal money won't I suspect be forthcoming.' This discouraging response, if hardly unexpected, was a disappointment made all the keener by the fact that this year Rosamond could not even look forward to coming south for Christmas: it had been decided that instead she would accompany her husband and Wogan Philipps for some stalking in the north of Scotland, where Wogan's family owned a shooting-lodge.

On 22 December 1925 the three of them left Newcastle to go by sleeper to Inverness, where the following morning they changed trains for Lairg, a small town on the edge of a loch deep in the Highlands. It had been snowing heavily, and they were met by the news that they could travel no further that day as there had been a blizzard and the lodge at Altnaharra thirty miles away was completely cut off. But by early the next morning, Christmas Eve, the wind had dropped and they decided to risk going on, piling into an ancient lorry with the men who were taking the mail. The road was buried in deep snow, and before long the lorry toppled over into a drift, the men at once setting to work with ropes and spades to dig it out. Rosamond did what she could to help but the snow falling into her boots turned into thick cakes of ice, causing such pain that she lost consciousness. When she came round both Leslie and Wogan were hanging over her, anxiously calling her name and plying her with whisky. With immense difficulty they were able to continue another few miles by motor, stopping at an inn for dry socks and a reviving lunch of Irish stew, but for the last six miles the road was impassable, except on foot. Rosamond, alight with whisky and a determination not to be left behind, set off ahead of them all into the moonlit, snow-bound landscape. 'There was a complete triumph of will over flesh. My feet felt winged. I outwalked them *all*, never stopping for a minute, and was entirely unconscious of fatigue until the moment I arrived at the front door.' At the lodge they were welcomed by the housekeeper with hot baths, a meal and bed, waking next morning to a brilliant blue sky, the sunlight gold, rose and mauve on the mountain peaks. There followed several perfect days, the men out stalking from early morning, in the evenings big fires, huge meals, and on the last night highland reels at the ghillies' dance. 'You would love it,' she told her mother.

What she did not tell Alice was that by the end of this magical Scottish Christmas she and Wogan Philipps had fallen in love.

5

'The Kind of Novel That Might Have Been Written by Keats'

During her bleak period of exile in the detested north of England, Rosamond had returned to her long-held ambition to write a novel. In this she had been encouraged by her husband – 'you'll be glad of an inexpensive occupation here,' Leslie had written to her from Liverpool shortly before their wedding – but her first attempts were unsatisfactory, and after completing a few 'feeble' chapters, she tore them up. But now everything was altered. 'Suddenly, a deeper level of consciousness seemed to open up. I wrote rapidly, with extreme diligence, with scarcely an erasure.' At Altnaharra while the men were out shooting, she had sat from morning till night covering page after page, 'extremely happy', and returning to Newcastle she continued to work inspired. 'Something happened and the [flood]gates burst and the whole of this extraordinary book came pouring out.' Now instead of bemoaning her solitude, Rosamond ruthlessly guarded her time to herself. 'I am more and more deluged with invitations to be on committees & organize bazaars, etc. etc. I am refusing them *all* firmly now,' she told Alice. 'I *will* live my own life and not be Runcimanized.' In this she was helped by the fact that in April, as she was not feeling well, Leslie had agreed to go without her to Italy, sailing there with his grandfather on the yacht, thus leaving his wife at liberty to work on her novel – and to pursue her love-affair with Wogan Philipps.

Since their return from Scotland at the beginning of January 1926,

Rosamond and Wogan had continued to fall ever more deeply in love. Always susceptible to appearances, Rosamond was captivated by Wogan's striking handsomeness, as well as by his gaiety and emotional candour, very different from Leslie's stolid reserve; she was touched, too, by his trustfulness and vulnerability, by his willingness to put himself under her tutelage: admitting having wasted his education, he told her, 'You opened up new thoughts, new worlds.... [I] want to improve myself with your aid.' On his side Wogan was ravished by her beauty and surrendered completely to what he described as the 'cool balm' of her gentleness and boundless sympathy; she was ready to listen to him for hours, and, in awe of her superior intelligence, he was intensely excited by their long discussions about books and music and personal philosophies. Her world seemed infinitely superior to his 'hopeless past life, vile & animal', as he dramatically phrased it, and her love and approval restored his damaged self-esteem, providing him with the resolution to 'try to climb up to you with all your purity & cleanness'. They snatched meetings whenever they could, and over discreet suppers talked and talked, insatiable for the smallest detail of each other's lives. Wogan's first intimation that Runciman's wife might become important to him, he told her, had come during the voyage on *Sunbeam* to Scandinavia. 'It was all so peaceful and calm, till – Stockholm – you beside me leaning on the side of the ship watching the sun, causing my blood to beat a little faster in slight anticipation & a faint feeling of mutual understanding.' Rosamond for her part remembered 'thinking in a ruthless way, this is how I get out of my marriage'.

Rosamond learned that Wogan, when he arrived in Newcastle the previous year, had been far from the well-adjusted, cheerful young man she had taken him for. In fact he was wretchedly unhappy, having been compelled by his father to break off an engagement to a beautiful young woman, Daphne Vivian, because the Vivian family was believed to be tainted with insanity. Wogan's father, Sir Laurence Philipps, founder and chairman of Philipps' Insurance and of the Court Line shipping line, was a self-made millionaire, an inspired and aggressive adventurer who had amassed several fortunes by means of taking colossal but carefully calculated risks which no one else in the City would touch: during the war, for instance, he had made huge profits by offering comprehensive insurance for shipping at six guineas per cent when all other policies excluded the risk of being torpedoed. Both literally and figuratively he was a giant of a man. Powerfully dominating, he controlled every detail of his adored eldest son's career, meticulously moulding the boy as heir to the Philipps baronetcy and estates and to the family's commercial interests.

Wogan, passionate, excitable, by no means remarkable for intelligence, had little sense of direction and was easily swayed, unquestioningly accepting the path laid out for him by his father. He had been sent to Eton and then Oxford, but was removed after only two years as Sir Laurence regarded higher education as a waste of time and the university valuable only as a source of profitable contacts. By his own account, Wogan was an idle, spoilt young man, but he also had charm, outstanding good looks, and an exuberance which many found immensely attractive. Hanning Philipps, one of Wogan's younger brothers, complained that when they went together to a party, all the pretty women wanted to dance with the charismatic Wogan, leaving only the plain ones for Hanning; and according to a woman friend, 'He always enjoyed himself enormously: if you went with him to a hunt ball, he was the life and soul of the hunt ball. He threw himself into anything and everything and everybody loved him. But clever he was not.' Sociable, and a gifted sportsman and athlete (one of the best oarsmen in his college), he was pursued by men as well as women, in particular by some of the older undergraduates who had fought in the war and who found his Byronic beauty and high spirits irresistibly appealing. 'At Oxford I was wild, mad, drunk with success and freedom,' as he described himself then. 'I picked up – dropped – & trampled over person after person.' Emotionally he remained intact until, shortly after coming down, he had a brief but passionate affair with a young woman which ended abruptly when he was despatched by his father to India to work in the Forestry Commission. Since childhood Wogan had been unusually accident-prone and vulnerable to illness: once while playing hide-and-seek he leapt over a wall and landed on a spike which injured him so badly he had to have several operations to repair the damage (and according to his mother, 'had been a bit mad ever since'). In India he fell seriously ill with malaria and was sent home, his life in the balance.

Once recovered, Wogan was enrolled in Philipps Insurance, a line of business that held no appeal for him at all: cannily, he worked out a simple system of truancy involving two hats, one to be worn on his head when he went out, the other to hang on the peg in his office so that anyone seeing it would assume he was in. Penned in his City office, he was restless and bored. Unlike his philistine parents, he loved music – would weep while listening to Wagner – but his great passion was for painting, and he nursed a secret ambition to be a painter which he dared not voice to his father. He would go off for days by himself into the country to sketch, took drawing classes under Bernard Meninsky, and his lunch hours were often spent wandering round galleries: he was so excited after seeing a Van Gogh exhibition at the Leicester Gallery that instead of returning to work, he rushed home, as 'I *had* to hurl as many colours on to a canvas as I could before it got dark'. In London society Wogan was naturally in great demand; pursued by hostesses and the mothers of marriageable daughters, he joined energetically in the antics of the Bright Young People, of whom Daphne Vivian was one of the loveliest and brightest. After breaking off his engagement to her, he was sent for a year to South America on a long sporting vacation – during which he was nearly killed in a train accident – all the time haunted by the fact that he had not been allowed to explain to Daphne the reason for his rejecting her, forced to write in a lying letter that he no longer loved her.

On his return to England Wogan found he could not endure London, could not endure the prospect of working again in the City office, where he sensed dislike and resentment of himself as the boss's son, and arranged instead to go for a year to learn the shipping business in Newcastle. Here for the first few months, he told Rosamond, he was more miserable than ever. 'I became so lonely, so morbid, so desperate that I can swear I was nearly mad. . . . Several nights I did not dare turn off the light, or lie down, & had to walk round the town to find another human being to make one remark to, or to watch something intently to distract me. My horror & nerves got the better of me & I couldn't be alone.' No wonder, therefore, that friendship with Leslie Runciman was so welcome. The two young men had sufficiently similar backgrounds and interests to provide common ground, and although Wogan found Leslie rather staid, he liked him well enough and was glad of his company in town during the week and on sporting weekends. Unlike Leslie, Wogan had little interest in commerce and all his energies were reserved for rowing and for hunting, shooting and fishing, with Leslie and also at Blagdon with Matt Ridley, with whom he had been at school and university.

Apparently without confrontation, indeed without anything much being said on the subject at all, it became accepted by Leslie that Wogan Philipps was Rosamond's lover. Believing that his best chance of keeping his wife was to condone her infidelity, Leslie made no overt objection, and whatever his real feelings, in the main his bearing remained one of civility and good humour. For obvious reasons the affair had to be conducted with the greatest secrecy in public, but in private the lovers enjoyed an unusual licence, which they owed entirely to this extraordinary degree of complaisance on Leslie's part. Rosamond was happier than she had ever been, intoxicated by her love affair and deeply immersed in her novel. Sometimes Wogan came to the house and kept her company while she worked, 'when, in your brown linen dress, you sat writing at the table, your face plunged in thought & mental effort, never still or calm for an instant. I used to lie on the settee, pretending to read, but really watching you. You would suddenly raise your head, our eyes met, & you would relax into a divine tender encouraging smile.' When Rosamond announced that she needed to go away in order to finish her book, Leslie motored her down to Dorset where she had taken a room in a farmhouse, fully aware that soon after he headed back home Wogan would be joining her. During those few weeks in her beloved south, in a whitewashed thatched cottage with a sunny garden surrounded by cornfields, Rosamond wrote quickly and for hours a day. She had, she said, 'discovered my true path, what I truly am and can do'. When Wogan arrived to stay for a week, he told her the time had come to make decisions: he declared that he could not live without her, that he wanted to marry her, and that she must make up her mind to leave Leslie.

Returning to Newcastle with her novel all but completed, Rosamond entered a strange sort of limbo. As before, little was said, but 'it was quite understood that our marriage was over, and Leslie appeared not to mind in the least'. Stranger still, Leslie and Wogan came up with a plan to rent a place together for the summer at Hexham, near Hadrian's Wall. 'This summer is going to be so terrific that it can never never end,' Wogan wrote blissfully to Rosamond, and indeed 'it was a lovely summer', as she herself recalled. At the beginning of May 1926 in high spirits she moved to Anick Cottage, an attractive old house surrounded by beautiful country on the banks of the upper reaches of the Tyne. To begin with she had the place to herself as the start of the General Strike that same week meant that Leslie, enrolled as a Special Constable, was unable to leave Newcastle, while Wogan was in London working as a mounted policeman in the East End. The strike ended within a few days, however, and both men were soon spending as much time as they could in their *ménage à trois* at Hexham, bringing relays of friends with them. 'I have reached my last chapter, & two or three days should see the whole thing finished,' Rosamond wrote to her brother John, 'but the house is crammed with visitors, & . . . I am completely overwhelmed.'

Among the visitors were John himself, who had just left Eton, and Beatrix, 'full of high spirits and devilry'. Bea was beginning to make a career as an actress, causing her mother a certain amount of anxiety in consequence. Alice had been worried about the influence on her youngest daughter of some of the more emancipated actresses, Elsa Lanchester, for example, whose part Beatrix had taken over in *The Way of the World*, and now Tallulah Bankhead, whom she had recently been understudying. 'I don't think you ought to worry about her friendship with Elsa,' Rosamond wrote reassuringly. 'The fact that Elsa has lovers will no more incline Peg to want to emulate her than the fact of, say, Elsa's marriage would make her want to marry'; as for Tallulah, 'She is a most warm-hearted & generous person, & a really good friend to Peggy in her own way. I know she has a reputation – but it's mostly only talk.' For her own part Beatrix was enjoying life in the theatre, sending her sister amusing descriptions of sharing digs with eccentric colleagues under the eye of warm-hearted theatrical landladies. '[I] have dropped into the ways of touring as if I'd been through it all in a past life!' she told her. '[Although] I'm sick of painting my face three times every night!'

Among other guests at Anick Cottage were Wogan's brother, Hanning, and his 9-year-old sister, Gwen; the Ridleys drove over from Blagdon, and from Wiltshire that exotic young man Stephen Tennant, son, by her first marriage, of Lady Grey of Fallodon. Grizel Hartley came for a few days, as did Steven Runciman, and a friend of Leslie's from Cambridge, George ('Dadie') Rylands. Dadie, old Etonian and King's man, protégé of Maynard Keynes and member of the elite 'Apostles', was a brilliant young scholar who had distinguished himself by taking a starred first in the English Tripos as well as becoming a celebrated member of the Amateur Dramatic Club, where he specialised in women's roles (his Duchess of Malfi was talked about for years). Blond, blue-eyed and a magnetic personality, Rylands had a feline wit (as undergraduates, he and Steven Runciman had been leaders of a set known as the 'Tea Party Cats'), and was much given to swift changes of mood, swinging between exhilaration and prolonged sulks. Dadie and Rosamond took to each other at once: 'O Rose of Grace,' he called her, 'my curds and cream.' It was through Dadie that, to the Runcimans' excitement, Lytton Strachey, on his way north to Edinburgh, was persuaded to break his journey for a few days at Anick Cottage. 'Leslie is to me extremely attractive, in character, even, as well as appearance,' Lytton reported to his devoted companion, Carrington.

> He is pompous, moody, flies into tempers, and is not mentally entertaining by any means. . . . But oh! he's so strong, and his difficulties are so curious – and his eyelashes . . . there's a childishness about him that – I daresay all grown-up people are childish in some way or another – I find endearing. Rosamond is a much brighter character . . . though not as good-looking – gay, enthusiastic, and full of fun. She and Dadie get on like a house on fire. Wogan lies vaguely and sympathetically at their feet. And dear Leslie makes a pompous remark, to which no attention is paid, looks divine, scowls, until I long to fling my arms round his neck.

'You were a great success with Lytton, dearest, – so clever of you,' Dadie purred to Rosamond, while Lytton himself told his hostess that the few days at Hexham had seemed 'almost incredibly civilised & delightful', and suggested a visit to his house Ham Spray later in the year.

According to Dadie, Leslie had been flattered by Lytton's flirtatious attentions, perhaps grateful for any distraction from the highly charged atmosphere existing between Wogan and his wife. 'It became quite clear to all concerned that she and Wogan were obsessed with each other,' said Dadie, 'and Wogan really was a great personage and a darling. Leslie was a chilly fellow rather, and she was madly romantic, and it became clear that the marriage would break up.' The complicated situation was complicated further by Dadie developing a passion for Wogan. To begin with, Wogan was sympathetic – he was not entirely inexperienced in homosexual affairs, having while at Oxford enjoyed a fling with Roger Senhouse, who became a love of Lytton's. Later, after his return to Cambridge, Rylands grew self-pitying and exigent, and Wogan losing patience went to see him to tell him to pull himself together. From Floors Castle in Scotland, where he was miserable in a job tutoring the surly son of the Duke of Roxburghe, Dadie complained bitterly to Rosamond of Wogan's treatment. 'Wogan came uninvited and gave me a thrashing. His cruelty and stupidity shattered me.' The friendship recovered, however, Dadie's amorous attentions were soon directed elsewhere, and both Rosamond and Wogan remained devoted to the volatile Rylands, as he to them.

It was Dadie to whom Rosamond first talked in detail about her novel, at his request showing him the manuscript, which he read with 'deep concentration', and incorporating several of his suggested alterations. Dadie had contacts in publishing, having worked briefly for Leonard and Virginia Woolf at the Hogarth Press, and he promised to show the finished work to Harold Raymond at Chatto & Windus, publishers of Lytton Strachey as well as of Stevenson, Trollope, Hardy, Chekhov and Proust. Raymond was reportedly 'bowled over', and a letter was sent to Rosamond expressing Chatto's interest: the book, they said, 'shows decided quality', and they would be delighted to take it if the author were willing to make certain changes, in particular a considerable cut in length. The poet and critic Robert Nichols was shown the manuscript and enthusiastically endorsed Raymond's response. 'O Lord! What a beautiful book! It has great distinction. She is thrilling – she really does know about love ... and what characterisation!'

With the summer over, the curious arrangement was maintained whereby the Runcimans and Wogan continued to meet with every appearance of amicability, to the bemusement of those of their friends in the know. 'Leslie at that time was full of theories about "you mustn't mind". I thought it frankly silly myself,' said his brother Steven. '[But] he was really in a vicarious way still very much in love with Rosamond, but in a very strange way, and wanting to do the best by her.' When Wogan, having completed his apprenticeship, left Newcastle and returned to work in the City, he and Leslie lunched or dined whenever Leslie had business in London; when Leslie and Rosamond went south for a week, Rosamond engineered an invitation for Wogan to join the party at Fieldhead. 'I'm sure you'd like him,' she told the unsuspecting Alice. For Wogan this was an intoxicating adventure. 'My own littleone,' he wrote:

> I was wildly happy seeing you & being with you again. I have a collection of vivid flashes, photographs on my brain. Catching your eye as we sat at opposite ends of the room; a deep draught of your eyes as you spoke fully at me at dinner; . . . the drive down & your eyes looking up at me as you nestled close. . . . Then I find myself in bed with you; after ages & ages our bodies meet, & from head to foot we mould into one; – calm security, fierce passion, & calmness again, which in turn is gradually dispersed by the dawn telling me to go . . . it was the most beautiful, beautiful night. . . .
>
> Little beloved, cling to me for protection. I am holding you. . . . I love you, I love you.

Soon after this Wogan asked the Runcimans to stay at Llanstephan, his family seat in Wales, and at New Year they were invited to the Philipps house in the south of France. All this while Leslie, the ever-tolerant husband, when absent from home was writing as affectionately as ever to his 'darling wife', pleasantly expressing the hope that her 'male companions . . . do properly comport selves', while sending her 'all the love in weirld'. Trusting that their marriage would survive if he let the affair run its course, Leslie's priority was to persuade his father to allow him to leave Northumberland, as with Wogan now in London, Rosamond's loathing for Newcastle was growing daily more intense: living there, she said, was making her physically ill. Nerving himself for confrontation, Leslie wrote to his parents.

> This Newcastle question is not a recent fancy born of tired nerves & I frankly am not impressed by your not being impressed by the aversion. For the matter of that I share it. . . . Its principal characteristics especially in winter are the two which Rosamond stands worst, wind & cold. . . .
>
> Probably you think we're a pair of spoilt children. If you do I'm

sorry. Please don't think I'm unappreciative or Rosamond either for all you've done for us both. We're not ... [but] if it came to a Rubicon I should of course go across it with Rosamond right or wrong.

It was during the holiday in the south of France immediately after Christmas that it became clear that matters could not continue in this manner. On one level it was very enjoyable: Primavera, the Philipps villa on Cap Ferrat, was luxurious, the weather warm, and everybody in a light-hearted mood. Rosamond declared Sir Laurence 'an angel' and the rest of the family 'terribly nice'. She herself 'in a great burst of rather feverish excitement' was starting work on a new novel, while 'Wogan has suddenly begun painting quite marvellously. The last two days we have simply gasped at the results'; even Leslie, not wishing to be left out, 'has bought a box of water colour paints & a block & is very busy!' Just before their return to England, Rosamond was taken ill with tonsillitis, and on arrival in London went straight into hospital for an operation. Immediately afterwards she moved down to Fieldhead to convalesce and never returned to Newcastle again. During the following months she stayed either at Bourne End or with friends – at the Rylands family home in Gloucestershire, with Lytton and Carrington at Ham Spray, and in Cambridge with Dadie's old tutor, F. L. (Peter) Lucas, and his wife Topsy. Still nothing decisive was said, but her brief marriage to Leslie Runciman was indisputably over.

Dusty Answer, dedicated 'To George Rylands', was published at the end of April 1927, a year that saw the publication of Elizabeth Bowen's first novel, *The Hotel*, and Virginia Woolf's *To the Lighthouse*. The title is taken from the end of George Meredith's bitter poem of marital jealousy, *Modern Love*, 'Ah, what a dusty answer gets the soul / When hot for certainties in this our life!' In various permutations the themes of the novel reappear throughout Rosamond's fiction, the themes of love betrayed, of expectation disappointed, of the painful discovery that life is as it is and not as the heroine/narrator's idealistic imagination believed it ought to be. 'Imagination at least had been fecund,' she writes, 'but the reality was as sterile as stone.' The innocent natures of her young women with their fatal passivity are a constant, and so is the type of man with whom they fall in love, dashing, aristocratic and unattainable. Here the roots lie bedded in definitive areas of emotional experience: an intense nostalgia for her childhood; a perception of herself as permanent outsider, which was to shadow her all her life; and specifically, the anguish of her rejection by David Keswick.

Steeped in the fiction of the last century ('I was singularly ill-read in fiction published in the twentieth century,' she admitted. 'I thought of the nineteenth-century literary giants as my great ancestresses, revered, loved, and somehow intimately known'), Rosamond saw herself continuing in the same tradition. Her heroine, Judith Earle, undertakes the journey to self-knowledge in much the same manner as Emma Woodhouse or Dorothea Brooke, although unlike those two more fortunate young women she is denied the eventual safe haven of a happy marriage. In a further departure from precedent, the story is told not as an unbroken narrative but in five discrete episodes, each covering a separate period of time, a construction possibly derived from May Sinclair's bleak and brilliant portrait of misguided self-sacrifice, *Life and Death of Harriet Frean*, which Rosamond read on its publication in 1922 and much admired. The manner in which the inner life of the heroine is revealed, her thoughts and feelings explored with unsparing intimacy and minuteness of detail, recalls the stylistic techniques of Dorothy Richardson, Katherine Mansfield and Virginia Woolf, all three greatly looked up to by Rosamond.

With the very first sentence of *Dusty Answer* – 'When Judith was eighteen, she saw that the house next door, empty for years, was getting ready again' – the reader is drawn irresistibly into the story. Judith is an only child whose solitary existence is periodically transformed by the Fyfe children next door who come from time to time to stay with their grandmother, mysterious, thrilling children, carelessly dropping over the wall to weave a glittering web of enchantment around the lonely little girl. Two, Charlie and Julian, are brothers, cousins to the other three, Martin, Roddy and Mariella of the fair hair and mermaid's eyes. From Judith's dazzled perspective they are all wrapped in glory, but it is Charlie, 'beautiful as a prince', by whom she is helplessly enslaved, indulging in luxuriant fantasies about saving Charlie's life and marrying him when she grows up. For long periods the house is closed, then comes the war and with it the news that Charlie and Mariella have married;

91

soon afterwards Charlie is killed at the front, leaving Mariella a young widow with a baby son.

Time passes: Judith, now 18, hears that the house is to be reopened, thus returning us to the start of the novel. One night, standing on the bank after swimming naked in the river at the bottom of the garden, she sees a canoe glide past in the darkness, and with a shock of excitement she recognises Roddy. In that dreamlike moment she falls hopelessly in love.

Next day Judith is swept up once more into the lives of these fascinating companions, although now she has eyes only for the elusive Roddy, who alternately charms and snubs her, uninterested 'in the warm little paths of childish reminiscence' with which she attempts to engage him. But then there is an intoxicating evening when the two of them dance after dinner and Roddy holds her close: as the record comes to an end Judith is left 'flushed, throbbing and exhausted with excitement'. Roddy, however, moving to switch off the gramophone with his usual idle grace, remains as 'pale and composed as ever'. The summer passes idyllically with picnics and boating, and then in the autumn the little group disperses, Roddy to study drawing in Paris, Judith and Martin to Cambridge.

The central section of the novel covers Judith's career at university. Like her creator, she is at first bewildered by collegiate life ('"I am lost, lost, abandoned, alone, lost," thought Judith wildly') and feels a fastidious distaste for her fellow students. She pines for her companions from home, but Martin rarely comes near her and Roddy is glimpsed only briefly, always in the company of Tony Baring, an effeminate and possessive young man, overtly hostile to Judith. While trying to find her way through the wilderness, Judith is befriended by the repellent Mabel Fuller. 'Earnestly her eyes beamed and glinted behind their glasses . . . her skin was greasy and pink was not her colour; and her lank hair smelt; and when she talked she spat.' Judith is rescued from the glutinous Mabel by Jennifer Baird, a golden-haired beauty, sophisticated, artistic, with a dashing contempt for the ugly, the vulgar and the mundane. The two young women form a passionate relationship, with Judith soon in a state of 'uncontrolled rapture' over Jennifer, to whom she confides everything except, instinctively, her love for Roddy. ' "You mustn't love anybody," said Jennifer. "I should want to kill him. I should be jealous."

Her brooding eyes fell heavily on Judith's lifted face. "I love you." '
Jennifer, however, turns out to be no more attainable than Roddy,
eventually abandoning the heart-broken Judith for an older woman of
unarguably lesbian tendencies.

The next section begins with Judith down from Cambridge, preparing
to leave for a picnic with Mariella, Julian, Martin, but not, to her secret
dismay, Roddy who has remained in the house with a headache.
Returning at the end of the afternoon, Judith finds him recovered,
charming as ever, his manner mocking and indifferent, but just as she
turns to go he kisses her hard; that night he takes her on the river, and
in a clearing among the willow trees makes love to her. Now Judith's
whole world is transformed, and she wakes next morning in such a state
of ecstasy that she sends Roddy a letter telling him how deeply she has
always loved him, how devotedly she will wait – years if necessary – until
he is ready to marry her. The following day, she unexpectedly
encounters him walking along the path between their two houses, and in
an agonising scene he makes chillingly clear his distaste for her ill-
judged outpourings.

'I was very much surprised at the way you wrote,' he said.

'How do you mean, surprised, Roddy?' she said timidly. . . .

'Well' – he hesitated. 'If a man wants to ask a girl to – marry him
he generally asks her himself – do you see?' . . .

'But why, Roddy, why did you take me out . . . behave as you did
. . . kiss me so – so . . .' . . .

'I thought that was what you wanted: what you were asking for,'
he said. . . . 'I thought you knew pretty well what you were about.'

From this moment Judith feels her emotional life is over, and the rest
of the novel records her descent into despair before her eventual arrival
at a new tranquillity, resigned to the fact that the golden promise held
out by her childhood companions has come to nothing, a 'dusty answer'
indeed.

Dusty Answer, although undoubtedly flawed, is a novel of extraordinary potency. Just as the children next door weave a spell over Judith, so
does *Dusty Answer* over the reader, mainly by means of its unerring
psychological truth and the mesmerising, lyrical quality of its language.

Rosamond may have come to regard with scorn her youthful attempts at composing poetry but it is in a poet's prose that much of the story is told, revealing a highly developed visual awareness, particularly of the natural world – the river predominantly, but also gardens, fields, the changing seasons, all depicted with a richly sensuous feeling for colour, light, form and texture.

> The sinking sun flooded the lawn. Its radiance was slit with long, narrow shades, and the great chestnut trees piled themselves above it in massed somnolence. The roses were open to the very heart, fainting in their own fragrance; and around them the dim lavender-hedges still bore white butterflies upon their spear-tips. The weeping beech flowed downwards, a full green fountain, whispering silkily.

Much of the sense of enchantment stems from the uncanny sensitivity, an almost extrasensory perception with which the characters are drawn: there is a universality about Judith's emotional experience that gives it a wide relevance, from the rages and intense emotions of childhood to the agonies and anxieties of adult love. So minutely accurate is their description that the reader is immediately convinced that this is what it feels like to fall in love, to be happy, to be sad, to be kissed, to suffer rejection. (For the rest of her life Rosamond was to receive letters about *Dusty Answer* from women readers exclaiming, 'Dear Miss Lehmann, How *did* you know? This is my story exactly!') Nowhere is this more true than in the early sections of the novel. With an unusually direct access to her own childhood memory, Rosamond Lehmann creates a kind of optical illusion by which Judith the child is seen through the eyes of a child and simultaneously by a more detached and clear-sighted adult narrator. This is often very funny, as in the scenes when Judith imagines the melodramatic manner in which she might win Charlie's heart, either by nursing him through fever and delirium, or by falling mortally ill herself.

> Charlie came to her and with tears implored her to live that he might show his gratitude. Sometimes she did; but sometimes she died; and Charlie dedicated his ruined life to her, tending her grave

and weeping daily. From the bottom of the grave she looked up and saw him pale and grief-stricken, planting violets.

Nothing in the least like that ever really happened in spite of prayers. He was quite indifferent.

There are weaknesses in *Dusty Answer*, and they are clearly apparent; but in fact they detract little from the power of the whole. As well as a lushness of tone and an unrestrained romanticism that occasionally become overpowering, there are flaws in the structure, especially in the final section which trails off with little defined sense of direction. There are problems, too, with the character of Jennifer. Rosamond clearly saw her as fascinating, although in fact she comes over as affected, snobbish and insufferably self-important.

[Jennifer] stared impressively at Judith; then broke into loud whistling. . . . 'It's terrible to be so swayed by appearances. . . . Ugly people rouse all Hell's devils in me, and beautiful ones make me feel like the morning stars singing together. I want beauty, beauty, beauty . . .' . . . Leaning heavily on the mantelpiece she continued. 'Are these photographs your people? They look divinely aristocratic. You're not an Honourable are you? You look as if you might be.'

Her friendship with Judith, too, struck many readers as far less innocent than its author intended: indeed, it is difficult not to interpret the highly-charged scenes between the two women as evidence of a full-blown lesbian love-affair, an interpretation which shocked Rosamond, who saw in it no more than the kind of innocuous emotional relationship she herself had had at Girton with Grizel Buchanan.

Judith and her creator are twin souls. (*Dusty Answer*, Rosamond wrote years later, '[was] my only absolutely-innocently-written book.') Dark-haired and beautiful, both are naive, insecure, emotionally needy and painfully vulnerable; both are imaginative and voluptuously romantic; both are passive, yearning for male domination; and Judith's longing to be accepted on equal terms by the children next door finds a parallel in Rosamond's belief that even as a child she never 'belonged'. The boys, Roddy, Charlie and Julian, are similar in type to the glamorous Grenfell brothers whom Rosamond used to see and never forgot on the precious occasions when she was invited by the Desboroughs to Taplow Court, their godlike good looks and innate self-confidence influencing for ever her image of the heroic ideal. Both Roddy and Charlie take the role of romantic lead in only slightly different guises throughout her fiction, with Mariella, lovely, vapid, carelessly indifferent to the enviable advantages of her patrician birth, appearing as their exquisite appendage. In the character of Julian, cleverest of the cousins and most difficult in temperament, are clear echoes of Leslie Runciman. Contemptuous of religion, Julian suffers from a general resentment at having been born. 'I have the misfortune to be doubtful of the objective value of life, and especially of its pains,' he tells Judith; and like Leslie, Julian was less self-assured than he appeared. 'The others thought him conceited, and he was; yet all the time he was less conceited than self-abasing and sensitive, less overbearing than diffident.' Significantly, Julian is a minor figure in Judith's story, which reflects the extent to which, by the time Rosamond wrote the novel, she had emotionally distanced herself from her husband.

Although its author was later to state that her first novel was 'quite remarkably *invented* – imagined: the characters not portraits from life at all', the autobiographical parallels are numerous. The Earles' house and garden are modelled on Fieldhead, and like Rosamond, Judith idolises her father, who 'had known how to stir mystery in a child. . . . He had seemed to forget her for weeks at a time, but when he had remembered, what a more than compensating richness had come into life! She had planned to grow so beautiful and accomplished that he would be proud of her and want her with him always.' Judith's mother, although more chic and worldly than Alice Lehmann, shares Alice's lack of maternal feeling; and like Alice's, '[Mrs Earle's] remarks had generally a faint sting in their tails'.

Reviews were slow to appear and at first Rosamond had little to go by except the reactions of relations and friends. The one opinion she would have valued above all others, that of her father (whose name in her professional persona she proudly continued to bear), was unavailable to her – 'He was a vegetable, bed-ridden, didn't recognise anybody' – but the rest of the family were quick to respond. Helen wrote that she had adored the book, and that 'all the dear dead things of our childhood carried in that first part has touched me beyond words'. Alice, too, was impressed, confiding to John that she thought that '[Rosamond's] style is really first class except just now & then, and that she ought to write a next book of the *very first* order'; she added, however, that in her view the novel would never have a big sale as it was not sufficiently 'startling' for the general public – a judgement which on both counts could not have been more wrong. John, who of all the family most admired and understood his sister's talent, wrote a letter of detailed appreciation. '[*Dusty Answer* is] quite unlike anything else ... in its sort of poetical design – offering no philosophy, only a shot-silk web of feeling, all seen from the one angle, as all real poetry. ... I like it so tremendously, & feel it's very "special" and "intimate" ... I think I almost like the first two parts more than anything I have ever read.' His perceptive reading touched Rosamond, particularly as she valued her brother's literary judgement and expected much from his own efforts in the same direction.

> I shall never have a better letter than yours from anyone about my book. It isn't for the praise I value it (though of course I loved that) but for the understanding of what I was driving at, & the feeling I had of wanting it to seem like poetry, and half-unreal. ... I know I shall never write anything else like it: I'm not that person any more, but I want to write things approximating more & more to poetry.

By the end of the first week the only review to have appeared was a short notice in the Darlington *Northern Echo*. Harold Raymond did his best to sound encouraging. 'I notice that Bowes & Bowes of Cambridge took another six today,' he wrote, 'and Mawson, Swan & Morgan of Newcastle have already sold over two dozen. I think this is a promising week's work, but it is too early to make any prophecies as yet. What we really want now, of course, is a few really good reviews.' Two weeks later his wish was abundantly granted by publication in the *Sunday Times* of a eulogy by Rudie's old friend, the distinguished poet and critic Alfred Noyes.

It is not often that one can say with confidence of a first novel by a young writer that it reveals new possibilities for literature [wrote Noyes]. But there are qualities in this book that mark it out as quite the most striking first novel of this generation. . . . The modern young woman, with all her frankness and perplexities in the semi-pagan world of today, has never been depicted with more honesty, or with a more exquisite art. The style is lucid and simple, and it has the subtlety of those great qualities. It is the kind of novel that might have been written by Keats if Keats had been a young novelist of to-day.

Thanks to this ecstatic encomium, *Dusty Answer* almost overnight became a best-seller, going into seven impressions within the first year. Harold Raymond could hardly believe his luck, that a first novel by an unknown author was suddenly being talked and written about every-where. 'The Noyes review has swept us off our feet,' he told Rosamond delightedly.

The telephone in our manufacturing department was very busy indeed ordering paper for the new impression and harrying printers and binders to put on an extra spurt. We have now sold over 1,000 and have orders for almost the entire balance of the first edition. The Times Book Club alone has ordered 300 copies during the last three days, and our hopes are so high that we are actually ordering paper for a third impression.

Following the lead set by the *Sunday Times*, other papers began to take serious notice. Christopher Morley in the *Saturday Review* wrote, 'We have not had since *The Constant Nymph* a first novel of such brilliant, cruel and tender beauty,' while in the opinion of *Country Life* the novel was 'rich in humanity, in understanding, in pictures, material and spiritual . . . [and contained] some of the most exquisite, lightly touched in glimpses of English scenery that have been given in any modern novel.' It was not all unadulterated praise, of course, some of the most distinguished critics voicing the more serious reservations. Leonard Woolf, writing in the *Nation*, thought that the book had great promise, although 'Miss Lehmann shows the clumsiness and lack of economy which so often accompanies freshness and exuberance in the work of inexperienced novelists,' while Desmond MacCarthy, under his by-line of 'Affable Hawk' in the *New Statesman*, expressed the view that *'Dusty Answer* is far above the average novel, but its merits are not those which make one confident that the author will write a better one'. Arnold Bennett, who patronisingly made clear that he had not troubled to read more than a hundred pages, complained to the readers of the *Evening Standard* that, 'I can perceive little or no originality in the work, and no genuine distinction. . . . I left the book with respect, and even liking, but without regret.' It was Rose Macaulay writing in Rudie's old paper, the *Daily News*, who launched the wittiest but also the most wounding attack. *'Dusty Answer* is a very readable novel,' she began, before going on to pour scorn, in particular disparaging the unattractive self-absorption of the heroine. 'The only question Judith asked of life was "Does he, or she, love me?" and the answer was, usually (as might be expected in such cases, for the intensely personal are not as a rule the most beloved), "No, not very much."' But after condemning the weakness of the Cambridge section, Miss Macaulay finished on a more kindly note. 'A little humour and more variety of vision would have made it a very good book; as it is, it is a very promising one.' Rosamond, stung by such an insensitive interpretation, was soothed by Raymond who, unwilling to have his young star upset, replied placatingly that the reviewer was plainly jealous. 'Rose Macaulay is a delightful person but unco' spinsterish, & she ought never to be allowed to review the work of any author of the same gender as herself.'

Delighted by her astonishing success, Rosamond was also unnerved by the unaccustomed attention. She shrank from the sudden 'terrifying' intrusion into her private life of journalists and photographers, and came to dread the daily avalanche of letters from unknown members of the public. 'It would be less than true to pretend that I did not experience pleasure, gratification, from my sudden change of status,' she recalled, 'but all the reviews and publicity made me feel as if I'd exposed myself nude on the platform of the Albert Hall.' By temperament a subscriber to her father's view of women as delicate and subservient creatures, she was appalled to find herself hailed as one of the new post-war breed of liberated feminist. 'I was simply horrified. I thought, What have I done? . . . Like the old woman in the nursery rhyme I wanted to exclaim: "This is none of I!"' Worse was the other side of the coin, when a number of readers accused her of obscenity, of grave offences against womanly decorum, of dwelling indelicately on unhealthy subjects such as carnal love and unnatural passion.[1] One letter signed, 'Mother of Six', stated simply, 'Before consigning your book to flames, would wish to inform you of my disgust that anyone should pen such filth, especially a MISS.' For a sensitive, gently-nurtured young woman to be the source of such hostility was profoundly agitating, and Rosamond thought back enviously to the androgynous disguises assumed by the Brontës and George Eliot, 'the masculine masks they had adopted for the sake of moral delicacy'. Particularly painful was the disapproval shown by older members of her own family, some of whom were shocked and dismayed that the innocent child they had once known should now be responsible for 'the outpourings of a sex-maniac'. As a result of this unlooked-for notoriety, Rosamond wrote years later, 'an incurable ambivalence developed in me with regard to my profession after the smash-hit of *Dusty Answer*'.

Intensifying her feelings of anxiety were the agonies and uncertainties about the immediate future. '[I was] quite uninterested in fame because all I wanted to do was to get divorced and marry Wogan.' Since their return from the south of France in January, relations between Rosamond, Leslie and Wogan had continued harmoniously; there had been some frank but friendly discussions, during which Leslie had at last agreed that there was no further point in trying to prolong his marriage, and that according to gentlemanly custom he would do the decent thing and allow his wife to divorce him. It was at this point that Rosamond received an invitation from her father-in-law who, unaware of what was going on, asked her to join him for a short holiday on the island of Eigg. Convinced that his marked fondness for her would guarantee his sympathy, she wrote explaining that she and Leslie had amicably agreed to part. Walter Runciman's response was as swift as it was unexpected: 'he sent my letter straight to the King's Proctor as evidence of collusion, and never wrote or spoke to me again.' From that moment the situation changed very much for the worse. Under the terms of the law then in force, a woman could be divorced by her husband only on grounds of

---

[1] The very next year, 1928, saw the publication and subsequent prosecution of Radclyffe Hall's novel of lesbian love, *The Well of Loneliness*.

adultery, and collusion, the conspiring between husband and wife to bring about a divorce, was a criminal act. There could be no further possibility of civilised co-operation, and Runciman and Philipps were forced into position in enemy camps. Furthermore as it was considered scandalous in 1927 for a woman to be the guilty party in a divorce, Rosamond and Wogan had to be scrupulously careful not to give rise to any damaging gossip. 'I haven't seen Wogan for a horribly long time,' Rosamond wrote miserably to Dadie on 10 May. 'I practically never do see him now, & everything seems empty & I go back & back on the past since I daren't go forward into the future.'

The future may have been indistinct, but the lovers were determined that one way or another they would eventually become man and wife. '[Before] it all seemed so dream-like, & unreal,' Wogan wrote. 'Now I feel that an enormous machine has begun to slowly revolve & that we are all being caught up in it. Darling, darling, am I really going to marry you? . . . Even now I can only half believe it.' At a loss what to do next, Wogan turned to his father for advice in the complicated process of releasing Rosamond from her marriage without ruining her reputation. To Sir Laurence the whole affair was distasteful, first, that Wogan should have fallen in love with a married woman, and second, that that woman should be the daughter-in-law of his old friend, Walter Runciman, who had done him the favour of taking his son into his own business. He promised none the less to do everything in his considerable power to help. 'Daddy is being simply wonderful to me; so kind & sympathetic that I want to throw my arms round him & cry,' wrote Wogan histrionically. Having consulted his lawyers, Sir Laurence issued instructions that Rosamond must ask Leslie for a separation, after which it would be comparatively straightforward to proceed towards divorce. On one issue, as Wogan explained, his father was adamant: if there had to be a divorce, then 'Leslie *must be* divorced, not you'; to this end it was crucial that,

> whichever way this thing goes through, it is better for you, & for me, if we do not appear as friends even before strangers. It saves your reputation considerably if I come along, meet you & fall in love with you after you have been separated from your husband. . . . After you are separated we are to begin to meet casually &

gradually get very intimate & fall in love. By that strategy you are exempted from deserting Leslie for me & I am a little bit saved from running away with another man's wife.

There was an additional point to bear in mind. 'If my father knew that we had slept together, even with Leslie's knowledge, he would never understand. That part we *must* keep quiet.'

The one obstacle to this otherwise commendable scheme was that although Leslie had originally been prepared to play along, his father, to whom the very word divorce was anathema, was so enraged by Rosamond's behaviour that he absolutely forbade his son to co-operate in any way whatever: it was out of the question, said Mr Runciman, that the blameless Leslie should have to act the guilty party to oblige his unfaithful wife. The only alternative was for Leslie to divorce Rosamond, in theory condemning her to live beyond the pale, never to be received in respectable society. With neither side prepared to yield, the situation seemed to have reached stalemate, until suddenly a new element was introduced by Leslie's embarking on an affair with a cousin of Wogan's, Honor Philipps, daughter of Lord Kylsant. This was welcome news to Wogan and Rosamond, both of whom promoted the relationship vigorously, but unfortunately Leslie soon lost interest and the affair petered out. Leslie continued to live and work in Newcastle, doing nothing either to further or prevent divorce, while Rosamond remained based at Fieldhead, discreetly meeting Wogan whenever she could at safe houses and in the company of friends.

For both, it was a time of great anxiety. Intensely in love, they longed only to be with each other, and the frustrations of their situation inevitably caused strain and quarrels between them. 'Discussions, lawyers, family, gossip of friends & acquaintances have all combined to sap me,' Rosamond wrote.

The spiritual ecstasy is there all right, wells up often: but it *is* a terribly difficult relationship now. You must be patient with me darling, & remember, remember, remember that that cold lecturing is absolutely no good. . . . I know perfectly well what's happening to me when I'm in one of those awful moods, & can get straight in time. But the more you go on the more I go on. . . . If only you needed me to comfort & strengthen you a little more often, how it would help.

Once or twice Wogan lost his head, frantically begging Rosamond to throw her reputation to the winds and run off with him before he was driven to insanity by the impotence of his position – 'Are we ever ever ever going to be together? . . . Oh God, the strain of all this! I shall die before it is over, or else go mad' – but he was always brought back to his senses by his father's moderating influence. 'Poor Daddy. He goes on saying "Don't leave a stone unturned. Only run away with her as a last resort. You have no idea what a difference it would make to you both if you got it this other way."'

A further source of tension was the jealousy each felt about that part of the other's life which existed independently. Wogan suffered from the usual lover's possessiveness, resenting Rosamond's old friends and the time she spent with them when he was not of the company. Her jealousy was more complex, partly on account of her far more precarious position, which led her to feel uncomfortably insecure. She was envious not only of Wogan's friendships, in particular, with ex-girlfriends, but of his whole sophisticated social world, of his glamorous London life, his evenings at night-clubs, at the ballet and opera, his weekends at amusing house-parties, when she was dismally marooned at Bourne End. When he could not see Rosamond, Wogan considered it only natural that he should try and pass the time as pleasantly as possible, take his mind off missing her by the distractions of his old way of life, while in her eyes it was bitterly unfair that he should be off gambling at Le Touquet when she throughout the summer was bored and lonely in the depressing nursing-home atmosphere of Fieldhead. Predictably these issues led to some reproachful exchanges. 'Darling don't be jealous of my other life as you call it,' Wogan wrote to her:

> You accuse me of gadding about. . . . I dare not ring you up. I dare not write to you. We merely discuss my easy life, accuse one another of forgetfulness & get harsh & more miserable. Complete silence & separation would be much easier. . . . This is a horrid letter, & you will go on saying 'he doesn't understand' to my 'I do, I do, I do'. . . . But we don't belong to each other yet, & . . . we

mustn't be impatient, jealous, mistrusting. . . . Oh God darling I can assure you that I am as jealous of Cambridge, Stephen Tennant, John, Lytton, Dadie as you can ever be of anything of mine.

Dadie was the one person they knew who was equally a friend to both. In his role as her novel's 'onlie begetter', he had become a close confidant of Rosamond's, while Wogan, once Dadie's infatuation had evaporated, came to feel deep affection for this clever, quicksilver young man. 'Our relationship is far the most important thing I have got outside this vast overwhelming love for Rosamond,' he told him, while to Rosamond herself he wrote: '[Dadie] seems very happy with me & our relationship is perfect according to my standard.' Having recently been awarded a fellowship at King's, Dadie lived in rooms in college but needed regular escape from the austerity of the university, and with this Wogan was more than ready to assist, giving him an open invitation to stay at the family house in Hill Street, off Berkeley Square. 'We did have such fun watching Dadie dress this evening to go out,' he wrote. 'Powder, eyelash grease, eye brows, rouge, lip stick – etc – he rivals Stephen Tennant.' In the morning there was usually a highly dramatised rendering of the events of the night before, whether of an 'orgy at the Horse Guards' or of a fashionable first night. 'I was woken by an excited raving uncontrollable figure clad in a pink bath towel dancing round my room. . . . [Dadie with Lytton] had gone to the Maughams' party after the first night of Noel Coward's play . . . [and] met Noel Coward & his mistress & his boy sleeping partner, & met Ivor Novello & all the other gods. . . . He said it had been like drinking nectar.' Up one minute, down the next, Dadie was suffering miserably over an affair with Peter Morris, an acquaintance since childhood of Rosamond's. 'The Peter affair looks terribly bad,' Wogan reported. 'It does give me a queer taste, like sulphur, to help a person who six months before was experiencing the same anguish over myself.'

Rosamond, still based at Bourne End, was aching to escape from her mother. It was not that Alice was unsympathetic, even if in principle she disapproved of divorce – although it is unlikely that she knew the full story behind the marriage, she knew enough to realise there was no question of Rosamond's returning to her husband – but her brisk and bracing attitude was grating to the nerves, as was her expressed opinion that Wogan was too highly strung to provide the steady emotional support her daughter needed. Longing to be away, and financially independent for the first time in her life, Rosamond at the end of July took a restorative holiday in St Jean de Luz accompanied by Dora, Peter Morris's elegant sister, after which for the rest of that exceptionally hot summer she stayed as often as she could with friends where Wogan could visit her. 'Oh! those three wonderful nights! . . . Going over them again in my brain fires me,' he told her after one such weekend. In counterpoint to the happiness of these reunions was the constant fear that Rosamond might become pregnant, which would present a problem of appalling dimensions. As the summer wore on and the tension increased, Rosamond grew thin and vulnerable to infection, with the result that her menstrual periods, referred to in code as 'Jane', grew irregular, giving rise to a number of false alarms. 'Oh darling I am terrified of Jane. I should have thought you were too weak and ill to conceive after flu,' Wogan wrote anxiously on one such occasion. 'I have got panic about starting a baby. Do take some steps to encourage Jane – please. It would be the end of everything. Those pills, sweetheart, can't you take them? Shall I send you some?'

Meanwhile *Dusty Answer* continued its dizzying climb up the bestseller list, and 'a torrent of letters' flooded in, many from complete strangers. John Galsworthy declared that he had been 'deeply impressed'; Archibald MacLeish asserted that '*Dusty Answer* is a much better book than the most favourable of your critics make it, because it establishes for you a free & viable road over any kind of country (unlike Mrs Woolf's sea-mist which can only blow over vague sea & breaks up at once on the cliffs – in the hot sun). . . . You will write better novels. But you will write them because you wrote this one.' Compton Mackenzie wrote of the delight she had given 'to a brother writer who is at the same time quite a sensible reader and feels as if he had been walking about in a magical dawn'. Soon afterwards Mackenzie invited Rosamond to dine with him at the Gargoyle, an occasion which marked the beginning of what he was to describe as 'a friendship which has been one of the privileges and pleasures of my life'. One of the most treasured opinions was that of Lytton Strachey, who, it was reported, regarded *Dusty Answer* as remarkable for a first novel. 'The disadvantage to my mind is that it is too romantic and charged with sunset sentiment', wrote Lytton to Roger Senhouse. 'But very well and carefully done – without horrors in taste (a rare thing nowadays) and really at moments moving.' Chatto had sold the book in America to Henry Holt & Co. for publication on 1 September 1927, and now Holt telegraphed the news that the novel was to be Book of the Month Club choice for that month. Harold Raymond was beside himself with excitement. 'I am so bubbling over with joy that I can't think of anything to say,' he told Rosamond. 'If Holt sells only 45,000 to the Club, you would draw on that alone at least £1200. But that's a small matter compared with the value of this selection on the ordinary bookstore sales of the book. Moreover, its value to your future is immense.[2] Here you are, an absolutely established author on your first novel.' The size of the British market could not, of course, begin to compete with the American. 'I feel almost ashamed now of mentioning your sales in this mingy book-borrowing little island but they have very nearly reached 6000 & go on very steadily . . . with luck we might reach 10,000 before Xmas.' Anxious to capitalise further on the novel's phenomenal success – 23,000 copies printed by the end of the year – Raymond added that he very much hoped Rosamond would seriously consider Holt's suggestion of visiting the United States.

With her distaste growing for the furore caused by her novel, by the letters and reviews and the unaccustomed publicity, the prospect of crossing the Atlantic to face more of the same, and leaving Wogan perhaps for months, seemed to Rosamond unbearable: she almost wished she could disown the book altogether. Of course she was pleased by aspects of her triumph, particularly by the Book of the Month selection, but as she confessed to Harold Raymond, 'It's rather terrifying somehow when a thing you have made yourself, very privately, becomes so very public'; and in a magazine interview she confessed, 'I feel I have outgrown *Dusty Answer*, that I have cast it off as a snake casts off a dead skin.' However, as it became increasingly clear to both Wogan and Rosamond that a lengthy separation would undoubtedly help their cause, it was reluctantly decided that she should go. 'I just burst into

---

[2] Such was the novel's enduring reputation that thirty years later Rosamond was to write that only now was she 'beginning at last to resign myself to the probability of being remembered, if at all, as the author of *Dusty Answer*'.

tears when the word America is mentioned,' she wrote miserably to Dadie. 'I can't bear it. I am leaving everything hopelessly wrong & I can't see the future at all.' Wogan, too, was in a frenzy of melodramatic despair. 'My nerves have completely gone & at the slightest thing I scream. I know I might kill you at any moment. I am in a hideous nightmare. . . . Oh God, how I shall long for you. . . . How are we going to say goodbye! While you were in France I too was circling round that awful picture, "How were we going to say goodbye?" . . .'

On 25 August 1927, four months after her novel's publication in England, Rosamond left for the United States on board RMS *Scythia*. The weather was bad, and all the way across the Atlantic, she wished 'this hateful ship . . . was going very fast indeed the other way'. As they sailed up the Hudson, 'I remember standing on deck and seeing the Statue of Liberty and tears absolutely pouring down my face.' In New York she stayed with Helen and Georgene Davis, spinster daughters of Alice's brother, who were kindness itself, 'the essence of thoughtful, concentrated, virginal femininity turning to old-maidishness . . . I tell them nothing'. Rosamond's anguish at being parted from Wogan made it impossible for her to enjoy her new experiences. 'I want to come home so badly that, if I let myself think for two minutes, I can hardly refrain from dashing to book my passage on the next steamer.' The sales of *Dusty Answer* had already exceeded 72,000 and reviews were excellent, but Rosamond remained unmoved. 'The extravagance of the reviews I get really does sicken me. . . . What a queer country! – clever schoolboy judgments, schoolboy politics, schoolboy enthusiasms, emotions & extravagances. Every original work hailed as a work of genius.' After New York, she went to Dedham, Massachusetts, to stay with Rosamond Hamlin, one of the Peabody girls Alice had tutored, now married with children, and from there to relations in Pittsburgh, before going to the Davis family farm in Northwood – 'very elementary people, very New England, totally uninterested in literature or my work. They weren't at all impressed.'

Returning to New York in the warm October weather, Rosamond explored the city, taking long bus rides through Manhattan. 'Those threatening buildings pressing in on you, the noise & rush, the view of all those mighty shapes piling themselves terrace on terrace into the sky . . . New York is thrilling, appalling,' she wrote to Wogan. The notices

were extravagantly complimentary, demands for interviews were incessant, and the sales were still climbing, 100,000 copies by the beginning
of December, with news from England of 14,000 copies sold, and
translations, handled by the literary agent Curtis Brown, under way into
French, Danish and Norwegian. As word went round of the young
Englishwoman's celebrity, invitations began to arrive, including one
from a wealthy couple with a house on Long Island, described in detail
to Wogan, where among others she met Edna Ferber, 'a very metallic
witty Jewess (you remember she wrote "Show Boat") & the [Pulitzer
Prize-winning] writer Louis Bromfield. . . . It was so ridiculous the way
they took no notice of me till they discovered I'd written "D.A." &
then —!' To Harold Raymond she wrote, 'Wherever I go people are
discussing Judith & weeping over her. I think the real secret of its
success is the Englishness of it.' Her publisher, delighted with the impact
she was making, arranged several parties for her,

> or tried to, but it was Prohibition and entertaining was at a very
> low ebb. Twice I was rung up by Elliot Holt who said, 'No point in
> coming: everybody's under the table.' People used to drink raw
> alcohol and pass out. I went once to a big dinner party given by
> Holt. . . . For the first course a soup cup came with a lid on,
> presumably cold soup, but it was alcohol. Most of the conversation
> was about Sacco and Vanzetti. There were some literary people
> invited, Archibald MacLeish, for instance, and his wife, one or two
> literary critics, who were reviewing my book in a very ecstatic way.
> But I was in a state of despair because I couldn't bear all my
> publicity. I couldn't bear wandering around America where I never
> found a congenial companion, and I was always in dread of missing
> Wogan's next letter.

Wogan, meanwhile, was tormented by Rosamond's desolate tone, and
tormented even more by the long intervals when no mail arrived from
the States at all. 'Oh darling, darling: this is too much to bear. No letter
from you since last Saturday week. . . . Five mail boats! Five times have I
read "Mail may be expected & will be delivered in London to day from
the following countries: – U.S.A. etc".' But then in November came
good news. Leslie, from whom Rosamond had now been separated for

nearly a year – 'Please address me by the noble name of Lehmann, to which I have decided to revert,' she wrote to John – suddenly emerged from stasis and agreed to start divorce proceedings, on condition that he did the divorcing. Although originally the Philippses had refused to countenance Rosamond being put in the position of guilty party, the events of the past twelve months had led them to realise they had little alternative: the Runcimans were immovable, and it was clear that whatever happened now the lovers were not to be parted. Wogan was exultant. 'Oh my God, I am alive again,' he wrote to Rosamond. 'It is over: I am going to have you all to myself for ever & ever. . . . Life is only just going to start. The curtain is going up. I feel I have fought a terrific battle, & have won. I have convinced all my family. . . . And they are so happy at seeing me happy again. We have won, darling.' Excitedly he poured out plans for their reunion: when Rosamond sailed home in mid-December, he would meet her at Cherbourg, they would go straight to Paris, and then have two or three weeks secretly in France before returning to England to face whatever they had to face. 'Six more weeks before I see you. I am burning & burning with impatience. . . . God knows how I am going to pass the time. Sleep is right out of the question. I just toss about, & kiss & kiss & kiss you!' If all went smoothly, he told her, she would have her decree nisi by February, and they would be free to marry at the end of the summer.

On 5 November Rosamond was at a dinner party on Long Island when a cable was handed to her: 'WOGAN PHILIPPS SERIOUSLY ILL GASTRIC ULCER VERY WEAK AT MOMENT BUT IMPROVING AND EVERY HOPE RECOVERY'. Terrified by this and by a letter which swiftly followed from Beatrix explaining more fully that Wogan had suffered a massive internal haemorrhage which had dangerously weakened him, Rosamond was thrown into panic, convinced Wogan was about to die, frantic to get home. Immediately cancelling all engagements she managed to book a passage on the *Mauretania* sailing a week later. Again the crossing was rough and she was wretchedly seasick. Her mother, who met her at Plymouth on a dark November morning, was shocked at how thin and ill she looked. In London, Rosamond went first to Hill Street to call on Sir Laurence. Calmly she told him that she would not agree to any further separation from Wogan, that from now on they were going to be together. Sir Laurence, unwilling to put his son under further strain, agreed, asking only that she not upset the patient with too intense a display of emotion. Then at last she went to the nursing-home to see Wogan, who was overjoyed at her return. 'He is very weak,' she reported afterwards to John, '[but] he is miraculously better considering that 12 days ago they didn't think he could live.'

6

Ros and Wog

By April 1928 Wogan was at last well enough to leave his nursing-home, and he and Rosamond travelled down to the south of France to stay with Matt and Ursula Ridley, who had taken a villa at Ste Maxime on the Côte d'Azur. For the first few days, exhausted by the months of nervous strain, the lovers could do little more than sleep; but soon reviving, they began to enjoy the spring weather, reading in the garden, strolling into the village to drink vermouth under the plane trees, and as a mean mistral abated and the temperature rose, sunbathing on the beach and swimming, Rosamond protecting her fair complexion with dark glasses and a large hat. 'It's so extraordinary to be able to be with Wogan day after day,' she wrote blissfully to Dadie. 'I feel very well and safe and happy and lucky. . . . I'm beginning to feel "married" to Wogan now. It takes a lot of one's energies moulding & hammering the relationship into shape & trying to learn how to make it really good & not just ordinary . . . I really think I should die if I failed this time.'

As their vitality returned, both she and Wogan started to work, Wogan, freckled and sunburnt, 'painting wildly' from dawn to dusk, while Rosamond continued with her new novel. 'Now I am stuck, but only lazily so,' she told Dadie. 'I mean I know what I want to do, but I haven't the energy.' The Ridleys were ideal companions, providing not only essential cover – the divorce could still be jeopardised by blatant evidence of adultery – but sympathetic companionship, Ursula wickedly

111

amusing, Matt clever and flirtatious. 'We get along very happily,' Rosamond reported. 'They are both as nice as can be.' Ursula, however, cynical by nature, viewed the idyll in a slightly less roseate light. '[Rosamond] is *so* attractive & I'm devoted to her but she has no sense of humour, & is desperately intense & serious. She wanted to read poetry aloud in the evenings – but we insisted on P. G. Wodehouse – which she reads as if it was poetry! . . . Then she takes Wogan's painting so seriously, is always driving him to it, & making him "follow his art" – whereas really he can't paint at all.'

On 11 May came news that Rosamond's decree nisi had been granted, and a fortnight later she and Wogan returned to England. Although beginning to tire of the Riviera she was depressed by the knowledge that coming home meant again living apart, until her decree absolute came through in six months' time. Wogan went back to Hill Street and his office in the City, while Rosamond, determined to avoid Fieldhead and wishing to be on her own to write, rented the Mill House at Tidmarsh in Berkshire, a house which had once belonged to Lytton Strachey. In spite of having turned down, at Wogan's high-minded insistence, a film offer for *Dusty Answer* worth $15,000, she was now financially independent, the money earned from her book enabling her over the past year not only to support herself but to refuse any financial assistance from Leslie, a refusal which had distressed her ex-husband considerably. At Tidmarsh Wogan appeared at discreet intervals, but as being seen together might endanger the divorce, great care had to be taken: 'we always had to be looking out for the King's Proctor, so his visits had to be rather secret.' It was another hot summer and the two of them made the most of their brief interludes together, by day swimming in the mill pond and lazing in the garden, making love most of the night. 'Last night was the most marvellous thing I have ever ever known,' Wogan wrote in early July 1928. 'It was the utmost happiness a human being can endure without dying. . . . The walk to the station this morning was so lovely . . . wrapt up in the ecstasies of love & you: & the hedges smelt so divine & everything shone in the early, wet light.' The contrast of this to his life at home with his parents was a painful one: their company was now perceived to be 'unutterably boring' and their philistinism deeply wounding to his artist's soul. 'My whole spirit is starved there,' he declared. 'I have a tremendous craving for something very beautiful &

spiritual. I long for some music . . . I long to paint or draw, but what? Where?' His previous unquestioning dependence on his father was disintegrating fast, with irritated exasperation taking the place of admiration and respect. '[Daddy] is too *bloody sensible* in all his outlooks,' he complained to Rosamond. 'Here, neither writing or painting is mentioned. Painting is never suggested as a possible profession, & they never think of you having a profession at all. It is a family without any idea of art.'

Under such stress the same cracks and strains began to appear as in the long separations of the year before, with Rosamond resenting Wogan's social life in London when she was stuck down in the country on her own. 'It is no use accusing & accusing each other. We will wear each other down, as last year,' Wogan warned her. Soon the scenes became so wearing that he dreaded telephoning her, dreaded coping with her moods when they met. 'Darling, there is one thing I feel I must try & explain. . . . It is the *way* your misery comes out – it drives me away. . . . I daren't admit things, daren't talk to people, daren't enjoy things because they raise this kind of jealousy in you, which isn't jealousy at all, but unhappiness because I am away from you, & you can't follow me. I seem to have to defend all I do.' Part of the trouble was Rosamond's uneasiness about her position as a divorced woman (at heart she was too respectable to take pleasure in being regarded as 'fast'), but much of her jealousy stemmed from the old embedded conviction that she did not rightfully 'belong', that her place in Wogan's world was somehow precarious and unmerited. Although he wished to be sympathetic, Wogan was impatient by nature and his temper was tried by the incessant complaining; driven to the limits, he would explode, and then they would quarrel bitterly.

In August Wogan again fell ill: as before, his symptoms were attributed to a burst stomach ulcer – and as before the diagnosis was wrong. (It was years before the actual cause of the trouble, a hiatus hernia, was discovered.) For a time they remained in London with Rosamond devotedly nursing him, until he told her he could no longer endure having her in the room. She 'wore him out & got on his nerves – and he much preferred his awful, stupid, but competent nurse to look after him', he told her. 'In the end,' she said, 'I went away feeling injured and miserable! [But] directly he was well the whole thing was just as before.' As Wogan began to recover, his doctor advised Sir Laurence that there should be no question of his son returning to work in the City for at least a year: he should live in the country, have plenty of rest, and be allowed to do very much as he pleased. In compliance with this agreeable prescription, Rosamond took Wogan to convalesce in Quainton, a village near Aylesbury, in a rented cottage which for propriety's sake they shared with Beatrix and an American friend of hers, the rich and dashing Henrietta Bingham. As Wogan's strength was restored, he turned to his painting while Rosamond wrote. Among their visitors at Quainton were Lytton Strachey and Carrington. 'Rosamond lives in an absurd little cottage with roses, and arbours', Carrington reported. 'She and Wogan look like that picture of Alice in Wonderland enlarged. They can scarcely move in and out of rooms and their heads touch the ceilings ... the village looks exquisitely beautiful ... with shining thatched cottages in the sun and great windmill dominating all the little houses like a broody hen, on the green.' For once the fairytale imagery was apt: with Wogan by her side, her work going well, and the final decree imminent, Rosamond had her every wish fulfilled. 'I know I know how monstrously lucky I am,' she wrote to Dadie. 'I am the one living example of a person who has got what she wants. The gods must surely punish me.'

After an autumn in the country Wogan and Rosamond returned to London, to be married quietly on 21 November 1928 at a register office in Victoria in the presence of both their families.[1] 'I'm glad that W & R are at the end of the difficulties which have involved us all in so much unhappiness,' Alice remarked feelingly to John. Immediately afterwards the couple left for a brief honeymoon in Paris before returning to London to set about house-hunting. Sir Laurence was prepared to be generous, telling Wogan that he intended to leave him handsomely provided for in his will. 'He wants me to take Llanstephan & entail it in our family. He also leaves me Hill Street with liberty to sell, let or pawn. I told him we wanted to live in the country & he agreed.' More than simply agreeing, Sir Laurence offered them the use of the dower house on his property at Dalham, near Newmarket, which he would pay to have enlarged as it was too small comfortably to accommodate a family.

---

[1] In her entry in *Who's Who* Rosamond makes no mention of Leslie, listing only her marriage to Wogan.

This was an offer eagerly accepted, Rosamond in particular attracted by the proximity of Dalham to Cambridge. Meanwhile as a temporary measure the couple rented an old grey-stone house with a garden, in the village of Kidlington, near Oxford. 'A slightly invalidish ménage . . . very early hours, gentle talk – a dreadful little dog etc,' was the description given by Lytton Strachey after a brief stay there.

Almost as soon as they had moved into the Old Rectory Farm, Rosamond was summoned to Fieldhead, where her father died on 22 January 1929. Rudie had been a helpless invalid for over ten years, for the last two or three wholly unrecognisable as his old self; by the time he died he had long been lost to his family, and much of their grieving for the fascinating father they once knew was already done. By this stage, 'death', as Rosamond observed, 'was kinder than life'. With her children gone, Alice, though her day still stoically revolved around tending her husband, had made some independent life for herself by undertaking voluntary work for the county, eventually becoming a county councillor, a JP, a governor of several local schools, and serving for thirty-five years on the Buckinghamshire County Education Committee. Nonetheless it was a sad time for them all as they gathered for the funeral at the church in Wooburn: Helen, now living in Marlow, drove over with Mounty, Bea came down from London, and John from Cambridge. Flags were flown at half-mast in Cambridge and the Union held a minute's silence; the Leander Club at Henley sent a standard to drape over the coffin. Rosamond, reflecting on Rudie's glamour and that dazzling early promise, never to be fulfilled, wrote, 'When I look at the startling beauty of his face in early photographs I seem to detect in it a fatal excess; and it occurs to me that, though he lived to be 70, and was my father, he died of his fabulous youth.'

The occasion of her father's death was made harder to endure by the debilitating bouts of nausea Rosamond suffered in the early stages of pregnancy. Although she and Wogan were delighted by the idea of a baby, the actuality was fraught with problems: prostrated with morning sickness, she was tormented by memories of her earlier experience. 'Leslie haunts me in an absolutely pathological way – with all his horror of offspring – & his horror of *me* for wanting them.'[2] As winter turned

---

[2] In 1932 Leslie married again and two years later fathered a son. Rosamond writing to

into spring, she continued to feel ill and depressed, able to read only for half an hour at a time or occasionally tinker with her manuscript. As the weather grew warmer, Wogan would disappear all day sketching while she sat in the garden in a trance, watching the rooks cawing in the elms, the pigeons fluttering on the lawn. 'Wogan works at fever heat,' she wrote to her brother, 'but I, alas, still feel like a none-too-fresh vegetable, & begin to think I shan't recover the use of my head till September. It *is* depressing.'

For Wogan, on the other hand, life was more than satisfactory, married to the woman he loved, a baby on the way, and finally free to follow his chosen path as a painter. This last had been a contentious issue with his father, in whose view painting was all very well as a hobby but in no sense could it be considered a career. Now, however, with Wogan unable to return to business for the immediate future, Sir Laurence offered him a deal: he would subsidise his son for two years, but if at the end of that time he was unable to earn a sufficient income as an artist, then he must find some more profitable profession. Determined to prove himself, Wogan threw himself into his new life with passion; he enrolled at the Ruskin School of Art in Oxford, where he was taught by Gilbert Spencer and John Nash, and at home worked for hours a day in his makeshift studio.

By the summer Rosamond was feeling better, and in July she and Wogan took a short holiday in Cornwall before going up to London to await the birth, renting from Violet Hammersley a house in Tite Street which had once belonged to the painter John Singer Sargent. On 25 August 1929 she went into labour, attended by a monthly nurse and a fashionable young gynaecologist, Hugh Taylor. The arrival of her son was traumatic.

> I had the most appalling labour anyone's ever had, going on for two or three days and nights. Then it was a forceps delivery. The gynaecologist blamed the anaesthetist for giving me anaesthetic too soon, which stopped the contractions. He panicked and shook

---

congratulate him asked if his attitude had changed. 'Honestly, no,' Leslie replied. 'But one gets older & better equipped, more cynical & much more tolerant, more interested in what is & less in what should be, so I didn't really think it would.'

me and said I wasn't trying, and the nurse was very indignant on my account, and my mother downstairs, not the most tactful person, giving Wogan hell, poor Wogan marching up and down, almost off his head, and just as things were beginning to start again I heard the gynae say, 'The baby's heart-beat's slowing, and if we don't get it out very soon, he'll be dead.' Then I was put right out and he called his brother in to help. Poor Hugo was torn out, a high forceps delivery. When I came round Hugo, blue, was put in my arms. He hadn't breathed for 40 minutes. They thought at first he was still born. I was torn to pieces. The baby was huge with an enormous head, and goodness knows how many stitches I had. I could not move hand nor foot for several days. From the waist down I was paralysed. They'd given me chloroform. When Wogan finally came in he said, 'And darling, the best of it is you've had the worst time any woman's ever had!'

A month later the baby, Hugo John Laurence, was christened at Dalham. His mother was enchanted by him. 'Hugo is full of divine smiles,' she told her brother. 'He has exquisite features & enormous eyes – in fact altogether *un spécimen bien réussi*.'

By the beginning of the following year, 1930, with health and energy restored, Rosamond returned thankfully to her work. 'I am writing 5 hours a day, & have given up all correspondence,' she told John, while to Dadie she confessed, 'When I think of the future, I think mostly of my work, my work, my work! I do so long to be settled at it. I know it could be good if I can manage it – this new novel.' She was not allowed to settle at it for long, however, as Sir Laurence suddenly announced that he had changed his mind about the house at Dalham, deciding that it was too small and not worth enlarging. It was 'a shattering blow' to Rosamond and Wogan, both furious with the old man as they prepared to start again looking for somewhere to live. And then, 'a miracle dropped into our laps'. In the tiny Oxfordshire village of Ipsden, near the Thames between Wallingford and Goring, they found the perfect house, a large, beautiful Queen Anne manor house which had once belonged to the novelist Charles Reade. Built of mellowed red brick, it was peaceful and remote, with a big shady garden, surrounded by woods and cornfields; down the hill a quarter of a mile away was the single village street of tiny, flower-fronted cottages, and in the distance could be seen the red-gold beech hangers of the Berkshire downs. 'It's a dream house,' Rosamond told Dadie, 'L-shaped on a hill, with a view for 40 miles, huge old trees on the lawn and a rookery – and an old dove house.'

While Rosamond moved between Fieldhead and Llanstephan, engaging servants and going up to London to shop for fabrics and furniture, Wogan camped at Ipsden to oversee the work in progress. He himself was engaged on a portrait of Rosamond's beloved Dandie Dinmont terrier, Sheltie, 'in a prospect of tulips'; Carrington was commissioned to paint six panels depicting exotic animals for the nursery door, and the young surrealist, John Banting, painted a mural in the hall (which privately Rosamond never cared for) and designed some wittily surrealist curtains made out of sackcloth edged with a giant tape-measure. Under Banting's fashionably contemporary influence, aluminium tables and tubular steel chairs were introduced as innovative contrast to the more traditional chintz and mahogany. '[Ipsden] is completely absorbing us – and *is* going to be pretty, I think,' Rosamond told Dadie. '*What* fun I propose for myself this summer, filling the house with people!'

It was at Ipsden that Rosamond and Wogan properly began their married life. They were an exceptionally attractive couple, devoted to each other, glamorously good-looking, both artists, both amusing, hospitable and relatively well-off. Rosamond, after years of anxiety and disappointment, was in high spirits, happy with her husband, doting on her baby – '[whom] I loved overwhelmingly from the beginning' – thrilled with the house, making good progress with her book. Those who met her now for the first time encountered a lovely, lively young woman, with her dark hair prematurely threaded with grey and a deliciously voluptuous figure – her only flaw thick calves and ankles; she was full of warmth and vitality, and possessed a much-appreciated talent as mimic and raconteur. Frances Marshall, who had known Rosamond slightly at Cambridge, and who now as the lover of Ralph Partridge was part of Lytton Strachey's complex *ménage* at Ham Spray, found her transformed.

She had been a pretty, round-faced girl; she was now a *stunning* beauty, tall and slender, with a low musical voice and a gurgling laugh. . . . When Ralph and I first visited them in their own house their little boy Hugo was about two, and the family was completed by Ros's unattractive but adored dog Sheltie. . . . I had asked her in what order she would save her loved ones in case of fire, and she replied without hesitation, 'Oh, Sheltie first, then Hugo, then Wogan!'

Wogan himself, although very different in temperament, was equally appealing: good-natured, immensely charming, given to wild bursts of enthusiasm, with an almost childlike eagerness for new ideas and experience. 'Ros and Wog' soon became the focus of a wide circle, and Ipsden a centre for comfort and good talk. The social stigma of divorce, which had been so ominously predicted, was barely detectable. 'I heard that one or two ancient crones living in big houses round about debated whether they should call on us and decided they shouldn't . . . [but] our friends were all very jolly about it.'

Among those who came regularly to lunch and dine or to stay for the weekend, Dadie was naturally one of the most welcome. He was deeply devoted to both Philippses, although the path of his friendship with Rosamond never did run 'altogether through flowers'. The trouble was that Dadie was touchy, given to quarrels and pettish feuds; affectionate by nature and the loyallest of friends, he was also thin-skinned and jealous, quick to see desertion and betrayal in his friendships where none existed. Now he had chosen to take as a personal affront the decision to abandon Dalham and settle so far from Cambridge, and had retreated into a sulky silence out of which he had had to be lovingly wooed. 'Don't don't say, Dadie, that we will drift away from you', Rosamond coaxed him. 'If you only would realise what you mean to us – but you do really – & you are being naughty & cruel.' Thanks to Dadie's initial introduction, both Lytton Strachey and Carrington had become close friends, and as Ham Spray was less than twenty miles away, there was a frequent to-ing and fro-ing between the two houses. Lytton's russet beard and lanky form became familiar features, sunk deep into a sofa or deck-chair; he was regarded with affection, respect and not a little awe for his cynicism, wit and phenomenal erudition; Rosamond was always avid for his judgements, delivered in the squeaky Strachey voice, while Wogan loved Lytton unreservedly, looking up to him as his mentor. 'Lytton Strachey made a tremendous difference to my life. . . . He educated me, really, telling me what to read and discussing it.' With Carrington,

119

Rosamond had a more intimate relationship. This shy, self-deprecating woman with her pit-pony fringe, sandals and quaint cotton frocks gave the impression of a childlike innocence; but there was a changeling quality about her: the big blue eyes had a curious blankness, and she possessed an emotional elusiveness and ambivalent sexuality that were magnetic and disturbing. 'She was so vulnerable,' Rosamond wrote of her, '[and also] comic, loving, childlike, devious, anxious, faithful, tricky.' Carrington herself was fascinated by Rosamond, admiring her beauty and claiming to be envious of her luxurious clothes. 'Hateful Rosamond to have drawers of clean new silk stockings, and crêpe-de-chine underclothes!' she wrote teasingly to Lytton's niece, Julia Strachey. Carrington courted the young woman expertly. According to Diana Guinness, a friend and neighbour, 'Carrington wielded an extraordinarily powerful weapon which she used with unusual skill. It was flattery.' 'Do tell me,' Carrington wrote flirtatiously on one occasion, 'which dress you are wearing when you write to me. – If I dressed you I should make you look slightly Russian, with an astrakhan Pea jacket, & a white woolen [sic] dress. . . . And your hair in a great knob at the back of your head.'

Through Lytton and Dadie the Philippses were introduced into the heart of Bloomsbury society. For Rosamond the atmosphere was familiar, an extension of the bookish world known from childhood, but for Wogan it was a revelation: disaffected with the landed upper classes in which he had been brought up, he found the company of this intelligentsia, left-wing and literary, profoundly exciting. 'I absolutely took to it. I at last found [people] who made sense to me, [and] I moved right away from my old friends.' Although he was never on the same plane intellectually, Wogan charmed and entertained them. He was an amusing story-teller, even if his stories could not always be completely believed – what was referred to as his 'Welsh double-facedness' had always to be taken into account; but his openness and naivety were beguiling, and so, too, his readiness to be instructed, and the energy with which he hurled himself into arguments and discussions. Much of the talk went over his head, but this never bothered him. 'Oh, fuck-a-doodle-do!' he would crow cheerfully when in his opinion the conversation grew too elevated or intense. Lytton was enchanted by him, and so were Leonard and Virginia Woolf. 'The Woolfs loved

Wogan,' said Rosamond. 'They were tremendously amused by him. He could be very malicious himself and often saw the Bloomsberries as comic figures. Except Lytton, for whom he had the deepest respect and affection. But he could say shrewd and very biting things about some of them.' Rosamond was slightly less at ease with the Woolfs, especially with Virginia. Her masterpiece, in Rosamond's opinion, was her biography of Roger Fry, although the novels were also revered – *To the Lighthouse* above all – even if some of the stylistic tricks were sometimes found to be irritating: 'There are moments when the quivering antennae of her senses seem too receptive, and almost stifle one with minute impressions. Blinds sway, brooms tap, chairs creak too frequently.' (In person Virginia could be daunting, and her notoriously sharp tongue and hyper-critical judgements made Rosamond nervous. She suspected, wrongly as it turned out, that the older woman considered her novels banal. 'Perhaps that's why she was so nice to me: she never thought of me as an aspirant. She always was adorable, delightful company.'

Through her old friendship with Stephen Tennant, Rosamond became devoted to his lover, Siegfried Sassoon, whose work she much admired; an added bond was Sassoon's uncritical adoration of her little dog, Sheltie. Among the younger members of the coterie were Lytton's adored Roger Senhouse, in Rosamond's view 'one of the most attractive, handsome, debonair young men I've ever seen', Eddie Gathorne-Hardy, whom Wogan had known at Oxford, the Francophile Raymond Mortimer, and Eddy Sackville-West, 'a perfectly *awful* character, only saved by his glorious capacity for jokes and laughter'. These witty, literary, effeminate young men were all old friends, and liked to spar with and spark off each other, showing off to their hosts. A 'raffish lot', as Rosamond referred to them, '[they] seemed to enjoy coming [to Ipsden], though the cooking was very poor, very basic . . . [and] they were food snobs, with a great vogue for French cooking. But there was plenty of good wine: Wogan saw to that. There was a lot of drinking and a lot of fun. I looked after them and worked hard at making them comfortable and giving them plenty of food.'

John Banting came down to paint Rosamond's portrait, as did Henry Lamb, one of the few unquestionably heterosexual members of the group. Wogan, too, painted his wife again and again, with an almost fanatical zeal. A recent, and slightly younger, newcomer into the circle, the poet Stephen Spender, whose father had been a colleague of Rudie's on the *Daily News*, remembered that the house was full of Wogan's 'wild, somewhat childish paintings, amongst which were many portraits of Rosamond. Although these were not good portraits they brought out something grandiose, almost Byzantine, mosaic-like about her appearance.' Stephen, tall, fair, blue-eyed, a contradictory mix of innocence and tough ambition, quickly fell under Rosamond's spell, succumbing to her beauty and sweet nature and, even more, to her interest in himself. 'I think him so full of promise & charm that I forgive him his egotism, which is colossal,' she wrote to Dadie. Having had 'that absolute lunatic Stephen' staying in the house for a whole week, 'Wogan & I feel we have won through an exhausting struggle to being very fond of him – and oh! he is so eager for affection'. Impressed by his poetry, she took him to Ham Spray at Christmas to meet Lytton. '[Stephen] was a great success & rose rapidly to the seventh heaven of ecstasy, especially after Lytton had put on a pink paper cap and joined in "Up Jenkins".' Less successful was her attempt to foster a relationship between Stephen and her brother John whom she brought together during that same Christmas: with so much in common, it seemed these two attractive blond giants must take to each other, both poets, passionate about literature, politically in tune, travelling in the same direction sexually; but although they were to remain closely connected all their lives, the friendship remained uncomfortably competitive and quarrelsome, with Rosamond usually left in the middle trying to make peace between them. During that first meeting at Fieldhead, John and Stephen went for a walk together along the river towards Marlow; all Rosamond could hear of their conversation, she said, was an egotistical chorus of 'I,I,I,I, – like a flock of cawing crows'.

Distant in every sense from this bohemian society was Wogan's family, based at Llanstephan, in Wales. The Philippses were proud of their ancient Welsh ancestry – several members of the tribe lay buried in St David's Cathedral in Cardiff – and it was Sir Laurence who in 1915 had purchased the beautiful Llanstephan estate in Radnorshire, as well as later buying back nearby Picton Castle, built and continuously inhabited by Philippses since Norman times. The youngest of six sons, Sir Laurence was one of the eleven children of Sir James Erasmus Philipps, prebendary of Salisbury Cathedral. His wife, Ethel, was also from a clerical family, the only daughter of the Rev. Benjamin Speke, rector of Dowlish Wake in Somerset, her uncle the Hanning Speke who discovered the source of the Nile with Richard Burton. The Philippses had six children, five boys, Wogan, Hanning, James, the twins William and Geoffrey, and one girl, Gwenllian ('Gwen'), much the youngest. As well as Llanstephan, a great modern block of a house, there was the house in London, Dalham with its stud farm – Sir Laurence had become keenly interested in racing – and the villa in the south of France. The family was always moving restlessly from one to another, for social life in London, fishing at Llanstephan, shooting and racing at Dalham, winters on Cap Ferrat.

Rosamond had little in common with her parents-in-law, but she made it her business to be agreeable to them, and they, if they could not quite approve of her or her work (her novels reportedly had Sir Laurence 'swooning with horror'), nevertheless accepted her – particularly after the birth of Hugo – as one of the family. So much so that when a trip of Sir Laurence and Lady Philipps to India coincided with one of their sons, Geoffrey, falling ill, Rosamond was asked to stay at Llanstephan to look after him. This was no hardship as she was fond of Geoff, enjoyed the comfort of a well-run house, and with Hugo in the care of his nanny most of the day, was able to make good progress with her novel.

Less satisfactory was the fact that her husband had declined to accompany her. In pursuit of his painterly ambitions, and despite the lack of any discernible talent, Wogan had decided that he could not be a proper painter without sampling the life of an art student in Paris, studying drawing, living in picturesque squalor, and as Rosamond sourly recounted to Dadie spending every evening in seedy bars 'roaring out songs at the top of his voice & standing all the other students drinks'. He kept in touch only sporadically, and when Rosamond went over to visit him she was made to feel unwelcome and out of place. 'He put me into an awful little bug-infested hotel, and made it clear he thought my coming was an awful nuisance. I didn't fit in at all, and went back very depressed indeed. I didn't know if he was ever going to appear again.' In fact he returned only when it became clear that his brother's nephritis had taken a dangerous turn: his parents came back from India just before Geoff died. Rosamond's kindness during the crisis did not go unappreciated by her mother-in-law, who wrote to thank her for being 'such a dear to us'; she was glad, she added, that during this sad time, at least Wogan had had the chance to reacquaint himself with Llanstephan. 'Wogan really had forgotten it. We wish he would come & take charge of it & make it his interest as well as the painting.'

But Wogan was enjoying his bohemian existence far too much to pay attention to any future responsibilities as landed gentleman – or even, it seemed, to his obligations as husband and father. He did join his wife for a short motoring holiday in Brittany with Lytton and Dadie, but soon afterwards went off again by himself, this time sketching in Corsica, while Rosamond was left to take Hugo ('that not *altogether* unmixed blessing') for a bucket-and-spade holiday with Helen and her children on the Isle of Wight. This was enjoyable enough in its way, and it was a relief that Wogan was absent for some of the little boy's more terrible tantrums – 'he would have simply thrown him into the sea' – but Rosamond missed her husband and felt lonely returning to Ipsden without him. As she pointed out, 'Here we were, newly married and he supposed to be the devoted husband, very proud of his infant son, and in fact he was always going off at a tangent, neither to have nor hold'.

The trouble, as always, lay with both sides. Both Wogan and Rosamond were self-absorbed and demanding, and Wogan in particular, though charming and affectionate, was emotionally immature. (After visiting Ipsden one day, Lytton Strachey was asked, how was Wogan? 'He used to be *ten*,' said Lytton, 'now he's *eight*.') During the tense and harrowing period before their marriage, when sexual and emotional frustration was at its height, neither could imagine any greater happiness than spending the rest of their days peaceably together, writing, painting – and bringing up their children. Rosamond passionately wanted children, and Wogan liked the idea of having them, but when the first arrived he found the reality uncongenial. Like many men, he was bored by babies and resented his wife's absorption in motherhood. While Rosamond doted on her little boy and was blissfully happy in his company, either in the nursery or sitting on a rug on the lawn where she could 'watch Hugo's flawless piece of life playing in the sun', Wogan was often irritated by his son's presence. 'Wogan gave me a great scolding after you'd gone for having Hugo down to breakfast so spoiling the conversation,' Rosamond wrote to Frances Marshall in February 1932. 'I am so sorry! I do quite see he must have been a fearful bore . . . I am afraid I never thought about it.' A free and irresponsible spirit, Wogan wanted to go wherever the inclination took him, and the fact that with a small baby to look after, a nursery and nanny to supervise, Rosamond was often unable to accompany him, he regarded as unreasonable. 'What Rosamond wanted more than anything else was children, and I was thrilled [when we had them]. But then it took her away from me so much. We couldn't go abroad: the children came before *anything*; they became a bloody nuisance. And she totally lost interest in me.'

Wogan's sense of grievance was not wholly unjustified: to an extent Rosamond had lost interest. 'I never ceased to love Wogan, but after Hugo was born I stopped being *in* love with him.' This was partly a consequence of the birth itself, which had left her in a state of physical shock. 'After being torn to pieces like that, I simply couldn't *bear* the idea of sex. Much as I continued to love Wogan and wanted to share a bed with him, I couldn't bear the thought of being touched. He couldn't understand it and thought I'd turned against him. I don't know if I ever would have got over it, but I certainly never, never wanted to go to bed with him in that sense ever again. . . . He felt terribly rejected.' With Rosamond making only too clear her distaste for their increasingly infrequent love-making, and with neither willing nor apparently able to understand the other's point of view, they each blindly nursed a sense of injury and inevitably began drifting apart.

From the outside, however, the marriage still appeared idyllic. Certainly Wogan was warmly encouraging when his wife's second novel, *A Note in Music*, was published, again by Chatto & Windus, in September 1930. He himself drew a design for the cover, which was turned down, although his woodcut of two lovers kneeling by a pool remains on the title page. '[Wogan] thinks it infinitely better than "D[usty] A[nswer]",' Rosamond reported triumphantly to Dadie.

The title of *A Note in Music* is taken from a quotation from Landor: 'But the present, like a note in music, is nothing but as it appertains to what is past and what is to come.' As in *Dusty Answer*, the theme is of an imaginative but naive woman seduced by the glamour of a world to which she knows she can never rightfully belong; but as if in deliberate antithesis to the lush romanticism of the earlier novel, here the colours are dark and subdued, the mood sombre and austere. The story has two sources, both substantially transmogrified in the process of creation –

Rosamond's unhappy first marriage and life in Newcastle, and her experience of falling in love with Wogan, to whom the book is dedicated. Her heroine, Grace Fairfax, born and brought up in the south, loathes the drab, cold, ugly environment of the northern industrial city where she lives with her dull husband Tom, with whom for ten years she has been locked into a stagnant marriage, little now holding it together except habit and good nature. Tom is out all day at his office, while Grace, bored and lethargic, contemplates 'the mud-flats' of her featureless existence. 'How far indeed from gay was this life!' Grace dispiritedly reflects, trying to cheer herself up by thinking of the small pleasures ahead, 'when Annie drew the curtains, heaped the fire, and left her with a great cup of coffee and a toasted bun, and a new novel from the library. . . . Fish-pie and chocolate shape for supper. She had been looking forward to chocolate shape ever since ordering it this morning.' Grace has one friend, Norah, married to an embittered and highly strung academic, but unlike Norah, who has two little boys, Grace is childless, her one pregnancy having resulted in a stillbirth.

Suddenly into this bleak landscape fly two birds of brilliant plumage, a glamorous young man, Hugh Miller, nephew of the owner of the firm where Tom is employed, and his sister, the chic, sophisticated Clare. Like the Crawfords in *Mansfield Park*, Hugh and Clare dazzle their provincial acquaintance and cause excitement and upset in about equal proportions. 'They resembled each other . . . in a certain lordly and careless demeanour, as if they were accustomed to some sort of natural privilege.' After long years of nothingness, Grace feels herself coming to life as she begins to fall in love with the much younger Hugh, who considerably increases his attractions by introducing her to an aristocratic family, cousins of his, living at the nearby great house, closely modelled on Blagdon. For Grace this is a magic place, and she recognises at once that Hugh is at home here in a way that she herself could never be. 'Gentle birth, property, family, the stately homes of England – she told herself that Hugh's appearance suggested such terms. He was "above her station". . . .'

By the end of the novel twelve months have passed but little outwardly has changed: Hugh leaves for foreign parts unaware of the emotions he has inspired; Clare, having carelessly captivated Norah's husband, returns to her smart life in London; while Grace's brief

126

flowering shrivels with Hugh's departure and the coming of winter. Yet all is not quite as it was: Grace has learned that at least she is capable of love, and consequently is able to resign herself in tolerable tranquillity to the rest of her life with the unsatisfactory Tom.

Although *A Note in Music* is in a minor key, it has some remarkable qualities, recognisable as a lesser work by an accomplished novelist, rather than as a poor novel. Its main influence is clearly Virginia Woolf, specifically *Mrs Dalloway*, but the work is no imitation. The characters are drawn with subtlety, especially the dreamy Grace, her endearing and pathetic husband, Tom, and Hugh, who underneath the charming manner is inhibited and sexually unresolved, dismally sealed inside the courteous carapace of his privileged existence. In his last meeting with Grace, this immaturity is made painfully obvious. 'He simply could not help despising, recoiling from any one who wanted pity. . . . [But] after all, she was not going to tell him (as more than one woman had) what a failure her married life was. . . . He was not going to be forced to mutter "Bad luck", and offer a handkerchief (or, as upon one ghastly occasion in London, a most reluctant shoulder).' Technically, too, *A Note* is interesting, the narrative perspective moving from one character to another, carrying a story-line which is cleverly constructed – in spite of its partial undermining by a dire sub-plot involving a brave little prostitute with a flowerlike face and tubercular cough, with whom both Tom and Hugh become separately involved. The vengeful portrait of the dark, grimy city is memorable, a grim contrast, with its sour streets and screeching trams, both to the lavish luxury of the local mansion and to the warm and fertile southern countryside to which Grace escapes for a brief holiday. 'In this northern town the light had no colour. She thought of the little park with its deserted bandstand, hopping robins, struggling shrubs, keep-off-the-grass signs, silent nursemaids, dejected dogs on leads . . . even in midsummer it never quite lost its look of grieving wintry sadness.'

In an interview given many years later, Rosamond stated that in this second novel it was her deliberate intention 'to get away from any sort of self-identification, and when I began to write about Grace Fairfax, I couldn't identify her with anyone I knew, and particularly not with myself'. Her tracks are clearly visible, none the less. Grace, although not a beauty, shares a number of characteristics with her creator – thick ankles, dark hair streaked with grey, a tendency towards physical inertia, and a love of comfort and of stodgy nursery food; and like Rosamond, Grace is spell-bound by the aristocratic world, which tantalisingly she can enter but of which she can never be part. Grace, it is made clear from the beginning, has married beneath her; but just as she feels herself socially superior to her husband, so does she recognise her own inferiority in that respect to Hugh. It is a potent part of Hugh's fascination that, 'He seemed to have a secret of mastery, of confidence, of being at home in the world,' which Grace attributes to his background and breeding; as much as by his person, she is mesmerised by the appurtenances of his class, by his 'well-bred hand' with its engraved signet ring, by his gold cigarette case. 'She opened it and read the inscription: Hugh George Miller Esq., Presented by the Tenants of the Willowfields Estate on the occasion of his Twenty-first Birthday. . . . The imposing words opened a window into a world closed to Grace Fairfaxes.'

Although Hugh bears only traces of Wogan's personality – his exuberance, his moodiness and lack of focus – Rosamond's experience of falling in love with him is faithfully reproduced in Grace's falling in love with Hugh. After dinner at the great house, Grace watches Hugh walk out on the lawn. 'Why should one young man, drinking sherry and smoking, be so absorbing and mysterious?' (Wogan himself, uneasy at the unconditional admiration for the upper classes in Rosamond's fiction, later admitted that it had come as a shock when he first realised how important a part his background had played in his attraction: the fact that he came from an old landed family and was the son of a baronet 'meant a very very great deal to her'.)

After the acclaim which greeted *Dusty Answer*, the chilly response to its successor could not but be disappointing. Several critics reacted with distaste to the novel's defeatist air and in particular to its social emphases. 'A faintly snobbish book,' said V. S. Pritchett in the *Spectator*, 'banal, blasé and pretentious.' Although it had a few half-hearted supporters ('a book which no intelligent person can read without respect', remarked Harold Nicolson kindly in the *Daily Express*), the majority condemned it for lack of imagination, absence of humour, and the sheer dullness of the material. Describing the story as 'a poor wisp of a thing' and the book as a whole as 'exceedingly dull', Gerald Gould in the *Observer* wrote that he 'read it through without much enjoyment, and cannot help wondering whether the previous book was not over-praised'. The reviewer in the *Times Literary Supplement*, exasperated by such 'a disappointing second novel', briskly gave it as his opinion that 'If Grace Fairfax had not ordered and eaten with positive enjoyment such horrible suppers as fish-pie and chocolate shape her married life would have been happier, her husband thinner, and her own mind less stagnant'. (Lytton Strachey, who saw what he described as this 'really crushing review' just before going on holiday with Rosamond and Wogan, wrote to Roger Senhouse, 'I have suppressed all knowledge of [it] – no point in anticipating this bit of unpleasantness.')

As might be expected, friends were more charitable, although several expressed reservations. 'Rather too many trees for my individual taste,' wrote Raymond Mortimer, 'but I enjoyed it very greatly.' Helen in a letter to her brother damned with faint praise by saying that she thought *A Note in Music* 'a marvellous story about dull people, which is, I suppose, true art', while the novelist Charles Morgan sent his earnest congratulations to Miss Lehmann for '[being] without what is nowadays called a sense of humour, a blessed lack in a serious writer'. Stephen Spender, who wrote a long letter, purportedly about the book, but more about himself, decided that there was too great a stress on the negative side of life, even though he accepted that the key to the story was the failure of any of the characters to make contact with each other ('I suffer most terribly from this myself . . . indeed I have thought that it was this neurosis which made me an artist' . .)

Rosamond felt 'quite bludgeoned' by the critics, complaining to Dadie that she was convinced she would never be able to write again. She was consoled, however, by kinder treatment from the American papers, forwarded to her by Holt after publication in the United States, and also by some opinions from nearer home. She particularly treasured words of approval from Virginia Woolf ('I am reading R. Lehmann, with some interest & admiration,' Virginia noted in her diary. 'She has a clear hard mind, beating up now & again to poetry'), a courteous expression of appreciation from Morgan Forster, and an excited letter from the distinguished French painter and critic of *Les Nouvelles Littéraires*, Jacques-Emile Blanche. Predicting a 'flabbergasting success' for *A Note in Music*, Blanche wrote that the novel deserved comparison with *Anna*

Karenina, Sons and Lovers and *Mrs Dalloway*. 'In French we at present can boast of nothing that compares with your natural gifts and accomplishments,' he assured her.

Unlike Grace, who ends the novel resigned to her empty life with a dull husband in an ugly town, Rosamond through marrying Wogan had effected her escape. And yet if infinitely desirable when viewed from outside the pale, inside, the prospect was not entirely pleasing, and there were some stretches of very rough ground indeed. One such was the crisis which now blew up: a savage quarrel between Wogan and his father. Sir Laurence, impatient with his son's failure to persuade anyone to buy his pictures, decided the time had come to make a visit of inspection. Sweeping up to Ipsden in his large motor, he walked over to Wogan's studio, emerging shortly afterwards red in the face with fury at having seen a painting of a nude woman, complete with pubic hair. Angrily describing the work as 'obscene' and swearing that he would no longer support the production of such filth, he returned immediately to Llanstephan, where he was followed by a letter of abuse from Wogan so violently offensive that Sir Laurence refused to have any further communication with him. 'Dear Rosamond,' he wrote:

> I much regret that I cannot have anything more to do with Wogan until he apologises for the letter he has just written me. He wishes to cut himself off entirely from me & to be disinherited – I am obliging him & regret that this must hit both you & the boy. I shall always be delighted to see you & to help you or Hugo in any way I can. . . . I have nothing more to add. I look on him as a weak fool – but there are limits to what I will stand from my son.

So began the long-drawn-out hostilities that were eventually to result in complete rupture. 'The dramas that went on at Llanstephan were part of a saga with which we would entertain our friends,' Rosamond recalled, 'although it wasn't all that funny for us really.' Entirely on her husband's side in the affair, Rosamond nevertheless wrote an emollient letter to her father-in-law – but to no effect. 'I have to thank you for a very charming letter, but too late. Wogan has killed any desire in me to see him or help him or have anything to do with him again.' Lady Philipps, angry at what she regarded as her son's abominable behaviour, none the less tried to defuse the situation, writing to both Wogan and Rosamond in an attempt to make them see her husband's point of view: 'How you do misread Daddy (both of you).' Wogan failed to understand, she felt, that it was entirely for his own good that his father had wanted him 'to show & prove that you could *do* something & be successful', a statement that was instantly perceived to be typically and despicably mercenary.

The quarrel and her anxiety about their financial state put a considerable strain on Rosamond; unwell for some weeks, she was suddenly rushed into hospital in Reading after a haemorrhage and operated on in the middle of the night; soon afterwards she suffered an early miscarriage. Perhaps fortunately, she was distracted from much grieving by her indignation at Wogan's treatment by his parents. 'It is fantastic & wild & awful,' she told Dadie. Rosamond went to see Sir Laurence, but in spite of her persuasiveness, the old man was as intractable as his son, both of them still in a state of boiling rage. In thanking Stephen Spender for sending him a book of Baudelaire's poems, Wogan wrote, 'I have so much in common with Baudelaire's outlook & views. Only I hate, hate, hate. Destroy everything, smash, shoot, lust. . . .' He continued to hurl accusations at his father, said he wanted no further dealings with him, and had not the slightest trace of affection left. When Rosamond in a frantic attempt at damage limitation tried to argue that Hugo's future was being put at risk, Sir Laurence told her she was talking 'bosh'. Wogan, he said, 'seems to be living in some fantastic world of his own creation. . . . It seems to me that you have put him into an atmosphere too rare for him – mental & moral indigestion. Let him come back to earth where he & I were meant to live & we could understand one another. Until then I can see no solution of all our difficulties.'

This time, however, although neither side was prepared to retract, a state of armed neutrality was negotiated whereby Sir Laurence stopped Wogan's allowance, and Wogan resigned from his directorship of the family shipping company, but channels of communication were left open, allowing for the resumption of occasional visits between Ipsden and Llanstephan. Once Wogan was free of his father's financial control, or as he put it, 'Now that the terrible thorn of finance is rooted out from between us,' he was prepared to assume a more civil aspect. 'I shall crawl all right in the end,' he admitted to Rosamond, 'but I think if I hold out another month he will respect me more.' Meanwhile, with their joint income no more than £300 a year, Ipsden must be let and Wogan find salaried employment, two desperate strategies which in the event were pursued half-heartedly: a tenant was found for the house but only for a few months, and Wogan, with an instinct for impracticality amounting almost to the surreal, tried, and fortunately failed, to land the post of honorary attaché at the British Embassy in Warsaw.

Such disruptions in their domestic life made it hard for Rosamond to settle down to serious work, although she did complete one minor project, an essay in the Hogarth Press series of *Letters*. This was agreed to in support of her brother John, who in January 1931 had been taken on by Leonard and Virginia Woolf as manager of the press. John was thrilled at the prospect, and Rosamond tactfully refrained from expressing her doubts: Leonard was a notoriously exacting and despotic boss, who had had unhappy relations with all three of John's predecessors, Dadie among them; and John himself was far from easy. Tall, blond and strikingly handsome, John was touchy and notably lacking in both humour and charm; he was highly intelligent, well-informed, and had a passionate love of literature, poetry in particular, but was inclined ruthlessly to instruct his audience, completely insensitive to whether that audience desired to be instructed. 'He is sweet but Lord what a bore!' Wogan exploded after a visit of John's to Ipsden. 'This frightful German Encyclopaedic knowledge on every subject – this quoting of his own poems – his frantic woodcut talk . . . – his type writer! . . . We go for long walks: John thunders Greek, Latin, German & French at me – I cannot speak one word of any of them.' John idolised Rosamond, and for all his faults she loved and admired her brother, convinced that he had a future, if not as a poet, then as a critic or publisher, and to this end it was important that he make a success of working with the Woolfs. He is 'painfully loyal already', she told Dadie, '[but] what I fear is that he'll get on their nerves'.

Published in August, *A Letter to a Sister*, a lyrical meditation on domesticity, on the joys of summer in the country, the potency of nostalgia, of early intimations of mortality, was well received by Leonard. 'This is such a relief to me,' Rosamond told her brother. 'Nothing has ever given me so much trouble! – I mean in proportion to its length.' Virginia's influence on the piece was spotted by at least one reviewer, Vera Brittain, who wrote that the author 'has become a little uncertain whether she is Virginia Woolf or herself', going on to say that although she admired the 'luscious pen-pictures', it was unfortunate that the Letter's keynote was struck 'in the significant phrase which refers to "the anguished self-importance of our ego"'.

With the *Letter* out of the way, Rosamond planned to return to the novel that had been in the back of her mind for some time. But now a new crisis loomed.

By the end of 1931 it had become distressingly apparent that Lytton Strachey, who for some time had appeared increasingly unwell and withdrawn, was now seriously ill. 'We motored over to see Lytton & Carrington yesterday,' Rosamond told Dadie at the beginning of the year. 'Lytton was so dim as to be scarcely visible, not speaking above a whisper & sitting with his head in his hands.' It was unthinkable that anything should happen to Lytton. For the Philippses, the household at Ham Spray had become an integral part of their lives. As well as Lytton and Carrington themselves, Rosamond had grown fond of Carrington's husband, Ralph Partridge, and in particular of his lover, Frances Marshall, who through her relationship with Ralph had become part of Lytton's extended family; she had also come to know Lytton's nieces, Julia Strachey and Janie Bussy, as well as Virginia Woolf's sister Vanessa, Vanessa's husband Clive Bell, Philip and Ottoline Morrell at Garsington, the painter Duncan Grant, and David ('Bunny') Garnett, married to Frances's sister Ray. As Lytton grew weaker, there were few people whose company he could tolerate, but gentle Rosamond, with her soft voice and soothing manner, was one whom he was always glad to see. At Christmas, the situation suddenly seemed to improve when the patient, whose life had been despaired of, miraculously appeared to rally. 'I feel now he will live, though the danger is still acute,' Rosamond wrote to John. 'The bottom would fall out of the world for us if Ham Spray was no more. And I do so love the old boy.' But the revival of hope was short-lived, and on 21 January 1932 Lytton died, to the great grief of both Wogan and Rosamond. 'I just can't believe that he with all he stood for is gone,' she wrote.

The immediate and urgent concern was now for Carrington, who, convinced she could not endure life without Lytton, had been rescued from attempted suicide only a few hours before his death. Refusing all offers of help for her own part, she asked instead if Rosamond would take pity on Ralph Partridge, whose inconsolable grief she found difficult to bear. 'I think he would be happy with you, & Wogan,' she wrote. 'By being kind to Ralph you will be helping me more than I can say. Your love for Lytton, & me meant so much these last two months.' As Ipsden was let, Rosamond and Wogan took Ralph with Frances to Llanstephan for a few days, a respite which seemed to help restore Ralph, and which marked the beginning of a life-long friendship with Frances. 'Your visit & Ralph's was an undiluted joy to us,' Rosamond wrote to her afterwards, '& my only regret is that I haven't known you till now.'

In spite of the devoted attention of her friends, Carrington finally succeeded in killing herself, with a borrowed shot-gun, on 11 March. Rosamond, shocked and anguished, declared to Siegfried Sassoon, 'I never loved any other woman, excepting sisters, half so well; and never shall';[3] while to Frances she wrote,

> It is bitter to think one loved her so much and yet could be deceived about her state of mind. Her serene smile when she came to see us a fortnight ago, her humour and affection, and the discussions of character just as usual. But now I look back and see how in every detail it was a farewell. What a supreme and perfect actress she was. . . .
>
> It was such an exciting joy to be with her, always, for me. Nobody has ever enriched me as she did, & I counted much too much on her love and support – and the intimacy I thought I had with her. And to think how many others felt the same! One is pricked in a futile selfish uncontrollable way by indignation at her cruelty. . . . She had a genius for life – yet she could do this; while I for instance with not a speck of what she had, could never *not* live. Could you?

It was a desolate period, wretchedly unhappy for all concerned. 'With those two gone, it seems as if exactly half of life has been taken away,' Rosamond told Siegfried Sassoon. Wogan left almost at once for a

---

[3] Nearly forty years later Rosamond still felt the same. 'I never loved any woman as I loved her,' she wrote to David Garnett in October 1970.

walking holiday in France, together with his old friend John Strachey and the sculptor Stephen ('Tommy') Tomlin, husband of Lytton's niece, Julia. For once, Rosamond was glad to see him go, as 'we have both been feeling at too low an ebb to do each other any good'. The immediate future, however, promised a definite improvement: Sir Laurence had relented so far as to let Wogan have a third of his original allowance of £300, which meant they could afford to return to Ipsden for the summer; and Rosamond had at last finished her new novel. 'It is called *Invitation to the Waltz*,' she told Dadie. 'I'm longing to show it to you.'

7

At the Very Heart of Bloomsbury

Invitation to the Waltz was published on 6 October 1932. After the disappointing reception of Rosamond's second novel, much rested on the third. Certainly its writing took longer than before. The first mention of the project appeared in a cheerful letter to Harold Raymond as far back as July 1930, two months before the publication of *A Note in Music*, when there was as yet no indication of the critical cudgelling to come. A few weeks later, Rosamond reported that she had decided on the form of '[a couple of] long-short stories with a slight connection between them', this eventually evolving into a novel 'about two young girls . . . a lighthearted affair'. Interestingly, the sentence that follows – 'The next story is about them 10 years later, and means to be rather dramatic' – indicates that already she had in mind the sequel, which was to make its sensational appearance four years later as *The Weather in the Streets*.

Divided into three discrete sections, *Invitation to the Waltz* spans a single week in the lives of two sisters, Kate and Olivia Curtis, daughters of a retired businessman, living in modest prosperity in the village of Little Compton in 1920. The story opens on the morning of Olivia's 17th birthday: almost her first thought on waking is that in exactly a week is the Spencers' dance, to which she is looking forward with a mixture of excitement and dread, for this will be her first experience of adult society outside the family and village. The first part of the novel is devoted to preparations for the dance, all undertaken strictly within the unchanging confines of domestic routine. First there is breakfast with her parents and Uncle Oswald, a semi-permanent visitor, with Kate, her older sister, and with her much younger brother, 7-year-old James. Mr Curtis, frail and asthmatic, is a dry, sardonic man who keeps aloof from the normal banter and barter of family life, reserving most of his attention for his Pekinese, Simpkin, while Mrs Curtis, kind but severe, is a model of domestic efficiency, 'queller of giggling-fits, detector of subterfuges, swift snubber, just admonisher'.

One of Olivia's birthday presents is a length of flame-coloured silk, to be made up into an evening dress by Miss Robinson, the local dressmaker. Youngest of three unmarried sisters living with a monstrous old mother, Miss Robinson is a gallant, pathetic creature, the only one of her dire family possessing any spirit or imagination. 'Gay-hearted, quivering, hysterical . . . she was sinking, fatally enmeshed, struggling feebly and more feebly as youth slipped from her year after year, and old Mrs Robinson continued to be alive, and virginity, like a malignant growth, gnawed at her mind and body.' She is generously enthusiastic about Olivia's material, however – 'Scrumptious!' – and full of suggestions for cunning drapes and panniers, agreed to rather doubtfully by Olivia, who is still a little on the plump side. The rest of the day passes according to custom: dining-room tea with birthday cake, then a peaceful hour with Olivia reading in the schoolroom while Kate sews, supper with their parents and Uncle Oswald, after which the two girls in their long-sleeved velveteens fill in the time before bed playing ludo.

'Time crawling by at length delivered up the evening of the dance', is the opening sentence of Part II. The overwhelming anxiety for Kate and Olivia had been a lack of partner to accompany them, but Mrs Curtis, for once sympathetic to her daughters' predicament, had finally come to the rescue by dredging up a forgotten godson. Reggie Kershaw, who now arrives, is instantly perceived to be the wrong sort of young man. 'His skin was smooth, pinkish, rather shiny – not a healthy rough shine, but a sort of surface glisten, very unappetizing. His mouth shut like the two halves of a muffin.' Mrs Curtis welcomes Reggie warmly, but as Kate despairingly observes, 'Mum's standards are so shatteringly low.' However, as they wallow in a scented bath, their spirits rise, and even Olivia's misgivings about her dress – 'there was a queer place in the waist where, owing to a mistake in the cutting, Miss Robinson had had, in her own words, to contrive it' – are temporarily subdued. Great efforts have been made with dinner, roast pheasant and trifle, candles on the table, Mrs Curtis in black velvet, Mr Curtis impressively doing duty with the port and asking Kershaw questions about Oxford. Excited, the girls take their place in Walker's taxi, Reggie between them, for the half-hour drive to Meldon Towers.

Here, in Part III, they enter another world, a world of wealth and privilege, of thick rugs and chandeliers, of marble pillars, statues, white chrysanthemums in tubs, the whole presided over by Lady Spencer, regal in silver brocade with diamond tiara and parure. Kindly greeting the Curtis girls, Lady Spencer casually lets drop the intoxicating news that Rollo, son of the house, 'came down at the last moment with a whole batch of brother officers. So we're well off for young men.' His sister Marigold, with whom Kate and Olivia once shared lessons in the schoolroom, comes flying over with a little basket of dance programmes, fair-haired and ravishing in a divine frock of cream-coloured net. 'Isn't it fun?' she asks them. '"Rollo's come. Isn't it gorgeous?" They agreed enthusiastically, looking with diffidence towards the piano, over which her brother leaned in the midst of a laughing group, strumming with one finger and joking with the pianist. Rollo was not for them.'

Fortunately the sisters are rescued from humiliating neglect by the unexpected appearance of their cousin Etty, chic, frivolous, sophisticated Etty, down from London with her current admirer, Podge, both staying with neighbours, the Heriots, for the dance. Kate is blissfully swept up by handsome Tony Heriot, for whom she had long been nursing an unspoken infatuation; Olivia, less fortunate, is pushed round the floor by the patronising Podge – '"And is this her very very first dance?" "Yes, it's my first dance." "Having a wonderful time, are you? Mm? Heu, heu! You jeunes filles are rather pets." He squeezed her hand again. . . .' Podge is only one of a series of disappointing encounters, among them Peter Jenkin, a pretentious young poet furiously contemptuous of the glittering scene – '"What a spectacle!" He snorted. "Makes one sick"' – a lecherous old buffer; a blind man, casualty of the war; and a good-looking cousin of the house, remembered with a thrill from the Spencers' children's parties, with whom Olivia had fallen in love at the age of 10: dancing with Archie, surely, will transform the whole evening into something magical? But Archie, drunk, forgets the promised dance, and remains glassy-eyed at the entrance to the ballroom, glancing at Olivia without recognition as she positions herself hopefully beside him. 'It's too much to bear. How can I live if things like this are going to happen?'

As the dance moves towards its close, Olivia wanders dejectedly outside onto the terrace. A man is ascending the steps from the garden: Rollo. '"I have met you before, haven't I?" he said. . . . "But I've forgotten your name." . . . Their voices dropped into the air one after the other with an impersonal lost sound, as if they reached one another from a distance; yet the sense of isolation seemed to enclose them together in a kind of intimacy.' Rollo is charming, taking her indoors to talk to his father, Sir John, discovered reading by the fire in a small private sanctum. Immediately Olivia's evening, up till now a disappointment, becomes enchanted. 'How extraordinary to be here with them; from being outcast, flung beyond the furthest rim, to have penetrated suddenly to the innermost core of the house, to be in their home. The dancing, the people beyond were nothing, a froth on the surface, soon to be blown away.'

The next morning, with Reggie's departure, life reverts to normality; and yet, subtly, much has changed. Kate, in the process of falling in love with Tony Heriot, exhibits a new-found independence: when the telephone rings with an invitation from the Heriots to a hunt ball, Mrs Curtis out of habit says, 'We must talk it over,' but Kate replies simply, 'I said I could,' and leaves the room. Olivia, striding alone across the fields admits to herself that Kate has moved on, while she is left behind. But with a lurch of excitement she realises that she too, has taken the first steps over the threshold; and that for her also, 'Everything's going to begin. . . .'

Invitation to the Waltz is a novel almost without flaw: delicate in structure, beautifully written, minutely observed, moving and frequently very funny. Undoubtedly Rosamond's best work, it is on this and on its distressing sequel, *The Weather in the Streets*, that her reputation must ultimately rest. Alone of all the Lehmann novels, *Invitation* is light and optimistic in tone, its inspiration drawn not from disappointment and betrayal but from the prospect of love requited and future contentment. Significantly, it is also the most outward-looking, least self-concentrated of Rosamond's novels, written during that brief period of time when she was fulfilled in her marriage, anticipating years of happiness with Wogan, of bringing up children, and of productive work; as for Olivia and Kate, so for her: everything was about to begin. From this sunny perspective, she was able to look back serenely to the memories of childhood, to the comedy as well as the agony of the intense emotions of adolescence. Although Rosamond the novelist is identified by her empathetic understanding of the female broken heart, in fact one of her greatest and most under-rated gifts – under-rated by herself as much as by her critics – is for comedy, in particular her subtle use of comic irony. In *Invitation*, there are dark undercurrents, of lust, of drunkenness, of loneliness and grief to come, but above all this is a comedy of manners, directly evolved from the comedic tradition of Fanny Burney and Jane Austen.[1]

In the transmuting of life into fiction, many of the autobiographical elements remain visible beneath the surface: Rudie and Alice appear little changed as Mr and Mrs Curtis; Kate is an affectionate portrayal of Helen, brisk, capable, courageous, full of common sense, while the dreamy and emotional Olivia is in all important features an accurate picture of the youthful author. Their brother James, a clever, lonely little boy, is John to the life. James's most important appearance is at breakfast, when he anxiously presents Olivia with a hideous china ornament, purchased with his pocket money and chosen with care.

'Look out of the window, James dear,' said Mrs Curtis. . . . 'Two dear tomtits in the new cocoanut. Isn't that nice?'

But James did not look out of the window. His perforating gaze was bent upon the parcel which Olivia was undoing. He took a sharp breath.

'That's from me.'

'Oh, James! . . .' . . .

He sighed and turned away. It had been a long job, but it was

---

[1] Perhaps it should be said here that Rosamond was never an unreserved admirer of Jane Austen. '[Jane Austen] is *far* from being my "favourite" author', she wrote. 'She is truly witty, and ironic, and I admire her mocking enjoyment of the absurdities & pomposities & hypocrisies of human beings. . . . But I don't feel in the least passionately about her (as some do), and do get bored and put off by the endless stress on rank, station and income'.

over. The expedition to Holloway's had been solemn, notable, the choosing dramatic, the paying anxious, the concealing tense. Each night a serpent voice had whispered: 'Keep it yourself. . . .' But now the final placing by the plate had been accomplished: all was over.

The intense interior life of the two sisters is the focus of the novel, their raptures and miseries, their frantic hopes and bravely assumed cynicism, the story dominated by Olivia – innocent, tender-hearted, agonisingly self-conscious and brimful of enthusiasm. In conveying character through dialogue Rosamond displays perfect pitch and a tight economy of style, telling everything that needs to be told sometimes in only a few brief lines of conversation, whether of Lady Spencer's stately patronage, Etty's fashionable frivolity, or of the good-natured Martin sisters with their hilarious, coarse-fibred normality – 'Good old Martins. When all else was lost, their presence could always be counted on at the buffet. "First in as usual!" cried Phyl.' The terrible moment of Olivia's great gaffe is told almost entirely in dialogue: sitting out after a dance with one of the hunting fraternity, a young man introduced by Lady Spencer herself, Olivia, who knows nothing of hunting, is unsuspectingly lured into a shameful exposure.

'Were you out to-day?'
  'Oh yes.'
  'Jolly good day, wasn't it?' . . .
  'Yes, it was nice.' Rather surprising. It had been so very wet. . . .
  'Going out on Saturday – ?'
  'I expect so.' Rather mystifying. 'I go out every day, really.'
  'What? Do you honestly?' He looked very much impressed. . . .
'You must be awfully keen. I suppose some days you have a jolly good distance to motor?'
  'Oh no. We haven't got a car.'
  He looked absolutely staggered.
  'But I didn't know there were more than two packs within fifty miles.'
  Bombshells. Death and damnation. Hideous light in darkness. Consternation. Humiliation.

141

Although the theme of alienation is very much present, as in *Dusty Answer* and *A Note in Music*, here it is treated more cheerfully and without anguish. The difference in standing between the solidly middle-class Curtises and the aristocratic Spencers is clearly indicated (precisely the same as that which existed between the Lehmanns at Fieldhead and the Desboroughs at Taplow), with the former showing a finely calculated deference to the latter, both acknowledging that they moved, just, within the same social sphere. While Kate and Olivia accept without question that Rollo, Marigold and the rest of the Spencer house-party are 'not for them', it is Olivia who is most acutely aware of her exclusion, gazing with a pang at the gilded youth, rich, confident and secure, who live within the charmed circle. Towards the end of the evening she goes upstairs to tidy herself in preparation for her dance with Archie. Here she finds Marigold's old Nanny on duty,

> short, trim, sober, self-effacing in the respectable black silk and cairngorm brooch, the flat strong heels of service. . . .
> A plump fair girl in yellow burst into the room.
> 'Oh, Nannie angel, my stocking's exploded into ladders. What shall I do?'
> 'Gracious, Miss Hermione. I can't mend that. . . . You shouldn't wear your suspenders so tight. I'm always telling Marigold the same.'
> One of the house-party; one of the inner circle, the initiated.

Olivia's fantasies are fixed, of course, on the magnificent figure at the very centre of the magic circle, on Rollo, the romantic hero, 'Rollo superb in his pink coat, tall, ruddy, chestnut-haired, commanding, surrounded by his companions, every inch the only son of the house'. But Rollo is out of Olivia's class, and, it is tacitly indicated, already spoken for: there is a dark beauty in a white satin sheath who exerts a mysterious hold over him. Olivia watches in awe as the exquisite Nicola descends the stairs. 'She stood half-way down, looking about her, then catching sight of Rollo, from what seemed an immense distance, raised her hand slowly, summoning him. . . . There was less of appeal than assurance in the deliberate gesture; she knew he would come.'
It is the brief conversation with Rollo on the terrace, and his taking

her in to make a cosy trio with his father, that for Olivia is the climax of the evening. Coming within a few pages of the novel's end, there is little else to follow; and yet its significance is not in doubt, a significance that became clear to Rosamond herself only as she wrote the passage in question. 'I thought, I see! This is what all this is about! . . . I realised there was an awful lot more to say about Olivia's life – an awful lot that I didn't yet know, and must wait to find out; and that that meeting was unrealised, it was broken off. But I knew that *that* was what I'd got to deal with later.'

Reviews of *Invitation to the Waltz*, although less hyperbolic than for *Dusty Answer*, were almost universally favourable, with some of the soberest critics waxing rhapsodic over Miss Lehmann's exquisite prose. One of the most ecstatic was Rosamond's old enemy, Gerald Gould of the *Observer*. 'How to describe Miss Lehmann's delicate and delicious *Invitation to the Waltz*? As well attempt to describe the petals on a sun-provoked flower: or the gleam a candle gives to the wings of a moth! . . . All is in the atmosphere, the sensitiveness, the style – and the very fragrance and sweet fatuity of youth. . . .' In the United States the acclaim was even more enthusiastic, with the *New Yorker* stating unequivocally that, 'Rosamond Lehmann is the greatest living woman novelist', and Hugh Walpole writing in the *New York Herald Tribune* that '[Rosamond Lehmann's] work . . . gives me more pleasure than the work of any living English novelist save Virginia Woolf, George Moore and E. M. Forster'. The novel was chosen as American Book of the Month for November, and an offer was received from the RKO Studio for a three months' script-writing job in Hollywood, a proposal which although financially attractive was eventually refused as the terms were considered too vague.

From such plaudits Rosamond was abruptly brought down to earth by the recommencement of hostilities between Wogan and his father. During the past year relations had remained relatively amicable, with Sir Laurence confining himself to making helpful suggestions for his son's future employment. 'Wogan had an interview with his father which ended in his advising him to look into the question of bee-farming. . . . We don't get much further than shrieking with impotent laughter about it,' Rosamond reported in May 1932. In August she and Wogan went to stay at Llanstephan, where almost immediately a furious quarrel broke out, ignited by Wogan's airing of his provocatively left-wing views. 'It started with an argument about capital punishment (W. against, papa for, of course) and developed at lightning speed into communism, filthy painting, being in a filthy set, rotten intellectuals, intention of making Wogan squirm & beg for every penny etc. etc.' Blazing with temper, Sir Laurence challenged Wogan to demonstrate his political commitment, first by finding a job as an ordinary mechanic in the Morris motor works in Oxford, then by going to Russia to see how he liked it there. Again Rosamond acted as mediator, but as they made their now customary hurried departure, she felt convinced that the situation between father and son must soon deteriorate past saving.

Her greatest fear was that if Wogan's allowance were again stopped, Ipsden would have to go. Desperately casting round for any suitable scheme to bring in money, Rosamond approached her brother, who to nobody's surprise had fallen out with Leonard Woolf and in September 1932 abandoned his job at the Hogarth Press. Rosamond was annoyed on John's behalf; 'I only hope you have left Leonard in the lurch,' she told him, before going on to introduce her proposition: would he consider starting a publishing business of his own in partnership with Wogan? Wogan was said to be keen, and Sir Laurence would certainly finance it; she herself would let them have her next book, and promised to use her influence to bring in writer friends.

The plan, however, came to nothing as John had already made up his mind to take a new direction entirely and was on the point of leaving England for Vienna. Since coming down from Cambridge, John had been restless and unhappy, partly because as the adored only son he felt suffocated by his mother's possessiveness, but chiefly on account of his sexual orientation, which made him impatient to escape from laws which frustratingly restrained his activities: supplied by Stephen Spender with delectable detail concerning the way of life available to expatriates such as Spender himself, Isherwood and Auden in Berlin, he chafed at the puritanism prevailing in his own country. While at university John had had at least one serious homosexual affair (with the young actor, Michael Redgrave) and already there had been an embarrassing incident when a working-class boyfriend had turned up at Fieldhead in his absence and demanded money from Alice. Rosamond had been sympathetic towards John's love life – the little she knew of it – ever since Dadie privately confirmed what she had for some time surmised: 'I'm so thankful to know for certain. . . . It's been going on for years – extraordinary – ever since J. was a pretty little shrimp his first term at Eton'; and Wogan, too, was supportive, offering practical advice when trouble arose ('I do know a solicitor all the boys go to . . .'). But the lure of liberty on the Continent was too great, and within days of leaving the Press, John was off.

Despite the ever-precarious financial situation, the threat of giving up Ipsden began to fade. With every month that passed, Rosamond grew to love the place more: she loved the house and garden, and she loved the surrounding country, the willow-lined river, the narrow lanes, the beech woods, the rose-coloured, lichen-covered barns and farmhouses. In no real sense a countrywoman, she yet had a finely tuned sensual and aesthetic response to the natural world: she was acutely aware of the changing seasons, of scent, colour, sound and texture;[2] and although not faintly interested in pruning or planting, there was little she enjoyed more than sitting in the garden in summer, or on a fine autumn afternoon walking with the dogs across the fields. It was the same with the house: prettiness and comfort were paramount, soft lighting, deep sofas, vases of fresh flowers, she herself never happier than when sunk in an armchair in front of the fire with a book and a delicious tea. And yet the domestic side of life bored her profoundly and was resented, especially when it interfered with her working. It was not so much the pram in the hall that got in the way – there was always a nanny to take care of that – but 'the various footling & infuriating household occupations', the dull daily routine of dealing with the servants (a cook and housemaid, and gardeners), ordering meals, and balancing the household books, not to speak of the tedium of the minor crises inseparable from running a house, which for some reason always seemed to fall to her share. 'A vast patch of damp has appeared in the nursery wall,' she complained to Dadie at the end of 1932, '& to-day the gale is

---

[2] An awareness richly reflected in her writing: in *Invitation to the Waltz*, Olivia, walking through the wintry kitchen garden, 'admired the cabbage bed – its frosty sea-blues and greens, the modelling of the huge compact rosettes with their strong swelling curves and crisp-cut edges. The looser outer leaves held sparkling drops and violet shadows. She shook one, listening to its silky creak, watching the transparent water-beads slip and race like quick-silver.'

blowing sulphury fumes from the boiler all through the house & the cook is obviously going to give notice'; and a few weeks later, 'Here all is exactly as usual. The cook's given notice. Dry rot's developed in the gardener's cottage. The plug won't pull. . . .'

But Ipsden offered great compensations, chief among them that it was a delightful place in which to entertain. Large and rambling, the house was pleasingly proportioned, an early eighteenth-century façade having been built over its Jacobean origins; three-storeyed and L-shaped, it was light and airy, with two elegant bay windows as well as French windows opening onto the garden, creeper and climbing roses trained luxuriantly up the walls. Dadie Rylands, who was often there, said that 'Ipsden was a tremendously happy house to be in', and Stephen Spender, also a frequent visitor, remembered it as 'beautiful Ipsden House. . . . It had a garden partly surrounded by a screen of trees . . . [and] the house and garden sheltered by the trees had their own closed-in atmosphere of lawn and paths and old brick walls.' Apart from the disappointing food – a monotonous diet featuring shepherd's pie and milk puddings made by a succession of incompetent cooks whom Rosamond was herself too inexperienced in culinary matters to train – visitors to Ipsden could be sure of a high level of conversation and comfort. The Philippses were sociable, and almost every weekend they invited guests to stay, with local friends often coming in to lunch or dinner during the week. Lytton and Carrington were painfully missed, but their old circle was intact, Dadie of course, and Roger Senhouse, Ralph Partridge and Frances, the Bells, Leonard and Virginia Woolf.

Since John's sudden departure from the Hogarth Press, Rosamond had been afraid there would be an awkwardness in her relations with the Woolfs – 'I don't see how I can see them again without feeling a horrid pit yawning beneath us,' she told Clive Bell – but in fact the friendship continued as agreeably as ever, even if Rosamond never quite lost her sense of wariness with regard to Virginia, was never quite sure how to respond to the older woman's unsettling combination of teasing and flattery. In November 1933 the Woolfs came to spend the night, a prospect which made Rosamond nervous for days beforehand. 'To my despair the central heating broke down and I knew whatever I did it would be cold, and I knew that was just the sort of thing she'd be spiteful about.' Virginia did indeed comment in her diary on the coldness of the house, but she also noted how much she preferred Rosamond to her brother ('not so much ego in her composition'), what good gossip there had been, and 'how nice, easy, mobile, affectionate, & humane it all was'. Rosamond for her part was relieved that both Woolfs had been 'at their most charming. . . . What an angel Leonard can be! Also I never realized that V. can be really human – almost cosy to talk to.' Inevitably Lytton and Carrington were much discussed, Wogan telling the story of how after Carrington shot herself, he had been sent for twice in one day by Frances to talk to Ralph, who was himself threatening suicide. 'Wogan has a shrewd worldly sense for all his patter,' observed Virginia. In a lighter vein the Philippses described Ralph Partridge's habit, when they stayed at Ham Spray, of bringing in their tray of morning tea while stark naked. To Virginia the influence of Lytton on the company was apparent in more ways than one. 'They all comment eternally on "parts" & breasts – a kind of rough parody of the old Ham Spray. . . . It's Lytton played by bumpkins – Lytton acted in the kitchen.'

Less daunting to Rosamond were the friends of her own generation, some of whom she had known during her first marriage. One such was Stephen Tennant, with whom, shortly after moving to Ipsden, she had met his lover, Siegfried Sassoon. 'I had the most strange & fascinating week-end with Stephen & Siegfried . . . they are a neurotic pair!' she wrote to Ottoline Morrell in 1930, and since that time she had spent many hours patiently listening as Sassoon poured out the details of his tormenting affair with the exotic and elusive Stephen. Going back even further was her friendship with the editor and critic John Hayward, who had come up to Cambridge while Rosamond was in her last year at Girton. Now crippled with muscular dystrophy, Hayward was a prickly, spiteful little man, but although Rosamond dreaded his rages, and even more the prurience of his tone when talking alone with her, she pitied him and enormously admired his powerful intelligence. A newer acquaintance was David Cecil, who came several times to stay at Ipsden – 'beautifully mannered and delightful . . . a tremendous aristocrat' – as did Cyril Connolly and his wife, Morgan Forster, Joe Ackerley, and the quiet, bespectacled William Plomer, the poet ('My Sweet William,' Rosamond used to call him, after the flower of that name in her border).

Stephen Spender was a regular visitor, bringing over from Oxford another poet, Bernard Spencer. Spencer became infatuated with his beautiful hostess, which was gratifying in a way, but tiresome in another: 'he's hopeless – so dreary & boring, so depressed and convinced of his own hopelessness,' she complained to Spender. Among her female friendships, one of the liveliest was with Hester Chapman, a cousin of Dadie's whom Rosamond remembered first meeting at a party of Duncan Grant's. 'It was very late and as I was about to go home, tripping over people lying on the stairs, I passed Hester sitting alone with her head in her hands. I asked, "Are you all right?" And she said in a slurred voice, "I'm very, very, very, drunk."' Before her marriage, Hester had shared a flat with Julia Strachey, and now both she and Julia came as guests to Ipsden, Julia sometimes with, sometimes without, her attractive but dangerously destructive husband, Tommy Tomlin. 'I long to tell you how I loved being with you,' Julia wrote affectionately to Rosamond after staying for a week. 'I am so awfully glad we have got to know each other at last.' Julia introduced a girlfriend of hers, Barbara Ker-Seymer, an avant-garde photographer with a studio in London – one room above Asprey's in Bond Street – in which Julia was currently employed as part-time secretary. Described as birdlike by one of her many boyfriends, '[with her] bright sharp eye and high clear voice', the bohemian Barbara appealed to Rosamond, who thought her comic and original, and commissioned her to take portraits of herself and Wogan.

Particular favourites with Rosamond were a couple known as 'the Tidcombe boys', Paul Cross and Angus Wilson, friends of John Banting, who lived in the nearby village of Tidcombe. Both keen gardeners, it was Angus, a professional horticulturist, who had the talent, Paul the money, and their pretty house, with its avenue, swimming-pool and large, immaculately kept garden, was something of a local show piece. '[They are] affectionate, sympathetic, artistic, sensitive, with that womanly knack women generally lack for making a house cosy and congenial with nice curtains, comfortable beds, latest books, gramophone records, good food & drink etc.' The boys were popular: gregarious, amusing and, if not particularly clever, always prepared, with the help of generous quantities of drink, to make a party go. Rosamond was fond of them both, but it was the handsome Paul, dark, tall, with a marked resemblance to the film star Gary Cooper, to whom she was drawn, and ever susceptible to masculine beauty and yearning for romantic love, convinced herself she saw in his well-mannered attentions a romantic affinity. Soon she was confiding in him about her anxieties over Wogan, and somehow allowed herself to believe that their long, intimate, emotionally charged conversations were a prelude to a deeper relationship.

For the Bloomsberries parties were an essential feature of life. There were so many parties, dressing-up parties, bottle parties, dinner parties, musical parties, parties where everybody sat about on the floor till the small hours drinking and talking. Fuelled by quantities of alcohol, behaviour was unconstrained and no topic of conversation taboo. During one frank discussion about sexual matters, Virginia tapped Rosamond on the shoulder and said, '"Remember: we won this for you" – meaning the freedom to discuss sex without inhibition in masculine society.' Wogan had rented a studio from Tommy Tomlin at 10 Fitzroy Street, and there the Philippses could stay the night when they came up to London – a practical, if not ideal, arrangement for Rosamond, who found the place 'a bit bleak and smelly'. For Wogan, these liberated evenings were in every sense intoxicating: while Rosamond preferred to sit in a small group with a cigarette quietly talking, Wogan, in flannel trousers and scarlet jersey, would leap about the room in a frenzy of excitement, drinking, dancing, playing the fool and kissing any pretty woman he could lay hands on, often sending his wife home by herself while he stayed to be swept out at dawn with the crumbs and spent matches. 'We went to a glorious party in somebody's studio last week,' Wogan wrote after one such occasion to Stephen Spender. 'I got beautifully drunk, kissed everybody, male & female, & danced with all sexes. Oh it was glorious. I was in heaven. Rosamond went home at 4 a.m., leaving me in the height of my bliss. I stayed till 7 a.m. Poor Rosie.'

In the eyes of most of their friends, both Philippses were at the very heart of Bloomsbury. But for Rosamond, well aware of the effect of her striking appearance but in other areas shy and lacking in self-confidence, it seemed always as if she were on the outside looking in. 'I sometimes wonder if I wasn't very boring at those Bloomsbury parties,' she said in retrospect. 'I wasn't a rebel, I wasn't a Communist, I hadn't been to prison, I wasn't a loose liver, I didn't get drunk. . . . It never occurred to me to get drunk or have affairs, all that sort of bohemian behaviour.' Sometimes she was even made to feel shy by the inevitable spotlight on her beauty. 'Rosamond wore her beauty modestly and with humour,'

Christopher Isherwood noted but added that he thought it made her uncomfortably self-conscious, 'as though she were embarrassed at being overdressed'. Highly intelligent and widely read, she was yet in many ways naive, temperamentally unsuited to the Bloomsbury tradition of intellectual debate, with its emphasis on cynical debunking and sceptical enquiry. Certainly not prudish, she was often entertained by the group's candour and contempt for euphemism, yet equally could be affronted by the insistently flippant tone in which serious subjects were discussed, uneasy when the conversation turned, as it often did, to Freud and psychoanalysis and the exploding of established theories and traditions.

Wogan, on the other hand, in a permanent state of rebellion against almost everything, revelled in such iconoclastic talk, but far from bolstering his wife's fragile confidence, he now deliberately began to undermine it. It was at a party in Vanessa Bell's studio, also in Fitzroy Street, that Virginia Woolf shrewdly observed that 'W[ogan] lives a little – but lives joyously, & I daresay wantonly – in the shadow of R[osamond] who, modest I think, is yet a best seller'. In her shadow he was, but far from living there 'joyously', he was jealous of his wife's success, in such painful contrast to his own lack of it. To him his painting was a serious matter, but unfortunately his talent failed to match his enthusiasm – 'only a scampering terrier brained painter', as Virginia called him – and there was little interest in his work. To begin with, Rosamond had encouraged him as best she could; when he held a solo exhibition, she begged Lytton to use his influence to persuade Roger Fry and Clive Bell to look at it, but to no avail: not a single picture sold, and one critic went so far as to say it was inexcusable that such an ungifted amateur should have an exhibition at all. For Wogan, desperate to prove himself, this was embittering, and he started to take out his disappointment on his wife, telling her that her books were despised by their friends – Virginia in particular 'roaring with laughter' at the very mention of her novels – and turning on her with violent verbal attacks. His aggressiveness was made more ferocious by sexual frustration. It was an agony to Wogan that his voluptuous wife, while still sharing a bed, should refuse to let him touch her. She failed to understand, he told her, how he was 'driven crazy & dangerously on-edge by desire. Yours is the only body that I go mad about. To live with it is, & has been for ages, hell.'

With all these pressures, it was to be expected that Wogan should grow increasingly resentful of Rosamond's close friendship with Paul Cross, from whom, it seemed, she was rarely apart. Paul was her close confidant, and Wogan could not bear to see how elated and happy she was in his company; he suspected, too, that Paul was leading her on, although both emotionally and physically he was unlikely to provide what he appeared to be offering. Miserable, Wogan turned for advice to his friend and fellow artist, Tommy Tomlin, a man on the surface well balanced, but inwardly unstable, 'strong & poisonous meat', as Rosamond soon discovered. It was at this stage that, according to Wogan, 'Tommy became my father confessor. . . . He made me give up all hope of you & me ever becoming right.' Indeed Tommy made no secret of his conviction that Wogan should leave his wife. Once while dancing with Tommy at a party, Rosamond told him how fond she felt of him. 'Oh, you do, do you?' he said, looking coldly at her. 'Well, you'd better not, because I'm doing all I can to break up your marriage.'

Inevitably the Philippses began spending more and more time apart, Rosamond remaining at Ipsden while Wogan was based in Tommy's Fitzroy Street studio. In an unusual show of independence Rosamond took two trips abroad without her husband, the first in August 1932 with Helen to Germany and Austria. 'She and Helen had a marvellous time,' Beatrix reported. 'Mounty vows he'll never let Helen out of his sight again. . . . Wogan, of course, barely noticed the absence of his wife.' The second, in January the following year, was a far more significant departure, six weeks in the West Indies staying with the Tidcombe boys on Tobago, where Paul Cross owned a house. In spite of the obvious impediment of his relationship with Angus, Rosamond by now had developed a serious infatuation for Paul, and in her mind there was a strong, if unrealistic, expectation of romantic involvement; she saw herself sailing off to an idyllic affair with a handsome man on a tropical island, a rose-coloured picture which would somehow compensate for all the inadequacies of her life at home. Unexpectedly Wogan made no objection to her going, indeed seemed delighted, and he, Julia Strachey and Barbara Ker-Seymer saw her off on the boat-train to Southampton. 'She looked very happy waving out of the window at us,' said Barbara. However, six weeks later she returned in a mood of deep depression, completely disillusioned '[because] she felt there was no hope for her with Paul Cross'.

Meanwhile, in a situation convoluted even by Bloomsbury standards, while Rosamond was pursuing the homosexual Paul, Wogan had started an affair with Julia Strachey, while still heavily dependent for support on her husband, Tommy. As he later explained it, 'Julia & Tommy between them were giving me new, permanent values, & offered me new hopes. I could hardly separate them into two people – Julia gave me the female side, & Tommy the male.' Restless and unhappy, it was only natural that Wogan should be drawn to Julia, who was in a similar state over the deterioration of her own marriage. Julia, sexy and stylish, was extremely pretty in a feline way, with a long-legged, boyish figure. In high spirits she could be very funny – outspoken and unconventional; she was also self-centred, neurotic and profoundly lazy: when asked once to describe her ideal way of life, she replied, 'Lying on a pink fur rug doing absolutely nothing.'

Wogan's affair with Julia started in the summer of 1932, and at first Rosamond suspected nothing, Julia continuing to come down to Ipsden where she made a point of acting girlish best friends with Rosamond. During the week Wogan would go to London, returning at weekends, 'generally in a foul temper, because he felt guilty'. When Rosamond went to Tobago, Wogan was relieved because he felt the burden of guilt lift, and when she came back depressed and disappointed, he was furious with her for making him feel again the one at fault. Relations between husband and wife became increasingly antagonistic, with Rosamond, miserable and frustrated, unable to stop herself goading Wogan into savage quarrelling. 'Rosamond loved scenes', said one observer, some-what unfairly, 'and in that respect Wogan gave as good as he got.' During their frequent fights, Rosamond accused Wogan of irresponsibil-ity, selfishness and an indifference to the truth, humiliating him by deliberately showing up his intellectual shortcomings in front of other people; he retaliated by complaining of her vanity, her bourgeois respectability and her habit of constantly finding fault. 'I think you are a difficult person to love,' he told her. 'I always have felt you'll find a rucked rug or a crumpled pillow to spoil the most sublime moments.' In frustration at their inability ever to hold a conversation without mutual recrimination, Wogan wrote his wife a long letter, analysing their destructive relationship, for which he largely blamed himself. 'I don't believe you will ever be able to estimate my loathing of myself over my behaviour to you.... And I now *can't* stop. The sight of you is a reminder of my loathsomeness & I feel I must leave you. Yet I *can't* leave you.... I feel you can't bear me & I don't know what to do.'

To be apart was a relief to both, and on more than one occasion Wogan took off secretly with Julia, telling his wife he was going away to paint. On one of these expeditions, when the two of them had gone for an illicit few days to Dorset, Matt Ridley arrived on his own at Ipsden, in an unhappy state on account of an affair (one of many) with a married woman. Looking for consolation, he turned to Rosamond, who had always adored him and found him 'terribly attractive'. Tall, elegant, moustachioed, Matt bore more than a passing resemblance to Rudie Lehmann, who to his daughter always remained the ideal of English manhood. Infinitely susceptible to Matt's gallantry and charm, Rosamond now read into his amorous manner a deeper feeling, unique to herself, and was willingly convinced by Matt's passionate declarations that he was seriously in love. 'He always said he was in love with me.... All his life, to the end of his life, [he said] I was the one and only, if only he could have married me, he would never want to look at anybody else.' She herself was half in love with him, flattered by his admiration and touched by his sweet nature and vulnerability. But more than that, she saw in his handsomeness and aristocratic demeanour a type of masculine ideal, the epitome of the patrician hero. Their time together was necessarily brief, and apart from one weekend later on in Germany, when for a heady twenty-four hours Matt declared he never wanted to leave her (an event later reproduced in a crucial scene in *The Weather in the Streets*), there was no question of the relationship going any further. And yet those few days retained a poignancy and glamour that for ever stayed with Rosamond untarnished, with Matt indelibly established in her imagination as the model of the romantic, upper-class lover. 'My relationship with Matt ... constituted one of the deepest and least mixed-up happinesses of my life ... there was something kingly in his nature: I can't think of any other word: kingly, magnanimous, highly distinguished, highly vulnerable,' she wrote. 'He became for me almost an archetype; and he haunted most of my subsequent work.'

Wogan knew nothing of what had taken place in his absence, and when he returned to Ipsden the painful drama continued, intensified by the fact that during his weekdays in London he was now having to cope with equally emotional scenes from Julia, who, desperate to leave the heavy-drinking, manic-depressive Tommy, had started pressuring Wogan to divorce Rosamond and marry her. But Wogan, although in love with Julia, at this stage had no wish to dissolve his marriage. Hysterical rows ensued, and Wogan in panic confessed the whole story to his wife. 'It was shattering, an appalling shock,' said Rosamond. '[At first] I just couldn't believe it, which was very stupid of me.' Angry and deeply wounded, almost as much by Julia's betrayal as by Wogan's, Rosamond's sense of justice none the less forced her to admit that she was in part to blame for her husband's defection. 'I saw it was quite natural to find somebody else to go to bed with. . . . At first I thought it was the end. He was ashamed and aghast and sheepish, and I thought, Oh well, I must forgive him. Which I did.' Wogan was grateful to her, promising to give up his affair, and both resolved to put every effort into making their life together work – the immediate result of which was that Rosamond again found herself pregnant.

But despite good resolutions and some candid discussion, Rosamond continued to underestimate the importance of the sexual aspect of her marriage, and made it clear she had no intention ever of resuming regular relations. In an injured tone, she complained to Barbara Ker-Seymer, '[Wogan] is so terribly important to me in every way but one – & because of that one not working properly, I am no use at all to him, it seems.' Certainly there was no question of allowing him near her now. As in her first pregnancy, she felt wretchedly ill, but Wogan was too hurt by and too angry at her recent rejection to show her much sympathy, returning to his old habit of spending most of his time in London, where he was starting a course of analysis with Lytton Strachey's brother, James. Alone at Ipsden, Rosamond felt frightened and depressed, aware that this was a far from ideal time to be having a child, and suffering not only from nausea but from a nervous exhaustion which left her barely able to move. She was plagued, too, by the excess salivation which occasionally accompanies pregnancy, having to carry with her a little black cup at all times. Certainly she was in no state that summer to travel with Wogan, nor did he show any desire to accompany her and Hugo for the annual holiday on the Isle of Wight. Instead, desperate to escape the tearful accusations of neglect, he went off on his own to paint, staying in a small inn by the River Orwell in Suffolk. 'I am so incredibly tired emotionally & mentally, & candidly fucking miserable,' he wrote to her.

> Mentally & in our approach & views of life, I suppose we are wide apart, but that ought not to matter. It ought to be more thrilling & interesting. However we have both got vast grievances against the other. But I can't do without you even then. . . . I do so love you. You attract me so mightily too. . . . I can't get away from my love of you & this cruel attraction, so that a mistress I have discovered is right out of the question.

This last statement, that a mistress was out of the question, was reassuring, and Rosamond believed Wogan's promise that he was no longer seeing Julia. But in this she was mistaken. 'I thought it was all over. But it wasn't over.'

The truth was that Julia had no intention of letting Wogan go, and few inhibitions either about telling him exactly how she felt about Rosamond. While she still believed the affair to be finished, Rosamond had misguidedly tried to effect a reconciliation with Julia, sending her one of her evening dresses as a present. This Julia had found enraging: immaculately chic herself – before her marriage she had modelled for Poiret in Paris – she despised Rosamond's conventional dress sense and was infuriated by her assumption that this second-hand garment could repair a friendship that no longer existed. Having written an offensive letter to Rosamond, she told Wogan she was disgusted by the pregnancy and that he was diminished in her eyes for continuing to feel affection for such a ghastly woman. Wogan hardly knew which way to turn in his dangerous balancing act between wife and mistress. The affair with Julia had now been continuing for a year and a half, but it was no nearer a solution. His dilemma was that although physical relations between himself and Rosamond were virtually non-existent, that they had little in common and he was irritated by her ladylike ways, he still loved her and hated making her unhappy. On the other hand he was obsessed by Julia, even if he had no wish to marry her, and could not bring himself to give her up. He was being torn apart, by Julia in London insisting that he leave his wife, and Rosamond at Ipsden, weepily imploring him not to leave her and swearing that she hoped and believed she would die in childbirth.

In the new year of 1934 Rosamond went into a nursing-home in London, as after her previous experience it was considered too risky for her to give birth at home. This time her labour was far less traumatic, and on 14 January 'a very nice daughter' was born; 'she is called Sarah Jane,' she told Dadie, 'but is already known as Sally.' The baby's father showed little pleasure in the happy event, 'coming only once in the evening when all the husbands came to see their infants, and in a glowering mood, very disagreeable. . . . He wasn't a bit thrilled with Sally.'

Back at Ipsden, with Rosamond absorbed in the new baby, husband and wife continued to move apart, the tension between them gradually giving way to a calmer, friendlier relationship. The two of them made a striking pair at Gwen Philipps's débutante ball in May, dancing till four in the morning, Wogan handsome and sunburnt in white tail and tails, Rosamond ravishing in a ball dress of iris-coloured chiffon. Wogan, at last in the process of detaching himself from Julia, was frequently away, deliberately absenting himself on various excursions, a motor tour of Wales with Augustus John, a painting holiday in Normandy, cruising in the Adriatic with Napier Alington. Rosamond, meanwhile, feeling full of creative energy, had embarked on a new project, a play, which she wrote quickly in a matter of weeks. 'I felt rather pleased with it at the time,' she told Stephen Spender, 'but now the thought of it wearies me so much I can hardly bear to revise it.' In August she and Beatrix took the children down to Cornwall, while Wogan, accident-prone as ever, was laid up at home with two broken ribs and a bad cut on his head resulting from diving onto a submerged rock in the river. Feeling sorry for himself he was pleased to be visited by Julia's chum, Barbara Ker-Seymer, who paid him a great deal of cosseting attention. Barbara, who had conducted many love-affairs of her own, was sympathetic and affectionate, prepared to listen for hours to Wogan talking about Julia. Only gradually did it occur to him that there was more to her generosity than simple friendship.

In September 1934 Wogan was in Greece on the final leg of a luxurious if debauched holiday with Napier ('Naps') Alington, with whom both Philippses had recently spent a heady few days at Crichel, his palatial eighteenth-century house in Dorset. Among a cosmopolitan group of guests had been Naps's current lover, a handsome young airman, as well as a very drunk Augustus John, and that living work of art, the flamboyant Marchesa Casati, mistress of Gabriele D'Annunzio, subject of nearly 200 portraits (several by John himself), and famous for giving the most extravagant and spectacular parties in Europe. The Marchesa was vividly described by Wogan in a letter to Barbara. 'She is too wonderful . . . [with] tousled carrot coloured hair, black eye lashes glued on an inch and a half long . . . black rings painted under the eyes right down to her cheek bones. An *enormous* scarlet mouth with wonderful flashing teeth.' Soon after this, he and Alington left for the Continent, where they indulged in an unbridled couple of weeks in Paris, Venice and Athens. Everywhere they went, Wogan delightedly reported, Naps was on the most familiar terms with gigolos, waiters, porters, barbers, policemen; even on the cross-Channel boat 'Naps knew all the ship's crew by their Christian names & the curves of their bottoms'. In company with a wide selection of fashionable international society there was heavy drinking, drugging, all-night parties and (on Naps's part) wild homosexual orgies. In Venice 'we were asked to at least ten parties . . . Roger Senhouse appeared . . . Prince Dimitri & other Russians, Austrians, Turks, Americans. . . . I fell wildly in love with Nikitina, more lovely off than on the stage, behaved madly, passed out in a glorious sexy dream roaring with laughter & adoring the world.' In Athens, perhaps in reaction to the wild dissipations of the previous fortnight, a more sober mood descended. From here Wogan wrote to his wife, 'I don't believe you realise how married I really am. . . . God, how I should mind if you wanted to try lovers, because I want you back so badly myself. . . . Oh darling! I do think of you such a lot, I really do. I miss you frightfully, & long for you.'

But despite such heartfelt expressions of affection, the time had long passed for any significant change in attitude on either side. They had grown too far apart, Rosamond wrapped up in her children and her literary life, Wogan being drawn more and more into a serious involvement in politics. As a very young man, Wogan had rejected the Liberal loyalties of his father in favour of the far right, but had undergone a form of Damascene conversion during the General Strike of

1926, which, like so many young men of his class, he had regarded primarily as a tremendous lark, excitedly volunteering for the once-in-a-lifetime chance to work as a bus-conductor or policeman. But while in the London docks preparing to unload the lorry he had been driving, he was surrounded by a group of dockers who at first threatened to attack him as a strike-breaker, then explained to him the shocking realities of their situation. Having joined the Labour Party, Wogan was further influenced in his move to the left by his old friend, John Strachey, a nephew of Lytton's, and a contemporary of his at Eton and Oxford. Strachey in Ramsay MacDonald's Labour government had been parliamentary private secretary to the future leader of the British Union of Fascists, Sir Oswald Mosley. When Mosley in 1931 resigned from Labour and created the socialist-tending New Party, Strachey followed him, and it was in the New Party that he now encouraged Wogan to join him. Wogan, increasingly horrified by the effects of the slump, by the widespread poverty and unemployment, the growing menace of Fascism in Germany and Spain, was interested, and the Philippses twice went to stay with Mosley at Savehay Farm in Buckinghamshire, where politics were energetically discussed every waking hour. (Rosamond was piqued that her host, well known as a connoisseur of beautiful women, paid her no attention. 'I was totally out of the group . . . I don't remember Tom [Mosley] even looking in my direction.')

Wogan always claimed that Rosamond was uninterested in politics, but this was not entirely accurate. True, she was bored by economics and political theory, and exasperated by the fanaticism with which in her view Wogan and friends such as Strachey and Stephen Spender were all at once talking politics to the exclusion of everything else. 'She resented it very much when we all became political,' said Spender. 'There we were in a world in which the serious things were literature and ideas, and the rest was amusing things like gossip, and then suddenly came this intrusion of politics, like some terrible leak in the water pipes.' Rosamond herself admitted that she was able to take no clearly defined political stance. 'My head, what there is of it, is with the Left, my heart is entirely with the people I love, my tastes, traditions, etc. etc. are with the centre-leaning-to-Right,' she told Compton Mackenzie. 'Vaguely Liberal' by upbringing and temperament, she saw the political situation overwhelmingly in human terms. While John was in Germany in 1933, for instance, she asked him to tell her 'all about Nazis & Berlin. . . . Today I'm haunted by a photograph in the "Herald" of a Jewish socialist walking barefoot through the streets with an armed bevy of Hitlerites round him & a placard round his neck saying: I will not complain any more to the police. The look on his mild spectacled face, the indignity of that heavy placard, those bare feet – I feel sick.'

But her main intellectual interests were as always literary, and as a novelist she was predominantly engaged in the business of reading and writing, with a keen critical interest in the works of other writers. She read avidly, modern poets such as T. S. Eliot, Roy Fuller, Auden and Cecil Day Lewis, and contemporary novelists, admiring in particular the work of Faulkner and Ford Madox Ford, Virginia Woolf, Ivy Compton-Burnett, Sylvia Townsend Warner, Jean Rhys and Elizabeth Bowen.

Jean Rhys's bleak, beautiful novel *Voyage in the Dark*, published in the same month as *Invitation to the Waltz*, had much impressed Rosamond, who invited its author to tea, with Beatrix and Violet Hammersley, all three intensely curious to meet this exotic creature – born and brought up in Dominica, on the stage in England, vagabond existence in Paris, heavy drinking, unhappy love-affairs – but it was a disappointing occasion as their guest, neatly dressed and demure, spoke hardly a word. Rosamond none the less was intrigued, and suspecting that Rhys was shy with new people, arranged to meet her again, this time on her own. But the second occasion was no more successful than the first, with the novelist deeply depressed and nursing a black eye, the result of a drunken fall; on the third date she never appeared at all, leaving Rosamond sitting waiting at the Café Royal until Jean's husband, Leslie Tilden Smith, turned up with a tale about a car accident constructed to conceal the real facts, that he and Jean had been involved in a drunken brawl for which they had been arrested and detained overnight. Rosamond, believing the accident story, tried one more time, but when she arrived at the flat in Bury Street, the door was opened by Tilden Smith to reveal his wife lying on the sofa in an alcoholic semi-coma. It was clear that the friendship was going nowhere, and Rosamond never made contact again.

With Elizabeth Bowen, whose first novel appeared at the same time as *Dusty Answer*, the initial stages of the friendship were considerably more rewarding. Elizabeth, tall, large-boned, almost handsome, was very much a product of her Anglo-Irish ancestry, generous, sociable, fastidious and highly strung; she dressed with elegance, smoked without cease and talked rapidly in a low, musical voice, jabbing the air with her cigarette for emphasis. Fascinated by personal relationships and capable of 'flashes of insight like summer lightning', she was also an intensely private person; she once described her life in terms of a long career of 'withheld emotion', and Rosamond was quick to sense her complexity. '[Elizabeth] had a passionate and primitive, even a ruthless streak, strictly controlled, beneath the persona of an Anglo-Irish gentlewoman she presented to the world.' Although a dedicated and disciplined writer, she had a wide and devoted circle of acquaintance whom she entertained generously, setting great store by intimate friendships with both men and women. She loved good talk, in spite of a tendency to shyness and a slight stammer which '[added] an edge at once comical and endearing to the marvellous wit, irony and incisiveness of her conversation'. Her husband, Alan Cameron, at that time director of education for the city of Oxford, was devoted to her, but although highly intelligent he was inclined to be ponderous, and Elizabeth while remaining extremely fond of him looked outside her marriage for a wider range of intellectual and emotional stimulus.

She and Rosamond were first introduced in 1933, immediately liked each other, and started to meet fairly often, not difficult as the Camerons were then living at Headington, on the outskirts of Oxford. The two women found they had a number of acquaintances in common, Cyril Connolly, Raymond Mortimer, Maurice Bowra, Isaiah Berlin, John Hayward and William Plomer among them, and through Elizabeth Rosamond made several more: one was the poet Cecil Day Lewis, whose sex appeal and romantic good looks made a notable impression. 'I met Cecil Day-Lewis ... at a party of Elizabeth Bowen's,' Rosamond told Stephen Spender in March 1936. '[I] rather lost my heart to him. He's beautiful, isn't he?'

Elizabeth came to stay at Ipsden, and in August 1935 invited both Philippses to her family house in Ireland, an invitation that was regretfully refused as Wogan had gone off sailing in the Scilly Isles leaving Rosamond stranded at home with the children. Her admiration for Elizabeth's new book, *The House in Paris*, published that year, was profound. 'You lucky clever woman to write so much & so well,' she told her, complaining of her own difficulties with trying to work while supervising the household. Elizabeth was sympathetic, and when at the end of the year she and Alan moved from Oxford to London, she offered a solution. 'If you ever want to combine being in London with working, if that's possible for you, come here, as there are several writing tables during the day and a reasonable silence.' But domestic responsibilities and Wogan's frequent absences made it difficult to leave Ipsden for more than the briefest intervals and still there was the new novel to be written.

Rosamond started work on *The Weather in the Streets* in the autumn of 1934, almost exactly two years after the publication of *Invitation to the Waltz*. Composing the sequel – 'like trying to haul a grand piano out of a bog single-handed' – she found a great effort. 'The machine was an infinite labour to get going,' she told John. 'The complexities of what I wanted to say bothered me dreadfully, & I couldn't get the rhythm – & also I think the difficulties of my own life – I mean all the daily things I have to do here – interfered.' The novel was finally finished at the beginning of January 1936, and came out on 6 July – published not by Chatto & Windus but by Collins, a change of imprint which not unnaturally had resulted in some uncomfortable exchanges between Rosamond and Harold Raymond.

As far back as 1933 Rosamond, through the literary agency J. B. Pinker & Son, had received a generous offer for her future fiction from Collins, which, although tempting, she was obliged to turn down because of an option clause in her American contract. On reflection, however, and in spite of the smaller advances, she was relieved to be staying with Chatto, she told Harold Raymond, with whom, and with whose wife, Vera, she was by now on the friendliest terms, '[although] I'm almost tempted to wish we weren't friends when it comes to talking business as it is *so* embarrassing!' Raymond was understanding, and suggested she should employ an agent, '[so that] you would certainly be saved from the least feeling of discomfort over any negotiations between us two'. Unfortunately, the opposite turned out to be the case, and it was Rosamond's agent, Ralph Pinker, who was entirely responsible for the trouble that now ensued.

J. B. Pinker, the firm's founder, had been a distinguished figure in the book world, but his son, who took over the business, was a crook whose eventual conviction for fraud was to lead to the firm's demise. It was Pinker junior who on Rosamond's behalf now duplicitously agreed a contract with Collins without informing Chatto until the deal was done. Harold Raymond, assuming Rosamond had been privy to the plot, was shocked and angry. 'Yes, I *do* feel badly treated,' he told her. 'I have never yet known an author leave her publisher for no other reason but one of terms without telling him what she had been offered elsewhere and giving him a chance of equalling it. And the fact is that I do not to this day know what terms you have accepted nor who is to be your next publisher.' In fact Collins's terms were generous, offering an advance of £750 for *The Weather in the Streets*, over twice the amount (£300) Chatto had paid for *Invitation to the Waltz*. None the less Rosamond was appalled: she had had no idea that Raymond and Pinker had not been conferring all along. 'I must have told Pinker 10 times, without exaggeration, to put all the cards on the table,' she wrote. 'Of *course* I assumed it had been done. . . . What do you take me for? . . . Pinker assured me all had passed off with perfect good feeling.' Sad but mollified, Raymond invited his former author to a conciliatory lunch, after which the two parted amicably, Raymond returning to his office privately convinced that Rosamond would come to regret leaving the publisher of Lytton Strachey and Proust for a firm which owed its huge commercial success to the Bible, school textbooks, thrillers, *Little Grey Rabbit* and the British rights to Walt Disney.

Rosamond never again employed a literary agent, from this time onwards consigning all business matters to the Society of Authors, of which she had been a member since 1928. It was the Society which during the war uncovered the fact that the disgraced Pinker had quietly continued to take his 10 per cent commission on all the Lehmann royalties, an unsatisfactory state of affairs which was abruptly ended in 1943 with his being brought to trial at the Old Bailey and sentenced to twelve months' hard labour. 'I think he was really a dishonest idiot rather than a scheming villain,' wrote Denys Kilham Roberts, the Society's secretary-general, 'but his fate will be a warning to other literary agents with glue on their fingers!'

The story told in *The Weather in the Streets* takes place ten years after the close of *Invitation to the Waltz*, its title intended to convey the impression of 'a crowd of people of today, unprotected, ordinary &

various, moving along in the streets in every sort of weather, stopping to talk, lingering to make love, disappearing to be sad, to die'. Olivia, separated from a feckless young husband, is lodging with frivolous cousin Etty in London while earning a meagre living as assistant to Anna Cory, a photographer friend. Summoned home to see her father, dangerously ill with pneumonia, she meets Rollo Spencer on the train, and during the course of their flirtatious conversation it becomes clear that the love-affair indicated at the end of the previous novel is now about to happen. Rollo invites her to dine at Meldon – there are the family much as before, the formidable Lady Spencer, Sir John, now drifting into senility, the disturbing and elusive Marigold – and while driving her home at the end of the evening he arranges to meet her in London. His wife, Nicola, the beautiful girl in the white dress glimpsed at the dance, is a semi-invalid and spends much of the time with her mother in the country.

So begins a time for Olivia of supreme happiness. Deeply in love with Rollo, she surrenders wholly to him, keeping herself free in case he calls, revelling in the unaccustomed luxury of expensive restaurants, the comfort of his large motor-car, sheltered by his wealth from the cold and the rain, from the weather in the streets. With Rollo, 'it was always indoors or in taxis or in his warm car; it was mostly in the safe dark, or in half-light in the deepest corner of the restaurant. . . . Drawn curtains, shaded lamp, or only the fire.. . .' Occasionally there is more: playing house in Etty's absence ('He said he was hungry so I sent him out for a couple of sausages and fried them for him. That delighted him. "You are a domestic little creature, aren't you?" I suppose he'd never seen a woman put on a kettle or use a frying-pan in his life, it moved him'); an idyllic night at a country inn; a party in Fitzroy Square with Olivia's bohemian friends. This last is a great failure with Rollo who goes home early. Olivia, unable to let the evening end on such an unhappy note, takes a taxi to his house, and shivering in a bitter wind watches him through a gap in the curtains as he stands smoking his pipe. 'From outside the room looked warm, rich and snug – a first-class comfortable home. I saw that . . .' From this moment her innate insecurity, only temporarily subdued, resurfaces as she realises that she is the eternal outsider, and that Rollo, pampered, prosperous, protected, belongs to a world in which she exists only on sufferance.

As Olivia's feelings for her lover intensify, she cannot stop herself making tearful demands, all of them distasteful to Rollo, an amiable, easy-going chap who cannot understand why she must spoil the lovely times they have together. Subliminally Rollo had made the rules clear to Olivia even before the affair had properly started, during the dinner-party at Meldon.

> He helped himself to fish before saying with a rueful twist of an eyebrow: 'I can't bear women to cry. I do deplore it.'
> 'Yes, it's a bad habit.'
> He said quickly:
> 'That's what I think –' checked himself; added vaguely: 'No . . .'
> 'What does it make you feel when people cry?' she asked lightly. 'Sorry? Irritated? or what? Does it melt you, or freeze you?'
> He thought a moment.
> 'Donno. A mixture, I suppose. Damned uncomfortable anyway. I want to rush off *miles* . . .'

The affair continues, punctuated by illness on Olivia's side, a long absence of Rollo's in America, and, unexpectedly, a glorious ten days in Austria during which Olivia is convinced that at last Rollo is 'utterly in love'. But the moment passes, and back in England she finds to her horror she is pregnant. Rollo has disappeared for the rest of the summer, leaving her alone in the hot, dirty, airless city. 'To be alone, sick, in London in this dry, sterile, burnt-out end of summer, was to be abandoned in a pestilence-stricken town.' Olivia's desperate telegram begging Rollo to make contact is intercepted by Lady Spencer, who calls on Olivia and with lethal civility makes clear that the relationship with her son must finish.

> '*May* I come in? Just for a very short time.' The tone was pleasant, but all-concealing; the old cordial note one's ear was tuned for absent. . . .
> 'What a charming little house.' Peeling off her lavender gloves, Lady Spencer looked about her. . . .

After the brief interview is concluded, Olivia realises she is left with no alternative but to go through the ultimate degradation of an illegal abortion. This is not the end of the novel, nor indeed of the affair, but it marks the point at which Olivia finally abandons all hope that she is anything more than a delightful pastime to the man who is the love of her life.

The Weather in the Streets is anguished, uncompromising, deeply felt, and in autobiographical terms painfully revealing. Bigger and more ambitious than its predecessor, structurally sophisticated, seamed with ironic humour, it is a more complex work, its emotional temperature deriving both from Rosamond's memories of her first marriage and the loss of her child, and from her painful experience of Wogan's infidelity. Olivia is a true Lehmann heroine in her vulnerability, passivity and eagerness to sacrifice everything for love, while Rollo is only a slightly older version of the 'wonderful young man' who from girlhood featured so prominently in Rosamond's fantasies. Handsome, good-natured and blandly charming, Rollo is also spoilt, complacent and weak; dismissive of intellectuals, contemptuous of Olivia's artist friends, and distrustful of any kind of introspection, to the reader he can appear something of a boor, although never to the besotted Olivia, who remains dazzled by him to the end. Rosamond was always defensive of her portrayal of Rollo, firmly refusing to see his spineless behaviour as caddish. 'Rollo isn't a cad,' she explained in an interview. 'He's trapped by conventions, and yet he's also very charming and rather touching. People of his class have always fascinated me because they are in such a muddle.' For Olivia, as for Rosamond, a potent part of his appeal is his social position, the effortless assurance that is such a seductive concomitant of money and rank: the large chauffeur-driven Sunbeam with its thick fur rug that collects him from the station, the prosperous aroma that clings to him – 'cigars, expensive stuff on his hair, good soap, clean linen' – all act as a powerful aphrodisiac. Although the Spencers' way of life is seen as sterile and stultifying, it still has an enchantment for Olivia, who, only too conscious of the shameful economies necessitated by her threadbare existence, is aware that she will never be accepted as an equal.

It is here that the major motif in Rosamond's fiction, as in her life, comes strongly to the fore. Standing in front of the fire after dinner at Meldon, Olivia wonders, 'Can they sniff out an alien upon this hearth? Or is it disguise enough, simply to be here, in an evening-dress?' On this occasion Olivia is so alight with the electricity between herself and

165

Rollo that she carries off the deception with panache, giving a consummate performance of a confident young woman entirely at home in her sumptuous surroundings. In a deftly witty scene she conducts a sophisticated dialogue with the cosmopolitan Sir Ronald, her neighbour at the dinner-table.

> She turned towards him, breaking the ice with a radiant beam. He said in a surprisingly high, feminine register:
> 'I feared vis uvverwise delightful meal was going to slip by in vain proximity.'
> 'I feared so too.' She continued to beam, disarming him. . . .
> 'No pudding?' She raised her eyebrows at his empty plate.
> 'No . . . [sic] No . . . [sic]' he said doubtfully, rather anxiously. He stuck his eyeglass in and eyed the pink-and-white cherry-scattered *volupté* she was engaged upon. 'No, I fink not.' . . .
> 'I love puddings,' she said, in the style of pretty confession. . . .

The theme of the outsider, a constant in Rosamond's novels, has a specific relevance to *The Weather in the Streets*, in which the imprint of Taplow and the Desboroughs is particularly distinct. Olivia's perception of Rollo as forbidden fruit evolved from an incident when Rosamond as a girl of 18 was invited to a party at Taplow, where she caught the eye of Ivo Grenfell, one of the dashing sons of the house. 'Ivo took a tremendous fancy to me, and we danced and danced, and he was very attentive. Then I suddenly caught sight of Lady Desborough sitting watching, and I saw her hooded eyes staring at us, and I thought, She wouldn't like it if Ivo fell in love with me. I should no longer be a favourite.'

Although Rosamond boasted to Barbara Ker-Seymer that this time 'the portrait seekers' would be frustrated, there are as ever a number of identifiable origins, Barbara herself contributing to the character of the photographer, Anna Cory, Rollo directly derived from Matt Ridley, and as in *Invitation*, Olivia's family, Mr and Mrs Curtis, brother James and married sister Kate closely based on the Lehmanns. The Curtis sisters' good-natured alliance against their mother is a close reflection of that of the Lehmann girls against Alice. When at the beginning of the novel

Olivia arrives home to see her father, Mrs Curtis swings into efficient action.

'Olivia, if you run through and just ask Ada she'll make you some bovril. . . .'

Mrs Curtis reflected an instant, then set off energetically up the stairs again.

'I don't want any bovril,' said Olivia, low.

'Want must be your master,' said Kate. 'Can't you stop kicking against the pricks for *one* morning? Ada's to make it and Violet's to bring it up and we're to drink it and we'll all be doing our bit. I'll go and order it. Meet you in the schoolroom.'

'Put a swig of something in mine. Port or sherry or something.'

But the door had swung to.

The least successful parts of the novel are those depicting Olivia's bohemian friends, drawn from Rosamond's knowledge of young men such as John Banting, Eddy Gathorne-Hardy and others, painters and writers on the fringes of Bloomsbury. It is essential that Olivia be shown to have work and friends of her own, and this raffish group makes a necessary contrast to the snobbish, conventional society in which the Spencers move; yet none of the artistic chums properly comes to life, mainly because there are too many of them too sketchily delineated, and their jolly, drunken antics, lengthily described, detract more than they add to the powerful pull of the main narrative.

Inevitably, the section that gave rise to some appalled reaction was that dealing with Olivia's abortion, based on Rosamond's own experience during her first marriage. Hers was not the first novel to deal openly with this painful topic – Jean Rhys writes of it in *Voyage in the Dark* published only two years earlier – yet its impact was shocking, less from any startling explicitness than from the uncompromising manner in which the nature of Olivia's predicament, her acute mental and physical distress, is described. Indeed so harrowing was this part of the story considered then that Rosamond's new American publisher, Reynal & Hitchcock, at first insisted that she remove all mention of it, which she refused to do, eventually agreeing to excise one short passage of barely half a page. Ironically, the cut was never made as the edition was rushed through before the author's final corrections could be incorporated. 'Imagine my feelings,' she wrote to John Hayward. 'All my precious final corrections have gone for nothing. All sorts of alterations & eliminations – minor, but dear to me. 85,000 copies of it!'[3]

The novel, energetically promoted by Collins with a showy advertising campaign, was the Book Society choice for July and sold briskly, in spite of a batch of mixed reviews. Some critics applauded: according to the *Illustrated London News*, 'it was impossible to praise [it] too highly', Ralph Straus in the *Sunday Times* declared it 'a triumph' and Cecil Day Lewis in the *Daily Telegraph* described Miss Lehmann as 'a very talented writer indeed', concluding in a curiously flirtatious final sentence that *The Weather in the Streets* was a notable achievement, 'for many reasons, not least its power to put any number of ideas into the head of a jaded reviewer'. Others, including (predictably) Gerald Gould in the *Observer*, claimed they found the work hard to stomach, Gould describing its author as a victim of 'fictional elephantiasis. . . . I cannot, I cannot, if I am to save one scrap of belief in my own honesty, pretend to think this sort of thing other than tedious and unreal.' Queenie Leavis was another detractor, who in a sneering review in *Scrutiny* took the opportunity to condemn the entire Lehmann *oeuvre* as bourgeois and immature, and the writer herself as typical of 'the pseudo-sophisticated would-be cynical actually sentimental emotionally vulgarising middlebrow novelist who goes down so well nowadays with the educated public'. In America where the book had been published a month earlier, it met with unqualified enthusiasm. 'The American reviews are mostly highly praising, but silly,' Rosamond told Stephen Spender. 'The sales are large.'

One of the first to read *The Weather* had been Rosamond's sister Beatrix, to whose letter of congratulation Rosamond replied, 'Oh I'm so glad, *glad* you like it. . . . I *know* some of it's all right, because it was imposed on me in a shape like iron: the abortion & the last quarrel in the "Wreath of May" – & the last few pages of all – also the night in the awful pub, when they had their first scene.' There were more congratulations, from among others Stephen Spender, Elizabeth Bowen,

[3] The passage exists also in the novel's French translation, an observation I owe to Gillian Tindall in her *Rosamond Lehmann: an Appreciation*.

who also reviewed it, and Morgan Forster, the latter describing in detail his reactions. 'The book moves me a good deal,' he told her. '[Olivia's] bitterness in Part IV is excellent and very sympathetic: one never feels she is tiresome. Sir Ronald made me laugh the most. Etty, Kate, Lady S, and Mrs C. – very good, and how you bring out the horror of the English country house. Were they ever not horrible?' He went on to complain that he found Rollo 'vulgar', which was certainly far from the author's intention, and he showed an unexpected interest in Olivia's symptoms in pregnancy. '[I didn't know] that the longings for e.g. prune-juice still went on – I thought that stopped in the 17th century! . . . [and] I wonder whether the sickness is *always* so bad.' There were a few dissenters, one of the most vehement David Garnett who, possibly influenced by the comic caricature of Vanessa Bell's daughter, Angelica, whom he adored, told Barbara Ker-Seymer, 'I have always stood up for Rosamond's work, but this has really left a very nasty taste. . . . Better not let Wogan see this letter as I suppose he thinks everyone thinks like Miss Bowen.'

David Garnett may not have agreed with Miss Bowen's view but to Rosamond the older woman's good opinion was paramount. In an appreciative letter about the novel, Elizabeth had again suggested a visit to Ireland, an invitation eagerly accepted as Rosamond not only looked forward to spending time with Elizabeth herself but had recently discovered good reason to wish to be away from home.

Over the past year or so, up to the early summer of 1936, relations with Wogan had been somewhat easier, he seeming calmer and more cheerful than before. 'Everything is much peacefuller and happier,' Rosamond had written to Dadie with relief. 'The unending process of adaptation which is marriage goes on successfully, I dare hope.' In April 1936 they had both joined Ralph and Frances Partridge for a holiday in Spain, starting with the Easter fair in Seville, moving on to Madrid, and from Madrid to Barcelona. Rosamond fell ill with influenza soon after leaving England, but she enjoyed herself nevertheless, her abiding memory that of going on her own to see the cathedral in Seville. 'No woman went out alone in Spain in those days, and I was about twice as tall as any Spanish woman, and very, very slender, and I wore an enormous hat. I was walking back to the hotel, and I began to be followed by crowds and crowds and crowds of people, saying, "Who is she? Who is she? Is she a goddess? Beautiful! Beautiful!"' For her this was an intensely moving, quasi-religious experience, but when in solemn tones she described the incident to the others, they merely laughed.

Back home, Rosamond returned to her writing in the intervals of her domestic duties. As always there were friends to stay every weekend. One Sunday in June, when Beatrix and Matt Ridley were at Ipsden, the famous American aviator Charles Lindbergh and his wife were brought over for the day. Rosamond was enchanted by them, although appalled by the knowledge of what they had endured over the kidnap and murder of their baby son. 'The agonizing fact remains. There is between them & the rest of the world the kind of barrier there is between, say, us and the blind.' Her own children were a source of endless fascination. Hugo, now 7 and at a prep school in Dorset run by Hester Chapman and her husband, was an independent little boy, wary of strangers, while 2-year-old Sally, with peachy complexion and white-blonde curls, was an angelic child, a cheerful, smiling little creature who welcomed the world: 'pink, plump, gay & amusing,' her mother described her, 'the joy of my life'. In *The Weather in the Streets* she draws an endearing portrait of Sally as Kate's 16-month-old daughter, Polly.

The baby attentively examined the mulberry upon her cushioned palm. After a moment of trance she cried, 'Away!' and as a bowler towards the wicket, plunged immediately into a gallop, swept her arm up and back, and hurled it from her. 'Gone!' she announced. She began forthwith to search over the grass, croaking 'Where? Where? Where?' in urgent reiteration.

'There it is,' said Kate languidly, pointing with her toe.

'Dere tis,' she cried rapturously. Knees flexed, she bent forward from the hips to examine it once more, then fell on it, stamped it to pulp, her face contorted with disgust, an eye on Kate. 'Ach! Ach! Ach!' She was hoarse with loathing.

'She's very good about not putting things in her mouth,' said Kate.

'She's terribly engaging.' Olivia watched the legs, a couple of burstingly stuffed pegs, start off once more towards the mulberry tree.

Doting on them both, particularly on her small daughter, Rosamond was annoyed with Wogan for his lack of interest in his offspring, although grateful that in general he seemed so much more content.

One morning while Wogan was working in his studio, Rosamond answered the telephone to Barbara Ker-Seymer, asking to speak to Wogan. Rosamond dialled the studio extension to put her through, and staying on the line to listen, heard Barbara in a low voice ask, 'Did you mean what you said?' to which Wogan made 'a tremulous reply. And I thought, "My God, surely not Barbara!" I slammed the receiver down, and thought, "Now, really! this is too much!"' Shortly afterwards Wogan came in and sheepishly confessed that the affair had been going on for some time. As before Rosamond felt cruelly betrayed: Barbara, like Julia, had been *her* friend, and it was intolerable that Wogan should have deceived her yet again. True, he was not in love with Barbara, as he had been with Julia – he described this new relationship as 'a cuddly friendship' – but the discovery was humiliating and depressing, none the less.

To Eddy Sackville-West, who had become a confidant, Rosamond poured out her woes, trying to analyse what exactly had gone wrong in her marriage. 'If I were different or had managed better this wouldn't have happened,' she wrote miserably.

> What doesn't seem to count with him, & what I wanted so much, was the gradual growing together of our lives: the *habit* of marriage, so to speak. But he wants endless stimulus: he always says I don't stimulate him. It is almost impossible to believe he doesn't really feel my great love for him – but whatever I do isn't right: if I let him rip and 'understand' then it's made to be that I don't care; if I collapse, it is mere possessive jealousy, beneath his notice. . . . Lately he has told me I once gave him all he wanted, that I helped him over his transition period, but that now he has passed on beyond me. . . . Oh, what will be the end of it all. . . .

Wogan for the moment did indeed seem to be beyond the reach of reason, wildly volatile, and towards his wife both guilty and defiant. There seemed little any of their friends could do to help the situation. 'Rosamond is having troubles,' Beatrix told John. 'W[ogan] is all too truly the young man of her novels! She really behaves *so well*, and these miseries have been going on for years, and she never breathes a word.'

With this new unhappiness in the background, it was with particular pleasure that Rosamond accepted Elizabeth Bowen's invitation to Bowen's Court, her austere and beautiful Georgian house in County Cork. At the beginning of September 1936, Rosamond, accompanied by Roger Senhouse, took the night ferry, arriving at Bowen's Court the following morning to find Elizabeth and Alan with a house-party which included Isaiah Berlin and two of his Oxford colleagues, Stuart Hampshire and Con O'Neill, and a young cousin of Elizabeth's, Noreen Colley. After two days of good food and a great deal to drink, with walks, visits and sightseeing by day, intellectual parlour games in the evening after dinner, a new guest arrived, the strikingly handsome writer and academic Goronwy Rees. The young man who walked into the drawing-room that late summer's day made an impressive entrance. Bare feet in sandals, shirt-sleeves rolled up, collar Byronically open at the throat, a lock of dark hair falling carelessly over his forehead, he strode into the house, said Isaiah Berlin, 'like the Toreador in *Carmen*, jangling all his bells and terribly excited'. Elizabeth the past couple of days had been noticeably on edge, chain-smoking, restless, her slight stammer more pronounced than usual, for she had fallen in love with the much younger Goronwy, a dazzling contrast to her kind but dull husband, and believed he and she were poised on the verge of an affair. To everyone else, it became instantly apparent that Goronwy had eyes only for Rosamond, sitting on the arm of her chair, caressing her hands, talking intently to her and to her alone; and Rosamond herself was observed to be 'very amorous'. As soon as their hostess came into the room the two sprang apart. After Rosamond went upstairs to bed, Goronwy followed, wanting to make love to her, which she would not allow, feeling it would not be right for them to spend the night together while under Elizabeth's roof. They agreed that for both it had been a *coup de foudre*, and they made plans to meet as soon as they were back in England.

After a couple of days Rosamond departed, leaving Goronwy behind. In his curious, backward-slanting hand, he wrote to describe his visit to Barbara Ker-Seymer, with whom until recently he had been having an affair; perhaps wishing to keep his options open with Barbara, he told her that although during the last few days he had felt 'frightfully excited all the time', he had made 'no wonderful emotional relationship'. Rosamond, he said, appeared 'very beautiful full face but side face looks rather pert & hard. She is extremely nice to everyone ... [but] extraordinarily unreal, like a character in one of her own books.' His hostess was presented with a different version: he had fallen in love with Rosamond, Goronwy confessed, and wanted to make her his mistress. Elizabeth was shocked and hurt, her hurt turning to fury at what she now learned from Noreen Colley. Noreen, sleeping in the room next to Rosamond's and hearing the two easily identifiable voices talking hour after hour, had assumed the worst, and having waited a few days had decided to tell Elizabeth what, mistakenly, she believed to have been going on. Elizabeth insisted on Goronwy's leaving at once, then in deep distress wrote an impassioned ten-page letter to Isaiah Berlin, giving full vent to her feelings of outrage and disgust. The weekend, she said, had been sullied '[by] the violently advancing intimacy between G. and Rosamond. This advanced by leaps and bounds and became very physical – unnoticed, which was strange, only by me. . . . Apparently, only my presence unhooked them from one another.' She was horrified, she went on, that they obviously considered the place and the occasion proper 'for the prosecution of a love-affair so ruthless that it crashed across the sensibility and dignity of everyone else here'. A few days later 'a long and *very* embarrassing letter' arrived from Rosamond full of gushing gratitude and tentative apology, to which she decided not to reply. 'If I felt that Goronwy and Rosamond could shake down into any kind of happiness I should be glad,' she told Berlin with less than complete conviction, 'but I cannot see that anything happy or healthy can begin with such ruthless incontinence.'

When Rosamond arrived back at Ipsden, she felt transformed, in a ferment over the prospect of her new love-affair and impatient for it to begin. Immediately she began writing long letters to Rees at Bowen's Court, the fat blue envelopes with their distinctive handwriting arriving, as Elizabeth sourly phrased it, 'with injudicious frequency'. Blithely Rosamond told John Hayward that she had adored her time in Ireland – 'I do SO love Elizabeth' – while to Isaiah Berlin she wrote, 'There never has been such an astonishingly pure & concentrated emotional & intellectual pattern as we all were making there with Elizabeth to hold & direct the weaving.'

With the future so bright, the familiar problems of her relationship with Wogan faded temporarily into insignificance – fortunately, perhaps, as Rosamond was now faced with his announcement that he was on the point of leaving to join the Republican side in the Civil War in Spain.

8

A *Split* Life

On her way to Ireland at the end of August 1936, Rosamond spent a week at Llanstephan, having arranged to leave the children with their grandparents during her absence. Wogan was planning to join them there the day before she left, and his presence was anticipated with a certain amount of apprehension. 'Wogan arrives to-day & then I suppose the fur will fly as usual,' Rosamond predicted. 'My guess is that Spain will be the rock they crack on this time.' Her guess was entirely correct. The Civil War in Spain, which had broken out a month earlier, was a topic which possessed the left-wing intellectuals with whom Wogan aligned himself, friends such as Stephen Spender, Cyril Connolly, John Banting, Rosamond's brother John, Vanessa Bell's son Julian. On 17 July the right-wing military had rebelled against the legitimate Republican government. Although the Nationalists, as the rebels came to be called, were at first in much the weaker position, powerful armed reinforce-ments were quickly despatched in their support by the two great Fascist powers of Italy and Germany, action strongly censured by the democracies of England and France, and to a lesser extent by the United States. Among the politically left-wing, such as Wogan, there was a passionate commitment to the Republican side: for them the issues were clear, a struggle between Fascism and the left, between an exploitative capitalist elite and a progressive intelligentsia in alliance with the working masses: it was unthinkable that any decent individual should be pro-Fascist, and support for Franco was seen as degenerate and damnable. It therefore came as little surprise to Rosamond to receive a telegram at Bowen's Court informing her that Wogan once again had been thrown out of the house by his father. On her return to Ipsden she found him in a state of feverish excitement, able to talk about nothing but the situation in Spain, the struggle against Fascism and his own whole-hearted dedication to the cause. During the following weeks Wogan immersed himself in frenzied political activity – meetings, speeches, fund-raising – and in February 1937 he left England as a volunteer for Spanish Medical Aid, driving a lorry as part of a small convoy ferrying medical supplies south through France to Barcelona.

Although Rosamond was heavy-hearted to see him go, in a sense Wogan's departure provided a necessary respite, an acceptable reason for a lengthy separation which both Philippses by now urgently needed. For too long their relationship had been miserably dissonant. Of the two, Wogan despite his extramural activities was the more determined to keep the marriage going, still loving his wife and looking up to her, although frequently provoked to anger and frustration. Rosamond, on the other hand, while needing the security of the married state, had grown bored with her husband's limitations and was tired of the pattern of explosive scenes and dramatic reconciliations: she had had enough, she said, 'of being the object of hate–love . . . [of] fighting a defensive battle & being the battleground at one and the same time'. At first sexual infidelity was more a symptom than a cause of their growing distance. Her discovery of the affair with Barbara Ker-Seymer was naturally a shock – 'I never thought of such a perky little creature as a *femme fatale*' – but in a way Rosamond was relieved that her husband was occupied with someone who appeared to pose no serious threat. 'I'd no *idea* there was any "situation," – though often I'd thought it would be only natural if there were,' she wrote amicably to Barbara. 'Anything would be better than the present deadlock between W. & me – so I hope you & he –' However, by the time he left for Spain Wogan's 'cuddly friendship' with Barbara had inevitably become more complicated. Whereas in the beginning they had both treated the affair light-heartedly, Barbara's affectionate nature and cheerful bohemianism providing a welcome relief from the constant nagging and reproach to be met with at home, she was now making serious demands, going so far as to threaten suicide if Wogan left her. He for his part had grown very fond of Barbara, while stopping well short of wishing for any long-term relationship. Rosamond still came first. Much as he resented her, frequently as he was irritated by her, he still loved her, and was correspondingly jealous of her infatuation with Goronwy Rees.

Soon after Rosamond's triumphant return from Ireland, Elizabeth Bowen had telephoned Wogan and demanded that they meet. Scarcely able to contain her fury, she described the goings-on between Goronwy and Rosamond at Bowen's Court, but other than providing mutual consolation, there was little either of them could do, Goronwy irretrievably lost to Elizabeth, and Wogan forced to accept that his wife was embarking on an affair, to which, as she made crystal clear, he was in no position to object.

The whole situation – the Philippses' estrangement, Wogan's affair with Barbara, Rosamond's with Goronwy, Goronwy's abandoning Elizabeth – had provided weeks of delicious gossip for their friends, but as Goronwy and Rosamond from the beginning conducted their affair openly, and as Wogan appeared to condone it, there was in their bohemian society little scandal attached. Rosamond, radiant, declared herself 'frightfully in love'; and indeed the first months of her relationship with Goronwy were intoxicating. On the surface at least he had everything to offer. Although small in stature, he was magnetically attractive, brimming with Celtic charm and fluency, a delightful companion and attentive lover, flirtatious, sensitive and fun. Before they met, Goronwy had had a number of love-affairs, drawn towards literary ladies rather older than himself; an Oxford colleague, A. L. Rowse, observing the impact he made on both sexes, categorised him as one of the 'deadly irresistibles'. True to the traditions of his Welsh temperament, he was prey to moods of melancholy, but they never lasted long and Rosamond became adept at coaxing him back to his customary high spirits. Of particular importance to Rosamond was the fact that his knowledge and love of literature were as deep as hers – he was a poet and had published two novels – and that he enjoyed talking about books and writing. Instead of undermining her, like Wogan, he flattered and inspired her, and she found him intellectually stimulating. 'He taught me a lot,' she said. 'He was so brilliant . . . and made me feel I had a new life. He gave me a lot of self-confidence.'

As they grew closer, Rosamond became increasingly fascinated by Goronwy and his (to her) exotic background. Born in 1909 in Aberystwyth, the son of a Calvinist minister, Goronwy had shown early brilliance at his grammar school in Cardiff, going on to win a scholarship to Oxford, followed by a first-class degree and election to the prestigious First Prize fellowship at All Souls. At the time they met, however, he had abandoned academe for journalism, and was currently working on the *Spectator*, living in a rented flat in Ebury Street, where he and Rosamond met frequently during the week, at Ipsden at weekends. Rosamond could not but be aware that Goronwy had a mysterious side to his nature, an instinctive elusiveness – 'Secrecy was Goronwy's habit and nourishment,' said the American critic Diana Trilling, who knew him in later life. 'Like a familiar perfume, it announced and trailed him' – and subconsciously she may have suspected that for such a consummate charmer monogamy was unlikely; she was careful, there-fore, not to put the relationship at risk by enquiring into his movements too closely. It was enough that they went about together and were accepted as a couple, each burnishing the other's standing and prestige, Rosamond proud to flaunt a talented young lover, Goronwy basking in the reflection of her literary celebrity.

After the critical acclaim of *The Weather in the Streets*, Rosamond's reputation stood high in her own country and even higher in France, where since the early success of *Dusty Answer* she had had an enthusiastic following, her particular brand of lyrical romanticism appealing to a nation who rated highly novels such as Alain-Fournier's *Le Grand Meaulnes*. The novelist and critic Edmond Jaloux in his monograph on the English novel, *Au Pays du Roman*, published in 1931, had devoted an entire chapter to *Poussière*, 'ce grave, profond et ravissant roman', and there had been a steady stream of letters from a growing fan base. 'You wouldn't believe how many long long LONG letters I get from French jeunes filles who have read *Poussière*,' Rosamond wrote wearily after the novel's publication in Paris. According to the critic Jacques-Emile Blanche, one of the earliest and most fervent admirers of her work, among the French the most popular of the English women novelists were Mary Webb, Margaret Kennedy and Rosamond herself, the last in his mind unquestionably superior to Virginia Woolf. Relations with Gabriel Marcel, Rosamond's editor at her French

Rudie and Alice with the children,
from left to right, Beatrix, Helen, John and Rosamond

Fieldhead

Rosamond at Girton, *c.*1920

Helen

Beatrix with her dog, Krusty

John with his mother

(*Left*) Leslie Runciman. (*Above*) Aboard 'Sunbeam':
Wogan second from left, next to Leslie and Rosamond

(*Below left*) Walter and Hilda Runciman on 'Sunbeam'.
(*Below right*) Leslie, Rosamond and Dadie Rylands

Matt and Ursula Ridley
with Rosamond in the
South of France, 1928

Wogan and Rosamond
at Tidmarsh, 1928

Dadie, Rosamond and Wogan
in France, 1930

Rosamond picnicking with
Lytton Strachey and Dadie

Carrington

Frances Partridge and Dadie
with Raymond Mortimer

(*Below left*) Stephen Spender
(*Below right*) Sir Laurence Philipps

Rosamond and Paul Cross
in the West Indies, 1933

Julia Strachey

(*Below left*) Barbara Ker-Seymer
(*Below right*) Matt Ridley

Ipsden

Rosamond at Ipsden, 1934

Rosamond with Sally and Hugo

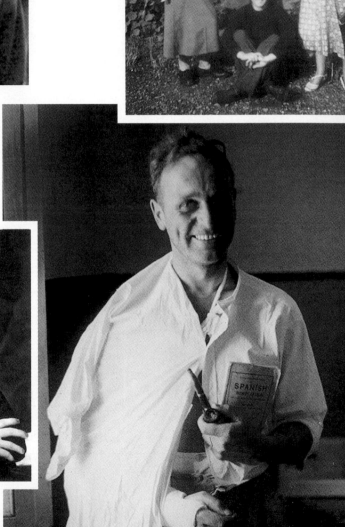

(*Above*) Goronwy Rees
(*Above right*)
Elizabeth Bowen (centre),
Goronwy Rees (sitting)
and Rosamond (right)
at Bowen's Court, 1936.

Elizabeth Bowen

Wogan on his return
from the Spanish Civil
War, 1937

publisher Plon, were extremely cordial. Marcel, writer and philosopher, was a significant figure in intellectual circles, responsible for making known in France many important writers from abroad, and his approval was an important mark of distinction. It was, however, her translator, Jean Talva, to whom Rosamond owed the most.

Jean Talva was the pseudonym of Marthe L'Evêque, a quiet, scholarly woman in late middle age who had worked as a translator mainly for the publishing firm of Stock. Rosamond's first novel was also Mme L'Evêque's first commission for Plon, and it was she who had effected the tricky transposition of the title, from *Dusty Answer* into *Poussière* ('the opposite of what I really meant,' Rosamond admitted, 'but you couldn't call it *Réponse Poussereuse. . .* so it was a beautiful translation but a silly title'); since then her sensitive renderings into French of Rosamond's fiction were much admired by its author. 'Really I think you are extraordinary, the way you convey every "nuance" – and more – of the English,' she told her after the publication of *Une Note de Musique*. 'As with *Poussière*, you have made me think better of my own works.' Mme L'Evêque had done an equally skilful job with *The Weather in the Streets* – 'Now I know for certain you do love what I write,' Rosamond assured her. 'To have the essence of what one has written shown to one is an extraordinary experience' – and the notices for *L'Intempéries* in France were little short of rapturous. 'I am soaring & planing far far above all others, even Mary Webb,' Rosamond wrote delightedly to John. 'Now there are only les soeurs Brontë & me.'

In February 1937, Rosamond went over to Paris to enjoy a couple of weeks of the headiest adulation. Her hostess was the legendary Princesse Edmond de Polignac, whom Rosamond had met for the first time at a luncheon in London a couple of months previously. Born Winaretta Singer in 1865, the only daughter and joint heiress of the immensely rich inventor of the sewing machine, 'Aunt Winnie', as she was irreverently known behind her back, was an enormously influential patron of the arts, close friend of Anna de Noailles and Colette, she herself an amateur painter and pianist of note. Ravel, Satie, Stravinsky, Milhaud, Poulenc and Fauré were among the composers who had dedicated works to her, and she regularly sponsored concerts in her magnificent mansion on the Avenue Henri Martin. Masculine in appearance, her voice a deep-throated growl, Mme de Polignac was invariably dressed in severe tailored costumes, her predilection for members of her own sex (among them Romaine Brooks, Clara Haskill and Vita Sackville-West's self-promoting girlfriend, Violet Trefusis) was widely known, and Rosamond was well aware that she herself had caught the eye of the formidable but kind-hearted old lady. 'The Princess plays me Bach preludes & fugues on the organ,' John was told. 'She is a grand old girl . . . – & likes me very much!' The Princess's current favourite was Alvilde Chaplin, a vivacious young married woman with whom Rosamond struck up a friendship that was to last, through a number of permutations, for the rest of her life.

Princess Winnie's entertaining was conducted on an opulent scale, her guests a combination of artists, intellectuals and nobility, and Rosamond, in a state of permanent gratified astonishment, found it intoxicating to be the focus of so much extravagant attention. The French, she discovered, appreciated her work far more and far more seriously than the English, and France is the country 'where apparently my (literary) existence has the most importance'. To her brother John she described her ecstatic reception.

> [I] have had the most fantastic time that ever was . . . [I] feel like a sleepwalker or an opium addict. Yesterday I lunched with Valéry. To-day with Cocteau. I suppose I've met 500 people at the least. They stare at me as if I were a new animal, they crowd round exclaiming & admiring. They remember my books, especially the last, far better than I do myself. I am great, but great! A genius! Et ma beauté! mes yeux de faunesse! . . . Tonight I meet Colette. Really I don't know where I am, what with Mauriac, Morand, Maurois, Giraudoux, Jaloux, Gabriel Marcel etc etc. I am going back with a *very different opinion* of myself, I can tell you.

An habitué of Mme de Polignac's, present at one of the soirées given for the distinguished English writer, gave an eye-witness account of such homage being rendered. Miss Lehmann, he wrote, fair-skinned and statuesque, resembled

> *une belle minotière hollandaise. Elle était assaillie d'admiratrices qui formaient autour d'elle un essaim bourdonnant. Une de ses lectrices,*

*accrochée à ses mains, les baisant presque, la regardait avec ferveur, en
répétant d'un ton plaintif: 'Ah! Madame, vous ne pouvez pas savoir ce
que* La Valse *a été pour moi. . . . Ah Madame, vous ne pouvez pas
savoir ce qu'*Intempéries *a été pour moi . . .* [sic] *Et* Poussière *. . .* [sic]
Ah! Madame, vous ne pouvez pas savoir ce que Poussière *a été pour
moi.*[1]

Only once was a different note sounded. An elderly and very
aristocratic lady, politely commiserating with Rosamond over Wogan's
absence in Spain, remarked that she hoped Franco would be victorious
and that Madame would soon have her husband home, to which
Rosamond replied, quietly but distinctly, that her husband was fighting
on the opposite side. 'A long frosty silence ensued.'

In complete contrast to this glittering *galère* was the evening
Rosamond spent at the apartment of her translator, with whom she had
corresponded for years but never met. Marthe L'Evêque, reserved,
quietly spoken and extremely shy, had at first been reluctant to agree to
an encounter, claiming that Rosamond would find her too dull, too
timid, and that she was quite incapable of conversing in English. But in
the event the occasion was a success, and the two women found
themselves immediately in sympathy. Tiny, pale, dark-haired, Mme
L'Evêque left most of the talking to her guests – as well as Rosamond,
her daughter Louise and Gabriel Marcel – but none the less she was
impressive with her dignity and gentle charm, possessed of 'a great deal
of heart as well as head'. Unlike the sophisticated *mondains* at the
Princesse de Polignac's, shamelessly gushing their fulsome flattery, she
never expressed any personal opinion of the novels on which she worked
with such meticulous precision; all she would say on the completion of a
translation was, '*J'ai fait de mon mieux; puisque vous êtes satisfaite, je suis
contente.*'[2] And yet Rosamond knew that in Jean Talva she had found

---

[1] 'a beautiful Dutch miller's wife. She was assailed by admirers who crowded round her
like a buzzing swarm. One of her readers, clasping her hands, almost kissing them, gazed at
her fervently while saying plaintively over and over again, "Ah! Madame, you don't know
what *Invitation* meant to me. . . . Ah! Madame, you don't know what *Weather in the Streets*
meant to me . . . And *Dusty Answer* . . . Ah! Madame, you don't know what *Dusty Answer*
meant to me."'

[2] 'I've done my best; as long as you are pleased, I am happy.'

excellence and empathy and she trusted her completely. As she wrote after her death, 'Ce n'est pas une question de connaissance approfondie de la langue originale . . . [c'est] une mystérieuse sympathie auriculaire. Cette faculté, Jean Talva l'avait: elle semblait entendre avec mes oreilles.'[3]

Returning to England Rosamond resumed her routine, moving between London and Ipsden, seeing Goronwy as often as he made himself available. Together they dined one evening with Cyril and Jean Connolly, Cyril noting uncensoriously that the pair of them were drunk. To Ipsden a new acquaintance was invited, Stevie Smith, whose *Novel on Yellow Paper*, published the previous year, carried a warm recommendation from Rosamond on its jacket. Stevie came down to spend the day, and was found to be '*extremely* talkative and amusing'. The friendship was not pursued, however. When a few months later Stevie sent Rosamond her next novel, Rosamond wrote that although she 'revelled' in the first part, she felt the second part had not quite come off, a criticism which offended Stevie who wrote a huffy letter, to which Rosamond replied with too brisk a rejoinder – 'Oh don't be so cross and snappish' – naturally provoking Stevie to further complaint. This time '*die schöne Rosamund*', as Stevie mischievously referred to her, apologised profusely, but although Stevie accepted the apology and Rosamond continued to admire her work, the two never came together again.

At Ipsden Rosamond was hostess and breadwinner, and with Wogan away she was also head of the household and sole parent. During one half-term for a treat she took Hugo to the Tower of London. 'It gave me claustrophobia & filled me with despair, but Hugo lingered long by the block & axe in a pleasurable dream.' For the Easter holidays of 1937, their mother took Hugo and Sally, accompanied by cook and housemaid, to the Isle of Wight, as the two children were only recently recovered from whooping cough and it was thought the sea air would do them good. One day the entire party embarked on a trip in a motor launch, an alarming excursion later described in a memorable sequence in Rosamond's autobiographical work, *The Swan in the Evening*. 'A storm sprang up and we nearly got drowned,' she reported to John Hayward. 'I

---

[3] 'It isn't a question of a profound knowledge of the original language ... [it is] a mysterious aural understanding. That faculty Jean Talva possessed: she seemed to hear with my ears.'

have a heavy cold to-day as a result of having to wrap the children in my coat to keep them dry. They looked so fresh shining beaming & rosy peeping out of the wrappings in their sou'westers. Oh dear, little they guessed the feelings in my breast.'

Little could they guess their mother's feelings, either, on the subject of their absent father, whose lengthy sojourn in Spain was the source of increasing resentment. According to Rosamond, Wogan had promised to return within a month and already he had been away for over three. 'I mind so much not having been told the truth,' she complained in April 1937 to Stephen Spender, who was himself in Spain reporting for the *Daily Worker*. 'It seems he *must* have known he was leaving for the duration of the war – & not to give me a hint of this seems too cynical.' She was furious with him not only for leaving her to cope with house and family, but also for leaving her to face the erupting volcano at Llanstephan. Wogan's departure for Spain had been the final straw for Sir Laurence, who had immediately instructed his bankers to cancel his son's allowance, a forceful statement undermined only by his then arranging for exactly the same sum, £100 a month and money for school fees, to be paid to Rosamond – on the strict understanding 'that none of it directly or indirectly is used to help either side in Spain'. All this and more was reproachfully relayed in letters to Wogan by his wife, with maximum emphasis laid on the personal injury and inconvenience inflicted by his extraordinary lack of consideration. But if Rosamond hoped to induce remorse, she was to be disappointed. '[I] shall give up this farce of writing him "news from home",' she told Spender bitterly. 'Obviously nothing exists for him but the work in hand.'

And this was true: Wogan, caught up in the huge momentum of the Civil War, stretched to the limits of endurance physical and mental, coping daily with danger, extremes of temperature and unimaginably harsh conditions, was unable to sympathise with what he could only regard as his wife's petty domestic worries.

Arrived with his convoy in Barcelona in the third week in February 1937, Wogan at first found himself in the midst of a lively and exhilarating scene, the city gay with the red banners of the Communist Party, the International Brigaders exuberantly welcomed by the locals, everyone bound together in brotherhood, full of optimism and wholly committed to the common cause. Excited by the atmosphere, Wogan boyishly took pleasure in being addressed as 'Comrade', taking every opportunity to give the clenched-fist salute. 'I am completely caught up in this new revolutionary world,' he wrote fervently to Barbara. At last he had found a movement in which he could wholeheartedly believe. To him, the Republican side was the side of the people and liberty, and Republican Spain everything that was good and noble. His Spanish co-workers, by whom he was known as '*el ingles grande*' on account of his height, possessed none of the British capitalist's corruption and greed. 'It is the first time I have ever realised the real strength & greatness of the working class. In England their one idea is to better themselves into the bourgeoisie. . . . These people have no such aim. Everything can be done – there is somebody who can tackle each job, & it goes with a glorious gay efficiency. Factories are taken over & work with a swing. They *are* the lawful owners.' In Communism Wogan found not only an ideology, not only the prospect of utopia and a bulwark against Fascism, but the discipline and direction which up till then his rudderless existence had lacked. Too young to have fought in the war, too long a rich, spoilt young man, Wogan for the first time in his life discovered that he was needed and relied upon, accepted as an ordinary but integral part of a close and beleaguered community. 'I seem at last to have linked myself up to life, to the meaning of history,' he wrote to Rosamond in an attempt to explain what was happening to him. 'I think I see what to do, & don't feel pointless & floating about. . . . I see what the world could be like – will be. I believe in humanity again & feel happy. . . . But I hate England, the English press, English liberalism, bourgeoisism, intellectualism.'

Moving from Barcelona to Valencia, Wogan deliberately distanced himself from most of his compatriots, friends like Spender and Connolly, who were seen as self-indulgent dilettanti, poseurs more interested in sitting around in cafés talking than helping the war effort; the same went for the big boys from America, 'Hemmingway' and John Dos Passos, 'a cheap horror, like his books'. In Valencia Wogan was put to work ferrying doctors to and from hospitals, carrying messages and delivering medical supplies. In March he joined the Popular Front Spanish Army as an ambulance-driver, picking up the wounded after air and ground attack and helping when necessary in the makeshift operating theatres. His duties were dangerous and frequently harrowing. During operations, often carried out under canvas or in caves on the edge of the battlefield, he disposed of amputated limbs and administered anaesthetic on a sponge while the surgeons managed as best they could in the primitive conditions. 'Moans and cries. Often a ghastly shriek. The smell made one feel sick. Flies covered everything.' The job of ambulance-driver was no less demanding: the terrain was rough, and the ambulances themselves easy targets for Fascist planes and artillery. In the account he later wrote of it, Wogan vividly conveyed the distressing nature of his experience. 'My ambulance was very small. The heads of the wounded, as they lay on the stretchers, were level with me as I drove. I could talk to them, encourage them, or hear if they asked for anything . . . sometimes a man would break down completely, and scream he was dying. Another would cry for water. . . . Sometimes they died on the journey.' Nothing daunted him, however, and he took in his stride the harsh conditions – sleeping in fields and ditches, short of food, exposed to intense heat and cold – revelling in the comradeship, proving himself courageous, hardy and resourceful. For his work with the wounded at the terrible Battle of Jarama near Madrid, during which two-thirds of the British contingent of the International Brigade were killed, he was promoted to the rank of sergeant, a recognition which gave him intense gratification; and as the weeks turned into months and his clumsy Spanish became more fluent he identified ever more closely with the other members of his battalion, many of them illiterate young peasants from whom in appearance he became almost indistinguishable: bearded, sunburnt, black with motor oil, a revolver in his belt, round his head a red bandanna, his shirts sleeveless, his trousers cut off at the knee.

After the urgency and confusion of the first few weeks and during the long intervals between periods of action, Wogan thought long and hard about the state of his marriage, holding lengthy debates with Rosamond by letter as to the direction of their future. Infidelity had been condoned on both sides, but the balance was unequal, Rosamond continuing to insist that she was blissfully happy with Goronwy, whereas Wogan, although sincerely attached to Barbara, felt unsure that he wanted to enter into any more permanent union. Deep down he longed for reconciliation with his wife, whom he still loved, 'though it has been a very difficult twisted thwarted path', as he frankly told her. The more he dwelt on the situation, the more he tormented himself, writing long, melancholy letters full of self-lacerating introspection, gloomily analysing the causes of breakdown, veering between remorse and accusation, between a longing to be free and a yearning to return to what they once had had – 'I think we can fall in love with each other again, & dumbfound the world.' He implored her to think carefully what it was she really wanted, as when he returned to England he must put an end to what he called his 'split life'. If she did want to start again, he told her, she would find him easier to cope with than before, 'because my frantic physical love for you has cooled & died'. Yet later in the same letter he writes, 'I want to make love – yes – hold you in my arms & make gentle close wonderful love ... I long & long to be in your arms making love, talking to you Rosie.'

Although he had not yet joined the party, for Wogan Communism was now his creed, and it was essential that Rosamond understand and accept this, even if she could not herself become a convert. A natural crusader, a religious character who had found his religion, he was exasperated by her political passivity; as she was the first to admit, 'I was not, never have been, a political animal.' Of course Rosamond supported the Republicans in the Civil War and understood Wogan's desire to participate; she had even started collecting books to be sent out for Spanish Medical Aid hospitals, but the job was time-consuming and the project soon allowed to lapse. Then Wogan was put into 'a dither of excitement' when he learned his wife had agreed to take part in the International Writers' Congress in Madrid, and correspondingly disappointed when she withdrew because of a change in date. As she explained to Compton Mackenzie, 'The fact is I don't see that I really belong in the left wing *actively* – although morally I do.' In order to impress on her the realities of the situation and generally to further her political education, Wogan ill-advisedly asked her to see a friend of his, a Communist Party member recently returned from Spain. Cristina Hastings, daughter of the flamboyant Marchesa Casati whom the Philippses had met in 1934 while staying with Napier Alington at Crichel, was married to Viscount Hastings, a young man who had followed a path very similar to Wogan's own – Eton and Oxford, then rebellion against a reactionary father, becoming a painter, and swinging towards the extreme left in politics. Passionate anti-Fascists, Jack and Cristina Hastings had come out to Spain, and Cristina while driving an ambulance for the Red Cross had been often in company with Wogan. What could be more natural, therefore, than that when she returned to England Wogan should ask her to act as emissary to his wife? However, when Lady Hastings obligingly turned up at Ipsden, full of messages and news, she received a frigid reception. 'I didn't take to her. I sensed that she'd got her claws into Wogan.... [She was] very friendly, full of passionate pro-International Brigade propaganda, exactly the sort of thing Wogan would swallow hook, line and sinker. But I suspected she was in love with him.'

Yet for the Philippses the chief obstacle to any hope of permanent reunion was Goronwy Rees, whose perfections were meaningfully paraded by Rosamond in her letters, and for whom Wogan not unreasonably nursed a deep loathing. 'I now know how I hate Goronwy,' he wrote to his wife in April 1937. Although in theory he accepted her absolute right to take a lover, in fact he found it extremely painful, and when he discovered that she and Goronwy had stayed with the Ridleys at Blagdon it was almost more than he could bear. 'It was Blagdon that was the match that blew me up,' he told her after one furious explosion of jealousy. 'I have always looked on Blagdon as a special sanctuary of ours.... I could never have gone there with a mistress.' Even more galling was the realisation that under Goronwy's influence Rosamond was developing a keen political awareness. 'I have always felt that you weren't really deeply honestly interested in things like politics, history etc,' Wogan wrote to her bleakly. 'It needed romance & love to wake you & couple you to them, perhaps.' And indeed it was true that while she had been bored and irritated by Wogan's activities, with Goronwy it was different and, infatuated with the man, she was swept up in the excitement and fervour of his ardently held beliefs, suddenly fired with enthusiasm for the cause in Spain, as Wogan observed with some sourness. 'Rosie, surely it doesn't need Goronwy to make you believe in me & what I am doing. Without him explaining to you about Spain would you be all personal bitterness & give me no support at all? Have I really got to be thankful to him for that?'

Although they largely travelled along the same track, politically Goronwy was far more subtle and sophisticated than Wogan, his tenets more intellectually grounded. As a very young man, he had been formed by his experience travelling widely in Europe, where he had seen for himself the grim actuality of Nazism; he had visited Russia, and nearer home had been deeply disturbed by the effects of the slump in the mining valleys of his native Wales. Convinced of the urgent necessity of defeating Fascism, he was a member of the anti-Fascist, left-wing Association of Writers for Intellectual Liberty (popularly known as FIL), and was dedicatedly anti-Franco in the Civil War, if stopping short of personally volunteering for active service. It was Goronwy who had encouraged Rosamond to accept an invitation to the conference in Madrid, in which he himself took part, and while under his tutelage that she contributed to a questionnaire, originally devised by Nancy Cunard, addressed to 'Writers and Poets of England, Scotland, Ireland and Wales', and posing the question, 'Are you for, or against, the legal Government and the People of Republican Spain? Are you for, or against, Franco and Fascism?' Above her signature Rosamond wrote:

> With all my mind and heart I am against Franco and Fascism, and for the legal Government and the people of Republican Spain. As a mother, I am convinced that upon the outcome of the struggle in Spain depends the future, the very life of my children. Up till now a pacifist in the fullest sense, I have come to feel that non-resistance can be – in this case, is – a negative, a sterile, even a destructive thing. . . . Not only as an internationalist, but as an English writer, I must choose to bear my part in the defence of culture against Fascism.

In the middle of one night at the end of June 1937, Rosamond at Ipsden was woken by the telephone: it was a reporter from the *Daily Express* informing her that her husband had been wounded. Frantic, she tried to find out what had happened, but with Wogan being moved from one casualty station to another, it was impossible to discover where he was. Then suddenly a few days later he walked into the house, thin, gaunt, sun-blackened, his right arm in a sling: a shell had exploded between two ambulances parked side by side, wounding the driver of one, Wogan, and killing the other. 'The shock & relief have made me feel very ill & I can't stop my heart beating all wrong,' Rosamond told Marthe L'Evêque. 'I listen painfully to accounts of his experiences & all he has been through.' To Eddy Sackville-West she wrote that Wogan on his return was 'fanatically calm and for the first few days quite impersonal . . . for the first time in his life he is fulfilling himself heart and soul in his work'. Predictably, the atmosphere between husband and wife soon became strained. Rosamond was repelled by Wogan's thumping out of his intractable party line – 'I can follow him intellectually & with my imagination but it's all so against what I am by nature that I can only feel full of conflict & exhaustion,' she told Sackville-West; while Wogan, alight with revolutionary fervour, was full of plans for change and contemptuous of the old way of life and all the old friends, 'the Ralphs, Raymonds, the weekly papers, Stephen. *None* of them even knows what the International Communist Party is.' ('Wogan too silly,' Cyril Connolly noted with his cool, clear eye, 'too much the Tolstoy-inspired Moujik, the cracky and obstinate rebel but no intellect.') During the week Wogan toured the country, raising money for Spanish Medical Aid and drumming up support for the Republicans, and at weekends he filled the house with 'ghastly Comrades', all of whom Rosamond found utterly abhorrent. '[Wogan] came back from Spain a true blue, hundred per cent Communist, and I couldn't follow him in that new life he'd found for himself,' she said. 'I couldn't, *couldn't* take it or take to it. . . . It was a hopeless [situation].'

Wogan, too, recognised that a crisis had been reached, and when after a couple of months' frenetic activity he announced that he was returning to Spain, he issued an ultimatum: either Rosamond leave the children and come with him, or they must work out some method of trial separation. As she refused even to contemplate the former, he made the following suggestion. 'The only thing for you to do is to go & live with G., as much as you can anyway – for a year, say. Give him a chance, & I'll give B a chance, too. . . . If you and he fail, & I and B, then you & I can really try again.' On paper this was straightforward, but once away from home, again Wogan began to waver. If only they could work together! His new ambition was to stand as a Labour candidate for Parliament, and could she not support him in that? 'I long to be home – painting – reading – gardening; & if I stand for Parliament I shall have the hell of a lot to do. It *is* exciting, & could be very helpful to *us*, if you want it to be. . . . Rosie darling, I do feel so frantically loving.'

For Rosamond, however, a future as the wife of a socialist MP could not compare with the pleasure and stimulus of life with Goronwy, who was so clever and amusing, so gregarious, so quick to respond to atmosphere, always ready to drink and talk, with few subjects on which he was not prepared to hold forth, often brilliantly. Louis MacNeice said of the famous Rees charm, that '[it] takes an ell if you give it a millimetre', continuing tellingly that '[Goronwy] would have made a wonderful travelling salesman'. During weekends at Ipsden, Goronwy was jolly with the children, playing football with Hugo, and often brought down friends from London, like the novelist Henry Yorke (Henry Green), or old chums such as Anthony Blunt and Guy Burgess. Rosamond never cared for Blunt, whom she considered aloof and too coldly intellectual, but she became devoted to Henry Yorke, while Burgess, handsome, warm-hearted, permanently dishevelled, she found immensely engaging. Working as a producer at the BBC, Burgess would arrive at Ipsden, bathe noisily in the river, then sit smoking and drinking, avidly talking politics until far into the night, arguing for a form of intellectual Marxism, pro-Communist and violently opposed to any form of appeasement with Hitler. Himself promiscuously homo-sexual, Burgess regarded Goronwy as one of his three closest non-homosexual menfriends. 'I think he is generous, appreciative, sympa-thetic, loyal, trustworthy,' Guy wrote to Rosamond, adding teasingly, 'With him as you know charm & looks are left out.' Many years later, Rosamond wrote that she had loved Guy and found him a most stimulating friend. 'We discussed Victorian novels – he urged me to read Mrs Gaskell and *Middlemarch*. One time, however, he overstepped the mark, and expressed his hopes of seducing the gardener's handsome son. I forbade it. "Oh, Rosie, Rosie," he cried, "can't I?" "No," I said.'

One evening when Rosamond had arranged to dine with Goronwy, she arrived to find him in a state of considerable agitation. 'I'm going to tell you something,' he said, 'but if you ever mention that I've told you, I'll kill you.' Burgess, it transpired, had just confided that he was a Comintern agent and had asked Goronwy to join him. Would he decide to work with Guy? Rosamond asked, but Goronwy looked uneasy and prevaricated, and so she let the subject drop. 'I didn't think it was such a shocking announcement. . . . All the young men were going off to fight for the International Brigades in Spain, and I thought that this was just Guy's way of helping . . . his way of fighting Fascism and Hitler. Russia, we thought, was the great bulwark, and we were disgusted and horrified by the supineness and feebleness of Chamberlain and Baldwin.'

With Goronwy, Rosamond was far more concerned with emotional than political loyalty. It is possible that briefly she had hopes of marrying him, but that such hopes were swiftly quashed (in a letter to Marthe L'Evêque at this time she makes what might be a reference to the subject: '*J'ai vu ce que me semblait un grand bonheur que je désirais et auquel je devais renoncer. C'est bête.*'[4]); but common sense told her that Goronwy was shy of commitment, and deep down she may have suspected he was not entirely faithful. Such suspicions would have come as little surprise to a number of her friends, who were made uneasy by Goronwy's chameleon qualities, his almost uncanny ability to adapt himself to whatever company he was in. Elizabeth Bowen, who eventually took her revenge by portraying him as the treacherous Eddy in *The Death of the Heart*, described the character as always 'trying to get the pitch', in the musical sense of the word. 'His appearance was charming: he had a proletarian, animal, quick grace. His manner, after a year of trying to get the pitch, had become bold, vivid and intimate. . . . What security he had rested so much on favour that he could not really afford to annoy anyone.' Others saw him variously as lightweight and irresponsible (A. L. Rowse), unscrupulous (Dadie Rylands), frivolous (Stephen Spender), self-conscious and underbred (Virginia Woolf); Barbara Ker-Seymer, who adored him, confessed she had always been wary of him, had 'seen the red light the first time I met him', while Diana Trilling, describing him as sexually irresistible, admitted that she distrusted his lack of spontaneity and the fact that he seemed always on guard: 'His smile was frequent and brilliant but ultimately lacking in mirth . . . it was gone as fast as it had appeared.' Within the Lehmann family the feeling was much the same. 'Oh dear, oh dear, I don't like him,' Beatrix confessed to John. 'I fear [he] is nought but bitter material for a novel about yet one more futile intellectual. But so long as she's happy . . .'

To Wogan in Spain, now operating as a political commissar, Goronwy continued to be presented as the masculine ideal, with Rosamond never missing an opportunity to compare the inadequacies of the one with the

---

[4] 'I glimpsed what seemed a great happiness which I much desired and which I had to give up. It was a shame.'

sensitivity and tenderness of the other. When Wogan finally returned home at the end of 1937, depressed by the Nationalists' unstoppable advance, it was to find his wife more absorbed than ever in Goronwy and busily occupied with literary and political causes, helping to organise a vast meeting at the Queen's Hall for writers to speak against Fascism, joining the panel of judges for the prestigious Prix Femina-Vie Heureuse. '[Rosamond] has become such a public figure,' he wrote miserably to Barbara. 'She is on all committees etc. Goronwy has certainly given her new interests ... [and] by being so beaming & pleased with himself when I have seen them together – and Rosamond's happiness ... have added to my sense of "a failure" so enormously that I can't bear to see his success, & so can't meet him ... Goronwy is a symbol of my failure.' Although he largely blamed himself for Rosamond's alienation, admitting that he was nothing but 'a carping hindrance' in her life, he still hoped that they might save the marriage, at least maintain a home together for the children. It was thus a shock to be told that 'Rosamond wanted to chuck everything up & live in a flat in London'. Riding high on her glamorous love-affair, she now appeared determined on separation. The Ridleys were asked to act as mediators, and at Blagdon, scene of so many happy episodes in the early days of their relationship, a crucial meeting was convened at which the Philippses discussed alternatives and argued over terms. Wogan eventually agreed that he would give up Barbara on condition that Rosamond promise never to see or write to Goronwy again. 'There was a deathly silence,' Ursula reported. 'I prayed & prayed for her to say yes quickly, without hesitation; but she didn't. After 5 minutes she said "I shall have to think it over." She obviously can't & won't.' Without this vital concession it was clear there was nothing to be done except to arrange the practical details of dissolving the marriage, with Rosamond insisting on staying at Ipsden with custody of both children, which as Ursula observed, 'did seem like more than her share'.

Then all at once both jumped back from the brink. 'The crisis is past & we have agreed on a united front,' Rosamond told Frances Partridge.[5]

[Wogan] reversed every 'irreversible decision' suddenly last week,

---

[5] Frances Marshall had married Ralph Partridge in 1933.

but I know he really means it & wants it, and so of course I agreed.
I think it will work: I shall try my best to make it, & I know he will.
The basis is different & more rational. I hope we'll be able to live
from day to day for a bit & quietly tick over. I don't can't bear to be
plunged into any more abysses & dragged out of them. Perhaps you
will mention this to any inquirers. I don't want to discuss it, as you
will understand.

A crucial factor in reaching this decision, glossed over by Rosamond,
was financial. According to Julia Strachey, '[Wogan] says Rosamond is
handing out the reconciliation stuff to everybody but it is really nothing
of the sort. He said that they literally had not got the cash to live in
separate establishments.' Thus, until a tenant could be found for Ipsden
– increasingly unlikely in the uneasy economic climate – there was little
alternative but to agree to share the house, Box and Cox. In this way
Rosamond was able to continue seeing Goronwy, and Wogan, whose
affair with Barbara was still half-heartedly continuing, was free to spend
time with her in London, to paint, and to pursue his political career.
The first step in this was his adoption as Labour Party candidate for
Henley-on-Thames; this was not, as he made clear, because his primary
loyalties were with Labour, but because he believed in any anti-
nationalist government movement, '& am prepared to stand for any
popular front party   which includes Labour'. He was becoming
increasingly interested in the children, particularly in Hugo, his son and
heir, and was concerned that their mother was too possessive and
indulgent, an attitude that she not unnaturally resented after all those
years of paternal indifference. It was agreed, however, that for the
immediate future, Hugo should go to school in Newcastle with one of
the Ridley boys while Sally attended baby classes in Ipsden village. Sally
was fond of her nanny, Sindy, but it was her mother whose company she
wanted most. 'I am absolutely certain Sally must go to school,' Wogan
had told Rosamond. 'I want to crack her complete fixation on you. You
are the *whole world* to her.'

Rosamond, meanwhile, remained very much in the public eye. In
April 1938, at the invitation of the surrealist writer and Communist
Louis Aragon, who, himself a novelist and poet, was an enthusiastic
admirer of her work, she went over to Paris with John to speak at an

international conference organised by the Société des Intellectuels Antifascistes. Although she always acquitted herself well, Rosamond never enjoyed these public exhibitions. 'That speech in Paris nearly killed me,' she said afterwards. 'It was wicked Aragon who would inflate me – because he thought I had more sex appeal than Amabel [Strachey] or Rose [Macaulay].' Of this nerve-racking ordeal she retained many strange images, including one of La Pasionaria (Dolores Ibárruri), 'bellowing like a sea-lion and hurling to the ground a bunch of red roses presented to her by Aragon'.

Two months later, on 8 June, Rosamond was one of the speakers at a meeting at the Queen's Hall in London, advertised as 'Writers Declare Against Fascism', of which she herself had been one of the chief organisers, persuading over fifty well-known writers to speak or have their names read out in protest specifically against the Nationalist rebels in Spain. Two of the most memorable participants were Goronwy Rees and the chairman, Cecil Day Lewis. According to Louis MacNeice, who also took part, 'Day-Lewis spoke first, in his tired Oxford accent, qualifying everything, nonplussed, questioning. Then Goronwy, who was just as Oxonian as Day-Lewis, took over and spoke like a revivalist, flashed his eyes, quivered with emotion.' When Rosamond, looking marvellously beautiful in purple and silver, went up to compliment Day-Lewis, who had been sitting near her on the platform, the poet fervently grasped her hand. Her own speech, written from the point of view not of a writer but of a mother, was considered one of the best of the evening. 'What gives my life its deepest reality is my children . . . [and] I believe I speak for everybody in this hall who is a parent,' she began.

> The worst grief would be to have to see our children grow up defeated: morally, physically, intellectually warped & stunted. . . . At this moment, in Germany & Austria, Jewish parents, who have perhaps stronger family ties than any other race, are forced to submit to the segregation of their children in school & playgrounds; to seeing them degraded to the position of something subhuman, to be stamped out like vermin from the community. . . . Under the Fascist dictatorships children start to be soldiers at the age of 3. . . . Their education is a deliberate fostering of a mass

slave-mentality. . . . They are trained in the crudest, most barbaric and aggressive forms of patriotism and leader-worship.

The following month Rosamond went again to Paris, this time for a rally organised for the Popular Front by the International Association of Writers for the Defence of Culture, its theme, 'For Peace and Against the Bombardment of Open Cities', with a number of familiar faces present, including brother John, Goronwy, Day Lewis, Stephen Spender and Guy Burgess. And at the beginning of 1939 she took part in a deputation to the Prime Minister, Neville Chamberlain, to demand positive action against Franco. 'To my pained surprise I found myself committed to walking in a procession down Whitehall, holding a placard,' she wrote to John. 'We were stopped at No. 10, delivered a protest by letter to a flunkey, were bidden to stand on the corner & shout "Arms for Spain!" – when I escaped, & jumped into a taxi & came home.'

Such demonstrations were not in character for Rosamond, as she herself was well aware. 'I've not become a Communist & it's a pretty safe bet that I never shall,' she told Eddy Sackville-West. 'Only these horrors and threats to freedom and culture and life itself have overwhelmed me rather, and, though it goes hideously against the grain, I have felt myself forced to be more active. . . . But I shan't be drawn into party politics or journalism. I shall emerge for a bit & hope it will toughen me up morally & intellectually – & then I shall write another book!'

Although public life left little time or energy for writing, the previous year, 1938, finally saw the production of the play Rosamond had completed four years earlier. Like many theatrical enterprises, *No More Music* had had an eventful pre-production history. Beatrix, the first to read the manuscript, had liked it and shown it to Noël Coward, who had suggested a number of alterations. Soon afterwards Rosamond was excited to learn that the producer Bronson Albery had bought a six-month option and that John Gielgud was pencilled in for the lead. Nothing came of this and the option expired, only to be bought again the following year, 1935, this time with Gielgud himself intending to direct. Nothing came of this plan either, and over the next couple of years several managers showed interest, including Rupert Doone of the Group Theatre, but none going so far as actually to put up any money.

Then suddenly at the beginning of 1938, when Rosamond had almost abandoned hope, the play was taken up by the recently formed International London Theatre Club, to be given three Sunday performances in February and March at the Duke of York's Theatre in St Martin's Lane, under the direction of the distinguished Viennese playwright and director Berthold Viertel, with Beatrix in one of the two female leads.

Beatrix was currently receiving immense acclaim for her performance in Eugene O'Neill's *Mourning Becomes Electra*, which had opened in the West End the previous November, the distinguished critic James Agate leading the chorus of praise for the actress who, he wrote, 'has for some time been knocking at the door marked "Great Acting Only" –' Although she had had some good parts and a few notable successes, Bea's career had been erratic, her unconventional looks and strong-minded refusal to compromise resulting in lengthy periods out of work. 'I get continual offers of horrible and useless, arty plays, the last being a poetic whimsey by Humbert Wolfe which was like a baby dribbling,' she had written to John some months earlier. 'I'm quite firm though and unshaken by nearly two years out of the theatre proper. I won't and can't do these tea-shop lyrics.' It was after a particularly bleak period professionally that Beatrix had followed her brother to Vienna in 1932, later moving on to Germany, lodging in cheap *pensions* and barely managing to survive on her tiny savings while she took lessons in the language in the vain hope of finding film work in Berlin; she was also writing a novel, her second, encouraged by one of her few friends from home, Christopher Isherwood. When she returned to London the following year, Isherwood introduced her to Berthold Viertel, then in England to direct a film for Alexander Korda. Although she was to work with him later, this time Bea failed to land the hoped-for part; she did, however, fall in love with Viertel, a bear-like man of enormous energy and charm, and the two of them began a serious affair, which ended unhappily when Viertel eventually left Europe to join his family in California.

Relations between Beatrix and Rosamond were loving and close, if not as close as they had been in childhood. Inevitably, Bea had maintained greater contact with John while they were both living on the Continent, the two of them sharing a more European outlook as well as finding themselves in step politically, as Marxists. John and Beatrix frequently made fun of their older sister's tendency to imperiousness, although they very much relied on her critical judgement and support, John sending Rosamond his poems for comment, and Bea submitting her two novels, both published in the early 1930s, *But Wisdom Lingers* (1932) and *Rumour of Heaven* (1934). Concerning the last, Beatrix wrote to her friend Henrietta Bingham, '[Rosamond's] advice was invaluable and pointed out various vital changes that *had* to be made. . . . She was evidently much struck with "Hector" and kept on repeating in the screamingly funny tactless and malicious way of hers: "But I don't see how *you* ever thought of him . . . but he's so *good* . . . !"' A brilliant mimic with a dry sense of humour, Bea when in the mood was immensely entertaining, although her fiercely independent spirit and complete lack of sentimentality could make her an awkward companion at times, and her stoicism in conducting her almost invariably unhappy love-affairs – 'my cynicism & bullet-biting', as she herself described it – was very different to Rosamond's emotional performance. None the less they had much more in common than either felt they had with their eldest sister, Helen, who with her hunting and shooting, was wholly wrapped up in husband and children, completely content with the life of a busy and capable county lady.

Rosamond's play, *No More Music*, is set in a small private hotel on an unnamed island in the West Indies, a quiet place where little ever happens to disturb the routine of swimming, superficial chat and an occasional walk along the beach. The guests are all of a certain age, set in their ways and incurably bourgeois, with the exception of Mrs Bloxham's niece, Hilda, a fierce, virginal young woman obviously in a state of acute frustration bordering on breakdown. As in the similarly titled novel, *A Note in Music*, two worldly newcomers arrive to overturn the status quo, a good-looking young painter, Jan Loder, and his mistress, Miriam. Theirs is an uneasy relationship, weary and disillusioned, made more so when Jan amuses himself by paying half-hearted attention to Hilda, who, instantly awakened, falls deeply in love; when towards the end she realises how little she means to him, she rushes out into the night and drowns herself. Although the mundane exchanges of the hotel guests are amusing and their characters well observed, much of the action is melodramatic, with neither Jan nor Miriam emerging from caricature, and the part of Hilda, played by Beatrix, frankly ludicrous – as an otherwise appreciative first-night audience was quick to pick up. 'It was hard on Peg [Beatrix], because the audience chose to think of her as a figure of fun,' Rosamond wrote in dismay to John. 'I think *only* an English audience would think a sex-starved inhibited passionate awkward virgin comic – but they did – and my feelings were indescribable. I felt I'd exposed her to a sort of devlish mob-mockery.' By the critics Rosamond was treated relatively kindly over what was generally regarded as a creditable failure, with well-deserved praise being heaped on the excellent cast, on Beatrix especially, as well as on Jack Hawkins as Jan and Margaret Rutherford as Miss Leith, manageress of the hotel.

During the following year, 1939, as the international situation deteriorated so did relations between Rosamond and Wogan. Incredulous and appalled, they watched the impending catastrophe – 'It's snowing here, and I await the fall of Barcelona with feelings to match the leaden skies,' Rosamond wrote to John in January – but the crisis instead of uniting them acted to drive them further apart, and they quarrelled rancorously over the news in the paper every morning and on the wireless at night. '[Wogan] is frantic about the war,' Rosamond told Beatrix, 'and of course identifies me with it. I *am* Chamberlain and all the "Imperialist gang of war-mongers"', an accusation with an ironic aspect in view of Rosamond's own loathing for Chamberlain and his government, 'filthy rubbish', as she contemptuously described them. '[Wogan] tries me almost to murder point with views from the *Daily Worker*, & the impossibility of making him see what the result of a Nazi victory would be on the socialist movement.' They fought, too, over the children, Rosamond wanting to keep Sally at home but to send Hugo to America, a plan which Wogan vetoed absolutely. Indeed there was little on which they could agree, Wogan in particular raging against the world in general, looking back in horror on a decade that had started with slump and was ending in war, convinced that all hope for democracy had been crushed by the Republican defeat in Spain. Having decided to return to his course of analysis with James Strachey, he was finding it painful in the extreme, the process inducing anger, black depression and violent alternations in mood, so that one moment he was berating Rosamond and vindictively insisting on divorce, the next begging her to forgive him and swearing he would do nothing to impede her happiness with Goronwy. To Rosamond such behaviour was swiftly becoming intolerable. 'I cannot describe to you what seems to be going on. I suppose the fact is there is a more or less complete schizophrenia,' she told Beatrix. '[At the moment] I am visited with bombs whirlwinds and infernal flames. . . . I got so frantic last night I rang up his analyst, but all that cautious old bird would say was that he was "not unduly anxious".'

The chief source of Wogan's anger was jealousy of Goronwy, aggravated by the corroding of his own relationship with Barbara; he also acutely resented Rosamond's refusal to support him in his political career – she turned up at public meetings only to laugh at him, he claimed, and made no attempt to conceal her dislike for the Comrades who congregated at Ipsden at weekends, filling the sitting-room with tobacco smoke and putting their boots up on the chairs and sofas. 'Our weekends were *ghastly*. . . . They were lower middle class, doctrinaire Communists, proclaiming that the war was an imperialist plot. Wogan was deeply in love with it all.' Cyril Connolly, who witnessed one of these Ipsden weekends, relished the grotesque nature of the scene, comparing Rosamond to the Alcazar of Toledo, 'an irreducible bastion of the bourgeoisie entirely surrounded by Communists'.

For her part Rosamond was painfully missing Goronwy. Earlier in the year he had joined the Territorial Army, and was now mobilised as a gunner in the Royal Artillery, turning up on his occasional days of leave looking very dashing in his uniform – as Hugo later drily remarked, 'One of the few of my mother's friends who did make it into uniform.' At the end of September, Goronwy was posted to Sandhurst for training as an officer cadet, which meant that opportunities for meeting were briefer and even more infrequent, Rosamond never knowing till the last minute whether or not he would be able to see her. 'I always feel worried when I have irrevocably booked up my weekends in case G. gets a sudden bit of leave & I am dished! I have 5 more months in which to see him fleetingly, and then – !' Her brother John when staying at Ipsden went with her once to meet Goronwy's train, and recorded in his diary, 'Her joy when G., very smart in long khaki coat & a white tab in his forage cap, appeared outside Reading station, was touching to see.' Friends were led to believe that all was still supremely well between them – she had recently bought a cottage in the nearby village of Aldworth in which she hoped they could eventually set up home together – but in private there were some brutal displays of bad temper on Goronwy's part, and it is unlikely that his lack of availability was entirely due to the demands of the military. Rosamond was nearing 40, Goronwy still only 29, and although he loved her and was often happy in her company, for him the affair was beginning to lose its lustre. Gentle and feminine, she was also a powerful personality, whose emotional neediness and sense of insecurity made her tenaciously possessive; her dependency chafed him, and aspects of her that once were appealing he now began to find tedious. Yet whenever he tried to distance himself, Rosamond became exigent and reproachful, and this in turn made him feel cornered. In his convoluted letters he apologises for his hostility, caused, he explains, by feelings of guilt and anxiety. 'I have hurt you so much that I wonder if such wounds can heal. I know I have humiliated you; yet now I think such things may be unimportant when compared with loving you.'

The actual outbreak of war on 3 September found Rosamond in a nursing-home recovering from a miscarriage. The pregnancy had been in its very early stages – 'a thing the size of a thrush has just come out of me', as she described it at the time – but profoundly upsetting nevertheless: 'the effect on one's body & spirit is so far-reaching & frightful.' Wogan came to visit her, but after his sitting by her bedside lecturing her on Communist policy, she felt weaker and more despondent than ever. Wogan himself had recently been involved in a car accident, and his right hand was in plaster. 'I don't know why he always has this faculty of displaying symbols of catastrophe about his person at the appropriate moment,' Rosamond wrily remarked.

Returning to Ipsden, she was confronted with a scene of indescribable confusion: Wogan assisted by Barbara Ker-Seymer ineffectually attempting to cope with eleven evacuee children sent down from the East End. 'They were so miserable,' said Barbara. 'They slept on the floor, and they peed everywhere and were sick, and they'd never cleaned their teeth in their lives. Rosamond got lovely meals for them, which they wouldn't eat because they wanted fish and chips.' Rosamond noticed almost immediately a fact unremarked by everyone else that two among them had scarlet fever. In a state of terror for Hugo and Sally, who were instantly sent away, and furious with Wogan and Barbara, she forgot her own fragile condition and swung into action, arranging amid fumes of disinfectant to have the evacuees removed, the two stricken children taken off by ambulance, and calling in doctors and sanitary inspectors to oversee the household. Luckily the disease had not spread and the panic subsided.

In such untranquil conditions and surrounded by the 'physical & spiritual black-out' of the beginning of the war, it was rather to her surprise that Rosamond found she was able to write. 'I feel clearer about what I want to say than ever before,' she told Marthe L'Evéque, '[although] it's very difficult to have the strength of mind to concentrate – or to believe it worthwhile.' It was not a novel this time, she continued, 'but some stories based on recollections of childhood. . . . It isn't quite like anything I've ever done before, and will clear a pile of queer memories out of me, I hope!'

The first story, 'The Gypsy's Baby', is a powerfully evocative re-creation of Fieldhead and the world of Rosamond's childhood, in particular her uneasy relations with the large family in the slum cottage that stood in the lane running along one side of the Lehmanns' house. Rebecca, the youthful narrator, is both fascinated and repelled by the Wyatts.

> All but one, they took after Mr Wyatt, and had flat broad shallow skulls, sparse mousish hair – foetus hair – coming over their foreheads in a nibbled fringe, pale faces with Mongolian cheek-bones and all the features laid on thin, wide and flat. Their eyes were wary, dull, yet with a surface glitter. They were very undersized, and they wore strange clothes ... done up in bits of cloth, baize or blanket; and once I saw the baby in a pink flannel hot-water bottle cover. There was something sharp, gnawing, rodent about them; a scuttling quietness in their movements.

Rebecca finds herself reduced to a state of helpless semi-paralysis as the Wyatt children relentlessly encroach on her beloved nursery world, hitherto protected by friendly domestics and the impregnable safeguard of parental authority. Tenacious and intent the little Wyatts take possession, securing their toe-hold in the well-appointed schoolroom by ruthlessly warning off intruders. One such is fat little Ivy, daughter of the head gardener at Lady Bigham-Onslow's, who is invited to tea one day by Isabel the nursemaid.

> Little Ivy, dressed in her best and feeling a wee bit shy, bless her, but innocently trusting to be met as arranged by Isabel at the back door, had come tripping across the fields at the appointed time. But at the turn of the lane, who should be lurking in wait pressed up against a small wooden side door in our garden wall – who but Chrissie? And then what happened? Chrissie Wyatt had had the downright demon wickedness to declare to Ivy she wasn't wanted inside, that she, Chrissie, had been specially posted there to tell her so . . .

Maintaining a fine line between the subtly comic and the sinister and tragic, Rosamond demonstrates a remarkable ability to understand the state of being a child while maintaining an adult's perspective on it, an ability she shared with that other great purveyor of stories about children, E. Nesbit, whose novels no doubt she was reading aloud to Sally at the time, and whose influence is clearly detectable. (*The Treasure Seekers* is actually mentioned in the text, and in a couple of cheerful letters written to Beatrix around this time Goronwy is referred to as 'the Psammead'.)

After 'The Gypsy's Baby' came 'The Red-Haired Miss Daintreys', inspired by memories of pre-war holidays on the Isle of Wight. Again closely autobiographical, it is a vivid impressionistic account of the spell exerted by the Daintreys over Rebecca, the exact image of the author as a child. Staying at the same small seaside hotel as Rebecca and her parents, Pa and Ma Daintrey with their four intriguing grown-up daughters are a cheerful, unpretentious family, well-off, slightly vulgar ('cockney genteel'), and of absorbing interest to Rebecca and her siblings.

> Miss Viola sat before the mirror in her bedroom, and I sat curled up on the bed watching her.
> 'I wish I had red hair like you,' I said.
> Miss Viola smiled at herself, at me, mysteriously in the glass.
> 'My hair is auburn,' she said. . . .

I said:

'I always have thought it's not very nice to be the middle one of the family . . . [*sic*] like you and me.'

'Really?'

'Yes, because you're not the eldest . . . [*sic*] and you're not the youngest . . . [*sic*]'

She paused in the act of twisting her back hair and looked at me thoughtfully in the glass.

'Yes,' she said. 'But on the other hand it's like the jam in a sandwich. Snug. You'll find there are advantages.'

Minutely observed, related with spirit and a subtle humour, the story is undoubtedly a miniature masterpiece, as was widely recognised on publication. 'My redhaired Miss Daintrey story has so far brought me more praise than I've had for years!' Rosamond exclaimed, while John told her that 'I think it is one of the most *beautifully written* things you have ever produced . . . almost like the background for a novel which you haven't given us, and for which you rouse a tantalising hunger.'

These two stories and the three that followed were eventually published after the war under the title *The Gypsy's Baby*, all first appearing under the aegis of her brother in his literary magazine, *New Writing*.

Since 1932, when John had left England to live in Austria, he had continued with his own writing, sending his work to Rosamond for comment, depending on her encouragement and sympathy not only with his literary but also in his emotional affairs. Although naturally she was told nothing of the rampant promiscuity indulged in by John, Christopher Isherwood, Wystan Auden and others in their circle of homosexual expatriates, she was confided in about her brother's more serious relationships, in particular with Toni Sikyr, a young man with whom John had lived in Vienna and whom he had had to leave behind when he returned to England in 1939. His unhappiness over this, and his depression over Isherwood's departure at about the same time for America, had made him touchier and more irritable than usual. 'John has no outlets for what amounts I know to real anguish of mind,' Rosamond wrote to Stephen Spender. 'I suppose Toni is the only person he loves apart from his family & he is utterly cut off from him & has the torture of picturing his state of mind & the more than possibility of his being killed, while he can do nothing, or even write to him. . . . He misses Christopher horribly too.' Isherwood's decision to move to the United States had been a serious blow to John as not only was he a close friend and mentor, but it was primarily with Christopher that he had been planning the launch of a small literary magazine, initially concentrating on the work of young and unknown writers from England and abroad. Rosamond, who had always thought more of her brother's talents as critic and editor than as poet or novelist, had been enthusiastic about the scheme and when the first two issues of *New Writing* were published in 1936 she had given it her whole-hearted support, contributing to the autumn number a translation from the French of 'Letter to Cousin Mary' by Jean Cassou. She promised that when John returned permanently to England she would work with him as an associate editor. And so she did, although the experience had its trying side: John was so pompous and so quick to take umbrage. 'I wish I had some of John's power & drive!' she told Spender, 'but on the other hand I wish he didn't oppress me with that feeling of enormous hollowness which coming Men of Power generally give me. It is that feeling of being treated officially as if one were part of the Agenda at a board meeting.'

Spender knew exactly what she meant as he had witnessed Lehmann's dictatorial manner all too frequently. Immune to John's steely beauty, he was irritated by the challenging, competitive nature of his friend's attitude towards himself, and bored by the jealous tantrums and frequent sulks which left the more easy-going Stephen too often in the position of appeaser. 'John had a sort of love–hate relationship with me. Before we met even, he had the idea that we should be partners, probably lovers as well, and that there would be a firm of publishers called Lehmann & Spender, and so on. The fact that I didn't live up to this, that I didn't want any of these things to happen, was regarded as a kind of treachery. He was peculiarly nasty towards me: I knew practically nothing that was nice about John.' With John's sister, however, Stephen's relationship was genuinely affectionate. Like her brother, he, too, confided in her about his affairs, both literary and amorous: she constructively criticised his work, and got on well with his long-term boyfriend, Tony Hyndman; when in 1936 Stephen suddenly changed tack and decided to marry, she did her best to feel well disposed towards his exotic but temperamental wife, Inez Pearn. In her eyes Stephen was a talented, sweet-natured, rather silly young man whose main fault was an overwhelming egotism, a view of his character which ran almost parallel to his of hers: '[Rosamond] was such a delightful person, very sympathetic, very charming: the most puzzling thing about her is that she was a total egoist. . . . Everything about her was very nice except for the superstructure of this enormous egotism.'

The winter of 1939–40 was exceptionally cold. In January the Thames froze over and the country was hit by one of the worst storms of the century, with snow, followed by a brief thaw, then a sudden ferocious freeze. For weeks Ipsden was under snow, as one by one the whole household came down with influenza, Rosamond, then Wogan, followed by Hugo (at school), Sally, and finally the cook and housemaid. The persisting cold and frequent plumbing emergencies for a time took precedence over the daily more ominous news from abroad, over the Soviet invasion of Finland, the relentless German advance on Paris. 'In a way I think the icy spell got us through the winter,' Rosamond told Frances Partridge. 'It absorbed one completely & there was very little energy left over to brood about the war.' She was also enchanted by the fairytale beauty of the frostbound countryside: even the Brussels sprouts brought into the kitchen were frozen inside blocks of ice, '[looking] like tiny Victorian paperweights', and there was a memorable story in the paper of four peacocks frozen to the ground, each encased from crest to long tail in a crystal shell. Meanwhile she and Wogan were on friendlier terms, each going their separate ways, Wogan spending most of the week in London, Rosamond keeping to the house, except for the rare occasions when she was able to meet Goronwy on leave from Sandhurst. 'I miss him enormously,' she told Frances, '& often ask myself what horrors will continue to separate us & for how long.'

In March 1940 Goronwy was commissioned as 2nd Lieutenant in the Royal Welch Fusiliers and posted to the regimental Infantry Training Centre at Wrexham in Wales. Here Rosamond spent occasional Sundays, which were sometimes enjoyable, sometimes not, and more than once Goronwy felt compelled afterwards to attempt to explain his complex antagonisms. '[Last] Sunday was lovely & I was absolutely happy, as I am always with you when I feel I'm not concealing anything;

only always it seems difficult that I should cause you pain by being truthful . . . I love you more genuinely, & when I cease to lie, I see you truthfully too, and don't have to invent imagined grievances to compensate my guilt.' In April they spent a 'heavenly' week together in Devon, before Goronwy was posted to Abergavenny in Wales and then to Avonmouth, near Bristol, before returning again to the north. Towards the end of June, Rosamond enjoyed a day of 'pure happiness', picking up Hugo from his prep school in Gloucestershire, then taking him on to meet Goronwy in Bristol, where they spent the afternoon wandering round the Zoo. After returning Hugo to school, she went back to dine 'with my precious G. and we were happy together, and I took him back to his billet along the river by moonlight, and went back & slept in a hotel in Bristol. . . . I wonder how many more times I shall see him. He looked so handsome and was so calm and confident and loving.'

The fact that his wife's lover was on active service can have given little satisfaction to Wogan, who had recently suffered the humiliation of rejection by the Home Guard, which regarded his political affiliations with the deepest suspicion. Instead he joined the Merchant Navy Reserve, which gave him further good reason for going up to London: not only was there a gunnery course to be taken, but he was starting to see a great deal of the handsome Cristina Hastings,[6] who, as Rosamond had suspected when she met her a couple of years earlier, had fallen in love with Wogan, her own marriage having been in serious difficulties for some time.

In June came the shocking news of the fall of France and of the near-miraculous rescue of the British Expeditionary Force from Dunkirk. Rosamond by chance witnessed the moving aftermath. 'I saw trainloads of the B.E.F. coming through Reading on Saturday. It haunts me day & night. Carriage after carriage in total silence, *stacked* with khaki forms, their bearded faces utterly serene in the sleep of exhaustion. One could only weep. God blast & curse our criminal rulers and all of us in this country.' So bitter was her contempt for the government that she was moved to write an impassioned attack on it in the *Daily Worker*,

[6] Now Cristina Huntingdon, her husband having succeeded as Earl of Huntingdon in 1939.

condemning 'the present official complacency, neglect and cynicism with regard to the protection of the people', and arguing that it was vital for the artist to engage in the struggle against Hitler and in support of the democracies. 'I have grown to believe it is nonsense to speak of the "inevitable loneliness" of the artist,' she wrote, 'or to make a virtue of "resisting the temptation" to join a political movement' – a statement of belief that caused much sucking of teeth among the Bloomsbury pacifists and their associates. 'I find it difficult to understand how people like you, who will certainly be exterminated in the event of a German victory, are ready to try and hinder the government,' David Garnett wrote reproachfully.

The war had entered Rosamond's personal orbit in March the same year, 1940, when she was persuaded by Guy Burgess to accompany him to France on an ill-defined mission which in the event turned out to be wholly abortive. Burgess was working for the Joint Broadcasting Committee sponsored by the Foreign Office, and the idea was that Rosamond, one of the few contemporary English writers well known to the French, should make a propaganda broadcast from a radio station in Paris. The flight over was hazardous owing to fog, Paris cold and semi-deserted, the staff at the radio station had no idea who she was or why she was there, and Burgess turned up only briefly, muttered a quick apology and disappeared. Most of the day Rosamond spent sheltering from an air-raid in the cellars of the Hôtel Crillon before catching her plane back to London. Four months later, with Paris under occupation, Rosamond was asked by the BBC to give a series of short broadcasts in French to the women of France, a request to which she agreed, although she described the project in a published 'Lettre à Jean Talva' as grotesque. '*Un honneur certes, mais qui ressemblait à une humiliation à cause de l'enorme futilité, me semblait-t-il, de ce geste.*'[7] It was on leaving Broadcasting House one day that she caught sight of the gaunt figure of General de Gaulle, recently arrived in London.

At home the war was encroaching everywhere. So monotonously depressing was the daily news that Rosamond could barely bring herself to do more than scan the headlines, and even her beloved George Eliot and the other, familiar nineteenth-century novelists provided scant

[7] 'An honour, certainly, but one which seemed a humiliation because of the immense futility, as it seemed to me, of the undertaking.'

nourishment. 'When war broke out I turned avidly to Flaubert, Stendhal and the great Victorians, and found much comfort in them; but just now the idea of them makes me depressed ... that broad, humanitarian, romantic, expanding scene gives me a nostalgia that has more pain in it than pleasure,' she wrote in an essay entitled 'Letter to a Friend'. The war was making increasing and unfamiliar demands on her time. A plan to turn Ipsden into a convalescent home for soldiers, conceived mainly in order to avoid more evacuees, had fallen through, and Rosamond now had billeted on her a brother and sister from Stepney. 'The girl is quiet, sensitive, plain & serious, the boy is a fearful exhibitionist & attractive, a child actor, full of bounce, oblique answers & Jewish wisecracks. They sing me Hebrew songs, & are fond of me, & I of them. ... At night I think of them tucked up in the attic above my head, so alien & glittering & alive & black – & I *can't* believe it.' To add to the burden, Alice Lehmann was in hospital in Oxford with a broken leg, the duty of daily visits devolving almost entirely on her second daughter, as Beatrix was on tour in the provinces, John working in London, and Helen, to the surprise and admiration of her siblings, had enrolled as a machinist in an aeroplane factory. Of the Philipps family, Hugo was away during term-time, while Sally at Ipsden was 'wholly absorbed in puppies, kittens, riding lessons, ice creams and clay modelling – trotting off to her kindergarten with her gas mask over her shoulder'; Wogan came home at weekends, his behaviour much more stable, his 'violent, half-baked fanaticism' kept mostly under wraps. Rosamond, knowing but not greatly caring that he was spending much of his time with Cristina, was glad of the peaceful atmosphere.

The period of tranquillity did not last. Looking through *The Times* one morning, Rosamond saw to her astonishment the announcement of Goronwy's engagement to an unknown young woman, one Margie Morris. Having heard nothing, suspected nothing, she was transfixed with horror, utterly distraught.

Beatrix, who had come to stay for a few days, was obliged to watch helplessly as her sister writhed in anguish, refusing all offers of comfort or consolation. 'I had hoped that as the agony *came out* so violently (beating of head, lying senseless on the floor, calling for brandy, screams and cries) that it might be soonest mended,' Beatrix wrote to her brother. 'But this is a tremendous ego and it doesn't mend. I begged her not to see him. She agreed. Two days or so later he was here.' The account given by a sheepish Goronwy did a great deal to restore Rosamond's equanimity: yes, he had been seeing this girl, but it was her family, not he, who without his knowledge had taken matters into their own hands and put the announcement in the paper. Rosamond still meant everything to him and, she was led to believe, he fully intended extricating himself as quickly as possible from an extremely embarrassing situation. By the time Goronwy left, it having been forcibly impressed upon him that such a marriage would be doomed to failure, Rosamond was in a much calmer frame of mind. 'Today at least I am out of the condemned cell, where the walls close in on you hour after hour, and every remembered act & word cries Treachery!'

Expecting daily to hear that the engagement had been called off, she was soon reduced to a state of frantic misery when time passed without a word. Desperately she tried to make contact with Goronwy. Letters were written, wires sent, telephone calls placed that never got through; Guy Burgess, summoned to a council of war, was made to write, as was Hester Chapman, both of them sympathetic, if privately unhopeful of success. Burgess was the first to receive a reply, the gist of which he conveyed, as promised, to Ipsden: Goronwy, stung by Rosamond's conviction that in marrying he could only fail, had immediately made up his mind that it was his one possible course of action. A letter to Rosamond quickly followed. He had seen his girl again, he said, and this time knew for certain that he loved her without qualification. 'I shall marry Margie as soon as I can. . . . She makes me happier than I've ever expected to be. . . . I know what this will mean to you, and I know it will mean my losing you, which is the greatest loss I shall have ever had. . . . I try not to think of your unhappiness, but it haunts me; only there is nothing I can do.' As his words of rejection sank in, Rosamond's helpless grief turned to fury: she would spike his guns! Denounce him to Margie's parents! Write to Margie herself! Discredit him with his commanding officer at Aldershot! *Why* should he be allowed to get away with it? Beatrix, herself emotionally self-contained, was shocked and alarmed, while doing her best to understand. For a personality like their sister's, she wrote perspicaciously to John,

[one for whom] the *personal life* is the be all and end all . . . [this is a] dreadful, agonising illness. Really serious and never to be quite cured. She looks deadfully, *is* dreadfully ill. All her friends notice this and that excites her very much. . . . The *world* chaos is a small tinkling side issue to her. A mean attack on her world and Sally's rations. There it is. Writing endless letters lying prone in a chair reading a novel or watching life galloping past as in a glass darkly has so long been her habit of life that one wonders how, and if, she can shake herself into real productivity again. Any change has to come from within herself – one can't really help. I often feel that a personal example only makes her think that activity is an inferior brand of living. My one hope is that her strong, healthy instinct for survival will triumph.

That same instinct for survival now directed Rosamond to appeal to Wogan. It was all over with Goronwy, she told him, and the world was falling apart around them: could they not try once more to make a life together? According to Rosamond's own account,

> a most terrible look came over Wogan's face, and he heaved a sigh, and struck me a blow on the chest so forceful that I fell through the French windows, and he shouted, 'Too late! Too late! I'm leaving you and I'm marrying Cristina!' It was agony for him. He didn't want to; not really. But he said that the Communist Party authorities had told him he must choose between me and Cristina, and put his private life in order or he'd be no good to them. And he chose Cristina because she was a Communist. He'd tried in vain to persuade me to join the great Cause, and I couldn't and wouldn't, so he must leave me.

The 'tremendous ego' identified by Beatrix may well have enabled Rosamond to ignore the fact that Cristina's Party membership was not her only attraction in Wogan's eyes, but whatever the motives behind his decision, his marriage to Rosamond was over.

In despair, Rosamond turned to Dadie, asking him if he could find her somewhere to live in Cambridge. She had lost her husband and her lover, and with Ipsden about to be let was soon to be without a home. 'I feel that in Cambridge, & near you, and with work, I might build up my life again,' she told him. 'I am *utterly* crushed.'

9

'The Beginning of a Tremendous Affair'

In later life Rosamond claimed that her affair with Goronwy Rees had never been 'a very deep relationship'. Even when they were at their happiest, at the back of her mind she suspected it would not survive, that he would never stay faithful, and she herself, although fascinated by him, was never wholly enamoured. At the time he had presented a golden opportunity, so charming, good-looking and clever, arriving on the scene just when her relations with Wogan were at their most unsatisfactory. When Goronwy left her, she was devastated; but her suffering stemmed as much from wounded pride and the terror of being left on her own as from grief over the loss of her lover. Part of the trouble lay in the disparate nature of their expectations: to the roving young Welshman, his association with Rosamond was just another affair, delightful certainly, but never intended to last; for Rosamond, who fed avidly on all the most rose-coloured illusions of high romance, it had to be seen as a great love-story. Being in love was a vocation, just as important as – if not more important than – her vocation as a writer. Referring to romantic love, she wrote, 'I can't believe I could live myself without love – giving it and receiving it – I doubt if I could even write much or for long without it. I would wither up.' Her image of herself was that of an anima figure, of a *femme fatale*, and she needed to see this image reflected by the lover paying homage. Without such homage her fragile self-confidence was eroded, and she felt lost and unhappy. Her remarkable beauty was the currency with which she acquired what she most needed, the affirmation that she was loved. As her old friend Grizel Hartley said with greater accuracy than she knew, 'Your loveliness is your life.'

Undoubtedly one of the beauties of her generation, Rosamond at 40 was more striking than ever. Her girlish figure had filled out to a full-bosomed shapeliness, and with her large eyes, pale skin and thick wavy hair turned prematurely grey, she exerted a potent attraction. Countless men found irresistible not only her face and magnetic sexuality, but the mildness of her manner: her voice was soft, almost breathy, she spoke hesitantly, and her shyness made her reluctant to look anyone in the eye, glancing sideways and slightly downward as she talked. Her admirers compared her to an orchid, a rose, a basket of ripe peaches, to a statue in alabaster lit from within; one declared that it was as impossible to describe her angelic qualities as to put a rainbow into a matchbox. Painters wanted to paint her, sculptors to sculpt her handsome head. She was well aware of the impact she made.

> [To a great many men] I was the image of the ideal woman. Over and over again the effect I had even on people I'd only just met was as if they'd been hit by something. I never knew at the time that T. S. Eliot, for instance, said to others that I was the most beautiful woman he'd ever seen. I suppose I enjoyed being a beauty, but I always got a shock, was frightened when I saw this tremendous effect I had on men. It was so startling – and it often brought with it frightful jealousy from their wives.

Because of her beauty, she was accustomed to men falling at her feet – and at her feet she expected them to stay. Goronwy's defection thus dealt her a double blow: she was no longer loved; and she was bitterly affronted that he had had the presumption to reject her.

Perceptive and sympathetic when advising lovelorn friends, Rosamond was destructive in her behaviour towards her own lovers: when happy she was gentle and giving, but she also required a great deal of attention, and at the first sign of preoccupation or detachment she quickly became accusatory, carping and in emotional terms voraciously demanding. The paradox was that in periods of calm she was often clear-sighted about her own failings and intelligently analytical on the phenomenon of being in love, as her novels clearly demonstrate. 'The important thing to remember about love,' she wrote to her brother before the end of the affair with Goronwy, 'is that it's one's *own* enormous need for the *other* person that exposes one so terribly and makes one's unhappiness.' And to Dadie, one of the many to whom she confided her misery over Rees, she admitted that unfailingly, 'I select love-objects who must bring me to disaster!' – an apt confession from one who claimed that Steerforth, the heartless, handsome bounder in *David Copperfield*, was her favourite figure in fiction. Dadie was appalled by Rosamond's suffering, but he, like Beatrix, knew very well that she would not allow herself to be consoled; he saw the mistakes she was making, but was resigned to the fact that she would be impervious to counsel. The trouble was, as he said, she '*overlaid*' the men who loved her: being loved by Rosamond 'was like being suffocated by a great eiderdown of rose petals. . . . She was too demanding, you see.'

With Goronwy, 'that seductive semi-cad', gone for good, and with Wogan irretrievably bound to Cristina, Rosamond was in a pitiable state, 'rejected and isolated and hoping I'd be killed by a bomb'. Believing herself on the brink of breakdown, she postponed her plan to move to Cambridge while she consulted Oswald Schwartz, a fashionable Viennese psychotherapist practising in London. 'If once I can understand how it all happened I may be able to be free of it,' she wrote to Dadie. 'I never imagined such unhappiness could go on without any relief.' No sooner was this course decided upon, however, than she received a letter from Goronwy so enraging that she was instantly jolted out of black despair into fury. Goronwy, newly married, was himself moving to Cambridge, having been appointed to a job as instructor in the Intelligence Centre based in Trinity College. Wouldn't it be fun, he cheerfully suggested, if he and Rosamond were to resume relations and see something of the beauties of Cambridge together? 'Dadie, isn't it INCREDIBLE?' she exploded: here was 'little Goronwy', bouncing in full of glee, and at a stroke not only completely ruining the one place in which she wanted to live, but having the inexpressible cheek to barge in on *her* friend, Dadie, his plan clearly 'to swim straight in to the delights of Cambridge society through you & over my discarded corpse'. Such behaviour was positively indecent, and what made it infinitely worse was 'oh! a bitter indignation that he will get away with it all – as he will – and can't suffer *one single pang*, not even uneasiness, over me. . . . I *cannot* bear it.'

Feeling very sorry for herself, Rosamond in March 1941 returned for the last time to Ipsden, to clear the house for the incoming tenants, a gloomy task which she had to undertake on her own as Wogan was in London with Cristina and both children were away, 11-year-old Hugo in his last year in prep school, Sally, aged 6, now a boarder at the tiny school in the village. The cottage purchased the previous year at nearby Aldworth was currently let to Barbara Ker-Seymer, and thus Rosamond was left with no alternative but to move herself, and during the holidays the children, into Fieldhead. This was a depressing solution as Alice had turned the house into a convalescent home for the duration, and there were only a couple of cramped servants' rooms available. More seriously, she made no attempt to conceal her disapproval of her daughter's situation: divorce for any reason was scandalous, but she had supported Rosamond over the breakdown of her first marriage, accepting that the fault lay predominantly with Leslie; a second divorce, however, was too much, particularly when, very late in the day, Rosamond had explained the nature of her relationship with Goronwy. Alice was strait-laced and conventional, and what was accepted as the norm in Bloomsbury went down very badly indeed at Bourne End.

Fortunately alternative accommodation was offered by that black-haired, sardonic figure, Henry Yorke, who put at Rosamond's disposal a room in his house in Rutland Gate, an offer gratefully accepted, especially as she now needed to be in London two to three days a week to work with her brother on *New Writing*. It was she, with Goronwy's backing, who had originally persuaded Henry to show John his novel, *Party Going*, which had been left languishing in a drawer after some discouraging rejections; impressed, John had suggested running extracts in *New Writing* before publication in book form by the Hogarth Press, with which he had recently renewed his association. 'The arrival of Henry Green as a Hogarth author', John wrote in his memoirs, 'gave me confidence in the future.' The success of *Party Going* also confirmed John's confidence in his sister's judgement, and he recorded in his diary how pleased he was by her editorial opinion. 'Clear she is going to be an excellent reader-adviser over mss,' he wrote after one of their initial meetings. And indeed the two of them collaborated usefully on the whole, as their tastes and literary background were sufficiently similar, and Rosamond's own contributions were considered by her brother to be 'exactly what I had in mind at its best'. Unfortunately, she was unable to regard his own productions in the same light, and as John was super-sensitive to criticism she quickly learnt to tread with extreme caution. 'Oh, I'm in TROUBLE,' she told William Plomer. 'John sent me his ballad, & I don't like it. It is to my mind, sentimental & imprecise. The sailor seems to me a most impure apparition with his apple cheeks and background of tulips and sundials. . . . I wrote tactfully but firmly. Back came the answer; just as was predicted. . . . I do genuinely want to prevent John publishing poor stuff, but it isn't worth the trouble & irritation involved.'

The arrangement at Rutland Gate worked well, and Rosamond looked forward to her couple of nights a week in town, in spite of queues and the black-out and the almost nightly bombardment of the Blitz. Both John and Beatrix had experienced narrow escapes: '[Beatrix] spent Monday night *alone* in a cellar in Charlotte Street with a rat and her dog,' Rosamond reported, horrified, after one heavy raid. Henry as a member of the Auxiliary Fire Service spent every third night fire-watching, and would come off duty begrimed with soot and still in uniform to join Rosamond for breakfast; he then retired for the rest of the day to write, and in the evening they would meet again for a drink before Henry, whose wife preferred to stay in the country, went off to a night-club with '[one of] his rota of ridiculous young girls . . . – never with me: there was never any question of my having an affair with Henry'. Years afterwards she described him at this time as 'an eccentric, fire-fighting, efficient, pub-and-night-club-haunting monk, voluble, friv-olous, ironic, worldly, austerely vowed to the invisible cell which he inhabited'. It was a relief to Rosamond that she could talk as much as she liked about Goronwy, a subject on which sympathy had been in short supply at Fieldhead. Later on she wrote to Henry of 'your perfect goodness to me at the time when sirens, chaos and death seemed my only companions, and every hour another proof of waste and exile. I thought I was done for. Your figure re-appearing at intervals, so remote yet so friendly, gave me a little focus of re-assurance and stopped the unending pinch under my ribs.' It was an important bond between them

215

that they admired each other's work. 'You are one of the very few, the two or three, I will take praise from,' Henry told her, and Rosamond in turn, revering Henry's formidable talent and ground-breaking originality, was particularly gratified by his encouragement. After reading a short story of hers, 'A Dream of Winter', he wrote, 'It's the best I've read of that length since Chekov. . . . I really do mean it & I hardly ever feel like this, once in 12 years, about someone else's work.'

It was rather to her surprise that Rosamond had been able to work at all. So deep was her depression after Goronwy left her that she thought for a time she would never write again, and that she should find some other occupation. In a moment of madness she decided she wanted to train as a doctor, and even went so far as to request an interview with the head of the Oxford Medical School, who fortunately lost no time in telling her she was hardly suitable material. It was at this point that she was brought back to her proper path by John asking her for another story for *New Writing*. He himself described his tactics as those of a 'merciless slave-master', but he knew that such tactics were necessary to galvanise his sister into action. '[Rosamond was] one of those complex imaginative artists whose whole creative being wilts at the merest hint of the regular production-line obligations of the journalist, as surely as a dahlia at the first touch of frost.' Her response to his request, 'A Dream of Winter', was completed in November 1940, at exactly the time when her anxiety over Goronwy was at its most critical, after the engagement announcement had appeared in *The Times*, but before his final letter. In her wretchedness, she told her brother, the writing of it 'seemed like getting one's head & hand out of a swamp to do it, for about an hour a day – then going down again in the foul sticky mud. . . . The only thing I could bear was to fix my mind on impersonal images & try to make something of them.'

The story describes an actual episode that took place at Ipsden – the removal from the house of a bees' nest – during the winter of 1939–40. The event is given an almost surreal subjectivity by the protagonist's own semi-hallucinatory state as she lies in bed with a high fever. 'In the middle of the great frost, she was in bed with influenza; and that was the time the bee man came from the next village to take the swarm that had been for years buried in the wall of her country house; deep under the leads roofing the flat platform of the balcony outside her bedroom window.' As in a dream she watches the strange procedure, which she finds almost nightmarishly disturbing – the digging out of the desiccated comb, the murmuring black swarm, the coral-like atolls of pale honeycomb. In robust contrast, her two children, John and Jane, the picture of pink-cheeked normality, appear from time to time outside her window on top of the bee man's ladder, a couple of spirited comedians thrilled by the adventure. The final scene, as if reflecting her own anger and unhappiness, is shocking: a small bird, found half frozen by John, is brought in to be revived beside the fire.

Jane came and knelt beside him.
  'Isn't it a *sweet* little tiny bird?'
  Suddenly it flew straight up out of his hands, dashed against the mantelpiece, fell down again upon the hearth-rug. They were all perfectly silent.
  After a moment his hand went out to pick it up again. Then it flew straight into the fire, and started to roast, to whirr and cheep over the coals. . . .

For the Easter holidays of 1941 Rosamond took the children to Llanstephan, where in spite of kind treatment by her parents-in-law, she was overwhelmed by unhappy memories, and not only of Goronwy: the terrible news had just broken of Virginia Woolf's deliberate death by drowning in the River Ouse, a tragedy which not only deprived Bloomsbury of its linchpin but brought back all the horror of Carrington's suicide nearly ten years earlier. From Wales Rosamond moved on to Blagdon, where she struggled with an essay on Virginia for *New Writing*. 'I am worried to death about my Virginia article. . . . I can't "see" it at all or make any headway,' she complained to her brother. She persevered, however, concluding that Virginia for all her extraordinary talent 'was not equipped for a broad grasp of humanity, she had not the kind of richness and sanity, the rooted quality which comes from living a completely fulfilled life as a woman and mother'. Interestingly in the next sentence she attributes to her subject a perspective that precisely mirrored her own: 'her conception of the governing classes, of rank, fashion, titles, society – all that – was perhaps a shade glamorous and reverential.' At Blagdon Rosamond's spirits improved as she talked over

217

the events of the past few months with the Ridleys, who encouraged her to start planning for the future. Arriving back at Bourne End on 1 May ('looking so much better and more her old self altogether,' John noted in his diary), she wrote at once to Henry Yorke to ask if she could stay at Rutland Gate for a few nights the following week. It was then to her surprise that she received a note from Cecil Day Lewis, currently working in London at the Ministry of Information, inviting her to dine, an invitation in all likelihood inspired by a recent favourable review by Rosamond in the *New Statesman* of two volumes of his verse. Describing him as 'a moving and a memorable poet', she had praised his lyricism and his sense of the spiritual. 'He is a writer with a profound and happy experience of love,' she had written, '[who] appears to have left confusion and mental distress behind him, and to have rediscovered his peace of mind.'

Delighted at the prospect of an evening in the company of a man so attractive and intelligent, Rosamond accepted with pleasure, and under the influence of her host's flattering attention found herself pouring out her woes, describing the pathos of her situation, left with nothing, no marriage, not even anywhere to live. 'You had better come and live with me,' Day Lewis said, looking at her intently. 'Do you mean that?' 'Of course I mean it.' There was, it appeared, a small service apartment available on the floor immediately below Cecil's borrowed flat in Buckingham Gate, the street running alongside Buckingham Palace. 'You can see as much or as little of me as you want. Please.' 'I said, "I will."' Immediately Rosamond's entire perspective was transformed. 'I felt, this is a way out, and this is perhaps going to be wonderful.' Excited, she returned to Fieldhead for a few days to pack her belongings before moving to Buckingham Gate. Here she dined a couple of times more with Cecil, and after the second occasion, 'I stayed the night with him, and from then was the beginning of a tremendous affair. . . . It never crossed my mind this would happen, but it had a sort of smooth inevitability. I was out of black despair into happiness. He just was madly, madly, madly in love with me.'

Cecil told her he had been in love with her from a distance for years, although they had seen each other only infrequently. At their first meeting in 1936 at Elizabeth Bowen's house in Regent's Park, when Rosamond had been so struck by the poet's good looks, Cecil, then a schoolmaster at Cheltenham Junior School, had asked her if she would come down to address the Cheltenham Literary Society, of which he was chairman, adding that he and his wife Mary would be delighted to put her up for the night. The experience proved unrewarding. The audience consisted of 'dozens and dozens of elderly ladies with iron-grey perms & pince nez', and Rosamond's fellow celebrity was the poet and critic Humbert Wolfe, whom she disliked. Wolfe and Cecil took it in turns to declaim their poems while Rosamond, sitting behind them on the dais, was never invited to speak at all. Returning to the Day Lewises' tiny cottage expecting to be offered a drink and some discussion of the evening, she was disconcerted when husband and wife wished her goodnight and immediately disappeared upstairs to bed. When she came down the next morning, Cecil had already gone, and she was left to have breakfast while Mary fed the two small boys, after which Rosamond helped her make the children's beds before leaving for the station. Mary 'was very shy but obviously terribly nice, a typical English schoolmaster's wife. . . . One couldn't see a sign of her ever having been even pretty, but she was obviously a very good wife.' After this unpromising encounter, Rosamond had met Cecil again at the Queen's Hall in 1938, when they had both been on the platform, and the following month at the Popular Front rally in Paris. These occasions apart, she had come across him only at committee meetings of the Society of Authors, '[when] he used to sit at the other end of the table and I saw his eyes fixed on me in a very meaningful way'.

At the time Cecil began his love-affair with Rosamond, he had left schoolmastering behind him, having established himself as a poet, supplementing his income by writing popular thrillers under the pseudonym Nicholas Blake. Indeed it was mainly Nicholas Blake who supported the family, although it was C. Day Lewis[1] who was distinguished in literary circles, in particular for his lyric and pastoral poetry. Cecil had begun writing poetry at school, publishing his first slim volume, *Beechen Vigil*, at the age of 21. By far the greatest influence on his early work was W. H. Auden, a fellow undergraduate at Oxford

---

[1] Cecil hated his Christian name, and for reasons he later described as inverted snobbery had removed the hyphen from Day-Lewis – later restoring it as he disliked even more being addressed as 'Mr Lewis'.

whose willing disciple he became. 'I knew very soon that he was and would be the best poet of my generation and I have never had any reason to change my mind.' By the mid-1930s, Day Lewis, with Auden, Spender and Louis MacNeice, formed one of that predominantly left-wing group of poets – public school, Oxford – known as 'the Auden Gang', or as their contemporary Roy Campbell derisively lampooned them, 'MacSpaunday'. From then on critics tended to refer to the four of them as a movement, but as Day Lewis protested, 'It was not a movement at all. . . . We did not know we were a Movement until the critics told us we were.'

It was during the early 1930s, while Cecil was teaching at Cheltenham, that he became politically active, joined the Communist Party and devoted much of his time to local propaganda; but it soon became apparent that his Communism was too mild and idealistic to fit the party mould, and he found the drudgery of distributing leaflets, selling the *Daily Worker*, and speaking at public meetings increasingly distasteful. Ashamed to discover at the outbreak of the Spanish Civil War that he lacked the courage to volunteer for the International Brigade, he soon afterwards decided to give up politics to concentrate on poetry, moving his family from Cheltenham to Devon, where in his own words he quietly 'slipped the painter' from the Communist Party. At Musbury on the Devon–Dorset border, near the country of his beloved Thomas Hardy, Cecil found peace and inspiration. He loved the lush Devon landscape, the woods, the sheltered valley, the sight of buzzards circling over Castle Hill; and he enjoyed the company of the local people, the carters and farm-labourers he talked to of an evening in the pub. At the beginning of the war, he had joined the Musbury Home Guard and was soon commanding the platoon, a job he enjoyed enormously, rollicking about the countryside with his men, camouflaging pill-boxes and leading night operations carefully planned to end up at the Red Lion exactly fifteen minutes before closing time. Aware, however, that his Home Guard duties would not indefinitely exempt him from call-up, which he was fervently anxious to avoid, Cecil slightly shamefacedly applied for a post at the Ministry of Information, generally recognised as a safe haven for writers and journalists who shrank from more active participation. It was shortly after this that the affair with Rosamond began.

The few weeks at Buckingham Gate were for both an idyllic period in spite of the war. In 1941 huge areas of London were ruined and smoking after the recent terrible damage inflicted by the Blitz, and the whole city was looking shabby and battered, with paint peeling off the stucco houses, piles of rubble marking the places where a house or shop had taken a direct hit. It was a period, Rosamond wrote later, that was like '[plodding] on through an interminable, suffocating, over-crowded tunnel, and from time to time [we] saw one another's faces lit by lurid and scorching flares; and sometimes the tunnel roared and rocked as if it were about to fall down upon and bury us altogether'. And yet for many of those living and working in the capital there was a highly charged atmosphere, a tacit admission that in the violent disruption of routine rules had been suspended and anything could happen. Elizabeth Bowen captured the feeling in *The Heat of the Day*: 'The very temper of pleasures lay in their chanciness, in the canvas-like impermanence of their settings, in their being off-time – to and fro between bars and grills, clubs and each other's places. . . . There was a diffused gallantry in the atmosphere, an unmarriedness: it came to be rumoured about the country . . . that everybody in London was in love.' Revelling in their own 'unmarriedness', Rosamond and Cecil existed in a state of heady intoxication. Their first parting came with the summer holidays, when Rosamond returned to Fieldhead to be with the children. Once or twice, Cecil came down to Bourne End to see her, his courteous manner making a favourable impression on Alice, who said he reminded her of her brother; Hugo refused to be charmed, but Sally immediately adored him, and Cecil, with sons but no daughter, for a time became almost like a second father to the little girl.

Rosamond could hardly believe in the rapturous nature of her changed circumstances. Cecil, at 37 only three years younger than she, seemed to possess all the qualities of her ideal lover, handsome, responsive, clever and kind; he had a wide knowledge and love of literature, and read poetry aloud in a soft, musical voice with an attractive hint of an Irish intonation (although brought up in England, he was born in Ireland of Irish parents, and as a boy had spent most of his holidays in Ireland); even by Rosamond's high standards he was exceptionally good-looking, with thick brown hair and a lean, sensitive face; tall and slender, he was something of a dandy and always elegantly dressed. 'You can't imagine how marvellously beautiful he was then, how romantic-looking.' His charm was legendary, and although some were aware of a sense of hidden detachment, 'a reticence about him, lying just below a genial surface', most of his admirers would have agreed with the words of the young writer and fervent fan, Michael Meyer, that 'Cecil was magic!' Rosamond who had been the unhappiest of women was now one of the most fortunate, she wrote to Dadie. 'And oh! I do appreciate it & savour every moment of it, & shall never never get used to it or take it for granted. It is like a miracle. It is not only being given back my life – it is being given a thousand times more than I ever dreamed possible. I thought it had been proved that love was no use, & everything I lived by, and for, a blind alley, a waste and a hideous joke. But it isn't so. I don't see what the future will be – but I don't think it can go wrong through lack of love and trust.' When apart, the two of them exchanged long letters almost daily. 'It has been beautifully sunny these last days,' Cecil wrote to her from his Devon valley, 'but oh the sunshine has a fearful effect on me – it makes me want to take you into a wood over the hill, & undress you & kiss the leaf-shadows moving over your body, & love you till you are quite quite dead. . . . Little love, you ask me to tell you my thoughts; I only seem able to think about you, & they would make you blush so happily.'

At the end of summer Cecil wrote to Rosamond, 'I must live with my darling this autumn, the time is so short, every day & minute without her is something lost irretrievably, *nothing* can make up for it.' With London half empty, accommodation was not hard to find, and in September 1941 they moved into a small rented house, 31 Gordon Place, off Kensington Church Street, which, Rosamond later wrote, 'always remained the most romantic of London oases in my memory – despite the bombs'. Here they were again completely happy, Rosamond revelling in Cecil's devotion and thrilled by his possessiveness. One evening at a party an acquaintance of Cecil's, John Garrett, strode up to Rosamond saying, 'Come on, you great big beautiful bitch – dance with me,' and fox-trotted her off across the parquet. Cecil was outraged and it was months before he could bring himself to speak to Garrett again. The one cloud on their horizon was the fear that Cecil might be called up. He had already had one bad fright, receiving orders to report to the Royal Corp of Signals at Catterick, but to his intense relief after only twenty-four hours he was given a temporary discharge and allowed to return to the Ministry of Information. However, he hardly hoped to be so lucky again. 'I'm still evading the draft,' he wrote nervously to a male friend, 'but cannot feel I shall get many more deferments.' To Rosamond it was unthinkable that Cecil should be put at risk, and taking matters into her own hands she approached Harold Nicolson, then head of the MOI. Did he really want to lose one of his most valuable people? she asked him. 'He said, "Who do you mean?" I said, "Cecil Day Lewis." He said, "Good God, of course I want him," and scribbled a note. So Cecil was able to stay.'

With the Christmas holidays approaching, Rosamond decided that she must establish a permanent base in the country for herself and the children, and so, having given Barbara Ker-Seymer notice to leave, she moved into the cottage she had bought before the war in Aldworth, a small village in the Berkshire downs only a few miles from Ipsden. Diamond Cottage was a plain little house with whitewashed walls and a tiled roof, the front door under a porch to one side, with a good-size garden behind, the house backing on to the road leading downhill into the village. Less than a mile away was the aerodrome where at night could be heard the throb of engines as the bombers took off for their nocturnal raids over Germany. The routine was established that during term-time Rosamond should go to London for a day or two in the week while Cecil came down to Aldworth every weekend – except occasionally when he felt obliged to visit his family house, Brimclose, at Musbury. His wife was kept in complete ignorance of his relationship with Rosamond: Mary Day Lewis, unworldly and naive, had no contact with literary London, knew little about her husband's job, and as Cecil always took care to write to her on MOI-headed paper, she had no reason to suspect that his long absences were not entirely due to the demands of his official occupation.

'I felt completely married to him,' Rosamond recalled, 'as he did to me.' During the early stages of their affair, unwelcome reminders that this was not in fact the case largely remained submerged in their blissful absorption in each other. But as time passed the pressures of Cecil's double life were to cause grave trouble between them.

Trouble meanwhile was materialising from a different direction. Wogan for some time had been pressing Rosamond to divorce him,

223

anxious as soon as possible to marry Cristina, whose own divorce was now under way. So far Rosamond had refused to co-operate, reluctant for a second time to go through such a publicly humiliating process, and with no prospect of marriage for herself, not particularly inclined to oblige her husband. In taking this stand, she found a powerful ally in her father-in-law. Lord Milford, as Sir Laurence now was, having been created Baron Milford in 1939, had finally been driven past endurance, and had decided formally to disinherit his son: not only had Wogan joined the Communist Party – 'He should be put up against a wall and shot!' was the response to this piece of news – but he had deserted his innocent family to live in sin with another man's wife, who was herself a foreigner and a Communist. Believing Rosamond to be blameless, Lord Milford promised to give her and the children every support on condition she hold to her course, even trying to persuade her to sign a statement swearing that she would never give in to Wogan's demands. But when Rosamond started living with Cecil, Wogan saw his chance: he at once threatened to divorce her, cite Day Lewis as co-respondent, and petition for custody of the children – leaving Rosamond with no option but to do what he had wanted all along and sue him for divorce on the grounds of his adultery with Cristina.

Lord Milford was appalled. Not only had Rosamond gone back on her promise, as he understood it, but he was profoundly shocked to learn the truth about her own situation. 'Dear R,' he wrote, 'W's conduct is absolutely rotten & his present Woman worse – but remember that the first time he broke all decent codes was for your sake & at your instigation. My right to tell you plainly what I think was earned when we accepted at your hands the greatest injury decent minded (Victorian if you like) parents could receive. That's all.'

Incensed with Wogan for informing on her, Rosamond was none the less obliged to work with him in order to secure a financial settlement, brokered by Wogan's brother, Hanning, who undertook all direct dealing with Lord Milford. 'These communists are very set on the principle of inherited income, I find,' Rosamond sourly remarked after a particularly tough bargaining session. Both children remained in their mother's custody, although from this time on Hugo was to be drawn more and more into the orbit of his Philipps grandparents, who now looked upon him, rather than on his disgraced father, as their heir. Half of every school holiday Hugo spent in Wales, and Rosamond was glad for his sake that when at Llanstephan at least he would have the benefit of limitless supplies of butter, cream, eggs and meat from the home farm. Hugo had now left prep school and had just started at Eton. He seemed an intelligent boy, his housemaster wrote to Rosamond at the end of the first half, and was well liked by his contemporaries. 'I also much like what I have seen of him so far, and feel I am beginning to know him better. This takes some doing – as you told me it would; for he is reserved and sensitive, and sometimes wears a mask which is not easy to penetrate. Behind the mask a good deal goes on.'

Rosamond loved fiercely and was immensely proud of both her children, although it was Sally who was the child of her heart: Hugo was too independent and self-contained to allow his mother to take possession of him as she did of her blithe, enchanting daughter. In appearance and personality they could hardly have been more dissimilar, Hugo dark-haired and pale, Sally a bonny blonde, pink-cheeked and plump, doting on animals and with her mother's love of the sweet and starchy. ('If only Sally would eat vegetables!!' her Aunt Beatrix exclaimed when in charge of the children for a few days. 'She's a *castle* of milk puddings.') During the holidays, while Hugo went to Wales, Sally preferred to stay at Aldworth, '[growing] more & more to look like a large luxurious dahlia', and happily absorbed in playing with the village children, among whom her favourite companion was a little girl of her own age, Angela Holland, whose mother, Olivia, became a dear friend of Rosamond's. The children's letters home exemplify their contrasting personalities: Sally's correspondence, artless, cheerfully affectionate, studded with pencilled kisses, usually beginning 'Darling darlingest Mummy', is full of copious detail of her school day and tender enquiry after the household pets, usually starting and ending with requests for sweets and cake; Hugo's communications are stoical, practical, unemotional and terse. 'Dear Mother, This has been a very unfortunate week,' he wrote at the age of 12. 'As you probably already know Mr Evans died quite suddenly at five to twelve on Thursday. Not only that but three of my rabbits have died. . . . When you come down on the 21st will you please bring a pair of Belgian Hares about three months old. I am going to try once more and if this fails I'll take up tortoises.'

Eager to imbue in her children a love for the literature she as a child

225

had devoured with such passion, she had started by reading to them from her own favourites, Hans Andersen and the charming moral lessons of *Les Petites Filles Modèles*, but these were contemptuously rejected as 'tich stuff' and 'cissy', with Hugo demanding stories about aeroplanes and racing cars while Sally announced she had 'gone off' books in favour of comics. 'I rather think of the older authors, only E. Nesbit and Beatrix Potter . . . will weather all fluctuations and stand immortal,' wrote their mother resignedly.

In spite of the war, the four years at Aldworth Rosamond described as 'about the happiest time of my life . . . with the children there, [and] Cecil coming whenever he could'. By now she was as deeply in love with Cecil as he with her. Not only was he protective and adoring, but their tastes in literature ran along almost exactly similar lines and she admired him unreservedly as a poet. In 'The Lighted House', a sonnet written to celebrate his falling in love, Cecil compares Rosamond to Primavera:

> One night they saw the big house, some time untenanted
> But for its hand-to-mouth recluse, room after room
> Light up, as when Primavera herself has spirited
> A procession of crocuses out of their winter tomb.

They shared a love of music, too, and many evenings at the cottage were spent with Cecil singing in his light tenor the Irish melodies of Thomas Moore – ''Tis the Last Rose of Summer', 'The Minstrel Boy' – accompanied rather stiffly by Rosamond on the piano. They lived for their weekends together. 'Darling, darling, darling love,' Cecil wrote from his office in Russell Square, 'build yourself up next week – plenty of food, rest & exercise – you'll need all your strength at the weekend – I shall come at you like a tiger, a cloud burst, a toppling mountain, an arrow out of the sun.' In a letter to John Hayward, Rosamond confided, 'I am so peaceful & happy – I think I feel confidence in myself for the first time in my life. I never thought it could happen, but he has given me this by the incredible goodness & patience of his love. You've no idea what a true, reliable, grown-up character he is.'

Although among critics Cecil had his detractors, chief among them that notorious scourge Geoffrey Grigson, he was highly regarded as a poet and much in demand for broadcast talks and readings. He was not,

226

however, part of the sophisticated society of literary London, of which Rosamond was a leading member, acquainted with almost everyone in the book world and a familiar figure on the literary party circuit. Until he met her, Cecil still inhabited the persona of the provincial schoolmaster, insular in outlook, suspicious of intellectuals and nervous of going abroad. When William Plomer first came to know Cecil in the mid-1930s he remembered being shocked by his narrow outlook and lack of curiosity about his surroundings, and Cecil in an interview given in 1968 said of himself in those days, 'I didn't go abroad because I was afraid of making a fool of myself speaking a foreign language and people laughing at me.' The Paris conference of 1938, at which he was noticeably ill at ease, had been his sole excursion outside his own country.

But then Cecil came from a more modest background than the Lehmanns'. His paternal grandfather was the son of a railway clerk, his father a Church of Ireland parson who married a civil servant's daughter, through whose family was proudly claimed remote kinship with Oliver Goldsmith. His parents left Ireland for England in 1905 when Cecil was 1, and three years later his mother died, leaving the boy, an only child, to be brought up by his father and a much-loved maiden aunt. He was educated at Sherborne and Wadham College, Oxford, where he came under the influence of the Provost, Maurice Bowra, who, Cecil later recalled, 'took great pains to "bring me out" and make me less of a barbarian socially'. Coming down from Oxford with a disappointing third-class degree, Cecil found a job teaching at an Oxford prep school, then at a school near Glasgow, and finally, in 1930, at Cheltenham Junior School, meanwhile continuing to write poetry and to publish, gradually establishing himself as one of the more prominent poets of the 1930s. When his collection From Feathers to Iron came out in 1931, it was hailed in Poetry Review as 'a landmark, in the sense in which Leaves of Grass, A Shropshire Lad, Des Imagistes, and The Waste Land were landmarks'.

In 1928 Cecil had married Mary King, daughter of one of his old form-masters at Sherborne, by whom he had two sons. Although Cecil was fond of his wife, the marriage had not been altogether successful. When they met, Mary was a winsome young woman who talked to trees and had a 'faery fanciful way' of writing, traits which in the early days

227

Cecil found adorable; less so later. A countrywoman, she was private and reserved, devoted to her husband, her children and her home, but although she gave Cecil all the cosseting he required, she was in no way an intellectual companion. Only once did she try to talk to him about his poetry: 'You know nothing about it,' he told her, and she never mentioned it again. Mary shrank from emotional confrontation and physical contact, and by nature was drawn more to her own sex than to men, for years conducting a close relationship with a woman friend at Musbury. In his autobiography, Cecil wrote of his wife that, '[she was] inclined towards the austere. Plenty of fresh air in the bedroom, and single beds; wash, not wall paper; in furnishings, the plain and simple preferred to the fussy or elaborate.'

Soon after moving to Devon, Cecil began a passionate affair with the wife of a local farmer. Beautiful Billie Currall released in him 'a wildness of sensual violence that hitherto had been confined to phantasy, a certain nostalgie de la boue, a taste for the unrespectable ... and a positive relish for the stratagems and effronteries required by the Boccaccian situation'. The affair ended when Billie became pregnant and gave birth to a son, a child never publicly acknowledged by her lover. It was a little over six months after this that the affair with Rosamond had begun.

During the first half of 1942, while Rosamond was establishing herself at Aldworth, Cecil went to Musbury for only three weekends, dividing the rest of his time between London and Berkshire. At the start of the summer holidays he went home for ten days, but otherwise when not at the MOI he was at Diamond Cottage, where Rosamond was working hard to give Hugo and Sally, who was now at a new school, Westonbirt in Gloucestershire, as jolly a time as wartime restrictions allowed. Hugo remained frostily detached when Cecil was in residence, but Sally adored having him there and accepted him completely. 'I've just seen Cecil in bed with Mummy,' she announced one morning to one of her playmates, remaining serenely undisturbed by the picture. Rosamond herself revelled in her new-found happiness. 'I am pretty contented and peaceful these days,' she wrote to Henry Yorke, '[and] very much a part of this village community.' The village community regarded the new arrival with some fascination. Most of the men in the area – the Home Guard officer, the retired bank manager, the baker, the vicar – had quickly succumbed to the famous Lehmann seductiveness and were eager to offer assistance and advice, even the occasional present of local produce. Six hens were bought and the untidy garden given over to growing vegetables, although Rosamond, inexperienced and impractical, had only the smallest grasp of how to sow broad beans or dig over potatoes. Her immediate neighbour, the fashion journalist Anne Scott-James, watched with amusement as the statuesque beauty, her white hair rinsed with blue, went ineptly about her chores dressed in cherry-red trousers and an angora sweater which revealingly outlined her voluptuous figure. She was, said Miss Scott-James, 'as surreal a vision in our quiet village as a magnolia in a cornfield'. When Cecil was in residence, the sight was even more bizarre as when out walking the poet wore a dark city overcoat and carried an umbrella.

One of the most interesting of her neighbours was the poet and art-historian Laurence Binyon, who lived in retirement with his wife, Cecily, on the outskirts of the village. Rosamond was particularly pleased to make the acquaintance of such a distinguished scholar – Binyon had been curator of prints and drawings at the British Museum, and was famous to a wider public as the author of the poem 'For the Fallen' ('They shall grow not old, as we that are left grow old . . .'). There were a couple of agreeable evenings at Westridge Farm House, Binyon reading aloud from Dante and from his own work, but before the friendship had a chance to progress, on 10 March 1943 the old man died. Rosamond had been so touched by him that she wrote a moving elegy, published in *Horizon*, which by common consent was the finest of all the memorial tributes:

> . . . He went ahead,
> Casting his torch-beam towards the garden gate. . . .
> Across the grass we went. Then suddenly
> From dead of dark the apparition! . . . White
> Aerial spirit broken from bare wood,
> Prunus in bloom. . . . 'How beautiful by this light!'
> Over the boughs he threw its mild dim shower.
> So thus they stood –
> Sweetly illumined she
> By him; but he

Folded in winter dark impenetrably, –
Silently shining one upon the other:
The old man and the young tree, both in flower.

Rosamond was more fortunate than most in that at least she had some domestic help, in the shape of an ancient part-time gardener and an equally elderly and much-loved cook-housekeeper, Mrs Wickens. She bought a shabby little second-hand Ford in which she would 'chug & choke along' fulfilling more distant errands, but even so hours had to be spent in housework, gardening, and standing in food queues. 'An exhausted prisoner' of household duties, she sometimes described herself, 'all day struggling with coke buckets, wood chopper, brooms, pails, scrubbing brushes etc. Also hens . . .'; was it any wonder that 'writing is always being squeezed out'? As well as domestic duties, there were contributions to the war effort, which for Rosamond as for the other village women meant rolling bandages, taking turns to organise fund-raisers for the armed forces, and volunteering for first aid duties.

Tomorrow I have to start at 9.30 for an A.R.P. exercise at Yattendon. . . . I'm to be made up as an air-raid casualty, smeared with red paint & grey powder, & laid under a pile of debris in a shed until rescued. . . . Colonel Brett, our A.R.P. controller, a wild man, tells me with savage glee down the telephone to prepare to have my slacks ripped up the seam, my shirt torn off me to bandage me with, all my legs & arms in slings & perhaps a broken back, a stomach wound, a fractured scalp & a dislocated jaw thrown in.

However, once the children were back at school after the summer holidays of 1942 she was able to get down to work, this time on another story, 'a long complicated story which I don't yet understand the import of myself'.

Rosamond's trilogy of wartime stories[2] must be judged among the very best of her fictional compositions; indeed, except for her brief

---

[2] In 1946 these were published by Collins, to mixed reviews, in a collection under the title *The Gypsy's Baby*, which included the eponymous story as well as 'The Red-Haired Miss Daintreys'.

experiment in autobiography, *The Swan in the Evening*, she never wrote so consistently well again. But at this period in her life she was settled and happy, and although the war in many ways made daily life arduous, it also intensified emotion and provided new and interesting types of experience. And unlike many of her contemporaries, she was fortunate in being able to continue in a stable and reasonably comfortable way of life. As she put it in a letter to Rayner Heppenstall, an old FIL colleague, 'Although my life has completely changed, I am still in the country, under my own roof, with my children, within reach of my friends, and have privacy, and leisure to write.'

The wartime stories, all three commissioned by John for *New Writing*, are moving, funny and impressionistic, giving a vivid picture of domestic life at Aldworth under the wearisome restrictions of war. They also provide a touching celebration of maternal love, with lifelike portraits of Hugo and Sally (John and Jane), she cheerful and impulsive, he sensible and resourceful, barely managing to control a masculine exasperation with the silliness of the womenfolk. Like 'A Dream of Winter', the second story, 'When the Waters Came', also deals with the hard winter of 1939–40, this one describing the day of the great thaw, which turns the village street into a torrent of mud-brown water. The children's mother takes them out to see the phenomenon, an expedition which almost ends in disaster. 'Jane, rushing forward to seize a branch, went down. Perfectly silent, her astonished face framed in its scarlet bonnet fixed on her brother, her Wellingtons waterlogged, she started to sink, to sway and turn with the current and be carried away.'

The third and longest, 'Wonderful Holidays', a superb piece of work, closely founded in fact, was serialised in four issues of *New Writing* during 1944–5, and describes the somewhat hectic staging of a revue to be performed in front of the village to raise money for Salute the Soldier week. John and the boys from a neighbouring family, the Carmichaels, are in charge, with the much younger Jane and her friend Meg allowed to take minor roles, their mother, Mrs Ritchie, constantly on call to provide meals and deal with emergencies.

At 10.30 p.m. the telephone rang. John's voice came through, more than usually clipped.

'Look here, Mummy, I can't get back tonight.'

231

He had been absent since morning at the Carmichaels', a quarter of a mile away, and had rung up at intervals throughout the day to announce ineluctable non-return. . . .

'Can't get back?'

'Not possibly.'

Duty, said the voice, is paramount. No need, I presume, to point that out? . . .

'What's happened?'

'Well, I've got to turn the horse.'

'Turn the what?'

'Turn the horse. Gerald's horse – Conker.'

'Why must Conker be turned?'

'He's got colic. The vet. says there's a hundred to one chance for him if he's turned every four hours.'

'Couldn't Gerald turn him?'

'Single-handed?' inquired the voice, sick of foolishness.

The war is always in the background, rationing, petrol shortages, with at night the familiar drone of bombers overhead, and there is a taut and wonderfully comic sub-plot involving a lost school trunk, but nothing can detract from the excitement of the production. Jane develops a childish crush on an older boy staying with the Carmichaels, Roger Wickham, who elevates the schoolboy capering of the revue by his masterly playing of the violin. At his very first appearance Roger reveals himself as a familiar Lehmann type, a 'wonderful young man' in embryo. 'Roger Wickham, tall, slight, walking with the uncertain grace of his eighteen years, came through the trees towards them, carrying a huge sheaf of flowering cherry branches. . . . They all looked at him smiling, and he smiled back, looking at none of them.' Already Roger is embarking on a career as *homme fatal*, a Rollo Spencer in the making, even at this early stage committing an act of careless betrayal, although it remains undiscovered by its victim, Jane, until after the end of the story. The bond between mother and daughter is beautifully defined in the final pages: the older children, still high on the success of their show, whoop off into the night to walk the dog, but Mrs Ritchie insists on taking her exhausted daughter home.

'Where've they gone?' said Jane, dazed, walking at her mother's side.

'Only just a little way up the lane with Puffles . . .'

'Did Meg go?'

'No, no, I'm sure Meg's going to bed this very moment.'

'I thought I saw her dash out of the door.'

'No.' Mrs Ritchie suppressed an identical image. . . .

Jane pressed her hand. They crossed the lane and climbed the steep withy bank into the pasture, where open space made a faint lightening of the deep darkness.

'We forgot to bring a torch,' said Jane. 'Never mind. I like being out at night with you. Walking, walking, walking in nowhere. It doesn't seem as if we were in the world at all.' She squeezed her hand tightly again.

The seductive figure of Roger Wickham is in part based on a young man who had recently come into Rosamond's life, the Gloucestershire poet Laurie Lee. Laurie, like Roger, 'had a pale long cool-looking face, a fine head covered with wavy light-brown hair, beautiful secretive lips and clear eyes like aquamarines'; like Roger, he was charming, complex and elusive; and also he played the violin. Rosamond knew and admired Laurie's work, some of which had been published by John in *New Writing*, and she took to him immediately when they met in September 1941 at the BBC. Soon afterwards Laurie was invited to Gordon Place to meet Cecil, Laurie noting afterwards that Rosamond '[was] as tender and sentimental as her books'. Next day Cecil gave Laurie lunch at his club, thus laying the foundations for an enduring friendship between the two poets, a relationship which Rosamond cherished as one of the few that did not date from Cecil's previous life, before she knew him. Soon Laurie was a frequent and favourite visitor to Aldworth, helping weed the vegetable bed and saw up logs for the fire. Both Hugo and Sally adored him, regarding him as an honorary elder brother who would play with them by the hour, tell them jokes, and sing to them on his guitar. His presence was always much in demand during the holidays. 'My children dote on you,' Rosamond told him, 'but I don't want them to suck your blood.' With the children back at school, the evenings were less boisterous, with Laurie playing his violin, or listening while Cecil sang or Rosamond read aloud from Jane Austen. 'You are my brother, and I love you,' Rosamond wrote to him fondly. 'I have never in my life felt such perfect ease, affection, lack of friction with any member of the opposite sex.' At that time Laurie was going through a difficult love-affair of his own and was often unhappy; Rosamond was quick to sympathise, and in the course of this new-found intimacy, Laurie found himself almost against his will pushed into the role of confidant over her relationship with Cecil. 'I was a sort of page-in-waiting,' said Laurie, 'attendant on her great romance.'

When Rosamond described the years at Aldworth as some of the happiest of her life, she was speaking the truth. There is no doubt that Cecil was passionately in love with her, as she with him, and that most aspects of their life together were fulfilling at the profoundest level. 'Dear love, I think you do know & believe now how deeply & truly I love you,' Cecil wrote to her during this time. '[I would like to] wrap you up in peace & be a land-locked harbour for you. "I love the fond, the faithful & the true": I shall always be all that to you.' Soon after their affair began, he had composed a poem entitled 'The Album', which describes his feelings of regret as he looks at scenes of her past and his envy of all those who knew her when he did not:

> Courted, caressed, you wear
> Like immortelles the lovers and friends around you.
> 'They will not last you, rain or shine,
> They are but straws and shadows,'
> I cry: 'Give not to those charming desperadoes
> What was made to be mine.'
>
> One picture is missing –
> The last. It would show me a tree stripped bare
> By intemperate gales, her amazing
> Noonday of blossom spoilt which promised so fair.
> Yet, scanning those scenes at your heyday taken,
> I tremble, as one who must view
> In the crystal a doom he could never deflect – yes, I too
> Am fruitlessly shaken.
>
> I close the book;

But the past slides out of its leaves to haunt me
And it seems, wherever I look,
Phantoms of irreclaimable happiness taunt me.
Then I see her, petalled in new-blown hours,
Beside me – 'All the love most there
Has blossomed again,' she murmurs, 'all that you missed there
Has grown to be yours.'

With her divorce about to be finalised (she received the decree nisi on 22 December 1943), Rosamond was anxious to marry as soon as possible. In theory, so was Cecil; but there was his family in Devon to consider, Mary, who still knew nothing about the situation, and the two little boys, Sean 12, Nicholas only 9. Cecil would never forgive himself for hurting Mary and breaking up the home while the children were still so young: surely Rosamond would agree that they should wait till the boys had left school? On one level of course Rosamond did agree; but on another, more visceral plane she hated the arrangement and resented it bitterly. Jealous of Cecil's 'other family', she could not stop herself making scenes, even though Cecil spent far more time with her than he did with his wife and children at Musbury. However angry she felt, Rosamond had to be careful what she said about his marriage, as Cecil was apt to adopt an injured, defensive tone at any hint of criticism: boundaries were set, which Rosamond was not supposed to cross. 'Ah, those boundaries,' she wailed, '& the feeling they give one of being the other person's prisoner – in their power.' When apart, she and Cecil corresponded almost daily. His letters to her were full of expressions of devotion – 'It's a lovely, sunny, cloudy, windy day, the grass is sparking & oh my darling sweet, I wish we were going for a walk together & then having a huge tea & then going to bed & loving each silly' – although there was sometimes rather too much for the recipient's taste about the exhilaratingly hard work he was doing in the garden and the tremendously jolly times he had with his boys ('Blast those boys!'). It rankled that he was still refusing to tell Mary of her existence, and she continued to harp on this, privately hoping that a confrontation might force Cecil's hand, that if he revealed the truth about his split life Mary might be shocked into demanding a divorce.

But confrontation was precisely what Cecil wished to avoid. He adored his beautiful Rose, yet he was strongly rooted in his family life at Brimclose. He dreaded scenes and would do almost anything to avoid them, and he covertly undermined Rosamond by declining to take responsibility for the situation and showing no desire to change the status quo. If she compelled him to make a choice, he told her, he would try to settle down again with Mary, which would probably make him so unhappy that all their lives would be ruined. He realised that he could not give her what she wanted, and it worried him, he said, that he was destroying her chances of marrying again. Such apparently rational arguments drove Rosamond frantic, but as soon as she became exigent and emotional, Cecil would simply withdraw, often physically putting an end to the exchange '[by] the paralyzing act of getting up and going away'. As Laurie Lee observed, 'Cecil had the fatal quality of indifference, which was more damaging even than cruelty; but irresistible to Rosamond'. While to her his 'aspen hesitation' was maddening, he found her hysterical behaviour increasingly wearisome. 'Good God, Rosamond,' he burst out after one particularly trying episode, 'do you need *convincing*, *still*, after all we have suffered & loved through, that I hold you the most precious blessing of my life?' Hardest to endure was the fact that her attacks were always at their most ferocious when he arrived down from London on a Friday night, exhausted after a week of long hours at the Ministry and a journey in a blacked-out train that was cold, dirty, overcrowded and late. 'I'm often so deathly tired now at the end of the week,' he told her, 'no stamina, no emotional reserves to face those bad hours at night when a demon seems to enter you & makes you say cruel, stabbing things to me in a voice I can't recognise, & a demon comes into me & makes me just as bad.'

More trouble arose when Cecil invited Laurie to accompany him on one of his Musbury weekends. To Rosamond this was a betrayal on both their parts: how *could* Cecil wish to involve Laurie in his other life, and how could Laurie have agreed to go? If Laurie were to be taken up by the family in Devon, then her friendship with him must end, 'because it would be too painful for me to see you shared'. But Laurie refused to be blackmailed; he continued to visit Brimclose, where he was soon as popular with the Day Lewis boys as with Hugo and Sally – 'Laurie was the grown-up boy who made us bows and arrows and taught me how to use a telephone box without paying,' Sean Day Lewis remembered –

while simultaneously maintaining his friendship with Rosamond, who increasingly depended on him as confidant. 'I get terrified that wanting more than I can have will cause the destructive element to get the upper hand ... and that the end will be disaster all round,' she miserably explained to him. '[But] what I want isn't [at] all abnormal or unnaturally greedy. I want to live with him & look after him, and build mutual responsibilities, etc etc. In fact what women do want with the person they completely love & trust. ... I am very good three quarters of the time, & then I am very bad – and I am terrified of these crises coming quicker & quicker like capitalist wars, till disintegration is complete.' Her main fear was that eventually Cecil would find the strain of his double life too great, and that 'in the end he will prefer to retire to the bosom of his family, & lose me & relinquish me for ever & write beautiful poetry about separation'.

In the autumn of 1943 a serious crisis arose with the appearance of Cecil's new collection, *Word Over All*. These were his first poems to be published since 1938, inspired, as he wrote later, by the 'seismic disturbance' of a private emotional crisis which together with 'the violent happenings of the war ... had like an earthquake thrown up strata of my early experience which, till then, had not been available to me as a poet'. As the book was dedicated to Rosamond, there was no possibility that Mary could remain in the dark, and Cecil arranged to go down to Musbury to talk to her. Shortly before he left, he wrote to Rosamond from his office, attempting to be as honest and dispassionate as he could. 'You can be sure that, when I talk to Mary, I shall not attempt to make light of the bond between you & me, any more than when I talk to you I can make light of the bond between her & me,' he wrote. But as the letter continues, his tone, far from conveying the love and reassurance which Rosamond craved, grows increasingly resentful as anger at his predicament rises to the surface. 'I just don't know how much I need you – or Mary: how essential you are to me. Probably I never should know till I had lost you, or her. ... I begin to *hate* romantic love, to feel it should be bracketed with gunpowder as man's most disastrous invention.' Significantly, a similarly violent image of romantic love appears in *Word Over All*:

Love's the big boss at whose side for ever slouches

The shadow of the gunman: he's mortar and dynamite;
Antelope, drinking pool, but the tiger too that crouches.

During the course of this crucial weekend, Rosamond at Aldworth remained in a state of acute apprehension, divided between terror that Mary would persuade Cecil to stay with her and the children, and a wild hope that he might decide to leave Mary and come to her for good. In the event a compromise was reached: Mary was prepared to accept the situation, she said, as long as Cecil kept in regular touch with the family and did not try to break up the home. When Rosamond learned the outcome, she was enormously relieved and at the same time disappointed – 'I suppose because I had hoped, feared, imagined so many things,' as she told Olivia Holland. 'My trouble is that the unregenerate half of my nature resents this compromise & doesn't *want* to make it work. But the alternative – trying to do without each other – is too unbearable, so there we are.'

In fact once Mary had been told the truth, tensions for a time were considerably eased. With patient devotion Mary continued to welcome her husband when he came to Musbury, never reproaching him, and making sure Sean and Nicholas knew nothing of their father's double existence. (Accustomed to the forwarding of his letters while their father was away, the boys assumed 'the Hon. Mrs R. N. Philipps' to be his landlady.) Always attentive to his well-being, at regular intervals she posted off to Aldworth little boxes of home-made cakes, which Cecil, who had a sweet tooth, would squirrel away to eat by himself. So relieved was Cecil by the comparatively harmonious atmosphere that he even wrote a poem that on one level referred to the delicate balance between his two lives. Rosamond remembered how 'he tossed the poem over the table to her with a flick of the wrist and a mock-modest smile':

> *Shall I be gone long?*
>   For ever and a day.
> *To whom there belong?*
>   Ask the stone to say,
>   Ask my song.[3]

---

[3] These lines were later to be carved on Cecil's gravestone.

> Who will say farewell?
> The beating bell.
> *Will anyone miss me?*
> That I dare not tell –
> Quick, Rose, and kiss me.

As before, Cecil came to Diamond Cottage most weekends, and for six weeks that autumn Laurie moved in as lodger, having left his job in London to recover from a nervous breakdown caused by his unhappy affair with the beautiful Lorna Wishart. Laurie, by nature extremely private, preferring to cover his tracks and live concealed behind an emotional smoke-screen, had been led by Rosamond while at his most vulnerable into confiding a great deal more about his feelings than he intended, and later regretting it, he slightly withdrew from her, allowing his distaste for her insistent probing to show. Registering the snub, she reproached him with a failure in friendship. 'I don't like the feeling that you are keeping me at arm's length. . . . In fact, you make me feel you no longer trust me as you once did.' Tactfully Laurie replied that he loved her and was grateful, but that she must not expect him ever again to be so openly confessional. 'Last autumn the weight of my misery and your very dear understanding, both together, opened floodgates of confidences such as could not have occurred at any other time, or could again. . . . It made all the difference to my capacity for enduring. But that sort of thing *is* unnatural to me.'

The friendship remained solid none the less, and the following February Laurie went with Rosamond and Cecil when they rented a little house in Hasker Street, South Kensington, an arrangement that suited everybody, Laurie, living in the basement, able to retain his independence while at the same time acting as chaperon for his friends, a necessary precaution against the day when Cecil would initiate proceedings for divorce. Jokingly, Laurie became known as the King's Proctor. '[In those days] it made divorce more difficult if you were living together alone. . . . In a sense I was the guardian of their friendship because I made it impossible for them to be "loose".' Cecil found Laurie a job in his office, the MOI Publications Division, and when Rosamond came up to town they often went out as a trio, to a play, a concert, or a quiet dinner at Odennino's. One night during an air-raid when all three were sitting in a shelter, Rosamond suddenly remembered she had left the manuscript of her work in progress in the house: she became agitated, Cecil tried to soothe her, but it was Laurie who bravely dashed back to retrieve it. During the summer of 1944 Rosamond's visits became less frequent as the first of the flying bombs, the V1s, had appeared over London and Cecil was frightened for her safety, 'so I've been stuck in the country, gnawing my fingers & unable to concentrate on anything, & feeling lonely because I'm worried all the time'. In June, however, all three were at a party at John Lehmann's flat in Shepherd Market with a group of old friends, among them William Plomer, Rose Macaulay, Eddy Sackville-West, Louis MacNeice and Henry Yorke. There was also the poet and novelist Rex Warner, a close friend of Cecil's since Oxford days of whom Rosamond had become especially fond. 'He is a wonderfully nice man, full of goodness & intellectual vigour, pouring down pints & pints of beer all day,' she described him. 'No one ever suffered less from angst, & it's so refreshing.'

It was to Rosamond's relief that relations with John were continuing so smoothly, as recently the news had had to be broken that she and Cecil were planning to start a literary magazine of their own. It would not, of course, compete directly with *New Writing*, she assured him, but none the less she expected some acrimony, and was pleased when after only a little preliminary bristling, John behaved well, wishing her luck and welcoming her to 'the pleasures, the ardours, the intrigues and the bitterness that lie in wait for an Editor'. With the insatiable appetite among the wartime public for good reading matter, Cecil and Rosamond had been inspired to try to follow the path trodden by John himself, by Cyril Connolly (*Horizon*), Reginald Moore (*Selected Writing*), Henry Treece (*Transformation*), and by the latest in the field, Peter Quennell, new editor of *The Cornhill*, and launch something of the sort themselves. With two associates, the poet and critic Edwin Muir and Denys Kilham Roberts of the Society of Authors, whose original initiative it was, they established an office in Manchester Square where they met to discuss content and format. As a name, Cecil favoured *Albion*, Rosamond *Avenue*, but *Orion* was eventually decided upon as the title of a literary magazine that should be unpolitical and dedicated to culture, planned to appear in book form three times a year. The first issue, published by Nicholson & Watson and on sale in January 1945, included some distinguished names, among them Day Lewis himself, Walter de la Mare, Maurice Bowra, Edith Sitwell, Stephen Spender, William Plomer, Leonard Woolf, Rose Macaulay and Ivy Compton-Burnett. Great care had been taken with layout and design, but the arrival of the first copies came as an unpleasant surprise. 'I can scarcely speak about *Orion*, & nor can Cecil,' Rosamond fumed to John. 'After all our efforts & rages & frustrations what should those f——ing publishers dare to do but produce it on filthy shiny *paper* with revolting paper cover instead of the binding we had chosen. . . . All this will give you immense schaden-freude, I fully realize!'

In all, four issues of *Orion* made their appearance, two in 1945, one in 1946, the last in 1947, with contributions from little-known writers as well as from the well-established. The quality of the writing on the whole was high, with Rosamond in particular working hard at editing and at finding good material. Promising newcomers as well as famous names were solicited for contributions, although Denys Kilham Roberts strongly advised against inviting submissions within the magazine itself, advice which was ignored by Cecil who ran just such an advertisement, then retired to the country unwell, leaving Kilham Roberts to deal with the resulting avalanche. Kilham Roberts was not pleased. 'Under separate cover I am sending you three lots to have a look at,' he wrote to Rosamond. 'Cecil himself mustn't I suppose be bothered at present, but in due course I feel that he must shoulder the major part of this burden with which he has landed me.' On a practical level Rosamond's labour was considerable, as for some time there was no typist in the office and all letters and reports had to be written by hand. But her pleasure when she came across an accomplished piece of work was always enthusiastically expressed, the more so as she had to read so many manuscripts in which 'the illiteracy & flat ugliness & lack of talent for writing . . . makes me sick at heart.' She was particularly excited by a piece of literary self-analysis by Ivy Compton-Burnett, by a short story from Margaret Lane, 'far better than anything else we've had', poems by Denton Welch, and a work of youthful autobiography by Eric Bligh. With some of the newer writers she was generous with constructive criticism as well as with her friendship, two in particular benefiting from her encouragement, the young novelists Margiad Evans and Jean Howard.

In spite of this, the magazine failed to prosper, due mainly to disagreement among the founders. John had warned his sister that Kilham Roberts was a tricky character and that they were unlikely to get much work out of Muir, and so indeed it turned out, with Muir resigning after the second issue, and after the third so did Cecil and Rosamond as Cecil found himself unable to work with Kilham Roberts. But even without this incompatibility, Cecil was unlikely to have persevered much longer: as an editor he lacked John Lehmann's dedication and single-mindedness, and was soon hankering to return full-time to his own work.

On 25 September 1944, while the first issue of *Orion* was still in preparation, Rosamond's fifth novel, *The Ballad and the Source*, was published by Collins, its title suggested by Cecil, and dedicated 'To CDL'. Begun at the end of 1942, and originally intended as another 'Rebecca' story to follow 'The Gypsy's Baby' and 'The Red-Haired Miss Daintreys', the plot took on an impetus of its own, and 'the last story of the trilogy turned suddenly into a novel'. The child Rebecca is again the narrator, but the figure who dominates the book is that of the fascinating and witchlike Mrs Jardine. Sybil Jardine is modelled on Ménie Fitzgerald, mother of Rosamond's discarded first suitor, Nigel Norman, and like Ménie, Mrs Jardine is a woman with a past, regarded with disapproval by Rebecca's father, as Ménie had been by Rudie Lehmann. Like her original, Sybil Jardine had been an actress, a novelist, and had run away from her husband, leaving behind a child to whom she was then denied all access, in London secretly watching her small daughter play in the park just as Ménie used to haunt the playing-fields of Winchester. Both women were manipulative and possessed of a potent charm, but there the similarity ends, for Mrs Jardine is a vindictive and voracious personality, possessive, self-dramatising and self-obsessed.

The book opens in a manner reminiscent of the opening of *Dusty Answer*, with the sudden coming to life of a nearby house whose owners have been long away. 'One day my mother told me that Mrs Jardine had asked us to pick primroses on her hill, and then, when we had picked as many as we wanted, to come in and have tea with her.' The elderly lady who welcomes them inside is like a figure from a fairytale.

She was dressed in a long gown of pale blue with wide sleeves embroidered thickly with blue, rose and violet flowers. She had a white fleecy wrap round her shoulders, and on her head, with its pile of fringed, puffed, curled white hair, a large Panama hat trimmed with a blue Liberty scarf artistically knotted, the ends hanging down behind. She was small and rather stocky, with short legs and little feet shod in low-heeled black slippers with tongues and paste buckles.

Of the three children, it is Rebecca who is selected by Mrs Jardine to act as audience, the little girl held spellbound as she listens to the harrowing history unfolded by her exotic new friend. Mrs Jardine's delivery is unrelentingly histrionic – 'The source, Rebecca! The fount of life – the source, the quick spring that rises in illimitable depths of darkness and flows through every living thing from generation to generation. It is what we feel mounting in us when we say: "I know! I love! I *am*!"' – and the naive interjections and commonsensical perspective of the 10-year-old Rebecca provide a welcome light relief to the portentous style of this female Ancient Mariner. Her story is a shocking one, a gothic tale of hatred and betrayal, the tormented mother's desperate attempts to reclaim her daughter immersing three generations in hatred and revenge, and in their dreadful consequences, suicide, incest, madness and despair.

The story is long and the plot difficult to follow through all its convolutions; at one point even the enthralled Rebecca is obliged to admit, 'My head was whizzing round, hectically active but at the same time hopelessly confused.' Although parts of Mrs Jardine's 'ballad' do have a powerful, hypnotic effect, a major obstacle to enjoyment is that so much is conveyed at second hand: out of a total of 317 pages, 179 are in indirect speech, which has the effect here of thickening and dulling the narrative flow. Mrs Jardine is by no means the only offender, for there are three others, the worst Tilly, a chirpy little seamstress (closely modelled on the Fieldhead seamstress, Dickie), talking page after page in a dire version of an educated lady novelist's idea of Cockney; worse still, she and Mrs Jardine lengthily quote each other, 'imitating' each other's voices so that the reader sometimes has to cope with Cockney imitating refined imitating Cockney, and vice versa.

As always Rosamond is faultless in her treatment of children and in her understanding of the child's point of view; and substantially the best parts of the novel are those describing Rebecca's thoughts and feelings, her relations with her sisters, and their interaction with Sybil Jardine's three grandchildren, fierce, incorruptible Maisie, her brother Malcolm, and the youngest, the spoilt, manipulative Cherry. For the rest, despite the undoubted quality of the writing, it is hard for a modern reader to comprehend how such 'a thumping melodrama', as even its author referred to it, could have been taken seriously, let alone praised and enjoyed. But as Rosamond remarked with satisfaction, *The Ballad* was a Book of the Month Club selection, its sales were 'electrifying', and the reviews on the whole 'gorgeous', several critics remarking on the visible influence of Henry James, in particular of *The Turn of the Screw* and *What Maisie Knew*. Although some balked at the improbability of Mrs Jardine's confiding so uninhibitedly in Rebecca – 'A woman tells a child of ten how she sent a discarded lover to seduce her seventeen-year-old daughter!' – there were many ready to sing the novel's praises. The *Observer* described it as 'a charming, if dangerous, experiment'; Edwin Muir in *The Listener* wrote that the book was 'full of poetic imagination and of acute observation', adding that 'it holds a very fine balance, at least until near the end'; and in America the *New Republic* praised it as 'a beautiful, impressive and strangely moving romantic novel by one of the most important writing talents of our time'. The *New Statesman* remarked appreciatively on the author's technical sophistication, as well as 'the contempt for all modern inhibitions . . . the high-flying at every fence, the luxuriance of incident, and, above all, the impetus with which she models the over life-size figure of Mrs Jardine'. It was, the reviewer added, an especial joy 'to escape with her from the dingy interiors and cabbage-water smells now fashionable into châteaux and lime avenues where beautiful creatures in bright velvets parade their exorbitant personalities'.

The Ballad is the least subjective of all Rosamond's novels, the most highly coloured and furthest removed from the actuality of personal relationship, and the one most unrestrainedly imaginative – even if the imagination in question seems to have been influenced less by Henry James, more by Elinor Glyn and Mrs Braddon. Rosamond herself regarded it as her 'first grown-up book', and her finest work so far. 'I don't believe I shall ever do anything better & more concentrated,' she told William Plomer. 'If it isn't good, then I really am no good.'

Like her narrator Rebecca, Rosamond was possessed by Sybil Jardine, to such an extent that she immediately began planning a sequel around her. The character intrigued and mystified her, and although she recognised that Ménie had provided the original inspiration, she had no idea where the rest had come from. The intention, she said, had been for the book to be half fiction, half recollection, growing from '[some] childhood memories of picking primroses on a round green hill with a church on top and a garden wall with a small blue door in it'. Behind the blue door she expected to find 'a darling old lady in a wheelchair, crippled with arthritis'; instead, out burst Mrs Jardine. Some of Rosamond's friends were bewitched by her, others regarded her as 'a beastly wicked vile *fraud*'; but few could resist speculating about her 'real' identity, Henry Yorke detecting a resemblance to Ottoline Morrell, Roger Senhouse convinced she was based on Stephen Tennant, while Violet Hammersley saw only herself: '*Of course* Mrs Jardine is me!' she exclaimed proudly to Nancy Mitford. The young writer Michael Meyer, who had come to know Rosamond through contributing to *Orion*, and who had found her daunting, immediately assumed it was a self-portrait. 'That tormented, predatory, praying-mantis sort of woman was exactly who Rosamond was,' he said. 'Mrs Jardine seems to be affecting people violently, in all sorts of extraordinary ways,' wrote Rosamond, bemused. 'I've never had such a spate of letters about any book since *Dusty Answer* – including 2 or 3 informing me that never in their lives have they read such a *dull* stupid *boring* book. . . . I didn't know where or what I was when I'd finished it, – I wondered if I'd produced a monster. Indeed, I think I have.'

After the flurry over the book had mostly died away, Rosamond settled down to domestic routine at Aldworth. The last winter of the war was a hard one, week after week of snow, ice and polar temperatures. Rosamond, looking out 'on this iron landscape, this mineral sky', bemoaned the difficulties of keeping the cottage warm. 'Oh, the cold, I mind it so . . . I can't get the pipe to the cistern unfrozen & I am up on a beam, very dangerous, in the loft, half the day & night, burning things to thaw it; and then it freezes again and the cistern empties, empties . . . & the ballcock sticks up stark with a coronet of ice on it. When I die, you will find the word ballcock engraved upon my heart.' While shovelling snow in the loft Rosamond put her foot through her bedroom ceiling, '& now the wind keens & whistles down on me through a cavern of broken lathes & plaster'. To add to her worries, Beatrix had been seriously ill and was staying at Aldworth to convalesce, while Cecil was stuck down in Musbury, so unwell that he was under doctor's orders not to move. This was particularly anguishing as recently relations between Rosamond and Cecil had again grown uncomfortably tense, with Cecil in an agony over his hopelessly divided loyalties. John after a long talk with his sister had received the distinct impression 'that the passion was turning now, gradually, a little sour because of the enormous tension the whole situation had put him under for so long'. But eventually the view on the immediate horizon began to improve: the invalids recovered, the sun came out, snowdrops could be seen piercing through the drifts, and on 8 May 1945 came the declaration after nearly six long years that hostilities in Europe had ceased. On VE night, Rosamond took Sally up on the downs to see the bonfires being lit across the south of England, 'the same that were lit during the Spanish Armada time, & in the Napoleonic Wars. One felt part of history: & all the people who came over the downs & gathered round the beacon might have come out of The Dynasts. I shall never forget it.'

10

'The Terrible Decision'

The enormous success of *The Ballad and the Source* in Britain was as nothing to its rapturous reception in the United States: over 600,000 copies sold and the film-rights bought by the producer Walter Wanger for the immense sum of $250,000. Wanger's first choice for the role of Mrs Jardine had been Greta Garbo, but the star having refused to be lured out of retirement, Wanger then pursued the project as a vehicle for his actress wife, Joan Bennett. In November 1946 Rosamond was invited to meet the Wangers in London. 'Walter Wanger is an angel,' Olivia Holland was told, '& Joan Bennett extremely well-bred and lady-like & agreeable. Pretty my word! She literally looks 25, and has a daughter of 18. The scent of flowers & perfume in the room caused my head to start spinning, & I had to ask for an open window.' When the casting of Bennett proved impracticable, Wanger approached Ingrid Bergman, but Bergman turned down the offer on the grounds – ironical in the light of her subsequent behaviour – that she could not possibly play the part of a woman who deserts her child and leaves her husband for another man. Wanger, to Rosamond's relief, failed, too, in persuading either of his other choices, Joan Crawford and Anna Neagle, to take the part. Reluctant to abandon so expensive a property, Wanger then pitched the story to half a dozen studios, all of which rejected it, as did some big-name producers, one of whom, Darryl Zanuck, admitted that he agreed with the general view that the story was dull and heavy-going, and that '[it was] not the kind of story I would ever personally produce, mainly because it is the kind of story that for *money* I would never go to see'. Despairing of Hollywood, Wanger then struck a deal for the film to be made in England, but here he ran into trouble with the British censors who rejected the script's 'positive' portrayal of adultery, a rejection that finally brought to an end all attempts to realise *The Ballad* on film.

In spite of the unprecedently high levels of taxation recently introduced by a Labour government, from these ill-fated film-rights Rosamond earned more than she had ever done before, and with £12,000 of the proceeds bought a beautiful bow-windowed house in the village of Little Wittenham, on the Berkshire–Oxfordshire border. Almost equidistant between Oxford ten miles to the north and Ipsden to the south, Little Wittenham sits under the edge of the Chilterns, in the heart of that country of tree-lined tributaries that characterises the upper reaches of the Thames valley, a region which Rosamond, like her father, loved above all other. The Manor House, as it was called, although the actual manor house had been pulled down a hundred years earlier, was an old farmhouse, 'a dream house, late 18th century, a long, low, red-brick house smothered in roses'. (In one of his Nicholas Blake novels Cecil described it as 'A perfect Queen Anne house . . . [in] a cataleptic trance of white and yellow roses'.) Surrounded by a large, blossomy garden encircled by trees, the house was next to an ancient church, beyond which were meadows, the river and quarter of a mile upstream a lock and a weir. To the north across the fields could be seen the outline of Dorchester Abbey, while immediately facing was the gentle sheep-cropped slope of Wittenham Clumps, with a narrow single-track road running between the low garden wall and the hillside. To one side of the house, across a grassed courtyard shaded by an enormous chestnut tree, were a row of farm buildings and a magnificent tithe barn, intended for conversion into a retreat for Beatrix.

The move from Aldworth in April 1946 had been chaotic – a burst boiler in the new house, Mrs Wickens collapsed with heart trouble – and with rationing still in force there was little to be found in the way of pretty fabric or good furniture. But friends were generous, Stephen Tennant donating some curtains and a double bed upholstered in ice-blue satin, while the distinguished art historian Kenneth Clark, an ex-colleague of Cecil's at the Ministry of Information, gave a bookcase and lent several pictures. Another stroke of good fortune was finding domestic help, rare in that period of post-war austerity. Mrs Wickens, who died soon after leaving Aldworth, was going to be difficult to replace. 'I miss her dreadfully,' Rosamond wrote to Laurie. 'She was one of the best friends I shall ever have.' But contrary to her fears of having to cope on her own for the foreseeable future, a promising prospect appeared almost at once. 'I have actually got an extremely nice couple,' Rosamond delightedly told Olivia Holland. 'Gentlefolk, ex-Major, jobless, & his charming cultured wife. . . . They came to see the place & adored it, & have selected me from dozens of others in spite of my having no cottage. I am furnishing the attics for them. . . . The bliss of finding someone who talks the same language, & who isn't greedy or hoity-toity!'

By the end of May, although there was still a great deal to be done, Rosamond confided to William Plomer that, 'I adore my house, in spite of all. I've never had this feeling about a house before, since I left Fieldhead.' Cecil reported to Laurie that Rosamond's new home 'is all that there is of the most chic', and in celebration he wrote a poem entitled 'The House-Warming', in which he portrays himself as a phantom warming her 'dove-treed house' with his love:

> Curtaining, carpeting, lighting all
> Your rooms with a love ineffaceable.

And Rosamond was indeed happy, delighted to have exchanged the cramped quarters of Diamond Cottage for the spaciousness and elegance of the Manor House, with its large, leafy, green-lawned garden. As at Aldworth, her style was exotically different from most of her country neighbours, and thanks to the Ipsden furniture and the various gifts and loans she was able to create a comfortable, almost opulent interior. The drawing-room was lined in yellow silk, the lamps were rose-shaded, there was an Adam fireplace, rosewood and walnut furniture and a grey silk divan, with curtains and carpet 'the faded magenta of Christmas roses, bowls of roses all over the place, a luscious Renoir above the mantelpiece'. Books were everywhere. John Bayley, later Warton Professor of English Literature at Oxford and husband of Iris Murdoch, remembered as an anonymous young conscript being invited into the house for tea. 'Women everywhere in those days were accustomed to giving tea to soldiers, who were known to have an insatiable thirst for it,' he recalled. '[We went] into a large room filled with books in shelves and on chairs and tables, and decorated in a dashingly flamboyant manner. . . . *Horizon*, *Penguin New Writing* and Walter de la Mare's new anthology *Love*, with its stylish but romantic cover, were strewn over a wide elegant marble table with a raised bronze edge.' At first unaware of his hostess's identity, he nevertheless recognised that, 'This was clearly no ordinary country lady. . . . She was a big tall woman with fair hair and a strikingly large face and long neck. Much later I was to hear Lord David Cecil . . . remark that she seemed to loom over you like a ship's figurehead. So indeed she did.' The colour of Rosamond's hair, by now pure white, changed periodically, sometimes white, sometimes fair, sometimes rinsed with pink or violet. She was always carefully made-up, and indoors often wore silky pyjamas patterned in pinks and greens; on her wrist hung a bracelet with a heart-shaped locket given her by Cecil containing one of his poems. Her sense of well-being added lustre to her beauty: Julia Strachey observing Rosamond at a party remarked that '[she] glowed like a gorgeous peach with hoarfrost on its head'.

The new house was not the only source of Rosamond's contentment, for it was now that a fervently desired but unexpected development in her relationship with Cecil suddenly seemed to put within reach everything she had craved for so long.

Since the end of the war the old balance had been precariously maintained, with Cecil commuting between mistress and wife, the tensions of dividing himself between the two bleakly referred to in his poem 'Departure in the Dark':

> It was hard to be sure
> If home were prison or prison home: the desire
> Going forth meets the desire returning.

Inevitably the strain was beginning to tell. Like the hero of one of his Nicholas Blake novels, '[he] was torn between the two women. . . . And a man so divided, whose conscience is perpetually working overtime, is liable to crack.' Cecil knew very well that he was making both women unhappy; consequently he felt guilty most of the time and this was affecting his health: his physical collapse at the end of 1944 had undoubtedly been caused as much by the stress of his double life as by overwork at the Ministry – from which he had resigned with relief at the end of January 1946. The problem was that Cecil could not make up his mind whom to desert. Although Mary never pretended to be an intellectual equal, she was in a sense his bedrock. He felt he needed her docile, unquestioning devotion as much as he needed the passion and stimulus of his relationship with Rosamond, the calm domesticity of Brimclose providing an essential retreat from the high-powered social and literary life of London and Wittenham.

As a couple Cecil and Rosamond were much in demand, both successful, spirited and exceptionally good-looking, Cecil with his distinguished, haggard features an intriguing foil to Rosamond's white hair and creamy complexion. As neither was lacking in personal vanity, they enjoyed the attention and revelled in their celebrity status. 'I liked being in the limelight,' Cecil wrote in his autobiography, admitting that if at a party he were not regarded as 'the centre of the picture' he would be overwhelmed '[by] a sort of unfocused depression'. Such disappoint-ments were rare in those days, however, and Rosamond had the added satisfaction of knowing that she was the guardian of the gate through which the distinguished poet could be reached, that it was mainly through her that lesser mortals were obliged to seek access to Day Lewis. Almost always at Cecil's side when he gave poetry readings and lectures, yet Rosamond had her own high profile. In R. A. Scott-James's critical survey of the first half of the twentieth century, *Fifty Years of English Literature*, published in 1951, he wrote, 'I do not think there is any living English novelist whose work, at its best, and within its limits, so nearly reaches artistic perfection as Rosamond Lehmann's.' She was considered to be in the top rank of women writers, her critical reputation on a par with that of Elizabeth Bowen and Ivy Compton-Burnett, on a higher level than other well-respected but less innovative novelists such as Margaret Lane and Pamela Hansford-Johnson, from whom she was set apart by a superior artistry and technical daring as well by the quality of her style. By the 1940s she was besides one of the great and the good within her profession, an active campaigner for authors' rights and for the protection of persecuted writers abroad. Since the late 1930s she had been a member of the Society of Authors, of FIL and of the

251

International Association of Authors. In 1942 she joined the PEN Club, founded in 1921 to defend freedom of expression and to promote friendship between writers internationally; under PEN's auspices she devoted considerable time, effort and sometimes money to helping individual writers escape from Austria and Germany and find asylum in England.

Rosamond's admiration for her lover's work was unreserved, and under her influence Cecil wrote some of his best poetry. *Word Over All*, for instance, received greater critical praise and sold five times more copies than any of his previous volumes, and John Lehmann was not alone in judging the collection 'far and away the most striking . . . that Cecil Day Lewis ever wrote'. That same year, 1943, the Apollo Society was launched, its object to renew interest in spoken verse through the staging of poetry recitals accompanied by music; Cecil was one of the founder members, together with Dadie Rylands, Peggy Ashcroft, the pianist Angus Morrison, and Stephen Spender and his second wife, Natasha Litvin. In 1946 Cecil was asked to deliver the prestigious Clark Lectures at Cambridge. His chosen subject was 'The Poetic Image', with which Rosamond helped him considerably, as he acknowledged in his foreword when the lectures were published in book form, paying tribute to 'the one who, from first to last, with gentle encouragement and delicate criticism helped me over the exacting course I had set myself'. In his autobiography, he later made oblique reference both to the strain and the inspiration which were consequent upon his divided life and his association with Rosamond. 'Under stress such as I had never known and sweet influences that for long enabled me to bear it, my life seemed to grow again . . . while my work was enhanced by the joy and the pain which seemed to purify vision and enlarge it, to show me poetry everywhere.'

For Rosamond there was no division, no doubt: she wanted to marry Cecil, and his ambivalence left her baffled and resentful. 'Rosamond's pressure on Cecil to marry her was constant,' said Laurie. 'That demanded a great deal of physical, moral and emotional strength, which he was not able to maintain.' The more she threatened and implored, the further he withdrew, his ability to detach having been well developed in childhood when he had had to learn to protect himself from his father's exorbitant demands for love. As he later described it, 'I had little by little built up within myself a resistance to emotional pressure. . . . I developed a habit of shutting off my attention, letting my eyes glaze or staring into remote distances, as though I were meditating a poem or getting in tune with the Infinite.' For Rosamond Cecil's dispassion was a source of intense frustration, and in despair at the beginning of 1946 she turned for help to that worldly figure, Kenneth Clark, who she knew found her attractive[1] and would interest himself in her predicament. Clark advised her to give Cecil an ultimatum, 'to put all to the touch'. The results were surprising and dramatic.

Saying nothing of his intentions beforehand, Cecil in the middle of February went down to Musbury and announced to Mary that he had finally decided to leave her. Rosamond was ecstatic. A miracle had occurred, she told Laurie: anticipating nothing unusual she had arranged to meet Cecil for a drink at her club, the Sesame in Grosvenor Street, and completely out of the blue he had declared 'that he realized overwhelmingly that he could not go back [to Mary], & face a future without me, & had at last told her so the night before. She seems to have taken it calmly.' In compensation Cecil had agreed to spend the next three months mainly at Brimclose to help Mary prepare for his departure, and this Rosamond was willing to accept. 'I must wait & be patient & make no demands. Which of course is easy,' she told Kenneth Clark. Cecil had sworn that he was absolutely certain he had chosen the right path, although naturally he felt shaken to his depths and was in a state of violent crisis. 'But he is already writing poetry about it, so his fundamental state must be healthy . . .[2] I *hope* we may start to be together in the summer. . . . To think I have got a future after all! – I mean the kind I want & believe in.'

During the following three months Cecil and Rosamond managed to meet several times, the most bizarre occasion being one on which all three participants found themselves in the same room. The event was a grand one, a poetry recital organised by the Society of Authors at the

[1] 'When I first saw you,' Clark wrote to Rosamond many years later, 'you seemed the most beautiful human being I had ever seen & I fled. . . . I have a poor opinion of myself then.'

[2] According to one of his later lovers, Elizabeth Jane Howard, 'Cecil never felt emotion very deeply, but what he liked best, what he needed, was to be unhappily in love but unable to do anything about it. In such situations he wrote some of his best poetry.'

253

Wigmore Hall in the presence of Queen Elizabeth and both the Princesses. Performing with Cecil were the Poet Laureate, John Masefield, as well as Walter de la Mare, T. S. Eliot, Edith Sitwell, Louis MacNeice and Dylan Thomas. It was an honour for Cecil to have been asked to take part and there was no question of Rosamond not being present to witness his moment of glory. But Mary, too, had been invited, and she, too, wished to see her husband perform. As Rosamond reported to Olivia Holland, 'To my horror (and his) his wife elected to come at the last moment. I didn't know where she sat, & nor does he. I kept my seat rigidly, & didn't dare look to left or right; and he read *The Lighted House*[3] ... [*sic*] It is all AWFUL, this position, for everybody. She retired again to Devonshire afterwards, & he and I spent the night with my brother & attended a large dinner party of Edith Sitwell's.'

The poetry reading was in the middle of May 1946, towards the end of the period after which Cecil had promised to come to Rosamond for good. But as the weeks passed and no mention was made in letters from Musbury of any plans for the future, Rosamond grew uneasy. She knew that Mary never referred to the subject – 'I think she is a clever tough woman & understands him very well' – but it began seriously to worry her that Cecil seemed reluctant even to think about what lay ahead. Eventually, in July, she asked William Plomer, wise, discreet and a loyal friend to both, to talk to Cecil. Dutifully Plomer tackled the subject, reporting to Rosamond that the meeting had gone well and that Cecil claimed still to have every intention of leaving his wife. 'I want to say how very glad I am you broached the subject of our "situation" to C.,' Rosamond wrote to him gratefully. 'He will never discuss it & it has done him a power of good to air it to someone like you, of sense & sensibility, who can understand his feeling that he could have done & can do no other. It was like a burden rolled off him – so it helped *me*. He feels the dilemma acutely, & is always afraid my friends may be criticizing him.'

Reassured of Cecil's commitment, Rosamond realised she must now tell the children of her intention to remarry. Sally, recently settled at a new school, Cranborne Chase in Dorset, welcomed the news, but Hugo's reaction was very different. 'Little did I know that Hugo loathed Cecil

[3] The poem in which Rosamond is celebrated as Primavera, 'the sprite fire-fingered who came / To lighten my heart'.

always, *loathed* him, and never said.' Now in his last year at Eton, Hugo came up to London for half-term, suspecting nothing and looking forward to being taken out to lunch by his mother. 'I said, "How would you feel if I married Cecil?" He burst into howls and said, "You're not to! You're not to! You're not to! He only wants you for his poetry!"'

For the time being, however, Hugo had little cause for anxiety. Cecil, becalmed at Brimclose, was sunk in a state of moral paralysis and incapable of decisive action. As it was clear that nothing could be achieved while he was in this condition, it was agreed that for the immediate future he would return to the old compromise of shuttling between Wittenham and Musbury, but this time staying two consecutive months at each. However much she disliked it, Rosamond had little choice but to accept the arrangement, and with the prospect of marriage still on the horizon was prepared to be accommodating. 'I must try to start work & forget my private troubles,' she told Olivia Holland. 'It isn't too difficult, when I consider his appalling predicament, & his unhappy face, & remember that he totally depends on me for comfort.'

To fill Cecil's lengthy absences, Rosamond kept herself fully occupied. Friends came every weekend – Dadie, Laurie, William Plomer, Cecil's old friend Rex Warner, Hester Chapman and her second husband Ronnie Griffin – and there was a busy social life to organise for the children during the holidays. That summer Rosamond took them to Llanstephan, where she had finally been received back into the fold, 'restored to my former position of favourite daughter-in-law'. For at least one week during every holiday Hugo and Sally stayed with their father and Cristina in Gloucestershire, where Wogan divided his time between farming, painting and his work for the Communist Party. Cristina, who had a daughter of her own from her first marriage, was an affectionate stepmother, and Wogan, if sometimes forgetful when it came to birthdays and outings from school, was proud of his children, although with him as with Rosamond, it was Sally who was the favourite. Implacably hostile as he was to his own father, Wogan none the less had been bitterly hurt by Lord Milford's disinheriting him in favour of Hugo, and his feelings towards his son were as a result ambivalent. This did not prevent him from expressing some highly critical opinions about the intensity of their mother's relationship with both children. She was, he felt, too possessive, too emotionally demanding, and although Hugo, independent by nature, had become his own man and would soon be out of range, Sally, it was clear, was entirely dominated by Rosamond, who regarded her daughter as a prodigy, the most beautiful, the cleverest, the most gifted. When Sally was still at Westonbirt, Wogan had been summoned by her headmistress. 'I went over, and she said, "Look, Rosamond is ruining Sally by trying to make her out a tremendous genius, and the fact is that she's a very nice, ordinary, intelligent girl enjoying life like anything." I tried to get Rosamond to understand. Their relationship was crazy.'

Although the new novel was only in the earliest stages of planning, Rosamond tried to keep to a writing routine, contributing regular book reviews, of novels, letters and literary biography, to the *Times Literary Supplement* and the *New Statesman*. She was increasingly involved, too, with her brother, who in 1946 had set up his own publishing firm, John Lehmann Ltd, for which she acted as reader and consultant as well as being a shareholder and director. The terms were clearly laid out between them, with Rosamond making herself available, all expenses paid, one morning a week at the office in the basement of John's house in Egerton Crescent, in between agreeing to read at the rate of two guineas for a long manuscript, one guinea for a short one. 'Revision jobs are apt to be hell & to take a long time: we could discuss them no doubt as & when they arose.' Rosamond's reports were perceptive and precise, and some interesting material passed through her hands. 'Engrossing and brilliant,' she wrote of Tennessee Williams's novella *The Roman Spring of Mrs Stone* (adding fastidiously, '[but] I do wish it wasn't necessary for the anonymous young man to urinate so frequently??'). And of Paul Bowles's novel *The Sheltering Sky*, having complained crossly about the state of the typescript ('Tell him with my compliments I don't know how he has the nerve to send in such a mess'), she concluded that although 'the opening chapters are lacking in grasp, interest, authority', Bowles was a remarkable talent, and 'a very persuasive even dangerous philosophical writer'.

In the new year of 1947 while Cecil was at Brimclose, Rosamond went to Paris at the invitation of the British ambassador, Sir Alfred Duff Cooper, to stay at the magnificent embassy in the rue du Faubourg Saint-Honoré. Duff Cooper and his beautiful wife Diana were delightful company, they entertained lavishly, and their guests, both French and

English, were all that was most sophisticated and amusing. Certainly it was exciting and much of it enjoyable, 'but the fearful ordeal of being "on show" perpetually for five days half paralyzed me,' Rosamond admitted to Marthe L'Evêque. She was haunted, too, 'by the contrast between the luxe & chauffage of the Embassy & the painful conditions of existence of the people of Paris. . . . It gave everything an edge of nightmare.' But this was nothing to the nightmare that unfolded after she returned home.

On 1 February Cecil arrived for his two-month tour of duty at Little Wittenham. Since the autumn of the previous year he had been working as a reader[4] at Chatto & Windus under Rosamond's old mentor, Harold Raymond, commuting to London for a couple of days a week to lodge with Hester and Ronnie Griffin in their little house in Percy Street, near Fitzroy Square. The part-time nature of the job at Chatto was specifically designed to give Cecil plenty of time for his own work, but this had not been going well: he had recently scrapped a long poem – 'the best part of a year's work wasted' – and was feeling abnormally tired and dispirited. His arrival at the Manor House coincided with the start of the great snowstorms of that notoriously severe winter, and as the Arctic weather tightened its grip, so did Cecil's melancholy deepen as he remained frozen fast into what Rosamond described as one of his 'black ice' moods. These moods were nothing new, described by Cecil as arriving periodically and 'drenching me with misery and rendering me so morally impotent that I could not descry any gleam of reassurance through their mirk, nor make the least move to free myself'. This present affliction, however, seemed worse than any that had preceded it. '[Cecil] is very far from well, with a gastric ulcer boiling up, & dreadfully thin & depressed,' Rosamond wrote anxiously to Olivia Holland. In the middle of a blinding blizzard, with the house snowbound, a crisis arose when the gardener's wife, heavily pregnant, went into labour. It was, said Rosamond, the most frightening experience of her life. 'I was up for most of 2 nights, & it didn't go straightforwardly, & on the 2nd night Cecil got chains on the car & heroically ploughed 8 miles through the drifts &

---

[4] A more prestigious job in those days than it may sound now, it being accepted practice then for publishers to employ at least one established writer to read manuscripts and give advice. William Plomer did a similar job for Jonathan Cape, having taken over from the formidable Edward Garnett.

fetched the Nurse! Together she & I delivered a superb 9lb female child'
– an episode that was to be used with ominous significance in
Rosamond's next novel.

By the time Cecil returned to Brimclose at the beginning of April, his
depression was almost suicidal. Even his beloved Devon countryside
gave him no comfort, as he disturbingly described in a poem written at
this time, entitled 'The Neurotic':

> I will not lift mine eyes unto the hills
> For there white lambs nuzzle and creep like maggots.
> I will not breathe the lilies of the valley
> For through their scent a chambered corpse exhales.
> If a petal floats to earth, I am oppressed.
> The grassblades twist, twist deep in my breast.

Finally on 26 May Cecil broke down and poured out his misery to Mary,
telling her that his double life had become insupportable and that he
could bear the strain no longer. Next day he went to London where he
saw Rosamond, and together they decided that this time there must be
no going back. Two days later he returned to Musbury to inform Mary
that their marriage was over and that he was going to live permanently
with Rosamond. Somehow Mary managed to maintain her stoicism,
recording simply in her diary, 'Cecil in state bordering on insanity . . .
life becoming intolerable.' Early on the morning of 2 June, Cecil packed
his bag and asked Mary to drive him to Axminster to catch the train. In
the car Mary's restraint finally broke down and she began to sob
uncontrollably, begging her husband to stay, imploring him not to
abandon her and the boys. Grey-faced and silent, Cecil at first said
nothing, then suddenly shouted at her to turn the car round and drive
home. Once inside the house he exploded with rage, accusing Mary of
having made it impossible for him to leave: it was all her fault, he
shouted: she had ruined everything and robbed him of the love of his
life. Then he telegraphed to Rosamond at Little Wittenham to say that
he would not be coming to her after all.

Utterly wretched, Cecil in desperation sent for Laurie. 'The hideous,
destined thing has happened,' he began. 'I've had to write & tell
Rosamond we must part; God knows if it's the right decision. . . . It has

just about finished me.' Rosamond at Wittenham was also in an agonised state over what she described as 'the terrible decision'. To the publisher Rupert Hart-Davis, a confidant of hers as well as of Cecil's, she wrote,

> Rupert, tell him . . . that there is not one of us, *not one*, of his true, his adult friends who thinks this 'decision' is the right one. . . . He will make wonderful poetry out of his self-torture & my torture – but he will never be a whole human being now – if he does this. I *cannot* lose him to this criminal course – he will say he's got to murder someone, & he's decided it's to be me, & he can't help himself. . . . He tells me he is 'stretching his arms to me from the further bank, longing to help & comfort me, powerless'. Tell him he must find the power in himself to cross to the other bank before it's too late & I'm gone. . . . Tell him . . . that I'm worth staying with, & worth something better than being thrown on the dust heap.

In spite of all, Rosamond remained convinced that it was she, not Mary, whom Cecil loved the more, and she refused to accept defeat. It was unbelievable that Cecil could give up all that life with her had brought him in favour of a sterile marriage, in which, as she saw it, he and Mary were 'like two wheels of a bicycle propelling the stark frame of their life together, never meeting'. To Kenneth Clark she confessed, 'This state is miserably ignominious . . . I have grown so dependent on him for personal happiness during these 6 years, & he on me: the only time I've ever had "an equal love". Plenty of people must do without it, I know, but I hope not to have to be one of them.' Determined to retrieve the relationship, she persuaded Cecil to meet her in London. The two of them talked, and afterwards she felt calmer. 'My heart can beat & my breaths come and go,' she told Laurie. 'I kept off any discussion of the future but I know, finally this time, that there will be one.'

As Cecil urgently needed a respite from the appalling tensions of his situation, it was arranged that he and Laurie should go together for a fortnight to Denmark. While he was away Rosamond went to France for a few days to stay with Alvilde Chaplin and her husband at Jouy en Josas near Versailles. It had been ten years before that Rosamond had first met Alvilde, who, chic, lively and outspoken, had been a girlfriend of the

Princesse de Polignac's – the little house at Jouy had been left her by 'Aunt Winnie' on her death in 1943 – and it was at the Avenue Henri Martin that she and Rosamond had formed their friendship. Rosamond also took the opportunity to call on Marthe L'Evêque, with whom communication had been impossible during the war. Mme L'Evêque looked frail and ill, in a state of anxiety over her translation of *The Gypsy's Baby* stories (*L'Enfant de la Bohémienne*), which she had been working on for some while without being able to complete. And indeed she never did finish, dying in July 1947, only weeks after Rosamond's visit.

The Danish trip had been a success, the two men returning home in high spirits, as Laurie described when he wrote to Rosamond to report on Cecil's improved state of mind. She was particularly grateful to him for this, she told Laurie, as his 'sweet letter' had been far more informative than anything Cecil had sent her. 'When he's in a bad mental state his little missives are like so many shadows falling over me: they say nothing, mean nothing.' Relieved that Cecil had emerged from the worst of his depression, she knew that there was still a great deal of ground to be won; but in this she was constantly frustrated by her lover's fatalistic attitude,

which is rooted, I think, in his colossal instinct for self-preservation; and his habit of speaking in metaphors makes it seem awfully difficult to come to grips with reality. Directly I think we have established an emotional truth he splits it in half ... I am sick, SICK of hearing him say 'I can't face' – or 'daren't risk' – etc etc. I am sick of hearing him talk of his 'roots' – as if roots were always healthy, as if they didn't often bind & strangle – as if the flower & the fruit weren't the proof of a relationship.

Well aware that her recently established beachhead was resting on fragile foundations, she summoned Rex Warner and despatched him to Musbury with instructions to reason with Mary and stiffen Cecil's resolve.

Rex's mission was only partially successful. After two days of intensive discussion, it was decided that yet again a return to 'the old compromise' was the only possible solution, with Cecil going back to spending most of the holidays at Musbury, most of the school term at Little Wittenham. Rosamond was so thankful not to have lost him altogether that she accepted the conditions without a murmur. There was an emotional exchange of letters in which the two of them renewed their declarations of unswerving devotion, with Rosamond promising to abandon all thoughts of marriage, 'anyway for the moment', while Cecil swore that he would love her and be faithful to her for ever. 'He said, "However unsatisfactory it is for you, you've got somebody who'll never never never hurt you. And if you left me, I'd kill you and kill myself." And to me it was like having taken vows for life.'

The crisis, although painful, had been short-lived. By the end of July, after '4 very happy days' with Cecil at Wittenham, Rosamond felt completely restored, too relieved at the cessation of her anguish to wish to look beyond the immediate present. 'It is more wonderful than words can say to be with Cecil again,' she wrote to Laurie. 'As for the future, I mustn't brood about it. Some doors must be closed & locked, for ever, & maybe it's for the best.'

Now that the traumatic events of the past months were behind her, Rosamond felt able to return to her work. After *The Gypsy's Baby* stories and *The Ballad and the Source*, she was anxious to change direction, to move away from writing about children, about her own childhood as well as about Hugo's and Sally's, and to write 'a grown-up book about adults'. An idea for a novel had been in the back of her mind for a couple of years, and as the story was to be set in the West Indies she persuaded her publisher to advance her the air-fare to Jamaica, as she needed '[to crack] the crust off the old images & memories of 15 years ago'. Leaving London in an icy February, Rosamond arrived at the Richmond Hill Inn at Montego Bay for a 'heavenly' two weeks of swimming, sunbathing and some glamorous social life. 'I have plenty of male companions!' she wrote in a letter to Sally brimming with ecstatic descriptions of palm trees, orange groves, silver sands and crystal blue seas. Most attractive of these companions was the debonair Ian Fleming, whom Rosamond had known slightly on the London literary scene for some while: she claimed that it was she who encouraged him to take up the pen after reading an article of his in *Horizon*. Fleming was involved in a passionate love-affair with Ann Rothermere, whom he was soon to marry, but Lady Rothermere was in New York, and 'the Don Juan of the

Islands', as she sardonically referred to him, was no believer in sexual self-denial. He and Rosamond embarked on a brief romance, which Rosamond found intensely gratifying – he was delightful company '[and] did claim to be very fond of me', she later told Violet Hammersley. For Rosamond, the affair was well timed: she was far from home, in a dreamlike, exotic setting, and Fleming's admiration went a long way towards restoring her fragile self-confidence, so painfully undermined by Cecil's chronic inability to commit.

The Jamaican experience contributed to a short story published in 1956, and to a novel twenty years after that, but when Rosamond returned home, instead of drawing on her recent experience she decided to begin on a different project altogether, one which had grown insistent in her mind. 'It seems unlike anything I've ever tried before,' she wrote, 'though it is about sisters & family relationships.'

This letter was addressed to a new correspondent, the renowned art-historian Bernard Berenson. Berenson had written to congratulate Rosamond after reading *The Ballad and the Source*, to which his attention had been drawn by his old friend Sibyl Colefax, who was a friend also of Rosamond's. (Lady Colefax never failed to make time in her crowded diary for one weekend a year at Little Wittenham.) Intrigued, Berenson invited Rosamond to stay at I Tatti, his house at Settignano outside Florence, famous for its collection of Renaissance masters. Thrilled at having attracted the attention of such an illustrious scholar and excited at the prospect of a holiday in Italy, where she had never been, Rosamond gleefully accepted, asking if she might bring with her Cecil Day Lewis, with whom, Mr Berenson should know, she 'lived a devoted, as-much-married-as-possible life'. Berenson was agreeable to the sugges-tion; Cecil less so: he had been given 'blood-curdling accounts' by Maurice Bowra of what Berenson was like as a host, and he was distinctly apprehensive, as he frankly admitted. 'My own feeling is that, if B.B. is as painted by Maurice, seven days with him would be as intolerable as ten.' But Rosamond was not to be deflected. Keen to present her lover in the best possible light, she sent Berenson a copy of *Word Over All* and the recently published *The Poetic Image*, 'which seems to many others besides myself to go further into the nature and the springs of poetry than anything other . . . [*sic*], I was going to say since Coleridge'. Furthermore, '[Cecil] is very musical . . . has a ravishing singing voice . . . is a superb reader, & loves being called upon' – recommendations unlikely to have roused much enthusiasm in Berenson, accustomed, always, to taking centre stage himself. He was, however, too polite not to concur with Rosamond's breathless assurances that at Settignano 'we will have glorious séances'.

Rosamond and Cecil flew to Rome on 11 May 1948, where they spent a few enthralling days sightseeing before continuing by bus to Siena, then Florence, and thence to Settignano. The Villa I Tatti, high in the hills above Florence, is a converted fifteenth-century farmhouse approached by a long avenue of cypresses set with marble statuary, and surrounded by an extensive walled garden. The house was comfortable and efficiently run, thanks to the ceaseless efforts of Berenson's devoted, and much younger, woman companion, Nicky Mariano. The garden, designed before the First World War by Cecil Pinsent, was a famous showpiece and featured a series of terraces and parterres, lily ponds, a green garden, a wisteria walk, and a limonaia, or lemon house, where guests could sit and talk, sheltered from the wind or sun. Berenson himself was now in his eighties, but although slight and frail, he remained a commanding presence. His dapper, dandified figure was dressed with elegance and panache, by day in a pale grey suit with a flower in the buttonhole, sporting when out of doors a cloak or shawl and a cane, his dark eyes and neatly trimmed beard shaded by a wide-brimmed hat. Berenson had held court at I Tatti for nearly half a century, revered for his scholarship and expertise, the focus of a constant stream of admiring visitors, mainly from England and America, who came to pay homage to the sage of Settignano. Immensely vain, BB, as he was known, enjoyed his exalted position, enjoyed being treated, in the words of John Lehmann, as 'a mixture of the Oracle of Delphi and God the Father'. In his younger days an inveterate philanderer, he much preferred the company of women, his speciality in old age the conducting of a series of *amitiés amoureuses* with beautiful ladies whom he pampered and flattered with his exquisitely courteous attentions.

Predictably, BB and Rosamond were enchanted with each other, and instantly embarked on a delightful display of cultural pyrotechnics heavily spiced with amorous flirtatiousness. They soon discovered some interesting affinities, among them a similarity in family background,

Rosamond with her part-Jewish descent and New England relations pleased to find a parallel with Berenson's Jewish American upbringing. Within days the two of them were caught up in what Rosamond described as '[a] condition of the most agreeable in-loveness', a *coup de foudre*, they agreed. She revelled in his admiration and played up perfectly to her host as mentor, drinking in every word of his dazzling lectures on history and painting, and eagerly questioning him on his friendship with Edith Wharton, one of her literary idols. Day Lewis remained rather less impressed. He resented the deference paid to Berenson, resented the uninterrupted monologues at luncheon and dinner, and generally regarded his host as little more than a conceited poseur. With his own fondness for the limelight, he disliked being side-lined, and although BB obligingly remembered to request the advertised party-pieces – the reading aloud of a sonnet sequence, the singing of some Tom Moore ballads – Cecil was well aware that it was Berenson, not he, who was indisputably the cynosure.

Although Berenson's own reaction to Cecil was lukewarm – 'as a personality you attracted & interested me so much more than he did', he told Rosamond, adding that he had, however, enjoyed her lover's company 'in so far as possible for one who, like me, is so exquisitely aware of sex in woman, & so little in man' – he perceptively observed to a friend that in his view it was Day Lewis who was the more mature character, while Rosamond herself '[gives] the vague impression of a person not completely her own self'.

In her letter of thanks Rosamond told BB, 'Watching what you, and all of it, did to Cecil – apart from my own happiness – was one of the greatest achievements!' And indeed for all his reservations, the sojourn in Italy profoundly affected Cecil, who shortly after returning to England started work on *An Italian Visit*, a long verse sequence in which he gives expression to the many and varied facets of his experience, his intoxicated delight in the Tuscan countryside, his passionate response to the overwhelming beauty of Florence and Rome. The whole leads up to a long meditation, 'Elegy Before Death: At Settignano', dedicated to 'R.N.L.', in which the poet portrays his lover and analyses the nature of their love against a background of azaleas and lemon blossom, cicadas and nightingales:

... on a living night
When cypresses jetted like fountains of wine-warm air
Bubbling with fireflies, we going outside
In the palpitating dark to admire them,
One of the fireflies pinned itself to her hair.

Gradually, however, the sensuous idyll transmutes into something different, as the image of Rosamond as 'all woman' – 'Brutalizing, humanizing, / Pure flame, lewd earth was she, imperative as air / And weak as water, yes all women to me' – changes to ghost, shade, a wraith, and an ominous note of valediction is introduced:

... Again we are baffled who have sought
So long in a melting Now the formula
Of Always. There is no fast dye. Always! –
That is the word the sirens sing
On bone island ...

I imagine you really gone for ever. Clocks stop.
Clouds bleed. Flames numb. My world shrunk to an echoing
Memorial skull ...

But the completion of *The Italian Visit* was still in the future, and as Cecil worked slowly at his composition Rosamond basked in the prospect of her reflected glory. 'It is a major work, of immense richness freshness & variety,' she wrote proudly to BB in May 1949, exactly a year after their stay at I Tatti.

That same May 1949, almost exactly eight years after their affair began, Rosamond and Cecil went abroad again, this time to the south of France at the invitation of Somerset Maugham. Maugham had been an admirer of Rosamond's work from the publication of *Dusty Answer* in 1927, and had known her slightly ever since a summer shortly after the First World War when he, with his wife and daughter, had shared a house with the Lehmann family on the Isle of Wight. The Villa Mauresque on Cap Ferrat was 'beautiful & packed with treasures', Rosamond reported to Sally. There were no other guests, and the day's routine was expressly designed to suit the working writer. Every morning a maid brought Rosamond breakfast in bed, 'a glass of orange juice, a glass of yoghourt, coffee, toast, butter & jam. Then I slowly get up & go into another room where I find Cecil already working at his long poem – & I try *not* to stare out of the window but concentrate on writing a few pages of my novel. Then we go down about 12.30 & Willie appears from his writing room & we drink cocktails and eat a delicious lunch.' After a siesta, there was a bathe, and then Alan Searle, Maugham's companion, took the guests for a drive along the coast. The painter Graham Sutherland and his wife came to dinner, but most evenings were spent alone with their host and Alan Searle – the Duke and Duchess of Windsor and Greta Garbo, who had been promised, were discovered to be away, to Rosamond's regret. After a few days, work was abandoned as the weather grew warmer and hours were spent swimming and sun-bathing, interspersed with a couple of shopping expeditions to Nice. While Cecil was occupied elsewhere, Rosamond took the opportunity of confiding her anxieties over her troubled relationship, to which Maugham listened sympathetically. The visit was judged a success on both sides. 'Willie is a perfect host & delightful company: one of the most intelligent people I've ever known,' Rosamond told Sally, while Maugham after their departure wrote, 'You & Cecil are two of the pleasantest, most agreeable & sanest of all the guests I have ever had.'

If Rosamond had hoped that this idyllic interlude would effect any change in her situation she was to be disabused, as Cecil continued to shuttle tormentingly between wife and mistress. When in 1948 a new collection of his was published, *Poems 1943–1947*, Rosamond found they made painful reading, written as they were 'at the height of the emotional crisis'. She had, however 'to some extent accepted what cannot be mended or altered and we do manage to go on loving one another. I don't see how it could ever stop, now.' As Cecil needed to be in London for a couple of days a week for his work at Chatto & Windus, he and Rosamond took rooms in a house in Hampstead, before moving into a pleasant pied-à-terre in Charlotte Street belonging to Rex Warner's soon-to-be second wife, Barbara Rothschild.

Rex, tall, dark, 'hawk-faced', had been one of Cecil's closest friends since they had been Oxford contemporaries at Wadham. Like Cecil, Rex had first earned his living as a schoolmaster, since when he had published two highly acclaimed novels, *The Wild Goose Chase* and *The Aerodrome*. Married with three children, Rex had asked Rosamond to find him a house for the summer in or near Little Wittenham, which she did, delighted to have such congenial company so close at hand. During this period Rosamond at a party in Oxford introduced the Warners to the recently divorced Lady Rothschild, rich, restless, predatory, with a wicked wit and a lethal sexual magnetism. 'Barbara took everyone's man away,' one onlooker recalled. 'She was absolutely wonderful.' Rosamond had first met Barbara in 1946 at a dinner given by Dadie in Cambridge at the time of Cecil's Clark Lectures. 'Her reputation had gone before her, and I was told that she was a bad, bad girl and had endless lovers. I saw her eyes on Cecil, as if to say, "You're my next", [so] I was wary of her.' But Barbara having decided to spare Cecil, Rosamond grew devoted to her, admiring her charm and sophistication, and relishing her dry sense of humour and unconventional outlook.

A few weeks after the Oxford party, it became clear that Rex and Barbara had fallen in love, and in 1949, Rex having obtained a divorce, they married. Rosamond was pleased for both – although overcome by self-pity at the wedding, as she saw Barbara effortlessly granted what she herself had so far dismally failed to achieve. Cecil, on the other hand, was appalled, shocked at the break-up of his old friend's marriage and covertly hostile towards his new wife – a hostility he may have failed to conceal, for Barbara never cared for Cecil.

I never liked him. I didn't like anything about him, including his looks. He made me feel uncomfortable. I didn't trust him. Rex liked him enormously. They were rather tiresome together actually, always slapping each other on the back and going to pubs and talking about cricket. Rather self-consciously brotherly. He was very fond of Rex, and much more at ease with Rex than he would be with a woman. I don't think it was very easy for him to be friends with a woman.

However, both Cecil and Barbara maintained a good front, and during the renovations at Tackley, Barbara's big house outside Oxford, the newly married Warners stayed at the Manor House.

Meanwhile Rosamond continued to struggle with her novel, which had been occupying her sporadically since 1945. 'I am in the thick of it, chasing the flick of its tail through smoky caverns and black echoing tunnels, and half dreading to catch up with it and spear it, – and find, as ever, it's not the impressive animal I took it for,' she wrote to William Plomer at the beginning of 1949. By March she had finished the first half, her plan to complete the whole by the end of the year, but as always there were difficulties in keeping to a regular timetable. Most demanding was her work for John Lehmann Ltd, and in May she wrote to her brother, 'I am progressively getting into a state of internal crises & anxiety with a portion of the novel done and the worst still to face. If I could look forward to 6 months hard labour without interruptions I could finish it – but constantly having to break off to read & report for J.L. makes me terribly harrassed & overtired, on top of the drain of running this place & my correspondence etc.' John was sympathetic, and it was arranged that Julia Strachey, currently working as a reader for Secker & Warburg, should take over most of her duties. Julia, with whom Rosamond was once more on amicable terms, had married again, Tommy Tomlin having died over ten years earlier. Her second husband was the painter Lawrence Gowing, from whom during the war Rosamond had commissioned a portrait of Cecil. Gowing's shadowy, brooding portrayal had startled Rosamond. '"It's very *dark*," I said. "Yes," said Lawrence reflectively, "I think I've conveyed his ruthlessness."'

Social and domestic responsibilities were less easy to delegate. Beloved Mrs Wickens had been replaced by a series of married couples, each one needing to be time-consumingly trained in the ways of the household. And as at Ipsden, there were guests to stay almost every weekend, Laurie, Dadie and William Plomer among the most regular. Elizabeth Bowen was another welcome visitor, friendly relations having been restored since the débâcle over Goronwy more than ten years ago. Always an admirer of Elizabeth's work, Rosamond had been enormously impressed by her latest novel, *The Heat of the Day*, and had written several ecstatic letters of congratulation. 'Elizabeth, darling Elizabeth,' began one, 'I've never written this sort of letter to any writer before . . . [The book] is embedded deep deep in my consciousness: an overpowering experience for which I am eternally grateful.' Not only did she herself identify strongly with the heroine, Stella, but she saw in Stella's son the double of Hugo, while her traitor/lover, Robert, bore, she thought, a resemblance to Cecil.

When Cecil was away, Rosamond talked obsessively about her

situation, bemoaning Cecil's failure to leave his wife, and endlessly asking for advice on how to make him marry her. Dadie recalled one typical weekend, when he, Maurice Bowra and Barbara Warner were at the Manor House, and

> there was a great discussion about her whole relationship with Cecil. . . . In a way Cecil was a cruel fellow and a feeble fellow. I was devoted to him, but he was a cruel man really, and a vain man and highly sexy. . . . We all said exactly the same thing: 'Half a loaf is better than no bread. For God's sake, hang on to Cecil who adores you, and with whom you'd got so much in common. . . . Let him do what he likes, but enjoy the half you've got.' She paid no attention.

It may have been after this occasion that Bowra, exasperated, told Edith Sitwell that 'if she [Rosamond] had *one* more affair, he was either going into the lunatic asylum or was going to shoot himself, because he couldn't stand being kept up all night while R. examined her and everybody else's motives'.

Of the family, Helen and John came frequently to Wittenham, usually also taking the opportunity to visit their mother. Alice, having finally admitted in her mid-seventies that Fieldhead was too big to manage on her own, was now living just outside Beaconsfield in a smaller establishment, Little Fieldhead, looked after by a housekeeper. John as head of the family dutifully supervised her affairs, Alice taking pride in his reputation as a distinguished man of letters, his louche private life neither suspected nor revealed. In her eyes he was everything that was honourable and fine. The same could not be said of her daughters, Rosamond twice divorced and living in sin with a married man, and Helen now also divorced, Mounty Bradish-Ellames having left her for another woman. Helen, who had spent most of the war stationed near Salisbury working as a driver for the American army, had behaved with dignity and restraint throughout all her troubles, moving to London where Rosamond found her a position with the Society of Authors, a job at which she proved herself outstandingly proficient. Her boss, the same Denys Kilham Roberts with whom Cecil had had such trouble on *Orion*, said of her that it was impossible to believe Mrs Bradish-Ellames did not have a degree in law, so great was her knowledge and her application.

But it was Beatrix who was the cause of most concern. After the war, Beatrix, who in 1944 had served a term as president of Equity, the actors' union, had continued to make a moderately successful living. In 1946 she took over as director-producer at the Midland Theatre in Coventry, then in 1947 joined the Shakespeare Memorial Company for a season at Stratford, during which she played four leading roles, Portia, Viola, Isabella and the Nurse in *Romeo and Juliet*. But soon after this, offers of work started to dry up. High-principled and uncompromising, Bea since her Marxist days in Vienna had moved even further to the left, joining the Communist Party and sitting on the editorial board of the *Daily Worker*. Intractable political beliefs coupled with an open distaste for most contemporary productions resulted in a general reluctance on the part of producers to employ her. Even John, who had travelled at least some of the way along the same political path, was appalled by what he described as her 'violent half-baked fanaticism', worried by 'the terrible harm Peg is doing herself and her career with her blind continuing adherence to Communism & the D[aily] W[orker]'. He analysed her conversion as a result partly 'of her struggle to get work in a corrupt theatre world ... & partly the frustration of her personal life'. And indeed Beatrix's personal life could fairly be described as disastrous, a number of unsatisfactory affairs, with both men and women, one culminating in a terminated pregnancy. From this time on, her strong maternal instincts were directed towards a series of dreadful little dogs, loathed by family, friends and colleagues alike.

With long periods 'resting', Beatrix spent much of her time at Little Wittenham, where the large barn to one side of the house had been converted into a comfortable dwelling for her. Although John after lunch one day with 'Peg' in her barn was disturbed to see her 'looking so lined and without bloom – and without work', Beatrix loved the place. Her presence was a delight to Rosamond, who was devoted to her sister, even if, as Barbara Warner observed, '[Bea was] the exact opposite of Ros ... very amusing, very astringent, not at all feminine, no nonsense. They got on in a way very well. Ros used to get rather querulous about Bea, and Bea would get rather fierce about Ros, but it was all affectionate. They were so different, but they had an unbreakable bond.'

The elder sister was amused and touched by the younger's passionate absorption in the local fauna. 'She is entirely obsessed by the Natural Phenomena of Country Life,' Rosamond told John,

> the latest being the Great Bat Saga. Anything up to 200 bats have made their home in among the joists of the Barn. As dusk falls, they begin to emerge with maniac chatterings & squeakings from a minute aperture in the wall, under a beam. They drop down one after another like parachutists at the word of command. Last night we counted 121 before it got too dark to see. She woke me at 4 a.m. this morning to watch them return, in a whipping wild circling cloud & pop in again, one after another, like ghosts at cockcrow.

Beatrix was far and away the favourite aunt of both Hugo and Sally, Hugo in particular relishing what her old friend Christopher Isherwood described as her 'gallows humour'. Indeed they got on so well that Rosamond always suspected Hugo loved his tomboy aunt more than he did his mother. With Beatrix, Hugo knew it was he, not Sally, who was the favourite, and it was an enormous source of pleasure to him having her in residence while he was at home during the holidays. But in 1947 Hugo had left Eton and almost immediately received his call-up, sent for training in Northern Ireland before being posted to Kenya as an officer in the King's African Rifles. 'This is the first time it's really come over me that his boyhood is over, along with my ability to protect him in any way,' Rosamond lamented. In Kenya, as Hugo laconically described it to his anxious mother, 'My job is to fly with a platoon to wherever the palsied Kenya Government have got the jim-jams worst.' Although he liked his fellow conscripts, peacetime soldiering bored him and he counted the days till he could leave the army. 'We are no longer in a state of emergency, and Africa has quietened down without enlisting the services of that undoubtedly capable, though somewhat lethargic young officer, Ensign Philipps,' he wrote in March 1949. 'One realises that any tribesman from the reserve could do one's job and enjoy it! I feel like throwing away my musket and shouting "I will soldier no more."' Cambridge was the next step, and to his joy King's College agreed to apply for his early release so that he might attend the summer course for ex-servicemen prior to starting as an undergraduate in the autumn of 1949. Hugo returned home thin and sunburnt, much more mature and self-possessed than the schoolboy who had left two years before. '[It's] most peculiar to realise that I produced this handsome giant who teases me and coaxes me and treats me with offhand affection,' Rosamond wrote to Berenson. 'I feel so detached from him – and yet if he is ill when he's away, I know at once: the Cord tugs immediately.'

Sally, who hero-worshipped her good-looking brother, was still at school. During term, Rosamond missed her painfully – 'As usual,' she wrote to Mrs Hammersley after the end of the summer holidays, '[I] am hating her vacant chaotic bedroom' – and she took every opportunity to visit her daughter at Cranborne Chase, to which, aged 12, Sally had transferred, having become unhappy at Westonbirt. (During her last term at Westonbirt, the summer of 1946, she had written desperately to her mother, 'I am *not* happy here. I am not the only one either, many people hate it here (and I don't blame them either as it's just like a prison). . . . Please, PLEASE don't think this is just a faze.') At 15, Sally was as cheerful, pretty and plump as she had been when a little girl. Her stepsister, Moorea, who saw Sally on her visits to Wogan at Butler's Farm, said of her, 'Sally looked wonderful, with the most divine complexion, honey-coloured, breath-taking it was, and this funny disposition, always laughing and fun. . . . [She] was very tall and big and very clumsy: if Sally was going up or down stairs you could hear it.' Sally's letters home, still addressed to 'My darling, darlingest Mummy', were in many respects much the same as before, with pleas for cake and chocolate, concern for the welfare of her pony, Jack Frost, and earnest requests to convey her love, first to various pets, then to Cecil and Laurie. She was a loving, if not a pliant character, and she could be obstinate and uncooperative when she chose. 'There was a granite streak in her,' Rosamond wrote. 'The capacity she had for developing stubbornness, for instance, was a family joke: Miss Resista was one of my nicknames for her.' To her mother's pride, Sally was musical, played the piano and violin, and possessed a beautiful singing voice, which led to prominent participation in school concerts and recitals. Despite a lack of parental example, Sally had recently become religious, and just before her fifteenth birthday was christened at Little Wittenham, her godparents her cousin Nina Drury and Compton Mackenzie. Mackenzie had become as good a friend to Sally as to her mother, who loved him for 'his energy, his humorous yet humanitarian, comedic view of life ... his loathing & mockery of pomposity ... his passion for gardening, music, libraries'. Rosamond was sympathetic to her daughter's beliefs, but as she explained to Mackenzie, himself a Roman Catholic, 'I myself hold no dogmas of theological doctrines of any sort – indeed I am an agnostic, believing only that Love might mean God, or god might mean Love.'

By her mid-teens Sally's interests had naturally begun to change, and requests for lipstick, big-band records and dance frocks were regularly posted home. 'In case you are wondering, I also want an evening dress and an accordion for Xmas,' she wrote to her mother in December 1949. 'Don't you think black net over some other colour taffeta might be nice?' Boys, too, were becoming a major preoccupation. Boys from the nearby public school, Bryanston, were occasionally bussed over to Cranborne Chase for carefully monitored social functions, and Sally confided to her mother with a touching openness her hopes and misgivings over various Andrews and Nigels. To celebrate her fifteenth birthday in January 1949 Rosamond gave a dance for forty teenagers at the Manor House. 'I wish you could have been there to see the Budding Grove,' she wrote to Compton Mackenzie, 'and especially your goddaughter, in flowing silvery-white net with an off-the-shoulder fichu, looking quite heart-wringingly dreamy and gentle and peach-faced. She is going to be such a beauty in another two years.' Of course Sally had her anxieties – extreme short-sightedness, a continuing struggle to lose weight, and in particular the looming menace of School Certificate – but by nature she was an optimist who enjoyed her life and was rarely worried or depressed for long. 'She is a heavenly creature,' Rosamond told Berenson, '& a Child of Fortune (so far).'

During the months when Hugo was at Cambridge and Sally back at school, Rosamond enjoyed an increasingly crowded social life mid-week in London, with Cecil in attendance as often as possible. 'Oh you are so lucky going to all these parties,' Sally wrote enviously. 'I want to meet all these distinguished people.' Chief among the party-givers was brother John, who at his house in Egerton Crescent saw it as an important part of his role as literary impresario to entertain regularly, bringing together writers from all over the country, as well as visitors from Europe and America.

273

It was through John that Rosamond had achieved a long-held ambition to meet the Sitwells. She had encountered Osbert briefly during the war at committee meetings of the Society of Authors, and both Osbert and Edith had written admiring letters about *The Ballad and the Source*. At one point Osbert, using Denys Kilham Roberts as emissary, had suggested Rosamond should come to stay at Renishaw, the Sitwell family house in Derbyshire, but when her excited acceptance was conveyed to him, he changed his mind. '[I] don't want her here,' he told Kilham Roberts. With Edith, on the other hand, Rosamond was soon on the most affectionate terms. 'I fell flat for Edith Sitwell: she is glorious!' she told John after their first meeting in 1944, and the older woman was gratified by the younger's appreciation of her poetry, and in any case well disposed towards a sister of John Lehmann, who for years had been a loyal promoter of her work. Rosamond and Cecil lunched and dined several times at Edith's club, the Sesame, easily the most memorable of these occasions the dinner given there after the Wigmore Hall poetry reading in 1946. 'Dylan Thomas & his wife both arrived wildly drunk, fought & hit each other, & altogether presented a painful problem to Edith & all the distinguished guests, as they could neither be disposed of nor tamed,' Rosamond related. 'I shall never forget Mrs Thomas shoving a drunken elbow into her ice cream, then offering the elbow to T. S. Eliot & telling him to "lick it off".'

But friendship never could run smooth with someone as notoriously thin-skinned as Edith. In September 1949 there was a coolness after the publication of an article by Roy Campbell in *Poetry Review* attacking the poets of the 1930s, Day Lewis among them. When Rosamond sprang to Cecil's defence, Edith wrote contemptuously to Osbert of 'Rosamond's whining'. '*Really!*' she went on. 'It is the only harsh criticism any of these little pipsqueak poets have ever had – I mean softy Cecil and so forth.' She was further incensed by what she interpreted as a slighting reference made 'at my own luncheon table' by William Plomer who, also defending Cecil, had had the unspeakable impertinence to rate Cecil's poetry higher than her own. 'I shall not see Plomer again. After all, if I have to refuse to be defended, in order to please *all* the men Rosamond had dossed down with, my life would be a little difficult.' Shortly after this, some uncharitable remarks of Edith's about Rosamond's work got back to her, but Rosamond, recognising the vulnerability and kindness behind the forbidding façade, refused to allow it to damage the relationship. 'Faintly startled & also faintly depressed at Edith's reported comments on my work,' she wrote to John. 'When I think of her *dripping* letter, unsolicited, about *The Ballad* . . . [sic] Ah me! . . . [sic] which of us, though, would come out unscathed if our comments about our friends & their works & their characters were to see the light of day.'

It was William Plomer who was responsible for Rosamond's befriending another woman poet, Lilian Bowes-Lyon. Only six years older than Rosamond, Lilian, when they started corresponding in 1945, was already seriously ill, having had both legs amputated as a result of gangrene brought on by diabetes. Rosamond admired Lilian's brave spirit as much as she did her work, visiting her regularly at her flat in Brompton Square, and confiding in her about her troubles with Cecil. She was deeply moved by Lilian's stoicism in coping with the ferocious pain which accompanied her physical decline. 'Lilian, by her example even more than by what she said, helped to keep me in a "state of grace" when the difficulties, sadnesses and frustrations of Cecil's & my relationship threatened our love,' Rosamond wrote soon after Lilian's death in July 1949. She thanked William Plomer for giving her 'the precious and heart-rending experience of her friendship', and for months she kept a couple of Lilian's letters in her handbag.

One afternoon a visitor arrived at Lilian's flat just as Rosamond was leaving. Laurens van der Post, 'a kind of T. E. Lawrence of this war', was also an old friend of Plomer's, like Plomer born and brought up in South Africa. He was immediately struck by Rosamond's appearance. 'She looked so beautiful . . . a quite lovely, quite serene woman.' Rosamond on her side was greatly taken with van der Post, impressed by his sensitivity and charm, and by his blue-eyed, fresh-faced good looks. 'Didn't you think Laurens van der Post a tremendous cup of tea?' she asked Violet Hammersley soon afterwards. 'Ame bien née, if ever there was one.' Van der Post had adored Lilian Bowes-Lyon, and his grief over her death created an immediate bond with Rosamond. An even stronger link was that he had known Cecil since before the war, when Laurens was farming in the west country and Cecil, then a schoolmaster at Cheltenham, often used to come and stay. Rosamond, Plomer, Laurens and his wife, Ingaret, dined together, and the van der Posts were invited to Little Wittenham. This marked the beginning of what Rosamond was later to describe as a 'long, strange and deeply valued friendship', fonder and more emotional perhaps on her side than on Laurens's, to whom for the rest of her life she was to look increasingly for guidance and support. Much later she wrote to him of the early days of their relationship, 'I already knew . . . of the prolonged unimaginable ordeal which you had undergone in Japanese prison camps. I expected to feel the kind of awe and tension one is bound to sense in the presence of one who has endured intolerable suffering . . . but far more potent was the impression you gave of spiritual strength, sanity, humour, wisdom and integrity.'

It was van der Post who described the Lehmann/Day Lewis partnership as '[an] almost fairytale intellectual marriage . . . a very fine, good-looking young poet "married" to a very beautiful and remarkable novelist'; and there was no doubt that both participants enjoyed being so regarded in the eyes of literary London. But backstage all was far from well, and there were ugly tensions and increasingly stormy scenes. 'All my adult life I have been convinced that I am a man more scened against than scening,' Cecil wrote, 'and that, in spite of my moodiness and occasional fits of rage, I am really a person of most equable temperament.' And it was true that most of the quarrels were initiated by Rosamond, ever insecure; yet it was Cecil whose behaviour goaded her to frenzy, particularly over his interest in and attraction for the opposite sex. Cecil's was a highly sexual nature, and it is probable that by now the physical relationship with Rosamond had largely diminished, with the inevitable effect of making Rosamond more suspicious and more accusatory about other women. In a Nicholas Blake novel published in 1953, Cecil appears to be recalling this untranquil period with Rosamond when he writes, 'The truth is made for woman, not woman for the truth. One wouldn't mind that, if only they didn't make it so infernally difficult for men to be truthful with them: one's always being tempted to soften or sweeten or pare down or exaggerate the facts for them, so as to satisfy their vanity or avoid wounding their quivering sensibilities or bolster up their perpetually-crumbling egos.'

From time to time Cecil accepted invitations to give poetry readings at girls' schools, and his romantic susceptibility to maidens in uniform had long been a running joke between them. Now, however, even this amiable topic had turned sour. In April 1948 Cecil after one of his school visits wrote to Rosamond, 'It is sad to think you should have seen sinister jabs & pouncings in my reference to the Schoolgirl with Plaits – it was meant to be light, gay, amusing, with a gentle side-glance at my own well-known obsession with Sxxxxl-gxxxx . . . I shall have to confine my letters to fact, if tiny little jokes reach your end swollen in to great aggressions!' Not all their quarrels were conducted in private. One evening when Rosamond and Cecil had been invited to dine by Hester Chapman and her banker husband Ronnie Griffin, a bitter exchange was witnessed. 'Dinner was for 8.0,' recalled the Griffins' other guest, the writer Elizabeth Jenkins, 'and by half past eight they hadn't come, and Ronnie who'd had a cracking day at Hoare's Bank wanted his dinner. They did then come, and sat down, and Cecil Day Lewis was looking absolutely green – it was more than pallor – and he'd hardly taken up his soup spoon when Rosamond said, "We've been arguing as to how much men *lie* to women." Cecil just put his spoon down and said, "My *God*, I thought we'd gone through all that!"'

More and more it began to be noticed how drawn Day Lewis appeared, his complexion 'almost malarial', his thick hair 'lustreless . . . [and] donkey-coloured'. Cecil's looks quickly reflected his emotional state, and at this period, as he himself admitted, 'I was never long free from the sense of guilt, oppressive with disaster like the atmosphere before a storm that will not break.' Now the storm was about to break, and the premonition of disaster was etched on Cecil's face, plain for all to see. As early as January 1948, when he took part in a BBC poetry programme, *Time for Verse*, his fellow reader, Jill Balcon, noticed that he appeared 'like a ghost, ravaged and tortured'; and John Lehmann in his diary for August 1949 described Cecil at a tête-à-tête luncheon '[looking] more ravaged-faced than ever – more like a Victorian clergyman whose inner peace had been forever destroyed by the publication of Darwin'.

Before long Rosamond's ill-defined unease became specifically focused. Cecil, who was much in demand for poetry programmes on the wireless, over the past months had worked with and come to know Jill Balcon, a young actress who had been one of the early members of the Apollo Society. Rosamond, curious, suggested that Cecil bring this new colleague of his round for a drink so that she could meet her, but the proposal had failed to find favour. '"Oh, I don't think you'd like her," he said in a very off-hand way.'

277

Jill, in her early twenties and ravishingly pretty, with dark hair, huge dark eyes and a slender, sexy figure, was the daughter of the film producer Sir Michael Balcon, head of Ealing Studios. She had first seen Cecil at the age of 12 when he had judged a verse-speaking competition at her school, Roedean. 'He was', she recalled 'the most wonderful-looking man I'd ever seen in my life.' In July 1949 they had both taken part in the English Festival of Spoken Verse in London, and the following month Cecil, up from the country on his own, and without mentioning it to Rosamond, had taken Jill out to dinner. In September Cecil went to Venice with Spender and Auden for a PEN conference,[6] and soon after his return took part in an Apollo Society performance at the *Sunday Times* Book Exhibition at Grosvenor House. Cecil's elder son, Sean, awaiting call-up to the RAF, was present, and for the first time was introduced to both his father's 'other' women, to Rosamond and also to Jill, who kept discreetly in the background. 'There was', said Sean, 'a puzzling contrast between the warm responses of Cecil and Jill together, and the matter-of-fact calm which appeared to mark the relationship of Cecil and Rosamond.' A week later Rosamond invited Sean out to dinner, 'a simple, green, callow, ridiculously innocent creature . . . [who] never drew breath all evening'. Sean for his part was overwhelmed by her womanly beauty, her kindness and charm. 'She was obviously courting me, I now see,' he said later, 'and I fell completely for her.' She questioned him closely as to the cause of his father's persisting melancholia: it was probably, they concluded, no more than a natural apprehension over Sean's imminent call-up.

The next Rosamond heard about Jill was that Miss Balcon was reported to be very keen for the great Jacob Epstein, whom she knew, to sculpt a head of Cecil, and that there was to be a dinner for the two men to meet, to which Rosamond to her extreme displeasure was not invited. 'Didn't you say you were living with me? and that we didn't ever go out without each other?' she demanded of Cecil. 'I was froissée, and thought, "Oh, she's after him," but women were often after him – especially fawning schoolgirl fans.'

On the day of the Epstein dinner, Rosamond went to Cambridge to

---

[6] It was at this conference in Venice that the famous photograph, so often reproduced, was taken of Day Lewis, Spender and Auden together.

see Hugo, planning to take a late train back and arrive home about 11 p.m. Before leaving, she said to Cecil, '"MIND you're back! . . . *Swear* to me you'll be back." And he said, "Yes, of course."' In the train on the return journey she had a sudden presentiment that something terrible was about to happen.

But I thought, he'll be back in the flat when I get home and I shall know it's all right. I thought it was just jealousy and suspicion that had caused it. When I got back, he wasn't there. He came in looking very sheepish about an hour later. I was very cross, sulked, said, 'You promised!' 'Well, I couldn't help it,' he said. 'As it is I left long before the end.' Which was true. 'But you broke your promise to me.' 'Yes, I did.' It was a sort of lovers' quarrel, but not a bad one at all. I said, 'What about this famous head? When are you going to start?' 'It wasn't mentioned.' 'OH!' I thought to myself, 'that little so-and-so, Jill Balcon! She's after him!' I think I said, 'Miss Balcon's after you,' and he said, 'Oh, nonsense.' 'Of course she is!' 'You know I could never think of anybody but you.' So it faded away. I really don't remember having any conscious feeling of danger at all.

Towards the end of 1949, Sally in letters from school began excitedly to discuss plans for the celebration of her sixteenth birthday on 14 January. Instead of a party on the day itself, Rosamond had decided on something rather more special a few days later, an evening of music and poetry performed by three members of the Apollo Society, Cecil, his old friend and colleague Peggy Ashcroft, and the pianist Angus Morrison. Cecil had recently completed his long work, *An Italian Visit* – 'At last I've written something worthy of you,' he had told Rosamond – and no doubt she hoped he would read a passage from it.

As usual Cecil had been at Musbury over Christmas, he and Mary celebrating their twenty-first wedding anniversary on 27 December. His letters to Rosamond at Wittenham were 'very very brief and depressed'. When he arrived at the Manor House on the 30th it was instantly apparent that he was still locked deep into one of his black-ice moods, indifferent alike to Rosamond's pleading and recriminations. She for her part was in despair at her total inability to reach him. 'I thought, this is getting worse and worse. He *can't* go on like this, he must realise the only hope is for him to break away and come to me and make it permanent, and ultimately be married.' Laurens and Ingaret van der Post were staying for New Year's Eve, and after dinner the four of them went out into the garden. As midnight struck, the church bells began pealing all along the valley, and Rosamond, moved, took Cecil's arm. 'Isn't it wonderful to be together at this moment?' she asked him. But Cecil said nothing, and Laurens noticed him flinch, like an animal. '[It was] a spasm almost ... I was terribly perturbed by it, and I said to Ingaret, "There's something wrong."'

The next day the van der Posts left, and Cecil went for a few days to Musbury and then up to London. Here he was followed by a letter from Rosamond accusing him of coldness and irritability, and warning him that he must, despite his depression, put on a good face for Sally's party. 'I promise you I'll do my very best to sustain you through Sunday's ordeal,' he replied,

> be just as loving as I know how, not irritable (why should I be irritable? I'm depressed & nervous before these things, but surely not necessarily irritable), not cold; & I'll do my best not to be abstracted. And you must do the same ... I need to be given confidence & the feeling of being loved: and one way to give confidence to each other is not to remind of past failure & warn against their repetition.
>
> Well, all this sounds as if we were to face a horde of furious fancies instead of a pleasant group of your neighbours, all longing to see you & willing to be entertained by the Apollo troupe. It will be lovely, I promise you. I shall read & sing for you alone, remove your headache beforehand, fill you with love, dislodge the poisoned dart, & all will be well.

In the event the occasion was a triumph. Besides Hugo and Sally and friends from the neighbourhood, Rex and Barbara, with whom Peggy Ashcroft was staying, came over from Tackley, and Isaiah Berlin and Maurice Bowra from Oxford. The performers were magnificent, the audience enthusiastic. Only Rosamond knew that something was wrong. '[Cecil] was very gay but in a nervous, exaggerated sort of way ... [he]

looked white and as if there was some extraordinary internal struggle going on . . . I couldn't take my eyes off him. And I was frightened. I also developed the most appalling headache I've ever had in my life, and I felt he was giving me this.' The others, however, noticed nothing, and the evening was judged a great success.

The party was on Sunday 17 January 1950. On the following day Cecil went up to London as usual to his office at Chatto & Windus. From there he wrote Rosamond a long letter, telling her that he had fallen in love with Jill Balcon, and although he still loved his 'darling Rose' he had irrevocably made up his mind to leave her for Jill. 'I remember it said, "I can feel all your pain, every fibre of my being is conscious of your terrible pain, but I'm going to do it."' Rosamond was so shocked that she instantly threw the letter into the fire. 'I couldn't believe it.' Immediately she sat down and wrote him a brief note demanding to see him at once. 'In no sense did I say I understand. I was totally incredulous, telling myself this must be a form of madness. I had to accept the fact that he had been to bed with Jill, and I thought, well, ten years, it's been ten years[7] and it's quite natural, this kind of infatuation.' Cecil agreed to come the following evening, and next day in the afternoon Rosamond took Sally to the film *Bicycle Thieves* as a treat before going back to school. 'For some reason everything in the film was about stealing and betrayal, and I kept thinking to myself, my life has been stolen.' In the evening, Cecil arrived and the two of them talked for hours, but nothing Rosamond said seemed to make the slightest impression, Cecil, with a show of what appeared to be 'diabolical indifference', agreeing trance-like with every accusation. 'What about *me*?' she almost screamed at him. 'Oh, I can't think of *you*,' he replied matter-of-factly. 'I'm thinking of *her* now.' It was, Rosamond recalled, like talking to a total stranger. '[He] said he was now perfectly happy & had "forgotten me almost completely." When he spoke of the girl his voice showed a sort of satisfaction & tenderness. . . . He looked like a murderer. It was exactly as if you'd seen someone you'd liked and trusted split apart and a stranger emerging. Even the eyes, the colour of them, black, dark.

'And then he went away. Packed his suitcase and went back to Jill.'

[7] In fact their affair lasted just short of nine years.

Immediately Rosamond telephoned Barbara Warner at Wittenham with the devastating disclosure, but Barbara already knew, as Cecil had confided in Rex, telling him that he felt wonderful, that his life with Jill was a rebirth, a renewal, that he had never been happier. At the flat in Charlotte Street, Rosamond was in bed, unable to stop weeping when Cecil looked in at midday to collect one or two things he had forgotten. 'I was in floods of tears, and he kissed me quite affectionately and said, "Oh poor you!" I said, "You don't mean it! You *can't* mean it!" And he said, "Oh yes, yes, I do."' Desperately clinging to her conviction that this was no more than some powerful but short-lived infatuation, she begged him to promise that he would not see Jill again for three months, a period long enough, surely, to bring him to his senses. Amicably, Cecil agreed. He stayed for a few minutes more, and then he left.

The following day Rosamond returned to Little Wittenham, where she at once wrote to Mary Day Lewis to enlist her support. Cecil was already at Musbury, but had said nothing to Mary of his affair with Jill. He was surprised to discover, when after four days he broached the subject, that his wife, informed by Rosamond, knew all about it. Mary refused to give him the divorce he asked for. At the end of February Rosamond came up to London to meet Mary for the first time. They spent an afternoon at the Mayfair Hotel analysing Cecil's 'appalling brainstorm' and discussing tactics. Rosamond insisted that Cecil must be got to a psychiatrist, to which Mary, who saw not madness in her husband's behaviour but a simple off-with-the-old-love, on-with-the-new, somewhat sceptically concurred. Determined to comply with any reasonable demand from either of his wronged women, Cecil agreed to go to 'a Wimpole Street quack', but refused a second session, returning to Brimclose where he sat all day silent and remote, passively waiting out his three-month exile from Jill. After some weeks of this both Rosamond and Mary realised that the forcibly imposed separation was achieving nothing and lifted the ban.

On 20 March Rosamond at Wittenham asked Cecil to come once more to see her, ostensibly so that he might pack up his belongings, but desperately hoping she could persuade him to change his mind. It was a terrible few hours, Rosamond beside herself with grief and fury. But Cecil was no more approachable this time than before. He came, he stayed to supper, he listened politely while she ranted and implored, but his face remained shuttered. He was far away, detached, and 'it was exactly as if I didn't exist any more'. Finally he picked up his suitcase and asked her to drive him to the station. '"No, I won't," I said. I rang up for a local taxi and there wasn't one, so he went off after dinner and walked, quite a long walk, to the village and got a taxi there and drove to London in the taxi.'

11

'A Farewell to the World of Love'

To Rosamond, Cecil's defection was incomprehensible. Distraught, she continued to insist that he must be in a psychopathic state and that his passion for Jill Balcon was no more than a passing infatuation, a chimera, that he was suffering from a mental aberration from which with professional help he would in time emerge. Her agony and rage were terrifying to witness. To Dadie she wrote, 'This hasn't been, in any way, a decent human being, but a thing rising up from some hideous underworld in him that I never suspected.' Cecil was 'a destructive, death-cold character', who was 'reeling about morally & emotionally like a drunken person: most bewildering & distasteful. If ever he comes out of this . . . & I dare say he will – he will find scorched earth indeed. . . . God damn all suffering cripples.' Never for one moment did she allow herself to consider that some of the responsibility might be hers. 'If it turns out for the worst I shall be cruelly wounded but intact, because I shall have nothing tricky, cruel or treacherous to reproach myself with. His suffering will be different, – but after a while I shall no longer care about what becomes of him.' The most vituperative language was reserved for Jill Balcon, this 'grotesque little piece of human material . . . this ghastly, over-emotional, fawning creature who unrolled herself like a spaniel at his feet . . . and once he'd been to bed with her he called it "renewal", like a crazy, idiotic, stupid old man.' Mary Day Lewis, on the other hand, previously so despised and resented, was suddenly seen to

284

possess the most sterling qualities. 'His unfortunate wife & I are now standing shoulder to shoulder,' Rosamond stoutly declared, telling John that 'She sees it all as I do, and wants my help, as I need hers'. Mary's perspective was not quite the same as Rosamond's, however, her understanding of the situation considerably more realistic. 'Rosamond and I got on perfectly well I think. . . . But I just wondered which of us was going to have Cecil if we did get him back.'

John was one of a number of Rosamond's circle who was alarmed by the obdurate nature of her self-deception. 'She cannot believe that anyone could fall out of love with her, or feel that the possessiveness was too overwhelming,' he wrote in his diary. 'She is having to pretend that C. is out of his mind & can be restored by psychiatrists (of all people!) and an alliance of two noble women determined to rescue & stand by him – R. & C.'s wife (of all alliances!). It is tragic to see her feeding so recklessly on illusions.' He, like most of Rosamond's close friends, had been aware for some time that disaster was approaching. Barbara Warner, for instance, was surprised that the affair had endured as long as it had. In her view Rosamond was impossibly starry-eyed about men: 'she saw love as something absolutely perfect . . . [and] expected always to be courted'; insecure and insatiably demanding, she put constant pressure on Cecil to provide her with proofs of love. 'Men hate that: they can't take it,' said Barbara. Laurie, who had been an integral part of the *ménage*, understood that Cecil had been confronted with an impossible dilemma: wishing neither to marry Rosamond nor return to Mary, '[his] only solution was to . . . betray both . . . and Jill had given him the way of escape . . . When Cecil told me, he just leant back in his chair and gazed at the ceiling and said, "I feel so happy." The tension was broken. Brutally. He was a murderer, to use tabloid terms, and neither Mary nor Rosamond ever got over it.' And there was another consideration, said Laurie. Jill, unlike the older women, possessed 'a secret lechery . . . [and] she danced the dance of the seven veils through the gauzy chambers of his dreams'.

A particularly humiliating aspect for the jilted mistress was the lack of containment. Cecil's abandoning her had dealt a severe blow to Rosamond's pride, and at first she had hoped to keep the truth about the rupture quiet until, as must surely happen, Cecil returned. But suddenly it seemed that everyone was talking about it. She and Cecil had been too much in the public eye, their affair too widely known, and she herself too free with details of the various dramas and her volatile emotional state for the crisis to be kept to her intimates. Sibyl Colefax, although on her death-bed, was gamely issuing daily bulletins, Edith Sitwell went to the trouble of personally calling on John Lehmann for the latest news ('O I must tell Osbert!'), while Maurice Bowra with wicked wit was gleefully dining out on his recently coined nickname for Rosamond, 'the Meringue-Outang'. Even Bernard Berenson, who adored her, recorded in his diary that 'this marvel of a woman' was 'predatory, a Valkyrie . . . and I am glad that she and I met when I was beyond danger of walking into her parlour'.

Part of Rosamond's unhappiness was displaced on to Sally, to whom was attributed a grief almost as inconsolable as her own. Rarely was an opportunity missed to conjure up the heart-wrenching image of the young girl's anguish. 'Sally has taken it very hard, weeps every day. That is one of the worst things for me,' Rosamond wrote to Dadie, while Laurens van der Post was told, 'It is hard – for me – to feel the crime is to be forgiven when I see Sally weeping, unable to swallow the poison or to vomit it out.' The actuality was rather less harrowing. Sally, while undoubtedly shocked at Cecil's departure and distressed by what she saw of its effect on her mother, was far too absorbed in her own busy life to be disturbed for long. Although as a little girl she had become very attached to Cecil, in the last few years she had seen much less of him: he was nearly always away at Musbury during the holidays, at Aldworth or Wittenham when she herself was at school. Her letters home, sunny as ever, make very clear that although tenderly concerned for her parent, she herself was far more interested in plans for the immediate future. 'I'm afraid the holidays must have been an awful strain on you, Mummy,' she wrote at the beginning of the summer term of 1950. '[But] I did have a lovely time inspite of all.' She then proceeds to chatter on about her school work, the state of her tennis game, her new office as prefect, and the encouraging news that she has at last managed to lose weight, concluding, 'At the moment I'm living for half-term and Henley . . .'

For Rosamond another cause for resentment was the damaging effect of Cecil's betrayal on her work. Brooding bitterly over the past nine years, she began to resent more and more the time and effort she had put into helping and encouraging him with his career at the sacrifice of her own. She had learned the hard way, she told Berenson, that it was 'a great mistake ... to put too much creative energy into personal relationships'. Now his 'treachery' had left her with creative energy depleted and in such a wretched state that any attempt at writing demanded an almost superhuman effort. It made her feel quite savage, she told John, that 'every sentence has to be fought for'. She determined to struggle on none the less, and planned to use the next three months to address two major problems, the restarting of her novel and the healing of Cecil's damaged psyche. John's reply was badly received, though no doubt intended to be bracing. 'I feel that the idea of healing what has happened is vain,' he began. 'I do not myself see C's behaviour as psychotic, but only as the reaction of a man who has fallen out of this love as it was, or who cannot any longer [deal] with the tension of a situation when the other person's feelings continue far more undivided and possessive than his own.' The result was volcanic. Furious, Rosamond told her brother that he understood nothing of her 'appalling situation', and that it was intolerable he should depict her only 'as a howling possessive rejected female clutching at a lost love!!' So angry was she that she threatened to sever all professional contact between them. 'I cannot take any further interest in J.L. Ltd., and would prefer to resign unless our personal relationship is re-established. . . . I don't want to be part of the set-up at all until I know where I am with you. I don't want the passage between us to be overlooked as if it hadn't existed, and I don't want to be treated as any hystérique who will come to her senses if treated firmly and coldly.' For once it was John who acted as peace-maker, and for the time being at least the quarrel was patched up. 'It is a great load off my mind,' Rosamond told him gratefully. 'Meanwhile I know you will be glad to hear that I have been writing and writing – and writing well.'

By April Rosamond on the surface appeared to be regaining control, although still raw and seething underneath. She had had one last meeting with Cecil, during which he had destroyed any lingering hope of reconciliation. 'He is still set on what seems to all a mad and disastrous path,' she told Berenson. 'I have tried in every way honourably open to me to prevent it . . . but it is useless . . . I have lost him.' Finally forced to accept that Cecil was never coming back, Rosamond began to perceive that she must somehow construct a life without him. And this

287

eventually she did, although her anger barely abated, and for the rest of her days she remained in a state of entrenched vindictiveness: Jill's name could never be mentioned in front of her, and any reference to Cecil invariably provoked a violent eruption of bile.

During the Easter holidays that year, 1950, both Hugo and Sally had been at home. 'The children, though adorable, aren't much comfort – the young never are at these times,' their mother wrote, but at least when they were at Wittenham they provided a distraction from her miserable fixation.

Hugo, over six foot and handsome with his dark, Celtic good looks, was nearing the end of his first year at King's. Although inclined even with his friends to be somewhat taciturn and gruff, he could easily be coaxed into a more relaxed mood, and was famous for his lavish parties – thanks to his Philipps grandfather he had a generous income at his disposal. Like Rudie Lehmann a noted oarsman, Hugo spent much of his time on the river, as well as in the company of a circle of like-minded contemporaries, young men such as Ian Murray, Francis Haskell, Simon Raven, Mark Boxer, and the rich and dashing William Mostyn-Owen. The visits of Hugo's mother to Cambridge were always an event, and her impact on the male members of the university marked. 'She was a very great star at Cambridge. All the undergraduates were mad about her,' said one, while another, remembering her walking through the narrow streets with her queenly carriage, her height, her great head of white hair, compared her to a Boldoni portrait come to life. Dadie always made a great fuss of her, and there would usually be a party given in her honour.

During the vacations Hugo's young bloods came over to Wittenham, sometimes sweeping down to Cranborne Chase in Willy Mostyn-Owen's Rolls-Royce to take out Sally. Recently Hugo had fallen in love with the most beautiful girl of his generation, Margaret Heathcote, an undergraduate at Newnham, widely pursued and universally acclaimed as the Zuleika Dobson of her day, and it was at Easter that he brought Margaret to the Manor House for the first time to meet his mother. The occasion was not a success. Rosamond did not take to 'Hugo's Agitation', as she referred to Margaret, although she gave her credit for intelligence and for her remarkable beauty, with her dark hair, white skin and green mermaid's eyes. 'She is a very eccentric number & will give him many a headache I think,' she told Olivia Holland. For her part, Margaret, who came from a modest middle-class background, was made very conscious that she had proved a disappointment. Rosamond struck her as 'a *crashing* snob. . . . She hoped Hugo would marry someone grander, [and] I was not nearly grand enough to meet her standards.' She saw, too, that Hugo was painfully aware he took second place in his mother's affections. 'He always knew she preferred Sally, and that he was never quite as clever as she wanted him to be,' she recalled. 'What Hugo would have liked was a straightforward life with a landowning father and a nice tweedy mummy.'

Shortly after Sally returned to school and Hugo to Cambridge, Rosamond collapsed, and was ordered to bed for total rest. As her 'couple', her two living-in servants, chose this moment to give notice, she retreated to a health hydro in Bedfordshire, in the hope that a few weeks of steam baths and electro-therapy would help her overcome her emotional prostration. For the past months her feelings of shock and anger about Cecil had kept her galvanised, but now as the realisation sank in that her cause was hopeless, her defences disintegrated. 'Everything hurts so – every memory,' she complained. 'Oh how I wish I could find a nice kind man to look after me!'

Just such a man now appeared. Keith Millar-Jones, a solicitor and old friend of Laurens van der Post, tall, distinguished-looking, with a face like an amiable frog, was bowled over when he met Rosamond in the spring of 1950. At first she found him most agreeable. He, too, was recovering from a long love affair and was prepared to listen sympathetically and offer constructive advice. 'He has been very good to me, – rational & tough!' Rosamond told Laurens in May. Soon he proposed marriage, a proposal which Rosamond briefly considered accepting as a near-miraculous solution to her problems. But then she suddenly turned against Millar-Jones: he was too controlling, resented her stronger personality; and she could never imagine wanting to marry someone who kept his teeth in a glass of water and liked to go to bed at 10 p.m. 'It was all grotesque & infuriating,' she told Dadie. 'I feel he would have wished to teach me my Duty in the Bed.' Rosamond emerged from the affair distressed and humiliated, confessing that the whole experience had been strangely traumatic. Although the violence of her revulsion can in part be explained by a natural recoiling from any man who was not Cecil, no doubt she experienced a sense of private ignominy over her lack of fastidiousness in taking a new lover quite so soon, particularly one with whom she felt so little true affinity. After it was over she wrote sadly, 'Perhaps my trouble is I'm not interested in nice kind men!' while to Berenson she confessed, 'Au pays du tendre I am nowhere, darling. I tell myself: never again.'

None the less Rosamond as always was revived and invigorated by masculine attentions, and disappointing though the Millar-Jones episode proved, it did at least go some way to restoring her appetite for life. That summer she was able to report to BB that she was definitely beginning to recover, 'looking myself again, as they say, – and appearance is a great matter'. In July she went to Ireland to stay with Elizabeth Bowen, and in September took Sally with her when she travelled to Denmark to lecture to the Anglo-Danish Society in Copenhagen. At the beginning of the following year, 1951, for the third time she made the journey to the West Indies, again to stay with Ian Fleming on Jamaica. Fleming had issued the invitation during a weekend at Wittenham, and assuming that his lover, Ann Rothermere, would as before be away, he made it clear that at Goldeneye he hoped to continue the affair begun three years before, 'which I thought would be a wonderful distraction', said Rosamond. Unfortunately Ann Rothermere was not away, and when Fleming realised his mistake his nerve failed him and he neglected to mention Rosamond's arrival until the last possible moment. Rosamond, expecting a very different reception, was disconcerted and embarrassed. 'Oh dear, dear, dear. I didn't realise that (a) Ann was living with him, was installed, and (b) he hadn't told her I was coming out. She was *unbelievably* rude to me, unbelievably rude.' The atmosphere quickly became so awkward that Fleming went to his neighbour, Noël Coward, for help: would Noël please come to the rescue and take Rosamond off his hands? Coward was unsurprised as Rosamond had already been to see him to complain about her predicament. Relations with Ann were described as extremely sticky, and there had been an unamusing incident when Ian, ostensibly as a joke, had thrown a live squid into her bedroom. '[She is] none too comfortable and will probably be in this house soon,' Noël noted in his diary. The story that rapidly went the rounds was that Coward drove over to Goldeneye to assess the situation, caught sight of Fleming's expensive new Polaroid camera and quickly struck a bargain: he would take the unwanted guest in exchange for the camera. 'And tripod,' added Noël quickly. In his opinion, Fleming had not behaved well. 'You, my dear, are just an old cunt-teaser,' he told him.

Once Rosamond was installed at Blue Harbour, her mood lightened.

Noël was *terribly* sweet to me. He said, 'Come on now, this is all over and you must get on with your life. I promise you better things are to come.' I stayed with him for a week and had a very gay time. It wasn't like real life, but I was made a fuss of, with jokes and cocktails and playing on the piano and listening to his new play. Coley [Cole Lesley] was also very sweet to me and Oliver Messel came over, whom I always loved. It made me feel human again.

Noël also encouraged her to work concentratedly on her novel. As she told BB, 'I suddenly began to be able to write again, encouraged by his vitality, and by his seriousness about the art and craft of writing, and by the fact that he leads a regular working life wherever he is.' When Fleming and Ann Rothermere left the island, Ian, 'who I suppose felt very ashamed and embarrassed', suggested she move back into Golden-eye by herself for a further fortnight. 'I've been very lonely here, but at least I can get through the day without fear of collapse, and the beauty of the visible world no longer appals me,' she told Laurie. 'I've also written a good deal of the novel. I've also written a poem, which I enclose. Surely it's good, isn't it?' With its tone of plangent self-pity, the poem, 'The Bay', distils Rosamond's feelings of isolation and abandonment.

> . . . I alone,
> Expecting no one, not expected:
> Presence although of human flesh
> Abstract as water, bare as stone,
> Reflecting naught, and unreflected.
>
> Yet on this verge I still behold
> A weightless imprint, less than shade,
> Starker than moon, as soft, as cold, –
> Eternal ghost, forever laid –
> Once, by a double image made.

On her return to England, there were some unwelcome developments to be faced. Cecil, 'still basking in the worship of his little culture-puss', had been elected to the Professorship of Poetry at Oxford – galling information for an ex-consort forced to envisage him revelling in his distinguished position, with Jill Balcon at his side instead of herself. The election campaign had begun 'just at the time he transferred his overnight zip bag from my bedroom to Miss Balcon's,' Rosamond told Laurie, '[the appointment] a fearful shock to me, as he had told me he had made up his mind not – under the circumstances – to compete'. Only days after this came the news that Cecil had received his decree absolute, Mary Day Lewis having relented over the question of divorce. This was agonising: for nine long years Rosamond had been forced to accept that Cecil would not, could not ask for a divorce from his wife, but now here he was, apparently without a qualm jettisoning all for Jill Balcon, joyfully preparing to confer on Jill the longed-for status he had so tormentingly denied Rosamond. Deeply wounded, Rosamond attempted to conceal her more personal feelings by loudly declaring her overriding concern to be one of moral outrage that Cecil had failed to make public his impending divorce before his election, a fact which if known would almost certainly have put him out of the running. Now she could only feel bitter regret on his behalf for 'the squalor, the dishonour, the lost (I feel almost sure?) poet'. Less than a week later, on 21 April 1951, Cecil and Jill were married. 'The whole thing has an element of the grotesque and farcical,' Rosamond lamented to Edith Sitwell. 'Oh, when when will I stop feeling so shocked, and so lacerated with disappointment and incredulity?'

A few weeks later there was a shock of a different kind. On 7 June 1951 the news broke of the defection to the Soviet Union of Guy Burgess and Donald Maclean. This immediately brought to mind Rosamond's friendship with Burgess, dating back to before the war when he used to come down with Goronwy for weekends at Ipsden, and that mysterious evening when Goronwy had revealed that Guy was a Comintern agent. Convinced it was her urgent duty to go at once to the authorities and tell them what she knew, Rosamond telephoned the head of MI6, Sir Stewart Menzies. Surprisingly, Menzies seemed in no hurry to see her: today was no good as it was Friday and he was going away for the weekend. Monday, then? No, on Monday he was taking his little girl to Ascot. 'I felt that he was putting me off. He asked me if it was G[uy] B[urgess] – he didn't use the name, just the initials. And I said, yes. Then he said, Is it about A[nthony] B[lunt]? I said I knew nothing about AB. He said, Is it about G[oronwy] R[ees]? And I said, yes, in a certain connection.' The conversation ended and Menzies made no further contact. Determined to persevere, Rosamond asked Harold Nicolson to put her in touch with MI5, and this time she was taken more seriously, asked to go to a safe house in Mayfair where she was interviewed by two officers. 'They told me not to say anything about the meeting.'

Asking for complete discretion was asking for too much, and Rosamond was unable to resist telling John what had taken place. He was thrilled by the story, particularly as it gave him an opportunity to snub Stephen Spender, who had been 'jabbering away' that Burgess could never possibly have been a spy. John wrote to Spender to put him straight, and Stephen ill-advisedly gave the letter to the *Daily Express*, which on 11 June splashed it over the front page with the headline 'MYSTERY WOMAN PHONES M.I.5'. Immediately the Lehmanns were targeted: John's house in Egerton Crescent was besieged by reporters, reporters camped outside the stage door of the Duke of York's theatre where Beatrix was appearing, and Rosamond's telephone rang off the hook day and night. Understandably she was angry and upset, feeling doubly betrayed, by John for passing on the contents of a private letter, and by Stephen for going to the press. The tumult died down only after John successfully sued the paper for breach of copyright. 'Luckily, as soon as I took legal action, the persecution of R. and B. ceased,' he recorded. 'It had become extremely painful, because R. was in the end becoming extremely nervous and tragic about it & inclined to blame me.'

A curious coda was added a few years later. In 1956 Rosamond, by then living in London, was at a cocktail party in Eaton Square when she saw Anthony Blunt. He offered her a lift home, and in the taxi '[Blunt] suddenly burst out crying, and sobbed and sobbed. . . . He said: "Rosamond, can you ever forgive me?" When I said: "For what?", he just shook his head.' Her immediate assumption was that the man was drunk, but in the light of subsequent events she realised Blunt had been on the edge of breakdown as a consequence of several years of intensive interrogation, in a permanent state of anxiety that he, now in the prestigious position of Surveyor of the Queen's Pictures, was about to be revealed as a former spy. Recently the pressure on him had intensified with a sensational series of newspaper articles by Goronwy Rees about Burgess's treacherous activities. Rosamond at the instigation of Stephen Spender, who was appalled by Rees's intention to betray his old friend, had gone to see Goronwy to try to dissuade him from embarking on such a dishonourable course. Goronwy was 'very sheepish', she said, 'but would not change his mind'. Blunt on this occasion escaped identification.

For twenty years Rosamond saw nothing more of Anthony Blunt, until in 1979 his cover was finally blown by the publication of an exposé by Andrew Boyle, *The Climate of Treason*. The Prime Minister confirmed in the House of Commons that Blunt had been a Russian agent and he was publicly disgraced, although there was insufficient evidence to bring a criminal prosecution. It was at this point, in August 1980, that Blunt telephoned Rosamond to ask if he could come and see her. '[He] came for lunch and drank a great deal, and he asked me, "Did you know that Goronwy, Guy and I were together?" I said, No, I hadn't known but I'd rather suspected it. . . . I think Anthony was anxious to discover how much I knew about him . . . and whether, in any sense, I could still be dangerous to him. He was really only checking up on me.' At the end of a somewhat veiled conversation, Blunt took his leave and Rosamond never saw him again.

In May 1951 Hugo announced his engagement to the Cambridge beauty Margaret Heathcote, the wedding planned for the beginning of September. That summer Rosamond was in London a good deal, attending plays and parties and renewing some old acquaintances. 'I had a lovely time seeing Larry [Olivier] & Vivien [Leigh] again, both on the stage & behind. I also saw Kenneth Clark, Noël Coward, Joseph Cotton, Carson McCullers, Compton Mackenzie, Derek Hill, John Strachey, some American publishers, one distinguished American Judge, Graham Greene, Julian [Lezzard], and a number of others all in the space of two days,' she boasted after one trip to town. Inevitably, too, there was much activity at Wittenham, with groups of Hugo's friends cheerfully coming and going every few days. While Hugo occupied himself with his lovely fiancée, these high-spirited young men were more than willing to include Hugo's mother in their plans, taking her to the theatre at Stratford, out to dinner, and driving her about the countryside sightseeing. They cheered her up, teasing her and making her laugh, and she became fond of them, advising Quentin Crewe over an unhappy love-affair, lending money to Simon Raven, permanently penniless, and taking under her wing the unstable Ian Murray, having him to stay for weeks at a time and encouraging him to write. The 21-year-old Willy Mostyn-Owen, immensely tall, with fair hair and a pale, Plantagenet profile, was usually the prime mover in their expeditions. In his gleaming black Rolls he drove Rosamond and Quentin Crewe through the south of England, looking at churches and visiting National Trust houses. It was on a trip to Stratford that Quentin Crewe remembered Rosamond in full flood, fulminating against Cecil and Jill. 'I listened enthralled, but uncomprehending to Rosamond's tirades. It was beautiful to see her shake her leonine head and to hear her spit out her scorned fury against "that chit of a girl".' The two young men adored Rosamond and found her a delightful companion, both relishing, if slightly surprised by, her taste for risqué jokes. What she liked the most, she told them mischievously, was 'a clean-limbed, dirty-minded Englishman'.

In July, while Sally was in Italy with her father and Cristina, Rosamond, Willy and Ian Murray took off for the Mozart Festival at Aix-en-Provence, where they heard *Die Entführung* in the courtyard of the Bishop's Palace, lunched with François Mauriac and Leonard Woolf, and Willy took Rosamond for an immense walk up Mont Ste Victoire. She was still very weepy about Cecil, and Willy was kind and sympathetic, and during the few days at Aix they became lovers. In spite of the thirty-year age difference, Willy was entranced by Rosamond's beauty and touched by her unhappiness. 'It was a very strange and rather wonderful relationship,' he recalled. After returning to England, Rosamond wrote to him, 'Aix was the beginning of enjoying things again. I still see myself walking, or floating, arm in arm with you into the giant male torso of Mont Ste Victoire. . . . If I'd been alone I don't think I'd ever have come back. But then, the point is I wasn't for once alone – or lonely.' Over the next few weeks as the affair discreetly continued Rosamond felt happy and revived. 'How could I ever have dreamed you would let me cease, for a time, from being parched and scorched? The bewilderment, and my grateful love for you, when I discovered you were willing and equal to accepting all that was locked up in my – this is something I will never forget so long as I live,' she wrote to him, adding fervently, 'And I hope I'll never need to, or wish I could forget.' In August Rosamond took Sally up to Scotland to stay at Aberuchill, Willy's castle in Perthshire, where she made friends with his sister Liz, later standing godmother to Liz's baby daughter. Afterwards she wrote to 'My Precious Will' to thank him for 'all the joys and pleasures and sweetnesses you lavished on us at Aberuchill . . . all the happiness I've had since my life was destroyed has come through you. . . . It has come so suddenly, bewilderingly and unexpectedly that it is rather a heady draught – and I have to lecture myself all the time – and I do – about preparing myself to relinquish it if necessary.'

Meanwhile there were some pressing domestic duties waiting at home. Rosamond had decided to sell the Manor House and move to London. The house was no longer a pleasure and its upkeep, with only Kathleen the cook-general and a gardener, was becoming too much of a burden. 'It is a dreadful break to contemplate,' she told Dadie, 'but the place grows more & more posthumous, & I don't intend to settle down as a resigned Widow living for the occasional visits of my Young.' While fully engaged in the business of an imminent move as well as in plans for Hugo's wedding, she was suddenly interrupted at Wittenham by the arrival, uninvited, of 'two American alcoholics' in the shape of a very drunk Carson McCullers with her no less drunk husband, Reeves. When she had met them the previous year with Elizabeth Bowen in Ireland, Rosamond had liked Carson, whose work she admired. Now, however, she saw at once that a social visit was out of the question as the novelist's condition was serious, and when Reeves, unable to cope, returned to the States, she despatched Carson fairly swiftly to a doctor in London. The experience, she told Willy, had been 'like living in Blake's marriage of Heaven and Hell . . . I found her fascinating and lovable, but at the same time a terrific psychic drain . . . [and] her drinking habits made her a very difficult guest.'

Hugo and Margaret were married on 7 September 1951 at Holy Trinity, Sloane Street, with a reception afterwards given by John at Egerton Crescent. The party was described by John himself as

first class . . . with plenty of good champagne to keep it going, and all the bridegroom's relations looking very smart and distinguished and old friends like Rex & Barbara and Laurie to keep it intimate and gay. . . . Hugo himself pale and haggard with a large red pimple on his nose but full of beans, Laurie more mischievous every moment & finishing up by tying his own shoes with his own tie on to the back of the car . . . Rosamond and Wogan having a high old time together and everyone wreathed in smiles.

For Rosamond, in a haze of champagne and methedrine 'to keep up my morale', the occasion seemed remote and surreal, 'wondering if I had dreamed . . . I had a son who had grown up and married a completely unknown girl and left home for good without my being able to tell him, "Stop! Come back. It's all a mistake, I didn't mean you to go away just yet."' Watching Hugo's transformation into Margaret's husband was unsettling, but as he had since Sally's birth taken second place with his mother there was little reason to find the parting too painful: and she still had her enchanting daughter. As Rosamond wrote to Berenson, 'One has to try to enable one's sons to grow up to love other women, but one doesn't have to bother about that with the daughters – great comfort.'

With Hugo married and Sally enrolled at an Oxford crammer working for her university entrance, Rosamond was able to turn her attention to arranging the future of her 'sweet Will'. The first idea had been for the young man to go into business with John, who needed financial backing for his current project, the resuscitation of *New Writing*. But Willy, although initially interested, shied away from the scheme, wary of John's 'strange, closed character . . . [and the way] he looked at you through slit eyes, rather like an armoured car'. In fact he was more interested in the art world than in literary magazines and publishing, and so to further his ambitions in this direction Rosamond arranged to take him with her when for the second time she went to stay with Berenson at Settignano. She was sure the two would have much in common, she told Willy, adding whimsically, 'I'd like to write a story about a person like you at one end of the pattern, and a person like him at the other end, and a belle femme a little like me in the middle.'

BB, with whom Rosamond was closely in touch ('We must keep the shuttle gliding constantly between us,' he had written after her first

visit), had been warmly sympathetic over the ending of the affair with
Cecil, urging his 'Dear, glorious, wild woman' to come and stay at I Tatti
for as long as she wanted. 'You alone if you had the leisure, & the wish,
could replace for me the happiness I enjoyed in the company of Edith
Wharton,' he flattered her. Rosamond had been reluctant to return to
the place where she had been so happy; but now with a new lover by her
side she was more than prepared to confront any mournful memories. By
the end of November 1951, with the sale of the Manor House completed
and a lease taken on a flat in London, she and Willy left for Italy. The
visit was a notable success: Willy made such a good impression on
Berenson that the great man invited him to return in a few months to
study under his personal supervision; and Rosamond found to her relief
that Cecil, far from lurking in ambush in every corner of the house and
garden, was 'almost at once . . . a ghost'. Afterwards she wrote to her old
friend that at I Tatti she had experienced 'more peace of mind,
expansion of the senses and imagination and simple happiness with
every day that passed'.

On her return home Rosamond was greeted with the news that Sally
had won an Exhibition to St Hilda's College, Oxford. '[Sally] fell prone
on the floor,' her mother reported with amusement, 'and then started to
roll and somersault like some large blonde rosy marine animal, emitting
peals of laughter, and now and then rising to clasp me.' To fill in the
months before term began in October, it was decided that she should go
to the Conservatoire in Milan to further her musical studies and have
her singing voice properly trained. The suggestion had come from
Wogan, who was uneasy at the prospect of leaving Sally so much in her
mother's company, especially at a time when Rosamond had so recently
been in such a disturbed emotional state. And indeed, the atmosphere at
this period between mother and daughter was sometimes tense.
'Rosamond was glad when Sally went abroad,' Wogan recalled. 'She said
to me, "Thank God she's gone: I can't cope with her." And Sally said
exactly the same thing about Rosamond.' Cristina, who was fond of her
stepdaughter, offered to pay for the course and also to provide
accommodation: through her Italian family, the Casatis, she owned a
large apartment in the Palazzo Casati da Soncino on the Via Soncino,
and here Sally could stay, with another English girl, Connie Black, an
art student, as a companion; for at least part of the time Cristina herself

would be in residence and could keep an eye on Sally and introduce her to some suitable young people. Rosamond saw her daughter off at Victoria in the first week of January 1952, as always sad to see her go, knowing how much she would miss her cheerful presence.

Shortly after Sally's departure for Italy Rosamond moved into her new address, 70 Eaton Square, on the edge of fashionable Belgravia, an airy, two-roomed, first-floor flat at the western end of the square, with a long view over enormous plane trees and stately, creamy stucco houses. Here for the first time in her life she was obliged to manage without living-in domestic staff, her only helper a daily woman called May, whose arrival immediately after breakfast caused a considerable disturbance. 'May comes every morning and works (carolling lustily the while) like a Trojan. But she is so noisy and voluble and blows her own trumpet so clamorously that it is rather a relief when we bid each other a tender goodbye.'

Rosamond quickly settled into her new surroundings, although her pleasure in the move was marred by a rapid deterioration in her relationship with Willy. Spoilt, charming, with a wide circle of friends of his own age, Willy was beginning to chafe at Rosamond's ceaseless demands. 'I'm afraid I behaved after a time like the hero in *Dusty Answer*,' he said. 'She was insatiably vain, like a film star in that way. . . . "Am I looking beautiful, darling? Am I looking wonderful?" . . . She wanted total attention . . . [and] she wouldn't let go. She wasn't very subtle about letting you go and quietly bringing you back.' If Willy were off-hand, thoughtless or unpunctual, Rosamond would scold him as though he were a naughty schoolboy. 'You were my guest in the flat & you had no business to alter agreed plans to suit yourself without consulting me – nor to go off to see Geoffrey "for 10 minutes" and keep me waiting up for you an hour and a half,' she wrote crossly on one occasion. There had been an acrimonious exchange when Rosamond discovered that Willy, on the point of returning to Settignano, had bought a bracelet for another woman whose identity he stubbornly refused to reveal, saying only that it was for somebody who meant a great deal to him. In fact the bracelet was for Nicky Mariano, who had been particularly kind to him at I Tatti. The quarrel was soon made up, but Rosamond's resentment continued to rankle. 'I am bored with being thanked, over & over again, for "being so forgiving", when all I want is simple genuine proofs that you care enough for me & our relationship not to endanger it – and hurt me – so casually, so unnecessarily. You are planning to have life, including love and friendship, on your own terms entirely, – well, I don't think they're very good terms, though your remarkable charm & other gifts will take you a long way.' 'I began to find this sort of thing very difficult,' said Willy.

In fact even under the most propitious circumstances the affair was unlikely to have lasted as Willy for the next five years was to spend nearly all his time in Italy with Berenson. Without an attractive man to court her and with little sign of such a one in prospect, Rosamond sank back into depression. 'I have tried so hard for two years to accustom myself to living alone,' she wrote to BB, from whom the nature of her relationship with Willy had been carefully concealed. What she wanted, she explained, was what she thought she had had with Cecil, 'a hand in mine that, once taken and given, will never let mine go. . . . I don't want affairs with married men who think of me as a sort of luxury cake shop round the corner to be visited when domestic puddings pall.'

With no male companion to distract her, her thoughts returned obsessively to Cecil, circling round and round the well-worn track of his unforgiveable betrayal, endlessly attempting to find a satisfactory explanation for his behaviour. 'No doubt the chief clue [to his defection] lies in the fact that he didn't, in the end, find it suited the needs of his nature to go on sustaining a relationship with a stronger and in some ways more intelligent person than himself.' There was a serious rift with Dadie when Rosamond discovered not only that he was regularly seeing Cecil and Jill, but had talked of Rosamond herself in terms she considered offensive, referring to her 'sense of injury [and] self-pity . . . [her] imbecility' in regard to Cecil. John Lehmann commented gloomily on her peevishness and self-absorption.

> It has saddened me very much in recent weeks to see what heavy weather she has made over everything in her life, even getting into the new flat, how she has misjudged people and events . . . and still clings underneath it all to the shadow of Cecil . . . [sic] She talked a great deal of Jamie & Yvonne [Hamilton], how stupid they both were, how empty the conversation at their table, how snobbish and careerist K. Clark & Jane were, how there was nothing in the way

300

of a salon or centre in London today for wit and good conversation and intellectual stimulus (– and yet they have all taken so much trouble about her); and then of Christopher [Isherwood], how impossible she found it to talk to him now, how impenetrable, how uninterested in oneself, how fixed in immaturity. ... Yesterday I took V[iolet] H[ammersley] to Stratford ... & she said it was in her opinion like a grave illness, this need of flattery & worship, & how she remembered it was because C[ecil] was there and gave it her at a crucial moment that she took up with him – not falling in love, but the giving of the injection as it were.

For Rosamond the sterility of her plight was intensified by its contrast to Sally's riotous life in Milan, exuberant descriptions of which were arriving weekly in long airmail letters lovingly addressed to 'Mama carissima mia'. Sally at 17 had fined down to a slender-waisted, long-legged beauty, and as a blonde she was relishing the sensational impact she made on the young Milanesi. 'Oh bionda!' they called after her in the streets. 'A blonde can't fail here!' she wrote happily. 'The men are awful ...! – I think I shall have to get a wig!' In between a busy schedule of lessons for piano, violin and singing, she was enjoying a 'wild' time, eager Paolos, Ubertos and Giancarlos competing to escort her to the opera at La Scala, to parties, concerts, night-clubs, while with groups of student friends she made expeditions to Venice for the Biennale, to Rome, Florence, Naples and Pompeii. 'Life here gets gayer and gayer,' she exclaimed, '[and I] have been having a high old time. ... We all went to an extraordinary sort of existentialist night-club one night & danced the Charleston like fiends! It's known as a place where no self-respecting Italian girl would go, & is certainly an experience!' Of a short holiday in the mountains with a party of 'hilarious' young people she reported that 'we sang through meals & shouted & danced etc. The first few days we were there, there was another big party from Milan, & two of the men definitely thought they were Casanovas! ... Goodness we were a noisy lot – ceaseless practical jokes too!' 'Sally's letters are deliriously happy, but shockingly common,' Rosamond sourly observed.

Milan may have been gay but London was not. 'London is dark, dank, icy, soaking, and at present my spirits are leaden, leaden,' was the continuing refrain. But then suddenly everything changed. The new flat was found to be 'really rather beautiful, & I am very happy in it, contrary to my expectation', while the dark, dank city was all at once 'looking incomparably beautiful, full of soft green and blossoming trees and tulips'. The explanation for this altered perception appeared in a letter to Laurie. 'I have met an angelic man called Joshua Rowley,' she told him in March 1952, while the following month she wrote smugly to Willy, '[I am] enjoying my life & being dreadfully spoilt.'

Joshua Rowley, 'the nicest young man in the world', was 32, shy, genial and kind-hearted; deputy secretary of the National Trust, he was a keen countryman and conservationist, with a family seat, Tendring Hall, in Suffolk. Old Etonian and Trinity College, Cambridge, Joshua's interests were predominantly those of an old-fashioned country squire, although he was well read and widely experienced, having served in the Grenadiers and spent much of the war as a prisoner in Italy. Of medium height, with blue eyes and a pleasant, broad pink face, Joshua could not be judged good-looking, but he was a sweet-natured companion, and most important of all deeply in love with Rosamond. They had met at a party soon after the death of George VI in February 1952, and Rosamond had been impressed by the fact that Joshua had taken the trouble to go and see the King lying in state. In spite of the difference in age – Rosamond at 51 was almost twenty years older – Joshua was dumbfounded by her beauty and charm. 'She was so marvellous to look at, and I was so surprised that she took the slightest interest in me.' Although she was unable to reciprocate emotionally, Rosamond became immensely fond of her new young man, who was an adoring, if not particularly ardent, lover. 'It *was* a love-affair,' said Rosamond in retrospect. 'It wasn't very passionate, but it was very happy. . . . He became my escort and gave me a lovely time.' Immediately she felt her well-being restored, as though without love she was reduced to a state of chemical imbalance, an imbalance which could be corrected only by, in Mrs Hammersley's words, 'the injection' of a new love. No time was lost in informing the old love of his replacement: Joshua worshipped and cherished her, she boasted to Willy, and 'has brought me incredible, unexpected and unsought-for happiness. . . . Please say nothing to BB.'

Sally in Italy was also told of the change in her mother's fortunes, and expressed herself curious to inspect the new incumbent. She herself had fallen for 'a horrible handsome young Italian', as Rosamond told Dadie, adding that Sally's problems in love 'churned up' all kinds of feelings in her mother's breast, reminding her of her own unhappy experiences. But Sally's was a very different temperament: doted on from birth, an optimist by nature, feet planted firmly on the ground, she suffered none of the neuroses and insecurities, indulged in none of the illusions and self-deceptions that accounted for so much that was unsatisfactory in Rosamond's relationships. In August Sally left Milan for a short holiday in Genoa before returning to England, and her lively accounts of sleeping late, shopping, large meals and dancing every night until the small hours were hardly indicative of a broken heart. Shortly before leaving for home in September, she wrote to her mother, 'I can't believe that we parted at Victoria last January. What a lot I've seen & done since – I'm sure I must be much broader-minded now!' 'Sally came back glowing from Italy,' said Rosamond, who was overjoyed to have her daughter home, 'blooming, adorable, egotistical & exhausting'. In October 1952, after a few weeks' intensive party-going in London, Sally went up to Oxford to begin her undergraduate career at St Hilda's, a poignant reminder for her mother of the start of her own student days over thirty years before at Girton.

In this much happier frame of mind, Rosamond was able to complete her work long in progress, announcing with a mixture of pride and relief in October 1952 that she had finally finished her novel – 'at 8.30 pm on Oct 15th to be precise!' To reward herself, she went off with Joshua to Venice and Trieste for a couple of weeks, before going to Llanstephan for Christmas with Sally. This was a sad experience, with Lord Milford, her once formidable father-in-law, reduced to a pathetic old man who 'spends the waning of his days peering into his Television Set and chuckling over the Toddlers' Programmes'. In the intervals between, he 'broods over Wogan and fishes out all the letters written twenty years ago, and yearns for reconciliation, and generally wanders round and round the past like an old restless dog!'

The novel in question, *The Echoing Grove*, had been an unusually long time in gestation, but that Rosamond was never going to be either a speedy or prolific writer was reluctantly recognised by her publisher. After Ralph Pinker's disappearance from the scene in 1935, Rosamond's professional affairs had been taken over by the Society of Authors, with the society's secretary-general, Denys Kilham Roberts, acting as her agent. Although Kilham Roberts had a reputation for being difficult – as Cecil found when collaborating with him on *Orion* – he and Rosamond enjoyed the most amicable relationship, and not only through the office: Kilham Roberts and his wife stayed several times at Little Wittenham, and their daughter Jane had been at school with Sally. He was scrupulous in promoting his client's interests. In 1947, when negotiating the contract for the latest novel with Rosamond's publisher, William ('Billy') Collins, Kilham Roberts had agreed a new, more advantageous arrangement whereby instead of the usual payment of a single lump sum in advance (£750 for *The Weather in the Streets* and the same for *The Ballad and the Source*), for her next three novels Rosamond should be allowed to run an overdraft at any time of up to £1,250 on her Collins account. There was one proviso, Kilham Roberts warned her: bearing in mind his author's slow rate of production, Billy Collins had stipulated 'that before you exercised this prerogative, he would like to know that the next novel is taking shape. I imagine he has memories of the seven years or so which elapsed between *The Weather* and *The Ballad*. How, in fact, is the new book going, and can I give Billy a reassuring word about it?'

Billy Collins had reason to be wary. *The Ballad and the Source* was published in 1944, the new book, commenced the following year, was not delivered until October 1952. Partly, Rosamond's slowness was due to circumstances. During the years with Cecil, a great deal of her energy had been invested in helping him with his career and with *Orion*; there had besides been the constant emotional drain of the uncertainty of her situation, with all its dramas and upheavals, hopes raised and disappointed, culminating in the devastating blow of his departure. The novel's various stages can be traced through references in Rosamond's letters from 1945, when the process began, to 1952 when she finally finished. In October 1945, shortly before the move to Little Wittenham, she described the difficulty of getting started: 'Disparate scenes & faces & images go gnawing around in my head & won't fuse'; two years later the situation was little improved, with reports of 'terrible struggles with my writing'. The following year, however, after returning from the happy holiday with Cecil at I Tatti, she was 'about a third of the way through', making such good progress that in six months the first half was almost finished. But such optimism was premature, and four months after that, shortly after returning from staying with Somerset Maugham in 1949, there was a reversal: 'My novel goes hideously badly,' John was told. 'I've had to scrap Part 2 & re-start.' After Cecil left her at the beginning of 1950, Rosamond for a few weeks threw herself frenziedly into her work – 'The book is not very far from the end, but I am so physically exhausted it is hard to do good work on it or concentrate' – before breaking down completely and abandoning any attempt at composition for several months. By October 1950 she had pulled herself together, writing to Kilham Roberts that, 'picking up this novel again was a spiritual torment for which there are no words, but it will be better in the end for this break'. If he took this to mean that completion was imminent he must have been disappointed as it was another two years before the end was in sight. In March 1952 Rosamond was at last able to announce, in a letter to Laurie Lee, 'I am writing the last chapter.'

After her first novel, even under the most favourable conditions writing never came easily to Rosamund. When her work was going well she felt contented and fulfilled, knowing that this was what she was born to do. And yet, while defining herself as a writer, she never subscribed to the necessity of a regular discipline; unlike such novelists as Graham Greene, Evelyn Waugh and Somerset Maugham, who wrote daily, keeping to an inflexible working schedule, she had no such routine, preferring to wait until visited by impulse or inspiration. 'I just went on with life, and one day a novel would tap me on the shoulder. . . . There was no need for me to interfere or rack my brains. The book would come along or not, as the case might be.' She was stung when J. B. Priestley described her as an amateur, but this lack of routine, of compulsion to write on a daily basis, was probably what he was referring to. Rosamund was aware that her way of life was untypical of that of a professional writer, but she justified her low level of productivity by arguing that in her case quantity would come only at the expense of quality. 'I just can't produce a book a year,' she was later to say. 'In a way I do wish I had written more, produced more, regularly, like most of my colleagues. But there was always a feeling that if I did that I might write less well.' Most crucially, writing was not always her priority. Her financial situation was comfortable, thanks to her divorce settlement and a small income from a Lehmann family trust, and throughout her life love-affairs and domestic and social obligations could and did take precedence over her work. As she herself admitted, 'There are so many other things I enjoyed – children, friends, reading, music . . . I always found it very hard to withdraw and think that my writing was the most important thing.'

In the opening to her story 'The Red-Haired Miss Daintreys', Rosamond described the passive nature of her creative process.

I myself have been, all my life, a privileged person with considerable leisure. When asked how I spend it, I feel both dubious and embarrassed: for any answer implying some degree of activity would be misleading. Perhaps an approximation to the truth might be reached by stating that leisure employs me – weak aimless unsystematic unresisting instrument – as a kind of screen upon which are projected the images of persons – known well, a little, not at all, seen once, or long ago, or every day; or as a kind of preserving jar in which float fragments of people and landscapes, snatches of sound . . . there is not one of these fragile shapes and aerial sounds but bears within it an explosive seed of life . . . a spark catches, and the principle of rebirth contained in this cold residue of experience begins to operate.

She understood the necessity of listening to what she called 'the still centre' in the imagination from which every work of art must evolve, and she always emphasised the importance, particularly for the novelist, of an ability to love and feel compassion for human kind. 'Novelists must be able to love men and women. Their greatness depends on this.' Once the spark caught and the imagination was engaged, Rosamond was capable of bursts of concentrated effort, writing at her desk or sometimes in bed, covering page after page with her vigorous, spiky handwriting, in the early days working on loose sheets of exercise paper, later in folio notebooks, blue or black. A first draft in longhand was succeeded by a second, sometimes a third, before the book was sent off in sections to be typed.

The Echoing Grove, Rosamond's sixth novel, was published on 2 April 1953, the same year as *The Go-Between* by L. P. Hartley, *Hurry On Down* by John Wain, and just a year before Kingsley Amis's *Lucky Jim*. It is a lengthy, intricate work, unfolding not chronologically but in a fluid pattern of episodes moving between past and present, with the perspective shifting from one character to another. The story is of a love triangle, the love of two sisters, Madeleine and Dinah, for the same man, Madeleine's husband, Rickie. The young women are very different, Madeleine conventional and unimaginative, Dinah left-wing, rebellious and bohemian. The novel opens with the first encounter between the sisters for fifteen years: they last saw each other shortly before Rickie's death of an ulcer during the war, since when the knowledge of his clandestine affair with Dinah has made it impossible for them to meet. Now, however, enough time has passed, and Dinah, also a widow, visits her sister at her small house in the country. Awkward with each other, they take Dinah's dog for a walk, and in the churchyard he puts up a rat, 'flea-bitten, sodden, its belly blown; and all of it watchful, still, grey as damnation'. The rat, though moribund, fights fiercely, and the dog fails to kill it, leaving it to Madeleine to bludgeon it to death, a metaphorical slaying of the poisonous memory that gnaws at her own relationship with Dinah.[1]

From this shocking scene we are taken back to the bland, prosperous married life of Rickie and Madeleine, to the start of Rickie's affair with Dinah, then to Dinah's eventual pregnancy followed by a stillbirth. It is to help her recover from this that Rickie takes her for a short holiday in Wales, after which he tells Madeleine that he is going to leave her for her sister. Madeleine is devastated, but her husband ignores her pleading and walks out of the comfortable house in Montagu Square to go to Dinah's modest little flat in Stepney, intending as soon as possible to take her abroad. But this is not to be: at Dinah's, Rickie falls desperately ill and has to be removed to a nursing-home, where, weak and exhausted, he submits passively to Madeleine's control; indeed sees Dinah only once more before his death a few years later.

The focus of the book rests on the relationships between the three main characters, Rickie's with Madeleine and Dinah, the two sisters with him and with each other, each in turn subjectively viewed. Ruthless and destructive towards each other, individually they are to be

[1] Although no early drafts exist to show how *The Echoing Grove* evolved into its final form, there is correspondence between Rosamond and the BBC dating from 1948 which makes clear that the rat hunt was originally intended to form the first section of a long short story.

pitied. Even Madeleine, soignée, pretty, practical, a lover of dinner-parties and night-clubs, the most ordinary and superficial of the trio, is shown to have an unexpected capacity for mortifying self-knowledge, well aware of her inadequacy in the eyes of the husband she adores. A conscientious wife and mother, it is a torment to her that she is unable to penetrate his unfailingly courteous manner which, as she knows, conceals a chilling indifference. One evening at a night-club, Madeleine comments disparagingly to Rickie on another woman's showy dress:

> 'Have I ever had a penchant for showy clothes?'
> 'Have you? I do hope not.'
> 'You know I haven't. Quite the reverse.'
> 'Then we are at one.' He looked stonily ahead of him.
> After another long silence, Madeleine said:
> 'It might look better if we danced together once.'
> 'Oh, would you like to? Right. Let's dance.'
> To the strains of a curdling blues they took the floor. . . .

Rickie Masters like Rollo Spencer is an instantly recognisable version of the Lehmann wonderful young man, although older and more complex than Rollo, and unlike Rollo given to guilt and anguished self-analysis. Whereas the sisters are middle-class, Rickie is 'irrevocably out of the top drawer', and even though he has had to sell the family estate in Norfolk on which he was brought up, he remains well-off. There are a number of admiring references to his aristocratic upbringing – he reminisces nostalgically about '[the] blissful days alone with Marshall, our angelic keeper. . . . And the smell of fishing . . . I used to go fishing with Charlie; he was the chauffeur's youngest, a year or two older than me' – and he is frequently described in terms of the ease and self-confidence understood to be a concomitant of patrician birth. '[Rickie] had a way of running downstairs . . . an unbroken skidding run from top to bottom of the staircase, back straight, knees and ankles loose. . . . It's an upper-class thing: ways they invented in youth of playing with their ease of mind and body, decorating bored leisure with a flourish.' Like Rollo, he is charming, susceptible, elusive, irresponsible and weak, the quintessential betraying philanderer ('He was sick of seeing women lying in despair upon their beds'), quick to evade obligation by a disarming acknowledgement of his faults: ' "my quite outstanding ineffectuality as a feeler. . . . I'm a notable disappointer," he resumed. "Championship standard." ' There are further similarities: both Rickie and Rollo work in their family businesses, they live in the same neighbourhood, and Rickie taking Dinah to Wales is an almost exact reprise of Rollo taking Olivia to Austria. In both cases the experience is idyllic; towards the end of their time together, '[Rickie] was hopelessly in love with her again', just as Rollo in Austria is with Olivia: 'His eyes looked into my eyes, he was utterly in love with me then.' Rollo says, 'Listen, let's not go back,' while in Wales, Rickie and Dinah find 'they were one, they could not live apart, they knew it'.

Dinah, whom Rickie loves, is her respectable sister's opposite, proud, passionate, impoverished, wild-living and hard-drinking. Dinah's husband, acquired in a temporary break in the affair with Rickie, is killed in the Spanish Civil War; her friends are talented, disreputable and poor. Sibling rivalry, a theme familiar from *Invitation to the Waltz* and *The Weather in the Streets*, in which Kate and Olivia spar amicably in an alliance founded on love and mutual support, is here seen to be bitterly divisive, the sexual nature of the competitiveness between Dinah and Madeleine edging over into dangerous hostility. Even fifteen years after the final rupture over Rickie, the old resentments are in evidence.

'Are you a gardener?'

'I do garden,' said Madeleine.

'You find it soothing?' said Dinah.

'I find it a job of hard work,' said Madeleine, sharp and light. 'But I've quite taken to it. Had to.'

'Vegetables and all?'

'Of course. I don't potter about in embroidered hessian with a dainty trowel and a raffia basket, if that's what you mean,' said Madeleine, thinking: She hasn't changed. Still the cocked eyebrow, the guarded mouth firing off remarks designed to cause discomfort; as if to say no matter what the answer, she knew its fraudulence beforehand and would transfix it.

The contrast between the sisters is encapsulated in a couple of swift impressions of Rickie's. Leaving for a dinner-party with Madeleine, 'out of the corner of an eye he took in her appearance, thinking she looked a bit garish: petunia pink evening frock, a colour he disliked, white fur wrap, diamond clips and earrings, make-up overdone, blue-shadowed lids. . . . She was beginning to plaster it on, he thought'; while going out to lunch with Dinah, he finds her 'in her subdued way more chic, more delicately wrought than ever, in the kind of plain black figure-moulding frock that exactly suited his taste in women's clothes'.

The central theme of *The Echoing Grove* is narrated with hypnotic intensity, and the complex time scheme, moving back and forth between past and present, focusing on one protagonist, then another, is deftly accomplished. Every scene in which the reader is, as it were, present is striking and memorable: the meeting between the two sisters at the beginning, the disintegrating married life of Rickie and Madeleine, the start of the affair between Rickie and Dinah.

> . . . the night he had opened the door, closed it behind him like a thief, a murderer, a lover; and standing in the dark, called:
> 'Dinah.' Just above his breath.
> 'Yes.' She did not stir or switch the light on.
> 'You're not going through with this, you know,' Her engagement, so recently announced.
> 'I've got to.'
> 'You can't. You know why.'
> 'Yes.'
> 'Break it off.'
> 'Yes.' . . .
> Not one step towards her bedside, not another word. Turning from the threshold, swift the door open, noiseless closed again. Back along the passage to his dressing-room.
> And so it had all begun.

Unfortunately the main story is diminished by a series of weak sub-plots, several, fatally, conveyed ineptly in reported speech. One of these deals with Dinah's brief marriage to 'a Jew, called Hermann', sketchily realised, with whom she goes to live in the East End; after his death, Dinah, by now defiantly *déclassée*, becomes involved with another working-class boy, whose story, unsparingly narrated, again detracts from the main theme; as does Madeleine's lengthy entanglement with a younger lover, an equally unrealistic character who acts as little but a distraction. Even more damaging, in the second half of the novel there is a long sequence in which Rickie in wartime London takes refuge during an air-raid with Georgie, an attractive American woman first encountered at a brilliantly described disastrous dinner-party near the beginning of the book. The two of them dally on the brink of a love-affair, which gives Rickie ample opportunity to muse over his life and previous loves – and, regrettably, so does Georgie. (Gabriel Marcel of Plon, who read the novel in manuscript, immediately focused on this problem: '*je ne peux pas m'empêcher d'être gêné par l'immense scène entre Rickie et Georgie.* . . . *J'aimerais savoir pourquoi vous avez pensé que vous pouviez vous accorder cette sorte de licence.*'[2])

With *The Echoing Grove* Rosamond claimed that 'the wheel had come full circle' and that the story begun in *Dusty Answer* was now finished. In a radio interview given at the time of publication she said, 'I began to feel that, more than any of the others, this novel had something to do with the first I ever wrote. Not the same one in a fresh guise; not even a development from it; but more as if somehow – I cannot explain why – some cycle of experience that had opened when I was a girl was now coming to a close.'[3] In all probability this is a reference, only half understood as Rosamond admitted, to the cycle of emotional experience which began with her falling idealistically in love with David Keswick at Cambridge and ended in disillusionment with her abandonment by Cecil Day Lewis thirty years later. More specifically, 'it was really a farewell to a particular and in the main negative romantic view of the world of "love"'.

At the time Rosamond insisted that in this novel there were definitely 'no portraits from life', but this is transparently untrue, as she herself later conceded. Rickie, for example, is based on 'an amalgam of Matt Ridley and Wogan . . . a sort of tragic desperado, fascinating, selfish, cruel – well, not really cruel but what the French call *tête montée*, unable to cope with what he'd brought about'. His mistress, Dinah, in looks and

---

[2] 'I can't avoid finding tiresome the immense scene between Rickie and Georgie. . . . I would like to know why you felt you could allow yourself this kind of licence.'

[3] Perhaps this is why *The Echoing Grove* is dedicated to 'My Mother and My Father'.

personality derives from Beatrix: like Bea, Dinah is farouche, her attractiveness unconventional, and like Bea she is a passionate believer in left-wing causes, indifferent to material possessions and physical comfort. Interestingly, towards the end of her life Rosamond came to see Dinah and Madeleine as a kind of composite self-portrait. 'The two sisters are partly aspects of myself, I suppose,' she said, an observation which shows an awareness of two opposing sides of her character, that of respectable bourgeoise who craved marriage and security under a protective male wing, and her counterpart, the free-thinking, free-loving artist. Like their creator, both Dinah and Madeleine define themselves primarily in relation to men.

Of course there were those who were determined to read *The Echoing Grove* as a version of Rosamond's affair with Cecil, and of course this annoyed her a good deal. 'I have *never* written about Cecil Day Lewis, ever, ever,' she emphatically stated. But he is there, all right: as in a palimpsest Cecil is visible in ghostly form, 'a breath coming up again out of the buried day'. Indeed Rosamond had wanted to call the book *The Buried Day* (like 'dusty answer' a quotation from a poem by Meredith), but her publisher wisely warned her against it, the reference retained only in various translations, *Der begrabene Tag*, for instance, and *Le Jour Enseveli*.[4] Like Cecil, Rickie is 'a charmer . . . eminently fitted, in the matter of women, to get away with anything'; and like Cecil, he is able to retreat at periods of tension into an impenetrable detachment: 'not guilty or repentant or aggressive or on the defensive. Simply null and void . . . out of reach – stubbornly so: as if his will had operated a deliberate assumption of irresponsibility; an absolutely ruthless withdrawal into self-preservation.' When Rickie tells Madeleine he is going to leave her, she is paralysed by his manner. 'But for the fixed cold shadow in his eyes – that and his pallor – he seemed his everyday collected self. She told herself that what she was observing was a mental breakdown: he had gone quietly mad and must be humoured.' Throughout, Rickie remains apparently unmoved, 'wrapped in the cloak of a double life – rank cloak, invisible', and like Cecil he takes refuge in illness, withdrawing by means of physical or emotional breakdown,

---

[4] Unknowingly, Cecil was to choose just this title, *The Buried Day*, for his autobiography, published in 1960.

although significantly it is Dinah's collapse, when desperately ill in childbirth, that destroys the love-affair. The scene draws on the events of the severe winter of 1947 when Cecil, ill and deeply depressed, had to drive through the snow to fetch help for the gardener's wife who had gone into labour. Similarly Rickie has to drive for hours through snow to reach Dinah, who has retired to a cottage in Devon to give birth to their stillborn child. Dinah herself nearly dies, at the last moment given courage to live by Rickie: 'that was the crack-up. He saved her through the power of love, and that was the end of the power of love. There was no way out for it, it had so overreached itself; it burst against negativity and was extinct.'

A feeling of doom pervades the entire novel. The familiar Lehmann themes of betrayal and loss are here relentless and unrelieved. Death is everywhere: the dying rat in the opening scene, the dying marriage of Rickie and Madeleine, Rickie's death from a burst ulcer, the death of Dinah's husband, of a sinister doctor friend, Dr Selbig, of one of Madeleine's sons, of Georgie killed by a car, of Dinah's and Madeleine's father, and of Dinah's stillborn child. The evening when Rickie alone in London takes shelter with Georgie is full of ominous portent, of something terrible about to be unleashed.

> 'What are we waiting for?' she murmured. 'Something is going on. . . . Is it going to be a little more than we can bear?' . . .
> 'We shall be told,' he said, mild, reassuring. . . .
> He reflected carefully on what, by pure chance, he had seen go over, extraordinarily low, at the exact moment when he had emerged into the area. . . . An aircraft with a tail of fire, like a streaking comet. An aircraft engine with a thrumming and buzzing note. . . . He considered whether to mention it to Georgie now; decided not to. Time enough.

In a letter to Bernard Berenson about *The Echoing Grove*, Rosamond wrote, 'It may be that it will turn out to be only a novel *comme un autre*, but to myself I can truthfully say that every paragraph has come up out of the same level as poetry – and has had to be wrought line after line in the same way . . . everything I think I have discovered about the jungle of the human heart has gone into it.' She was particularly anxious that the book should not be categorised as a 'woman's novel', determined to show that with the character of Rickie she could create a convincingly masculine man, 'not just a woman novelist's idea of the male'. But from the critics the response to Rickie was disappointing. 'Sexually dim', said the *New Yorker*, like 'a soggy, half-deflated football', according to *Time*; the *Times Literary Supplement* found him 'strangely feminine', while Peter Quennell in the *Daily Mail* complained that 'Rickie remains an elegant tailor's dummy, all charm and chatter and rather bogus sexual attraction'.

Chosen as Book of the Month by the Book Society in Britain as well as by the Franco-British Book Selection Committee in Paris, *The Echoing Grove* was widely reviewed in Britain and France and in the United States, where it was the first of Rosamond's novels to be published by Harcourt, Brace, the firm which had taken over Reynal & Hitchcock six years before. Reactions varied as to the novel's quality, women reviewers on the whole responding more favourably than their male colleagues. There were a few exceptions – 'a great novel by any standards, ancient or modern', stated George Scott in *Truth* – but most of the men took John Betjeman's line, who wrote in the *Daily Telegraph* that he found the book less than compelling, 'partly because I am a man and this is very much a woman's book'. The *News Chronicle* agreed: 'Women luxuriate in these books as in hot baths, while men test them doubtfully with a tentative toe.' Bearing out the accuracy of this statement, Elizabeth Bowen was full of praise in the *New Republic*, Rebecca West stated it was the book she had most enjoyed that year, Elizabeth Janeway described the novel as 'a masterpiece' in the *New York Times*, and Marghanita Laski in the *Observer* declared that, 'No English writer has told of the pains of women in love more truly or more movingly than Rosamond Lehmann. . . . This is the book that Virginia Woolf wanted, the book that told what it felt like to be a woman.' But the sisterhood was not wholly united, and it was one of their number, Honor Tracy in the *New Statesman*, who of all the critics proved the most openly hostile. Describing the novel as a 'tedious affair', and Dinah and Madeleine as a couple of 'soulful bitches', she admitted she found the experience of reading from beginning to end almost unendurable. 'I must confess to having plodded along with an ever-growing exasperation,' she wrote. 'Exquisitely feminine readers . . . will probably receive the book with rapture. Others may feel as if they were making their way through a sea of toasted marshmallow.'

Rosamond prided herself on being able to take criticism well. 'I don't think reviews ever really shook me – good or bad,' she said once in an interview. 'I had a very solid core of self-criticism, that wouldn't let me be either too easily satisfied, or too deeply scarred.' But Honor Tracy's attack proved the exception. Infuriated, Rosamond made it widely known that she considered Miss Tracy's review malicious and offensive, and the New Statesman's literary editor, John Raymond, beneath contempt for his treachery in not suppressing such an unpardonable piece of invective. Friends and fellow novelists were lobbied and encouraged to write in protest, which many did, among them Stephen and Natasha Spender, William Cooper, Kay Dick and Pamela Hansford Johnson. Next the influential Raymond Mortimer was appealed to, but Mortimer refused to join the chorus of disapproval. 'I am afraid that as an ex-editor I cannot honestly share your view that John Raymond should have suppressed the critics,' he wrote. 'Will you be furious with me if I say that the admiration you have earned all over the world should enable you to disregard any word of dispraise, however odious?' The editor of the New Statesman, Kingsley Martin, took much the same line. 'Authors have a cross to bear: you . . . a very much lighter one than most people's,' he wrote briskly. 'In the case of the Honor Tracy review, I am, I confess, a bit surprised that you should still be bothered about it.'

Among Rosamond's own circle, as among the reviewers, responses to The Echoing Grove were far from uniform. The Spenders loved the book – 'very impressive and, at times, extremely moving', said Stephen – as did, among others, Rupert Hart-Davis, William Plomer, Somerset Maugham and Kenneth Clark, while Dadie, Raymond Mortimer, Eddy Sackville-West and, across the Channel, Gabriel Marcel confessed themselves disappointed. John Lehmann, always his sister's most attentive critic, wrote a long analytical letter on the subject. He admitted he found himself somewhat confused at times and dissatisfied by the portrayal of the two women as (in his view) remorseless man-eaters, but nonetheless the novel was a triumphant achievement. 'You make all other novelists writing today seem inarticulate or phoney . . . [and] you work with absolute freedom at a level where very few writers can operate at all,' he told Rosamond. Knowing the source from which it

315

sprang, the book had also profoundly dismayed him. 'It is terrific; and terrible; because such writing could only come out of the most terrible suffering. It is one of the most unmitigatedly painful books I have ever read: the almost total absence of that enveloping aura of the poetry of natural beauty which I have always loved so much in your writing, makes it seem like an inferno.'

The summer of 1953 was the summer of Elizabeth II's coronation, and London, gaily bedecked, was in festive mood. With the novel out of the way and Sally travelling on the continent with a group of friends, Rosamond felt free to enjoy herself, attending parties, dinners, the opera at Covent Garden, Benjamin Britten's Festival at Aldeburgh, with Joshua Rowley devotedly in the background ready to escort her when required. Only one cloud floated across this otherwise serene blue sky.

A couple of months before the publication of *The Echoing Grove* in April, Cecil's verse sequence, *An Italian Visit*, had at last made its appearance, delayed for nearly three years by Rosamond's withholding her consent for the publication of the sixth of the seven sections, 'Elegy Before Death: At Settignano'. At the end of 1952 she had finally relented, but the stirring up of memories of the visit to I Tatti five years before was agonising. 'It makes me feel like a ghost. . . . I mean, to be posthumously commemorated, so personally, nakedly too, in one's life time,' she wrote to Berenson. She suffered further anguish on the publication of Cecil's poem 'George Meredith, 1861', inspired by the story of Meredith's unhappy first marriage:[5]

> . . . He'd been the battlefield long enough
> As well as a combatant, when he withdrew
> Scorching the earth behind him thus . . .

Interpreting the poem as a gloss on the breakdown of their own love-affair, she wrote in outrage to Cecil, upbraiding him for his brutal insensitivity. In a dignified reply, Cecil apologised for having caused pain, which was far from his intention. 'What I thought I was doing was writing a poem about Meredith's heart & mind at and after the *Modern*

---

[5] This was also the subject of Meredith's poem *Modern Love*, from which Rosamond took the title of *Dusty Answer*.

Love time,' he explained. 'Inevitably some of myself & my experience went into the poem, as yours did into your last novel: but the poem is no more autobiographical in intention than (I imagine) the novel was.' Rosamond had a further grievance: she had been appalled to hear Cecil on the Third Programme reading some of his poems, including 'The Album', written expressly for her in their happy early days together, and relating them to his life. The performance had so incensed her that she was moved to compose a bitter little satire, 'Dirge for Rather a Nasty Spirit', parodying Richard Hughes's poem 'Burial of the Spirit of a Young Poet':

> . . . 'Relics! Mementos! All for hire!'
> Come Culture Lovers, B.B.C.,
> Come agents, publishers, conspire
> To offer a substantial fee;
> Come Sunday nights, when C.D.L.
> To all will bare his amorous past;
> When C.D.L., yes C.D.L.
> Will cry his wares – (who weeps? – or laughs?)
> An Album, several photographs
> That once were dear; but, quite a bargain now, upon the Air,
>   the air are cast.

To Cecil himself she wrote that the experience had been like listening to 'the embalmer discussing the technique of the operation in the case of loved ones'; his cruel indifference to her feelings could only mean that he thought of her as dead. 'Hardly a day passes that I do not think of you, but not as dead,' Cecil wrote; as far as he was concerned there was nothing more to be said, 'except that the answer to such questions as "have you quite forgotten that I am a real woman & that our love was once real?" is "No, & never shall."'

As these angry reactions demonstrate, Rosamond was far from reconciled to Cecil's having left her. At one level she had recovered a degree of equilibrium, able to take pleasure in a 'new feeling of release and revival and enjoyment of the love of friends'. Yet not far beneath the surface some bitter emotions continued to fester. Rosamond's greatest fear was of running into Cecil in the street or at a party, a fear far from groundless as he and Jill lived only a short distance away and moved in many of the same circles. By sheer good fortune the dreaded encounter had never taken place; but on 6 July 1955 it happened. Chatto & Windus threw a big centennial party which, as one of their distinguished authors, Rosamond was persuaded to attend. Cecil as a director was bound to be there, she knew, but with several rooms and in such a crowd she assumed it would be relatively easy to avoid coming face to face. And so it proved – until a mischievous guest decided as a prank to bring the two together, going up to Cecil and telling him that Rosamond wished to speak to him. Believing the message to be genuine, Cecil went to find her. The result was cataclysmic. According to one report, '[Rosamond] stood back, then hit him with a smack that resounded round the room.' Jill Day Lewis, who missed the actual encounter, recalled, 'I saw him come down the stairs *ashen*. I don't know what she said ... [but] she simply tore him apart. I had to take him home. It was terrible.'

Cecil in a subterranean way had provided much of the inspiration for *The Echoing Grove*, and Rosamond recognised that her next theme must take a different direction entirely. She began pondering an idea for a new novel, but in fact it would be many years before another full-length work of fiction, her last, would appear. For the present she immersed herself in short-term projects, a paper on Mrs Gaskell given at Leicester University in the autumn of 1953, and in November 1954 she undertook a tour in Switzerland for the British Council and PEN, reading from her novels and lecturing on 'The Theme of Innocence in English Fiction'.

Her most substantial undertaking was a translation of Jean Cocteau's novella *Les Enfants Terribles*. Rosamond enjoyed translating, regarding it as 'good mental exercise – makes me think about words – accuracy, precision, different ways of conveying meaning'. In 1936 she had translated Jean Cassou's story 'Letter to Cousin Mary' for *New Writing*, and in 1948, also for John Lehmann, a short novel by Jacques Lemarchand, *Geneviève*, for which she was awarded the Denyse Clarouin Translation Prize. Rosamond had first met Cocteau at a luncheon party in Paris in 1937 and been much taken with him: the great man had kissed her hand, told her he had come expressly to meet the author of *Poussière*, and assured her of the profound admiration of a fellow poet. 'His manners were so winning,' she said, 'he created an atmosphere so cordial and life-enhancing, that it was impossible to feel anything but ease and pleasure in his company.' She recognised that he and she had little in common, but nonetheless when she was approached by the Harvill Press she accepted the commission gladly, convinced that the experience would prove rewarding. It did not. The months spent working on *Les Enfants Terribles*, 'that *untranslatable* Greek myth in contemporary guise', turned out to be a 'hideous horrible nightmare task', with which Rosamond struggled miserably. 'Cocteau is utter total unremitting *hell* – because of his deceptive lucidity, his condensations, his ellipses, his opium-eater's intensity of vision that never relaxes & for which there is no equivalent,' she complained to Roger Senhouse. '[I] have, so to speak, to "invent" the whole thing over again from scratch, trying as I go along to penetrate the imagination of the creator *and* to listen with his or her ear; *and* to eliminate any suggestion of my own "rhythms" – and obviously this is not really possible.' In despair she was forced to engage an assistant, the estranged wife of Ignazio Silone who was a notable French scholar. 'She comes daily and I pay her £1 a day and together we wrestle groaning with this diabolical Laocoon.'

As might be expected, the results were far from satisfactory. Rosamond considered that with *Children of the Game*, as it was titled in English, she had eventually achieved a more than adequate rendering, and the Harvill Press were pleased, sending the manuscript to the francophile Raymond Mortimer in expectation of a flattering tribute. But none such was forthcoming. Mortimer was shocked by Rosamond's version, as he candidly told her: 'you have been working on a principle that I personally find strange and unacceptable,[6] he wrote. 'You have added and suppressed and changed so much that the result does not seem to me a translation, but a paraphrase, a different book. . . . I believe that Cocteau will be enraged, and that any critic who knows the original will be brutal.' Severely shaken, Harvill decided that the only way to deal with the problem was to keep silent: they must 'not on any account mention RM's view to anyone. . . . If we keep our nerve now we will bring that book out with a puff from Cocteau on the jacket saying how good it is.' Fortunately, Cocteau spoke not one word of English: '*Je vous*

---

[6] Mortimer had originally written 'odious', then crossed it out and substituted 'unacceptable'.

donne confiance les yeux fermés, incapable que je suis de pénétrer l'âme et les gestes de votre langue,[7] he had written to Rosamond before the work was begun. And on publication it was clear that his confidence remained intact: he obligingly supplied a graceful quote, and wrote charmingly to Rosamond herself: '*Chaque fois que je me sens découragé par l'immense sottise de l'univers . . . je regarde votre livre du coin de l'oeil et je pense: "J'ai tout de même gagné le Derby."* '[8] The reviews were 'none-too-gratifying', but so relieved was Rosamond to be done with the work that she cared very little what they said.

Meanwhile there were other, more pressing matters to claim her attention. The last couple of years had seen some major changes within the family. In the spring of 1953, Cristina, who for some time had been seriously ill, died agonisingly from cancer. Immediately it occurred to Rosamond that perhaps she and Wogan might remarry. He had come to see her after Cristina's death, and she was touched by how calm and sad he was, how dignified in the aftermath of his tragedy. 'He wouldn't go into how awful it had been, although I knew from Hugo it had been.' Soon she had convinced herself that Wogan was definitely coming back to her, and began talking of it almost as a *fait accompli*, which, said Hugo, 'I found frightfully embarrassing' – particularly as nothing could have been further from the truth: Wogan had already decided on this third wife, Tamara Rust, a Communist and widow of Bill Rust, former editor of the *Daily Worker*. They married the following year, 1954, the same year that Hugo's wife, Margaret, gave birth to a daughter, an event of unalloyed delight to Rosamond. Anna Margaret 'has a beautiful long head, very widely-spaced *long* eyes, and a look of intense alertness and sensibility which wrings my heart', she wrote to Dadie. But most momentous of all was the news that Sally, having fallen in love at Oxford with a fellow undergraduate, in October 1955 announced her engagement. The information was received by Rosamond with surprising calm. Sally's fiancé, Patrick Kavanagh, was 'a penniless, interesting, quiet, independent-minded young man'. He seemed to be very good for

[7] 'I trust you blindly, incapable as I am of understanding the soul and gesture of your language.'

[8] 'Whenever I feel discouraged by the immense foolishness of the universe . . . I glance at your book and think: "After all, I won the Derby." '

Sally, and Rosamond looked forward to arranging their wedding early in the new year. '[I] am really happy about the marriage,' she wrote to Berenson.

12

'The One Flawless Joy of My Life'

The romantic heroes who populated Rosamond's imagination were aristocratic, divinely good-looking, arrogantly at ease in their feudal, moneyed existence. It might, therefore, have been supposed that she would hope for just such a one, a Rickie or Rollo, to marry her daughter. And perhaps on one level she did. Yet from the moment Sally fell in love with Patrick Kavanagh it was clear she had found whom she wanted, and her mother was too happy for her daughter seriously to wish for anything different. Certainly Patrick – Irish, Catholic, in his own words 'genteel poor' – came from a very different mould. His father, Ted Kavanagh, was the scriptwriter for the popular radio comedy show *ITMA* (*It's That Man Again*). Patrick, an actor and poet at university, was three years older than Sally, having done his National Service before going up to Oxford, and he had seen more of the world than many of his contemporaries: after school in Switzerland he had worked in Paris, and while in the army was posted to Japan and Korea; after graduation came a year with the British Council in Barcelona, and it was not until his return from Spain that he proposed to Sally. Rosamond soon came to feel fond of the quirky, bookish young man, with 'his solitary rebarbative yet strong and loving nature'; she was touched by his devotion to Sally, and respected the fact that he was not remotely in awe of herself. 'He is a boy in a thousand,' she declared.

If the prospect of Sally's marrying inevitably brought its anxieties, there was also satisfaction in making arrangements on the young people's behalf. 'Although Sally is so sensible & independent and shouldering the main burden of her future (ie. seeing solicitors, builders, plumbers, going to furniture sales etc.) herself, I must be at hand to help and advise,' Rosamond wrote contentedly to Mrs Hammersley in January 1956. When Hugo had married, Rosamond knew she was losing her son, but in her uneasy relationship with Margaret could hardly claim she was gaining a daughter. In Patrick, however, there was much less of a threat. With as yet no settled direction, he was unlikely to assert too drastic an independence, and it seemed more than probable that the pair would remain under her wing for some time to come. Certainly their financial situation was precarious, Patrick earning a meagre salary as a production assistant at the BBC, while Sally supplemented the modest income made over to her by her mother with a variety of part-time jobs. Fortunately, a few weeks before the wedding, Aunt Gwen, Wogan's sister, came forward with a generous offer: she proposed to buy a house in London in which for the immediate future Patrick and Sally could live for a minimal rent. It was Rosamond who found the perfect property, a sweet little three-storeyed house in Clareville Grove, South Kensington, within walking distance from Eaton Square, 'with a tiny garden & a roof garden, & ultimately room for at least 2 grandchildren for me. . . . The two young creatures are so blissfully excited – it's a joy to see them.'

Rosamond's pleasure was genuine, but it is likely that there were other, subconscious reasons for her approval of the match. Since Sally's return from Italy in September 1952 her mother had found herself increasingly outshone. 'Sally was a honey,' as Laurie Lee said, and during the Oxford vacations the young men who came calling at the flat clustered round Sally, unthinkingly making it plain that it was the daughter, not the mother, who was the focus of their attentions. If never as striking as her mother, Sally, with her fair hair, green eyes and perfect smiling mouth had a freshness and innocence which were irresistibly attractive. Rosamond delighted in it, and at the same time she was acutely aware of the contrast to her own fading looks. Her beauty no longer made the impact that once it had, and as a consequence she craved even more the reassurance of male admiration. As she wrote to Berenson in a curious bilingual version of Baudelaire's line, 'it's a dur métier que d'avoir the reputation of being belle femme'. Laurie Lee, in the unique position of being equally a friend to both women, remarked on the shift in emphasis. Whereas previously Sally had been the satellite, now the situation was reversed, and Rosamond, to whom the supporting role was as uncomfortable as it was unfamiliar, needed to make strenuous efforts to maintain her position centre stage. When Sally's young men arrived, said Laurie, 'Rosamond would go into overdrive. She would sweep them off their feet and away from Sally, demanding their attention. I don't think Sally noticed really, but I noticed.'

If in one way a rival to her daughter, at another more fundamental level Rosamond was heavily dependent upon her. When Sally at 21 came down from Oxford she was a serene and well-adjusted young woman, already a stronger, more integrated personality than her mother. Sally not only loved her mother but she understood her anxieties and insecurities; understood them but never played up to them, never gave in to the superhuman demands for the homage and adulation that were exacted from others. With her daughter, Rosamond knew she was accepted for herself and loved unconditionally; there was no need for the destructive emotional games she indulged in elsewhere. With Sally, she finally achieved the profound, balanced and loving relationship that had through her life persistently eluded her. Of course there were rows – Miss Resista was far from biddable and liked to have her own way – but Sally's optimistic nature and firm grasp of actuality kept Rosamond anchored in the real world, and at the same time made that world enjoyable. She steered her mother away from the tragic view, from moroseness and self-pity, encouraged her to laugh and have fun – the two of them together were great gigglers, with a store of frivolous private jokes. From her earliest days Rosamond had looked for someone to lean on, and since Cecil left she had come to look primarily to her daughter for support. '[Sally] is more at home in the world . . . than I am,' her mother wrote of her. 'Just as I was born lost and searching, she was born found.'

The engaged couple had hoped for a quiet ceremony, but Rosamond's wishes prevailed, and the wedding, on 28 February 1956, was a grand affair. According to Vatican rules, Sally in order to marry a Roman Catholic was obliged to take instruction, although she had declined to be received into the Church as in her view her Anglicanism was quite good enough. For this reason the nuptial mass was conducted in a side chapel, rather than at the main altar of the Brompton Oratory, one of the most fashionable Catholic churches in London. Patrick's father, Ted Kavanagh, had suggested the reception be held at the Rubens Hotel immediately opposite the Oratory, but this was vetoed by Rosamond, who insisted on the hiring of an expensive house in Park Lane. Wogan was there to give his daughter away, and there was a large gathering of Lehmanns and Philippses, among them Sally's Lehmann grandmother, for whom this was to be the last appearance at a family reunion.

Although Rosamond was a dutiful daughter, her relationship with her mother had grown no warmer in recent years, with Alice remaining critical and undemonstrative, apparently more interested in her local committees than in the lives of her daughters. In 1954 her eightieth birthday had been celebrated by all four of her children taking her to the theatre, with supper afterwards at John's house in Egerton Crescent. John had remained his mother's darling; Alice doted on him, looked up to him, relied on him, and always gave generous financial support to his various publishing ventures. In August 1956 Alice, at 82 extremely frail, was taken to hospital in High Wycombe to be operated on for the removal of a cyst. Cancer was discovered, a second operation followed on 5 September, and two days afterwards she died. 'It was a blessing,' Rosamond told Mrs Hammersley. 'There would have had to be another operation the surgeon told me today & he feared a growth in the bowel.' She, her two sisters and John had been at the bedside, although only Helen was actually present at the end. Violet Hammersley, Alice's oldest friend, wrote a tribute to her for *The Times*, recalling the beginning of their friendship in the early days at Bourne End, 'when . . . through a little gate in the garden wall . . . I found, sitting on the lawn under the trees, a charming & pretty ash blonde, dressed in turquoise blue to match her eyes, elegant, quiet, but assured'. In reply to a letter of condolence from Rupert Hart-Davis, Rosamond wrote, 'My mother was an extremely impressive character, – the most *upright* I have ever known; and wonderfully benevolent and shrewd. . . . She was, I suppose, "proud of her children", as everyone assures me; but she never let on to *us*! and always made me feel I could have done better in every way if I'd tried harder. Too true!'

Shortly before she died Alice had made Rosamond promise that she would never quarrel with her brother, a promise that was nearly broken the very day after her death, while brother and sister were staying together at Little Fieldhead. '[Rosamond] succeeded in wounding me deeply by an incredible failure of tact and imagination,' John wrote in his diary. Rosamond's relations with John had suffered a sharp decline after Cecil's departure, when John not only refused to condemn Cecil but continued to see him socially and work with him, in 1955 collaborating with him in editing *The Chatto Book of Modern Poetry*. This had been regarded as a base betrayal which Rosamond found hard to forgive, although she did her best to put it behind her, continuing to support her brother in his professional activities. John had recently taken over the editorship of the *London Magazine*, his publishing house, John Lehmann Ltd, having collapsed under the weight of financial difficulty at the end of 1952. Three years later John published the first volume of an autobiography, *The Whispering Gallery*, infusing his childhood and youth with a rosy and romantic light which his sisters found ludicrous. 'It made Bea and me so furious,' said Rosamond, 'because the impression given is that we lived in this stately home, in a dream of glamour with adoring underlings, entertaining on a vast scale, as though we'd lived at Cliveden. He was an adored, marvellous-looking, spoilt little boy. He says over and over again how he adored me, and he did. And I adored him.'

The marvellous-looking little boy was now a tall, handsome, balding, middle-aged man of imposing presence. Most striking were his deep blue eyes, eyes like forget-me-nots in a skull, according to William Plomer who, like many of Lehmann's friends, admired the acumen and patience he showed in dealing with his contributors while acknowledging the extreme trickiness of his personality. Sexually voracious, John was emotionally cold and controlling, capable of gross insensitivity towards others while remaining thin-skinned himself, with a long memory for slights and offences. His sisters joked about his touchiness and pomposity, all three of them only too familiar with the sulks and bad moods, usually signalled by what they described as his narrow-eyed 'Interpol' expression.

As testified in his autobiography, his family meant a great deal to John, and it was Rosamond to whom intellectually he was closest, and yet of all the siblings John and Rosamond had the most tempestuous relationship, irritating and exasperating each other sometimes beyond endurance. The most violent explosion, mainly the result of long-simmering resentment dating from the time of Cecil's defection, occurred on a snowy day in March 1958, when John was driving Rosamond in London. She had been nagging him to take a different route when he suddenly erupted, shouting at her to be quiet, whereupon Rosamond completely lost control and hit him. Stunned, John stopped the car and pushed her out, leaving her to walk the slushy streets in search of a taxi. 'The amount of pain & distress incurred by both of us is obviously not measurable,' Rosamond wrote to him afterwards. Admitting that it was indefensible to have attacked him physically, she attempted to account for what had happened. 'A cry far back, deep-rooted panic and horror rose up in me when you were shouting; it wasn't only your shouting at me; it was Daddy shouting at Mother which is one of the deepest traumatic memories of my childhood. Probably you never witnessed it, but I did, more than once.' She was sad about their relationship, she continued, because she knew they loved each other, yet she resented John's self-imposed role of judge and censor. 'I so often am made to feel conscious of your disapproval – and that shrivels me up,' she complained. In particular she was hurt by his constant harping on her poor productivity as a writer, when in fact he made no attempt to understand the peculiar difficulties under which she laboured. 'You give me the impression that you ascribe my failure to turn out work to idleness or perversity or time-wasting. I do waste my time, I am lazy – but the reason is that I have lost my sense of direction and what self-confidence I ever had.'

If Rosamond hoped that John would be moved by this explanation she was to be disappointed. 'Of course, after what you write in your letter, I shall try and *get past* your assault on me in the car,' her brother replied. 'But I can't yet, because it was the most horrible and frightening thing that has ever happened to me. . . . I'm afraid I'm sure we ought not to meet each other for a while.'

Anxiety over her current lack of inspiration was very real, and Rosamond's suspicion that it indicated a failing of her powers as a writer had begun to haunt her. 'You *ought* to understand what anguish it is to feel one's creative powers blocked, or (as one naturally fears) petering out altogether,' she had written to John in the same letter. Characteristically Rosamond blamed much of her difficulty on her situation as a woman alone, a woman struggling to cope in a harsh world without the support of a loving man beside her. In this her outlook was strongly influenced by her father's anti-feminist attitudes, attitudes which, unfortunately for her peace of mind, were little tempered by her mother's New England spirit of independence. 'Every woman who is a poet or novelist is, I think, inclined to be melancholy and self-distrustful by nature. She needs a Leonard Woolf, or a G. H. Lewes, or a Maurice Goudeket or an Osbert – someone at the centre to encourage and support her. No doubt partly through my own fault I have never had this blessing in any of its forms, and see little if any prospect now of ever finding it.' Her examples – Virginia Woolf, George Eliot, Colette, Edith Sitwell – are carefully chosen to fortify her argument, and the fact that other names could as easily have been picked to demonstrate the opposite – Jane Austen, the Brontës, Rose Macaulay, Lilian Bowes-Lyon, Ivy Compton-Burnett, Stevie Smith – is largely irrelevant. In this area, Rosamond was not robust; she felt she needed male companionship, it was her due, and without it she would always repine.

Not unnaturally Rosamond felt she was in danger of becoming 'hopelessly neurotic' on the subject of her writing. In July 1956, in reply to a letter of friendly enquiry from Violet Hammersley, she wrote:

> You ask am I 'finishing a book?' . . . NO!! And never never never manage to isolate enough time and privacy for concentrated writing – and this drives me frantic. The unceasing telephone, and engagements, and meetings, and voluntary work for the Society of Authors and P.E.N. (not all that much but it takes time) and a correspondence which I can never manage to reduce or quite cope with, and a very stupid tho' willing antique maid in mornings only, quite incapable of taking the simplest message correctly, – and no cook – Why go on?

In fact there was one project Rosamond had managed to complete, a short story whose theme was distantly related to her ill-fated pre-war play, *No More Music*. Published by Macmillan in the *Winter's Tales* annual of 1956, 'A Hut, a Sea-Grape Tree' is, like the play, set in a small hotel on an island in the West Indies. On the beach beneath the hotel is a sea-grape tree, and in its shade a Victorian bathing hut, said to be haunted by bad spirits, or duppies. On the verandah sits a young woman, Margot Fielding, trying to write her journal but weighed down by loneliness and a strange, melancholy lassitude. There is a hint that she is unrequitedly in love with the husband of the couple with whom she travelled to the island. Also on the verandah is the hotel manageress, the eccentric Miss Stay, and a couple of guests, Captain and Mrs Cunningham, she silly but amiable, he a sadistic bully. In and out of the background wander a pair of nurses, glimpsed sunbathing or heard endlessly playing the gramophone in their room. The black maid, Princess, is the same as the maid in *No More Music*. Delicate and insubstantial, the story is in the form of an internal monologue of Margot Fielding's, interrupted by the resolutely banal conversation of the Cunninghams and Miss Stay. The young woman hears the voices of the others as if from a great distance. Her eyes focus dreamily on the sea-grape tree which idly she begins to draw. 'Suddenly, stealthily, in the dead centre something altered . . . there was something else there . . . a shadow shaped like a man . . . the ghost of a man . . . lost out of life and time, holding two things together with his shadow.'

Rosamond was pleased with the story, while at the same time aware that she was not yet done with the subject. '[I] very soon saw that it could and should be Part 1 of a longer piece of writing,' she told Denys Kilham Roberts. So convinced was she that there was more to be excavated from the roots of her sea-grape tree that shortly after the story's publication she began developing the theme into a full-length novel. 'It is wonderful to be working again, though infinitely pénible and exhausting,' she wrote to Berenson in July 1956. 'It is a different sort of thing, I really think, from anything that has gone before. The "I" who was always somewhere . . . seems to have disappeared – and the whole "vision of life" – to use an over-dignifying phrase, to have become reoriented. I don't a bit know what it is that is appearing on the page.' Certainly she can have had no conception that the work begun that summer was to be her last work of fiction, not to reach completion for another twenty years.

When John accused his sister of laziness in her working life, he was mainly referring to the dissipation of her energies in what he saw as a pointless round of entertaining and being entertained by people who meant little to her, a judgement unnecessarily harsh of someone who was fond of her friends and liked to treat them generously. Even John had to admit that the dinners she gave were enjoyable: '[she] always makes the flat look charming, has delicious food & good (ish) wine, and whenever I have been there excellently chosen company,' he wrote after dining at Eaton Square in August 1957 with the Kenneth Clarks and Tom Eliot and his new wife, Valerie. Rosamond described the same occasion in a letter to Frances Partridge, with whom her old friendship had recently been renewed. 'T. S. Eliot came to dinner mit Bride. She is a calm unpretentious friendly woman, intelligent and nice. . . . He seems blissful, & they hold hands all the time and dote on one another mildly rather than madly but certainly they dote.' That same year, 1957, there is mention of numerous theatre-parties amd dinner-parties – many given by Rosamond, often with Patrick and Sally in attendance; a luncheon-party of Edith Sitwell's at the Sesame Club; tea with the 'sublime and scarifying' Ivy Compton-Burnett; and in June to celebrate John's fiftieth birthday a picnic supper at Lake Cottage, his weekend retreat in Sussex, with the three sisters and John's long-time, long-suffering companion, the dancer Alexis Rassine. The year ended with a New Year's Eve party at Eaton Square, a riotous success in spite of the absence of Hugo as well as of Sally and Patrick. The New Year's Honours list had just been announced, with Rose Macaulay's DBE. 'Darling Rose Macaulay is a Dame. I heard just in time to spread the news,' Rosamond told Sally. 'I turned it into a sort of celebration party for her, which was lovely. In fact it was altogether a marvellous party, though I say it myself. . . . Not having you, Pat or H[ugo] there, I didn't ask any young things; and perhaps it was the absence of those critical, scornful and censorious young eyes that enabled us middle-agers to behave with extra recklessness.'

'Recklessness' here signified no more than drinking a little too much champagne, but there were other occasions when Rosamond pushed the boundaries further. Since moving to London she had struck up a close friendship with Patrick Trevor-Roper, distinguished ophthalmic surgeon and younger brother of the historian Hugh Trevor-Roper. Clever, sympathetic and amusing, he provided just the kind of male company Rosamond most enjoyed, and he soon became a regular visitor to Eaton

Square. Pat was a friend of Raymond Mortimer, who hearing about Gerald Heard's and Aldous Huxley's experiments with mescalin in California persuaded Pat to try something similar with him. When Rosamond was told of it, she became intensely curious and asked Pat to organise a similar session for her, just the two of them in the flat, with a young psychiatrist friend of Rosamond's asked in as an observer. 'It was fairly dramatic,' Pat recalled. 'Rosamond looked increasingly beautiful and statuesque, and her hair seemed to move in solid blocks. She kept saying, "The stone inside my womb is getting heavier and heavier. Oh, my womb is weighing so much." . . . It went on like that for two or three hours.' Rosamond was both intrigued and repelled by the effect of the drug, remembering

> a hard-edged semi-mineral disparate world of artefacts and coldness . . . phenomena that astonished me and yet had no meaning, and from which I was *horribly separated* so that I could feel no love for or pleasure in them. And the visual hallucinations I had for a time were of reptilian or crustacean forms of life i.e. P.T.-R.'s hands became crawling lobsters. His face and also the psychiatrist's looked *knowing*, crafty-eyed, although archaic images of stone.

In the middle of March 1957 Rosamond spent a week at I Tatti. 'Rosamond Lehmann arrived yesterday,' Berenson wrote in his diary, 'as magnificently beautiful as ever, even if a trifle stouter. Only her eyes begin to have the rusty look of age . . . As a spectacle, as a talker, as an artist, I know nobody so life-enhancing.' The few days in Italy were a welcome restorative as Rosamond before she left had had to cope with crises involving both her children, Sally having suffered an early miscarriage, and Hugo announcing that he and Margaret were to part as Margaret had fallen in love with another man.

Margaret's decision to end the marriage, although painful in the extreme for Hugo, was regarded by Rosamond as not wholly a disaster. Over time she had come to feel affection for her daughter-in-law, but was openly disapproving when Margaret took a job modelling for Vogue necessitating frequent absences in Paris, which was considered a dereliction of duty both as Hugo's wife and Anna's mother. Rosamond was besotted with her little granddaughter, who at least once a week was delivered by her nanny to spend the day; in between Rosamond took to dropping in at the Philippses' flat, only a few doors away at 65 Eaton Square, to check up on the baby and proffer advice about her upbringing. 'She started being rather criticising,' said Margaret, 'and that was a bit difficult.' As his marriage began to disintegrate, Hugo, true to his reticent nature, never confided and never complained, keeping his mother at arm's length, securely fenced off from his inner emotional territory. With his public-school upbringing reinforcing his natural reserve, Hugo took after the Philipps more than the Lehmann side of his family, remaining conventional, undemonstrative and intensely private. Although he had followed father and grandfather into the City, joining the family firm as an underwriter at Lloyds, Hugo was happiest in Wales, fishing and shooting and learning how to manage the estate. 'His grasp of estate management amazes me,' Rosamond wrote after Christmas at Llanstephan in 1957. 'He certainly loves the place & is extremely busy and efficient.'

Soon after her return from Italy, Rosamond wrote to Frances Partridge, 'My life is now agreeable and comfortable but somewhat pointless in my own opinion.' The reason for her dissatisfaction was the usual one. 'I have not a companion to look after & be looked after by – and without that, all seems peripheral and hard to find a focus for.' By now the relationship with Joshua had settled into a companionable friendship, a change in status which saddened Rosamond more for its reflection on her waning powers than because of any overwhelming passion for Joshua. He provided her with solace, and she relied on his devotion and dependability, even if she sometimes found him a little staid, lacking Willy Mostyn-Owen's sophistication and panache. (When Joshua first met Willy, Rosamond said, it was like seeing a bull-dog with a saluki.) Besides, Joshua had begun to show an unwelcome independence, insisting on his right to see other, younger women friends, in spite of the jealous scenes such behaviour invariably provoked. Now in her late fifties, Rosamond suffered all the insecurities of the ageing beauty, growing increasingly more importunate with her male acquaintance, her vanity, her neediness and her desire for a strong masculine presence leading her almost querulously to exact expressions of admiration that as a younger woman she was accustomed to receiving as a matter of course. A new friend, the writer and architectural historian James ('Jim') Lees-

Milne, who had recently married Alvilde Chaplin, remarked on this trait. 'Ros has a strong femininity with which I feel at times impatient. I am sure she does not expect or want a gesture of love from me, but I am occasionally made uncomfortable in suspecting that she would welcome the pretence of one.' (According to Rosamond's account, when Jim met her he became instantly enamoured, a version of events of which Jim himself had no recollection. 'I don't believe that I so fell for her that I exclaimed, Too late, too late!, having just married A[lvilde],' he wrote in his diary. 'Can it be true?')

All such frustrations were now overshadowed by the news, devastating to Rosamond, that in September Patrick and Sally were to leave England to live for two years in Indonesia. Patrick, having given up his much-disliked job at the BBC, had been working for a publisher, but office life bored and depressed him, and much as he and Sally loved the little house in Clareville Grove, they both felt that now, before they started a family and became too settled, was the time to try something different, to escape the dreariness of post-war England and go in search of adventure. Patrick had applied to the British Council for a teaching job, to be told they could offer a posting either to Istanbul or to Java. 'We hoped for Istanbul,' he wrote in his memoir. 'We got Java.'

All summer Rosamond remained in a state of dread at the prospect of parting with her daughter. A few weeks before the Kavanaghs were due to go she was unsettled further by learning of a chance encounter of theirs with Cecil. Patrick walking with Sally in the West End caught sight of Cecil buying cherries from a barrow in Davies Street. Sally, short-sighted, failed to recognise him, but Patrick urged her to go up to him, which after a moment's nervous hesitation she did, returning to her husband with a cheerful expression on her face. 'We were both pleased, I think,' said Patrick. 'A piece of the past had been brought out into the open and looked at, and that's usually a pretty good idea.' Cecil himself later described the exchange as 'affectionate'. Certainly as far as Sally was concerned, their brief conversation was enough to heal any lingering feelings of resentment, and thereafter she always referred to Cecil with fondness. But Rosamond when she heard about it was incensed, seizing on the fact that Sally had remarked how lined and haggard Cecil had looked. Sally, apparently, had been 'extremely shocked' by his changed appearance, telling her mother, 'I wish you could see him, you would feel better. He isn't a bit like the man we knew. His face is awful.'

The first part of September was spent by the Kavanaghs in a round of leavetaking. On the 10th, their last night in England, there was a farewell dinner at which Rosamond, suddenly distraught, rounded on Patrick, furiously accusing him of irresponsibility in taking Sally off to the other side of the world, to a country with a notoriously unhealthy climate, where the political situation was volatile and dangerous. Later she apologised for her outburst. 'Please put it down to primitive outraged maternal feelings plus drink and tiredness and dread of the prospect of the moment of parting,' she wrote to him. 'I was suddenly overcome with self-pity and wanted to accuse you of depriving me of my chief Prop and Comfort without giving me 100% fool-proof God-proof guarantees in advance that the whole venture was absolutely splendid and bound to Turn out for the Best.' Patrick and Sally sailed for Java on 11 September 1957, Rosamond seeing them off on the train from Waterloo, her last sight of her daughter that of '[Sally] looking intently at me from the window, not waving, white-faced'.

In retrospect Rosamond maintained that from the day Sally left, 'I didn't have one single happy moment,' but although there is no doubt that Sally was painfully missed and that her mother frequently felt rudderless and bewildered without her, there was enough going on, both absorbing and enjoyable, to prevent her life turning into the desert of despair that was afterwards depicted. The project dearest to her heart was the building of a little house on the Isle of Wight, scene of so many happy holidays in her own childhood as in Hugo's and Sally's. Rosamond had been encouraged in this by Violet Hammersley, who, for many years a widow, had become as close a friend to the Lehmann children, particularly to Rosamond, as she had been to their mother, all of them fascinated by her compelling, self-dramatising personality and her eccentric Spanish-duenna appearance, draped in black veils and shawls. Violet owned an 'enchantingly pretty bijou property' in Totland Bay, and it was the neighbouring plot, originally the Hammersleys' coachman's cottage and small garden, that Rosamond had bought the previous year with the intention of providing a tranquil retreat for the Kavanaghs when they came home on leave. The extension of the cottage and the building of a guest annexe at Little Eden, as the house

was called, was an absorbing undertaking, and Rosamond went over to
the Island as often as she could, sometimes taking Joshua with her.
'[Joshua] is really taking immense interest in the little house,' she
reported to Violet. And to Sally, to whom the house was legally to be
gifted, she wrote with satisfaction at the end of October, 'Great strides
made. Roof on, floors in, plumbing started.'

Soon the first letters began arriving from Java. The country was found
to be beautiful, although the capital Djakarta, currently under martial
law, had little to recommend it, and the stifling heat was proving hard to
bear. 'Oh so hot, hot, hot!' wrote Sally. 'My hair falls in unattractive
rats' tails round my face and I have a permanently beaded moustache.'
Insects were also a problem, large and ravenous mosquitoes, cock-
roaches, and others as yet unidentified – 'We have been unable to touch
the gramophone for two days since Patrick saw a vast hairy leg
disappearing into its innards.' For the present they were in temporary
accommodation which they were obliged to share, and were longing to
move into a house of their own. While Patrick was out most of the day
teaching at the university, Sally began giving classes in English to
students of a wide variety of nationalities, European, Indonesian,
Japanese. Although intrigued by the exotic nature of their surroundings,
neither of them was drawn to the ultra-conventional expatriate society,
mainly English and Dutch working for Shell. 'I really am going to
concentrate on making as much money as possible because I'm not really
sure how happy we're going to be,' Sally told her mother. 'The European
community is terrible and it will be very difficult to make Indonesian
friends at the moment . . . also I realise now how much I love England.'
At the end of the year the British Council at last provided them with a
house, 'but it's a horror,' said Sally, 'dark, airless, bathroomless, badly
designed and hideously furnished.' She was resolved, however, to make it
as attractive and comfortable as she could. 'A determined gleam came
into her eye,' wrote Patrick, 'and I almost heard the tapping of reservoirs
of resistance I might well envy.'

In London, Rosamond wrote long letters to her 'little Javas',
bemoaning their absence and increasingly anxious over the threatening
political situation. As she had done earlier with Sally over Cecil's
departure, so now she did with Anna, attributing many of her own
feelings to her 4-year-old granddaughter. No matter that Anna had

barely known Sally, who was already only a distant memory to the little girl, she was encouraged when with her grandmother to construct all her games around the fairytale figure of her absent aunt.

> Practically her first question (after: 'Can I have a sweet?') is always: 'Is Sally back yet?' . . . [sic] 'Why not?' . . . [sic] 'When's she coming?' . . . etc interspersed with plans for visiting you in Java . . . Her fantasies about you – and to a lesser degree Patrick – are assuming proportions beyond my control. Today she demanded to see all the photographs of you starting from babyhood. Various likenesses are set up and made to talk to one another or to *her* photograph.

The Christmas of 1957 Rosamond spent at Llanstephan. In the new year the news from Java was more cheerful as the Kavanaghs had managed to arrange a share in 'a charming, log-cabiny bungalow' in the hills where they could go at weekends. In answer to Rosamond's anxious queries about Sally's health, Patrick replied that he had never seen his wife looking better: she had just celebrated her twenty-third birthday, was playing tennis every day, and in spite of the difficult conditions was in excellent spirits – which was more than could be said for himself. 'I must say right away that among Sally's roses I am withered sedge,' he wrote. Indeed Patrick's health was beginning to cause some alarm as he suffered more than Sally from the heat, and was depressed by a bad skin infection on his hands which was failing to respond to treatment. However, there were other, pleasanter subjects to reflect on. In February Sally wrote to her mother, 'We're giving a great deal of thought to the problem of whether to start a baby yet or not . . .'

At the first mention of a possible pregnancy, Rosamond immediately determined that she must come out to Java to be with her daughter. In April 1958 she was due to leave for the United States on a long-planned lecture tour organised by the Institute of Contemporary Arts in Washington, and nothing could be easier than to divert her journey home via Indonesia. But Sally was not encouraging. Privately she and Patrick felt they needed more time on their own, away from family ties and obligations; and they were genuinely worried about the threat of insurrection, recently intensified by violent demonstrations against Dutch ex-colonials and an assassination attempt on the President,

Sukarno. 'I can't really say please come at the moment,' Sally wrote. 'The political situation has become very serious and everyone waits for the storm to break. . . . Yesterday there was a one-day general strike – banks, hotels, shops etc. and Dutch homes and firms are continually being invaded and taken over. . . . [And] I must warn you – travel round Indonesia would not be comfortable or luxurious by any means. Hotels are few and bad – no hot baths etc! . . . We should, of course, adore to see you but I'm worried that you might not enjoy it and might not be able to stand the heat.'

Disappointed, Rosamond agreed for the moment to give up the idea, and on 4 April she flew to New York and the first lap of her tour, her programme a combination of reading from her novels with lecturing on creative writing, to be delivered on campuses the length and breadth of the United States. 'I DREAD it,' she confessed to Sally. After a few days with Davis cousins in New York, she started on her itinerary, going first to Washington, to Johns Hopkins in Baltimore, Tulane in New Orleans, the University of Texas at Austin, and then to Seattle. The experience was a strange one. From New Orleans she wrote to Sally:

Feel curiously undignified and anonymous among all these vestigial souls. But they *are* kind, *are* hospitable, and in spite of all I've said, the academic world is very stimulating: such eagerness to learn, such yearning enthusiasm for Creative Writing; such good manners, such admiration & deference for British culture. If *only* it wasn't so lonely. But even that is exhilarating sometimes. I feel most curious *moments* of being equal to anything, and shedding my old skin.

From Seattle Rosamond went south to California to spend a weekend in Santa Monica with Christopher Isherwood 'and his dear little pretty little Friend Don Bacardi [sic]'. Isherwood, an old friend since the 1930s of John and Beatrix, knew Rosamond only slightly and had been less than enthusiastic about her arrival: Stephen Spender had only just left and he needed some uninterrupted time in which to work. 'The prospect of Rosamond Lehmann coming to stay with us next weekend, does not please. I only hope we can get rid of her soon. She asked herself. We're far too busy to be able to entertain guests at this time,' he wrote in his diary. Entertain her he did, however, and on the first evening to Rosamond's delight the Stravinskys and the Aldous Huxleys came to dinner. 'Igor became wonderfully oracular. . . . Aldous talked mescaline,' Isherwood noted. 'Rosamond did her best to keep up with the highbrow talk. She used phrases like "an organic whole." She wore a most elaborate grey dress and was covered with makeup.' The following night Christopher and Don took her to a party 'at the fabulous Beverly Hills "home"' of David Selznick and his wife, Jennifer Jones. Selznick was a great fan of *Dusty Answer* – he had changed his wife's name from 'Phyllis' to 'Jennifer' after the character in the novel – and was excited to meet the author in person. 'Ravishing visions gliding past my blurred line of sight, all gleaming & polished in their "sacks",' Rosamond told Sally, 'and sitting between Selznick (delightful emotional clever man) and Mel Ferrer (whew! – but with a beard alas! Because of making a film version of *Green Mansions* (?) – extraordinarily beautiful from head to toe, but somewhat inhuman –) with opposite me Lauren Bacall (a darling –) and Joan Fontaine (drunk). Well well! It was all a Beautiful Dream. We reeled away, with kisses and love all round, and left them all playing bridge and other indoor games.' On 28 April Rosamond left by train for Iowa, considerably to Isherwood's relief. 'Quite as I like her, her presence here was much more of an intrusion than Stephen's.'

While Rosamond had been revelling in the glamour of California, Sally and Patrick on the other side of the Pacific had also been enjoying a change of scene, spending a few days up country in Djogjakarta, a charming, lively little town surrounded by a lush landscape of woods and hills. Here while Patrick lectured, Sally explored the famous ruined temples at Borobodur. After a few days they returned to Djakarta, where with the heat worse than ever – 'we gasp like fishes all day & all night' – Patrick was feeling weak and unwell after a bad attack of dysentery. 'After endless tests and medicines he seems to have got rid of his bug at last,' Sally wrote. His hands were better, but he was suffering from bad sinus headaches. '[He] had lost a stone and looks dreadful. . . . I've also lost some weight, which is all to the good, and am blooming. . . . Still teaching hard. . . . Still keeping our peckers just above water. Still miss England, friends, civilised people, civilised conversation.'

From Los Angeles Rosamond travelled by train to Iowa City. 'I am in the Innermost Shrine and Birthplace of the New Criticism,' she reported, 'surrounded by tiny black-spectacled Troglodytes with very very quiet strangled voices and wives to match. I DON'T mind that they have never read my works & would despise them if they did: but they are so unpretty and chill-blooded and smoke menthol cigarettes and question me about Creative Writing over huge tepid cups of pseudo-coffee. Why am I here? I ask and there is not an answer.' The question might more pertinently have been put at her next stop, Chicago, where she found

> to my chagrin and embarrassment I was not expected!!! ... My supposed hostess, Mrs Adlai Stevenson, coped manfully with my arrival and made me feel welcome, instead of a nuisance; and Treat of Treats! I found that Robert Frost had just arrived, and I spent nearly all of two days listening to his inimitable conversation, hearing him read his poems, and watching his dearling face. I nearly cried when we parted, thinking how unlikely that I shall ever see him again. I adore him.

After Chicago, Rosamond went on to Boston, then at the end of six weeks once more to New York and Washington. From Washington on 17 May she flew back overnight to London, exhausted but proud to have emerged so well out of such an arduous experience. 'It has all been very very queer and bewildering indeed – but worth while, if only because of proving (DV) my unexpected powers of survival.'

At about the same time that Rosamond arrived back in London, Sally was writing from Djakarta with the exciting news that she and Patrick were shortly to go to Bali for a much-needed holiday. They flew out on 3 June, and were immediately entranced by the beauty of the island. 'We stayed in a little village with a sort of local sultan who has turned his palace into a guest house,' Sally described it to her mother. 'The palace consists of a series of courtyards filled with flowering shrubs & joined by huge intricately carved archways. Each courtyard has one or two little thatched bungalows where you live and eat, quite self-contained. ... The last two days we moved to a lovely hotel by the sea where our bedrooms opened onto the tropical beach – palm trees, white sand, coral, blue, blue water. It was all wonderful.' Patrick, too, described the perfection of the place. 'We arrived at evening and caught our breath.

White coral sand, pink sea, naked girls playing in it under the sunset. . . .
In the morning our room, which opened on to the sand itself, was filled
with a soft pink glow. We stepped out to watch dawn over the sea. . . . I
watched Sally. She sat in her nightdress on the warm soft sand, violet
and gold, staring out to sea, her knees drawn up to her chin.' A few days
after their return to Djakarta, he wrote for his wife a 'Dedication Poem':

> Curled in your night-dress on the beach,
> Corn-yellow ghost, pale with sleep,
> Head to the starry North, bare toes to the burning East,
> Tracking the sun's climb into our seaside perch,
> I watch you at the fringe of this other island
> Our public love makes private for us two . . .

Meanwhile on the other side of the world, Rosamond had been
engaged in overseeing the decoration of Little Eden. She hoped to have
it ready in July, she told her daughter after a visit of inspection at the
end of May. '*Wish* you were here to help me!' On 20 June, a Friday, she
went over to the Island again, this time taking Joshua with her.

The same week in Djakarta a terrible sequence of events was
unfolding of which Rosamond as yet knew nothing. On Sunday 15 June,
the day after the Kavanaghs' return from Bali, some friends had
unexpectedly turned up at the house with various suggestions how to
spend the evening. Patrick, nonplussed, had looked round for his wife,
who, strangely, was nowhere to be seen. He found her seated at the
dressing-table in their bedroom reflectively making up her mouth, and
when he asked her what she thought they should do – go to this bar, that
restaurant – she seemed uninterested, detached, unlike herself. She soon
recovered, however, and joined the others for dinner in the town, 'as
bright as I've ever seen her,' Patrick recalled. The next day Sally
complained of a headache, but deciding to ignore it went shopping in
the morning, then insisted on teaching her English class as usual in the
afternoon. In the evening the pain had become so bad that she went to
bed and the doctor was called, who diagnosed 'flu. After two more days
in bed there was no improvement so Patrick, worried, decided to take
her to the Tjikina Hospital. Here she was again examined, but this time
the diagnosis was different: not 'flu, but poliomyelitis. An iron lung was

put ready beside her bed. The Dutch doctors were reassuring, however, telling Patrick there was no need to worry, that as long as she was not moved the disease would probably pass off with no damage at all. 'I stayed with her while she slept,' Patrick wrote later, 'and at four o'clock in the morning, midsummer's day, Sally died.'

During her daughter's last hours on earth, Rosamond was busily occupied on the Isle of Wight. The weather was beautiful, and she and Joshua, staying at a small hotel in Totland Bay, had gone to Little Eden, and then taken Violet Hammersley for a drive along the coast. The next morning was overcast, with heavy rain threatening when they went again to the house, Joshua wandering out into the garden while Rosamond took measurements indoors. 'I was kneeling to measure the space between fireplace and kitchen door when there came a loud, sudden thud on one of the french windows. . . . I looked out and saw on the paved terrace beyond the tall glass door a dark blot upon the stone – a dead bird, a young blackbird.' Shocked, she asked Joshua to dispose of the corpse as she could not bear to see it. 'It seemed such an unpropitious omen.' On returning to the hotel, she was met by the manageress who told her brightly that her son had been on the line from London, leaving a message to ring him as soon as possible. She telephoned Hugo at once, and 'his voice on the other end of the line said that Sally was dead'.

Rosamond arrived in Eaton Square that evening to find two cables from Patrick, the first reading, 'SALLY VERY ILL COME IF YOU CAN', the second, 'MY DARLING STAY. SALLY GONE FOR EVER.' Hardly knowing what she was doing, Rosamond telephoned Laurens van der Post. 'Laurens, Sally's dead,' was all he heard, then silence as the receiver was replaced. Immediately he ran round to the flat. 'Rosamond was quite wild,' he recalled. 'I spent three or four hours with her, and it really helped that she could just pour out her grief, saying, "I wish I'd done this or that for Sally." There was a lot of self-reproach.' The next night Patrick flew in from Djakarta, and the following day Sally's last letter arrived, full of cheerful descriptions of the holiday in Bali. Looking back, Rosamond herself could recall very little of this period of engulfing unhappiness. 'I can't talk about the ensuing days and nights. There are no words there. There never will be. . . . It was such a terrible nightmare, I don't remember much about it, except that I wasn't *there* at all.' Her sisters were with her constantly, as was Hugo, who was '*utterly magnificent*'; the most practical help was provided by Rosamond's young doctor, Patrick Woodcock, who prescribed powerful sleeping pills and visited her daily. Friends, appalled, did what they could, but Rosamond, almost out of her mind with grief, was hardly aware of any of it, so great was her agony.

Over the next torturous few days the one solace lay in replying to the dozens of condolence letters, when the desperate woman could devote herself to communicating the depths of her feeling for Sally. 'From the day she first smiled at me at 10 days old we taught one another nothing but love,' she told her brother, while to Willy Mostyn-Owen's sister, Liz, she wrote, 'Nobody ever had a more beautiful good happy loving and loved daughter – and her life was, truly, a kind of miracle of perfected achievement. She died at the very peak of her married happiness.' The heart-broken words and phrases were poured out over and over again: 'This is the one thing that was always unimaginable . . . I did, do love her so enormously . . . the one flawless joy of my life. . . . My one joy and perfect achievement.' Hardest to bear, as she cried to Pat Trevor-Roper, was the realisation that, 'The streets are full of other people's daughters buying summer frocks, hurrying to parties, having babies'. Subject to the violent mood swings of bereavement, she found that, 'Strength and calm, joy almost, pour through me, drain out, leave me in howling wastes'. To Violet Hammersley she railed against the unintentional cruelty of many of her correspondents, the hundreds of letters 'speaking of loss, waste, unfairness, suffering without hope. These terrify me. Very very few life lines. I cannot go on unless I discover meaning and get her back. I do – but I lose her, lose her.' Her greatest consolation was knowing that Sally's short life had been untouched by suffering. 'I always managed to keep her out of suffering; and then she moved into a *perfectly* happy marriage – so "nothing is here for tears".'

There was one exception to this: Cecil, the demonic figure who even when she was *in extremis* was never far from the forefront of Rosamond's mind. '[Sally] had only one great grief,' her godfather, Compton Mackenzie, was told, '[and] that was what CDL did to me. She never could bear treachery, cruelty, coldness of heart. So perhaps it is as well she has been taken out of this world.' From Cecil himself there was no message, no letter. For a while Rosamond became irrationally convinced that in some way he was responsible for her daughter's death. 'I had an obsession for a long time that he'd caused her death. Perhaps he had. . . . I know I thought so at the time, that this was what he'd done.' When it came to her ears that Cecil had been devastated by the news ('The only time I ever saw Cecil weep,' wrote Jill Day Lewis later), she grew frantic at the thought that he might start writing poetry about Sally, and this she knew she would be unable to bear. As she had done once years before, she despatched Rex Warner as her emissary. 'I sent a message by Rex to say I forbade it, and that if he did [write about Sally] I'd come and kill him.'

It was with Rex that Rosamond took refuge in the country only ten days after Sally's death. Rex and Barbara had recently separated, and Rex was now living with a girlfriend, Liz Fyfe, dividing his time between a cottage in Wales and the house he shared with Barbara at Westwell, a tiny village in the Cotswolds. It was here on 4 July that Joshua brought Rosamond. Fond though she was of Rex, part of her was dreading being in the company of people who might not be sympathetic to her growing conviction, a conviction that was beginning to dominate her every waking thought, that Sally was still with her, that her daughter was not dead. As she had written to Violet Hammersley, 'I cannot go on unless I discover meaning and get her back,' and the more she dwelt on it, the more certain she became that in some way Sally was close at hand. So far, whenever she tentatively voiced her thoughts on the subject she had been met with embarrassment and evasion, but at Westwell, to her enormous relief, it was different. On her first evening, although she was unable to stop weeping, she had told Rex and Liz of her belief that in some mysterious manner Sally was present. 'Of course,' said Liz gently, and later going upstairs to bed she recounted some supra-normal experiences of her own. 'Hers was the first voice to make me feel that I was not alone, or out of my mind, perhaps.'

On the afternoon of the following day, as she was later to describe in her memoir, *The Swan in the Evening*, while the others went for a walk Rosamond lay on her bed to rest.

A blackbird was pouring forth his whole being just beyond my window; and from where I lay I could see elm tops moving against an intensely blue sky in billowing masses of unearthly greens and golds. Suddenly, a clear high-pitched vibration, like the twang of a harp-string, crossed my ears. . . . Then the humming faded out, and the song of the blackbird swelled, swelled, as if it was being stepped up a hundredfold. . . .

Now I was with Sally. She was behind my left shoulder, leaning on it. . . . There was no light, no colour, no external scenic feature: only close embrace, profound and happy communion; also the strongest possible impression of her individuality.

Then, with no shock or sense of travelling, I was back in my body, awake, cheerful as if I had just replaced the receiver after one of our long gossiping joking conversations. . . .

I looked at my watch and found that over an hour had passed. I sprang up, went to the window and looked out . . . [sic] and beheld a visionary world. . . . Most dramatic phenomenon of all, the climbing roses round the window-frame had 'come alive' – the red, the white. The beauty of each one of them was fathomless, – a world of love. I leaned out, they leaned towards me, as if we were exchanging love. I saw, I saw their intensity of meaning, feeling.

After tea, Joshua took her for a drive, when again the whole natural world was suffused with 'a softly gold effulgence. Hills, woods, groves, clouds, cornfields, streams and meadows – all were moving and inter-lacing buoyantly, majestically, as if in the ineffable rhythm and pattern of a cosmic dance . . . That evening, talk sparkled and rippled round the table as if the unimaginable death which had drawn us together were – not forgotten or ignored, but somehow overcome.' All three of Rosamond's companions were seen to be transformed by her mystical experience.

Everybody laughed and laughed. . . . Everybody talked as if the gift of tongues had visited them – Joshua particularly. He talked 'like an angel', with great clarity, fluency and point – tho' I can't remember what about. At one moment I let my eyes focus on him and saw that his face had dematerialized and was swaying and vibrating on a long swaying neck. Where were the jowls, where the fat cheeks? His eyes were large, luminous blue and his expression seraphic. This made me laugh with joy. I tried to see Liz but her face was dissolved in radiance, smiling radiance. Rex had no visual presence at all, or I couldn't see it. He was glorious laughter, 'the laughter of the gods.'

For a period of twenty-four hours Rosamond was transported, gloriously liberated from the dead weight of her misery. *'All things were pleasure to me and nothing could grieve me.'*

By contrast, the return to the bleak light of common day was almost insupportable. Writing to Pat Trevor-Roper of this vivid transcendental episode, Rosamond declared that during those hours she was 'more happy than I've ever been. . . . If only I could live on this level – but it all goes, & I'm left dry and deserted.' Not entirely deserted, however, for from this visionary experience came the *'blinding certainty'* that Sally was still very much with her and present in the world. To Rosamond this had the force of divine revelation, but she was well aware that to many others it would simply appear 'that grief and despair have driven me round the bend'. Frances Partridge with her rational Bloomsbury perspective was one whom Rosamond suspected might be dismissive, and when Frances invited her to Ham Spray for a couple of days, she replied that she would come only if 'you will accept the possibility that this knowledge is not hallucination or self-deception. . . . There are things I would like to tell you – but I am still too vulnerable and bewildered – and dread saying them to people who may look at me aghast. . . . I am more calm and sane, in fact, than I've ever been.' Neither Ralph nor Frances had any intention of pouring scorn, and they were besides curious about their old friend's new philosophy. 'The fact that it involved beliefs that neither of us holds made what she had to say no less tragic and interesting, and we went on talking far into the night,' Frances recalled. Rosamond was heartened by their kindness, and in thanking for the weekend she told them that driving home afterwards she had experienced 'one of those split-second reverberating intimations which (rightly or wrongly) I cannot doubt'. On the day of Sally's death when the blackbird was killed flying into the glass door at Little Eden, she now knew that the bird *was* Sally. 'She didn't *send* the bird with a message: she was *there*, (else why my bewildering irrational shock?), there as a super-sensible presence, on some intense vibration, and the bird flew into her. . . . Since realizing this . . . my superstitious dread of returning to the I of Wight has entirely vanished.'

With this fear removed, she made up her mind to go to the Island the very next week. Before that, however, she was to meet someone of whom she had only recently heard, a woman with extraordinary powers who would set Rosamond on the path she was to follow for the long remaining years of her life. 'Tomorrow I am going to see Cynthia Sandys, who lost her only beautiful daughter at the same age 18 months ago,' she told Frances. 'She says she can help me.'

13

'The Vast, Unshakable Consolation'

In Britain the great upsurge of interest in spiritualism occurred during and immediately after the First World War, when thousands of families were grieving for young sons and brothers lost at the front. Indeed it was during the war that Rosamond as a girl was first made aware of the subject, vividly remembering the day when Lord Desborough, after two of the three Grenfell boys had been killed within a few weeks of each other in France, came over to Fieldhead to see her father. He brought with him *Raymond, or Life after Death*, a book by the physicist Sir Oliver Lodge describing the author's communication with his own dead soldier son, which Rudie, harrowed by his friend's terrible bereavement, promised to read. He soon threw it aside in disgust. '[He] was *appalled*. He simply couldn't take it,' Rosamond recollected. 'He thought it all a fraud and nonsense.' Both her parents were atheists, members of 'the post-Darwin, lost-faith generation', but although always powerfully influenced by her father, Rosamond herself, imaginative, emotional, insecure, was drawn towards the solace offered by the Christian beliefs which Rudie and Alice rejected. 'I longed to have some kind of religion, a spiritual reassurance which my life and my friends, my background and my parents, didn't give me.' In adulthood the circumstances of her personal history made adherence to any such faith virtually impossible, both husbands uncompromisingly godless, as was the intellectual society in which they moved, with the Bloomsbury brand of scoffing scepticism

347

predominating. 'I thought of them as my intellectual superiors,' Rosamond said of the Bloomsberries. 'I thought they must know best.'

But now after the mystical phenomena experienced while staying at Westwell, Rosamond was finally in possession of the spiritual nourishment for which all her life she had been searching. Convinced that a great truth had been revealed to her, bringing her 'the vast, unshakable consolation' of knowing with absolute certainty that life continues after death, she became possessed by the idea of communicating with Sally. It was literally unendurable for her to continue living and breathing in a world in which Sally was not, and she grasped at what she saw as incontrovertible evidence that death did not mean extinction; instead, her daughter had simply passed over, to continue living, recognisably herself, in a different dimension on 'the other side'. Immediately, she began to be aware of indications that Sally was near, was lovingly providing signs of her spiritual presence: after Rosamond's return to Eaton Square, for instance, there was a 'scenting', a flowery fragrance that mysteriously pervaded the flat; on another occasion, a little potted plant, plainly dying, before her very eyes began to quiver and vibrate, then miraculously revived, going on to flourish in a way that could not possibly be accounted for by any natural law. 'It was brushed by the Breath. I was awe-struck. . . . You were there,' Rosamond wrote to Sally in a record she began keeping of her psychic experiences. Yet comforting though such manifestations were, Rosamond hungered for more direct contact, and when Rex Warner's girlfriend, Liz Fyfe, offered to put her in touch with a distinguished 'sensitive', who had herself recently lost a young, newly married daughter, she accepted eagerly.

Cynthia Sandys, wife of Arthur, Lord Sandys, was a member of an old county family, proud of a distant cousinship to Florence Nightingale. A capable woman with a strong sense of duty, she served locally in Worcestershire as a parish councillor and magistrate and as head of the County Commission for Girl Guides. Less conventionally, Lady Sandys practised as a clairaudient, having discovered her unusual gift – the hearing and transcribing of messages from the dead – on the demise of her father in 1937, later devoting her talents to assisting Air Chief Marshal Lord Dowding while he was collecting for publication postmortem messages from airmen killed in the Second World War. Less than two years before Rosamond's visit, the Sandyses had lost their elder daughter, Patricia, with whom her mother believed herself to be in close communication by means of her spirit writing. It was through Patricia that Cynthia Sandys intended to make contact with Sally.

When Rosamond arrived on 11 September 1958 at Himbleton Manor near Droitwich, she found that Lady Sandys, contrary to expectation, was no wispy-haired Mme Arcati but a commonsensical woman of 60, plain, portly, and with slightly protruding teeth. To her astonishment and delight there was already a letter waiting, full of comforting messages from her daughter about enduring closeness and love and the thrilling possibilities already being discovered by Sally since she had 'taken the ferry' to her new celestial habitation. 'Darling there is no death, it's life, more life, it's gorgeous and wonderful,' Patricia quoted her as saying. Strange and sublimely beautiful though these heavenly regions were, Sally was quick to assure her mother that she herself had undergone no visible change. 'I am SALLY, just the same Sally, I even look the same. . . . Eyes, nose and hair, all just the same . . .' She was even wearing some of her familiar old frocks, 'and as I wear them they became more me, as I now am. Pat is teaching me how to grow clothes! It's such fun. . . . One has all the colours in one's aura, did you know that I had an aura? We all love them and they are so lovely you've no idea. . . .'

There was not the slightest question in Rosamond's mind that this was genuine and she could hardly wait for the first session to begin. Intensely alert, she watched while Cynthia said a short prayer, meditated for a few minutes, then waited in silence for her pencil to start moving across the paper, seemingly under Patricia's dictation. Sally, she learned, though happy now, had been confused and miserable when she 'awoke'; alarmed at finding herself in an unearthly hospital, she called for her mother, at first unable to accept that she was dead. 'She couldn't believe it,' Rosamond related afterwards, 'and was calling for Patrick, and couldn't find him of course, and then was calling for me, and I did hear her. . . . It was Patricia who helped her most then.' According to Patricia, both she and Sally were among the chosen few, '[a group of] "young marrieds" who have left [the earth] according to a chosen plan, a pre-birth plan'. On this as on subsequent occasions there were many pages to be covered with the words of the two 'absent-present daughters', Cynthia's powers as a transmitter being exceptionally pure: she was able to 'receive' through an 'unsealed head centre, which is sealed in most of us,' Rosamond explained, '[and she] can actually hear the voice – its special individual tone – unmistakable'. Through Patricia, said Cynthia, 'I found it very easy to write for Sally. . . . You see, they aren't far away, and my daughter is a very good linker and I'm a good channeller.'

Rosamond returned to London enormously consoled, in an almost euphoric state at her great epiphany: 'I knew that Sally was not dead, not dead.' It was noticeable how much stronger she seemed, how much more positive in outlook. 'I have been – am being – given such spiritual help I couldn't sink,' she wrote to Violet Hammersley. Even the arrival of Sally's coffin by sea from Java, profoundly distressing although it was, failed to destroy her new-found courage. Rosamond had hoped the body would not come back, as 'I had this very strong feeling that the dead should not travel around but lie in peace,' but Patrick had wished his wife's grave to be in England. As Rosamond recoiled from the subject, and as Patrick, helpless with grief, was in no condition to make decisions, the necessary arrangements were left to Joshua Rowley. It was Joshua who had organised and paid for the passage home, and it was he who suggested that Sally should be interred in the little churchyard at Westwell, as during their short marriage the Kavanaghs had enjoyed some particularly happy times there while staying with Rex and Barbara. As Rosamond was 'too broken' to face the burial, only Patrick and Wogan, apart from the vicar, were present at the graveside. Wogan was utterly crushed by the loss of his daughter, and in time to come grew increasingly resentful of what he saw as Rosamond's overwhelming appropriation of Sally's death: it was, he said, as though only Rosamond had any right to grieve, as though she alone were Sally's parent, leaving her father with no claim to her at all.

As visits to Himbleton Manor were of necessity infrequent – Lady Sandys was much in demand by the recently bereaved – Rosamond, desperate for continuing contact, turned at the suggestion of a friend, Constance Sitwell, to the College of Psychic Studies in South Kensington. The College, originally known as the London Spiritualist Alliance, was founded in 1884 for the purposes of psychical research, the results of which, it was hoped, would 'proclaim to a world of increasing materialism that human personality survives bodily death and that this fact is capable of demonstration'. The premises, at 16 Queensberry

Place, were brought in 1925, immediately preceding the presidency of Sir Arthur Conan Doyle, most of the purchase price donated in gratitude by families who through the College had made contact with loved ones killed in the war. Constance Sitwell, a writer and kinswoman by marriage of Edith Sitwell, was a past president of the college, and it was she who promised to match Rosamond with a suitable medium. Rosamond was apprehensive, not at all sure that she cared for the idea. 'I had been brought up to think that mediums were all beads and robes and piano-shawl fringe and, well, fraudulent,' as she later admitted. Because of these doubts, when an appointment was made in January 1959 with the well-known medium Ena Twigg, Rosamond took the precaution of first attending a demonstration of clairvoyance to be given by Mrs Twigg at the College so that she could see something of what to expect. To her relief Mrs Twigg turned out to be a trim, well-spoken woman in her early forties. Addressing her audience from the dais in the first-floor lecture room, she almost at once picked out Rosamond sitting in the front row. 'There is a very young, beautiful spirit, somebody full of life building up behind you, my dear,' she told her. 'Why is she talking about the war god? She is saying she does wish the war god would believe she is alive. Can you understand?' Rosamond immediately realised that the reference to the war god, Wotan, was a corruption of 'Wogan', and she then knew for certain that this was Sally coming through.

At her first private sitting with Ena Twigg at the medium's home in Acton, Sally again was invisibly present. 'This spirit loves music,' Mrs Twigg reported. 'She is putting on records of Kathleen Ferrier.' During this session, as in further sessions with Mrs Twigg and others, Rosamond was given evidence not only that her daughter was with her, but that Sally herself was blissfully happy in her new-found world of light and joy. Her musical talents had brought her to the attention of St Francis, through whom she had gained access to the Bird World, where among other duties she was to teach the unborn birds how to sing. No less astonishing, Sally now had a baby – 'It's a little boy, Mummy, we've called him Pat . . . an *impish* little fellow' – and this spirit child was a source of much delight to others who were soon making their etheric presences felt. Alice and Rudie, as might have been expected, were among the first to come through; more surprising, perhaps, was the early arrival of Virginia Woolf, like Rudie full of regret for the scepticism so blindly adhered to during her span on earth. Virginia's spirit self was full of admiration and encouragement. 'Young and lovely, you were too generous-hearted . . . and I knew you were going to be hurt,' she told Rosamond. 'But tonight I am happy to tell you that all is well, you are safe. . . . You will be creative in love and better still creative in literary art.' Similar predictions were received through a variety of sources. One well-known medium, Geraldine Cummins, through her spirit guide, Astor, told Rosamond that she was a very unusual soul with great psychic potentiality; another, John Lovette, through his guide, Sha-mouni, an Eastern sage, assured her that the best was yet to come, and that she would shortly marry again. Repeatedly came the messages of love from Sally – or the Little Lady of Light, as for her special radiance she soon became known. 'I didn't love you enough, Mummy, please forgive me, I love you so much. . . . I didn't understand when you were so unhappy . . . [*sic*] please forgive me. . . .'

To Rosamond such communications were in the nature of divine revelation, and she devoured them avidly. 'I was greedy, hungry for endless proofs.' So desperate was she for any word from the other side, that both Cynthia Sandys and Ena Twigg felt obliged to restrain her by rationing her sittings, encouraging her instead to explore the subject by reading in the College library. In such a foreign field Rosamond was a complete beginner, although rarely can there have been a more eager apprentice. 'Needless to say, at that time I had never heard of the subtle or the etheric or the resurrection body; or of astral projection; or of the scientific likelihood that countless forms, worlds within worlds of them, are invisible simply because they are travelling on different energy levels, or at different vibratory rates.' She read with absorption, devouring the works of C. G. Jung, of F. W. H. Myers, Edmund Gurney, William James, J. G. Bennett, Douglas Fawcett, Geraldine Cummins, Jane Sherwood, C. Raynor Johnson, the Christian mystics, the Tibetan and the Egyptian *Book of the Dead*, numerous accounts of reincarnation, of life after death, and of continuing communion with the departed. No student can ever have raked the shelves of the small library more voraciously, as Rosamond recalled. 'My discoveries thrilled and astounded me . . . I became convinced – rightly or wrongly – that unimpeachably evidential records were available: these I absorbed and they became part of my thinking, feeling and breathing apparatus.' So effective a support did this apparatus become that by the end of 1959, only eighteen months after Sally's death, she was able to write that 'often I have more peace of heart and soul than ever before in my life – in spite of all the grief'.

Intoxicated by the implications of her new-found knowledge, it was a shock to learn that her discoveries were in the main met by open incredulity, most of her listeners responding not with the rapt attention she had anticipated but with a mixture of embarrassment, boredom and contempt. Of her family, John, Helen and Beatrix expressed themselves 'horrified' at the direction their sister was taking, while Hugo refused to discuss it at all, angrily dismissing the topic as 'bunk'. Predictably, some of the most vociferous derision came from the Bloomsbury old guard, that 'Stygian crew' as they were now described, who regarded all religious faith as fantasy and looked on a belief in spiritualism as downright pitiable. The Spenders, for instance, Duncan Grant and Vanessa Bell, Ralph and Frances Partridge, Maurice Bowra, Dadie, Julia Strachey, Hester Chapman, all refused to take the subject seriously, making clear that in their view their old friend had taken leave of her senses: not only was the whole premise utterly ludicrous, but almost more distressing was the banality of Rosamond's figuring of the 'au delà', as she chose to refer to it. 'I'm aghast', wrote Frances Partridge in her diary, 'to find how easily she soaks up any comforting rubbish about vibrations and higher spheres and finer forms.' Similarly James Lees-Milne in his diary wrote, 'Rosamond goes burbling on about the *occult*, which I find more irritating than the recognized sects because there is no dogma, no ethic, nothing in the way of discipline to be found in it to guide its followers.'

Laurie Lee, who had been devastated by Sally's death, was regarded by Rosamond as a convert, although in fact he was as taken aback as any by her extraordinary convictions. Soon after Sally died Laurie had gone round to Eaton Square, and Rosamond had called to his attention the wonderful flowery fragrance in the room. According to her, Laurie 'after standing for a time in silence said three words only: "Now I believe."' Privately, however, Laurie expressed his scepticism. 'Of course I didn't witness anything – but I couldn't hurt her feelings, poor woman. . . . It was self-deception on such a moving scale.' He was equally unimpressed when shown Sally's spirit messages. 'Anyone with a touch of awareness would know that Sally didn't write like that, didn't think like that.'

Although proclaiming herself disdainful of such shoddy old-fashioned props as ectoplasm and cardboard trumpets, Rosamond's own experience seemed little more evolved, with floral 'scentings' and spirit guides, and the various tappings and rappings and mysterious blue lights frequently reported in the flat. 'It was a mystery to me', said Natasha Spender, 'how someone so intelligent should have such an infantile view of the other world', an opinion shared by Dadie, who was appalled that a woman as intellectually sophisticated should have surrendered so speedily to the comforts of unreason. 'She was a very clever girl so it's difficult to see how she could have believed such childishness,' he said. 'It was totally idiotic.' Loving her as he did, it was particularly painful for him to witness her in the grip of what he saw as her pathetic delusion, and in consequence he was almost brutally uncompromising in his rejection of it. 'It cut her off from all her old Bloomsbury friends,' he said. 'Once she fell back on the spirit world, she was done for with us. None of us have any use for it at all. . . . We are not prepared to talk about it or think about it, except with shrieks of laughter. It's a great divide.'

It was indeed a great divide, and Rosamund soon began to realise the extent of her isolation. She learnt to be wary, careful not to bring up the subject of her 'secret life' unless she knew her audience was likely to be sympathetic. 'I used to feel so lonely,' she said, '[but] I learned it was best not to talk about it because either you frightened people or they thought you were mad.' Even more distressing, in some circles Rosamond's beliefs, far from engendering fear, were turning her into a figure of fun. Nancy Mitford, for example, had been the delighted recipient of a witty description by Raymond Mortimer of Rosamond's conversations with Sally, which she was now busily passing on with her own embellishments. 'I said bad luck on the girl – imagine a heavenly butler saying "The Hon. Mrs Philipps on the line again, Ma'am" just when one was gambolling in a green pasture.' Soon after this it came to Rosamond's ears that Violet Hammersley had talked to Duncan Grant and Vanessa Bell about her beliefs, which afterwards the two of them had taken much delight in maliciously mocking. 'It is very distasteful to be talked about in a "smearing" way,' Rosamond wrote reproachfully. 'I just want my inner life, my spiritual experiences and strivings to be respected and left alone. They are my own business.' Fortunately she never discovered the unholy alliance formed by Dadie and his cousin, Hester Chapman. Hester, an arch-sceptic who snorted with indignation at any mention of the supernatural, secretly subscribed to *Light*, the journal of the College of Psychic Studies to which Rosamond became a regular contributor. At Christmas, which Hester and Dadie always spent together, the year's issues of *Light* were produced on Christmas morning and delightedly scanned. 'We always read aloud Rosamond's nonsense at breakfast,' Dadie recalled, 'and it was absolutely glorious.'

Such cynical attitudes, if disappointing, failed to deter Rosamond when the occasion arose from trying to help even the most entrenched unbeliever – of whom one was Hester herself, whose adored husband had died in 1955. But when after Sally's death Rosamond tried to persuade her of Ronnie's continuing existence, Hester would have none of it. 'I don't want to see Ronnie in some hereafter,' she stubbornly insisted. 'I want him here, now, sitting beside me.' Another attempt at conversion was made after Bernard Berenson died at the age of 94, when Rosamond did her best to convince Nicky Mariano, despite knowing that Berenson himself had had no time for such things, a lack of accord which had resulted in a distance between them during the last months of his life. Nicky Mariano, while politely declining the offer – 'I do feel him very near to me and know what you mean even if I have not got your absolute faith' – assured Rosamond that BB's affection for her had in no way diminished on account of this disagreement, while doing her best tactfully to account for his distaste for the subject. 'Perhaps he was like Goethe he did not like to dwell on what he knew was beyond our comprehension.' Rosamond had no better success with Frances Partridge, whose son, Burgo, died suddenly in 1963. When Rosamond went to see Frances, primed with messages from Sally about Burgo's sunny reception in the au delà, Frances was repelled, recording in her diary the dismal nature of the occasion and Rosamond's 'hopeless woolly attempt to interest me in the spirit world'. Having in the space of three years lost both husband and son, Frances could not help noticing how Rosamond 'invariably speaks of Sally's death as unique among all bereavements'.

While most of Rosamond's friends recoiled from any mention of belief in the supernatural, there were a few, agnostic themselves, who were prepared to listen to what she had to say. Her son-in-law, Patrick, for example, understood only too well her desperate need to believe she was in touch with Sally, and although he was unable to follow on her chosen path, he was unendingly patient and sympathetic. Laurens van der Post was another always ready to discuss the possibility of life after death, as was Pat Trevor-Roper, both men whose intellectual curiosity was unusually wide-ranging. Remembering her mescalin experience and anxious to discover if access to the other side could be achieved by means of hallucinogenic drugs, Rosamond persuaded Trevor-Roper again to take it with her, but the experiment was a failure. 'It didn't bring Rosamond any nearer to Sally so she didn't go on with it,' said Pat. He continued to see her, however, and his kindly interest became so comforting that Rosamond began to rely on him completely. Eventually, she suggested they should marry. 'I think she slightly fell in love with me,' said Pat:

> but it was based on her need to have someone to lean on after Sally died, and on someone who would be able to talk about ESP and so on.... I might just have considered it.... I was fond of her company, fascinated by her.... But she would have been impossible to live with. She became increasingly as it were heavy, emotionally demanding and possessive, and the humour got less and less, and serious passions abounded. I couldn't handle it.

Others tried to help by steering her towards the Church, despite Rosamond's impatience with organised religion. Rose Macaulay referred her to a friend of hers who was an Anglican bishop, while Violet Hammersley did her best to guide her towards Rome. 'How marvellous it would be to be inside the fold,' Rosamond wrote to her, 'but I can't believe it will ever come about.' A more aggressive approach was adopted by Eddy Sackville-West, who himself had converted to Catholicism in 1949. 'He warned me in a very scolding way that if I went on in my wicked ways thinking I had had personal communication with Sally, which I *had*, that I should be punished by being cut off from her altogether. He was so cruel, you wouldn't believe.' Although Rosamond remained adamant that Rome had nothing to offer her – 'The Catholic Church utterly condemns communication with the dead. They try to prevent the truth being known because it will interfere with their authority. . . . It's difficult to believe how backward the Church is still' – Eddy was not prepared to give up, and in January 1959 he introduced her to the distinguished Jesuit, Philip Caraman. Father Caraman, small, dark and bespectacled, was himself a man of letters, responsible for bringing into the Church several distinguished writers, among them Edith Sitwell, and he was a close friend of Evelyn Waugh. Far too subtle to proselytise, Caraman concentrated on giving Rosamond reassurance. 'He used to come and see me,' Rosamond recalled, 'and have a little drink and smoke a little cigarette, and say, "Don't worry, you've been given a great grace." I told him what Eddy had said and he was simply furious.'

With Father Caraman Rosamond went to stay at Cooleville, Eddy's large, comfortable house in Co. Tipperary in the south of Ireland. Expecting a sophisticated house-party of the kind she remembered at Bowen's Court before the war, Rosamond was disappointed to find there was no one for her to meet except a group of 'absolutely uneducated' local priests in thick black boots who had no idea who she was, had read almost nothing ('most of the books one read oneself were on the Index'), and seemed interested only in consuming quantities of their host's superb food and drink. 'Eddy used to get frightfully sick of them and go off and play the piano. . . . The rest of the time he spent going to "*marse*" and receiving the sacraments. . . . Nobody took any notice of me.' This more or less marked the end of Rosamond's flirtation with Catholicism. Father Caraman came occasionally to call still, '[but] I think he realised it was no good. . . . He would say, "Just one leap in the dark and you'll be safe in the fold". And I'd say, "I just can't make that leap. I don't believe in any of your dogmas. I could never be an obedient daughter of the Faith. And I've got two husbands living."' Paradoxically, although Rosamond was never able to accept the doctrines of any established Church, and although her own religious belief, as it developed, must be regarded as unorthodox in the extreme, from the time of Sally's death she unquestioningly regarded herself as a Christian: 'the seed of faith has been granted to me at last,' she wrote in December 1958.

Despite her absorption in her daughter and in Sally's surreal activities in the spirit world, Rosamond was still much occupied with her responsibilities on the terrestrial plane. One of her most difficult decisions had been regarding the house on the Isle of Wight. Sally had never seen Little Eden, and yet all its associations were with her, which imbued the place with 'an element of dreadful pain'. At first determined to sell, Rosamond eventually decided to keep the property for the sake of her beloved grandchild, Anna, and also in the hope that Hugo would occasionally make use of it.

In July 1959 Hugo had married again, his new wife Mary ('Mollie') Makins. Rosamond was very taken with her 'adorable' new daughter-in-law, admired her prettiness and intelligence and responded to her cheerful, affectionate nature. Mollie earned great credit by producing a son, Guy, in 1961, followed by another, Roland, a year later, 'my two heavenly baby grandsons,' as Rosamond fondly referred to them; they were later joined by a girl, Kate (Katherine Nina) in 1964, and a third boy, Ivo, in 1967. Yet proud though she was of Hugo's second family (invariably described as outstandingly clever and astonishingly good-looking), Rosamond's relationship with Hugo himself was far from intimate. 'Hugo and I are light-years distant from one another,' she wrote regretfully to Patrick Kavanagh, '& tho' he is quite amiably disposed towards me I doubt if I would ever impinge again on his consciousness were I to vanish from his ken.' Her greatest delight as ever lay in the company of his eldest daughter, Anna. The little girl was endlessly indulged by her doting grandmother, who bought her sweets and pretty dresses and allowed her to sit up late at table when friends came to dinner. Anna returned her love and immensely enjoyed her visits to Eaton Square – except for the constant harping on Sally's ethereal presence. 'Rosamond used to spook me by saying, "Sally will come and sit on your window-sill", and I couldn't quite cope with that,' she recalled. But to Rosamond it was essential that the myth be maintained of a special bond between Sally and Anna, for Anna came closest to a replacement for her dead daughter. 'If *only* I could have her always to care for and bring up I should be "saved",' Rosamond declared.

Easily the most important link with Sally was Rosamond's son-in-law, Patrick, with whom for the rest of her life she maintained a close, if not always untroubled, bond. When in 1965 Patrick married again, to Catherine ('Kate') Ward, an Oxford friend and contemporary of Sally's, Rosamond regarded herself as an integral part of the family, arriving to stay several times a year, growing devoted to Kate, and interested in all the ups and downs in the lives of the Kavanaghs' two sons. After returning from Java, Patrick had for a while gone on the stage, continuing, while employed as an actor, to write. He produced two volumes of poetry at the beginning of the 1960s, and in 1964 published a prize-winning short memoir, *The Perfect Stranger*, which ends with an account of his courtship and marriage and of Sally's last days in Indonesia. It required all Rosamond's courage to read it, but after she had she wrote to him, 'Funny (*very*), moving, intelligent, truthful. . . . It seems to me that the truth, the reality of the portrait could not be excelled. Perhaps any words relating to Sally develop or generate a kind of centripetal force and write themselves.'

On 7 December 1962 Rosamond's father-in-law died. Wogan as eldest son inherited the title, although nothing else, the substantial estate divided among Laurence Milford's younger children and Hugo, who after his grandmother's death would take possession at Llanstephan. To Rosamond, who continued to spend Christmases in Wales, it was a matter of some regret that with Wogan having succeeded to his father's barony it was his present wife, Tamara, and not she who now had the right to style herself 'Lady Milford': 'the Hon. Mrs R. N. Philipps' was all very well, but 'Lady Milford' would have been better.

As to the Lehmann side of the family, Helen in 1960 had retired from her job at the Society of Authors and moved up to Peebles in Scotland. 'I feel that she is much better and happier – though still alas! chain-smoking and coughing like an ancient fog-horn,' Rosamond wrote after visiting her there. Kind-hearted under her gruff exterior, Helen was as independent and undemonstrative as ever, sometimes ruffling Rosamond's feelings with her fondness for plain speaking. 'I have for so long been the "inferior" member of the family, trying to bear up, I know, with too much asperity,' Helen wrote with touching candour, 'but please don't think I don't realise it – or moreover that I am insensitive.'

In August 1965, Rosamond was united with both sisters when Beatrix came up to Edinburgh to open in a new play at the Festival. Thin, grey-haired and prematurely lined, Beatrix in 1956 had resigned from the Communist Party, and was now enjoying the success that for some years had been eluding her, one of her most acclaimed parts in recent years that of Miss Bordereau in *The Aspern Papers*. Although she had had several serious relationships, the focus of Bea's emotional life was her dog, on whose account she refused ever to go abroad, usually managing to obtain special permission from reluctant theatre managements to keep Taffy with her in her dressing-room.[1] Beatrix was much-liked by her fellow-actors, who knew her to be generous and kind-hearted underneath an occasionally daunting façade; an excellent cook, witty and a brilliant mimic, Bea's sometimes riotous hospitality was much appreciated within the profession, although during her sister's visits she tended to keep her more raffish friends out of range of Rosamond's condescension. (When Rosamond came round backstage, said one, 'I always felt she was going to leave me a tip.')

Of all the sisters Beatrix showed the most sensitivity towards their brother John, whose private life continued on its promiscuous path. With unflagging energy John pursued his erotic adventures, while domestic matters were supervised by his patient partner, Alexis Rassine, both in London at the flat in Cornwall Gardens, where John had recently moved from Egerton Crescent, and at Lake Cottage in Sussex. In 1961 John had given up the editorship of the *London Magazine*, and had continued his autobiography, following *The Whispering Gallery* with two more volumes, *I Am my Brother* and *The Ample Proposition*. Depressed by the ending of his active career as an editor, John was to a certain extent mollified by his appointment to CBE in 1964, even though he had been hoping for the infinitely more prestigious Order of Merit. 'I notice, don't you, that men set more store on these matters than women?' Rosamond remarked to John's assistant, Barbara Cooper. For the moment her own relations with her brother were in reasonably good repair, John described as uncharacteristically 'mellow, serene and untouchy'.

In contrast to John's productivity, Rosamond's career appeared to be in a state of suspended animation, but gradually she was returning to

---

[1] Helen and John were also dog-lovers, and to a lesser extent so was Rosamond, although unlike her siblings she did not wish to be bothered with the responsibility of looking after a pet. The Lehmanns' love of dogs was inherited from their father, and when John's adored spaniel, Carlotta, died, he called her successor 'Rudie', but Rosamond was affronted by this, considering it *lèse-majesté* and an insult to their father's memory. In her novels she draws some memorable canine portraits, perhaps the most vivid Rollo Spencer's preposterous little lapdog, Lucy, in *The Weather in the Streets*. 'She had a coat like a toy dog and her eyes were weak with pink rims. Her nose also was patched with pink, and she wore a pinched smirking expression, slightly dotty, virginal, and extremely self-conscious.'

some semblance of activity, most publicly when in the summer of 1961 she agreed to become president of the English Centre of International PEN. When she proudly broke the news to John, 'he rocked and swayed with laughter like a poplar in a roaring gale, and tried to make my flesh creep by grisly descriptions of what the job would entail – but I believe I can do it, and feel it will be very good for me, and therefore I HOPE for PEN.' In this she was right, for four years proving herself a conscientious and popular president, particularly effective in her campaigning for authors' rights at home and in her efforts to help writers in political incarceration abroad. For some years she was chairman of the Writers in Prison Committee, until she eventually resigned in frustration at the ineffectiveness of her colleagues. 'Whereas from my own point of view the Writers in Prison aspect of PEN is of paramount importance,' she wrote to the general secretary, David Carver, in 1971, 'I feel that the Committee as at present constituted, is – chiefly for geographical reasons – too inert, and unable to cope with the pressing problems that constantly arise.' For instance, she continued, 'last year I wrote to Arthur Miller [president of International PEN] about certain pressing cases in S. America. He wrote an "interim" letter, saying he was considering what action to take and would shortly write again. Since when, I have never heard from him.' Nevertheless on the whole she found her duties rewarding, enjoying not only the social side, but also the committee work, at which she showed herself articulate, politic and tenacious, often acting as a valuable link between PEN and the Society of Authors. Despite complaining in private about the tedium of internal squabbles and intrigues, she told David Carver, 'I find the committee afternoons a most delightful change from my particular solitary and concentrated kind of work, and always feel relaxed and refreshed afterwards.' As president she frequently flew off to congresses abroad, to New York, Geneva, Oslo, Teheran, Belgrade and Budapest, even if the obligatory return hospitality was sometimes a source of 'intense boredom . . . trying to communicate with brown and black brothers, not to mention Iron Curtain delegates with stony faces, and observers for the USSR'. Her work did not go unappreciated: in 1968 David Carver wrote to her, 'I have never actually put it into words how I feel we are indebted to you for all you have done.'

Rosamond's activities at PEN were committed to promoting and protecting other writers, but by the mid-1960s her own writing appeared to have been left in abeyance. Part of the problem was that she suspected her present spiritualist preoccupations were unlikely to find a sympathetic readership, and her awareness of this distressed her, causing 'a well-nigh total seize-up in such powers of self-expression as I have'. Her frustration was intense, wanting to write but unable to visualise how, the unwritten book like a dead child in the womb. 'At times,' she said, 'I had the actual physical sensation of a solid book-like object bound in stiff boards with cutting edges and sharp corners stuck in my midriff.' The fact, too, that it was so long since she had last published – *The Echoing Grove* had come out in 1953 – made the prospect of resuming her professional persona all the more daunting. It was not encouraging, as she complained to her agents, that in her own country she seemed to be largely forgotten. There was still a certain amount of interest in the United States, and enthusiasm for her work in France was undiminished, but at home she was considered a back number, her once-prominent position now taken by younger women such as Brigid Brophy, Edna O'Brien and Margaret Drabble. 'Does it not seem beyond words strange to you,' she wrote to Anne Munro-Kerr at the Society of Authors, 'that my novels should continue to earn quite a handsome yearly income in French translations (well over £800 this year) – and in the original (English) language be mostly out of print?'

Sedate Eaton Square was only yards away from the King's Road, the very centre of the Swinging Sixties, but at Number 70 Rosamond was turning with nostalgia to the nineteenth century. 'I have just been dipping into the Victorian memoirs of one Walpurga Lady Paget,' she wrote in 1963, 'and wishing that the young beauties of today were arrayed like their grandmothers and great-grandmothers in white muslin or pink gauze caught up with rosebuds, and with wreaths of eglantine in their hair. How I would have loved it!' As always, Rosamond read voraciously and she admired much of the new fiction – by Iris Murdoch, William Trevor, Sybille Bedford – but when confronted by 'outspoken-ness' in novels and by newspaper accounts of free love and the pill, she declared, 'I'm getting to be an old lady & I simply don't want to be confronted with overt sexual description any more.' In a book review written as early as 1952 she had spoken yearningly of the previous century and its stricter moral climate, 'whose rigors and privileges I never knew, yet feel deprived of . . . [and] our present freedom to be writers or anything else we choose . . . seems to me, paradoxically, to have become a limitation: a loss of range, a dwindling of creative energy; a threat to full development'.

In fact Rosamond had not been idle, but the work on which she was engaged was not of a kind casually to be talked about to the uninitiated.

Through her studies in the paranormal Rosamond had made many new friends and contacts, most significantly Wellesley Tudor Pole, a retired major in the British army, who during the First World War had operated in Intelligence in the Middle East, and in the Second had won fame for having proposed the nationwide prayer for peace known as the Big Ben Silent Minute. Tudor Pole, an established expert on psychic subjects, had published a number of books dealing with astral projection, clairvoyance, precognition and post-mortem communication, and in 1959 had founded at Glastonbury the Chalice Well Trust, having himself purchased the site there of the holy spring in which the cup, or chalice, used at the Last Supper had supposedly been found. The Major, a spry old gentleman in his late seventies, lived in a modest semi-detached villa in Hurstpierpoint, Sussex. By day he was kept fully occupied by a global correspondence and by his numerous business interests, in particular the Chalice Well, but it was after dark that his real work was done. The Major was only a part-time visitor to Planet Earth; as he himself put it, 'I am a modest and anonymous ambassador from elsewhere.' At night, leaving his sleeping body on his bed, he saddled his steed and took off for distant regions, sometimes to his Rescue Station for those killed in accidents, sometimes to call on King Arthur and his knights, or to work in a spirit-operated laboratory on his discovery of a cure for cancer. Occasionally there would be an emergency – a big air-crash, for instance, or, in 1963, the heavenly reception to organise for the 'coming over' of Pope John XXIII – and then the peripatetic major would be hard pressed to complete his duties in time. Even under normal conditions he had to watch the clock, 'as I dare not overstep the five-hour period allotted to me each night; otherwise bodily life and work in daytime would suffer. . . . I return to my own home, stable my steed . . . disrobe, take a bath; put on my earth level garments, and prepare to re-enter my mundane frame.'

It was while inhabiting this mundane frame that during the winter of

1963 Tudor Pole first met Rosamond, over coffee at St Ermin's Hotel in Victoria. Tudor Pole, or 'TP' as he liked to be called, was about to embark on an important literary enterprise for which he needed a collaborator – far too busy to undertake the whole thing on his own – and Rosamond, who admired his published work, had been approached. Sitting opposite her she saw a lively old boy, bald, with bright dark eyes and fizzing with energy. 'I was in the presence of someone quite formidably *awake*,' she wrote later. TP's old-fashioned gallantry and waggish banter charmed her, and she was intensely excited by his project, nothing less than the putting into publishable form recollections of his personal association with Jesus Christ around the period of the Last Supper. Participation in such a momentous undertaking was an honour of which Rosamond felt scarcely worthy, embarking on her great task 'with hesitation and trepidation; above all with a genuine sense of being privileged far beyond my deserts'. To her, despite a contempt for organised religion, the person of Jesus, both in a historical and mystical context, was of immense significance. 'Nothing I had heard from pulpits, nothing I had been told by orthodox Christians of any denomination sparked a response in me. . . . [But] I believe that . . . the meaning of the life of Jesus on earth is of supreme importance to man's wholeness.' Within a couple of days she received from the Major a detailed outline of what the work would entail. 'TP to give you his unpublished scripts, to be written round and through,' he told her, adding that they should begin at once as he could not be sure how long his present sojourn on earth would extend. 'Delay would probably result in TP not being available to you in an advisory capacity.'

Three times a week long letters arrived from TP, mostly written in the third person ('Bless you, how tiresome TP can be, leaving you so little peace!'), and Rosamond found it was all she could do to keep up with his requirements. Yet the rewards of his friendship more than made up for his exigence, for 'he gave me fresh hope and courage, cherished me and made me laugh again; above all gave me the solid, acceptable metaphysical grounding I was seeking and had always lacked'. The major's correspondence ranged widely over all the subjects now closest to his pupil's heart. Addressing her as 'Alexias',[2] a name by which she

---

[2] A selection of these letters was published by Neville Spearman in 1979 under the title *My Dear Alexias*.

had allegedly been known in ancient Greece, he told her of her previous incarnations – not only in Greece, but in Egypt and Renaissance France – as well as of his own myriad theories and extraordinary experiences in this world and elsewhere. Most marvellous, once or twice while in excarnate form TP ran into Sally, 'looking so gay, and alive and beautiful on her white pony'. His letters are boyishly boastful, falsely modest, and brimming with arch humour ('What a joy to be naughty now and then!'), but the sprightly Major with all his eccentricity was not unendearing, and Rosamond had no difficulty in assuming the role of devoted disciple. They met fairly frequently, either in London or Sussex, or sometimes in Glastonbury at the Chalice Well, where several times Rosamond drove down to hear him talk. On one unforgettable occasion at his house in Hassocks Road, TP took her up to the attic room in which he had created a sanctuary for the sacred chalice itself, 'the wondrous mysterious sapphire bowl ... discovered in 1906 at Glastonbury after a vision experienced by TP while sitting in his Bristol office'.

Published in 1965 in an elegant small format by the specialist firm of Neville Spearman, A Man Seen Afar by Wellesley Tudor Pole and Rosamond Lehmann opens with an Introduction by Rosamond in which she briefly explains her involvement in the book and with TP. The main text begins with Tudor Pole's summary of his personal relationship with the Son of God, TP himself at that time pursuing an existence as a gentleman farmer on a substantial estate near Tyre; it then continues with a detailed description of the house in which the Last Supper took place, a location well known to TP, the section ending with Rosamond stating her belief in the authenticity of his account, adding that 'every subsequent reading has consolidated my primary conviction that the author had been "shown", accurately, in detail, the room in which the Last Supper was held'. After this there follows a dialogue between the two of them on a number of topics, including TP's recollections of Jesus and the apparently much-maligned Judas Iscariot; TP's other far memories and out-of-the-body experiences; and his unusually close association with all seven 'Kingdoms of Nature', as an example of which is included a memorable conversation the Major once conducted with a copper beech. The book ends with an exchange between TP and Rosamond on the subject of death, reincarnation and various forms of psychic arcana, from etheric shrouds and Akashic Records to the details of the seven Gateways of Initiation. On the last page is appended a form of *imprimatur* from Sally. 'Yes, I have seen and heard and met him [TP] in the inner planes during sleep. Yes, he has had many lives before, and has known the Mysteries . . .'

Tudor Pole, nothing if not shrewd in his terrestrial operations, may well have assumed that his association with Rosamond would bring his work into the mainstream, an outcome of which she on the contrary was distinctly nervous, knowing all too well how most of her acquaintance regarded her veneration for 'her crazy old colonel', as Tudor Pole was disrespectfully described. On publication TP was obliged to reassure her that although some of the 'ultra-orthodox respectables' might sneer at their little book, 'I am sure your reputation has suffered no damage from your collaboration with WTP; in fact, admiration of R.L. has been much enhanced'. In the event Rosamond had little reason to worry as *A Man Seen Afar* materialised quietly and dematerialised again with little notice from the world at large.

How most of Rosamond's friends would have reacted to the book had they known of it is not hard to imagine: shock at her credulity and dismay at the insipidity of her vision. But this was largely missing the point. With the death of her child, 'the cruellest and seemingly most unnatural of all human bereavements', Rosamond lost the only person who could keep her anchored to reality, the one firm foundation of her life. Without her daughter she was lost, incapable of seeing any way to continue. She had to have Sally back, in some shape or form, and if the price was the total and uncritical acceptance of what the rational world regarded as the simplistic imaginings of a group of mediums, then it was a price she was only too willing to pay. Sally would return to her, Persephone retrieved from the Underworld, but in exchange she must shut down her reasoning, hobble her imagination, and without demur swallow whatever she was given. And swallow it she did, the whimsical narratives of Cynthia Sandys, Ena Twigg and their ilk, with their vocabulary of 'rays', 'auras' and 'vibes' (or 'vibs', as Rosamond always spelt the word), becoming her essential nourishment. Of her sessions with Cynthia Sandys, she wrote, 'To me, the extraordinary news I get is like an occasional long comforting telephone conversation on a clear line, from the other side of the world.' Although she came to despise certain aspects of psychic practice – 'evidential' sittings,[3] for instance, which she herself had clamoured for in the early days, were now described as 'distasteful . . . like journalism of the lower sort' – subconsciously she knew, as Philip Caraman had told her when talking of Catholicism, that it needed only one leap in the dark and faith would be granted her. Now she had made the leap, if not quite in the direction Father Caraman had envisaged, and her belief was absolute.

Among her own friends there were a few who turned out, to a greater or lesser extent, to be fellow travellers, Elizabeth Bowen for one, Elizabeth Jenkins for another. Among the more adventurous in researching the realm of extra-sensory perception was Aldous Huxley, who after the death of his first wife in 1955 had explored the possibility of making contact with her through Eileen Garrett, an Irish medium and parapsychologist living in the south of France. He recommended Miss Garrett to Rosamond, who immediately flew out for a consultation, but when she excitedly returned with a message purporting to be from Maria, Huxley remained ambivalent.

> There are some things in it which Maria might have said, and others which she couldn't possibly have said – and the whole tone is profoundly uncharacteristic of her. . . . The fact that you had known Maria and me made a certain amount of free-floating information available to the sensitive. Some of the free-floating information was correct, some of it was incorrect. . . . Meanwhile I am happy that you are getting such unambiguous signs of life and love and understanding.

Some time after Huxley's death, his friend and biographer, Sybille Bedford, whose novels Rosamond immensely admired, suffered a painful bereavement from which she took a long time to recover. Rosamond was endlessly kind to her, and Sybille was so touched that in gratitude she agreed, if with some reluctance, to see a medium. However, shaken though she was by the communication she received (not, as expected, her dead friend, but Aldous himself), she remained ultimately unconvinced. Rupert Hart-Davis, on the other hand, who after the death of his

---

[3] Literally, providing evidence of the continuing existence of the departed loved one.

367

wife Ruth was introduced to Ena Twigg, became at least for a time an enthusiastic convert. 'My visit to Mrs Twigg has indeed changed everything,' he wrote. 'I truly do believe it all.'

If the sceptics were spared the more winsome descriptions of Sally's activities in the au delà, for instance her sterling work in the natural world – 'I can make plants grow & help trees to throw out branches,' she trilled via the pencil of Cynthia Sandys. '[As yet] I have been given only little things to do like moving stones on flower beds but to me it's all thrilling and marvellous, making things move without touching them!' – it was apparent to them all how significantly the image of Sally was being changed. The photograph of her daughter in her bridal veil had a permanent place on Rosamond's dressing-table, but while the picture remained the same the personality was constantly being reshaped, the flesh-and-blood Miss Resista having been replaced by an artless young creature blithely gushing about birdsong and flowers in between singing paeans of praise to her peerless mother, to whom she endlessly promises devotion, protection and support. As the years passed Spirit Sally became a more and more powerful instrument, ever ready like a genie in a fairytale to carry out her mistress's bidding. Spirit Sally's most active role was in helping new arrivals on the other side to settle in. For those among Rosamond's acquaintance who died in the belief that they were moving on to another life, the period of transition was relatively painless, and Sally had little to do but extend a welcome; those who died denying this knowledge, however, found themselves in a state of confusion and distress, grateful, therefore, when Sally arrived to assist and explain. Occasionally souls came over whose behaviour towards Rosamond had been so heinous that they must remain in excruciating torment until such time as forgiveness was granted; and for these Spirit Sally could do nothing except report sadly to her mother on the agonies of remorse with which the poor wretches were afflicted.

At the same time as acting as literary assistant to Tudor Pole, Rosamond was slowly developing an idea for a book of her own. Originally entitled Go, Said the Bird, after T. S. Eliot's lines from Burnt Norton, quoted at the book's beginning –

Go, said the bird, for the leaves were full of children,

> Hidden excitedly, containing laughter.
> Go, go, go, said the bird: human kind
> Cannot bear very much reality –

it was described as a 'sort of "spiritual autobiography"', the work intended as a tribute to 'my long, long relationship with Sally'. It was Laurens van der Post who came up with the idea of a three-tiered structure built of the 'three "youngnesses"', Rosamond's own childhood, Sally's childhood and life after death, and ending with the babyhood of Anna, to whom the book is dedicated. As Rosamond stated, it was to be 'an entirely personal testament . . . the only one of my books I would like to be remembered by'. The manuscript was delivered in May 1967, and Collins, with whom a £500 advance had been agreed, were reported to be 'thrilled', Rosamond told Dadie. 'I can't help thinking it has come out right but of course I am full of dread.'

This brief, beautiful memoir was published at the end of October 1967 under the title *The Swan in the Evening*, the phrase taken from a traditional Irish song, a favourite of Sally's, the words tracked down at Rosamond's request by Laurie Lee.

> She turned away from me, and she went through the Fair;
> And fondly I watched her move here and move there;
> And then she went homeward, with one star awake,
> As the Swan in the evening moves over the lake.

To her mother's mind, '[The song] somehow evokes her symbolically and subtly in more ways than one'.

Part 1 is a lyrical evocation of the prelapsarian early days at Fieldhead, moving, funny, passionately subjective. As always Rosamond is at her most sensuous and sensitive when writing of childhood, and some passages shimmer with an almost hallucinatory intensity as she recalls those primordial memories, of the garden, the river, her father with his dogs, the minor tragedies – the tears, the tears – and comedies of the nursery, the solitary ecstasy of versifying high up in the leafy branches of the walnut tree. The sequence includes her own early intimations of mortality, as well as childhood experiences of abandonment and betrayal, and ends by describing her first supernatural episode, when as a

369

child strolling along a garden path one autumn evening, 'I look up and see the moon quite high in the sky. ... I stop to stare at it. Then something extraordinary happens ... [*sic*] A flash ... [*sic*] as if an invisible finger had pressed a master switch and floodlit my whole field of vision. At the same time the world starts spinning, and I am caught up in the spin, lifted, whirled. A voice splits the sky. ... It is the Voice of God, of this I am certain.' The significance of this revelation is illuminated by lines from a poem by Ralph Hodgson, which might be taken to stand for Rosamond's subsequent philosophy:

> Reason has moons, but moons not hers,
> Lie mirror'd on her sea,
> Confounding her astronomers,
> But, O! delighting me.

The next section describes the events surrounding the time of Sally's death – the visit to the Isle of Wight with Joshua, the dead blackbird as ominous portent – and the mystical experiences, from the first crystalline vision during the weekend at Westwell.[4] Here tribute is paid to the lifelong influence on Rosamond's work and thinking of Eliot. 'I took down and re-read *The Four Quartets*, the sublime, unhopeful, consoling cluster of poems; and discovered, or rather re-discovered, that everything was there – everything that I have been trying, and shall be trying, to say.' This part is followed by fragments of Sally's childhood, of her marriage and life in Java, and includes an account of a powerful dream in which Rosamond comes face to face with Jesus himself in the Garden of Gethsemane. (But even this celestial apparition is insufficient to obliterate other, demonic forces: in the same dream another, far from beatific face appears, a face 'all too familiar, the expression cold, supercilious, smirking. He was watching me weep, examining my broken heart ...') The section ends with a little vignette of Anna, Part IV taking the form of a personal letter to Anna about belief in the after-life and Rosamond's own journey towards this belief. Addressing herself to her grandchild and recalling the poignancy of Anna's baby prattle – ' "I

---

[4] A version of this part first appeared in *Light*, the journal of the College of Psychic Studies.

(*Left*) Laurie Lee and
Cecil Day Lewis
(*Above*) Laurie at
Diamond Cottage

Rosamond and Cecil *c.*1943

FACING PAGE
(*Main picture*) Rosamond
at I Tatti (*Inset*) Nicky
Mariano and Bernard
Berenson

Laurens van der Post

Cecil, Rosamond and
Keith Millar-Jones

(*Below*) Marthe L'Evêque
(Jean Talva)
(*Below right*) Noël Coward

(*Above left*) Hugo on leaving Eton (*Above right*) Sally

Willy Mostyn-Owen

Hugo, Margaret, Rosamond and Joshua Rowley
at the Stork Club

E.M. Forster, Rex Warner and William Plomer
at a party of John Lehmann's, 1954
(*Right*) John Lehmann, editor
(*Below*) Writing *The Echoing Grove*

(*Left*) Patrick Kavanagh and Sally on their wedding day. (*Above*) Wogan and Rosamond at Sally's wedding

(*Below left*) Rosamond with Anna

(*Below*) Wellesley Tudor Pole

James Mossman

Rosamond, 1981

Rosamond with novelist Lettice Cooper

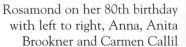

Rosamond on her 80th birthday
with left to right, Anna, Anita
Brookner and Carmen Callil

Rosamond with
Carmen Callil at the
opening of the Virago
Bookshop, 1984

Rosamond at Yoxford

wish Sally hadn't gone to heaven, why did she?" was a heart cry for a week, a month, more than a year' – Rosamond tells her that *The Swan in the Evening* is her book because 'at least, with you, I could talk about Sally'.

On publication day in October Rosamond was alone on the Isle of Wight, acutely apprehensive as to the book's reception, frightened that she had too unguardedly exposed herself to hostile opinion. 'One feels desperately vulnerable about such a "heart's blood" testimony,' as she confessed to Laurens van der Post. With the *Sunday Times* and *Observer* under her arm, she sat down on an unoccupied bench on the Turf Walk and nerved herself to open the papers. 'Presently, familiar names were swimming giddily before my eyes – Cyril Connolly Rosamond Lehmann Philip Toynbee Rosamond Lehmann . . . trembling uncontrollably, I forced myself to concentrate. Shall I ever forget the relief, joy, gratitude that flooded through me as I took in the sympathy and respect with which these two influential critics treated Sally and myself?'

Indeed the majority of critics treated the work with sympathy and respect, applauding its author for her courage and sincerity, even if most were unwilling to go along with her creed. Of the two influential reviews Rosamond read that Sunday morning, Cyril Connolly's was the more perceptive, his article beginning with characteristic panache. 'Time was when the Lehmanns, like the Sitwells and Stracheys, were a well-knit family full of torque and thrust. . . .' He then deals a very slightly back-handed compliment to the book's style – 'Unlike anything else she has written, *The Swan in the Evening* is a model of selection and compression' – before going on to say how much he enjoys what he describes as a combination 'of the earthiness of Colette with the imaginative insight of Virginia Woolf', ending by giving credit to the author for her refusal to proselytise on behalf of her personal beliefs. 'Miss Lehmann pleads, insinuates but never dogmatises on her psychic experiences.'[5] Philip Toynbee, equally atheistic, was equally impressed. 'Miss Lehmann does not offer very much which would pass for evidence among the

[5] Rosamond wrote to thank Connolly for his review, and they corresponded sporadically over the next few years on the subject of spiritualist belief, in which Cyril showed a mild if ambivalent curiosity. On one occasion, he told Rosamond that his mother had been clairvoyant, '"but I never mentioned it to anyone because I was ashamed of it." So I said to him: "You do believe in an afterlife, don't you?" He just turned away and didn't answer.'

incredulous,' he wrote. '[But] to my mind it would be both an impertinence and an intellectual impropriety to tell Miss Lehmann why she believes what she now believes, and to explain to her why she ought not to do so.' Over the next couple of weeks other reviewers recorded similar reactions: 'powerful, vulnerable, and brave', wrote Claire Tomalin in *The Times*; 'courageous . . . [and] moving', according to the *Times Literary Supplement*; while Sally Williams in the *Evening Standard* summed up the majority consensus when she wrote, '[Lehmann's] book may comfort some people, and embarrass others, but her courage in writing it is undeniable.'

Inevitably there were some who reacted less than favourably to *The Swan*'s message. One such was Anne Duchene in the *Guardian* who, asserting that sceptical readers 'will pretty easily explode' the significance of the psychic encounters, expressed her frustration at the 'mild, inconclusive allusions to Christian and Jungian belief, and so on, when Miss Lehmann claims that "no student can ever have raked the shelves of the library of the College of Psychic Science more voraciously" than she. The pity of the book, in short, is that . . . it was not cast in a sterner mould'. Such a negative view was no doubt easily dismissed: far more riling was a review written a couple of months later by Stevie Smith, in which Rosamond's idiosyncratic version of Christianity is openly deplored. 'Towards the end [of the book], Miss Lehmann has a vision of Christ in the Garden of Gethsemane. This vision turns Miss Lehmann's thoughts to the possibility of becoming a Christian, but, like many people in this position, she seems not fully acquainted with the tenets of Christianity.' The reviewer then turns her attention to what she regards as the errors of Rosamond's convictions. 'Miss Lehmann thinks that people who do not wish to traffic with the dead are cold, careless or timid. They may be more full of love than she thinks. . . . For if you believe in God, you will let the dying go. . . . Is it asking too much that we should love our dead and leave them alone, waiting for our own deaths to know what it is all about? Or to know nothing ever again.' Stung, Rosamond wrote to Stevie, accusing her of having given vent to a personal hostility, to which Stevie replied calmly but uncompromisingly.

To the idea of life after death I found in your book . . . I am hostile;

but not to you. I hoped I had made this clear, and also made clear how much I admired your courage, and the beauty of much that you have to say, and the way you say it. . . . I do not see the dead as a 'frightening and hostile society', but as being . . . [sic] either non-existent, or, in the hands of a loving God. . . . I love to think of the dead as in the hands of God and safe from us. So there we are, both · of us, I expect, so far as here and now goes, in the hands of our temperaments.

As might be expected, the responses of Rosamond's friends were in the main supportive, even if some expressed a measure of dissension. Noël Coward, Laurens van der Post, William Plomer, Rex Warner and Elizabeth Bowen were among those who wrote to congratulate, as did members of the family, whose reactions were naturally of especial interest. Rosamond's two sisters were profoundly affected. 'I read it at one gulp, the tears pouring down my face,' wrote Helen, while Beatrix said much the same. 'I read through the book in one swoop – all night! I found it almost . . . unbearably moving. . . . So unlike John's travesty, Helen's unforgiving infantilism, and my cynicism and bullet-biting.' John, while confessing he found the childhood fragments 'quite beautifully done', had reservations about some of the rest. 'There seems to me to be a profound inhibition lurking somewhere, which drags against the intention of the book. It very nearly breaks into three; and it is the third part – the Letter to Anna – which seems to be least satisfactory, because there is a didactic, almost patronizing tone that your record of Anna's Infant Sayings only brings out more sharply.' Much the most revealing response came from Hugo, who for once lowering his guard told his mother some of what he had gone through at his sister's death.

I lost a lot of foundation, underpinning, security I suppose, with Sally's death which came at the same moment as a lot of illusion-shattering, and my own life seemed to have had a watershed thrust on it which meant that to have a future the past must be excluded and switched off. . . . *Swan in the Evening* made me howl with despair at [the] waste, but . . . explained a lot which may shake my nihilism. . . . I know there was a reason for the transformation in

373

you and I now understand it. Objectively, I think it is a marvellous book.

One letter infuriated Rosamond, and that was a communication from Wogan, to which she fired off an angry reply.[6] Shaken, Wogan wrote to apologise.

I am terribly terribly sorry I upset you so much. How dangerous of me to write. I have taken long reflection before I dared write this. My letter to you completely reversed fire. It was a cry from me, not a reflection on you whatever. Our life together was terrific. You saved me from a shallow hopeless nothing. It was a tremendous love affair. You gave me so much, & I have never forgotten it for one moment & am grateful for ever. . . . *Please* never answer this or tell anyone I wrote.

In replying to the many, many letters received after the publication of *The Swan in the Evening*, Rosamond gave repeated assurances that she was now restored to health and happiness; and this was by and large true. There were still times when she felt crushed by grief, desperate for Sally's actual, physical presence, an 'eternal exile' in the world; but by the mid-1960s such descents into despair had grown infrequent, and in 1967 she was able to write robustly, 'The thing I never dared hope would happen *has* happened: I mean, the anguish of being with "other people's daughters" has gone entirely. I adore them, in fact.' To Stephen Spender she went further, declaring her conviction of the importance of concentrating on the earthly plane. 'We *must* resolve to live in this life, it is of paramount importance to do so, and it took me a long time after she left me to see this and act on it.' Certainly Rosamond took a keen interest in what was going on around her, not only busy at home, but staying with the Spenders in France, going on holiday with Hester Chapman in Egypt, with Barbara in Greece, with Frances Partridge in Sicily, with Hugo, Mollie and the grandchildren in Portugal. Yet still her overwhelming preoccupation was with spiritualist affairs, her activities in this sphere discreetly executed, unmentioned except to fellow

[6] Neither of these letters appears to have survived.

believers. She saw herself as inhabiting two separate worlds, and it was to the extraterrestrial world of the living dead that she was the more emotionally attached. A great deal of time was spent in Queensberry Place, not only in the College library and attending lectures and meetings, but she herself now counselling the bereaved. '"Counselling" is too grand a name,' she wrote modestly. 'I have come to feel that the best I can do is to *listen*: listen with a totally self-obliterating measure of attention. Sooner or later . . . a breath of spiritual fragrance steals in, quickening the air.'

During the decade Rosamond lost a number of old friends, Violet Hammersley and Matt Ridley in 1964, Ursula Ridley and Peter Morris in 1967, Wellesley Tudor Pole in 1968. It began to be noticed that she showed an intense, almost prurient interest in the mortally ill, attending the death-bed whenever she could, and if possible being present at the actual moment of departure, a white-haired, heavy-limbed Angel of Death, by no means always a welcome apparition. When Elizabeth Bowen lay dying in hospital in 1973 Rosamond's visits became so relentless and disturbing that eventually Elizabeth had to ask that they be prevented. Seeing Rosamond at the end of her bed, she said, was like seeing a great white mouse waiting to pounce. This morbid streak was commented on by several observers. According to Dadie, 'What she *loves* is for people to be ill and dying. What she likes best is to say, "Oh, of course, I was there at the last. The last words he ever spoke were in fact spoken to me."' Jim Lees-Milne also noted this trait. '[Ros] designates herself death-bed watcher-in-chief,' he wrote in his diary. 'She cannot keep away, revelling in death scenes.' The terminal illness of Peter Morris, a friend of Rosamond's since the 1920s and an old love of Dadie's, was a case in point. Morris, in the final stages of cancer, was slowly dying in the Royal Marsden Hospital in Fulham. Every day for three months Rosamond had gone to see 'poor precious Peter', insisting on sitting by his bedside morning and evening and towards the very end all night, to the intense irritation of Peter's long-term partner, Vail, who found it difficult ever to be alone with his lover. On the day that Peter finally 'slipped away', Rosamond took off for Cynthia Sandys's house in Worcestershire. Returning to London, she described to Dadie the comfort her lengthy vigils had given to the dying man, before going on bitterly to complain about Vail. 'The Vail part of my ordeal was unspeakably painful – & I'm afraid I can't get over it: I hadn't taken in the extent & quality of his jealousy and hostility until that night I watched by Peter. It became clear he thought I wanted to "steal" Peter's dying breath from him.

Whereas to some Rosamond's fixation on death and dying appeared unhealthy, if not downright dangerous, to others it was an irresistible lure. In October 1969 Rosamond was invited to dinner by Peter Adam, a young German film director who worked at the BBC. Having been introduced to Rosamond through her doctor, Patrick Woodcock, who had become a valued friend, Peter now wanted her to meet a colleague of his, James Mossman. Mossman, a highly regarded television reporter, the year before had suffered a personal loss from which he had been unable to recover. Rosamond was pleased at the prospect of meeting such a celebrity, whose public reputation owed as much to his outstanding good looks as to his undoubted ability and intelligence. The evening was a success, and a date was made for Mossman to come and dine alone with Rosamond the following week, an occasion to which, although on the verge of 70, she looked forward with an almost girlish excitement.

14

'A Woman Sitting Alone'

As Rosamond moved into her seventies she continued to pursue her double life, half in the world she had always inhabited, half with Sally on the other side. In her face could be seen vestiges of the celebrated beauty, but she had grown very stout, her love of rich food coupled with a distaste for exercise all too visibly affecting her figure. The American critic Diana Trilling, dining in her company one evening in the early 1970s, recorded how shocked she was by the change. 'Lionel and I were invited to dinner with her at the home of a London doctor, Patrick Woodcock. The only other guest was Christopher Isherwood.[1] . . . I had been warned that she had gained an extraordinary amount of weight but I could not have been prepared for her altered appearance: at Dr Woodcock's, she all but overflowed the little sofa in his sitting-room.' While mildly interested in clothes, Rosamond had always lacked chic, her style now growing increasingly singular, most of her wardrobe made by a local dressmaker of modest ability who constructed for her roomy jackets and skirts and, as her girth increased, a series of tent-shaped garments in pastel colours, in which, said Dadie, 'she would come sailing forth like a great balloon'. She had a penchant for costume jewellery, appearing with ropes of pearl beads wound round her wrists and heavy earrings pendant from her long lobes. The wonderfully thick head of hair

[1] The novelist L. P. Hartley was also there but his presence had made little impression on Mrs Trilling.

was as silky and luxuriant as ever, often rinsed with pink or Parma violet, while the large face was coated with a pale opalescent foundation, the cheeks vividly rouged, the mouth painted a bright crimson. She regarded herself very much as a reigning beauty still, and made it clear from her manner that she expected homage to be paid; when it was not she felt injured and cast down. Yet even in decline there was a certain magnificence about her: Frances Partridge, describing 'that over-lifesize, smooth, handsome face', compared her to 'a vast primitive goddess', while on Sylvia Townsend Warner, meeting Rosamond one Christmas in Wales, she made a similar impression, in appearance like 'an Indian God ... plump, suave, diamond candelabras swinging from her ears, smiling with indifferent benignity'.

Social life was of paramount importance to Rosamond, and she worked at maintaining her friendships, tirelessly arranging weekend visits and conscientious about keeping in touch on the telephone. In London she enjoyed most an intimate evening with one or two friends, or a play or concert followed by a cosy supper. She loved vigorous debate: politics or ethics if men were there, books, gossip and the confiding of love-affairs, preferably unhappy, if alone with an intimate of the same sex. As one of her female friends said of her, 'Rosamond was a friend to women, benign, tender-hearted, and concerned, and it seemed to make no difference to her what age they were. . . . Her conversation was always characterised by searching questions about one's feelings, for she was a woman of sensibility, and one who was interested in the emotional truth of situations.' With reluctance Rosamond had taught herself to cook, and although she never took pleasure in the process, her repertoire, if limited, was creditable. When entertaining, she gave a great deal of thought to selecting her company, taking pride when friends previously unacquainted with each other hit it off. Sometimes they hit it off rather too well, and she, the hostess, felt left out. Diana Cooper was a noted offender, monopolising the most attractive man at the table and totally ignoring Rosamond. Hester Chapman's conduct was even worse. 'Much as I love her, I think her behaviour as a guest . . . is unspeakable. There have been occasions when, quite literally, she hasn't looked at or spoken to me the whole evening. . . . Once I went & lay on my bed for half an hour, then did the washing up & came back at 1.30 a.m. She hadn't noticed my absence, & was still shrieking away.'

Of the family Rosamond saw as much as she could, staying with Hugo and Mollie at Llanstephan and in the house they had bought for holidays in Italy; but with four small children swirling about, these occasions were sometimes more exhausting than enjoyable, and Rosamond could not always be the centre of attention. The same was true of her visits to the Kavanaghs, who had moved to Gloucestershire, within easy reach of Wogan and Tamara at Butler's Farm. There were now two small boys, Cornelius and Bruno, and Rosamond sometimes felt herself edged to one side. 'What I really feel *always* now is that you don't take much trouble about me when I come to see you,' she complained to Patrick. 'Either you wander off, or play with Corn in an *excluding* way which doubtless you are not aware of. And then you and family are now integrated into the Wogan–Tamara unit. Can't you see how lonely this makes me feel?'

Far the most rewarding familial relationship was still with her granddaughter Anna, who had grown into a delicate dark-haired beauty. 'Ros certainly tried to make me into a substitute daughter,' Anna recalled, 'though I'm so unlike Sally: I'm not blonde, I can't sing. But she knew I liked nice things and she always bought me clothes. My first bikini came from her and my contact lenses.' Powerfully possessive, Rosamond tried to control every aspect of the young girl's life, and exacted from her, in exchange for abundant love and generosity, a heavy tribute in the form of extravagant expressions of affection and gratitude. Anna adored her grandmother, but found her emotional demands burdensome. 'She was wonderful – but the price you paid was very, very high,' she said. 'You could never, *ever* do enough for Ros.'

For a woman such as Rosamond, not only accustomed to being admired, but needing admiration, the absence of suitors in old age was a serious deprivation. But just as vanity protected her from the reality of her ruined appearance, enabling her to see herself as a beauty regardless of the reflection in the mirror, so vanity came to the rescue of her feminine self-esteem, and almost any presentable man who entered her orbit, married or single, was understood to be discreetly enamoured. 'In spite of having been left by at least four men,' Frances Partridge observed, 'she clearly nourishes in her heart a conviction of being universally beloved and desirable. . . . Julia [Strachey] once said she lived entirely by wish-fulfilment and I think this is true.' Many were the hints

379

and allusions to these secret idolators: Jim Lees-Milne, for example, was known to be nursing a hidden *tendresse*, as was Margaret Lane's husband, Jack Huntingdon, while Rosamond's own ex-husband, Wogan, never stopped privately regretting their divorce. The fact that all three were happy in their marriages and completely unaware of the feelings attributed to them was in no way allowed to impinge on the illusion.

There was one source of gratification that never disappointed. Over the years since Sally died, Rosamond had become an important figure in Queensberry Place. She sat on the editorial board of the College journal, *Light*, where she and the poet Kathleen Raine were valued as the only two professional writers involved; and in the late 1970s she was elected vice-president of the College, regularly presiding over meetings, introducing lecturers, and in company with Cynthia Sandys giving readings from their daughters' posthumous letters.[2] She also devoted a great deal of time to working with the bereaved. The publication of *The Swan in the Evening* had brought her an enormous new public, literally hundreds of readers – many of them mothers – writing to recount their own experience and implore her help in contacting their departed dear ones. Some she saw personally, others she referred straight to suitable channellers, but always taking the trouble to respond thoughtfully, always patient, always sensitive and understanding. In consequence she received quantities of heartfelt expressions of gratitude and adulation. 'Dear Miss Lehmann, I am on my knees to you for your heavenly kindness . . .'; 'Dear Miss Lehmann, I can't begin to tell you how grateful I am for your kindness to me yesterday . . . I could never have imagined that I could pour out my troubles to a stranger so freely.'

Rosamond counted a number of mediums among her personal friends, even if she rarely needed their services now, having developed the ability to communicate without the intervention of a third party. The one exception was Cynthia Sandys, through whom she continued to 'receive', but she frequently made contact with Sally on her own, writing letters to her in a dark blue notebook kept for the purpose. Often she

[2] In the 1960s the College of Psychic Studies published two pamphlets by Rosamond and Cynthia Sandys, jointly entitled *Letters from Our Daughters*, of which Part 1 comprised communications from Sally. Some of these were also included in *The Awakening Letters* (Neville Spearman, 1978), a selection of post-mortem correspondence received by Cynthia Sandys and edited jointly with Rosamond.

wrote simply for comfort. 'I wonder, shall we return together? How could we bear to be separated again? . . . Sometimes I wonder if we didn't both incarnate for just this reason – to prove death is only a myth – a tragic man-made myth.' At other times there was some specific problem on which she needed advice, for instance an anxiety about Anna, who had taken up with a Persian boyfriend of whom Rosamond disapproved. 'One or two worries . . . about which I know you will & can help,' this letter began. 'Anna's Persian boyfriend. How to detach them! I can't help feeling it is a left-over from another incarnation & should not have a future . . .' Sally was consulted, too, about the subject of Rosamond's next book. The president of the College, Paul Beard, had suggested she write a novel about relationships between the living and the departed, a theme which intrigued her – but did she know enough to describe convincingly conditions in the au delà? On Good Friday 1972, she wrote:

You know Sal, although you are the constant background – IF NOT THE FOREGROUND – to my daily & nightly thoughts & dreams, I find it very difficult to make what one might call Reality Pictures of your life 'over there'. If only I could it would be easier to write another novel. For instance, what are YOU doing when I am waking up in the morning, getting up generally with an aching back, making a cup of coffee, dressing, brushing my hair, making my face presentable. You don't use face creams, powder, lipstick etc., do you??

The extreme pathos of these private letters was far removed from Rosamond's confident public persona as an acknowledged expert in psychic study. It was because of her reputation in this field that James Mossman had asked to meet her. In his early forties, Mossman for ten years had been the leading foreign reporter for BBC Television's prestigious current affairs programme, *Panorama*. Tall and dark-haired, he had a lean, ascetic handsomeness that was slightly reminiscent of Cecil's; charming and self-effacing, he possessed, too, the quality of emotional indifference that, as Laurie Lee once observed, was always irresistible to Rosamond. In 1968 Mossman's male lover, Louis, had died, since when he had been sunk in a profound melancholy, out of which it was hoped Rosamond could somehow find a way to lead him. From their first encounter, Rosamond was dazzled by Mossman: 'Jim the Smasher', as she called him, 'rather takes one's breath away.' She confessed she was 'worried because I can't find anything wrong with him! Sensitive, serious, amused & amusing, immensely intelligent, hard-working, intuitive . . . [*sic*] Where is the catch?? I see I've left out the beauty! – which is very important.' Whenever she asked him to dine, he accepted; 'and when he comes I find him the nicest, easiest, most responsive company; but I'm sure that unless I go on taking the initiative I should never see or hear from him again.' It was this passivity that tantalised her. 'I'm uncertain about his capacity for loving,' she wrote to Jim Lees-Milne. 'I told him once I was glad I hadn't met him 20 years ago, when I should have fallen in love with him & he would have made me miserable, a confidence he received with an enigmatic smile.'

For a period of just over a year, from the beginning of 1970 to April 1971, Jim Mossman saw Rosamond regularly, usually spending the evening alone with her at Eaton Square, except when very rarely she invited some carefully selected friend to join them. Occasionally she went for a weekend to his house near Diss on the Suffolk–Norfolk border, where normally he took pains to ensure his solitude was undisturbed. The two of them intensively discussed Louis's death and life after death, Rosamond passionately persuasive on the subject, begging Jim to accept that Louis was present, waiting for him on the other side, and that their life together would blissfully continue in the spirit world. She sent him first to one medium, then to another, but somehow the experience was unsatisfactory, and it was with Rosamond herself that Mossman seemed to find most comfort and conviction. Gradually she began to believe he was emerging from his state of 'shattering melancholia. . . . He is *much* less depressed,' she told Jim Lees-Milne, one of the few who had been allowed to meet Mossman. 'I do rather think he looks on me as a sort of anchor & that I have slightly helped him out of black despair.' By now wholly captivated by this complex, unhappy man who seemed so touchingly dependent on her, Rosamond decided to sell her property on the Isle of Wight and buy a cottage in Mossman's part of East Anglia, eventually deciding on a minute doll's-house in the village of Yoxford, ten miles north of Aldeburgh on the coast.

On 5 April 1971, when the purchase of the Yoxford property was on the point of completion, news came that Jim Mossman had killed himself. He had taken an overdose of sleeping pills and left a letter saying, 'I can't bear it any more, although I don't know what *it* is.' Rosamond was devastated. 'I was well aware of the soul-sickness that had overwhelmed him. I *didn't* realize it had become irreversible,' she cried to Peter Adam. 'I thought the worst danger was over and that one day the splinter of ice in his heart would melt.' Peter Adam, responsible for introducing Mossman to Rosamond, was far from convinced that her influence on his friend had been beneficial. 'Rosamond drew Jim towards death,' he said. 'She promised him that life on the other side was infinitely superior. She encouraged him to die.' Despite the fact that almost at once messages started coming through from Sally that Mossman bitterly regretted not only his suicide but the fact that he had never told Rosamond how much he loved her, that he never while on earth gave her what she deserved, Rosamond was profoundly saddened by his death. 'I am in "a depression" which won't lift,' she wrote to Patrick Kavanagh in August that year. 'J.M.'s suicide knocked me backwards. ... It is very hard to come to terms with, & seems to get more distressing as it recedes in time.'

Earlier that year Rosamond had been warned of the imminence of another death, one that would affect her even more profoundly, that of Cecil Day Lewis, who was reported to be seriously ill with pancreatic cancer. Intimations of this 'nightmare event' had thrown her into a frenzy. 'Even if I didn't believe (or rather know) that death is *not* the end, I would I think have imagination enough to realize that one longs to be given the chance at least, for a reconciling word, after so much negative grief & pain. I don't know what to do, I don't know what to do. Unless he is already too ill and weak, he would want to see me, – that I'm almost sure of.' Spurred on by this conviction, Rosamond wrote to Cecil saying that she knew he was very ill and would he like her to come to him? Cecil was bewildered. 'Why is she writing to me now?' he asked. Then he understood. 'The moment I think he knew he was going to die,' Jill Day Lewis recalled, 'was when Rosamond wrote him that letter.' Far too weak to cope with such a stormy figure from his past, Cecil gently replied that he had been 'very glad' to get her letter, but that at present he was 'at a very low ebb' and too ill to receive visitors. Should he improve, however, 'it would be nice to see you'.

Two months later Cecil died, on 22 May 1972. For Rosamond, denied the opportunity to make her peace, his death opened all the old wounds, anguish over the love she had lost and red-hot rage at the memory of his perfidy. Well-intentioned letters of condolence did little to soothe her. 'Concentrate on the happiness of the past, and if you can bear it read the lovely poems that Cecil wrote to you and because of you. They are the children of your love,' Rupert Hart-Davis advised her; but such counsel was ignored as over and over again she rehearsed the facts of Cecil's treachery. It was like a murder, she said, and the evil came to show in his face; his beauty seemed 'gradually to disappear & become overlaid by a horrible, almost grotesque mask. One thought of *The Picture of Dorian Gray*.' Her one consolation lay in the belief that Cecil had known little happiness after he left her. 'There were awful scenes with Jill, I'm delighted to think, and he started having affairs left, right and centre. . . . In the middle of it all he was appointed Poet Laureate which was the kiss of death to him as a poet. I don't think he's one of the really good poets. . . . He hadn't a great gift.' A few weeks after he died, Rosamond was sitting with a medium whose 'control' suddenly became very insistent that she talk to somebody who was desperate to communicate. 'Cecil came through and said in a very dead voice how wretched he was, and implored me to forgive him. He said he now realised how wrong he had been to have scoffed at the after-life, and how miserable he was at having caused such terrible unhappiness.' Try as she might Rosamond was unable to feel one drop of compassion or forgiveness, with the consequence that Cecil was reportedly doomed to remain in purgatory on the other side. Still she continued obsessively to recycle her personalised version of his great betrayal. 'There is only one person in all my life I know I haven't (yet) forgiven,' in 1982 she told Patrick Kavanagh yet again, '& that is more because of the damage he did to Sally than to me.'

While most of her friends tried to offer comfort, her brother as usual succeeded only in infuriating. John had written an obituary tribute to Cecil, to which Rosamond had taken angry exception, regarding it as an act of base disloyalty which had 'stabbed me to the quick'. Refusing either to apologise or retract, John argued with justification that his friendship with Cecil had existed quite independently of hers, and that in his view he rather doubted 'the wisdom of trying to involve other people . . . however close to oneself, in one's own emotional disasters'. Such pontificating was bad enough, but as nothing compared to a 'nauseating' article that now appeared in the *Sunday Times*, a personal memoir of Day Lewis by the novelist Elizabeth Jane Howard. Rosamond knew that some years previously Jane Howard, much younger than she, a beauty, critically acclaimed, had had an affair with Cecil; this knowledge had rankled, and her bitterness intensified when she learnt that Jane Howard and her husband Kingsley Amis had arranged for Cecil and Jill to spend his last weeks at Lemmons, their large, comfortable house in Hertfordshire, where he could be most easily looked after; and it was at Lemmons that Cecil died. 'That was a very embarrassing piece you wrote about CDL,' Rosamond wrote angrily to Jane. 'I ought, I suppose, to be grateful to you for dismissing me as an "emotional involvement" . . . However, would it not have been better to keep silent rather than publish stuff which can only add to the bitterness and distress of those whom Cecil wounded most?'

From such tribulation, it was a continuing comfort for Rosamond to be able to withdraw to her cottage at Yoxford, which despite the absence of Jim Mossman became a source of much enjoyment. The Coach House, as it was called, was one in a row of tiny artisans' houses, early nineteenth-century, which stretched along the broad main street of the village. It had once been a shop, and immediately inside the front door there was a narrow parlour with a bow window, once the shop window, looking out onto the street; leading out of the parlour was a minuscule dining-area with kitchen beyond, and upstairs two little bedrooms and bathrooms. At the back was a small paved garden, planted with a pink-and-white Rosa Mundi rose, and the original coach house, now turned into an annexe for guests. The doll's-house proportions had a certain charm, although to some the sight of Rosamond's large form looming over the miniature sofa and chairs was comically reminiscent of the overgrown Alice in the White Rabbit's burrow. Jim Lees-Milne was also reminded of Alice. 'Her cottage in the village street incongruously tiny,' he wrote in his diary after staying at Yoxford in August 1974. 'It reminded me of the shop in *Alice through the Looking-glass*, and Ros of the old woman who turned into a sheep. She was dressed from neck to ankle in flowered chiffon and walked heavily leaning on my arm down the village street, a strange spectacle in such rural surroundings.' Most weekends friends came to stay, as did the grandchildren during school holidays, and of course Anna, but she was rarely available on her own, having married in 1975, her husband, Christopher Woodhouse, inevitably much resented by Rosamond. In Suffolk, the great event of the year was the June music festival at Aldeburgh, established in 1948 by Benjamin Britten, for which tickets were always taken and musical friends invited. (It was a source of particular pride when Rosamond's cousin, the distinguished conductor Steuart Bedford, was on the programme.) When Rosamond first moved into the area, some hopeful attempts were made to infiltrate the close circle around Britten and Peter Pears, but nothing came of it, Britten politely thanking for the copies of her novels while declining the suggested meetings. None the less there was an agreeable social life to be had locally, and Rosamond was made much of, particularly by 'a small circle of dear queer friends who are very kind to me & affectionate.' All in all, 'I am rather happy in Suffolk . . . where I feel peaceful and collected'.

Not long after the move to Yoxford, Rosamond was faced as well with a move in London, forced by the effects of the recession to give up her expensive flat in Eaton Square and look for something cheaper. Despondency soon gave way to delight when her ex-sister-in-law, Gwen Philipps, offered her at a modest rent the very same house in Clareville Grove in which Sally had lived when newly married. At once Rosamond felt that this had all along been 'meant', and in November 1976 she happily installed herself, with a reassuring sense of coming home. Number 30, at the end of the quiet, leafy street, is a narrow, three-storeyed house, two small rooms on each floor, with a minute garden enclosed behind a wall in front. 'Clareville Grove is a most civilized & charming little sort of village enclave,' she wrote to Dadie, '[I] have made it pretty & have *most* of my things still around me, and I long to show it to you.' Immediately inside the front door is a tiny hall, with a staircase on the left, to the right a snug sitting-room with two windows looking out onto the garden. The sitting-room was crammed with books, not only in shelves but piled on tables – new novels, poetry, recent publications of a spiritualist nature – leaving only just enough room for a small sofa and a couple of armchairs in front of the fireplace. In one of these chairs Rosamond spent most of the day, reading, writing on a tray balanced on her knees, and in the evenings with a glass of whisky beside her talking to friends who came to call. Leading off the sitting-room was a small dining-room, dominated by a sumptuous Edwardian portrait of a beautiful, bosomy young woman, one of the Pettigrew sisters by Théodore Roussel.

Earlier that same year, 1976, Rosamond finally finished the novel on which she had been working sporadically and with immense difficulty for four years. 'My novel is killing me,' she had told Jim Lees-Milne. 'But better to die of it than not to write it (I suppose!).' Described by its author as 'a love story plus a sort of ghost story . . . an account of loss of identity and its recovery', A Sea-Grape Tree[4] appeared on 28 October 1976, unlucky with the date of publication in that its publisher, Billy Collins, had died the previous week – which may partly account for the low-key campaign with which the firm publicised Rosamond Lehmann's first novel for twenty-three years.

Returning to the Caribbean setting of No More Music and of the short story 'A Hut, a Sea-Grape Tree', this last brief work of fiction is an evanescent piece full of ghosts and echoes, harking back to the themes and characters of The Ballad and the Source, a sequel having been long planned about the later life of Sibyl Jardine. The time is 1933, the place a modest guest house on one of the smaller of the Windward Islands, where Mrs Jardine had come to live and two years ago had died. Into this tropical paradise comes Rebecca Landon, a child no longer but a broken-hearted young woman recently betrayed by her married lover. Within the small, enclosed society in which she finds herself – among them familiar figures such as Captain and Mrs Cunningham, Princess the maid, the eccentric manageress Miss Stay – Rebecca prefers to be known as 'Anonyma', feeling her personality to have been fragmented and dissolved in her unhappiness. It is kind Mrs Cunningham, seeking to comfort her, who takes 'Anonyma' to meet the mysterious young man living at the water's edge on the far side of the bay, in an ornate hut

---

[4] Rosamond had wished the title to be An Accident in Time but A Sea-Grape Tree was preferred by Billy Collins.

underneath a sea-grape tree. Johnnie, mysterious, aloof, as handsome as
a sea-god (and member of an old landed family), was a flying ace in the
war, paralysed from the waist down after his plane crashed in France. In
spite of this affliction, he and Rebecca embark on a passionate sexual
affair, during which she discovers that while on the island he had known
and been loved by Sibyl Jardine, thus vividly recalling for Rebecca all
her childhood memories of the house on the hill and the children and
the terrible sequence of events unfolded by that sinister and mesmerising
presence. The spirit of Mrs Jardine herself then appears to Rebecca,
leading to a long exposition of that lady's entire history. The novel ends
with Rebecca preparing to leave the island, Johnnie having proposed
marriage and promising to follow her to England in a year's time.

It is difficult not to perceive *A Sea-Grape Tree* as the last faint
exhalation of a fine talent. According to Rosamond, the story balances
'on the brink, as it were, of another dimension, part poetic, out of time,
part realistic', and it is true that the atmosphere is marvellously infused
with a magical, visionary quality entirely appropriate to its other-worldly
theme. It is in the handling of this theme, however, that the novel fails:
not only is the love story ludicrously overblown (not to mention
physically impossible, given Johnnie's unfortunate disability), but the
vast tracts of flashback attached to Mrs Jardine's ghostly materialisation
fatally unbalance the narrative, and are in any case meaningless without
a thorough knowledge of *The Ballad and the Source*. In contrast, the
minor characters are solidly drawn, quirky, comic and infinitely more
tangible than either the moody, elusive hero, constructed from the thin
shavings left over from the wonderful young men of the earlier novels,
and Rebecca herself, passive, clinging, desperate for love. '"I *cannot* live
without love," she tells Johnnie, "without – you know, being in a state of
love. A loved and loving state.[5] Can you?" "I do," he muttered. "I told
you. I'm not loving – or lovable." He hung his head, idly picking at a
paint blister on the floor boards.' The island's lush vegetation is
sensuously delineated, and the bay depicted with a stereoscopic clarity,
its coral beach, driftwood and pounding breakers having obviously
remained fresh in the mind's eye over the years. Describing the bay
Rosamond draws on the words of the poem of the same name written

[5] Rosamond always regarded Rebecca Landon as being the closest she came to a self-
portrait.

after her visit to Jamaica in 1951: the line 'I alone, / Expecting no one, not expected . . .' is echoed in the novel by 'expecting nothing, no one; not expected anywhere, by anyone'.

In a postscript to a later edition, Rosamond wrote, 'A Sea-Grape Tree is generally considered an unsatisfactory work'; and so it was regarded by the critical majority, a consensus instrumental in her abandoning plans to write a third and final instalment of Rebecca Landon's story. By far the most wounding review was by Auberon Waugh in the Evening Standard, who mockingly referred to the love element as 'the sort of pulp romance which would nowadays make even Woman's Own blush'. Others were little more complimentary: 'unintentionally absurd', said The Times; 'Anonyma and Johnny, paper people,' concluded Lorna Sage in the Observer; while Valentine Cunningham in the New Statesman considered that 'A Sea-Grape Tree is disappointing from the start . . . It's set in 1933, and shows no signs at all that its author has the technical resources to write anything but the tritest of bestsellers à la mode of that year.' Some critics were kinder, notably, to Rosamond's surprise, Elizabeth Jane Howard in the Daily Express – 'immensely readable, acute, passionate, funny' ('Coals of fire!' Rosamond wrote to Patrick Kavanagh); kind, too, was Margaret Drabble in the Listener, who concluded: '[Miss Lehmann] must write more novels, for this is too full of life to be a swan song . . . her descriptive prose is more powerful than ever, her characters as enigmatic, as convincing.' When the novel was published in the United States by Harcourt-Brace the following year, it was treated with considerably more respect than by most of the English critics, but by that time Rosamond had lost heart, and although for a while she pondered writing a sequel, even going so far as to sketch the outline of a plot, the impulse went no further. Her career as a writer was essentially over.

From Rosamond's friends there had been an avalanche of congratulatory letters, some more genuine than others, with Sybille Bedford (who privately hated the book) and Stephen Spender among the most enthusiastic in their praise. But among the accolades, one sour note was sounded. 'Just had a typical letter from John about the book . . . rejecting both the love story and the re-appearance of Mrs J.,' Rosamond complained to Spender. The fact that John with his customary perspicacity had put his finger on the novel's two most serious flaws did little to impress his sister, who interpreted the criticism as a purely personal attack. 'However,' she went on, 'I dare say it's "only human" after what I said about *his* book.'

John's book had been published in September 1976, a month before *A Sea-Grape Tree*. The general assumption was that he had been working on more of the autobiographical sequence begun in 1955 with *The Whispering Gallery*, although Rosamond had had a hint that this final volume might be slightly different when she heard that her brother was intending to include something about his love life. '*Is* it true???' she asked him. 'If so, very interesting – but do tell me!' Indeed it was true; but everyone was taken by surprise when *In the Purely Pagan Sense* appeared. Under his well-known pseudonym of Jack Marlowe, John devotes the entire book to a detailed and mercilessly explicit first-person account of his sexual exploits from childhood to late middle age. John's avowed purpose was 'to write a serious, candid account of what it has been like to live a homosexual life in our time', but many besides Rosamond were appalled that this distinguished figure should not only have produced a work so frankly disgusting but one showing such a dismaying lack of literary ability. Rosamond declared herself 'heartsick'. 'If it weren't so suffocatingly boring it would be straight pornography: mostly brutish accounts of picking up boys and exactly what they did in bed, very complacent about his own equipment and prowess. I think he must have gone mad. I look on it as a deep family disgrace; and have been v. unhappy!' she wrote at the end of September. Two months later the shock-waves were still reverberating. 'I still feel incredulous – as if I'd seen him take off a mask & show a satyr's face. But he insists that it is "poetic" and "a spiritual search" and that for the sake of Truth he was "determined to tear off every fig leaf". That's one of the things he said at our last painful meeting. I dread my grandsons getting hold of it at Eton.' The meeting referred to had taken place in October, and had been found no less painful by John, who remained defiantly unrepentant. 'R. continues to rage like a jealous wife who has caught her husband out in squalid delinquencies. . . . Nothing to be done.'

The following year, 1977, there was a dinner given at the Garrick to celebrate John's seventieth birthday. Rosamond did not attend, but she composed an ode for the occasion, 'not written particularly light-heartedly, but from the heart'.

May all be mirth,
Feast intellectual, culinary as well,
To celebrate your seventy years on earth.
But should a sister swell
However proud, this hearty PUBLIC chorus?
Accept instead a (semi-) private page,
A backward glance with the long sight of age.
Let us remember how, the prospect all before us,
Softly sweet Thames began to run
Beside our parents' second daughter,
And not long afterwards beside their son.
Since then, how many bridges, how much water
Since you and I
Set out! . . . Let's not philosophize or specify.

The prospect dwindles now; and the running tide
Upon which we have travelled – sometimes side by side
Slackens. . . . And yet, how stealthily, still hurries us along;
Will bear away toys, trinkets, relics, prizes,
Pomps, medals, masks, and other old disguises;
Will sweep us out of Time and end our song.
Alone then, bearings lost, how will it be
For us! – how shall we fare! . . .
Striving to breathe an unaccustomed air,
Facing at last our hidden selves may we
Take hands again; laugh again; agree,
If not before, after we reach the sea.

John was touched, and for a while friendly relations between brother and
sister were re-established.

During the 1970s Rosamond suffered the loss of a number of her
oldest friends, Elizabeth Bowen, William Plomer, Hester Chapman, and
at the very end of the decade, Goronwy Rees. But far the most agonising
was the death of her sister Beatrix. In the early spring of 1979 Bea had
gone up to Manchester to play in T. S. Eliot's *The Family Reunion*.
During rehearsals she had felt unwell and had had trouble learning her
lines, finally collapsing with a stroke at the end of the first week of the
run. 'I can promise you that the last performance she gave in Manchester

was a feat of the greatest courage and brilliance,' her co-star Edward Fox
wrote to Rosamond. '[She] electrified the audience and her fellow
actors.' Beatrix was driven back to London by Shelagh Fraser, an actress
friend with whom for nearly fifteen years she had had a close
relationship, and it was Shelagh who devotedly nursed her at Bea's little
house in Canonbury. In May Bea's condition suddenly deteriorated and
she was taken into hospital, where a scan revealed the presence of a
brain tumour. It was decided to operate, but although she survived for a
further month she never recovered consciousness, and on 31 July 1979
Beatrix died. Rosamond was gratified by the number of tributes to her
sister she received from colleagues – 'Playing a scene with Bé [*sic*]', wrote
the actor Trader Faulkner, 'was like standing up to a very fast & *very*
accurate service from a Wimbledon champion' – although there was one
whose very existence she considered an affront. From the time she first
met Shelagh Fraser when Shelagh was in a play with Bea at the
Edinburgh Festival, Rosamond had resented her, jealous of her closeness
to Beatrix. When she discovered that it was 'that Fraser woman' who
was the main beneficiary of her sister's will, she was incensed, firing off a
couple of intemperate letters and insisting that Shelagh be forbidden
from attending the funeral.

These corrosive quarrels, about the will and then about the setting up
of a scholarship in Beatrix's name, rumbled on for some time, with John
making matters worse by siding against his sister; but fortunately
Rosamond was soon able to take comfort in consoling messages from
Beatrix herself. After an uneasy passage to the other side – 'very difficult
because she was a total sceptic' – Bea awoke to find Sally beside her,
ready to guide her through the initial stages of her new existence. 'Bea
didn't in the least want to look back on her earth life, and now she's
producing plays in the hereafter. She suddenly wrote quite a long letter
saying that she was beginning to understand what had caused so many
difficulties in her life, and how I'd really helped her, and helped her very
much during her last illness.'

With the start of the 1980s, and with her professional reputation
faded and diminished, it seemed to Rosamond that she was destined to
join the ranks of forgotten novelists. 'It is odd to think what a fantastic
best-seller I was before the war,' she wrote mournfully to her publisher in
New York. 'Maybe if I took to the bottle, like poor Jean Rhys, or

committed suicide dramatically, it would help?' Fortunately neither of these measures turned out to be necessary. In July 1977 Adrian House, Rosamond's editor at Collins, had received a letter from Carmen Callil, founder of Virago, a small new firm specialising in books by and for women; Callil wished to enquire about the possibility of licensing the Lehmann novels for reissue in paperback. Adrian House was unenthusiastic. 'They appear to be fairly pronounced feminists!' he told Rosamond. 'I would much rather find a paperback imprint which is more firmly established for your books and will explore this actively.' But nothing was done, and Callil was tenacious. In May 1978 she wrote again, only to receive another refusal, and yet another in answer to her third request three months later. Then suddenly in 1980 everything changed. A new editorial director, Christopher MacLehose, arrived at Collins, and he immediately gave instructions that Virago should be granted their request. 'He just stormed into the Rights Department and said this is ridiculous and that was that.' A luncheon was arranged at the beginning of May for Rosamond and Carmen Callil to meet, at which, said Callil, 'It was literally a case of love at first sight. . . . It was the most wonderful thing for both of us.'

And so indeed it proved. It was agreed that beginning in 1981 Virago should publish the complete works in their Modern Classics series at the rate of two a year, for an advance of £500 each and royalties, the exceptions being *Dusty Answer* and *The Echoing Grove*, which were to be reissued almost simultaneously by Penguin. The first titles, *The Weather in the Streets* and *Invitation to the Waltz*, appeared in November 1981, following the Penguin publications in July. Carmen Callil, a tough, clever and inspirational woman with enormous energy and flair, promoted the books with a vigorous campaign fuelled by her own personal enthusiasm for the author and her work, in marked contrast to the lackadaisical approach exhibited by Collins in recent years, whose neglect of Rosamond shocked her. 'Her publishers let her down, quite frankly,' said Callil. 'Her work was sitting on warehouse floors in good hardcover editions. . . . I think the reason I was not permitted to publish them [for so long was] . . . that they thought Virago was some peculiar sort of bra-less publishing company.' In fact Virago was one of the great success stories of the 1980s, and from the first the imprint had attracted a great deal of attention with its canny appeal to a large niche market.

Virago Modern Classics with their distinctive green covers and decorative period art work were prominently displayed on designated stands in bookshops throughout the country, and women everywhere were delightedly discovering high-quality fiction that had long been out of print. Through Virago Rosamond Lehmann was brought to the notice of an entirely new generation, a generation that in the late twentieth century inhabited a very different world from the world of *Invitation to the Walz* and *Dusty Answer*. A social and sexual revolution had taken place. Female emancipation had been fought for and won. Yet here was this most defiantly unfeminist writer issued by a stridently feminist publishing house, and proving herself as relevant to the 1980s – 'Oh Miss Lehmann, this is my story!' – as she had been half a century before. Critics new to her novels admired her ability to create the impression of a universality of emotional experience; at the same time they were confounded that Lehmann herself should choose to apply to her work such an outdated and discredited adjective as 'feminine'. But 'feminine' is how she saw it, and ' "feminist" labels and enquiries are driving me up the wall!' as she complained to Laurens van der Post. It was Marghanita Laski in *Encounter* who best summed up the conundrum. ' "Feminine" is the word to seize on,' she wrote, 'because it is, in today's climate, so startling. It is hard to think of any other woman writing seriously today who would choose this epithet to describe herself and, by implication, her work. But it is Rosamond Lehmann who has provided it, and the critic may fairly seize on it with relief, for without its use, fair assessment would be hard to make. Rosamond Lehmann is, essentially, a feminine writer.'

No one was more surprised than Rosamond to find herself once more in the public eye. She was dazed by the sudden change in her fortunes, in the glorious renaissance brought about by 'blessed Virago' and Carmen Callil, whom she described as 'my redeemer . . . my saviour'. The first two Virago titles, *Invitation* and *The Weather*, published in 1981, each sold just under 20,000 copies in less than three years. 'My resurrection as an "important" writer is making me feel very peculiar,' Rosamond wrote. 'Fan letters, requests for interviews etc. etc. pour in by every post, and ALMOST make me feel I could write another novel.' Articles appeared in newspapers and magazines by some of the leading journalists of the day, by Maureen Cleave, Victoria Glendinning, Lynn

Barber, Gillian Tindall, Janet Watts. There was a dramatisation for radio of *The Echoing Grove*, a television adaptation of *The Weather in the Streets*; Rosamond was invited to be a castaway on the BBC's prestigious radio interview series *Desert Island Discs*, she was the subject of profiles on the television arts programmes *Kaleidoscope* and *Bookmark*, and in 1981 she was named by the Book Marketing Council as one of the top twenty living British authors, together with Graham Greene, Victor Pritchett and V.S. Naipaul. In 1980 she was invited by the Browning Society to lay the wreath on the tomb of Robert Browning at Westminster Abbey, a poet particularly beloved by Rosamond because of his connection with the Lehmann family. In December 1984 Carmen Callil invited her to open the Virago Bookshop in Covent Garden. Less ephemeral distinctions were also bestowed. In 1982 she was appointed CBE, in 1985 made an honorary DLitt. by Leeds University, in 1986 elected to an Honorary Fellowship at Girton, and in 1987 to be a Companion of Literature by the Royal Society of Literature, among her fellow Companions Samuel Beckett, William Golding and Graham Greene. Several theses were written on her work, and in 1985 Chatto & Windus, of which Carmen Callil had become managing director, brought out a discerning study by Gillian Tindall, *Rosamond Lehmann: an Appreciation*.

For the most part Rosamond revelled in her revived celebrity, but in old age she had grown more thin-skinned about criticism and was quick to take umbrage at the expression of any opinion that diverged in the slightest degree from her own self-assessment. The major part of Gillian Tindall's book met with her approval, but the few adverse judgements made her bridle, and she resented what she regarded as the intrusiveness of some of the reviewers. 'I am SICK of all these assessments and re-assessments,' she wrote crossly to Dadie, while to Jim Lees-Milne she grumbled, 'The huge reviews of G. Tindall's book all dwelling . . . on my private life have made me feel sick & depressed, as if exposed on a dissecting table. Who are these impertinent beady-eyed young female journalists, busy making a meal of me??' A much more pleasing project, also commissioned by Callil, was the publication of *Rosamond Lehmann's Album*, a selection of photographs compiled with the help of her grandson, Roland Philipps, now working as an editor at Chatto. Designed to give a pictorial overview of the subject's life and friendships, with an Introduction and Postscript by Rosamond, the *Album* is more revealing than was probably intended. Among the quotations following the title page was a favourite line from Baudelaire, chosen with an unblushing lack of self-consciousness, '*C'est un dur métier que d'être belle femme*'; and accompanying one of the many striking portraits of the subject herself a substantial quotation from Stephen Spender's autobiography beginning, 'Rosamond was one of the most beautiful women of her generation . . .' There is only one photograph of Cecil Day Lewis, his face half hidden as he fires a gun. The book is a slightly eccentric affair, an impression compounded by the curious addition as Postscript of an outline for the sequel to *A Sea-Grape Tree*, which, as was admitted, 'will now never be written'. The *Album* nevertheless was a source of satisfaction to its author, and her return to Chatto & Windus particularly fitting, the publisher of her first book also publishing her last.

As the spotlight fell not only on her work but on her life, it began to be realised that Rosamond Lehmann was a rich historical source, and with the Bloomsbury industry in full swing biographers and thesis-writers began to light on Clareville Grove in the hope of uncovering original material about their chosen subjects. 'It makes me feel . . . like an old dredger,' Rosamond commented drily, wearying of the inevitable sameness of the questions. ' "Oh, Miss Lehmann, you must have known so many interesting people," they all start off, which means, "how well did you know Virginia Woolf?" ' Her attitude changed somewhat when Dadie suggested that she herself should be the subject of a biography. At first she was shy of the prospect, but over time the idea began to appeal, and when Dadie proposed a young academic, Philip Gardner, an ex-pupil of his, Rosamond agreed to see him. Several meetings took place, but then unfortunately it was discovered that Mr Gardner intended also talking to Jill Balcon – and that was the end of that. 'GOOD GOD!!!' she exploded to Dadie. 'The thought of that woman discussing me with P. G. made me feel physically sick.'

One of the most pleasurable consequences of Rosamond's late-flowering fame was the personal friendships she formed as a result. Of these the first and most important was with Carmen Callil, whose generous and ebullient nature endeared her to Rosamond, as did her outspokenness and refusal to be cowed by the ever-hovering threat of injured feelings. It was Carmen who introduced her to the distinguished contemporary novelist Anita Brookner, whose work Rosamond unreservedly admired – 'my favourite novelist' – and of whom she became extremely fond. Anita, elegant, fastidious, unusually perceptive, had certain reservations about Rosamond's writing, although she became devoted to her person. 'I adored her,' she said:

> She was very benevolent towards me ... [although] she never regarded me as an equal: that was not the game to be played. One always had to refer to her beauty, which was not apparent any more, of course. And she trailed a glorious past behind her, which didn't deceive me for one minute. She was very insecure and very innocent. I could see that she'd been abandoned. There were lots of names, lots of friends, she gave the impression of an extremely peopled world and life. And yet the impression I had was of a woman sitting alone, inconsolable.

Anita and Carmen sometimes dined together at Clareville Grove, when Rosamond would reminisce about her love life, encouraging the younger women to confide in her about their own. On a couple of occasions all three spent the weekend at Yoxford, 'Anita sternly going for walks and drinking tea, me insisting on singing in the motor car as we drove around Suffolk', as Carmen recalled it. In 1983 Anita paid the ultimate act of homage by dedicating a novel to Rosamond, the widely acclaimed *Hôtel du Lac*, always thereafter referred to with pride as 'my novel'.

Such rewarding new friendships were particularly opportune as they helped distract Rosamond from some depressing events within her immediate family. The first concerned Anna, upon whose support Rosamond depended more than ever. Despite the fact that Anna now had two small children, she was telephoned by her grandmother at all hours, demanding that she come and deal with every variety of domestic problem. But in 1982 Anna was suddenly struck down by a mysterious illness, eventually diagnosed as thrombosis in a spinal artery, which was to leave her always lame and for a time semi-paralysed. The following year came the announcement that Hugo's second marriage was to end in divorce, Mollie having fallen in love with John Julius Norwich, the son of Rosamond's old friend Diana Cooper. 'How *could* Mollie do this to *me!*' was Rosamond's first reaction, before recollecting herself and lamenting the rupture on Hugo's behalf. Not long after this, Helen, the eldest of the siblings, was diagnosed with lung cancer, of which in January 1985 she died in a nursing-home near Guildford. Rosamond, who for the last weeks was with her sister constantly, was deeply saddened by her death; although she had never been as close to Helen as she was to Beatrix, she remembered gratefully the many instances of Helen's awkwardly expressed kindnesses. 'Though she was never good at showing sympathy she was far gentler than the other two in 1958,' she wrote meaningfully to Patrick Kavanagh. Three months after Helen's death, John suffered a stroke, and he, too, was loyally attended in his nursing-home by Rosamond. 'Wonder of wonders! he is being very patient & stoical, & much improved in temper. In fact, as mild as a dove,' she reported with surprise to Dadie. John made what appeared to be a good recovery, but not for long, dying in hospital on 7 April 1987, after a fall. It was a comfort to his sister, the last remaining Lehmann, that she and John had been on good terms at the end, although in spite of persistent efforts on her part she failed to convert him to her spiritual beliefs. 'Poor old boy,' she remarked, 'he will be having a strange surprise now.'

The depredations of old age were taking an increasingly heavy toll as Rosamond moved into her middle eighties. Mentally she remained alert as ever, but physically the wreckage was cruelly apparent, 'collapsed like a big pudding . . . into mountainous landslides of stomach, neck and cheeks'. She had become stiff and arthritic, and most of the day was spent in her armchair, where she would sit with skirt above the knee, feet planted wide apart, revealing a view that dismayed some of the fastidious old gentlemen who came to call. 'Went to see Rosamond,' Jim Lees-Milne wrote in his diary. '[She] sits in the most ungainly manner, on a low armchair, her legs spread-eagled, displaying her not very attractive knickers up to the fork. Strange no one has told her about this.' She complained of feeling tired all the time, and that her eyesight was failing, making reading a strain. At the age of 85 she had been forced to give up her car, to general relief as at the best of times she had never inspired confidence behind the wheel; but this meant a considerable restriction of her movements, and although for a time she continued to go down to Suffolk whenever she could find somebody to drive her, the effort soon became more than she felt she could manage, and the little cottage at Yoxford was given up. At Clareville Grove, the top floor was converted into a self-contained flat for a housekeeper 'to live in & look after me a bit; because I am really growing old at last,' she wrote to Patrick Kavanagh in July 1985.

Patrick was as faithful as ever, writing regularly and often looking in to see her, as did many of her old friends, as well as her family. Hugo married again in 1989, his wife, Felicity Leach, enchanting Rosamond with her prettiness and high spirits. With or without Felicity, Hugo called round regularly to help with letters and bills; Roland, his second son, who since childhood had been unfailingly kind and attentive to his grandmother, came in at least once a week; and Anna drove over almost daily to cope with the latest requirements, her husband, Christopher, a pediatric surgeon, sometimes accompanying her as his medical expertise had a soothing effect. But none of it was enough. Rosamond was lonely; she felt aggrieved and abandoned. Buried in the mountainous form was still the little-girl-lost craving affection, and the deeper she sank into self-pity, the more difficult she became. 'I don't look forward very much to going to [see her],' said Dadie. 'It's always a little bit tricky; you never quite know whether she's going somehow to cut up rough about something. Her egomania is terrifying.' Although she could still be delightful company, too often now visitors were met with querulous accusations of neglect, and talk tended to circle round and round the old grudges and complaints, with a depressing running commentary on how everything in the world today was viler, more violent, more selfishly materialistic than in the pure, prelapsarian world of her childhood. 'She lost her sense of humour and required too much homage. In the end she became unlovable. It was no pleasure at all to see her,' said one friend, while another observed, 'The trouble with Rosamond is that she has been a star, and is now a decayed old lady whom a few friends visit out of kindness. Conversation is not easy.' In fact with a little effort and cunning she could be distracted from her grievances, even coaxed into laughter, and however dismal her situation she never lost interest in what was happening beyond her own personal boundaries: the Prime Minister, Margaret Thatcher, for instance, was an unfailing source of fascination, and anything touching on the royal family was pursued with passionate curiosity.

Unquestionably the most serious of her afflictions was her failing sight: although letters could be written by a secretary, not being able to read was a torment to Rosamond. Fortunately, however, when her eyes were examined it was found there were cataracts that could easily be removed, and in November 1985 this was done. The surgeon was pleased that the procedure had been entirely successful, and Anna, who accompanied her grandmother for the post-operative test, was delighted to hear him say that all she needed was a new prescription for spectacles and her sight would be almost as good as ever. But mysteriously, this appeared not to be true. In contradiction of the surgeon's report, not only could Rosamond not see to read, she could barely see at all. At the same time she found she could no longer climb the stairs, that almost any physical movement was beyond her. In this pathetic state, bed-ridden and virtually blind, she was truly to be pitied. She had to be helped in everything, in even the most intimate requirements, by her housekeeper, Maria, or by her doctor, Christian Carritt, who came nearly every day. Rosamond listened to the radio, but was unable to turn on the recorded Talking Books apparatus which Anna set up for her, and so was heavily dependent on the kindness of friends. She took the greatest pleasure in the visits of a young man, Alexander Norman, a distant cousin and descendant of Nigel Norman and Ménie Fitzgerald whom Rosamond had known in the 1920s. When Alexander discovered the link with his family and that Ménie had been the inspiration for Mrs Jardine, he had written to Rosamond, thereafter coming regularly to see her. 'He's very good looking, and I think just a *little* in love with me,' she simpered, pleased.

There was not one of Rosamond's acquaintance who did not feel immense compassion for her, and few days went by without one or two putting their heads round the bedroom door, bringing little presents of flowers or, even more appreciated, chocolates and cake, and staying to drink whisky and talk. The photograph of Sally in her wedding dress was prominently displayed on the dressing-table, although, surprisingly, there was little reference now either to Sally herself or to life on the other side.

But what none of these old friends realised, while sympathising with Rosamond's situation and listening to her lamentations, was that there was in fact very little the matter. The truth was she could see perfectly well. There was nothing to stop her getting up and going downstairs except her own decision that she would not. But such was her longing to be loved in her increasingly unlovable old age that, perhaps half-unconsciously, she devised this bizarre method of attracting sympathy. 'Rosamond didn't lose her sight at the end of her life,' said Patrick Trevor-Roper, who as an ophthalmic surgeon had been unofficially consulted for a second opinion. 'She told everyone she had, but it was hysterical attention-getting.' Dr Carritt, who had taken over as Rosamond's GP when Patrick Woodcock retired, had no illusions either. 'Rosamond had no need to be bed-ridden. She wasn't particularly depressed, but she was very, very lazy. She liked lying in bed. . . . And also she craved attention and thought she could get it by making increasing demands on people. . . . There was nothing physically wrong with her at all.'

Only towards the very end did Rosamond's mind grow less than clear, when she would wander a little in conversation. In the last months she looked beautiful again, her face thinner and unpainted, her pure white hair cut short. Several times she talked about a curious character who came to sit on the end of her bed, a tiny man about the size of a cat, with a face like a powder puff, wearing a green jacket and sometimes a hood. His name was Sir Frederick Quarles. He seemed benign and he watched her closely, and on occasion he seemed to have friends with him.

During the evening of Saturday 10 March 1990, Rosamond had difficulty breathing, began gasping for breath, and Maria, alarmed, sent for Christian Carritt, who diagnosed pneumonia. The next day she seemed better, and on Monday the 12th was responding so well that the crisis was thought to have passed. But that evening, with her supper tray on her knee, she again became breathless. Dr Carritt was summoned and gave her morphine, and very quietly Rosamond died, barely six weeks into her ninetieth year.

The funeral was held at Putney Vale Crematorium on 19 March. After a weekend of unseasonably warm weather, with temperatures in London reaching 72 degrees, the day was wet and windy, although not cold. The little chapel was completely filled; among the mourners were all Rosamond's grandchildren, as well as Hugo and Felicity, Patrick Kavanagh, and also Wogan, frail in a pin-stripe suit and brown muffler, leaning heavily on Patrick's arm. Afterwards there was a small gathering at Anna and Christopher's house in Clapham. Several people remarked on the fact that in the last months of Rosamond's life there had been little mention of Sally and of the blissful reunion so impatiently awaited. For years she had talked of it, the theme, as described in *The Swan in the Evening*, endlessly repeated. 'I have been taught . . . something of how it will be when I wake up after I have shed my body; so I look forward, I look forward. . . . No matter how far ahead of me Sally has gone – and I know she has – she will be waiting, as she promised. She will pull me through the door.' As Rosamond approached death, however, her thoughts seemed to have turned away from the spirit world; she dwelt instead on the world she remembered from her childhood, as though it were not to astral planes but to her early and innocent days on earth that she longed to return. In her last published work Rosamond wrote, 'I dream that I shall wake up after death sitting in a branch of the walnut tree, watching my father open the French windows of the library, step down, and start strolling towards the river accompanied by two or three high-spirited dogs. . . .'

15

Afterword

I feel it would be disingenuous to end this book without explaining a little of my own friendship with Rosamond Lehmann, and also of how this biography came to be written. In a sense Rosamond was almost part of my family: when her second husband, Wogan Philipps, left her it was to marry my father's first wife, Cristina Casati. My father then immediately married my mother, Margaret Lane, with whom he had discreetly been living for some time, and Rosamond became a friend, especially of my mother, who greatly admired her. Although there was a photograph, now lost, of Rosamond holding me when I was 3 months old, it was years before I properly became aware of her existence. I remember the occasion clearly, in June 1958, when I was 13. My parents had gone out for the evening and I was doing my homework while listening to the radiogram in the sitting-room at home when the telephone rang. A man's voice said, 'Margaret?', and I replied, No, it was her daughter, and could I take a message? and the man said, 'Sally's dead. Tell your mother we've just heard that Rosamond's Sally has died.'

After this a period of perhaps two years passed, and then I remember going to the ballet at Covent Garden with Rosamond and my mother, and during the course of the evening becoming aware that this beautiful person was someone remarkable, someone possessed of rare qualities of empathy and intuition. She was gentle and rather sad, and she looked wonderful with her white skin and thick white hair, and she told me that she liked my dress and asked me where I'd bought it. It was at this time that I started reading her novels, *Dusty Answer* and *Invitation to the Waltz*, returning to them over and over again, enthralled. I found both them and their author irresistible, and began to look on Rosamond as a sort of fairy-godmother, the member of the older generation I most wanted to see, who, I knew, would give me the spoiling attention that naturally I was denied by my heartless parents. She appeared so flatteringly interested in *me*, kindly creating the impression that she believed me an exceptional person with a fascinating future before me – heady stuff for a self-absorbed adolescent. And despite her long sadness over Sally there was an underlying gaiety which appealed to me enormously. She was capable of a surprisingly astringent wit and she loved to be made to laugh. In my twenties and thirties we used to go to the theatre, and I vividly recollect her giggling helplessly during a revival of George S. Kaufman's *That's Hollywood*, and just as helplessly at a dull and impenetrable play by Marguerite Duras starring her old friend Peggy Ashcroft. 'What on earth', asked Rosamond during the interval, 'are we going to say to Peggy afterwards?' Round we went backstage when the performance was over. 'Lovely to see you, darling,' said Dame Peggy. 'Sorry about the ghastly play. Have you any idea what it *means*?'

Occasionally Rosamond came to dinner at my flat or I with her in Eaton Square. Sometimes Hugo would be there, and once I was invited to meet her last attachment, James Mossman, although at the time I had no idea what an honour this was. 'A *great* cup of tea, isn't he?' she whispered as I followed her out to the kitchen. There were also weekends with her at my parents' house in Hampshire, and I went a number of times to stay at Yoxford, usually on my own, once, to my joy, with Dadie Rylands as my fellow guest. She took me to the Aldeburgh Festival, where I remember her unconsciously annoying her immediate neighbours during a concert by jangling heavy jet bracelets as she displayed her handsome white arms. She had made it clear in the neighbourhood that she liked to be invited out, and most days we lunched or dined with charming friends, mostly male couples in pretty period houses with immaculately tidy gardens. At the Coach House it was understood that I always did the cooking, and I quickly learned that what she loved was rich nursery food, particularly very sweet puddings with plenty of cream. The other day I came across a postcard from her – 'RL' in pink inside a wreath of roses – written after one such weekend. 'Darling, You left all that CREAM!! – I didn't mean you to. But of course I can't resist it.'

We shared, she and I, a love of gossip, and spent hours discussing the private lives of our friends. Wholly at the mercy of her own feelings, she was exceptionally sympathetic to the emotional life of others, and enjoyed nothing more than the recounting of an unhappy love-affair. Her eiderdown softness was infinitely seductive: one sank self-indulgently into it, fatally encouraged by the shining eyes and the little gasps of shock or sympathy from the armchair opposite. In low tones she would then unfold the sad stories of other young women who came to see her, and it was years before I realised that just as I was regaled with the intimate details of their hopes and disappointments, so they were being regaled with mine. On much the same level she was curious about the royal family, in particular Princess Margaret, admiring her prettiness and intrigued by reports of her difficult personality. For a time I had a boyfriend who was close to the Princess, so I was endlessly interrogated on the subject, no detail, however unrewarding, considered too mere for study and speculation. 'When Derek's alone with Princess Margaret,' Rosamond once asked after a thoughtful silence, 'does he call her "Ma'am"?' She was mesmerised, too, by the aristocracy, all of whom she was convinced possessed the key to a golden world of privilege and self-assurance which to her would always be denied. Her longing to be part of this exclusive society largely accounts, I think, for her ambivalence towards her Jewish ancestry: on the one hand she was proud of the talented Lehmanns' descent from the portrait-painter of Hamburg; on the other it made her uneasy, aware that among the upper classes of her parents' generation to be Jewish was considered 'common'.

In her old age my relationship with Rosamond became much trickier. Wallowing in self-pity, she was a prey to envy and chronically dissatisfied. Sometimes, it is true, she forgot her grievances and opened the door with a beaming smile, throwing up her hands in welcome like the fisherman's wife in the fairytale, but more often than not she seemed almost impossible to please. When I rang up I was met with reproach, addressed as 'stranger', and told, 'I'm surprised you still remember my number'; she said she watched Selina Scott on television as 'her' Selina came to see her so rarely. Laden with guilt, for there was a hefty element of truth in her accusations, I had to brace myself to make the next telephone call, the next visit, dreading the inevitable catalogue of complaint. She was haunted by the suspicion that she was being left out, that there was laughter in the next room, a permanent party elsewhere from which she alone was excluded. Sometimes, trying to distract her, I made the mistake of talking about something I had enjoyed. 'I went to a marvellous film last week,' I would begin. 'No one takes *me* to the cinema,' was the immediate gloomy response. I quickly discovered that the best way to cheer her up was to recount misfortune, either one's own or another's, it hardly mattered. Then after a good gloat – 'I knew it! I *knew* he would never go back to her!' – the old Ros would rise to the surface and we would end the evening in perfect harmony. But it never lasted, and the next time the entire process would have to be repeated.

Then out of the blue came Dadie Rylands's suggestion of a biography. Rosamond bloomed; she loved the idea, conjuring up an image of a wonderful young man who would sit worshipping at her feet while she narrated her long romantic history. Philip Gardner, whom I never met, failed in some way to fit this picture; yet all might have been well had he not accidentally left behind him one day a notebook in which he had jotted down the questions he wanted to ask. According to Rosamond, at the bottom of the page he had written, 'Check all this with Jill Balcon.' And thus Mr Gardner's goose was cooked. Rosamond couldn't, she simply could not, see him again, and at her insistence the publisher, Collins, terminated the arrangement. But her initial feeling of relief was soon succeeded by disappointment: who would write about her now? It was then that she telephoned me.

I accepted gratefully, flattered and very moved: she was making me a present of her life, even if at that stage I had little idea how rich a gift this would turn out to be. At the time I was working on a biography of Nancy Mitford, but that was seen as no impediment as Rosamond made it a condition that not a word should be published in her lifetime. It was agreed that I would come at regular intervals to record her recollections, and that she would give me any correspondence that was not already deposited in her archive at King's College, Cambridge. She furnished me with a list of friends whom I should see – and another list of those whom I was to go nowhere near as they would be incapable of telling the truth about her. For a while the arrangement worked beautifully. I spent evenings at Clareville Grove listening to Rosamond's story, and as I left I would be handed a couple of John Lewis carrier bags bulging with letters. And so matters might amicably have continued if it had not been for the appearance in the autumn of 1981 of Philip Ziegler's life of Diana Cooper. Rosamond admired Lady Diana, but was always a little jealous of her superior social standing and of her reputation as a beauty. When she read the reviews and the profiles, saw the enormous amount of attention Diana was enjoying as a consequence of Ziegler's biography, she could hardly bear it. Overnight the leisurely approach was abandoned and she demanded that I drop Nancy Mitford and start work on 'her' book at once: she wanted it published as quickly as possible.

For me, this was out of the question. Not only did I have a contract to fulfil, but it was as clear as day that any degree of objectivity would be impossible with Rosamond dictating the approach and attempting to control my every move. I told her I quite understood, but that, with regret, I would have to stand down and a replacement be appointed. My behaviour was not entirely selfless: prepared as a last resort to do as I said, I was fairly sure she would not want to start completely from scratch with somebody new. And so it proved. Reluctantly she retreated and agreed to return to our original pact. But now the atmosphere was soured. In place of pleasant evenings arranged at our mutual convenience, she began to pursue me as though I were an errant lover, telephoning crossly to demand my immediate presence, tape recorder at the ready, as she had something extremely important to divulge which could not possibly wait till next week. She was angry with me and resentful, and the more exigent she became, the more childishly stubborn did I, grudging my time and listening sulkily to what I told myself was nothing but egocentric self-indulgence. I had a vision of myself as the subject of a painting or short story entitled *The Captive Biographer*, with Rosamond, like Mr Todd in *A Handful of Dust*, keeping me for ever prisoner with her endless reminiscences. I remember one tense weekend when Rosamond came to stay at my parents' house in the country. She and I had had a long session on Saturday, consisting mainly of the rehearsing of grudges, Cecil as usual to the fore, and I had assumed I would have the next day off. But on Sunday morning after driving into the village to fetch the papers, I came back to find my mother waiting for me at the front door. 'You'd better go inside at once,' she said drily. 'Rosamond's pacing up and down demanding to be interviewed.'

As I continued to work on Nancy Mitford, Rosamond launched a series of guerrilla operations, clumsily camouflaged strategies designed to undermine any hopes I might have of finishing my book, that 'terrible assignment' as it was now described. She was extremely concerned about me, it suddenly appeared, because I looked so tired and ill, and with the Mitfords had obviously bitten off far more than I could chew. When I assured her I was fine, there was no need to worry about me, she said, 'Oh, I don't worry about *you*: I worry for *my* sake!' Foiled in this, she tried another tack. Nancy Mitford, of course, was a marvellous subject for a magazine article, but how exactly was I going to pad it out into a book? Then came the third assault. A friend of mine, Michael, was a fan of Rosamond's and had asked to meet her. I invited them both to dinner, and at the end of a successful evening during which Michael had been assiduous in paying homage, he ill-advisedly asked how I was getting on with my work. Before I could divert him, he said, 'I'm ashamed to admit I've never read anything by Nancy Mitford. What sort of thing did she write?' In a flash Rosamond answered for me. 'Rubbish – actually,' she said. This immediately led into what by now had become a familiar refrain. 'I think Selina's got paralysis. She'll *never* finish this awful book. She'll *never* be ready to publish me in my lifetime!' Every few months in order to clear the air I staged a confrontation, repeating that if she wished the biography done now, she must find someone other to do it. Each time she retracted, swore she wanted nobody else, was prepared to return to our original plan, and for a while the pressure would be off. But before long she would forget, and I would hear her on the telephone: '. . . Selina Hastings . . . my biographer. . . . Yes, isn't it exciting? . . . Yes, I think she's starting writing any moment . . .'

Eventually my book came out, and I behaved treacherously by immediately signing up to write another. I knew I could not write about Rosamond while she was alive; I knew I had to have distance and detachment, the distance and detachment that would come only with her death. Contrary to expectation she was sweet to me about my Mitford book, resigned to the fact that I was embarked on a further long project that had nothing to do with her. We continued to meet with my tape recorder, but she was growing frail, and it became increasingly difficult for her to focus. By the time she decided to take to her bed she showed little interest in talking about her past, preferring instead that I should read aloud snippets from the paper about the Queen and Prince Philip, or articles on the triumphant progress of the Prime Minister, Margaret Thatcher, in whom she took a personal interest because of a rumour going round, unfounded as it turned out, that Mrs Thatcher's mother was the illegitimate daughter of the dashing Harry Cust, a handsome sportsman friend of Rudie Lehmann's.

The last time I saw Rosamond was on 17 February 1990, three weeks before she died. She was wearing a lilac crêpe-de-chine nightdress and she looked pale and hauntingly fragile. I had brought with me a small basket with flowers, some geranium hand-lotion and a box of chocolates. The flowers and hand-lotion were inspected without much interest, but the chocolates were opened at once. She described the odd little man whom recently she had seen sitting at the end of her bed. 'His name is Sir Frederick Quarles,' she said, 'and he tells me I still have a long time to live. Many years, in fact, many, many years.' Strangely, this assurance seemed to give her pleasure, and she smiled contentedly as I kissed her goodbye.

Abbreviations

AL	Alice Lehmann
BL	Beatrix Lehmann
HL	Helen Lehmann
JL	John Lehmann
RL	Rosamond Lehmann
RCL	Rudolph Chambers Lehmann

JLD	John Lehmann's ms diaries Copyright the Executors of John Lehmann deceased (2002)
JLMD	James Lees-Milne's unpublished diaries Copyright Michael Bloch (2002)
RCLD	R. C. Lehmann's ms diaries

The following are the editions of Rosamond Lehmann's work used in the text:

A Hut	*A Hut, a Sea-Grape Tree* (Winter Tales Annual/Macmillan 1956)
Album	*Rosamond Lehmann's Album* (Chatto & Windus 1985)
BS	*The Ballad and the Source* (Virago 1982)
DA	*Dusty Answer* (Flamingo 1996)
GB	*The Gypsy's Baby* (Virago 1982)
IW	*Invitation to the Waltz* (Virago 1981)
NM	*A Note in Music* (Virago 1982)
SE	*The Swan in the Evening* (Virago 1982)
SGT	*A Sea-Grape Tree* (Virago 1982)
WS	*The Weather in the Streets* (Virago 1981)

Berg	Berg Collections, New York Public Library
Bodleian	Bodleian Library, Oxford
CPS	College of Psychic Studies, London
CUL	Cambridge University Library
DUL	Durham University Library
GUL	Georgetown University Library, Washington DC
HRHRC	Harry Ransom Humanities Research Center, University of Texas at Austin
I Tatti	Villa I Tatti, Harvard University Center for Italian Renaissance Studies
KCC	King's College, Cambridge
Lilly	Lilly Library, University of Indiana
PUL	Princeton University Library

RUL   Reading University Library
Tate   Tate Gallery, London
Tulsa   McFarlin Library, University of Tulsa
Yale   Beinecke Manuscript Library, Yale University

Source Notes

Chapter 1. Vestiges of Creation

1 'I was not . . .' BBC *Bookmark*, unedited ts November 1984, KCC
2 'I feel weak . . .' Elizabeth Jenkins in conversation with the author
'Time was when the Lehmanns . . .' *Sunday Times*, 29.10.67
3 '[My father] stands behind everything . . .' *Listener*, 26.3.53
'Of course the Lehmanns are of Jewish descent . . .' RL to George Rylands, 29.1.29, KCC
4 'I have eleven good reasons' *Memories of Half a Century*, p. 7
5 'It's sad that I never knew . . .' RL in conversation with the author
6 'To make the rhythm right . . .' *Style and the Oar* from *Selected Verse of R. C. Lehmann*
'dear lazy shining Thames' RCL to AL 15.7.1898, PUL
'one of the most spectacular . . .' RCL to AL 30.6.1897, PUL
'Dear Papa and Mama . . .' *The Whispering Gallery*, p. 33
7 'Miss Davis and I . . .' RL in conversation with the author
8 'a difficult trio . . .' AL ms PUL
9 'His mind was not on making . . .' *Out and About*, p. 86
'[Lehmann] has never been in reality . . .' *Sunlit Hours*, p. 156
10 '[He was] singularly unenterprising . . .' *Out & About*, p. 82
'a cherished (if sometimes feared) . . .' E. V. Lucas to BL 29.5.34, KCC
11 'I sing the sofa! . . .' *The Last Straw* from *The Vagabond and Other Poems*
'the Roman poet's note of sadness . . .' *Selected Verse of R. C. Lehmann*, p. viii
'I don't know if it will give you . . .' RCL to AL 29.9.03, PUL
'This is the last letter . . .' RCL to AL 23.10.03, PUL
'No one could give a better dinner . . .' *Sunlit Hours*, p. 221
12 'I believed Violet Hammersley . . .' SE, 49
13 'I know you'd rather die . . .' AL to RCL 24.8.12, PUL
'I'm sailing on the 3rd . . .' AL to RCL 19.8.12, PUL
'Really life is too short . . .' AL to RCL 24.8.12, PUL
'I suppose you will deny . . .' AL to RCL 5.3.06, PUL
'You played a noble part . . .' AL to RCL 14.7.10, PUL
14 '"And now," I said . . .' *Punch*, 18.7.17

'a hateful, bitter war' AL ms PUL
'Winston ignorant . . .' RCLD 22.2.06

Chapter 2. Prospero and His Magic Isle

17 'I am disappointed for you . . .' Laura Henderson to AL 11.2.01, KCC
   '*congrats* for I am so sorry . . .' Constance Browne to AL 20.2.01, KCC
19 'a nightmare (for me) . . .' RCLD 21.1.07
   'I could not face . . .' RCLD 12.12.10
20 '[was] on the whole . . .' RCLD 20.10.07
   'Helen and Rosamond are . . .' RCLD 1.10.03
22 'Don't forget the *one* thing . . .' AL to RCL 5.3.06, PUL
   'I was absolutely spell-bound . . .' RL in conversation with the author
23 'Hail, Caesar, lonely little Caesar . . .' *Punch*, 1.6.10
   'the wax-skinned reed-pierced . . .' GB, p. 81
   'This is a great day . . .' RCLD 14.7.11
   'the single sculler, the pair oar . . .' *SE*, p. 40
   'Both Helen & Rosie . . .' RCLD 27.5.10
24 'Come, Peggy, put your toys away . . .' *The Vagabond & Other Poems*, p. 64
   'In the garden I found . . .' *Punch*, 4.2.14
   'So I found Glumgold . . .' *Punch*, 17.10.17
   'I can't explain . . .' *Punch*, 27.5.14
25 'He was never one to blame . . .' GB, p. 14
   'Daddy, will the fairies come tonight? . . .' *SE*, p. 54
26 'As far as we were concerned . . .' *The Whispering Gallery*, p. 29
   'Everybody adored him . . .' RL in conversation with the author
27 'one of the deepest traumatic memories . . .' RL to JL 5.3.58, PUL
   'very unhappy sometimes . . .' RL in conversation with the author
   'I had the run of my father's library . . .' *Looking Back*, p. 149
   'The three girls became afflicted . . .' RCLD 22.5.05
   'No sooner tapped . . .' GB, p. 68
28 'I couldn't think what I was doing . . .' *Writing Lives*, pp. 150–1
   '[My father] helped me . . .' *Listener*, 26.3.53
   'It was, I remember . . .' RL ms KCC
   'This was trivial stuff . . .' *SE*, p. 58
29 'I don't think I've ever laughed . . .' RCLD 28.8.10
   'My mother had many a subtle way . . .' GB, p. 72
   'Rosie writes doggerel . . .' RL in conversation with the author
   'in a lovely white armchair . . .' *SE*, p. 39
   'People have no business . . .' RL in conversation with the author
30 'striding through the room . . .' RL in conversation with the author
31 'He was very beautiful . . .' *Looking Back*, p. 147
   'My constant worry . . .' BBC: *Woman's Hour* 18.6.57 RL, KCC
32 'an infant version of Mithras . . .' *SE*, p. 19

33 'I was brilliantly clever...' [et seq] RL in conversation with the author
34 '[although] I was pleased to discover...' *SE*, p. 75
35 'They were ... as different from ordinary life...' BBC script 14.4.46, HRHRC
   'That's how I saw the outbreak...' RL, KCC
   'Of the world crisis, I remember only...' *GB*, p. 82
36 'American ... and was all but arrested...' RCLD, 13.8.15
   'I was being shocked...' *Listener*, 26.3.53
   'In my teens I nearly always...' RL, KCC
   'The bath-water was always cold ...' [et seq] RL in conversation with the author

Chapter 3. The Castle of Otranto
39 'I am sure one gets more...' HL to AL 21.10.17, KCC
40 'Coming straight from a very sheltered...' *Listener*, 26.3.53
   'They thought I was queer as a coot...' RL in conversation with the author
41 'We have a scuttle of coal...' RL to AL 17.1.20, KCC
   'Alas! when I joined...' HL to AL 21.10.17, KCC
   'I simply don't know *what* I should have done...' RL to AL 14.10.19, KCC
   'fairly big, with (Thank heaven!)...' RL to AL 24.9.19, KCC
42 'Spotty complexion & greasy hair...' RL to AL 18.6.18, KCC
   'I went to a supper-party...' RL to AL 27.1.20, KCC
   'Oh, the bitterness of having to share...' RL to AL 14.10.19, KCC
43 'We had a very emotional friendship' RL in conversation with the author
   'like a particularly heady wine' RL to Grizel Hartley, 11.4.51, KCC
   'Not that we wish in any way...' *Cambridge Review*, June 1920
44 'a real old battle-axe...' RL in conversation with the author
   'Prof. Coulton is giving a series...' RL to AL 14.10.19, KCC
   'I've got to read aloud...' RL to AL 29.11.19, KCC
45 'Crowds of long-haired "literary blokes"...' RL to AL n/d, KCC
   'start a lot of dances...' *Evening Standard*, 7.10.20
46 'who seem to have an idea...' HL to RL n/d, KCC
   'The Cambridge dances...' [et seq] RL to AL 29.11.19, KCC
   'The amount of chaperonage...' RL in conversation with the author
   'It's agony having to have to leave...' RL to AL 29.11.19, KCC
47 'That dance I'm going to...' RL to AL 1.2.20, KCC
   'That would have been unthinkable' RL in conversation with the author
   'I was thoroughly startled...' RL to AL 21.2.10, KCC
   'The grand people, older men...' [et seq] RL in conversation with the author
   'To have a sensible view...' *Sunday Express*, 21.2.82
48 'Next week I'm going to 2 dances...' RL to JL 25.2.21, PUL
   'Do try to get hold of "The London Mercury"...' RL to RCL 13.11.19, KCC
49 'Myself is knocking at your gates...' *Cambridge Review*, 19.11.20
   'I'm sure you're right about the latest...' RL to RCL 8.2.20, KCC
   'which really *is* exciting' RL to AL 15.2.20, KCC

'I began to realise . . .' RL in conversation with the author
'I had this worrying feeling . . .' *Sunday Express*, 21.2.82
50 'that brutal business of being *forced* to seem silly' BL to RL 26.8.34, KCC
'Alas for the peach satin! . . .' RL to AL n/d, KCC
'The pink voile doesn't look nice . . .' RL to AL 26.5.20, KCC
51 'I want to take Trip. next year . . .' RL to AL 26.5.20, KCC
'We walked over a bit . . .' RL to JL 18.7.20, PUL
'I go to them whenever I like . . .' RL to AL 15.10.20, KCC
52 'My dear, I'm awfully, awfully glad' RL to HL, 31.10.20, KCC
'*Tell Helen*: any of her discarded clothes . . .' RL to AL 1.11.20, KCC
53 'Thursday was an unforgettable day . . .' RL to AL 23.10.21, KCC
'Oh, *how* I want to publish a book!' RL to AL n/d, KCC
'I honestly don't think . . .' RL to AL, 22.4.22, KCC
54 'Wicked, wicked Nina . . .' RL in conversation with the author
55 'White & trembling . . .' RL to AL n/d, KCC
'Such perfect weather . . .' RL to AL 22.5.22, KCC
'I spoke really marvellous French . . .' RL in conversation with the author
'There is no doubt . . .' Katherine Jex-Blake to RL 14.6.22, KCC
56 'I'm afraid I shall have to ask for more money . . .' RL to AL 15.5.22, KCC
'I do so want to keep . . .' RL to AL 22.5.22, KCC
'I dined out last night . . .' RL to AL 22.6.22, KCC
'I felt he'd deceived me . . .' RL to AL n/d, KCC
57 'very, very smitten' [et seq] RL in conversation with the author

Chapter 4. Into Marriage with a Sinking Heart

58 'Oh Mummie! . . .' RL to AL n/d, KCC
'She was fascinating, brilliant . . .' BS, p. x
59 'You cannot possibly know . . .' *Gallia*, p. xxxiv
'a wild 4 days . . .' RL to AL 16.8.22, KCC
60 'bound to be a writer' [et seq] RL in conversation with the author
'She was wrong . . .' My First Book (*The Author* 1983)
'I sat under them . . .' *Writing Lives: Conversations Between Women Writers* (Virago
1988) ed. by Mary Chamberlain p. 151
'I don't know that you'll ever . . .' *Sunday Express*, 21.2.82
61 'I had it lodged in my subconscious . . .' My First Book (*The Author* 1983)
'It was pretty quick . . .' Leslie Runciman in conversation with the author
'As I wanted above all things . . .' RL in conversation with the author
62 'You appear to have waded . . .' Leslie Runciman in conversation with the author
'You went down so terribly well . . .' Leslie Runciman to RL n/d, KCC
'Nobody was good enough . . .' [et seq] RL in conversation with the author
63 'Oh! I'm so terribly excited . . .' HL to RL 12.7.23, KCC
'You're preparing some nice seductive underclothes . . .' Grizel Hartley to RL,
KCC

64 'I'd never describe you . . .' Leslie Runciman to RL 1.6.23, KCC
    'He really should have been a don . . .' Steven Runciman in conversation with
      the author
    'This afternoon I spent . . .' Leslie Runciman to RL 10.11.23, KCC
65 'the little I have yet seen . . .' Leslie Runciman to RL 3.10.23, KCC
    'this revolting town' [et seq] Leslie Runciman to RL, 29.10.23, KCC
    'It was bloody & thoughtless of me . . .' Leslie Runciman to RL 13.9.23, KCC
66 '[my] own disbelief . . .' Leslie Runciman to RL 15.10.23, KCC
    'I refuse flatly . . .' Leslie Runciman to RL 8.10.23, KCC
    'The more I think of a church . . .' Leslie Runciman to RL 12.10.23, KCC
67 'If it were not that you, . . .' Leslie Runciman to RL 18.10.23, KCC
    'the pro children argument . . .' Leslie Runciman to RL 8.11.23, KCC
    '[While] it is impossible . . .' Leslie Runciman to RL n/d, KCC
    'My complaint against God . . .' Leslie Runciman to RL n/d, KCC
    'If I was 14 . . .' RL in conversation with the author
68 'remorseless undressers in public' RL in conversation with the author
    'You were so easily the kindest . . .' Leslie Runciman to RL 5.10.23, KCC
    'Other people (in this case me) . . .' Leslie Runciman to RL n/d, KCC
    'He thought it was an intellectual disgrace . . .' RL in conversation with the
      author
    'I never think of you . . .' Leslie Runciman to RL 5.10.23, KCC
    'I'm missing you so horribly . . .' Leslie Runciman to RL 25.10.23, KCC
69 'owing to the intolerance of others' Leslie Runciman 28.10.23, KCC
    'I go now to canvass . . .' RL to AL 3.12.23, KCC
    'I'm all in favour . . .' Leslie Runciman to RL 15.12.23, KCC
70 'wife . . . who do more & more love' Leslie Runciman to RL 20.10.24, KCC
    'Leslie has bought me an account-book . . .' RL to AL 15.1.24, KCC
    'Ham salad, Eggs à l'Aurore . . .' RL to AL 12.1.24, KCC
    'but they're very early ones . . .' RL to AL 31.1.24, KCC
71 'It's funny how she can't bear . . .' RL to AL 22.3.24, KCC
    'It makes me angry . . .' RL to AL 30.1.24, KCC
    'I get so angry with the office . . .' RL to AL 26.1.24, KCC
    'I can't describe how grim . . .' RL in conversation with the author
    'I simply perspire . . .' RL to AL 3.2.24, KCC
    'He really did sort of fall in love . . .' RL in conversation with the author
72 'Steven is sure to be a monster' Leslie Runciman to RL n/d, KCC
    'Steven – God, he was so awful . . .' RL in conversation with the author
    'They [the Runcimans] are a chattery . . .' JLD 20.8.23, PUL
    'Steven & Margie came to lunch . . .' JLD 9.8.24, PUL
    'I really think . . .' RL to AL 20.2.24, KCC
73 'Newcastle seems much like any other . . .' RL to AL 18.7.24, KCC
    'Oh!! how I hate it all . . .' RL to AL 9.7.24, KCC
    'It was an *awful* evening . . .' RL to AL 2.10.24, KCC
    'The house is marvellous . . .' JLD 8.8.24, PUL

74 'There were moments . . .' Leslie Runciman in conversation with the author
'I christened my ship . . .' RL to AL 2.10.24, KCC
'Prudence continues to flood the house . . .' RL to AL 2.10.24, KCC

75 'While we were living in Newcastle . . .' RL in conversation with the author
'My darling Wiggles . . .' Leslie Runciman to RL 20.8.24, KCC
'I never forgave her . . .' RL in conversation with the author
'Leslie says he's bound to admit . . .' RL to AL 17.12.24, KCC
'Our sex life . . .' [et seq] RL in conversation with the author

76 'trotting round race meetings . . .' RL to AL 28.3.26, KCC
'These accidents will happen . . .' WS 286
'I thought, I'm married . . .' RL in conversation with the author

77 'The more I think that Rosie is betterer . . .' Leslie Runciman to RL 19.1.25, KCC
'Don't think I'm unhappy . . .' Leslie Runciman to RL n/d, KCC
'somehow I'll make you happy . . .' Leslie Runciman to RL 1.2.25, KCC
'Come soon & cheer up Lellie . . .' Leslie Runciman 3.2.25, KCC

78 'I do really rather like him . . .' Leslie Runciman to RL 15.3.25, KCC
'Everybody in Northumberland . . .' RL in conversation with the author
'They are delightful . . .' RL to AL n/d, KCC

79 'Eigg is rather a marvellous place . . .' RL to AL 24.9.25, KCC
'the great yachts, including the king's yacht . . .' RL to AL 4.8.25, KCC
'It's a wonderful yacht . . .' RL to AL n/d, KCC
'South Bucks has its attractions . . .' Leslie Runciman to RL 9.7.25, KCC

80 'There was a complete triumph of will . . .' [et seq] RL to AL 26.12.25, KCC

Chapter 5. 'The Kind of Novel That Might Have Been Written by Keats'

81 'you'll be glad of an inexpensive occupation here' Leslie Runciman to RL 8.10.23, KCC
'Suddenly, a deeper level of consciousness . . .' My First Book (The Author 1983)
'Something happened and the [flood]gates burst . . .' RL in conversation with the author
'I am more and more deluged . . .' RL to AL 3.1.26, KCC

82 'You opened up new thoughts . . .' [et seq] Wogan Philipps to RL n/d, KCC
'thinking in a ruthless way . . .' RL in conversation with the author

83 'He always enjoyed himself enormously . . .' Moorea Black in conversation with the author
'At Oxford I was wild . . .' Wogan Philipps to George Rylands n/d, KCC
'had been a bit mad . . .' RL in conversation with the author

84 'I had to hurl . . .' [et seq] Wogan Philipps to RL n/d, KCC

85 'discovered my true path . . .' RL in conversation with the author
'it was quite understood . . .' RL in conversation with the author
'This summer is going to be . . .' Wogan Philipps to RL n/d, KCC

86 'I have reached my last chapter . . .' RL to JL 23.8.26, PUL
'full of high spirits and devilry' RL to JL 15.9.26, PUL

'I don't think you ought to worry...' RL to AL 16.2.25, KCC

'She is a most warm-hearted...' 26.1.26 RL to AL, KCC

'[I] have dropped into the ways of touring...' BL to RL 7.8.26, KCC

87 'O Rose of Grace...' George Rylands to RL n/d, KCC

'Leslie is to me extremely attractive...' *Lytton Strachey* by Michael Holroyd (Chatto & Windus, 1994), p. 565

'You were a great success...' George Rylands to RL 20.7.26, KCC

'almost incredibly civilised...' Lytton Strachey to RL 20.7.26, KCC

'It became quite clear...' George Rylands in conversation with the author

88 'Wogan came uninvited...' George Rylands to RL n/d, KCC

'shows decided quality' Chatto & Windus to RL 5.10.26, KCC

'O Lord! What a beautiful book...' Robert Nichols n/d, RUL

'Leslie at that time...' Steven Runciman in conversation with the author

89 'I'm sure you'd like him' RL to AL 30.5.26, KCC

'My own littleone...' Wogan Philipps to RL n/d, KCC

'male companions...' Leslie Runciman to RL 13.7.26, KCC

'This Newcastle question...' Leslie Runciman to Walter & Hilda Runciman 25.10.26, KCC

90 'in a great burst...' RL in conversation with the author

'Wogan has suddenly begun painting...' RL to JL 7.1.27, PUL

'Imagination at least had been fecund...' *DA*, 60

91 'I was singularly ill-read...' *SE*, 69

'When Judith was eighteen...' *DA*, 7

'beautiful as a prince' ibid. 13

92 'in the warm little paths...' ibid. 73

'flushed, throbbing and exhausted with excitement' [et seq] ibid. 76

'"I am lost, lost..."' ibid. 108

'Earnestly her eyes beamed...' ibid. 113

'uncontrolled rapture' ibid. 116

'You mustn't love anybody...' ibid. 130

93 'I was very much surprised...' ibid. 226–8

94 'The sinking sun...' ibid. 218

'Charlie came to her...' ibid. 14

95 '[Jennifer] stared impressively...' ibid. 117–9

'[was] my only absolutely-innocently-written book' RL to Shane Leslie 30.10.54, GUL

96 'I have the misfortune to be doubtful...' *DA* 63

'The others thought him conceited...' ibid. 18

'quite remarkably invented...' *Listener* 26.3.53

'had known how to stir mystery...' *DA* 104

'[Mrs Earle's] remarks had generally a faint sting...' ibid. 197

'He was a vegetable...' RL in conversation with the author

'all the dear dead things...' HL to RL n/d, KCC

'[Rosamond's] style is really first class...' AL to JL n/d, KCC

97 '[*Dusty Answer* is] quite unlike anything else . . .' JL to RL 1.5.27, KCC
   'I shall never have a better letter . . .' RL to JL 3.5.27, KCC
   'I notice that Bowes & Bowes . . .' Harold Raymond to RL 6.5.27, KCC
   'It is not often that one can say . . .' *Sunday Times*, 22.5.27
98 'The Noyes review has swept us . . .' Harold Raymond to RL 25.5.27, KCC
   'We have not had since *The Constant Nymph* . . .' *Saturday Review*, 14.5.27
   'rich in humanity . . .' *Country Life*, 4.6.27
   'Miss Lehmann shows the clumsiness . . .' *Nation & Athenaeum*, 10.9.27
99 '*Dusty Answer* is far above . . .' *New Statesman & Nation*, 16.7.27
   'I can perceive little or no originality . . .' *Evening Standard*, 18.8.27
   '*Dusty Answer* is a very readable novel . . .' *Daily News*, 25.5.27
   'Rose Macaulay is a delightful person . . .' Harold Raymond to RL 27.5.27
   'It would be less than true . . .' [et seq] *My First Book* (*The Author* 1983)
100 'the masculine masks they had adopted . . .' [et seq] SE, 67
   '[I was] quite uninterested in fame . . .' *Writing Lives*, p. 154
   'he sent my letter . . .' RL in conversation with the author
101 'I haven't seen Wogan . . .' RL to George Rylands 10.5.27, KCC
   '[Before] it all seemed so dream-like . . .' [et seq] Wogan Philipps to RL n/d, KCC
102 'Discussions, lawyers, family . . .' RL to Wogan Philipps n/d, KCC
103 'Are we ever ever ever . . .' [et seq] Wogan Philipps to RL n/d, KCC
   'Darling don't be jealous . . .' Wogan Philipps to RL n/d, KCC
104 'onlie begetter' RL to George Rylands 12.1.80, KCC
   'Our relationship is far the most . . .' Wogan Philipps to George Rylands n/d,
      KCC
   '[Dadie] seems very happy . . .' Wogan Philipps to RL n/d, KCC
   'We did have such fun . . .' [et seq] Wogan Philipps to RL n/d, KCC
   'I was woken by an excited . . .' Wogan Philipps to RL 26.10.27, KCC
   'The Peter affair . . .' Wogan Philipps to RL n/d, KCC
105 'Oh! those three wonderful night . . .' Wogan Philipps to RL 25.6.27, KCC
   'Oh darling I am terrified . . .' [et seq] Wogan Philipps to RL n/d, KCC
   'a torrent of letters' SE, 66
   'deeply impressed' John Galsworthy to RL 26.9.27, KCC
   '*Dusty Answer* is a much better book . . .' Archibald MacLeish to RL 28.11.27,
      KCC
   'to a brother writer . . .' Compton Mackenzie to RL 30.12.27, KCC
   'a friendship which has been . . .' *My Life and Times*, vol. 6, 166
   'The disadvantage to my mind . . .' Lytton Strachey to Roger Senhouse 11.5.27,
      Lytton Strachey, 569
106 'I am so bubbling over . . .' Harold Raymond to RL 23.7.27, KCC
   'beginning at last to resign myself . . .' RL to Anne Monro-Kerr 9.2.57, Society of
      Authors
   'I feel almost ashamed . . .' Harold Raymond to RL 23.7.27, KCC
   'It's rather terrifying . . .' RL to Harold Raymond 26.7.27, RUL
   'I feel I have outgrown . . .' *New York World*, 10.30.27

'I just burst into tears . . .' RL to George Rylands n/d, KCC

107 'My nerves have completely gone . . .' Wogan Philipps to RL n/d, KCC
'this hateful ship . . .' RL to Harold Raymond 31.8.27, RUL
'I remember standing on deck . . .' RL in conversation with the author
'the essence of thoughtful . . .' RL to Wogan Philipps 7.10.27, KCC
'I want to come home . . .' RL to JL n/d, PUL
'The extravagance of the reviews . . .' RL to JL 16.9.27, PUL
'very elementary people . . .' RL in conversation with the author
'Those threatening buildings . . .' [et seq] RL to Wogan Philipps 7.10.27, KCC

108 'Wherever I go . . .' RL to Harold Raymond 27.10.27, RUL
'or tried to . . .' RL in conversation with the author
'Oh darling, darling . . .' Wogan Philipps to RL 26.10.27, KCC

109 'Please address me . . .' RL to JL n/d, PUL
'Oh my God, I am alive . . .' [et seq] Wogan Philipps to RL n/d, KCC
'Wogan Philipps seriously ill . . .' 5.11.27, KCC

110 'He is very weak . . .' RL to JL n/d, PUL

Chapter 6. Ros and Wog

111 'It's so extraordinary . . .' RL to George Rylands 21.4.28, KCC
'I feel very well and safe . . .' RL to George Rylands 11.5.28, KCC
'Now I am stuck . . .' RL to George Rylands 21.4.28, KCC

112 'We get along very happily . . .' RL to George Rylands 21.4.28, KCC
'[Rosamond] is *so* attractive . . .' Ursula Ridley to Emily Lutyens 20.3.28, private collection
'[but] we always had to be looking out . . .' RL in conversation with the author
'Last night was the most marvellous thing . . .' Wogan Philipps to RL 4.7.28, KCC
'My whole spirit is starved . . .' Wogan Philipps to 20.6.28, KCC

113 '[Daddy] is too *bloody sensible* . . .' Wogan Philipps to RL 19.9.28, KCC
'It is no use accusing . . .' Wogan Philipps to RL 24.6.28, KCC
'Darling, there is one thing . . .' Wogan Philipps to RL 12.7.28, KCC
'wore him out . . .' [et seq] RL to Siegfried Sassoon 8.4.31, CUL

114 'Rosamond lives in an absurd . . .' *Carrington: Letters*, p. 399
'I know I know how monstrously lucky . . .' RL to George Rylandsf n/d, KCC
'I'm glad that W & R . . .' AL to JL 19.11.28, PUL
'He wants me to take Llanstephan . . .' Wogan Philipps to RL n/d, KCC

115 'A slightly invalidish ménage . . .' *Lytton Strachey: a Critical Biography* vol. II, p. 627
'death was kinder than life' RL to Harold Raymond 2.2.29, RUL
'When I look at the startling beauty . . .' BBC *Woman's Hour*, 18.6.57
'Leslie haunts me . . .' RL to George Rylands 29.1.29, KCC

116 'Honestly, no . . .' Leslie Runciman to RL 15.11.34, KCC
'Wogan works at fever heat . . .' RL to JL 28.4.29, PUL
'I had the most appalling labour . . .' RL in conversation with the author

117 'Hugo is full of divine smiles...' [et seq] RL to JL n/d, PUL
'When I think of the future...' RL to George Rylands 2.8.29, KCC
'a miracle dropped into our laps...' [et seq] RL to George Rylands 2.12.29, KCC
118 '[Ipsden] is completely absorbing us...' RL to George Rylands 14.5.30, KCC
'[whom] I loved overwhelmingly...' RL in conversation with the author
'She had been a pretty, round-faced girl...' Frances Partridge *Spectator*, 9.2.91
119 'I heard that one or two ancient crones...' RL in conversation with the author
'altogether through flowers' RL to George Rylands 26.6.70, KCC
'Don't don't say, Dadie...' RL to George Rylands 3.12.29, KCC
'Lytton Strachey made a tremendous difference...' Wogan Philipps in conversation with the author
120 'She was so vulnerable...' RL to Stephen Spender 6.11.70, private collection
'Hateful Rosamond...' Dora Carrington to Julia Strachey, *Carrington: Letters*, p. 429
'Carrington wielded...' *Loved Ones*, p. 22
'Do tell me which dress...' Dora Carrington to RL 15.3.28, KCC
'I absolutely took to it...' Wogan Philipps in conversation with the author
'The Woolfs loved Wogan...' RL in conversation with the author
121 'There are moments when...' RL *Penguin New Writing*, vol. 7
'perhaps that's why...' [et seq] RL in conversation with the author
122 'wild, somewhat childish paintings' *World within World*, p. 143
'I think him so full of promise...' RL to George Rylands 14.5.30, KCC
'that absolute lunatic Stephen...' [et seq] RL to George Rylands 29.12.30, KCC
'I,I,I,I, – like a flock of cawing crows.' Stephen Spender unpublished journal, private collection
123 'roaring out songs...' RL to George Rylands 3.4.30, KCC
'He put me into an awful...' RL in conversation with the author
'such a dear to us...' Ethel Philipps to RL 1.5.30, KCC
124 'that not *altogether* unmixed blessing' RL to Ottoline Morrell 25.7.30, HRHRC
'he would have simply thrown him...' RL to George Rylands 1.10.30, KCC
'Here we were, newly married...' RL in conversation with the author
'He used to be *ten*...' *A Life of Contrasts*, 83
'watch Hugo's flawless piece of life...' RL to Frances Partridge 17.13.32, private collection
'Wogan gave me a great scolding...' RL to Frances Partridge 22.2.32, private collection
125 'What Rosamond wanted...' Wogan Philipps in conversation with the author
'I never ceased to love Wogan...' [et seq] RL in conversation with the author
'[Wogan] thinks it infintely better...' RL to George Rylands 9.2.30, KCC
126 'How far indeed from gay...' *NM*, 7
126 'They resembled each other...' ibid. 80
'Gentle birth, property...' ibid. 128
127 'He simply could not help...' ibid. 241
'In this northern town...' ibid. 21

'to get away from any sort . . .' ibid. viii
128 'He seemed to have a secret of mastery . . .' ibid. 63
'She opened it . . .' ibid. 129
'Why should one young man . . .' ibid. 164
'meant a very very great deal . . .' Wogan Philipps in conversation with the author
'A faintly snobbish book . . .' *Spectator*, 27.9.30
'a book which no intelligent person . . .' *Daily Express*, 9.9.30
'a poor wisp of a thing . . .' *Observer*, 24.8.30
129 'a disappointing second novel . . .' *Times Literary Supplement*, 4.9.30
'really crushing review' Lytton Strachey to Roger Senhouse 9.9.20, Berg
'Rather too many trees . . .' Raymond Mortimer to RL 5.10.30, KCC
'a marvellous story . . .' HL to JL n/d, PUL
'[being] without what is nowadays . . .' Charles Morgan to RL 6.12.30, KCC
'I suffer most terribly . . .' Stephen Spender to RL 2.9.30, KCC
'I am reading R. Lehmann . . .' *Diary of Virginia Woolf*, vol. III, p. 314
130 'In French we at present . . .' Jacques-Emile Blanche to RL 15.12.30, KCC
'Dear Rosamond, I much regret . . .' Laurence Philipps to RL 29.5.31, KCC
'The dramas that went on . . .' RL in conversation with the author
'I have to thank you . . .' Laurence Philipps to RL 30.5.31, KCC
131 'How you do misread Daddy . . .' Ethel Philipps to RL and Wogan Philipps, 2.6.31, KCC
'It is fantastic & wild . . .' RL to George Rylands 22.6.31, KCC
'I have so much in common . . .' Wogan Philipps to Stephen Spender n/d, private collection
'seems to be living . . .' Laurence Philipps to RL 12.7.31, KCC
'Now that the terrible thorn . . .' Wogan Philipps to Laurence Philipps 12.7.31, KCC
'I shall crawl all right . . .' Wogan Philipps to RL 31.8.31, KCC
132 'He is sweet . . .' Wogan Philipps to Stephen Spender n/d, private collection
'This frightful German Encyclopaedic . . .' Wogan Philipps to George Rylands n/d, KCC
'painfully loyal already . . .' RL to George Rylands n/d, KCC
'This is such a relief . . .' RL to JL 29.7.31, PUL
133 'has become a little uncertain . . .' *Week-End Review*, 7.11.31
'We motored over . . .' RL to George Rylands n/d, KCC
'I feel now he will live . . .' RL to JL n/d, PUL
'I just can't believe . . .' RL to JL n/d, PUL
134 'I think he would be happy . . .' Dora Carrington to RL n/d, KCC
'Your visit & Ralph's . . .' RL to Frances Partridge 22.2.32, private collection
'I never loved any other woman. . . .' RL to Siegfried Sassoon n/d, CUL
'I never loved any woman . . .' RL to David Garnett 30.10.70, Lilly
'It is bitter to think . . .' RL to Frances Partridge 17.3.32, private collection
'With those two gone . . .' RL to Siegfried Sassoon n/d, CUL
135 'we have both been feeling . . .' RL to George Rylands n/d, KCC
'It is called "Invitation to the Waltz" . . .' RL to George Rylands n/d, KCC

Chapter 7. At the Very Heart of Bloomsbury

136 '[a couple of] long-short stories . . .' RL to Harold Raymond 13.10.30, RUL
'about two young girls . . .' RL to Harold Raymond 12.11.30, RUL
137 'queller of giggling-fits . . .' IW, 34
'Gay-hearted, quivering . . .' ibid. 44
'Time crawling by . . .' ibid. 117
'His skin was smooth . . .' ibid. 120
'Mum's standards are so shatteringly low', ibid. 37
'there was a queer place . . .' ibid. 133
138 'came down at the last moment . . .' ibid. 156
'Isn't it fun? . . .' ibid. 157
'"And is this her very very first dance? . . .' ibid. 222
'"What a spectacle!" . . .' ibid. 197
139 'it's too much to bear . . .' ibid. 264
'"I have met you before . . .' ibid. 272
'how extraordinary to be here . . .' ibid. 280
'we must talk it over . . .' ibid. 300
'everything's going to begin . . .' ibid. 301
140 '[Jane Austen] is far . . .' RL to James Lees-Milne 24.10.77, Yale
'look out of the window . . .' ibid. 22
141 'good old Martins . . .' ibid. 180
'were you out to-day? . . .' ibid. 209
142 'short, trim, sober . . .' ibid. 262
'Rollo superb in his pink coat . . .' ibid. 161
'she stood half-way down . . .' ibid. 283
143 'I thought, I see! . . .' ibid intro
'How to describe . . .' Observer, 2.10.32
'Rosamond Lehmann is the greatest . . .' New Yorker, 5.11.32
'[Rosamond Lehmann's] work . . .' New York Herald Tribune, 28.8.32
'Wogan had an interview . . .' RL to JL 29.5.32, PUL
144 'It started with an argument . . .' RL to Frances Partridge n/d, private collection
'I only hope you have left Leonard . . .' RL to JL 6.9.32, PUL
145 'I'm so thankful to know . . .' RL to George Rylands n/d, KCC
'I do know a solicitor . . .' Wogan Philipps to JL 16.9.32, PUL
'admired the cabbage bed . . .' IW, p. 78
'the various footling . . .' RL to JL n/d, PUL
'A vast patch of damp . . .' RL to George Rylands 30.11.32, KCC
146 'Here all is exactly as usual . . .' RL to JL 15.3.33, PUL
'Ipsden was a tremendously happy house . . .' George Rylands in conversation
with the author
'beautiful Ipsden House . . .' World within World, 143
'I don't see how . . .' RL to Clive Bell 7.12.32, KCC
'To my despair . . .' RL in conversation with the author
147 'not so much ego in her composition' Letters of Virginia Woolf, vol. V, p. 247

'how nice, easy, mobile...' *Diary of Virginia Woolf*, vol. IV, p. 188

'at their most charming...' RL to JL 25.11.33, PUL

'Wogan has a shrewd worldly sense...' *Diary of Virginia Woolf*, vol. IV, p. 188

'They all comment eternally...' ibid

'It's Lytton played by bumpkins...' *Letters of Virginia Woolf*, vol. V, p. 247

'I had the most strange...' RL to Ottoline Morrell, 11.8.30, HRHRC

'beautifully mannered and delightful...' RL in conversation with the author

148 'he's hopeless – so dreary...' RL to Stephen Spender 25.4.34, private collection

'It was very late...' RL in conversation with the author

'I long to tell you...' Julia Strachey to RL n/d, KCC

'[with her] bright sharp eye...' *Chapter of Accidents*, 129

'[They are] affectionate, sympathetic...' RL to Elizabeth Bowen 5.9.35, HRHRC

149 '"Remember: we won this for you"...' *Rosamond Lehmann's Album*, p. 53

'a bit bleak and smelly' RL to Clive Bell 7.12.32, KCC

'We went to a glorious party...' Wogan Philipps to Stephen Spender n/d, private collection

'I sometimes wonder...' RL in conversation with the author

'Rosamond wore her beauty...' *Christopher and His Kind*, 79

150 'W[ogan] lives a little...' *Diary of Virginia Woolf*, vol. IV, p. 140

'only a scampering terrier...' *Letters of Virginia Woolf*, vol. V, p. 247

'driven crazy & dangerously...' Wogan Philipps to RL n/d, KCC

151 'strong & poisonous meat' RL to Frances Partridge 30.5.83, private collection

'Tommy became my father confessor...' Wogan Philipps to RL n/d, KCC

'"Oh, you do, do you?"...' *Good Company*, 31

'She and Helen had a marvellous time...' BL to Henrietta Bingham 24.8.32, KCC

'She looked very happy...' Barbara Ker-Seymer to author 23.3.90, KCC

152 'Julia & Tommy between them...' Wogan Philipps to RL n/d, KCC

'Lying on a pink fur rug...' *Julia*, 97

'generally in a foul temper...' RL in conversation with the author

'Rosamond loved scenes...' Steven Runciman in conversation with the author

'I think you are a difficult person...' Wogan Philipps to RL n/d, KCC

153 'I don't believe you will ever...' Wogan Philipps to RL n/d, KCC

'He was very beautiful...' *Looking Back*, p. 147

'He always said he was in love...' RL in conversation with the author

'My relationship with Matt...' RL to Joshua Rowley 8.3.64, private collection

'He became for me...' WS, intro

154 'It was shattering...' [et seq] RL in conversation with the author

'[Wogan] is so terribly important...' RL to Barbara Ker-Seymer n/d, Tate

155 'I am so incredibly tired...' Wogan Philipps to RL 8.8.33, KCC

'I thought it was all over...' RL in conversation with the author

156 'a very nice daughter...' RL to George Rylands 24.1.34, KCC

'coming only once in the evening...' RL in conversation with the author

'I felt rather pleased with it...' RL to Stephen Spender 24.5.34, private

collection
157 'She is too wonderful . . .' Wogan Philipps to Barbara Ker-Seymer 6.9.34, Tate
   'Naps knew all the ship's crew . . .' Wogan Philipps to Barbara Ker-Seymer 20.9.34, Tate
   'we were asked to at least ten parties . . .' Wogan Philipps to Barbara Ker-Seymer n/d, Tate
   'I don't believe you realise . . .' Wogan Philipps to RL n/d, KCC
158 'I was totally out of the group . . .' RL in conversation with the author
   'She resented it very much . . .' Stephen Spender in conversation with the author
   'My head, what there is of it . . .' RL to Compton Mackenzie 23.10.38, HRHRC
159 'all about Nazis & Berlin . . .' RL to JL 15.3.33, PUL
160 'flashes of insight like summer lightning' *The Siren Years*, p. 143
   '[Elizabeth] had a passionate . . .' *New Statesman & Nation*, 10.10.75
   '[added] an edge at once . . .' RL to the *Times*, 26.2.73
   'I met Cecil Day-Lewis . . .' RL to Stephen Spender n/d, private collection
   'You lucky clever woman . . .' RL to Elizabeth Bowen 25.8.35, HRHRC
161 'If you ever want to combine . . .' Elizabeth Bowen to RL 19.12.35, KCC
   'like trying to haul a grand piano . . .' RL to Jean Rhys 21.1.35, private collection
   'The machine was an infinite labour . . .' RL to JL 11.8.36, PUL
   '[although] I'm almost tempted . . .' RL to Harold Raymond 26.11.33, RUL
   '[so that] you would certainly be saved . . .' Harold Raymond to RL 27.11.33, KCC
162 'Yes, I *do* feel badly treated . . .' Harold Raymond to RL 15.10.35, KCC
   'I must have told Pinker 10 times . . .' RL to Harold Raymond 16.10.35, RUL
   'I think he was really a dishonest idiot . . .' Denys Kilham Roberts to RL 19.2.43, KCC
   'a crowd of people of today . . .' RL to Marthe L'Evêque 12.4.36, private collection
163 'it was always indoors . . .' WS 145
   'He said he was hungry . . .' ibid. 168
   'From outside the room looked warm . . .' ibid. 184
164 'He helped himself to fish . . .' ibid. 76
   'To be alone, sick, in London . . .' ibid. 263
   'May I come in? . . .' ibid. 272
165 'Rollo isn't a cad . . .' *Radio Times*, 11–17 February 1984
   'cigars, expensive stuff on his hair . . .' WS, 68
   'Can they sniff out an alien . . .' ibid. 72
166 'She turned towards him . . .' ibid. 80
   'Ivo took a tremendous fancy . . .' RL in conversation with the author
167 'Olivia, if you run through . . .' WS, 33
   'Imagine my feelings . . .' RL to John Hayward 12.5.36, KCC
168 'it was impossible to praise [it] too highly' *London Illustrated News*, July 1936
   'a triumph' *Sunday Times*, 5.7.36
   'a very talented writer indeed . . .' *Daily Telegraph*, 11.7.36
   'fictional elephantiasis . . .' *Observer*, 12.7.36

'the pseudo-sophisticated would-be cynical...' *Scrutiny*, vol. 5, no. 1, June 1936

'The American reviews are mostly highly praising...' RL to Stephen Spender 25.6.36, private collection

'Oh I'm so glad...' RL to BL 8.7.36, KCC

'The book moves me...' E. M. Forster to RL 11.7.36, KCC

169 'I have always stood up...' David Garnett to Barbara Ker-Seymer 15.7.36, Tate

'Everything is much peacefuller...' RL to George Rylands 6.6.35, KCC

'No woman went out alone...' RL in conversation with the author

170 'The agonizing fact remains...' RL to Mina Kerstein Curtiss n/d, Berg

'pink, plump, gay & amusing' RL to Marthe L'Evêque 30.10.34, private collection

'The baby attentively examined...' *WS*, 243

171 'Did you mean what you said?...' RL in conversation with the author

'a cuddly friendship' Wogan Philipps to Barbara Ker-Seymer 12.2.35, Tate

'If I were different...' RL to Edward Sackville-West n/d, Berg

'Rosamond is having troubles...' BL to JL 16.8.36, PUL

172 'like the Toreador in Carmen...' Isaiah Berlin in conversation with the author

'frightfully excited all the time...' Goronwy Rees to Barbara Ker-Seymer n/d, Tate

173 '[by] the violently advancing intimacy...' [et seq] Elizabeth Bowen to Isaiah Berlin 23.9.36. Isaiah Berlin Papers, Bodleian Library, Oxford University

'I do SO love Elizabeth' RL to John Hayward 1.10.36, KCC

'There never has been...' RL to Isaiah Berlin 8.10.36. Isaiah Berlin Papers, Bodleian Library, Oxford University

Chapter 8. A Split Life

175 'Wogan arrives to-day...' RL to Sebastian Sprott n/d, KCC

176 'of being the object of hate-love...' RL to Laurie Lee 30.4.43, private collection

'I never thought...' RL in conversation with the author

'I'd no *idea* there was any "situation,"...' RL to Barbara Ker-Seymer n/d, Tate

177 'deadly irresistibles' *New Welsh Review*, no. 29/summer 1995, p. 31

'He taught me a lot...' RL in conversation with the author

178 'Secrecy was Goronwy's habit...' *Partisan Review*, 1996, vol. LXIII, no. 1, p. 11

'ce grave, profond et ravissant roman' *Au Pays du Roman*, p. 231

'You wouldn't believe...' RL to Marthe L'Evêque 31.3.36, private collection

179 'the opposite of what I really meant...' BBC *Bookmark* unedited ts November 1984, KCC

'Really I think you are extraordinary...' RL to Marthe L'Evêque 8.10.31, private collection

'Now I know for certain...' RL to Marthe L'Evêque 16.7.37, private collection

'I am soaring & planing...' RL to JL 1.12.36, PUL

180 'The Princess plays me Bach...' RL to JL 24.2.37, PUL

'where apparently my (literary) existence...' RL to Marthe L'Evêque 26.2.37, private collection

'[I] have had the most fantastic time . . .' RL to JL 24.2.37, PUL

'une belle minotière hollandaise . . .' *Vieille Angleterre de ma Jeunesse*, 105

181 'A long frosty silence ensued' *The Food of Love*, p. 202

'a great deal of heart . . .' RL to 'Mrs Whale' 26.9.38, CUL

'J'ai fait de mon mieux . . .' *L'Enfant de la Bohémienne* (Plon) iii

182 'Ce n'est pas une question . . .' ibid. vi

'*extremely* talkative and amusing' *Stevie* (Barbera & McBrien), 113

'Oh don't be so cross . . .' *Stevie* (Spalding), p. 143

'It gave me claustrophobia . . .' RL to JL 9.11.37, PUL

'A storm sprang up . . .' RL to John Hayward 20.4.37, KCC

183 'I mind so much . . .' RL to Stephen Spender n/d, private collection

'that none of it directly . . .' Laurence Philipps to RL 29.3.37, KCC

'[I] shall give up this farce . . .' RL to Stephen Spender n/d, private collection

184 'I am completely caught up . . .' Wogan Philipps to Barbara Ker-Seymer n/d, Tate

'It is the first time . . .' Wogan Philipps to RL 25.5.37, KCC

'I seem at last . . .' Wogan Philipps to RL 4.4.37, KCC

'A cheap horror, like his books' Wogan Philipps to RL 14.4.37, KCC

185 'Moans and cries . . .' *New Writing*, p. 31

'My ambulance was very small . . .' ibid

'though it has been a very difficult . . .' Wogan Philipps to RL 25.5.37, KCC

186 'I think we can fall in love . . .' ibid

'because my frantic physical love . . .' ibid

'I was not, never have been . . .' BBC *Bookmark* unedited ts November 1984, KCC

'a dither of excitement' Wogan Philipps to RL 26.5.37, KCC

'The fact is I don't see . . .' RL to Compton Mackenzie 23.10.38, HRHRC

187 'I didn't take to her . . .' RL in conversation with the author

'I now know how I hate Goronwy' Wogan Philipps to RL 4.4.37, KCC

'It was Blagdon . . .' Wogan Philipps to RL 25.5.37, KCC

'I have always felt . . .' Wogan Philipps to RL 10.5.37, KCC

'Rosie, surely it doesn't need Goronwy . . .' ibid

188 'Are you for, or against . . .' *Left Review*, November 1937

'The shock & relief . . .' RL to Marthe L'Evêque 5.7.37, private collection

189 'fanatically calm . . .' [et seq] RL to Edward Sackville-West 6.7.36, Berg

'the Ralphs, Raymonds . . .' Wogan Philipps to RL 31.10.37, KCC

'Wogan too silly . . .' *Cyril Connolly*, p. 246

'[Wogan] came back from Spain . . .' BBC *Bookmark* unedited ts November 1984, KCC

'I couldn't, *couldn't* take it . . .' RL in conversation with the author

'The only thing for you to do . . .' Wogan Philipps to RL 25.9.37, KCC

'I long to be home . . .' Wogan Philipps to 31.10.37, KCC

190 '[it] takes an ell . . .' *The Strings Are False*, p. 168

'I think he is generous . . .' Guy Burgess to RL 9.4.38, KCC

'We discussed Victorian novels . . .' *Album*, p. 84

'I'm going to tell you . . .' [et seq] RL in conversation with the author

191 'J'ai vu ce que me semblait . . .' RL to Marthe l'Evêque 1.12.37, private collection
'His appearance was charming . . .' *The Death of the Heart* (Vintage, 1998), p. 62
'seen the red light . . .' Barbara Ker-Seymer in conversation with the author
'His smile was frequent . . .' *Partisan Review*, 1996, vol. LXIII
'Oh dear, oh dear . . .' BL to JL 11.11.36, PUL

192 '[Rosamond] has become . . .' [et seq] Wogan Philipps to Barbara Ker-Seymer n/d, Tate
'a carping hindrance' Wogan Philipps to RL 23.10.37, KCC
'Rosamond wanted to chuck everything . . .' Wogan Philipps to Barbara Ker-Symer n/d, Tate
'There was a deathly silence . . .' [et seq] Ursula Ridley to Emily Lutyens n/d, private collection
'The crisis is past . . .' RL to Frances Partridge 10.7.38, private collection

193 '[Wogan] says Rosamond is handing out . . .' Julia Strachey to Frances Partridge 11.7.38, private collection
'& am prepared to stand . . .' Wogan Philipps to RL 8.11.37, KCC
'I am absolutely certain . . .' Wogan Philipps to RL n/d, KCC
'I want to crack . . .' Wogan Philipps to RL 3.10.37, KCC

194 'That speech in Paris . . .' RL to Rayner Heppenstall 18.9.43, HRHRC
'bellowing like a sea-lion . . .' RL to Diana Mosley 23.2.83, private collection
'Day-Lewis spoke first . . .' *The Strings Are False*, p. 168
'What gives my life its deepest reality . . .' RL ms KCC

195 'We were stopped at No. 10 . . .' RL to JL 25.1.39, PUL
'I've not become a Communist . . .' RL to Edward Sackville-West 13.5.38, Berg

196 'has for some time been knocking . . .' *Sunday Times*, 19.11.37
'I get continual offers . . .' BL to JL 23.4.36, PUL

197 '[Rosamond's] advice was invaluable . . .' BL to Henrietta Bingham 24.8.32, KCC
'my cynicism & bullet-biting' 16.10.67 BL to RL, KCC

198 'It was hard on Peg . . .' RL to JL 8.3.38, PUL
'It's snowing here . . .' RL to JL 25.1.39, PUL
'[Wogan] is frantic . . .' RL to BL 18.4.40, KCC
'[Wogan] tries me almost to murder . . .' RL to BL 3.6.40, KCC

199 'I cannot cannot describe . . .' RL to BL 29.4.39, KCC
'Our weekends were *ghastly* . . .' RL in conversation with the author
'an irreducible bastion . . .' *The Missing Diplomats*, p. 23
'One of the few . . .' Hugo Philipps in conversation with the author
'I always feel worried . . .' RL to JL 29.11.39, PUL
'Her joy when G . . .' JLD 4.12.39

200 'I have hurt you . . .' Goronwy Rees to RL n/d, KCC
'a thing the size of a thrush . . .' Barbara Ker-Seymer in conversation with the author
'the effect on one's body . . .' RL to Marthe L'Evêque 8.10.39, private collection
'I don't know why . . .' RL to ESW n/d, Berg

'They were so miserable . . .' Barbara Ker-Seymer in conversation with the author

201 'physical & spiritual black-out' [et seq] RL to Marthe L'Evêque 8.10.39, private collection

'but some stories based . . .' RL to Marthe L'Evêque 3.7.39, private collection

'All but one, they took after . . .' GB, p. 10

202 'Little Ivy, dressed in her best . . .' ibid. p. 33

'Miss Viola sat before the mirror . . .' ibid. p. 72

203 'My redhaired Miss Daintrey . . .' RL to BL n/d, KCC

'I think it is one . . .' JL to RL 19.11.39, KCC

'John has no outlet . . .' RL to Stephen Spender n/d, private collection

204 'I wish I had some of John's power . . .' RL to Stephen Spender 30.10.38, private collection

'John had a sort of love-hate . . .' [et seq] Stephen Spender in conversation with the author

205 'In a way I think . . .' RL to Frances Partridge 28.2.40, private collection

'[looking] like tiny Victorian paperweights' GB, p. 94

'I miss him enormously . . .' RL to Frances Partridge 28.2.40, private collection

'[Last] Sunday was lovely . . .' Goronwy Rees to RL n/d, KCC

206 'with my precious G . . .' RL to BL 22.6.40, KCC

'I saw trainloads of the B.E.F. . . .' RL to BL 3.6.40, KCC

'the present official complacency . . .' *Daily Worker*, 29.10.40

207 'I find it difficult . . .' David Garnett to RL 6.12.40, KCC

'Un honneur certes . . .' *Aguedal*, December 1943

'When war broke out . . .' *Penguin New Writing*, vol. 5, April 1941

208 'The girl is quiet . . .' RL to BL 18.6.40, KCC

'wholly absorbed in puppies . . .' RL to Compton Mackenzie 22.5.40, HRHRC

'violent, half-baked fanaticism' JLD 19.3.41

'I had hoped . . .' BL to JL 29.11.40, PUL

209 'Today at least . . .' RL to JL 19.11.40, PUL

'I shall marry Margie . . .' Goronwy Rees to RL n/d, KCC

'[one for whom] the *personal life* . . .' BL to JL 29.11.40, PUL

210 'a most terrible look . . .' RL in conversation with the author

'I feel that in Cambridge . . .' RL to George Rylands 16.12.40, KCC

Chapter 9. 'The Beginning of a Tremendous Affair'

211 'a very deep relationship' RL in conversation with the author

'I can't believe I could live . . .' RL to Jean MacGibbon 29.11.44, private collection

212 'Your loveliness is your life' Grizel Hartley to RL n/d, KCC

'[To a great many men] I was the image . . .' RL in conversation with the author

213 'The important thing to remember . . .' RL to JL 19.11.40, PUL

'I select love-objects . . .' RL to George Rylands 7.1.41, KCC

'was like being suffocated . . .' George Rylands in conversation with the author 'rejected and isolated...' RL in conversation with the author

'If once I can understand...' RL to George Rylands 7.1.41, KCC

'Dadie, isn't it INCREDIBLE?...' RL to George Rylands 25.1.41, KCC

'to swim straight in...' RL to George Rylands 7.2.41, KCC

214 'oh! a bitter indignation...' RL to George Rylands 2.2.41, KCC

'The arrival of Henry Green...' *The Whispering Gallery*, p. 329

'Clear she is going to be...' JLD, 2.3.41

215 'exactly what I had in mind...' *I Am My Brother*, p. 95

'Oh, I'm in TROUBLE...' RL to William Plomer 27.10.43, DUL

'[Beatrix] spent Monday night...' RL to Compton Mackenzie 13.9.40, HRHRC

'[one of] his rota...' RL in conversation with the author

'an eccentric, fire-fighting...' *Times Literary Supplement*, 6.8.54

'your perfect goodness...' RL to Henry Yorke 19.6.43, private collection

216 'You are one of the very few...' Henry Yorke to RL 14.3.45, KCC

'It's the best I've read...' Henry Yorke to RL 9.1.41, KCC

'merciless slave-master' [et seq] *I Am My Brother*, p. 95

'seemed like getting one's head...' RL to JL 19.11.40, PUL

'In the middle of the great frost...' *The Gypsy's Baby*, p. 101

217 'Jane came and knelt...' ibid. p. 111

'I am worried to death...' RL to JL n/d, PUL

'was not equipped...' *Penguin New Writing*, vol. 7, 1941

218 'looking so much better...' JLD, 14.5.41

'a moving and a memorable poet...' *New Statesman & Nation*, 29.3.41

'You had better come...' [et seq] RL in conversation with the author

219 'dozens and dozens of elderly ladies...' RL to JL 20.10.36, HRHRC

'was very shy...' [et seq] RL in conversation with the author

220 'I knew very soon...' *New Verse*, November 1937

'It was not a movement at all...' *The Buried Day*, p. 216

221 '[plodding] on through...' *Britain Today*, no. 122, June 1946

'The very temper of pleasures...' *The Heat of the Day* (Vintage, 1998)

222 'You can't imagine...' RL in conversation with the author

'a reticence about him...' Julian Symons *Sunday Times*, 28.5.72

'Cecil was magic!' Michael Meyer in conversation with the author

'And oh! I do appreciate it...' RL to George Rylands 4.2.42, KCC

222 'It has been beautifully sunny...' C. Day Lewis to RL n/d, KCC

'I must live with my darling...' C. Day Lewis to RL n/d, KCC

'always remained the most romantic...' RL to Francis King 29.2.80, HRHRC

'Come on, you great big beautiful bitch...' *C. Day-Lewis*, p. 144

223 I'm still evading the draft...' ibid. p. 146

'He said, "Who do you mean?"...' [et seq] RL in conversation with the author

224 'Dear R, W's conduct is absolutely rotten...' Laurence Milford to RL 21.9.42, KCC

'These communists are very set...' RL to Laurie Lee 14.1.44, private collection

225 'I also much like...' Geoffrey Nickson to RL 28.12.42, KCC

'If only Sally would eat . . .' BL to RL n/d, KCC

'[growing] more & more . . .' RL to William Plomer 15.9.45, DUL

'Dear Mother, This has been . . .' Hugo Philipps to RL 15.6.41, KCC

226 'I rather think . . .' *New Statesman & Nation*, 9.12.39

'about the happiest time of my life . . .' RL in conversation with the author

'One night they saw . . .' *Word over All, The Complete Poems*, p. 315

'Darling, darling, darling love . . .' C. Day Lewis to RL n/d, KCC

'I am so peaceful & happy . . .' RL to John Hayward 17.10.42, KCC

227 'I didn't go abroad . . .' C. *Day-Lewis*, p. 32

'took great pains to "bring me out" . . .' *The Buried Day*, p. 164

'a landmark, in the sense . . .' *Living in Time*, p. 29

228 '[she was] inclined towards the austere . . .' *The Buried Day*, p. 201

'a wildness of sensual violence . . .' ibid. p. 230

'I've just seen Cecil . . .' Gillian Warrender in conversation with the author

'I am pretty contented . . .' RL to Henry Yorke 19.6.43, private collection

229 'as surreal a vision . . .' *Sketches from a Life*, p. 102

'He went ahead . . .' *Horizon*, vol. 7, April 1943

230 'chug & choke along' RL to Edward Gathorne-Hardy 30.7.45, Berg

'An exhausted prisoner . . .' RL to Herman Ould 25.2.43, Tulsa

'writing is always . . .' RL to William Plomer 7.7.42, DUL

'Tomorrow I have to start . . .' RL to Denys Kilham-Roberts n/d, Society of
 Authors

230 'a long complicated story . . .' RL to William Plomer 7.7.42, DUL

231 'Although my life . . .' RL to Rayner Heppenstall 6.9.43, HRHRC

'Jane, rushing forward . . .' GB, p. 97

'At 10.30 p.m. the telephone rang . . .' ibid. p. 115

232 'Roger Wickham, tall, slight . . .' ibid. p. 155

233 '"Where've they gone?" . . .' ibid. 191

'had a pale long cool-looking face . . .' ibid. 155

'[was] as tender and sentimental . . .' *Laurie Lee*, p. 154

'My children dote on you . . .' RL to Laurie Lee 25.8.44, private collection

234 'You are my brother . . .' RL to Laurie Lee 1.12.43, private collection

'I was a sort of page-in-waiting . . .' Laurie Lee in conversation with the author

'Dear love, I think you do know . . .' C. Day Lewis to RL n/d, KCC

'Courted, caressed, you wear . . .' *Word Over All, Collected Poems*, p. 316

235 'Ah, those boundaries . . .' RL to Jean MacGibbon 28.1.45, private collection

'It's a lovely, sunny . . .' C. Day Lewis to RL 25.12.42, KCC

'Blast those boys!' RL to Olivia Holland 19.9.44, private collection

236 '[by] the paralyzing act . . .' RL to Laurie Lee 9.6.43, private collection

'Cecil had the fatal quality . . .' Laurie Lee in conversation with the author

'Good God, Rosamond . . .' C. Day Lewis to RL n/d, KCC

'I'm often so deathly tired . . .' C. Day Lewis to RL n/d, KCC

'because it would be too painful . . .' RL to Laurie Lee 23.4.43, private collection

'Laurie was the grown-up boy . . .' Sean Day-Lewis in conversation with the

author
237 'I get terrified that wanting more . . .' RL to Laurie Lee 23.4.43, private collection
'in the end he will prefer . . .' RL to Laurie Lee 30.4.43, private collection
'the violent happenings . . .' *The Lyric Impulse*, p. 147
'You can be sure . . .' C. Day Lewis to RL 28.10.43, KCC
'Love's the big boss . . .' *Word over All, Complete Poems*, p. 330
238 'I suppose because I had hoped . . .' RL to Olivia Holland 3.11.43, private collection
'My trouble is . . .' RL to Olivia Holland n/d, private collection
'he tossed the poem over . . .' C. *Day Lewis*, p. 156
'Shall I be gone long? . . .' *Poems 1943–1947*, p. 380
239 'I don't like the feeling . . .' RL to Laurie Lee 26.11.44, private collection
'Last autumn the weight . . .' Laurie Lee to RL 27.11.44, KCC
'[In those days] it made divorce . . .' Laurie Lee in conversation with the author
240 'so I've been stuck in the country . . .' RL to Jean MacGibbon 14.7.44, private collection
'He is a wonderfully nice man . . .' RL to Rayner Heppenstall 26.2.45, HRHRC
'the pleasures, the ardours . . .' JL to RL n/d, KCC
241 'I can scarcely speak . . .' RL to JL n/d, PUL
'Under separate cover . . .' Denys Kilham Roberts to RL 26.1.45, KCC
'the illiteracy & flat ugliness . . .' RL to Eric Bligh 3.9.44, Bodleian
'far better than anything . . .' RL to Denys Kilham Roberts 14.5.44, Society of Authors
242 'the last story of the trilogy . . .' RL to Jean MacGibbon 1.4.43, private collection
'One day my mother . . .' BS, p. 5
'She was dressed . . .' ibid. p. 10
243 'The source, Rebecca! . . .' ibid. p. 101
'My head was whizzing round . . .' ibid. 313
244 'A woman tells a child of ten . . .' *New Statesman & Nation*, 30.9.44
'a charming, if dangerous, experiment' *Observer*, 1.10.44
'full of poetic imagination . . .' *Listener*, 26.10.44
'a beautiful, impressive . . .' *New Republic*, 1944
'the contempt for all modern inhibitions . . .' *New Statesman & Nation*, 30.9.44
'I don't believe I shall ever . . .' RL to William Plomer 27.7.43, DUL
245 '[some] childhood memories . . .' BS, p. ix
'a beastly wicked vile *fraud*' RL to Jean MacGibbon 1.11.44, private collection
'*Of course* Mrs Jardine is me!' Violet Hammersley to Nancy Mitford 13.10.44, private collection
'That tormented, predatory . . .' Michael Meyer in conversation with the author
'Mrs Jardine seems to be . . .' RL to Jean MacGibbon 1.11.44, private collection
'on this iron landscape . . .' [et seq] RL to Grizel Hartley n/d, KCC
246 '& now the wind keens . . .' RL to JL 4.2.45, PUL
'that the passion was turning . . .' JDL 5.5.45, PUL
'the same that were lit . . .' RL to JL 16.5.45, PUL

Chapter 10. 'The Terrible Decision'
247 'Walter Wanger is an angel . . .' RL to Olivia Holland 23.11.46, private collection
'[it was] not the kind of story . . .' *Walter Wanger*, p. 266
248 'a dream house . . .' RL in conversation with the author
'A perfect Queen Anne house . . .' *Head of a Traveller*, p. 11–12
249 'I miss her dreadfully . . .' RL to Laurie Lee 11.1.47, private collection
'I have actually got . . .' RL to Olivia Holland 23.11.46, private collection
'I adore my house . . .' RL to William Plomer 22.5.46, DUL
'is all that there is of the most chic' C. Day Lewis to Laurie Lee n/d, private
collection
'Curtaining, carpeting, lighting all . . .' *Poems 1943–1947, The Collected Poems*, p.
376
'the faded magenta of Christmas roses . . .' *Head of a Traveller*, p. 13
250 'Women everywhere in those days . . .' *Iris*, p. 86
'[she] glowed like a gorgeous peach . . .' *Julia*, p. 208
'It was hard to be sure . . .' *World Over All, The Complete Poems*, p. 319
'[he] was torn between . . .' *The Dreadful Hollow*, p. 97
251 'I liked being in the limelight,' *The Buried Day*, p. 60
252 'far and away the most striking . . .' *I Am My Brother*, p. 231
'the one who, from first to last . . .' *C. Day-Lewis*, p. 168
'Under stress such as I . . .' *The Buried Day*, p. 234
'Rosamond's pressure on Cecil . . .' Laurie Lee in conversation with the author
'I had little by little . . .' *The Buried Day*, p. 138
253 'to put all to the touch.' RL to Kenneth Clark 21.3.46, Tate
'that he realized overwhelmingly . . .' RL to Laurie Lee 14.3.46, private collection
'I must wait & be patient . . .' RL to Kenneth Clark 21.3.46, Tate
'Cecil never felt emotion . . .' Elizabeth Jane Howard in conversation with the
author
254 'To my horror (and his) . . .' RL to Olivia Holland 16.5.46, private collection
'I think she is a clever . . .' RL to Laurie Lee 16.4.46, private collection
'I want to say how very glad . . .' RL to William Plomer 26.7.46, DUL
255 'Little did I know . . .' RL in conversation with the author
'I must try to start work . . .' RL to Olivia Holland 16.5.46, private collection
'restored to my former position . . .' RL to Olivia Holland 13.9.46, private
collection
256 'I went over, and she said . . .' Wogan Philipps in conversation with the author
'Revision jobs are apt to be hell . . .' RL to JL 17.11.47, HRHRC
'Engrossing and brilliant . . .' RL ms n/d, HRHRC
'Tell him with my compliments . . .' RL to JL 26.9.51, HRHRC
257 'but the fearful ordeal . . .' RL to Marthe L'Evêque 4.2.47, private collection
'the best part of a year's work wasted' C. Day Lewis to Rupert Hart-Davis, *C. Day-
Lewis*, p. 167
'drenching me with misery . . .' *The Burial Day*, p. 146
'[Cecil] is very far from well . . .' RL to Olivia Holland 1.6.47, private collection

'I was up for most of 2 nights . . .' RL to JL 11.3.47, PUL

258 'I will not lift mine eyes . . .' *Poems, 1943–7, The Complete Poems*, p. 400

'Cecil in state bordering on insanity . . .' C. *Day-Lewis*, p. 170

'The hideous, destined thing . . .' *Laurie Lee*, p. 237

259 'the terrible decision.' RL to Laurie Lee 12.6.47, private collection

'Rupert, tell him . . .' RL to Rupert Hart-Davis n/d, Tulsa

'like two wheels of a bicycle . . .' RL to Laurie Lee 11.8.47, private collection

'This state is miserably ignominious . . .' RL to Kenneth Clark n/d, Tate

'My heart can beat . . .' RL to Laurie Lee 12.6.47, private collection

260 'When he's in a bad mental state . . .' [et seq] RL to Laurie Lee 20.7.47, private collection

261 'anyway for the moment' [et seq] RL in conversation with the author

'It is more wonderful . . .' RL to Laurie Lee 27.7.47, private collection

'a grown-up book about adults' RL to Bernard Berenson 17.10.47, I Tatti

'[to crack] the crust . . .' RL to Bernard Berenson 11.2.48, I Tatti

262 '[and] did claim to be very fond of me' RL to Violet Hammersley n/d, KCC

'It seems unlike anything . . .' RL to Bernard Berenson 24.7.48, I Tatti

'lived a devoted . . .' RL to Bernard Berenson 15.9.47, I Tatti

'My own feeling is . . .' C. Day Lewis to RL 14.4.48, KCC

263 'which seems to many others . . .' [et seq] RL to Bernard Berenson 17.10.47, I Tatti

'is a superb reader . . .' [et seq] RL to Bernard Berenson 16.4.48, I Tatti

'a mixture of the Oracle of Delphi . . .' *The Ample Proposition*, p. 158

264 '[a] condition of the most . . .' RL to Bernerd Berenson 29.5.48, I Tatti

'as a personality you attracted . . .' Bernard Berenson to RL 4.4.50, KCC

'in so far as possible . . .' Bernard Berenson to RL 10.6.48, KCC

'[gives] the vague impression . . .' *Sylvia Sprigge and the 'Sage of Settignano'*, p. 17

'Watching what you . . .' RL to Bernard Berenson 29.5.48, I Tatti

265 'on a living night . . .' [et seq] *The Italian Visit, Elegy Before Death: At Settignano, The Compete Poems*, p. 465

'It is a major work . . .' RL to Bernard Berenson 8.5.49, I Tatti

266 'beautiful & packed with treasures' [et seq] RL to Sally Philipps 23.5.49, KCC

'You & Cecil . . .' W. S. Maugham to RL 19.6.49, KCC

'at the height of the emotional crisis' [et seq] RL to Frank Taylor 14.12.48, Lilly

267 'Barbara took everyone's man . . .' Wogan Philipps in conversation with the author

'Her reputation had gone before her . . .' RL in conversation with the author

'I never liked him . . .' Barbara Ghika in conversation with the author

268 'I am in the thick of it . . .' RL to William Plomer 24.1.49, DUL

'I am progressively . . .' RL to JL 2.5.49, PUL

'"It's very *dark*," . . .' RL in conversation with the author

'Elizabeth, darling Elizabeth . . .' RL to Elizabeth Bowen 14.2.49, HRHRC

269 '[The book] is embedded . . .' RL to Elizabeth Bowen 4.3.49, HRHRC

'there was a great discussion . . .' George Rylands in conversation with the author 'if she [Rosamond] had *one* more affair...' Edith Sitwell to Philip Caraman 30.1.59, Copyright Francis Sitwell (2002), KCC

270 'violent half-baked fanaticism' JLD 19.3.41
'the terrible harm Peg is doing...' JLD 3.4.49
'of her struggle to get work...' JLD 26.7.40
'looking so lined...' JLD 1.2.50

271 '[Bea was] the exact opposite...' Barbara Ghika in conversation with the author
'She is entirely obsessed...' RL to JL 1.7.49, PUL
'gallows humour' *Christopher and His Kind*, p. 91
'This is the first time...' RL to Denys Kilham Roberts 4.10.48, Society of Authors
'My job is to fly...' Hugo Philipps to RL 10.1.49, KCC
'We are no longer...' Hugo Philipps to RL 4.3.49, KCC

272 'One realises that any tribesman...' Hugo Philipps to RL n/d, KCC
'[It's] most peculiar to realise...' RL to Bernard Berenson 24.7.48, I Tatti
'As usual [I] am hating...' RL to Violet Hammersley n/d, KCC
'I am *not* happy...' Sally Philipps to RL 2.5.46, KCC
'Sally looked wonderful...' Moorea Black in conversation with the author
'There was a granite streak...' *The Swan in the Evening*, p. 98

273 'his energy, his humorous...' RL to P. J. Kavanagh 14.1.71, private collection
'I myself hold no dogmas...' RL to Compton Mackenzie 11.12.48, HRHRC
'In case you are wondering...' Sally Philipps to RL n/d, KCC
'I wish you could have been there...' RL to Compton Mackenzie 15.1.49, HRHRC
'She is a heavenly creature...' RL to Bernard Berenson 4.1.52, I Tatti
'Oh you are so lucky...' Sally Philipps to RL n/d, KCC

274 'I fell flat for Edith Sitwell...' RL to JL 31.10.44, PUL
'Dylan Thomas & his wife...' RL to Olivia Holland 16.5.46, private collection
'It is the only harsh criticism...' [et seq] Edith Sitwell to Osbert Sitwell 28.9.49, *Selected Letters of Edith Sitwell*, p. 313

275 'Faintly started...' RL to JL 3.10.49, PUL
'Lilian, by her example...' RL to Laurens van der Post 27.8.49, Laurens van der Post Estate
'the precious and heart-rending...' RL to William Plomer 27.7.49, DUL
'a kind of T. E. Lawrence...' RL to Compton Mackenzie 30.7.50, HRHRC
'She looked so beautiful...' Laurens van der Post in conversation with the author
'Didn't you think Laurens van der Post...' RL to Violet Hammersley n/d, KCC

276 'long, strange and deeply valued friendship' [et seq] *The Rock Rabbit and the Rainbow*
'[an] almost fairytale...' Laurens van der Post in conversation with the author
'All my adult life...' *The Buried Day*, p. 241
'The truth is made for woman...' *The Dreadful Hollow*, p. 164

277 'It is sad to think...' C. Day Lewis to RL 14.4.48, KCC
'Dinner was for 8.0...' Elizabeth Jenkins in conversation with the author

'almost malarial . . .' *The Years Between*, p. 120

'I was never long free . . .' *The Buried Day*, p. 240

'like a ghost . . .' *C. Day-Lewis*, p. 174

'[looking] more ravaged-face . . .' JLD 25.8.49

278 '"Oh, I don't think . . ."' RL in conversation with the author

'He was the most wonderful-looking . . .' Jill Day-Lewis in conversation with the author

'There was a puzzling contrast . . .' *C. Day-Lewis*, p. 180

'a simple, green, callow . . .' RL in conversation with the author

'She was obviously courting me . . .' Sean Day-Lewis in conversation with the author

279 'Didn't you say . . .' [et seq] RL in conversation with the author

'At last I've written something . . .' [et seq] RL in conversation with the author

280 'Isn't it wonderful . . .' Laurens van der Post in conversation with the author

'I promise you . . .' C. Day Lewis to RL 11.1.50, KCC

281 '[Cecil] was very gay . . .' *C. Day-Lewis*, p. 185

'[he] looked white . . .' [et seq] RL in conversation with the author

'diabolical indifference' RL to Laurens van der Post n/d, Laurens van der Post Estate

'What about *me*?' RL in conversation with the author

'[He] said he was now . . .' RL to Laurens Van der Post n/d, Laurens van der Post Estate

282 'He looked like a murderer . . .' [et seq] RL in conversation with the author

'appalling brainstorm' RL to Kenneth Clark 1.2.50, Tate

283 'it was very exactly as if . . .' RL in conversation with the author

Chapter 11. 'A Farewell to the World of Love'

284 'This hasn't been, in any way . . . RL to George Rylands 2.4.50, KCC

'a destructive, death-cold character' RL to Bernard Berenson 13.6.50, I Tatti

'reeling about morally . . .' RL to JL 3.2.50, PUL

'If it turns out . . .' RL to JL 14.3.50, PUL

'grotesque little piece . . .' RL to Laurens van der Post n/d, Laurens van der Post Estate

'this ghastly, over-emotional . . .' RL in conversation with the author

285 'His unfortunate wife . . .' RL to JL 16.2, PUL

'Rosamond and I got on . . .' *C. Day-Lewis*, p. 188

'She cannot believe . . .' JLD 18.2.50

'she saw love as something . . .' Barbara Ghika in conversation with the author

'[his] only solution was . . .' [et seq] Laurie Lee in conversation with the author

286 'O I must tell Osbert!' JLD 1.4.50

'this marvel of a woman . . .' *Sunset and Twilight*, 12.3.57

'Sally has taken it very hard . . .' RL to George Rylands 3.4.50, KCC

'It is hard – for me . . .' RL to Laurens van der Post n/d, Laurens van der Post

Estate
'I'm afraid the holidays . . .' Sally Philipps to RL 30.4.50, KCC
287 'a great mistake . . .' RL to Bernard Berenson 11.5.50, I Tatti
'every sentence has to be fought for' RL to JL 3.2.50, PUL
'I feel that the idea . . .' JL to RL 18.2.50, PUL
'as a howling possessive . . .' RL to JL, 19.2.50, PUL
'I cannot take any further interest . . .' RL to JL 14.3.50, PUL
'It is a great load . . .' RL to JL 19.3.50, PUL
'He is still set . . .' RL to Bernard Berenson 31.3.50, I Tatti
288 'The children, though adorable . . .' RL to Bernard Berenson 31.3.50, I Tatti
'She was a very great star . . .' Margaret Vyner in conversation with the author
'She is a very eccentric number . . .' RL to Olivia Holland 6.6.51, private
collection
289 'a *crashing* snob . . .' Margaret Vyner in conversation with the author
'Everything hurts so . . .' RL to Olivia 20.6.50, private collection
'He has been very good . . .' RL to Laurens van der Post n/d, private collection
'It was all grotesque . . .' RL to George Rylands 3.7.50, KCC
290 'Perhaps my trouble is . . .' RL to Olivia Holland 6.7.50, private collection
'Au pays du tendre . . .' RL to Bernard Berenson 18.3.51, I Tatti
'looking myself again . . .' RL to Bernard Berenson 4.8.50, I Tatti
'which I thought . . .' [et seq] RL in conversation with the author
'[She is] none too comfortable . . .' *The Nöel Coward Diaries*, 12.2.51
291 'You, my dear . . .' *Ian Fleming*, p. 211
'Noel was *terribly* sweet . . .' RL in conversation with the author
'I suddenly began . . .' RL to Bernard Berenson 18.3.51, I Tatti
'who I suppose felt very ashamed . . .' RL in conversation with the author
'I've been very lonely here . . .' RL to Laurie Lee 14.3.51, private collection
'I alone, Expecting no one . . .' *Listener*, 12.7.51
292 'still basking in the worship . . .' RL to Bernard Berenson 18.3.51, I Tatti
'just at the time . . .' RL to Laurie Lee 30.1.58, private collection
'the squalor, the dishonour . . .' [et seq] RL to Edith Sitwell 24.4.51, private
collection
293 'I felt that he was putting me off . . .' [et seq] *Conspiracy of Silence*, p. 362
'Luckily, as soon as I took . . .' JLD 22.6.51
'[Blunt] suddenly burst out . . .' [et seq] *Conspiracy of Silence*, p. 388
294 '[He] came for lunch . . .' RL in conversation with the author
'I think Anthony was anxious . . .' *Mask of Treachery*, p. 32
'I had a lovely time . . .' RL to William Mostyn-Owen n/d, private collection
295 'I listened enthralled . . .' *Well, I Forget the Rest*, p. 67
'a clean-limbed . . .' Joshua Rowley in conversation with the author
'It was a very strange . . .' William Mostyn-Owen in conversation with the author
'Aix was the beginning . . .' RL to William Mostyn-Owen 17.9.51, private
collection
'How could I ever . . .' RL to William Mostyn-Owen 5.8.51, private collection

296 'all the joys and pleasures...' RL to William Mostyn-Owen 3.9.51, private collection
  'It is a dreadful break...' RL to George Rylands 3.7.50, KCC
  'two American alcoholics' RL to William Mostyn-Owen 5.8.51, private collection
  'like living in Blake's marriage...' RL to William Mostyn-Owen 17.8.51, private collection
  'I found her fascinating...' *The Lonely Hunter*, p. 378
  'first class ... with plenty of good champagne...' JLD 8.9.51
297 'to keep up my morale' [et seq] RL to Laurie Lee 27.9.51, private collection
  'One has to try to enable...' RL to Bernard Berenson 6.3.52, I Tatti
  'strange, closed character...' William Mostyn-Owen in conversation with the author
  'I'd like to write a story...' RL to William Mostyn-Owen 17.9.51, private collection
  'We must keep the shuttle...' Bernard Berenson to RL 10.6.48, KCC
298 'Dear, glorious, wild woman' Bernard Berenson to RL 29.5.52, KCC
  'You alone if you had the leisure...' Bernard Berenson to RL 22.4.52, KCC
  'almost at once ... a ghost' [et seq] RL to Bernard Berenson 19.12.51, I Tatti
  '[Sally] fell prone...' RL to Bernard Berenson 19.12.51, I Tatti
  'Rosamond was glad...' Wogan Philipps in conversation with the author
  'May comes every morning...' RL to Elizabeth Mostyn-Owen 5.2.52, private collection
299 'I'm afraid I behaved...' William Mostyn-Owen in conversation with the author
  'You were my guest...' [et seq] RL to William Mostyn-Owen 2.1.52, private collection
300 'I began to find this...' William Mostyn-Owen in conversation with the author
  'I have tried so hard...' RL to Bernard Berenson 4.1.52, I Tatti
  'No doubt the chief clue...' RL to Bernard Berenson 4.1.52, I Tatti
  'sense of injury...' RL to George Rylands 13.2.54, KCC
  'It has saddened me...' JLD 21.1.52
301 'Yesterday I took...' ibid. 10.7.52
  'A blonde can't fail here!' [et seq] Sally Philipps to RL 12.2.52, KCC
  'Life here gets gayer...' Sally Philipps to RL 29.6.52, KCC
  'we sang through meals...' Sally Philipps to RL 5.4.52, KCC
  'Sally's letters are deliriously happy...' RL to William Mostyn-Owen 30.4.52, private collection
  'London is dark...' RL to Bernard Berenson 4.1.52, I Tatti
302 'really rather beautiful...' RL to Bernard Berenson 6.3.52, I Tatti
  'looking incomparably beautiful...' RL to William Mostyn-Owen 30.4.52, private collection
  'I have met an angelic man...' RL to Laurie Lee 23.3.52, private collection
  '[I am] enjoying my life...' RL to William Mostyn-Owen 30.4.52, private collection

'the nicest young man...' RL to William Mostyn-Owen 13.6.52, private collection

'She was so marvellous...' Joshua Rowley in conversation with the author

'It *was* a love affair...' RL in conversation with the author

'has brought me incredible...' RL to William Mostyn-Owen 13.6.52, private collection

'a horrible handsome young Italian' RL to George Rylands 25.5.52, KCC

303 'I can't believe...' Sally Philipps to RL n/d, KCC

'Sally came back glowing...' RL to Bernard Berenson 1.10.52, I Tatti

'at 8.30 pm on Oct 15th...' RL to Bernard Berenson 19.10.52, I Tatti

'spends the waning of his days...' RL to Quentin Crewe 21.12.52, private collection

'broods over Wogan...' RL to Violet Hammersley n/d, KCC

304 'that before you exercised...' Denys Kilham Roberts to RL 10.12.47, Society of Authors

'Disparate scenes & faces...' RL to Jean MacGibbon 26.10.45, private collection

'terrible struggles with my writing' RL to Michael Meyer 14.12.47, private collection

'about a third...' RL to Denys Kilham Roberts 28.9.48, Society of Authors

305 'My novel goes hideously...' RL to JL 1.7.49, PUL

'The book is not very far...' RL to George Rylands 3.4.50, KCC

'picking up this novel...' RL to Denys Kilham Roberts 29.10.50, Society of Authors

'I am writing...' RL to Laurie Lee 23.3.52, private collection

'I just went on with life...' Anita Brookner, *Spectator* 17.3.90

'I just can't produce...' [et seq] *Writing Lives*, p. 156

306 'I myself have been...' *GB*, p. 57

'Novelists must be able...' *Britain Today*, no. 122, June 1946

307 'flea-bitten, sodden...' *EG*, 24

308 'Have I ever had a penchant...' ibid. p. 65

'irrevocably out of the top drawer' ibid. p. 152

'[the] blissful days alone...' ibid. p. 257

'[Rickie] had a way...' ibid. p. 43

'He was sick of seeing women...' ibid. p. 106

309 '"my quite outstanding ineffectuality..."' ibid. p. 235

'I'm a notable disappointer...' ibid. p. 238

'[Rickie] was hopelessly in love...' ibid. p. 127

'His eyes looked into my eyes...' *WS*, p. 225

'they were one...' *EG*, p. 128

'Are you a gardener?' ibid. p. 10

310 'out of the corner of an eye...' ibid, p. 46

'in her subdued way...' ibid. p. 107

'the night he had opened the door...' ibid. p. 143

'a Jew, called Hermann' ibid. p. 22

311 'je ne peux pas m'empêcher...' Gabriel Marcel to RL 26.12.52, KCC
'I began to feel...' *Listener*, March 1953
'it was really a farewell...' RL to P. J. Kavanagh 12.6.75, private collection
'no portraits from life' RL to Bernard Berenson 15.4.52, I Tatti
'an amalgam of Matt Ridley...' RL in conversation with the author

312 'The two sisters are partly...' *Writing Lives*, p. 156
'I have *never* written...' RL in conversation with the author
'a breath coming up again...' *EG*, p. 51
'a charmer ... eminently fitted...' ibid. p. 56
'not guilty or repentant...' ibid. p. 73
'But for the fixed cold shadow...' ibid. p. 131
'wrapped in the cloak...' ibid. p. 174

313 'that was the crack-up...' ibid. p. 176
'What are we waiting for?...' ibid. p. 265
'It may be that it will turn out...' RL to Bernard Berenson 15.4.52, I Tatti

314 'not just a woman novelist's idea...' RL to Bernard Berenson 22.6.53, I Tatti
'Sexually dim' *New Yorker*, 23.5.53
'a soggy, half-deflated football' *Time*, 22.6.53
'Strangely feminine' *Times Literary Supplement*, 17.4.55
'Rickie remains an elegant...' *Daily Mail*, 11.4.53
'a great novel by any standards...' *Truth*, 10.4.53
'partly because I am a man...' *Daily Telegraph*, 10.4.53
'Women luxuriate in these books...' *News Chronicle*, 15.4.53
'a masterpiece' *New York Times Book Review*, 10.5.53
'No English writer has told...' *Observer*, 5.4.53
'tedious affair...' *New Statesman*, 11.4.53

315 'I don't think reviews...' *Writing Lives*, 154
'I am afraid that as an ex-editor...' Raymond Mortimer to RL 20.5.53, KCC
'Authors have a cross...' *New Statesman*, 2.2.54
'very impressive and, at times...' Stephen Spender to RL 12.6.53, KCC
'You make all other novelists...' JL to 10.3.53, KCC

316 'It makes me feel like a ghost...' RL to Bernard Berenson 25.2.53, I Tatti
'He'd been the battlefield...' George Meredith, 1861 from *Pegasus and Other Poems*, *The Complete Poems*, p. 504

317 'What I thought I was doing...' C. Day Lewis to RL 21.3.55, KCC
'Relics! Mementoes!...' RL ms KCC
'the embalmer discussing the technique...' [et seq] C. Day Lewis to RL 21.3.55, KCC
'new feeling of release...' RL to Shane Leslie 28.6.54, GUL

318 '[Rosamond] stood back...' Laurens van der Post in conversation with the author
'I saw him come down...' Jill Day-Lewis in conversation with the author
'good mental exercise...' RL to Bernard Berenson 5.12.53, I. Tatti

319 'His manners were so winning...' [et seq] *Adam 300* ed. Miron Grindea (Adam Books/Curwen Press, 1965)

'hideous horrible nightmare task' RL to Violet Hammersley 14.2.55, KCC
'Cocteau is utter total . . .' RL to Roger Senhouse, 6.12.55, KCC
'She comes daily . . .' RL to Violet Hammersley 14.2.55, KCC
'you have been working . . .' Raymond Mortimer to RL 11.6.55, KCC
'not on any account mention . . .' Martin Villiers to RL n/d, KCC
320 'Je vous donne confiance . . .' *Adam 300*
'Chaque fois que je me sens . . .' Jean Cocteau to RL 18.12.55, KCC
'none-too-gratifying' *Adam 300*
'He wouldn't go into . . .' RL in conversation with the author
'I found frightfully embarrassing' Hugo Philipps in conversation with the author
'has a beautiful long head . . .' RL to George Rylands 6.5.54, KCC
'a penniless, interesting . . .' RL to Bernard Berenson 18.7.55, I Tatti
321 '[I] am really happy . . .' RL to Barbara Cooper 28.12.55, HRHRC

Chapter 12. 'The One Flawless Joy of My Life'
322 'his solitary rebarbative . . .' RL to Stephen Spender 23.8.58, private collection
'He is a boy in a thousand' RL to Violet 19.1.56, KCC
323 'Although Sally is so sensible . . .' RL to Violet Hammersley 19.1.56, KCC
'with a tiny garden . . .' RL to Violet Hammersley 19.1.56, KCC
'it's a dur métier . . .' RL to Bernard Berenson 27.3.54, I Tatti
324 'Rosamond would go into overdrive . . .' Laurie Lee in conversation with the author
'[Sally] is more at home . . .' RL to Laurie Lee 14.3.51, private collection
'Just as I was born lost . . .' RL to Elizabeth Mostyn-Owen 28.7.58, private collection
325 'It was a blessing . . .' RL to Violet Hammersley 4.9.56, KCC
'when . . . through a little gate . . .' *Times*, 25.10.56
'My mother was an extremely impressive . . .' RL to Rupert Hart-Davis 22.9.56, Tulsa
326 '[Rosamond] succeeded in wounding me . . .' JLD 10.9.56
'It made Bea and me . . .' RL in conversation with the author
327 'The amount of pain . . .' RL to JL 5.58, PUL
'Of course, after what you write . . .' JL to RL 7.3.58, KCC
'You *ought* to understand . . .' [et seq] RL to JL 5.3.58, PUL
328 'Every woman who is a poet . . .' RL to JL 5.3.58, PUL
'You ask am I "finishing a book?" . . .' RL to Violet Hammersley 10.7.56, KCC
329 'Suddenly, stealthily . . .' A *Hut*, p. 166
'[I] very soon saw . . .' RL to Denys Kilham Roberts 8.5.56, Society of Authors
'It is wonderful to be working . . .' RL to Bernard Berenson 3.7.56, I Tatti
330 '[she] always makes the flat . . .' JLD 29.8.57
'T. S. Eliot came to dinner . . .' RL to Frances Partridge 29.8.57, private collection
'Darling Rose Macaulay . . .' RL to Sally Philipps 9.1.58, KCC
331 'It was fairly dramatic . . .' Patrick Trevor-Roper in conversation with the author

'a hard-edged semi-mineral . . .' RL to Patrick Trevor-Roper 15.7.58, KCC

'phenomena that astonished me . . .' RL ms diary, CPS

'Rosamond Lehmann arrived . . .' *Sunset and Twilight*, 12.3.57

332 'She started being rather criticising . . .' Margaret Vyner in conversation with the author

'His grasp of estate management . . .' RL to Sally Philipps 29.12.57, KCC

'My life is now agreeable . . .' RL to Frances Partridge 8.6.56, private collection

333 'Ros has a strong femininity . . .' *A Mingled Measure*, 20.4.53, p. 20

'I don't believe that I so fell . . .' 28.9.89, JLMD

'We hoped for Istanbul . . .' *The Perfect Stranger*, p. 156

'We were both pleased . . .' C. *Day-Lewis*, p. 198

'affectionate . . . [it] made me . . .' C. Day-Lewis to RL 25.3.72, KCC

334 'I wish you could see him . . .' RL in conversation with the author

'Please put it down . . .' RL to P. J. Kavanagh 9.11.57, private collection

'[Sally] looking intently . . .' *SE*, p. 82

'I didn't have one single . . .' RL to P. J. Kavanagh 2.3.82, private collection

'enchantingly pretty bijou property' *SE*, p. 77

335 '[Joshua] is really taking . . .' RL to Violet Hammersley 11.6.58, KCC

'Great strides made . . .' RL to Sally Philipps 27.10.57, KCC

'Oh so hot, hot . . .' Sally Philipps to RL 22.10.57, KCC

'My hair falls . . .' Sally Philipps to RL 20.11.57, KCC

'We have been unable to touch . . .' [et seq] Sally Philipps to RL 8.11.57, KCC

'but it's a horror . . .' Sally Philipps to RL 5.12.57, KCC

'A determined gleam . . .' P. J. Kavanagh to RL 8.12.57, KCC

336 'Practically her first question . . .' RL to P. J. Kavanagh 9.11.57, KCC

'Her fantasies about you . . .' RL to Sally 31.1.58, KCC

'a charming, log-cabiny bungalow' Sally Philipps to RL 27.1.58, KCC

'I must say right away . . .' P. J. Kavanagh to RL 6.2.58, KCC

'We're giving a great deal . . .' Sally Philipps to RL 6.2.58, KCC

337 'I can't really say . . .' Sally Philipps to RL 5.12.57, KCC

'[And] I must warn you . . .' Sally Philipps to RL 6.2.58, KCC

'I DREAD it' RL to Sally Philipps 8.3.58, KCC

'Feel curiously undignified . . .' RL to Sally Philipps 12.4.58, KCC

'and his dear little . . .' RL to Sally Philipps 4.5.58, KCC

'The prospect of Rosamond Lehmann . . .' Isherwood's *Diaries* 24.4.58, p. 747

338 'Igor became wonderfully oracular . . .' Isherwood's *Diaries* 28.4.58, p. 748

'at the fabulous Beverley Hills "home" [et seq] RL to Sally Philipps 4.5.58, KCC

'Quite as I like her . . .' Isherwood's *Diaries* 28.4.58, p. 748

'we gasp like fishes . . .' Sally Philipps to RL 23.4.58, KCC

'After endless tests . . .' Sally Philipps to RL 23.4.58, KCC

'I am in the Innermost Shrine . . .' [et seq] RL to Sally Philipps 4.5.58, KCC

339 'We stayed in a little village . . .' Sally Philipps to RL 14.6.58, KCC

'We arrived at evening . . .' *The Perfect Stranger*, p. 178

340 'Curled in your night-dress . . .' *The Perfect Stranger*, p. 178

'*Wish* you were here . . .' RL to Sally Philipps 29.5.58, KCC
'as bright as I've ever seen her' P. J. Kavanagh to RL 20.1.82, KCC
'I stayed with her . . .' *The Perfect Stranger*, p. 177
341 'I was kneeling to measure . . .' [et seq] *SE*, p. 80
'Sally very ill . . .' [et seq] RL to Compton Mackenzie, HRHRC
'Laurens, Sally's dead' [et seq] Laurens van der Post in conversation with the author
341 'I can't talk about the ensuing days . . .' *Ena Twigg*, p. 205
'From the day she first smiled . . .' RL to JL n/d, PUL
'Nobody ever had . . .' RL to Elizabeth Mostyn-Owen 28.7.58, private collection
'This is the one thing . . .' RL to Denys Kilham-Roberts 28.9.58, Society of Authors
'I did, do love her . . .' [et seq] RL to Elizabeth Mostyn-Owen 28.7.58, private collection
'My one joy . . .' RL to Rupert Hart-Davis 29.6.58, Tulsa
'The streets are full . . .' RL to Patrick Trevor-Roper 15.7.58, KCC
'Strength and calm . . .' [et seq] RL to Violet Hammersley 1.7.58, KCC
'I always managed to keep . . .' RL to Frances Partridge 8.7.58, private collection
'[Sally] had only one great grief . . .' RL to Compton Mackenzie 25.6.58, HRHRC
343 'I had an obsession . . .' RL in conversation with the author
'The only time I ever saw . . .' Jill Day-Lewis to author 23.7.01, KCC
'I sent a message by Rex . . .' RL in conversation with the author
'Hers was the first voice . . .' *SE*, p. 109
'A blackbird was pouring forth . . .' ibid. p. 111
344 'a softly gold effulgence . . .' ibid. p. 115
That evening, talk sparkled . . .' ibid. p. 117
'Everybody laughed and laughed . . .' [et seq] RL ms CPS
345 'more happy than I've ever . . .' RL to Patrick Trevor-Roper 15.7.58, KCC
'that grief and despair . . .' [et seq] RL to Frances Partridge 8.7.58, private collection
'The fact that it involved . . .' *Everything to Lose*, p. 311
'one of those split-second . . .' [et seq] RL to Frances Partridge 10.9.58, private collection

Chapter 13. 'The Vast, Unshakable Consolation'
347 '[He] was *appalled* . . .' [et seq] RL in conversation with the author
348 'the vast, unshakable consolation' *Album* p. 11
'It was brushed by the Breath . . .' RL ms CPS
349 'taken the ferry' *Ena Twigg*, p. 204
'Darling there is no death . . .' [et seq] RL ms CPS
'absent-present daughters' *Ena Twigg*, p. 207
'unsealed head centre . . .' RL to P. J. Kavanagh 3.2.69, private collection
350 'I found it very easy . . .' Cynthia Sandys in conversation with the author

'I knew that Sally . . .' RL in conversation with the author

'I have been – am being . . .' RL to Violet Hammersley n/d, KCC

'I had this very strong feeling . . .' RL to James Lees-Milne 5.2.69, Yale

'proclaim to a world . . .' CPS website

351 'I had been brought up . . .' [et seq] *Ena Twigg*, p. 208

'It's a little boy . . .' [et seq] RL ms CPS

352 'I was greedy, hungry . . .' RL in conversation with the author

'Needless to say, at that time . . .' *SE*, p. 110

'My discoveries thrilled . . .' ibid, p. 126

353 'often I have more peace . . .' RL to Barbara Cooper 31.12.59, HRHRC

'Stygian crew' JLD 19.8.72

'I'm aghast to find . . .' *Good Company*, p. 26

'Rosamond goes burbling on . . .' *A Mingled Measure* 11.4.64, p. 74

'after standing for a time . . .' *SE*, p. 119

'Of course I didn't witness anything . . .' *Laurie Lee*, p. 382

354 'It was a mystery to me . . .' Natasha Spender in conversation with the author

'She was a very clever girl . . .' [et seq] George Rylands in conversation with the author

'I used to feel so lonely . . .' *Writing Lives*, p. 158

'I said bad luck on the girl . . .' Nancy Mitford to Violet Hammersley 31.10.58, private collection

'It is very distasteful . . .' RL to Violet Hammersley 17.9.60, KCC

355 'We always read aloud . . .' George Rylands in conversation with the author

'I don't want to see Ronnie . . .' RL in conversation with the author

'I do feel him very near . . .' Nicky Mariano to RL 29.10.59, KCC

'hopeless woolly attempt . . .' *Other People*, p. 11

'invariably speaks of Sally's death . . .' *Good Company*, p. 26

356 'It didn't bring Rosamond any nearer . . .' [et seq] Patrick Trevor-Roper in conversation with the author

'How marvellous it would be . . .' RL to Violet Hammersley 16.12.58, KCC

'He warned me . . .' [et seq] RL in conversation with the author

357 'the seed of faith . . .' RL to Violet Hammersley 16.12.58, KCC

358 'an element of dreadful pain' RL to Violet Hammersley n/d, KCC

'my two heavenly baby grandsons' RL to Sybille Bedford 15.1.63, HRHRC

'Hugo and I are light-years distant . . .' RL to P. J. Kavanagh 27.7.64, private collection

'Rosamond used to spook me . . .' Anna Terrington in conversation with the author

'If *only* I could have her . . .' RL to Violet Hammersley n/d, KCC

359 'Funny (*very*), moving . . .' RL to P. J. Kavanagh 24.9.64, private collection

'I feel that she is much better . . .' RL to Violet Hammersley 25.9.63, KCC

'I have for so long . . .' HL to RL 15.10.67, KCC

360 'She had a coat like a toy dog . . .' WS p. 12

'I always felt . . .' Shelagh Fraser in conversation with the author

'I notice, don't you . . .' RL to Barbara Cooper 31.12.63, HRHRC

'mellow, serene and un-touchy' RL to Barbara Cooper 30.12.66, HRHRC

361 'he rocked and swayed . . .' RL to Barbara Cooper 8.8.61, HRHRC

'Whereas from my own point of view . . .' RL to David Carver 17.1.71, Tulsa

'I find the committee afternoons . . .' RL to David Carver 5.7.53, Tulsa

'intense boredom . . .' RL to James Lees-Milne 9.8.76, Yale

'I have never actually . . .' David Carver to RL 26.4.68, Tulsa

362 'a well-nigh total seize-up . . .' [et seq] SE, p. 89

'Does it not seem beyond words . . .' RL to Anne Munro-Kerr 12.8.64, Society of
Authors

'I have just been dipping into . . .' RL to Barbara Cooper 5.2.63, HRHRC

'I'm getting to be an old lady . . .' RL to P. J. Kavanagh 14.9.72, private collection

'whose rigors and privileges . . .' Three Giants: Charlotte Brontë, Mrs Gaskell and
George Eliot, New York Times Book Review, 21.11.52

363 'I am a modest . . .' My Dear Alexias, p. 2

'as I dare not overstep . . .' ibid. p. 103

364 'I was in the presence . . .' ibid. p. 3

'with hesitation and trepidation . . .' A Man Seen Afar, p. 16

'Nothing I had heard . . .' SE, p. 166

'TP to give you . . .' [et seq] My Dear Alexias, p. 16

'Bless you, how tiresome . . .' ibid. p. 17

'he gave me fresh hope . . .' RL ts CPS

365 'looking so gay . . .' My Dear Alexias, p. 112

'What a joy to be naughty . . .' ibid. p. 12

'the wondrous mysterious sapphire bowl . . .' ibid. p. 4

'every subsequent reading . . .' A Man Seen Afar, p. 27

366 'Yes, I have seen and heard . . .' ibid. p. 127

'her crazy old colonel' Good Company, p. 25

'ultra-orthodox respectables . . .' My Dear Alexias, p. 140

'the cruellest and seemingly . . .' SE, p. 29

'To me, the extraordinary news . . .' RL to P. J. Kavanagh n/d, private collection

367 'distasteful ... like journalism . . .' RL to P. J. Kavanagh 19.1.69, private
collection

'There are some things in it . . .' Aldous Huxley to RL 16.10.59, KCC

368 'My visit to Mrs Twigg . . .' Rupert Hart-Davis to RL 20.3.67, KCC

'I can make plants grow . . .' RL ms CPS

369 'sort of "spiritual autobiography"' RL to Barbara Cooper 25.8.65, HRHRC

'an entirely personal testament' RL to George Rylands 30.5.67, KCC

'the only one of my books . . .' Album, p. 11

'I can't help thinking . . .' RL to George Rylands 30.5.67, KCC

'[The song] somehow evokes . . .' My Dear Alexias, p. 183

'I look up and see the moon . . .' SE, p. 61

370 'I took down and re-read . . .' ibid. p. 70

'all too familiar . . .' ibid. p. 134

'"I wish Sally hadn't gone ..."' ibid. p. 154
371 'One feels desperately vulnerable ...' RL to Laurens van der Post 26.10.67,
    Laurens van der Post Estate
    'Presently, familiar names ...' *SE*, p. 161
    'Time was when the Lehmanns ...' *Sunday Times*, 29.10.67
    'but I never mentioned it ...' *Looking Back*, p. 167
    'Miss Lehmann does not offer ...' *Observer*, 29.10.67
372 'powerful, vulnerable, and brave' *Times*, 4.11.67
    'courageous ... [and] moving' *Times Literary Supplement*, 2.11.67
    '[Lehmann's] book may comfort ...' *Evening Standard*, 7.11.67
    'will pretty easily explode ...' *Guardian*, 3.11.67
    'Towards the end ...' *Listener*, 4.1.68
    'To the idea of life ...' Stevie Smith to RL 16.1.68, KCC
373 'I read it at one gulp ...' HL to RL 15.10.67, KCC
    'I read through the book ...' BL to RL 16.10.67, KCC
    'There seems to me ...' JL to RL 15.10.67, KCC
    'I lost a lot of foundation ...' Hugo Philipps to RL 31.7.67, KCC
374 'I am terribly sorry ...' Wogan Philipps to RL 12.12.67, KCC
    'eternal exile' *SE*, p. 118
    'The thing I never dared hope ...' RL to Margaret Lane 19.1.67, KCC
    'We *must* resolve to live ...' RL to Stephen Spender 25.11.67, private collection
375 'Counselling' is too grand a name ...' *SE*, p. 166
    'What she *loves* ...' George Rylands in conversation with the author
    '[Ros] designates herself ...' *Ancient as the Hills*, p. 15
    'The Vail part of my ordeal ...' RL to George Rylands 31.1.67, KCC

Chapter 14. 'A Woman Sitting Alone'
377 'Lionel and I were invited ...' *Partisan Review*, 1996, vol. LXIII, no. 1, p. 38
    '[in which] she would come sailing forth ...' George Rylands in conversation with
        the author
378 'that over-lifesize ...' *Good Company*, p. 16
    'an Indian God ... plump, suave ...' *Sylvia & David*, p. 172
    'Rosamond was a friend to women ...' Anita Brookner, *Spectator* 17.3.90
    'Much as I love her ...' RL to James Lees-Milne 4.8.73, Yale
379 'What I really feel *always* now ...' RL to P. J. Kavanagh 4.2.70, private collection
    'Ros certainly tried ...' [et seq] Anna Terrington in conversation with the author
    'in spite of having been left ...' *Good Company*, p. 23
381 'I wonder, shall we return ...' [et seq] RL ms CPS
382 'Jim the Smasher ...' RL to James Lees-Milne 6.8.70, Yale
    'worried because I can't find ...' RL to James Lees-Milne 20.4.70, Yale
    'and when he comes ...' RL to James Lees-Milne 3.4.70, Yale
    'I'm uncertain about the capacity ...' RL to James Lees-Milne 6.8.70, Yale
    'shattering melancholia ...' RL to James Lees-Milne 20.4.70, Yale

'I do rather think . . .' RL to James Lees-Milne 6.8.70, Yale
383 'I can't bear it any more . . .' *Daily Telegraph*, 7.4.71
'I was well aware . . .' RL to Peter Adam 10.6.71, private collection
'Rosamond drew Jim . . .' Peter Adam in conversation with the author
'I am in "a depression" . . .' RL to James Lees-Milne 2.8.71, Yale
'Even if didn't believe . . .' RL to Colette Clarke 23.2.71, KCC
'very glad . . . at a very low ebb . . .' C. Day Lewis to RL 25.3.72, KCC
384 'Concentrate on the happiness . . .' Rupert Hart-Davis to RL 23.5.72, KCC
'gradually to disappear . . .' RL to James Lees-Milne 23.6.72, Yale
'There were awful scenes . . .' [et seq] RL in conversation with the author
'There is only one person . . .' RL to P. J. Kavanagh 2.3.82, private collection
'stabbed me to the quick' RL to JL 1.6.72, PUL
385 'the wisdom of trying to involve . . .' JL to RL 3.6.72, KCC
'That was a very embarrassing piece . . .' RL to Elizabeth Jane Howard n/d, ms draft KCC
'Her cottage in the village street . . .' *Ancient as the Hills*, p. 187
386 'a small circle of dear queer friends . . .' [et seq] RL to James Lees-Milne 18.7.74, Yale
'where I feel peaceful . . .' RL to Hugo Manning 9.12.73, HRHRC
'Clareville Grove is a most civilized . . .' RL to George Rylands 6.2.77, KCC
387 'My novel is killing me . . .' RL to James Lees-Milne 9.11.72, Yale
'a love story . . .' RL to P. J. Kavanagh 27.4.76, private collection
388 'on the brink, as it were . . .' SGT, p. 162
'I *cannot* live without love . . .' ibid. p. 126
'expecting nothing, no one . . .' ibid. p. 67
389 'A *Sea-Grape Tree* is generally considered . . .' ibid. p. 162
'the sort of pulp romance . . .' *Evening Standard*, 2.11.76
'unintentionally absurd' *Times*, 11.11.76
'Anonyma and Johnny . . .' *Observer*, 31.10.76
'A *Sea-Grape Tree* is disappointing . . .' *New Statesman*, 19.11.76
'immensely readable, acute . . .' *Daily Express*, 28.10.76
'Coals of fire!' RL to P. J. Kavanagh 28.10.76, private collection
'[Miss Lehmann] must write . . .' *Listener*, 4.11.76
'Just had a typical letter . . .' RL to Stephen Spender 11.1.77, private collection
390 '*Is* it true??? . . .' RL to JL 4.3.73, PUL
'to write a serious, candid account . . .' *John Lehmann*, p. 252
'If it weren't so suffocatingly boring . . .' RL to P. J. Kavanagh 28.9.76, private collection
'I still feel incredulous . . .' RL to Rupert-Hart-Davis 25.11.76, Tulsa
'R. continues to rage . . .' JLD Oct 1976
'not written particularly light-heartedly . . .' RL to Lettice Cooper 4.7.77, private collection
'May all be mirth . . .' RL ms KCC
391 'I can promise you . . .' Edward Fox to RL 5.6.79, KCC

392 'Playing a scene with Bé . . .' Trader Faulkner to RL 29.12.81, KCC
'very difficult . . .' [et seq] RL in conversation with the author
'It is odd to think . . .' RL to John Ferrone 11.12.79, HRHRC
'They appear to be fairly . . .' Adrian House to RL 28.7.77, KCC

393 'He just stormed into the Rights Department . . .' [et seq] Carmen Callil in conversation with the author

394 '"feminist" labels and enquiries . . .' RL to Laurens van der Post 25.11.81, Laurens van der Post Estate
'"Feminine" is the word . . .' *Encounter*, 1.4.83
'My resurrection . . .' RL to James Lees-Milne 26.10.81, Yale

395 'I am SICK of all these assessments . . .' RL to George Rylands 12.2.85, KCC
'The huge reviews . . .' RL to James Lees-Milne 18.2.85, Yale

396 'Rosamond was one of the most beautiful women . . .' *World within World*, p. 143/ *Album*, p. 51
'will now never be written' *Album*, p. 107
'It makes me feel . . .' RL to James Lees-Milne 12.8.81, Yale
'"Oh, Miss Lehmann" . . .' RL in conversation with the author
'GOOD GOD!!! . . .' RL to George Rylands 28.3.82, KCC
'my favourite novelist' RL to P. J. Kavanagh 10.4.84, private collection
'I adored her . . .' Anita Brookner in conversation with the author

397 'Anita sternly going for walks . . .' Carmen Callil in conversation with the author
'How *could* Mollie . . .' RL in conversation with the author

398 'Though she was never good . . .' RL to P. J. Kavanagh 8.10.84, private collection
'Wonder of wonders! . . .' RL to George Rylands 4.6.85, KCC
'Poor old boy . . .' JLMD 8.4.87
'collapsed like a big pudding' JLMD 4.9.85
'into mountainous landsites . . .' *Through Wood and Dale* 8.11.77, p. 210
'Went to see Rosamond . . .' 20.1.83, JLMD
'to live in & look after me . . .' RL to P. J. Kavanagh 11.7.85, private collection

399 'I don't look forward . . .' George Rylands in conversation with the author
'She lost her sense of humour . . .' Josephine Filmer-Sankey in conversation with the author
'The trouble with Rosamond . . .' 17.2.87, JLMD

400 'He's very good looking . . .' RL in conversation with the author
'Rosamond didn't lose her sight . . .' Patrick Trevor-Roper in conversation with the author

401 'Rosamond had no need . . .' Christian Carritt in conversation with the author
'I have been taught . . .' *SE*, p. 167

402 'I dream that I shall wake up . . .' *Album*, p. 11

Chapter 15. Afterword
405 'Darling, You left all that CREAM!! . . .' RL to Selina Hastings 18.1.83, KCC

Select Bibliography

Books by Rosamond Lehmann

Dusty Answer (1927)
A Note in Music (1930)
A Letter to a Sister (1931)
Invitation to the Waltz (1932)
The Weather in the Streets (1936)
No More Music (1939)
The Ballad and the Sources (1944)
The Gypsy's Baby & Other Stories (1946)
The Echoing Grove (1953)
The Swan in the Evening (1967)
A Sea-Grape Tree (1976)
Rosamond Lehmann's Album (1985)

with Cecil Beaton: *Air of Glory: a Wartime Scrapbook* (1941)
with Wellesley Tudor Pole: *A Man Seen Afar* (1965)

Translations:
Genevieve by Jacques Lemarchand (1948)
Children of the Game by Jean Cocteau (1955)

Other works
Alexander, Bill, *British Volunteers for Liberty: Spain 1936–1939*, (Lawrence and Wishart, 1982)
Alexander, Peter F., *William Plomer*, (Oxford University Press, 1989)
Angier, Carole, *Jean Rhys: Life and Work*, (Penguin, 1992)
Annan, Noel, *The Dons*, (HarperCollins, 1999)
Barbara, Jack & McBrien, William, *Stevie*, (Heinemann, 1985)
Bayley, John, *Iris and the Friends*, (Duckworth, 1999)
Beaton, Cecil, *The Years Between: Diaries 1939–1944*, (Weidenfeld & Nicolson, 1965)

Bedford, Sybille, *Aldous Huxley: a Biography Vol. 2: 1939–1963*, (Chatto & Windus with Collins, 1974)

Berenson, Bernard, *Sunset and Twilight: from the Diaries of 1947–1958*, ed. Nicky Mariano (Harcourt, Brace & World 1963)

Bernstein, Matthew, *Walter Wanger, Hollywood Independent*, (University of California Press, 1994)

Blake, Nicholas, *Head of a Traveller*, (Collins Crime Club, 1949)

— *The Dreadful Hollow*, (Collins Crime Club, 1953)

Blanche, Jacques-Emile, *More Portraits of a Lifetime*, trans. by Walter Clement (Dent, 1939)

Bowen, Elizabeth, *Pictures and Conversations*, (Allen Lane, 1975)

Bowra, C. M., *Memories 1898–1939*, (Weidenfeld & Nicolson, 1966)

Boyle, Andrew, *The Climate of Treason: Five Who Spied for Russia*, (Hutchinson, 1979)

Bradbrook, M. C., *'That Infidel Place': a Short History of Girton College, 1869–1969*, (Chatto & Windus, 1969)

Brandon, Ruth, *The Spiritualists: the Passion for the Occult in the Nineteenth and Twentieth Centuries*, (Weidenfeld & Nicolson, 1983)

Chamberlain, Mary (ed.), *Writing Lives: Conversation Between Women Writers*, (Virago, 1988)

Chisholm, Anne, *Nancy Cunard*, (Sidgwick & Jackson, 1979)

Connolly, Cyril, *The Missing Diplomats*, (Queen Anne Press, 1952)

Cook, Theodore, *The Sunlit Hours: a Record of Sport and Life*, (Nisbet, 1925)

Costello, John, *Mask of Treachery*, (Collins, 1988)

Coward, Noel, *The Nöel Coward Diaries*, (Papermac, 1983), (eds. Graham Payn & Sheridan Morley)

Crewe, Quentin, *Well, I Forget the Rest: the Autobiography of an Optimist*, (Hutchinson, 1991)

Day Lewis, C., *Poems 1943–1947*, (Cape, 1948)

— *The Buried Day*, (Chatto & Windus, 1960)

— *The Lyric Impulse*, (Harvard University Press, 1965)

— *The Complete Poems*, (Sinclair-Stevenson, 1992)

Day-Lewis, Sean, *C. Day-Lewis*, (Weidenfeld & Nicolson, 1980)

Deacon, Richard, *The Cambridge Apostles: a History of Cambridge University's Elite Intellectual Secret Society*, (Robert Royce, 1985) de Cossart, Michael, *The Food of Love: Princesse Edmond de Polignac and her Salon*, (Hamish Hamilton, 1978)

De-la-Noy, Michael, *Eddy: the Life of Edward Sackville-West*, (Bodley Head, 1988)

Diesbach, Ghislain de, *Vieille Angleterre de Ma Jeunesse*, (privately pub., 1999)

Dowie, Ménie Muriel, *Gallia*, (Everyman, 1955) ed. Helen Small

Fowle, Frances, 'Sylvia Sprigge and the "Sage of Settignano": Berenson's First Biographer' (*Apollo*, November, 1996)

Garnett, David (ed)., *Carrington: Letters and Extracts from her Diaries*, (Cape, 1970)

Garnett, Richard (ed.), *Sylvia & David: the Townsend Warner/Garnett Letters*, (Sinclair-Stevenson, 1994)

Garrett, Eileen J., *Many Voices: the Autobiography of a Medium*, (Allen & Unwin, 1969)

Gelpi, Albert, *Living in Time: the Poetry of C. Day Lewis*, (Oxford University Press, 1998)

Glendinning, Victoria, *Elizabeth Bowen*, (Weidenfeld & Nicolson, 1977)

— *Edith Sitwell*, (Weidenfeld & Nicolson, 1981)

Grant Duff, Shiela, *The Parting of Ways*, (Peter Owen, 1982)

Grove, Valerie, *Laurie Lee: the Well-Loved Stranger*, (Viking, 1999)

Guppy, Shusha, *Looking Back*, (Paris Review Editions, 1991)

Hatcher, John, *Laurence Binyon: Poet, Scholar of East and West*, (Oxford University Press, 1995)

Hinshaw, Robert (ed.), *The Rock Rabbit and the Rainbow*, (Daimon Verlag, 1998)

Holroyd, Michael, *Lytton Strachey: a Critical Biography vol. II: the Years of Achievement 1910–1932*, (Heinemann, 1968)

— *Lytton Strachey*, (Chatto & Windus, 1994)

Howarth, T. E. B., *Cambridge Between Two Wars*, (Collins, 1928)

Isherwood, Christopher, *Christopher and His Kind: 1929–1929*, (Eyre Methuen, 1977)

— *Diaries: Volume 1: 1939–1960*, ed. Katherine Bucknell, (Methuen, 1996)

— *Lost Years: a Memoir 1945–1951*, ed. Katherine Bucknell, (Chatto & Windus, 2000)

Jaloux, Edmond, *Au Pays du Roman*, (R.-A. Corrêa, 1931)

Jones, J. D. F., *Storyteller: the Many Lives of Laurens van der Post*, (HarperCollins, 2001)

Kavanagh, P. J., *The Perfect Stranger*, (Carcanet, 1995)

Keir, David, *The House of Collins*, (Collins, 1952)

Lawrence, P. S. H., *Grizel: Grizel Hartley Remembered*, (Michael Russell, 1991)

Lees-Milne, James, *A Mingled Measure: Diaries, 1953–1972*, (John Murray, 1994)

— *Fourteen Friends*, (John Murray, 1996)

— *Ancient as the Hills: Diaries, 1973–1974*, (John Murray, 1997)

— *Through Wood and Dale: Diaries, 1975–1978*, (John Murray, 1998)

— *Deep Romantic Chasm: Diaries, 1979–1981*, ed. Michael Bloch, (John Murray, 2000)

— *Holy Dread: Diaries, 1982–1984*, ed. Michael Bloch, (John Murray, 2001)

Lehmann, John, *The Whispering Gallery*, (Longmans, Green, 1955)

— *Ancestors & Friends*, (Eyre & Spottiswoode, 1962)

— *I Am My Brother*, (Longmans, Green, 1960)

— *The Ample Proposition*, (Eyre & Spottiswoode, 1966)

— *In the Purely Pagan Sense*, (Blond & Briggs, 1976)

Lehmann, John (ed.), *New Writing: Autumn 1938*, (Hogarth Press, 1938)

Lehmann, Rudolf, *An Artist's Reminiscences*, (Smith, Elder, 1894)

Lehmann, R. C., *Selected Verse of R. C. Lehmann*, (Blackwood 1929),

— *The Vagabond and Other Poems*, (John Lane, The Bodley Head, 1918)

— *Memories of Half a Century: a Record of Friendships*, (Smith, Elder, 1908)

Lehmann, R. C. (ed.), *Familiar Letters: N.L. to F.L. 1864–1867*, (privately published)

Linklater, Andro, *Compton Mackenzie. a Life*, (Chatto, 1987)

Lycett, Andrew, *Ian Fleming*, (Weidenfeld & Nicolson, 1995)

Mackenzie, Compton, *My Life and Times Octave Six 1923–1930*, (Chatto & Windus, 1967)

McLeod, Kirsty, *A Passion for Friendship: Sibyl Colefax & Her Circle*, (Michael Joseph, 1991)

MacNeice, Louis, *The Strings Are False*, (Faber, 1965)

Marshall, Archibald, *Out and About: Random Reminiscences*, (Murray, 1933)

McWilliams-Tullberg, Rita, *Women at Cambridge*, (Gollancz, 1975)

Meyer, Michael, *Not Prince Hamlet: Literary and Theatrical Memoirs*, (Secker & Warburg, 1989)

Mosley, Diana, *A Life of Contrasts*, (Hamish Hamilton, 1977)

— *Loved Ones: Pen Portraits*, (Sidgwick & Jackson, 1985)

Partridge, Frances, *Julia: a Portrait by Herself*, (Gollancz, 1983)

— *Everything to Lose: Diaries 1945–1960*, (Little, Brown, 1985)

— *Other People: Diaries 1963–1966*, (HarperCollins, 1993)

— *Good Company: Diaries 1967–1970*, (HarperCollins, 1994)

Patmore, Derek, *Private History*, (Cape, 1960)

Penrose, Barrie & Freeman, Simon, *Conspiracy of Silence: the Secret Life of Anthony Blunt*, (Grafton Books, 1986)

Plomer, William, *The Autobiography of William Plomer*, (Cape, 1975)

Price, R. G. G., *A History of Punch*, (Collins, 1957)

Pryce-Jones, David, *Cyril Connolly: Journal and Memoir*, (Collins, 1983)

Raine, Kathleen, *Autobiographies*, (Skoob, 1991)

Rees, Goronwy, *A Chapter of Accidents*, (Chatto & Windus, 1972)

Ritchie, Charles, *The Siren Years: a Canadian Diplomat Abroad, 1937–1945*, (Macmillan, 1974)

Runciman, Sir Walter, *Before the Mast – and After: the Autobiography of a Sailor and Shipowner*, (Benn, 1924)

Scott-James, Anne, *Sketches from a Life*, (Michael Joseph, 1993)

Scott-James, R. A., *Fifty Years of English Literature, 1900–1950*, (Longmans, 1956)

Secrest, Meryle, *Being Bernard Berenson*, (Weidenfeld & Nicolson, 1980)

Sitwell, Edith, *Selected Letters*, ed. Richard Green (Virago, 1997)

Simons, Judy, *Rosamond Lehmann*, (Macmillan, 1992)

Spalding, Frances, *Stevie Smith*, (Faber, 1988)

Spencer Carr, Virginia, *The Lonely Hunter: a Biography of Carson McCullers*, (Doubleday, 1975)

Spender, Stephen, *World within World*, (Faber, 1977)

— *Journals 1939–1983*, ed. by John Goldsmith (Faber, 1985)

Staley, Thomas F., *Jean Rhys: a Critical Study*, (University of Texas Press, 1979)

Barbara Stephen, *Girton College 1869–1932*, (Cambridge University Press, 1933)

Thwaite, Ann, *A. A. Milne: His Life*, (Faber, 1990)

Treglown, Jeremy, *Romancing: the Life and Work of Henry Green*, (Faber, 2000)

Tudor Pole, Wellesley & Lehmann, Rosamond, *A Man Seen Afar*, (Neville Spearman, 1965)

Tudor Pole, Wellesley, *My Dear Alexias: Letters from Wellesley Tudor Pole to Rosamond Lehmann*, ed. by Elizabeth Gaythorpe (Neville Spearman, 1979)

Twigg, Ena, with Ruth Hagy Brod, *Ena Twigg: Medium*, (W.H. Allen, 1973)

Warner, Oliver, *Chatto & Windus*, (Chatto & Windus, 1973)

Woolf, Virginia, *The Diary of Virginia Woolf*, ed. Anne Olivier Bell, Vol. III: 1925–1930 (Hogarth Press, 1980); Vol. IV: 1931–1935 (1982)

— *The Letters of Virginia Woolf*, ed. Nigel Nicolson, Vol. V: 1932–1935, *The Sickle Side of the Moon*

Wright, Adrian, *John Lehmann: a Pagan Adventure*, (Duckworth, 1998)

Index

Works by Rosamond Lehmann appear directly under title; works by others under author's name. Titles and ranks are generally the highest attained in the period covered

the Dark', 250; 'Elegy Before Death: At Settignano', 264–5, 316; *From Feathers to Iron*, 227; 'George Meredith, 1861', 316; 'The House–Warming', 249; *An Italian Visit*, 264–5, 316; 'The Lighted House', 226; 'The Neurotic', 258; *Poems 1943–1947*, 266; *The Poetic Image* (Clark Lectures), 252, 262; *Word Over All*, 237, 252, 262
Day-Lewis, Jill *see* Balcon
Day Lewis, Mary (*née* King): RL stays with, 219; ignorance of Cecil's relations with RL, 223, 235; marriage and children, 227–8; and Cecil's double life, 235–8, 246, 251, 259–61; Cecil decides to leave, 253, 258; attends Cecil's poetry recital, 254; Cecil returns to, 258–9; twenty–first wedding anniversary, 279; and Cecil's commitment to Jill Balcon, 282, 284–5; divorce from Cecil, 292
Day-Lewis, Nicholas, 235, 238
Day-Lewis, Sean, 235–6, 238, 278
de la Mare, Walter, 241, 254
Denmark: Day Lewis visits with Laurie Lee, 259–60; RL lectures in, 290
Desborough, Ethel, Lady ('Ettie'), 30, 96, 142, 166
Desborough, William Henry Grenfell, Baron, 12, 37, 96, 142, 166, 347
Desert Island Discs (radio programme), 395
Diamond Cottage *see* Aldworth
Dick, Kay, 315
Dickens, Charles, 4–5, 60
'Dirge for Rather a Nasty Spirit' (RL; poem), 317
Doone, Rupert, 195
Dos Passos, John, 184
Dowding, Air Chief Marshal Hugh, 1st Baron, 348
Doxford, Northumberland, 72, 79
Doyle, Sir Arthur Conan, 351
Drabble, Margaret, 362, 389
'Dream of Winter, A' (RL; short story), 216–17, 231
Drinkwater, George, 19, 33
Drinkwater, John, 19

Drury, Nina (*née* Lehmann, Sally's cousin), 273
Duchene, Anne, 372
Duke of York's Theatre, London, 196
Duras, Marguerite, 404
Dusty Answer (RL): reception and success, 3, 97–100, 105–8, 128, 178, 245; publication, 90; plot and themes, 91–6, 142, 242, 311; RL declines film offer for, 112; French translation and reputation, 178–9; reissued, 393–4

Eaton Square, London: RL moves to, 299; RL entertains in, 330, 404; RL leaves, 386
Echoing Grove, The (RL): writing, 303–4; published, 306, 362; plot and themes, 307–13; Day Lewis and, 312–13, 318; title, 312; reception, 314–16; reissued, 393; radio dramatisation, 394
Edward VII, King: funeral, 22
Egypt: RL visits, 374
Eigg (island), 79, 100
Eliot, George, 5, 100, 207, 328
Eliot, T.S., 159, 212, 254, 274, 330; *Burnt Norton*, 368; *The Family Reunion*, 391; *The Four Quartets*, 370
Eliot, Valerie, 330
Elizabeth II, Queen, 316
Elizabeth, Queen of George VI, 254
English Centre of International PEN *see* PEN Club
Epstein, Sir Jacob, 278–9
Evans, Margiad, 241

Fairbanks, Douglas and Mary, 51
Faulkner, Trader, 392
Faulkner, William, 159
Ferber, Edna, 108
Ferrer, Mel, 338
Ferrier, Kathleen, 351
Fieldhead (house) *see* Bourne End
FIL *see* Association of Writers For Intellectual Liberty
Fitzgerald, Edward, 51, 58
Fitzgerald, Ménie (*earlier* Norman; *née* Dowie), 51, 56, 58–61, 69, 242, 245,

'Gwen'), 86, 123, 156, 323, 386
Philipps, Hanning (Wogan's brother), 83, 86, 123, 224
Philipps, Honor (Wogan's cousin), 102
Philipps, Hugo John Laurence (*later* 3rd Baron Milford; RL/Wogan's son): birth, 116–17; holidays with mother, 154, 182; schooling, 170, 193, 206, 208, 214, 225, 228; RL takes to Tower of London, 182; father's relations with, 193, 255–6; RL wishes to send to USA, 198; on Goronwy Rees's military service, 199; influenza, 205; reserve over Day Lewis, 221, 228; Philipps grandparents care for, 224–5; character and appearance, 225, 256, 288, 332; portrayed in RL's stories, 231–2; fondness for Laurie Lee, 233; protests at RL's intention to marry Day Lewis, 255; fondness for aunt Beatrix, 271; military service, 271; attends Cambridge University, 272, 279, 288; at Sally's 16th birthday celebration, 280; and Day Lewis's defection from RL, 288; rowing, 288; relations with RL, 289, 358; marriage to Margaret Heathcote, 294, 296–7, 323; marriage with Margaret ends, 331–2; dismisses RL's spiritualist beliefs, 353; and RL's Isle of Wight property, 358; second marriage (to Mollie Makins) and children, 358; on *The Swan in the Evening* and Sally's death, 373; RL visits Portugal with, 374; RL visits at Llanstephan, 379; divorce from Mollie, 397; third marriage (to Felicity), 399; at RL's funeral, 401; author meets, 404
Philipps, Ivo (Hugo/Mollie's son): birth, 358
Philipps, Sir James Erasmus (Wogan's grandfather), 122
Philipps, Katherine Nina (Hugo/Mollie's daughter; 'Kate'): birth, 358
Philipps, Sir Laurence (Wogan's father) *see* Milford, 1st Baron
Philipps, Margaret (Hugo's first wife) *see* Heathcote, Margaret

Philipps, Mary (*née* Makins; Hugo's second wife; *later* Viscountess Norwich; 'Mollie'): marriage to Hugo and children, 358; in Portugal with RL, 374; at Llanstephan, 379; marries Norwich, 397
Philipps, Roland (Hugo/Mollie's son), 358, 395, 399
Philipps, Sarah Jane (RL/Wogan's daughter; Sally) *see* Kavanagh, Sarah Jane
Philipps, Tamara (Wogan's third wife) *see* Milford, Tamara, Lady
Philipps, William (Wogan's brother), 123
Philipps, Wogan (RL's husband) *see* Milford, 2nd Baron
Picton Castle, Wales, 122
Pinker, J.B. & Son (literary agency), 161
Pinker, Ralph, 161–2, 303
Pinsent, Cecil, 263
Plomer, William: friendship with RL, 147, 160; and Elizabeth Bowen, 160; and RL's criticism of John Lehmann's writing, 215; on Day Lewis's narrow outlook, 227; at John Lehmann's party, 240; contributes to *Orion*, 241; and RL's *The Ballad and the Source*, 245; and RL's move to Little Wittenham, 249; negotiates with Day Lewis for RL, 254; visits to Little Wittenham, 255, 268; works for Jonathan Cape, 257n; letter from RL on novel writing, 268; offends Edith Sitwell, 274; and Lilian Bowes–Lyon, 275; praises RL's *The Echoing Grove*, 315; on John Lehmann's appearance, 326; praises RL's *The Swan in the Evening*, 373; death, 391
Plon (French publisher), 179, 311
Polignac, Princesse Edmond de (*née* Winaretta Singer), 179–81, 260
Portugal, 374
Potter, Beatrix, 226
Pottle, Mrs (nanny), 17
Priestley, J.B., 44, 305
Primavera (villa), Cap Ferrat, 90
Pritchett, Sir Victor S., 128, 395
Punch (magazine), 5, 10, 12, 19, 23

Orion, 241; in France, 295; as support
for Virginia, 328

Woolf, Virginia: as RL's mentor, 3; at
Hogarth Press, 88, 132; stylistic
technique, 91; MacLeish on, 105;
devotion to Wogan Philipps, 120;
RL's relations with, 121, 146–7;
influence on RL's writing, 127, 133,
371; praises RL's writing, 129; visits
Ipsden, 146; on sexual emancipation,
149; on Wogan's being overshadowed
by RL, 150; RL reads, 159; Blanche
on, 178; on Goronwy Rees, 191;
death, 217; and RL's The Echoing
Grove, 314; Leonard's support for, 328;
in RL's spiritualist experiences, 351–2;

Mrs Dalloway, 127, 130; To the
Lighthouse, 90, 121
World War I: outbreak, 35–6
World War II: outbreak, 200; conduct of,
205–7; ends in Europe, 246
'Writers Declare Against Fascism'
meeting, 1, 194

Yorke, Henry (Henry Green), 190,
214–16, 228, 240, 245; Party Going,
214
Yoxford, Suffolk: The Coach House, 382,
385, 397–8, 404

Zanuck, Darryl, 247
Ziegler, Philip: life of Diana Cooper, 407

that it's going to mean a litt[le]
meaning to write to you every
after lunch. I spend the who[le]
... scribbling paper, it makes it ...
written. ... ... and ...
... ... a wal[k]
... ... the day
... to work. You don't s...
ask us to lunch & tea inv...
... you going to Malaga[?]
Give Frances my best lo[ve]
by John Fothergill...